TOGETHER WE STAND

TOGETHER WE STAND

AMERICA, BRITAIN AND THE FORGING OF AN ALLIANCE

BY

JAMES HOLLAND

miramax books

HYPERION

NEW YORK

ISBN 1-4013-5253-7

First Edition
10   9   8   7   6   5   4   3   2   1

Contents

List of Maps   vii
Principal Personalities   xxxvii
Principal Commanders   xliii
Introduction   xlix
Prologue: Sidi Rezegh, Libya: November 1941   liii

PART I: NADIR • 1

1 Enter America   3
2 Calm Before the Storm: Monday, 4 May, 1942   19
3 Britain's Mistakes: A Brief Discourse on Tactics
  and Equipment   39
4 Missed Opportunities: 26 May–5 June, 1942   63
5 Into the Cauldron: 4 June to 10 June, 1942   89
6 Knightsbridge: 11–18 June, 1942   110
7 Surrender and Retreat: 19 June–1 July, 1942   127

PART II: COMING TOGETHER • 153

8 Parry: July, 1942, Part I   155
9 And Thrust: July 1942, Part II   177
10 New Faces: 1–12 August, 1942   193
11 A Victory at Last: 13 August–4, September 1942   214

12 Getting Ready Part I—September 1942   239
13 Getting Ready Part II—October 1942   261

PART III: ADVANCE AND RETREAT • 291

14 Into Battle—23–26 October, 1942   293
15 Attrition—26 October–3 November, 1942   314
16 Lighting the Torch—5–11 November, 1942   334
17 The Race for Tunis: November 1942   360
18 Harsh Realities: December 1942   382
19 Purse For Thought: January 1943   406
20 Conflicting Personalities:
     18 January–13 February, 1943   433
21 Rommel Strikes Back: 14–22 February   459

PART IV: SHOULDER TO SHOULDER • 483

22 Alex & Mary Take Control:
     22 February–20 March, 1943   485
23 Left Hook: 17–31 March, 1943   510
24 Joining Hands: 1–18 April, 1943   539
25 Endgame: 19 April–13 May, 1943   565

Postscript   591
Glossary   607
Notes   611
Bibliography and Sources   629
Acknowledgments   649

LIST OF MAPS

 1. Key to Maps   ix
 2. Middle East Theatre of War   x
 3. Gazala Line, 26 May 1942   x
 4. First Day at Gazala, 27 May 1942   xi
 5. Gazala, 28–9 May 1942   xi
 6. The Cauldron, 5–6 June 1942   xii
 7. Knightsbridge, 11–14 June 1942   xii
 8. Retreat from Gazala Line, 14–15 June 1942   xiii
 9. Fall of Tobruk, 21 June 1942   xiii
10. End of Rommel's Advance, 1–2 July, 1942   xiv
11. SAS Operations   xv
12. First Ruweisat, 14–15 July 1942   xvi
13. Second Ruweisat, 21 July 1942   xvi
14. Battle of Alam Haifa, 31 August 1942   xvii
15. Axis Sea and Air Transport Routes to North Africa,
    October 1942–May 1943   xviii
16. Eve of El Alamein, 23 October 1942   xix
17. Operation LIGHTFOOT, 23–4 October 1942
    (northern half of line)   xx
18. Operation LIGHTFOOT, early 24 October 1942
    (northern half of line)   xxi
19. Snipe and Woodcock, 26–7 October 1942   xxii
20. Seizure of Oran   xxiii
21. Plan of Operation SUPERCHARGE   xxiv
22. Final Attacks of Battle of Alamein   xxv
23. The Pursuit after Alamein, 4–7 November 1942   xxvi
24. TORCH Landings   xxvii
25. Seizure of Casablanca   xxviii
26. Tunisia   xxix
27. First Allied Attempt to Reach Tunis   xxx
28. Kasserine, 14–22 February 1943   xxxi
29. Von Arnim's Offensive in the North, February–March 1943   xxxii
30. Mareth and the Tebaga Gap, 20–28 March, 1943   xxxiii
31. US II Corps Operations, March 1943   xxxiv
32. Wadi Akarit, 6 April 1943   xxxv
33. Capture of the Tunis Bridgehead   xxxvi

MAPS

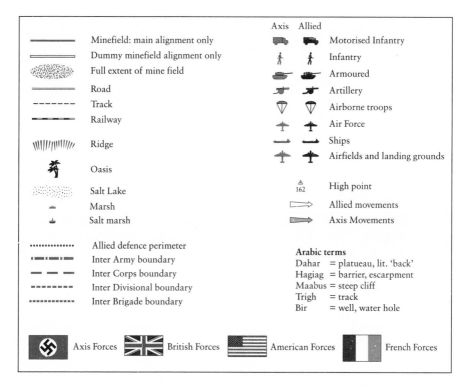

		Axis	Allied	
▬▬▬▬	Minefield: main alignment only	🚚	🚚	Motorised Infantry
▬▬▬▬	Dummy minefield alignment only	🚶	🚶	Infantry
🌫️	Full extent of mine field	🛡️	🛡️	Armoured
▭▭▭	Road	◄	►	Artillery
- - - - -	Track	▽	▽	Airborne troops
▬▬▬	Railway	✈	✈	Air Force
||||//||||////	Ridge	⬡	⬡	Ships
		✈	✈	Airfields and landing grounds
🌴	Oasis			
⋯⋯	Salt Lake	△ 162	High point	
⋏	Marsh	▷	Allied movements	
⋏	Salt marsh	▶	Axis Movements	

•••••••••••	Allied defence perimeter
▬•▬•▬•▬	Inter Army boundary
— — —	Inter Corps boundary
- - - - - -	Inter Divisional boundary
•••••••••••	Inter Brigade boundary

Arabic terms
Dahar = platueau, lit. 'back'
Hagiag = barrier, escarpment
Maabus = steep cliff
Trigh = track
Bir = well, water hole

卐 Axis Forces   🇬🇧 British Forces   🇺🇸 American Forces   🇫🇷 French Forces

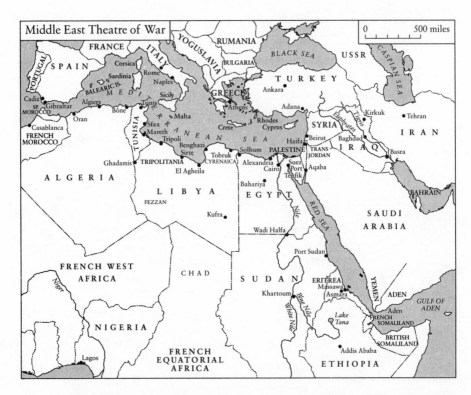

Middle East Theatre of War

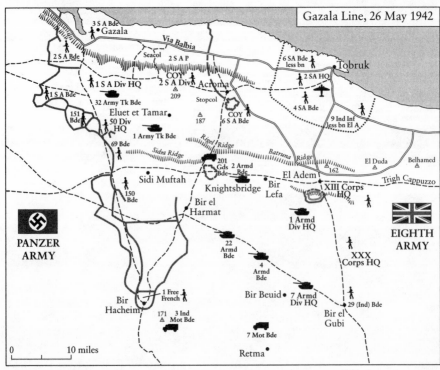

Gazala Line, 26 May 1942

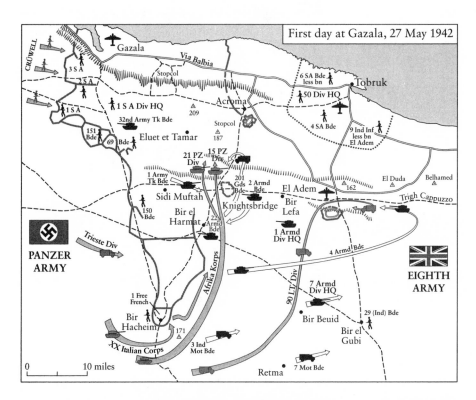

First day at Gazala, 27 May 1942

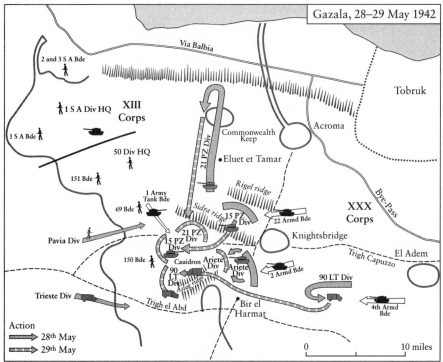

Gazala, 28–29 May 1942

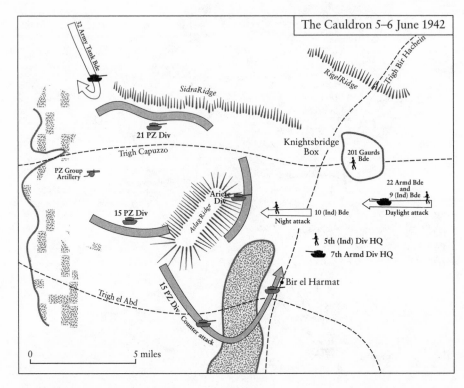

The Cauldron 5–6 June 1942

32 Army Tank Bde

SidraRidge

RigelRidge

Trigh Bir Hachein

21 PZ Div

Knightsbridge Box

201 Gaurds Bde

Trigh Capuzzo

PZ Group Artillery

Ariete Div

22 Armd Bde and 9 (Ind) Bde

15 PZ Div

Aslag Ridge

10 (Ind) Bde
Night attack

Daylight attack

5th (Ind) Div HQ

7th Armd Div HQ

15 PZ Div Counter attack

Bir el Harmat

Trigh el Abd

0   5 miles

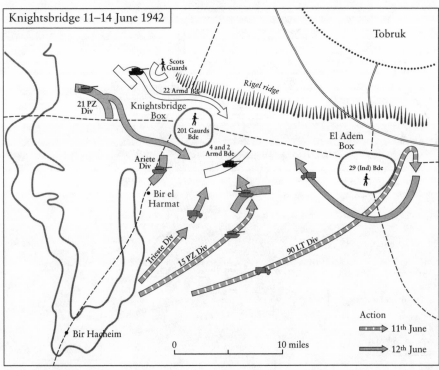

Knightsbridge 11–14 June 1942

Tobruk

Scots Guards

22 Armd Bde

Rigel ridge

21 PZ Div

Knightsbridge Box

201 Gaurds Bde

El Adem Box

4 and 2 Armd Bde

29 (Ind) Bde

Ariete Div

Bir el Harmat

Trieste Div

15 PZ Div

90 LT Div

Bir Hacheim

0   10 miles

Action

11th June

12th June

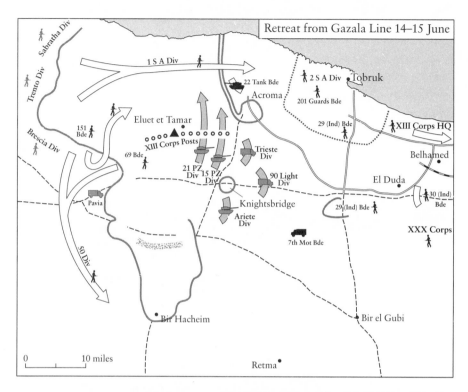

Retreat from Gazala Line 14–15 June

Sabratha Div
Trento Div
Brescia Div

1 S A Div
22 Tank Bde
Acroma
2 S A Div
Tobruk
201 Guards Bde
29 (Ind) Bde
XIII Corps HQ
Belhamed
Eluet et Tamar
151 Bde
XIII Corps Posts
69 Bde
Trieste Div
21 PZ Div
15 PZ Div
90 Light Div
El Duda
30 (Ind) Bde
Pavia
Knightsbridge
29 (Ind) Bde
Ariete Div
XXX Corps
50 Div
7th Mot Bde
Bir Hacheim
Bir el Gubi
0   10 miles
Retma

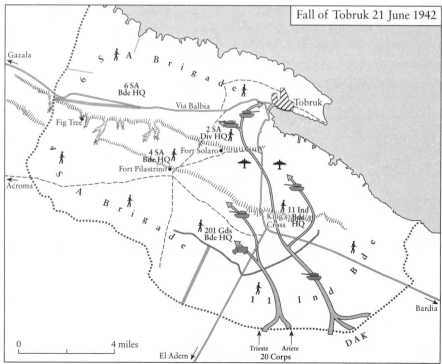

Fall of Tobruk 21 June 1942

Gazala
S A Brigade
6 SA Bde HQ
Via Balbia
6 SA Brigade
Tobruk
Fig Tree
2 SA Div HQ
Fort Solaro
4 SA Bde HQ
Fort Pilastrino
Acroma
S A Brigade
11 Ind Bde HQ
King's Cross
201 Gds Bde HQ
11 Ind Bde
Bardia
1 1 Ind
DAK
0   4 miles
El Adem
Trieste   Ariete
20 Corps

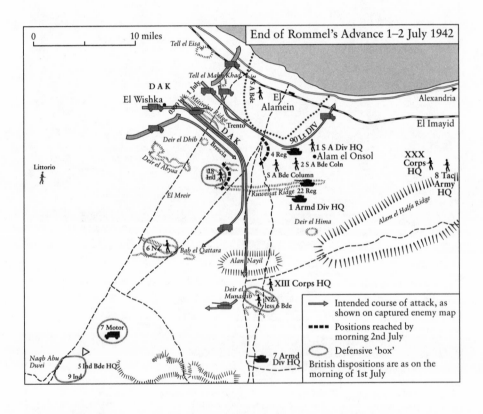

End of Rommel's Advance 1–2 July 1942

0   10 miles

Intended course of attack, as shown on captured enemy map

Positions reached by morning 2nd July

Defensive 'box'

British dispositions are as on the morning of 1st July

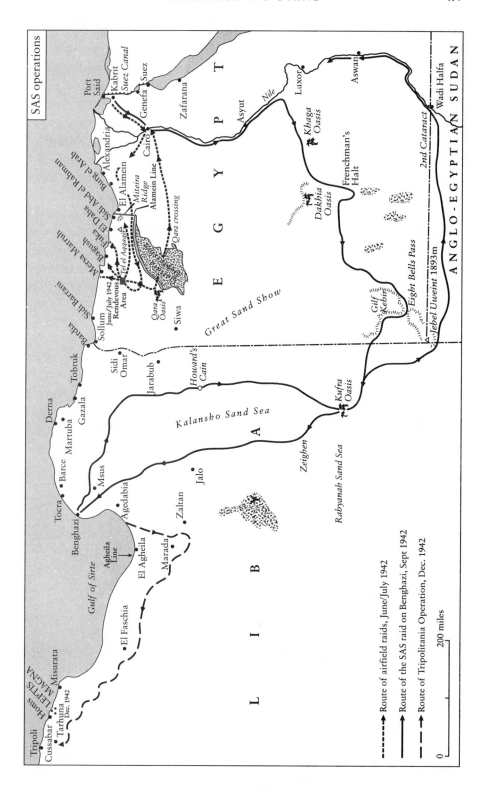

SAS operations

ANGLO-EGYPTIAN SUDAN

E G Y P T

L I B Y A

Route of airfield raids, June/July 1942
Route of the SAS raid on Benghazi, Sept 1942
Route of Tripolitania Operation, Dec. 1942

0   200 miles

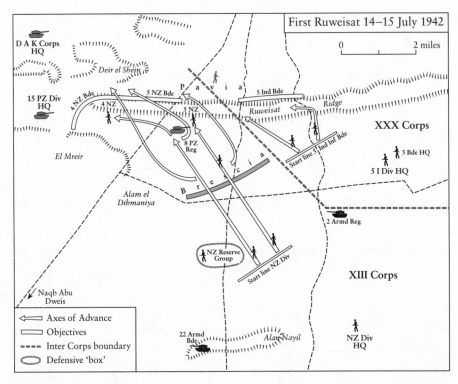

First Ruweisat 14–15 July 1942

0   2 miles

D A K Corps HQ

Deir el Shein

15 PZ Div HQ

4 NZ Bde

5 NZ Bde

5 NZ

4 NZ

5 Ind Bde

Ruweisat Ridge

XXX Corps

8 PZ Reg

Start line 5 Ind Inf Bde

5 Bde HQ

5 I Div HQ

El Mreir

Alam el Dihmaniya

B   r   e   s   c   i   a

P   a   v   i   a

2 Armd Reg

NZ Reserve Group

Start line NZ Div

XIII Corps

Naqb Abu Dweis

⇐ Axes of Advance

▭ Objectives

---- Inter Corps boundary

◯ Defensive 'box'

22 Armd Bde

Alam Nayil

NZ Div HQ

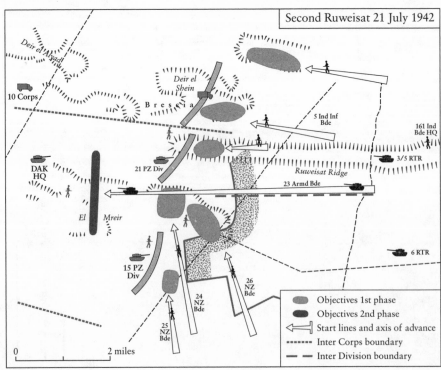

Second Ruweisat 21 July 1942

Deir el Abyad

Deir el Shein

10 Corps

B r e s c i a

5 Ind Inf Bde

161 Ind Bde HQ

DAK HQ

21 PZ Div

3/5 RTR

Ruweisat Ridge

23 Armd Bde

El Mreir

6 RTR

15 PZ Div

24 NZ Bde

26 NZ Bde

25 NZ Bde

◯ Objectives 1st phase

● Objectives 2nd phase

⇐ Start lines and axis of advance

······ Inter Corps boundary

–– Inter Division boundary

0   2 miles

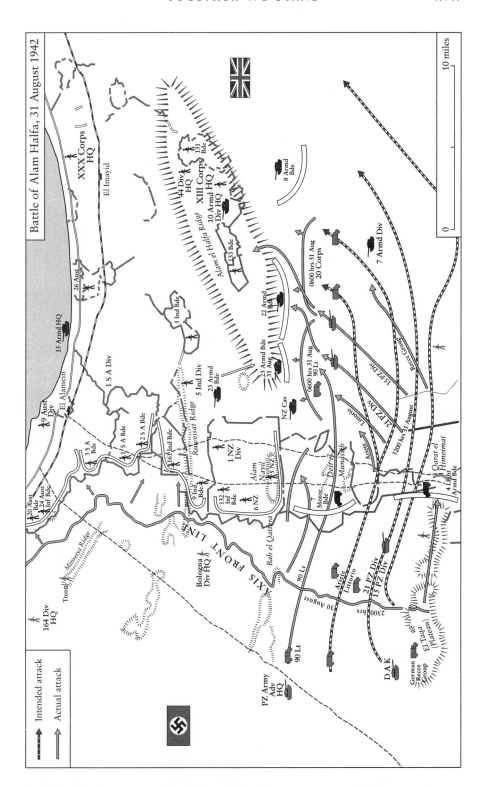

Battle of Alam Halfa, 31 August 1942

Intended attack
Actual attack

10 miles

0

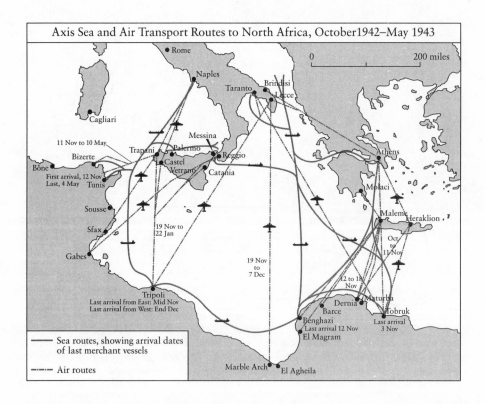

Axis Sea and Air Transport Routes to North Africa, October1942–May 1943

0   200 miles

Rome

Naples

Taranto

Brindisi
Lecce

Cagliari

11 Nov to 10 May
Bizerte
Messina
Trapani Palermo
Castel
Vetrano
Reggio
Catania

Athens

Bône
First arrival, 12 Nov
Last, 4 May Tunis

Molaci

Sousse

Maleme
Heraklion

Sfax

Oct
to
11 Nov

19 Nov to
22 Jan

Gabes

19 Nov
to
7 Dec

12 to 18
Nov

Tripoli
Last arrival from East: Mid Nov
Last arrival from West: End Dec

Maturba
Dernia
Barce
Benghazi
Last arrival 12 Nov
El Magram

Tobruk
Last arrival
3 Nov

—— Sea routes, showing arrival dates
of last merchant vessels

----- Air routes

Marble Arch
El Agheila

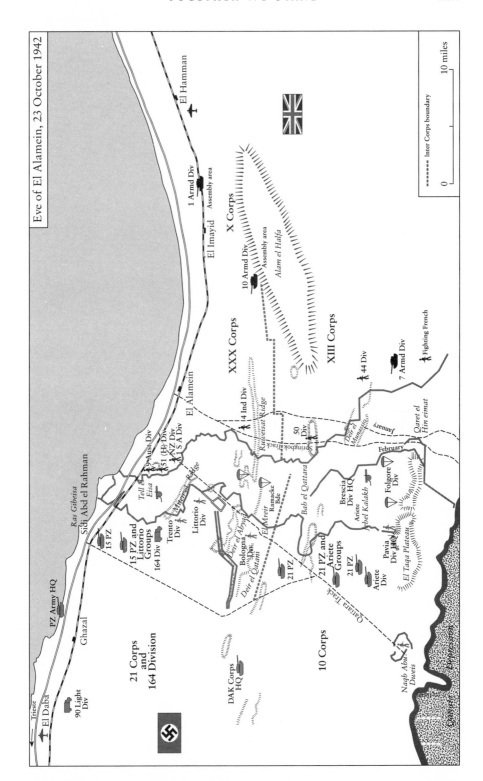

Eve of El Alamein, 23 October 1942

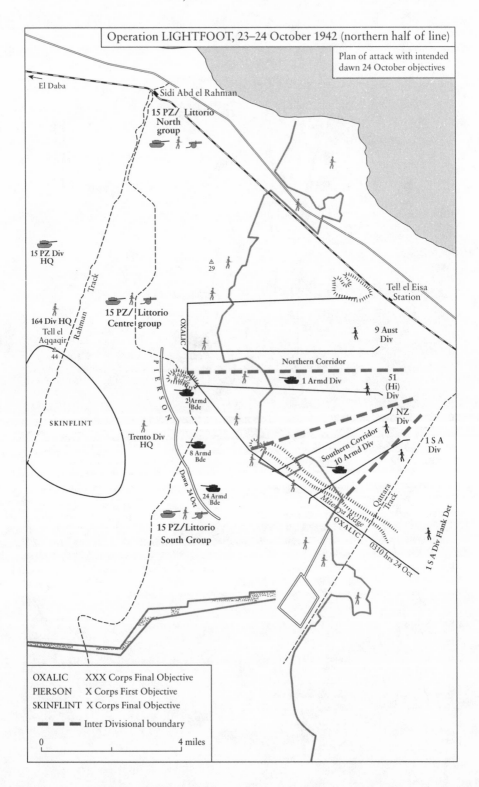

Operation LIGHTFOOT, 23–24 October 1942 (northern half of line)

Plan of attack with intended dawn 24 October objectives

El Daba

Sidi Abd el Rahman

15 PZ/ Littorio
North group

15 PZ Div
HQ

Tell el Eisa
Station

Rahman Track

△ 29

15 PZ/ Littorio
Centre group

9 Aust
Div

164 Div HQ
Tell el
Aqqaqir
△ 44

OXALIC

PIERSON

Northern Corridor

1 Armd Div

51
(Hi)
Div

2 Armd
Bde

SKINFLINT

NZ
Div

Trento Div
HQ

8 Armd
Bde

Southern Corridor
10 Armd Div

1 S A
Div

24 Armd
Bde

Dawn 24 Oct

Miteirya Ridge

Qattara Track

0310 hrs 24 Oct

1 S A Div Flank Det

15 PZ/Littorio
South Group

OXALIC

OXALIC   XXX Corps Final Objective
PIERSON   X Corps First Objective
SKINFLINT   X Corps Final Objective

– – –   Inter Divisional boundary

0   4 miles

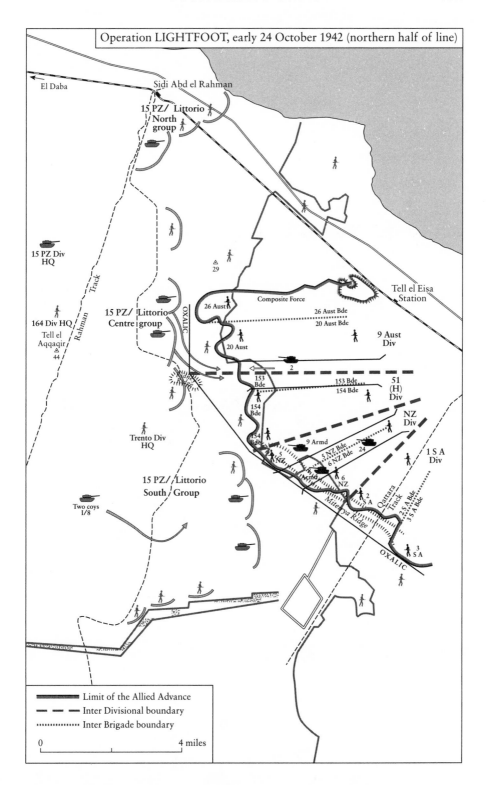

Operation LIGHTFOOT, early 24 October 1942 (northern half of line)

El Daba

Sidi Abd el Rahman

15 PZ/ Littorio
North
group

15 PZ Div
HQ

164 Div HQ

Tell el
Aqqaqir
△ 44

15 PZ/ Littorio
Centre group

Rahman Track

OXALIC

△ 29

26 Aust

Composite Force

Tell el Eisa
Station

26 Aust Bde
20 Aust Bde

9 Aust
Div

20 Aust

2

153
Bde

153 Bde
154 Bde

51
(H)
Div

154
Bde

NZ
Div

Trento Div
HQ

154
Bde

9 Armd

5 NZ Bde
6 NZ Bde

24

1 S A
Div

15 PZ/ Littorio
South Group

5
NZ

Armd

6
NZ

2
SA

Two coys
I/8

Mitenya Ridge

Qattara Track

2 S A Bde
3 S A Bde

OXALIC

3
S A

Limit of the Allied Advance
Inter Divisional boundary
Inter Brigade boundary

0   4 miles

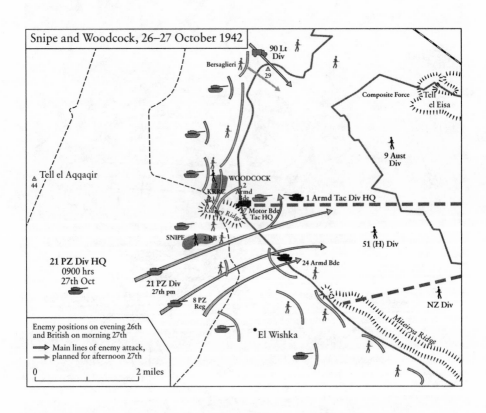

Snipe and Woodcock, 26–27 October 1942

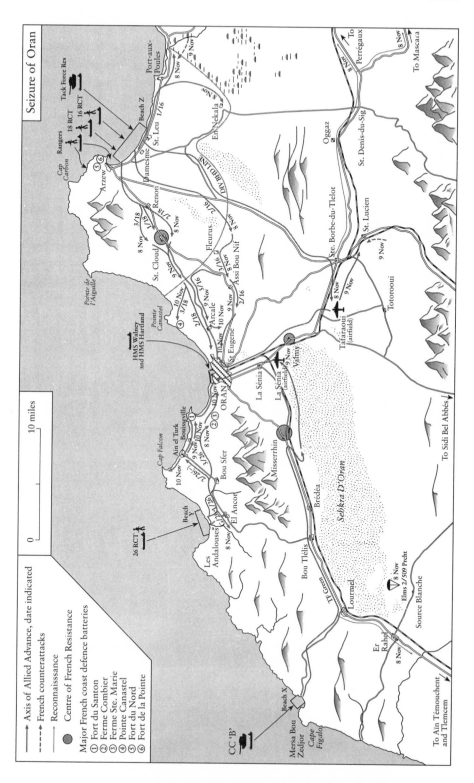

Seizure of Oran

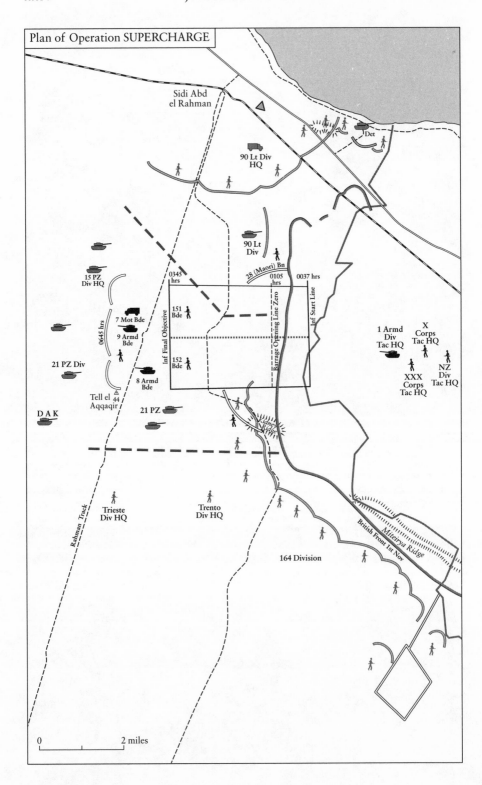

Plan of Operation SUPERCHARGE

Sidi Abd
el Rahman

Det

90 Lt Div
HQ

90 Lt
Div

28 (Maori) Bn

15 PZ
Div HQ

0345
hrs

0105
hrs

0037 hrs

Barrage Opening Line Zero

Inf Start Line

151
Bde

1 Armd
Div
Tac HQ

X
Corps
Tac HQ

7 Mot Bde

0645 hrs

9 Armd
Bde

Inf Final Objective

152
Bde

XXX
Corps
Tac HQ

NZ
Div
Tac HQ

21 PZ Div

8 Armd
Bde

Tell el
Aqqaqir

44

DAK

21 PZ

Kidney
Ridge

Trieste
Div HQ

Trento
Div HQ

Miteirya Ridge

British Front 1st Nov

Rahman Track

164 Division

0   2 miles

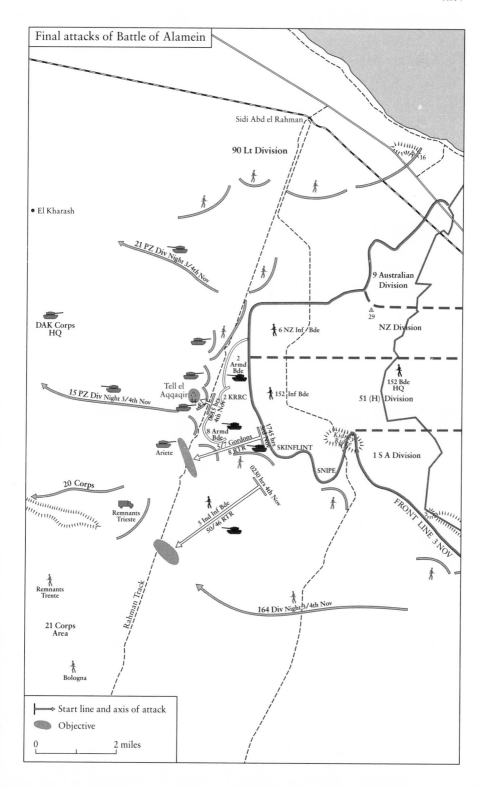

Final attacks of Battle of Alamein

Sidi Abd el Rahman

90 Lt Division

• El Kharash

21 PZ Div Night 3/4th Nov

DAK Corps HQ

15 PZ Div Night 3/4th Nov

Tell el Aqqaqir

2 Armd Bde

2 KRRC

8 Armd Bde

5/7 Gordons

8 RTR

Ariete

SKINFLINT

6 NZ Inf Bde

152 Inf Bde

1745 hrs 3rd Nov

0615 hrs 4th Nov

9 Australian Division

29

NZ Division

152 Bde HQ

51 (H) Division

Kidney Ridge

SNIPE

1 S A Division

20 Corps

Remnants Trieste

5 Ind Inf Bde

50/46 RTR

0230 hrs 4th Nov

FRONT LINE 3 NOV

Rahman Track

Remnants Trente

21 Corps Area

164 Div Night 3/4th Nov

Bologna

⊢—▷ Start line and axis of attack

⬤ Objective

0   2 miles

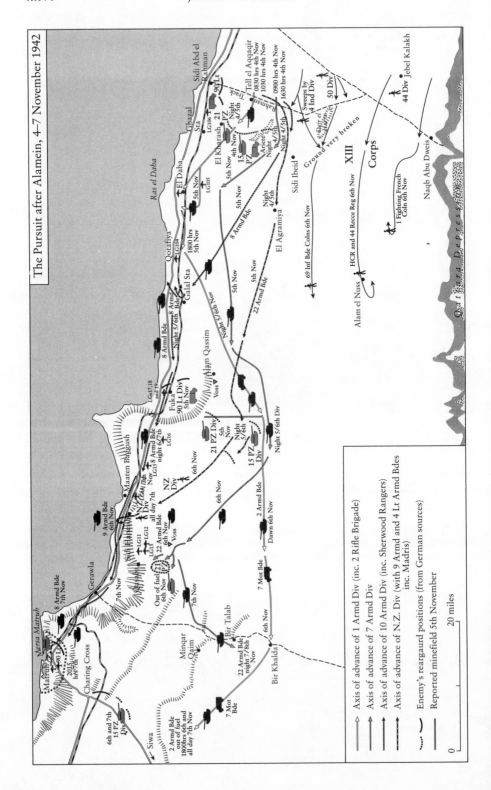

The Pursuit after Alamein, 4–7 November 1942

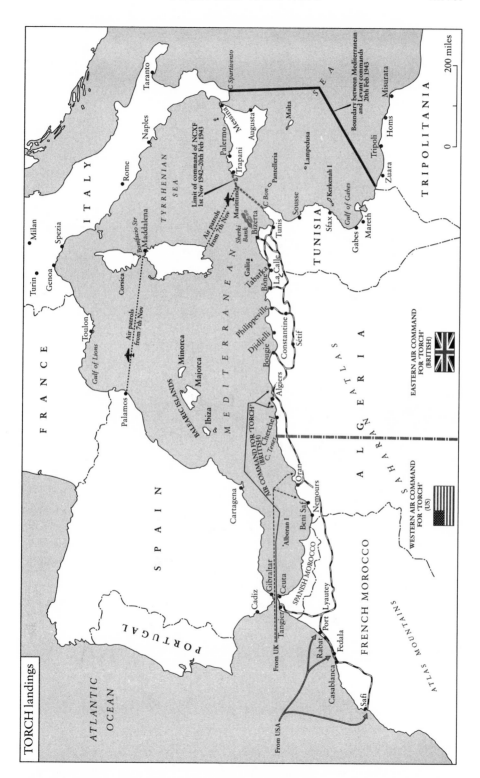

TORCH landings

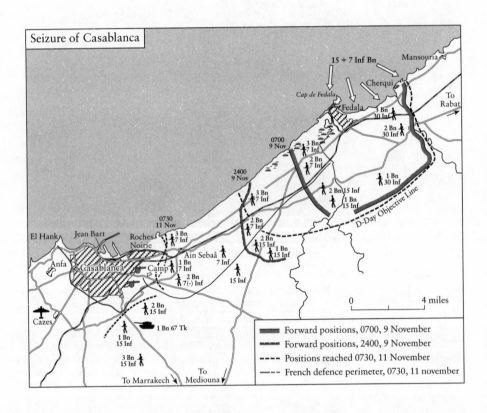

Seizure of Casablanca

15 + 7 Inf Bn

Mansouria

Cherqui

Cap de Fedala

To Rabat

Fedala

3 Bn
30 Inf

0700
9 Nov

3 Bn
7 Inf

2 Bn
30 Inf

2 Bn
7 Inf

1 Bn
30 Inf

2400
9 Nov

3 Bn
7 Inf

2 Bn 15 Inf
1 Bn
15 Inf

D-Day Objective Line

0730
11 Nov

2 Bn
7 Inf

El Hank

Jean Bart

Roches
Noirie

3 Bn
7 Inf

2 Bn
15 Inf 1 Bn
15 Inf

Anfa

Ain Sebaâ

7 Inf

Casablanca

1 Bn
7 Inf

Camp

15 Inf

2 Bn
7(-) Inf

Cazes

2 Bn
15 Inf

1 Bn 67 Tk

1 Bn
15 Inf

3 Bn
15 Inf

To
Medíouna

To Marrakech

0   4 miles

▬▬▬ Forward positions, 0700, 9 November

▬▬▬ Forward positions, 2400, 9 November

- - - Positions reached 0730, 11 November

–·–·– French defence perimeter, 0730, 11 november

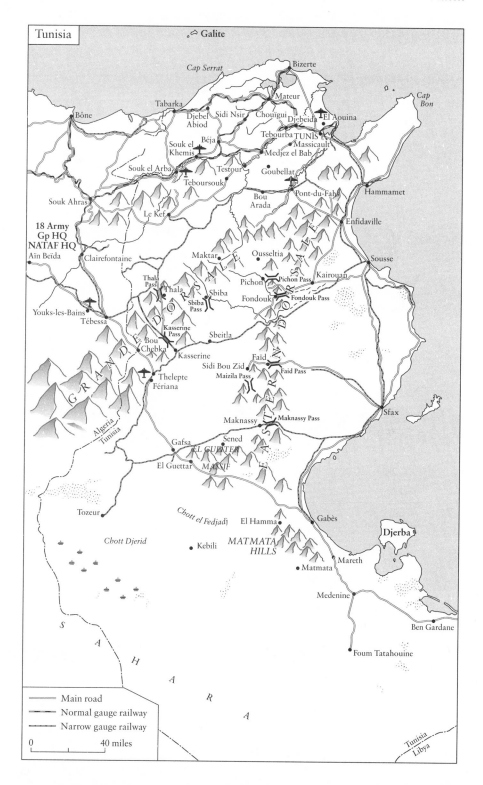

Tunisia

Galite

Cap Serrat

Bizerte

Cap Bon

Bône

Tabarka

Mateur

Sidi Nsir

Chouïgui

Djebel Abiod

Djebeïda

El Aouina

Béja

Tebourba

TUNIS

Souk el Khemis

Massicault

Medjez el Bab

Testour

Souk el Arba

Teboursouk

Goubellat

Hammamet

Souk Ahras

Bou Arada

Pont-du-Fahs

Le Kef

Enfidaville

18 Army Gp HQ NATAF HQ

Aïn Beïda

Clairefontaine

Maktar

Ousseltia

Sousse

Thala Pass

Pichon

Pichon Pass

Kairouan

Thala

Sbiba

Fondouk

Fondouk Pass

Sbiba Pass

Youks-les-Bains

Tébessa

Kasserine Pass

Sbeitla

Bou Chebka

Kasserine

Faïd

Sidi Bou Zid

Faïd Pass

Thelepte

Maizila Pass

Fériana

GRAND DORSALE

EL

Algeria

Tunisia

Maknassy

Maknassy Pass

Sfax

Gafsa

Sened

EL GUETTAR

El Guettar

MASSIF

EASTERN DORSALE

Tozeur

Chott el Fedjadj

El Hamma

Gabès

Djerba

Chott Djerid

Kebili

MATMATA HILLS

Mareth

Matmata

Medenine

S A H A R A

Ben Gardane

Foum Tatahouine

Tunisia Libya

Main road

Normal gauge railway

Narrow gauge railway

0   40 miles

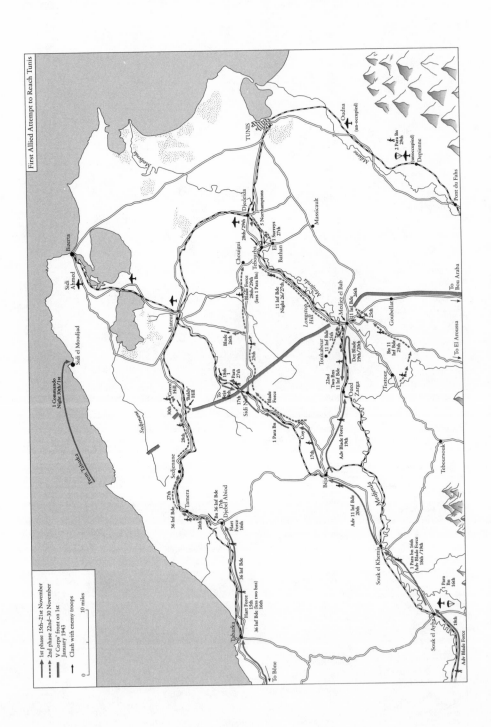

First Allied Attempt to Reach Tunis

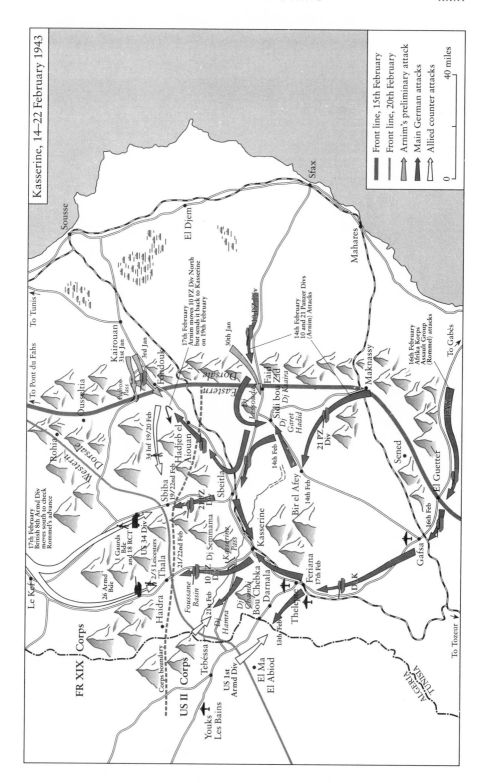

Kasserine, 14–22 February 1943

Front line, 15th February
Front line, 20th February
Arnim's preliminary attack
Main German attacks
Allied counter attacks

0   40 miles

To Tunis
Sousse
El Djem
Sfax
Mahares
To Pont du Fahs
Kairouan
31st Jan
3rd Jan
Oueslatia
Fondouk
Fondouk Pass
Eastern Dorsale
17th February
Arnim moves 10 PZ Div North
but sends it back to Kasserine
on 19th February
30th Jan
10 PZ Div
14th February
10 and 21 Panzer Divs
(Arnim) Attacks
Maknassy
16th February
Afrika Korps
Assault Group
(Rommel) attacks
To Gabès
Rohia
Western Dorsale
34 Inf 19/20 Feb
Hadjeb el Aioun
Faid
Dj Lessouda
Sidi bou Zid
Dj Ksaira
Dj
Garet
Hadid
21 PZ
Div
Sened
DAK
El Guettar
17th February
British 8th Armd Div
moves south to check
Rommel's advance
Sbiba
19/22nd Feb
21 PZ
Div
Sbeitla
14th Feb
Bir el Afey
14th Feb
14th Feb
16th Feb
Gafsa
Le Kef
1 Gaurds
Bde
and 18 RCT
US 34 Div
26 Armd
Bde
2/5 Leicesters
Thala
21/22nd Feb
Kasserine
Pass
Kasserine
Feriana
17th Feb
DAK
Haidra
Foussane
Basin
21st Feb
Dj Hamra
10 PZ
Div
Dj Semmama
Dj
Chambi
Bou Chebka
Darnala
Thelepte
13th Feb
To Tozeur
FR XIX Corps
Corps boundary
US II Corps
Tebéssa
US 1st
Armd Div
El Ma
El Abiod
ALGERIA
TUNISIA
Youks
Les Bains

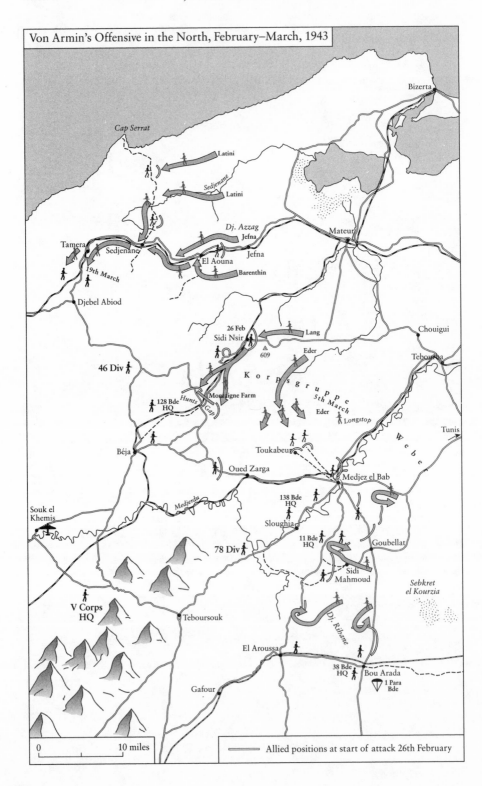

Von Armin's Offensive in the North, February–March, 1943

Bizerta

Cap Serrat

Latini

Sedjenane

Latini

Dj. Azzag

Jefna

Mateur

Tamera

Sedjenane

El Aouna

Jefna

19th March

Barenthin

Djebel Abiod

Chouigui

26 Feb

Sidi Nsir

Lang

△ 609

Eder

Teboursa

46 Div

Korpsgruppe

128 Bde
HQ

Hunts
(Gap)

Montaigne Farm

5th March

Eder

Longstop

Tunis

Béja

Toukabeur

Webe

Oued Zarga

Medjez el Bab

Souk el
Khemis

Medjerda

138 Bde
HQ

Sloughia

11 Bde
HQ

Goubellat

78 Div

Sidi
Mahmoud

Sebkret
el Kourzia

V Corps
HQ

Teboursouk

Dj. Rihane

El Aroussa

Gafour

38 Bde
HQ

Bou Arada

1 Para
Bde

0   10 miles   ———— Allied positions at start of attack 26th February

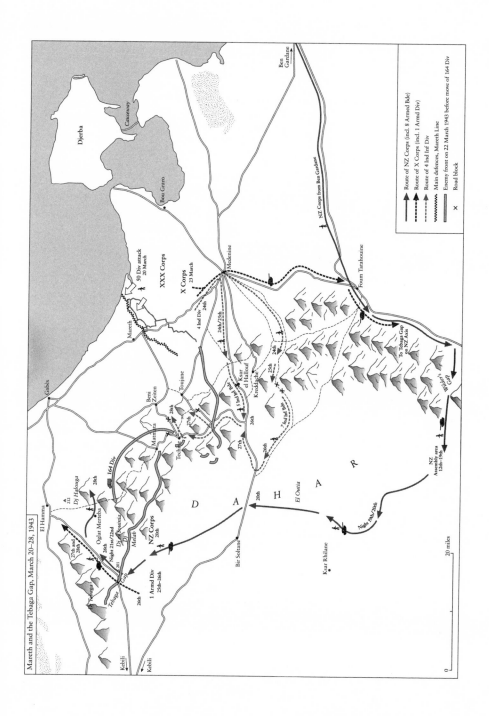

Mareth and the Tebaga Gap, March 20–28, 1943

Route of NZ Corps (incl. 8 Armed Bde)
Route of X Corps (incl. 1 Armd Div)
Route of 4 Ind Inf Div
Main defences, Mareth Line
Enemy front on 22 March 1943 before move of 164 Div
Road block

Djerba

Causeway

Bou Grara

Ben Gardane

NZ Corps from Ben Gardane

Medenine

50 Div attack
20 March

XXX Corps

X Corps
23 March

Foum Tatahouine

Mareth

4 Ind Div

24th

24th/25th

To Tebaga Gap
on NZ Axis

Gabes

Toujane

Beni
Zeiten

Ksar
el Hallouf

Kreddache

24th

25th

Wilder's Gap

5 Ind Inf Bde

7 Ind Inf Bde

26th

27th

26th

27th

26th

NZ
Assembly area
12th–19th

El Hamma

Dj Haïouga

112

Oglat Merteba

28th

164 Div

Matmata

Techine

D   A   H   A   R

El Outia

20th

Bir Soltane

Night 19th/20th

Ksar Rhilane

Night 21st/22nd

26th

201

Dj Soultni

Dj Melab

NZ Corps

20th

27th and
28th

Tebaga

201

Tebaga Gap

1 Armd Div
25th–26th

26th

Kebili

Kebili

0   20 miles

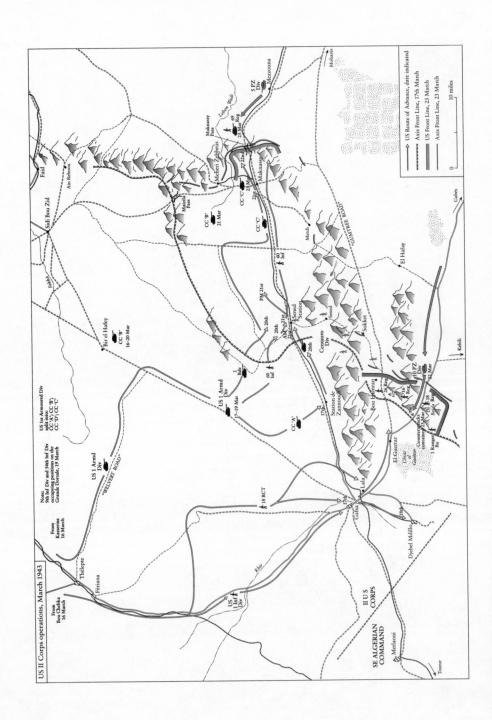

US II Corps operations, March 1943

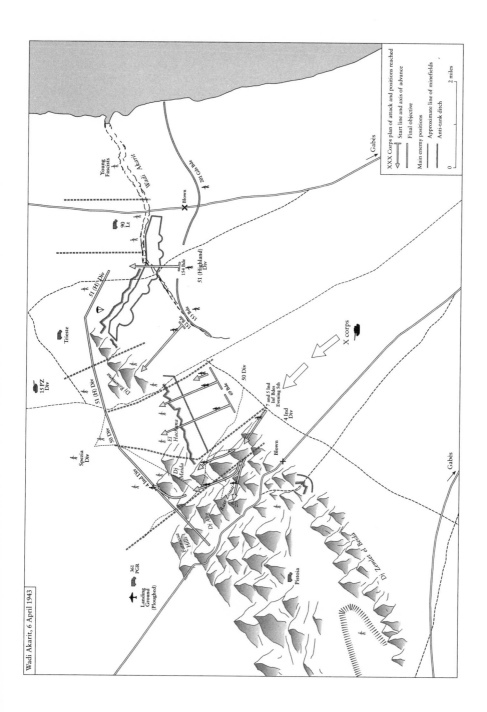

Wadi Akarit, 6 April 1943

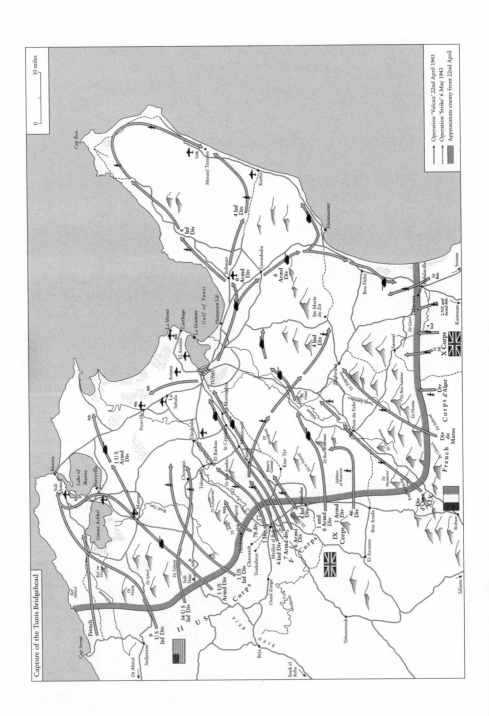

Capture of the Tunis Bridgehead

PRINCIPAL PERSONALITIES
FEATURED IN THE BOOK

(Note: ranks given are those at the end of
the North African campaign.)

Private Johnny Bain—British (Hertfordshire)

B Company, 5/7 Gordon Highlanders, 153rd Highland Brigade, 51st Highland Division, XXX Corps, Eighth Army. Johnny Bain arrived in the Middle East in September 1942.

Squadron Leader Tony Bartley—British (London)

Commanding officer of 111 Squadron, flying Spitfires. Tony arrived in North Africa shortly after the TORCH Landings and commanded 111 Squadron until the tour expired. He returned to England in January 1943.

Cecil Beaton—British (Wiltshire)

Photographer working for the Ministry of Information and in the Middle East March–July 1942, working principally on behalf of the RAF.

Privates First Class Henry and Tom Bowles—American (Alabama)

18th Infantry Regiment, 1st Infantry Division, US II Corps, First Army. Identical twins, Henry and Tom Bowles volunteered to join the Army before Pearl Harbor. Henry served in HQ Company, Tom in G Company.

Sergeant Sam Bradshaw—British (Merseyside)

B Squadron, B Echelon, 6th Royal Tank Regiment, 7th Armoured Division, XIII Corps, Eighth Army. Sam Bradshaw joined the army in 1938 and arrived in North Africa in 1940. He served in all the major engagements right up to the Battle of Alamein, in October 1942.

Bombardier Lieutenant Ralph Burbridge—American (Missouri)

Bombardier of the "All American," 97th Bombardment Group. Ralph Burbridge and the crew of the All American were one of the first B-17 crews to reach England in 1942, and flew in the first raid by the 97th over Europe in August 1942. The group was posted to North Africa in November 1942.

Commander Harry S. Butcher—American (Iowa)

Old friend and Naval Aide to General Dwight D. Eisenhower. Butcher kept a diary throughout the planning of Operation TORCH and during the North Africa campaign.

Lieutenant Willie Chapman—American (Texas)

415 Squadron, 98th Heavy Bombardment Group, USAAF. Willie Chapman joined the US Army Air Force in July 1941, and arrived in the Middle East in August 1942.

Flight Lieutenant Bryan Colston—British (London)

225 Squadron, 242 Group, RAF. Joined the RAF in 1940 and on completing training was posted to 225 Army Support Squadron. Reached North Africa in November 1942.

Private Petrus Dhlamini—Zulu (Natal)

Regiment President Steyn, 1st South African Division, XXX Corps, Eighth Army. Petrus Dhlamini reached the Middle East in June 1942 and returned home in January 1943.

Major Stanley Christopherson—British (London)

Nottinghamshire Sherwood Rangers Yeomanry, 8th Armoured Brigade, 10th Armoured Division, X Corps, Eighth Army. Stanley Christopherson served in the yeomanry before the war and was called up on the outbreak of war in September 1939.

Squadron Leader Billy Drake—British (London)

112 Squadron, 239 Wing, Desert Air Force. Billy reached North Africa in May 1942, and took over command of 112 Squadron until being posted in January 1943

Sergeant Bill Eadie—South African (Durban)

Brigade HQ, 2nd South African Infantry Brigade, 1st South African Division. Bill dropped rank from sergeant to corporal and switched regiments in order to serve in North Africa. He arrived in autumn 1941, and remained there until the division returned home to South Africa in January 1943

Lieutenant Edward "Duke" Ellington—American (Indiana)

65th Fighter Squadron, 57th Fighter Group. Duke Ellington was with the first American fighter pilots to reach North Africa, joining the RAF's Desert Air Force in August 1942.

Ray Ellis—British (Nottinghamshire)

425 Battery, South Notts Hussars, Royal Horse Artillery. Joined the regiment in 1939, reaching the Middle East in January 1940.

Lieutenant Sergeant Warren "Bing" Evans—American (South Dakota)

E Company, 1st Ranger Battalion, US II Corps, First Army; later Battalion Sergeant-Major, and then, in April 1942, was given a battlefield commission and appointed company commander in newly formed 3rd Ranger Battalion. Bing Evans joined the Rangers, the US Army's first Special Forces, in February 1942.

Flying Officer John "Johnnie" Fairbairn—British (Hertfordshire)

73 Squadron (Hurricanes). John Fairbairn was called up in 1940 and joined the RAF, becoming a fighter pilot. He reached North Africa in April 1942 and was posted to 73 Squadron in May 1942.

Private Joe Furayter—American (Pennsylvania)

Gunner with the 5th Field Artillery Battalion, Joe arrived in North Africa with the 1st Infantry Division and remained in North Africa until the end of the campaign.

Colonel John Frost—British (born Poona, India)

Commanding officer 2nd Parachute Battalion, First Army. Frost led the battalion from their arrival in North Africa shortly after the TORCH Landings until the end of the campaign in May 1943.

Sergeant Harold Harper—British (Nottinghamshire)

426 Battery and then 520 Battery, South Notts Hussars, RHA; July 1942, 107 Battery, 7 Medium Regiment, RA. Joined South Notts Hussars in 1939, reaching the Middle East in January 1940.

Lieutenant Stephen Hastings—British (London)

2nd Battalion Scots Guards and SAS. Commissioned into Scots Guards in 1939, joining Eighth Army in early 1941. Joined SAS in May 1942.

Lieutenant Margaret Hornback—American (Kentucky)

A nurse with the 48th Surgical Hospital (later 128th Evacuation Hospital), she landed with the 1st Infantry Division and remained in North Africa until the end of the campaign.

Lieutenant-Colonel Hamilton Howze—American (New York)

Assistant Chief of Staff G-3, HQ 1st Armored Division, US II Corps, First Army. Hamilton Howze reached North Africa as part of the TORCH Landings in November 1942. In April he became attached to the 81st Reconnaissance Battalion, then on 3 May took over command of the 2nd Battalion 13th Armored Regiment.

Pilot Officer Christopher Lee—British (London)

Intelligence Officer with 37 Squadron, 231 Wing, 205 Group, RAF Western Desert Air Force.

Corporal Joe Madeley—Australian (New South Wales)

A Company, 2/13 Battalion, 9th Australian Division, XXX Corps, Eighth Army. Joe Madeley reached the Middle East in 1941.

Rifleman Sergeant Albert Martin—British (London)

A Company, 2nd Battalion Rifle Brigade, 7th Motor Brigade, X Corps, Eighth Army. An Eastender, Albert Martin arrived in North Africa

in September 1940, and fought with the Rifle Brigade throughout the
three years the Desert Rats were in North Africa.

Captain Carol Mather—British (Cheshire)

SAS (L Detachment), Middle East Forces. Carol Mather reached
Egypt in March 1941, and after serving with the Commandos and GHQ
Liaison Squadron, joined the SAS in May 1942.

Sergeant Mangal Singh—Indian (Punjab)

4th Indian Division Signals Regiment, XXX Corps, Eighth Army.
Joined the Indian Army in 1936 and arrived in North Africa in November
1941.

Captain Pierre Messmer—French (Paris)

Joined the 13 DBLE in Britain after the fall of France and then went
with them to West Africa, East Africa, Syria and the Middle East. Reached
Bir Hacheim, south of the Gazala Line, in February 1942.

Lieutenant Peter Moore—British (Leicestershire)

B Company, 2/5 Battalion Leicester Regiment, 46 (North Midlands)
Division, V Corps, First Army. Peter Moore joined the army in 1941 and
was commissioned the following year. The battalion reached North Africa
in January 1943.

Alan Moorehead—Australian (South Australia)

Worked for the London *Daily Express*, and arrived in North Africa in
May 1940, just before the Italians declared war.

Rifleman Nainabahadur Pun—Nepali (Pokhara)

1/2 Battalion King Edward VII's Own Gurkha Rifles, 4th Indian Division, XXX Corps, Eighth Army. Nainabadr Pun joined the Gurkhas in
1941 and reached North Africa in 1942.

Captain Nigel Nicolson—British (Kent)

3rd Battalion, Grenadier Guards, 78th Infantry Division, V Corps,
First Army. Nigel Nicolson joined the army in 1940, and arrived in Tunisia
in January 1943.

Private Maiki Parkinson—New Zealander (Maori)

C Company, 28th (Maori) Battalion, 5th New Zealand Infantry Brigade,
XXX Corps, Eighth Army. Maiki Parkinson volunteered to join the 28th
Battalion, even though he was only seventeen at the time, and so four years
under age. He reached North Africa in August 1942.

Lieutenant Randolph Paulsen—American (New York)

Reached North Africa with the Western Task Force direct from America.
Initially with the 3rd Infantry Division, Randolph Paulsen joined G Company, 18th Infantry Regiment, 1st Infantry Division, US II Corps, First Army
in April 1943.

Ernie Pyle—American (Indiana)

A journalist with the *Washington Daily News,* Ernie Pyle began his daily column about "ordinary folk" before the war. He arrived in North Africa with the first American troops on 8 November, 1942.

Lieutenant James E. Reed—American (Tennessee)

Flight Lieutenant with 59th Fighter Squadron, 33rd Fighter Group. Landed on North Africa as part of the TORCH Landings, November 1942.

Private Ray Saidel—American (New Hampshire)

Private with G Company, 1st Armored Regiment, 1st Armored Division, II US Corps, First Army. Joined his regiment as a replacement in February 1943.

Sophie Tarnawska—Polish

Sophie Tarnawska reached Cairo via Poland and Greece, where she worked for the Polish Red Cross.

Flight Lieutenant "Tommy" Thompson—British (Norfolk)

Flight Commander with 73 Squadron flying Hurricane night fighters. Tommy Thompson flew in the Battle of Britain and on Malta with 249 Squadron, and was posted to 73 Squadron in September 1942.

Susan Travers—British (Devon)

Driver with the 13 DBLE (French Foreign Legion). Susan went to West Africa with the Free French, later following them to East Africa, Syria, and then, at the end of 1941, to the Middle East. She reached the front line at Bir Hacheim in February 1942.

Sergeant Edward "Bucky" Walters—American (New Jersey)

H Company, 135th Infantry Regiment, 34th Infantry Division, US II Corps, First Army. Bucky Walters was drafted in 1941, and reached North Africa on New Year's Day, 1943.

Lieutenant Ronnie Ward—British (Yorkshire)

Officer on the Royal Navy submarine HMS *Safari.* Ronnie Ward joined the crew as 4th Officer in July 1942. *Safari* joined the 1st Submarine Flotilla in August 1942, and then was attached to the 10th Submarine Flotilla in September 1942, before returning to the 1st Flotilla in January 1943.

Lieutenant Jack "Cobber" Weinronk—South African (Port Elizabeth)

Boston pilot with 3 SAAF Squadron; joined the squadron in July 1942 and flew with them until the end of the campaign.

GUIDE TO PRINCIPAL COMMANDERS FEATURED IN THE BOOK

(ranks at the end of service in North Africa)

Major-General Terry Allen—American

Commander of US 1st Infantry Division, the "Big Red One" from the TORCH Landing until the end of the campaign in Tunisia in May 1943

Lieutenant-General Charles Allfrey—British

Commander of V Corps in Tunisia from his arrival in December 1942. Remained so at the end of the campaign.

General Sir Harold Alexander—Irish

Commander-in-chief, Middle East, August 1942–February 1943, then Commander 18th Army Group, and Deputy Supreme Commander under General Dwight D. Eisenhower, February 1943.

General H. H. "Hap" Arnold—American

Chief of staff, US Army Air Force.

General Sir Claude Auchinleck—British

Commander-in-chief Middle East until August 1942, and also commander British Eighth Army June–August 1942.

Major-General Walter Bedell-Smith—American

Secretary to the US chiefs of staff February–August 1943, then Eisenhower's chief of staff.

Major-General Lewis Brereton—American

Commander US Army Middle East Air Force August 1942. From November 1942, commander 9th Air Force.

General Sir Alan Brooke—British

As Chief of the Imperial General Staff, Britain's most senior commander.

Lieutenant-General Mark "Wayne" Clark—American

Deputy commander-in-chief US Army Forces in Europe and then, for the TORCH Landing, deputy commander-in-chief Allied Expeditionary Force Mediterranean. From 1943, commanding general US 5th Army.

Air Marshal Sir Arthur "Mary" Coningham—New Zealander (born Australia)

Officer commanding RAF Western Desert Air Force and then, from February 1943, the North African Tactical Air Force.

Major-General Crocker—British

Commander of British IX Corps from its arrival in Tunisia in March 1943. Wounded during Operation VULCAN, he handed over command to General Horrocks for the final offensive.

Admiral Sir Andrew Cunningham—British

Commander-in-chief of the Mediterranean Fleet until April 1942, when appointed head of British Admiralty Delegation, Washington DC. Made Naval Commander-in-Chief, Allied Expeditionary Force (NCXF) in October 1942.

Admiral Francois Darlan—French

Commander-in-chief Vichy French Armistice Army until November 1942; the High Commissioner for French North Africa until assassination, December 24, 1942.

Major-General Freddie De Guingand—British

Director of Military Intelligence June 1942; chief of staff to Auchinleck, July 1942; chief of staff to Montgomery from August 1942.

General Dwight D. Eisenhower—American

Commander-in-chief Allied Expeditionary Force for TORCH; later appointed supreme Allied commander North Africa in February 1943.

Air Commodore Tommy Elmhirst—British

Officer in command of administration, the Desert Air Force, and also Coningham's deputy until he and Coningham took over the First Tactical Air Force in February 1943.

Major-General Vyvyan Evelegh—British

Commanding officer of 78th Division in Tunisia from the TORCH Landings and later CO of 6th Armoured Division.

Lieutenant-General Lloyd Fredendall—American

Commander of US II Corps from TORCH until March 1943.

Lieutenant-General Freyberg—New Zealander

Commander 2nd New Zealand Division and, from March 1943, New Zealand Corps.

Major-General Alec Gatehouse—British

Commander 10th Armoured Division, July–November 1942

General Henri Honore Giraud—French

Commander-in-chief French Forces in North Africa, November–December 1942, then Civil and military governor French North and West Africa.

Lieutenant-General "Strafer" Gott—British
Commander of British XIII Corps from Gazala until August 1942. Briefly commander of Eighth Army until death on 6 August, 1942.

Major-General John Harding—British
Director of Military Training, July 1942; commander 7th Armoured Division from September 1942.

Major-General Ernest Harmon—American
Commander Southern Landing Force (Safi), then commander 2nd Armored Division and, from April 1943, commander 1st Armored Division.

Lieutenant-General Brian Horrocks—British
Commander British XIII Corps from September 1942. From November 1942, took over command of X Corps.

General Alphonse Juin—French
Commander-in-chief French forces in North Africa, November 1942.

Brigadier Howard Kippenberger—New Zealand
Commander 5th New Zealand Brigade throughout campaign.

General Marie-Pierre Koenig—French
Commander 1st Free French Brigade (Fighting French Brigade) throughout campaign.

General Louis-Marie Koeltz—French
Commander French XIX Corps.

Brigadier-General Laurence Kuter—American
Assistant secretary War Department general staff, November 1941–March 1942; deputy chief of the Air Staff, March–October 1942; commander 1st Bombardment Group, October 1942–January 1943; commander Allied Tactical Air Force, January–February 1943; Deputy-Commander NATAF, February 1943.

Lieutenant-General Oliver Leese—British
Commander XXX Corps, August 1942 through to end of campaign.

Major-General Herbert Lumsden—British
Commander 1st Armoured Division, and then, from August–November 1942, commander of XXX Corps.

General George Marshall—American
Chief of staff, United States Army.

Major-General Frank Messervy—British
Commander 7th Armoured Division, March–June 1942.

General Sir Bernard L. Montgomery—British
Commander of British Eighth Army from August 1942.

Lieutenant-General Leslie Morshead—Australian
Commander 9th Australian Division.

Admiral Lord Louis Mountbatten—British
    Chief Officer of Combined Operations; joined Chiefs of Staff Committee, March 1942.

Lieutenant-General Willoughby Norrie—British
    Commander of XXX Corps until July 1942.

Brigadier-General Lunsford Oliver—American
    American commander of Combat Command B, 1st Armored Division for the TORCH Landings.

Lieutenant-General George S. Patton—American
    Commander of Western Task Force for the TORCH Landings. Appointed commanding officer of US II Corps March–April, 1943.

Major-General Dan Pienaar—South African
    Commander of 1st South African Division at Gazala and Alamein.

Air Marshal Sir Charles Portal—British
    Chief of the Air Staff.

Major-General William Ramsden—British
    Commander 50th Division, and then, commander XXX Corps, July–August 1942.

Lieutenant-General Neil Ritchie—British
    Commander of Eighth Army November 1941–end of June 1942.

Brigadier-General Paul Robinett—American
    Commander of Combat Command B (CC B), 1st Armored Division throughout Tunisian campaign.

Major-General Charles "Doc" Ryder
    Commander 34th "Red Bull" Division throughout campaign.

General Carl "Tooey" Spaatz
    Commander US 8th Air Force, May–December, 1942; commander American Air Forces European Theater, July 1942; commander US 12th Air Force and Allied Air Forces in Northwest Africa, December 1942–February; commander Allied Northwest African Air Forces, February 1943.

Air Marshal Sir Arthur Tedder—British
    AOC-in-C RAF Middle East, and from February 1943, Allied Commander-in-Chief Mediterranean Air Command.

Major-General Lucian Truscott—American
    American representative at Combined Operations HQ, May 1942; commander Northern Landing Force (Port Lyautey), and then field deputy to the Commander-in-Chief Allied Expeditionary Forces.

Major-General Francis Tuker—British
    Commander of the Fourth Indian Division. Took over in December 1941 and was still in charge at the end of the North African campaign in May 1943.

Major-General Orlando Ward—American
   Commander of the 1st Armored Division 1942–April 1943.
Air Marshal Sir William Welsh—British
   Commander RAF Eastern Air Command, Northwest Africa, November 1942–February 1943.

Letter from Lieutenant Paul Lunn-Rockliffe, written on the day the war ended in North Africa.

13 May 43
Dear Margaret,
   I find it very difficult to write about David as we were such good friends and got on so well together. His loss leaves a big gap in the Battery, where, beside his undoubted capabilities, he was most popular with officers and men alike. Death can be regarded as a catastrophe, but I prefer the old-fashioned outlook regarding it as an insignificant transition to another life and world. I know many find that faith very comforting, especially in battle. I mention this philosophy in case it is of any comfort as I fully realise that the hardest lot of all is for those left at home.
   I was the last to see David. We were together on the assault of "Longstop" on Good Friday. Casualties were heavy—several of our parties were wounded and killed, but David got to the top of the hill with me. I last saw him taking shelter in a trench. I was 30–40 yards away behind some rocks. When the fire had reduced I tried to contact him but failed at first. Later I found him. David's end had been instantaneous—shot through the head. His grave, with others, is up in the hills of Longstop. It has been cared for and is marked with a cross Dick had specially made. The campaign is over now and looking back, Good Friday and thereabouts saw some of the heaviest fighting. We lost 3 other officers at the same time.
   I never was very good at writing, but if you want any more details or to know anything about David's efforts in the previous part of the campaign then I shall endeavour to supply them. For the time being accept all my sympathy.

Yours very sincerely,
Paul Lunn-Rockcliffe

Part of a letter from Lieutenant Margaret Hornback, 128th Surgical Hospital, US Army Nurse Corps, Tunisia, to her childhood friend in Shelbyville, Kentucky, November 1943.

. . . I don't hear from Andy very often. He's a sensitive sort of a boy and gets terribly depressed during battle. Some of his best pals and mine have gone on. It will be many years before we know the depth of the wounds to these kids' souls. They'll be longer standing, I know, than those we treat with sulfabromide. They have had it pretty rough and when you mention battle hazards, you've only just begun. There is continual rain, cold and dirt, cold food etcetera, with only your thought for company. I feel better almost when he's in battle. He's a captain of artillery and when in action, his thoughts are kept occupied. That picture doesn't do him justice but he is good looking anyhow. To me it seems we as a nation and as individuals have been terribly short sighted, concerned with small things and letting them loom larger. I sometimes think we're as much to blame for this mess . . . we at least knew better, but so engrossed were we in our own affairs that we didn't help much. May gracious God give us the humility and wisdom to let Him use us in fashioning a lasting peace. I don't believe civilization can survive another war.

INTRODUCTION

IN NOVEMBER 2003, George W. Bush was preparing to embark on the first state visit to Britain of an American president, an occasion that was seen as an opportunity to reaffirm the Anglo-US nexus. Before his departure, the president invited a few British journalists into the Oval Office, where the bronze bust of Winston Churchill by Sir Jacob Epstein—loaned by the current Prime Minister, Tony Blair—was on display. "I thought he was a clear thinker," Bush said of Churchill to the journalists assembled before him, "the kind of guy that stood tough when you needed to stand tough; he represented values that both countries hold dear—the value of freedom, the belief in democracy, [and the] human dignity of every person."

Bush also likes to point out that he uses a desk that was once used by America's wartime leader, President Franklin D. Roosevelt; as the two nations have stood shoulder to shoulder once more, Bush has drawn inspiration from the part both Roosevelt and Churchill played in forging this alliance and the "moral leadership" he believes they both demonstrated.

Bush's fascination with Churchill is telling. It would be inconceivable for an American president to have the bust of any other national leader on his desk. It was Churchill himself who first openly talked of a "special relationship" between America and Britain, during his famous Iron Curtain speech of 1946. Yet, however deeply entwined many may believe the two nations to be, the truth is that the foundations of this alliance were laid down only comparatively recently, during the period outlined in this book. Before the Second World War, it would also have been unthinkable for an American president to have gazed at the bust of a British prime minister for inspiration. Until then, Britain was still seen by most Americans as the old enemy, the evil empire that had wished to stifle the American settlers under the yoke of imperialism. Britain was also the nation against which the United States fought its first two wars. In classrooms from Connecticut to California, schoolchildren were taught that the British redcoats had been the bad guys, the oppressors of freedom. True, the two nations had come together—briefly—during the First World War, but American troops entered the fray only at the end of that bitter conflict and even then were commanded by Americans only. There was little unity of command on the Western Front. Furthermore, Britain and America were culturally worlds apart, despite the link of a common language; there was no sense of an "anglosphere" existing in 1939.

This point needs to be borne in mind when considering the birth of the Anglo-US alliance. There was much suspicion between the leaders and commanders of both nations and while there were undoubtedly considerable disagreements, the success of their partnership was, unquestionably, an extraordinary achievement.

Much has rightly been made of the close partnership of President Roosevelt and Prime Minister Winston Churchill; their friendship and mutual understanding was crucial to the success of Allied fortunes, yet considerable credit needs to be given to the military commanders, General Dwight D. Eisenhower especially, for establishing a joint command structure and unity of purpose between two nations that was unprecedented in history. Significantly, President Bush also has a bust of Eisenhower in the Oval Office, the man who led the first major Anglo-US combined operation—the invasion of Northwest Africa in November 1942—and who later became the Allied Supreme Commander.

The relationship has been tested since Churchill's speech of 1946: during the Suez Crisis of 1956, and again when Britain resisted pressure to send troops to Vietnam. The US was angered by Britain's withdrawal from the Far East during the 1960s, while British concerns over the US invasion of Grenada in 1983 were ignored. Nonetheless, for over sixty years, America has had no greater friend within Europe, and the two nations have, in recent years—in Iraq, in the Balkans, and in Afghanistan—rekindled the military alliance that was forged in 1942–43.

Studies of the North African campaign have traditionally been hindered by national bias. British historians have tended to give the impression that the fighting there was all over half an hour after the end of the Battle of Alamein in November 1942, the first decisive Allied victory on land against the Axis. American historians, on the other hand, have somewhat blanked any military operations in North Africa *prior* to November 1942, when US troops landed in Northwest Africa. Few realize that there were a number of American forces helping the British in the Western Desert of Egypt and Libya, or that they made a considerable contribution to the victory at Alamein. Similarly, many Americans could be forgiven for thinking the war in Northwest Africa was an entirely American show. Our preoccupation with the subsequent D-Day landings and the campaign in Northwest Europe has also tended to belittle the Allied achievements earlier in the war.

Yet our knowledge of what was to follow should not cloud our judgment of what was a critical period of the war. May–June 1942 marked the nadir of Allied fortunes in the war against Germany and Italy. America was still a comparatively young nation, ill-prepared for the fight ahead, while Britain, for all her experience and two-hundred-year empire, was also woefully equipped for the kind of warfare Germany had developed. Only when the extent of these deficiencies are examined can the true scale of the remarkable turn-around that followed be properly appreciated. And this is the point: Allied fortunes turned only once Britain and the United States started to work closely together, and this only began in earnest during the summer of 1942. Materially, America's contribution to the British campaign against Rommel in the Middle East cannot be underestimated, but it is also worth pointing out that at the time, the TORCH Landings in Northwest Africa in November 1942 were the biggest seaborne invasion the world had ever seen. And they were planned and put into operation in just three months across thousands of miles of hostile sea.

It is also worth remembering that for all the trials and tribulations that followed the TORCH Landings, by the time victory was finally achieved in May 1943, the Allies had reclaimed all of North Africa and had captured *a quarter of a million men,* more than the total number of troops in the US Army in 1939, and more than were captured at the great Russian victory of Stalingrad. Significant tactical and doctrinal developments had also been made, developments that were carried through to Sicily, Italy, and Normandy. The use of air power in support of ground forces, as still used in Iraq and Afghanistan today, were developed during this period in North Africa; so too were many of the command structures.

This is why this critical period from the summer of 1942 to May 1943 is so important. In the corridors and offices of Washington and London, and in the sand, mud, and mountains of North Africa, one of the great political and military alliances was born, an alliance that has had a lasting and profound effect upon the history of the world.

James Holland
Wiltshire, England, May, 2005

PROLOGUE

Sidi Rezegh, Libya, November 1941

A LITTLE AFTER 6 AM, Friday, 21 November, 1941. Reveille for the men of the 6 Royal Tank Regiment. Trooper Sam Bradshaw was awake instantly. It was still dark, and cold too, in the encampment. The other men of the regiment were stretching, stiffly getting to their feet and picking up their blankets. Surrounding the camp were their tanks, fifty-two in all, their barrels pointing outward and forming a temporary steel barricade. This was the leaguer, as useful to the British Eighth Army now as they had been in the days of covered wagons.

In equally time-honored fashion, a camp still needed guards through the night, and each troop of fifteen men would take it in turns to walk around their tanks in pairs, armed with pistols and a Thompson submachine gun, listening and straining their eyes for any sign of trouble. This was known as "Prowler Guard," and the night before Sam had been on duty with a friend of his called Wilkinson. They'd lived close to each other back home in Crosby, a small town near Liverpool on the Lancashire coast, and had even joined their territorial unit on the same evening on 1 September, 1939, two days before war had been declared. Wilkinson's mother was German, a fact he had always kept closely guarded; he'd also never told anyone that he spoke the language too, and Sam was certainly not going to betray that secret. But that night, as they'd walked out ahead of their tanks, they'd heard the sound of digging, of picks hitting the rock, and voices too. In the stillness of the night it could be hard to tell distances, but Sam guessed they were coming from no more than six hundred yards. "They're Germans," Wilkinson whispered to Sam. "That's a German NCO giving instructions." Sam had hurried back to wake the troop officer but had been told to go back to guard duty and not to worry. But Sam *had* worried—and with reason. Before dawn, the newly arrived enemy troops, now dug in ahead of them, had opened fire with mortars and mobile 50mm anti-tank guns. It had caused pandemonium: an ammunition truck was hit and blew up, and in the confusion one of their tanks moved out of line and was hit by one of their own shells. Lieutenant Hancock and two of his crew had been killed. By 9:30 AM, the regiment was withdrawing to the south.

They had then spent that day, 20 November, patrolling the western edge of the airfield they'd captured the day before. Artillery duels had continued throughout the morning and afternoon, shells whistling across the sky, and although B echelon, the regiment's supply unit, was sent well back to the rear, it had later come under attack from a number of Stuka dive-bombers. Sam's troop from B Squadron had been busy for much of the day, but this was not the major action. That was still to come.

Sam had discovered just what that would be at a briefing later that evening. Few of the men were told about battle plans, but as a tank commander, Sam was put in the picture despite being only a trooper in the ranks. As he'd suspected, they would be going into battle the following morning. Their task was to be twofold: firstly, they were to help the 2nd Rifle Brigade secure the enemy lines that ran along the ridge west-east to their north, all the way to the large white Bedouin tomb known as the mosque. Having done that, they were to drive over the lines and drop down the other side of the ridge, a fairly steep slope of some fifty feet, into the valley and across the desert track known as the Trigh Capuzzo toward Ed Duda. There, if all went according to plan, they were to link up with the troops breaking out of the besieged seaport of Tobruk.

Sam had pulled the short straw that night: Prowler Guard at 2 AM, or "Dead Man's Hour" as they called it—the time of night when their exhausted bodies should be sleeping their deepest. Not that he found it easy to sleep the night before battle, no matter how tired. It had been quiet, though, in their corner of the desert that night. Nothing had stirred. Twenty miles away to the northwest, however, he could see Tobruk being bombed. The sky was lit with orange flashes, and then moments later he heard the distant crump of explosions and anti-aircraft fire as the sound carried its way across the empty desert air. He thought of all the Allied troops trapped there, as they had been for two hundred and forty days. "Don't worry," he thought, "we'll have you out of there tomorrow."

Returning to his bedding within the square of the leaguer, Sam struggled to get back to sleep. Too much nervous energy. In a few hours they would be joining battle again, and God only knew what that would bring.

It was now 6:15 AM on the morning of the twenty-first, and the camp was alive once more. The air was still dark, sharp, and fresh. Sam could see his breath in the day's first glimmer of light; he'd slept fully clothed and wearing his greatcoat. He kept it on now, as he walked over to his tank. The dull metal glistened with morning dew and Sam picked up his towel, now sodden. This was something of a ritual—a damp towel always proved a Godsend later in the day, for although in November temperatures remained cool throughout the day, it didn't take long for the inside of a tank to turn as hot as an oven.

His tank was called *Ferret*. They all had a name, and all began with the letter F: *Felicity, Fearless, Flippant*. The reason for this was simple: they were the 6th Royal Tank Regiment and F was the sixth letter in the alphabet. *Ferret*, like all the other tanks in the regiment, was a Nuffield A15 Crusader. Certainly it was sleek, and, as tanks went, speedy and nimble enough to deserve the name. But what advantage it had in speed, it lost in armament. The two-pounder main gun and Besa machine gun were adequate weapons so long as they didn't come up against German Mark IV tanks, with their 75mm gun, or the dreaded 88mm anti-aircraft gun, adopted to great effect by the Germans in an anti-tank capacity. Both had greater range, and could fire larger shells with greater velocity than either the Crusader or any other British tank. In practical terms, this meant they could knock out a Crusader with ease at 2000 yards, while the Crusader had to get within 600 to make any kind of impression. Such was the velocity of the 88mm, you simply couldn't hear it coming; the saying was, if you heard it, you were already hit.

There were only a few tasks to do now: testing the machine gun, running up the engines, and brewing some tea and a bit of breakfast. All mechanical checks had been done last thing the previous evening: oil levels tested, track bolts tightened, fuel and ammunition loaded. The supply team usually came up with the food wagon, so if there were any problems, the mechanics would, hopefully, be able to sort them out then. *Ferret* was in good mechanical order, however, despite the ninety-mile march—a regimental record—three days before and the action of the previous two days. On the nineteenth, the regiment had easily overwhelmed their first objective, the enemy landing ground of Sidi Rezegh. Three aircraft had managed to get airborne as C Squadron had stormed onto the airfield, but seventeen had been captured on the ground and then destroyed. The tanks had rolled over the tailplanes, crushing them as easily as cheese crackers.

John Billyard, Sam's driver, lowered himself into the driver's seat and began running up the engines. He was new—had only arrived the night before straight from the depot. He was older too, than the others—married with two children. John had arrived with new packets of cigarettes and had made himself popular by offering them around. Turned out he was from Manchester too, only down the road from Crosby. "Have you got any advice for me?" John had asked Sam. "Yes," Sam had told him. "When you find your marker, make straight for it, and if we have to make a run for it, for God's sake don't stall."

The sound of engines shattered the early morning quiet as the tanks rumbled and clanked forward a short way to allow the three-ton lorries, ambulances, and other soft-skinned vehicles that had leaguered within the camp enough room to move out. Their place was a mile or two back, well away from the front line. At the same time, machine gun fire tore into the sky as each crew tested their guns.

A quiet stillness returned once more. Sam sat on the flat flight deck above the engine at the rear of the tank, drinking his tea and eating some breakfast: bully beef and biscuit. It was now about 6:45 AM—more than two and a half hours to go before they started up their engines again. An hour later in the east, the sun was beginning to rise, casting a tangerine glow across the scrub. Without anyone really noticing it happen, the mist had gone and with it the cold of the night. Within the hour, the dew would have evaporated and the metal would start to bake once more. Sam hated this waiting; it was the worst thing about battle. He started to think about home, then chided himself and tried to think about something else: football, leave in Cairo. Anything but home and his family. Then, glancing down at the ground, he noticed a spider crawl out from underneath the sand. He wondered whether, given the opportunity, he would want to swap places with the spider. "By tonight," he thought, looking at the spider, "you will most likely still be alive, and I will probably be dead." He tried not to think about death too much, and for the most part felt a strong, overwhelming belief that, somehow, he would be all right. But before going into battle, it was easy for such self-belief to be shaken.

At 8:05 AM, 7th Armoured Brigade HQ received word that considerable numbers of enemy tanks were concentrating southeast of their position. As a result, it was decided that the 7th Hussars tank regiment would stay behind to face them, while the 6 Royal Tanks along with A Company of the 2nd Rifle Brigade and one battery of the Royal Horse Artillery would press ahead with their northern attack as planned. Command for these northern operations was handed over to Brigadier Jock Campbell. That was something in their favor, for Campbell was already something of a legendary figure within Eighth Army, known for his charisma, courage and daring leadership.

At 8:15 AM, Sam and his crew started up *Ferret* and a quarter of an hour later began moving across the start line. Firing the main two-pounder and Besa machine gun repeatedly, they soon reached their initial objective, the enemy lines along the ridge from Point 167 to the "mosque." Inside the tank, the noise of the firing was deafening, resounding around the cramped metal hull and turret. The cramped fighting chamber was also thick with smoke and the smell of fuel and cordite. Strictly speaking, Sam was supposed to keep inside the turret, alongside the gunner and loader, with a short periscope for seeing what was going on. In practice, however, this meant he could see next to nothing, his only view a narrow aperture clouded by sand and smoke, and so he frequently stuck his head through the hatch to try and get a better idea of where they were and what was happening. Even so, any action was always horribly confused and this was no exception. And although wearing earphones and still in radio contact with the squadron and troop leaders, Sam could only guess from the number of explosions and burning tanks around him that things were not going as well as planned.

What Sam certainly did not know, nor the British command, was that earlier that morning, at 6:30 AM, while it was still dark, the Axis commander himself, General Erwin Rommel, had stepped out of his command car a mere three miles north of where Sam was curled up on the ground trying to sleep. It was here, at Belhamed Ridge, with its commanding position over not only the Trigh Capuzzo valley, but also the forward lines around Tobruk to the northwest, that the artillery of General Bötcher was dug into prepared gun pits. Rommel, aware that the British were massing their forces both at Sidi Rezegh and at Tobruk, ordered Bötcher to turn the guns around, away from Tobruk and toward the airfield to the south—where Sam and various formations of the 7th Armoured Brigade would shortly be readying themselves for battle. Even worse, as the 6 Royal Tanks began moving over the start line two hours later, Rommel ordered four 88mm flak guns from a nearby German reconnaissance unit to take up position on the Belhamed Ridge alongside Bötcher's field artillery.

Against such well-trained firepower the Crusader tanks were sitting ducks, and so it was that half an hour after the attack had started, Regimental Headquarters of the 6 Royal Tanks had almost ceased to exist. The commanding officer, Lieutenant-Colonel Lister, and his adjutant were captured after their tank was destroyed. The second-in-command, Major Warren, and his intelligence officer were killed. The regiment continued forward without its headquarters. Soon after, Major Laing, commanding C Squadron, was badly wounded—he would lose his arm. Major Miller, Sam's commanding officer in B Squadron, was also captured. Tank after tank was stopped in its tracks. Some blew up completely, and many of those who tried to escape were machinegunned as they fled the burning wrecks. Others were incinerated where they were hit.

By late morning, however, both *Ferret* and the other two tanks in the troop were still in one piece, and in the course of their repeated attacks, Sam reckoned they must have done a fair amount of damage, with many men killed or wounded, and several of the 50mm anti-tank guns along the first ridge destroyed. He was now left with just 6 two-pounder rounds from the 110 he had begun the morning with, and down to just one box of machine gun bullets out of an original twenty-two. As far as Sam was aware, they were the only three tanks left in the Squadron—he had by now lost all radio contact with any of the others. He hoped not all had been destroyed; it was easy to lose your way in the heat of battle or to simply break down, but of the fifty-two they had set out with, his troop were the only two he could now see. Nor could he say how far they'd advanced—with all the dust and smoke and carnage around him, it was too difficult to tell. What he did know, however, was that they had broken through two lines of defense and were now approaching a further ridge. Although the ground was generally gently rising, it was also pockmarked with small dips and rises, large enough to offer some protection. Pausing behind a slight dip in the ground, he had maneuvered them into a classic "hull-down" position, whereby the majority of the tank, save the turret and gun, was shielded from enemy fire. Gingerly, he raised his head out of the hatch. Slightly ahead of him and to one side was the troop commander's tank. The second tank was on Sam's other side, on more open ground. Peering through his binoculars, he could also see the enemy guns up ahead on Belhamed Ridge. At that moment, the tank on his right was hit and erupted into flames.

It was against orders to pick up crew of another tank—too many had sacrificed movement or good defensive positions trying to help others. But at that moment, a court-martial was the last thing on Sam's mind. He could see some of the crew jumping from the burning wreckage—good mates of his—and he wasn't going to let the Germans machine-gun them while he stood watching. "Pull out and pick them up," he told Billyard, and so *Ferret* swung out of their safe position and raced across toward the two men running toward them. The first jumped onto the front and swung himself up by the Besa barrel, while the other leaped onto the flight deck behind the turret.

Sam neither saw nor heard the shell coming; all he was aware of was a sensation of everything stopping. His world, his existence, that moment in time, ceased. Then he felt a pain in his side, as though someone had taken a hammer and smashed it into him, and saw blood on his shorts. He fell from the driver's seat to the floor of the fighting chamber. When he came to, he wasn't sure whether he'd been out for minutes or only a few seconds. He was aware of the tank moving but not being driven, just jolting along very, very slowly. He looked around him, but the gunner and loader were both gone. Then he peered into the driver's chamber and saw that John Billyard was still there, in his seat. The problem was that there was no way of him getting out; the fighting chamber, which included the turret, operated independently from the rest of the tank. If the gun barrel was pointing straight ahead, there was a wide enough aperture between the fighting and driving chambers for the driver to get out; but the barrel was not dead straight. Rather, it was pointing at an angle—about 2 o'clock—and the gap was not wide enough for escape through the fighting chamber; the only way was through the hatch directly above the driver's seat at the front of the tank. "Come on Billy!" shouted Sam. "Get out son, we're going to burn!" Sam stretched his arm through the gap between them, but when he pulled it back, saw his hand was covered in blood. "Shoot yourself, Bill!" he shouted.

Conscious of his own urgent need to get out of there as quickly as possible, he hoisted himself up, only to discover his leg was completely numb, as though it had been amputated. Despite this, he managed to clamber back onto the commander's seat, and from there push himself up and out of the hatch. As he did so, he rolled down the back of the tank and ended up lying next to a severed leg and buttock, still fully booted.

The tank was still gently rolling forward, and Sam could clearly see the German guns ahead. Machine-gun fire spat out nearby—the Germans were always most efficient at finishing off fleeing crews. Realizing he needed to keep the tank between himself and the enemy, he slid off the back and began to run toward the cover of a small hillock and some scrub, although he hadn't gone far before he could run no more. His leg gave out and he was forced to cover the rest of the ground by crawling on his hands and knees instead.

He managed to reach the rise in the ground and hid behind a bush. He realized he was still wearing his beret—an obvious target in the desert—so took it off and put it inside his shirt. Ahead of him *Ferret* was still trundling forward, but now billowing smoke and flames. "My God," he thought, "I hope he's not still alive." He felt terrible about Bill, but what else could he have done? He'd never have been able to get him out.

Sam lay still for a moment. It was midday, the sun high in the sky. He still had his pistol, which he pulled out of its holster, but no water. He could see some knocked-out and burning tanks nearby, but otherwise not a soul. The battlefield suddenly seemed deserted. His wound was bleeding, but not too badly; even so, the hole was big enough to put two fingers in. Since his shorts were already fairly ragged, he tore off a piece and clutched it over his side. It didn't hurt; rather, he still felt numb. And terrified. His mind was frantic. Should he stand up and surrender? Without water he would soon be finished. But he couldn't do that, couldn't just hand himself over like that.

While he was still agonizing over what to do, he saw a patrol of nine men appear over the ridge in front of him, and past the still-burning tanks. The soldiers were German, but with them was a small two-man Italian tank. At each tank they stopped and looked around it. Sam thought they were bound to see him. Then that would be the end: they would see him, walk over and then shoot him. Or worse, bayonet him. He'd heard that's what a lot of Germans did. He lay there with his pistol clutched tightly in his hand. He thought: if they try to shoot me, I'll shoot them, because I'm going to die anyway. Or perhaps he should shoot them first? Or just shoot himself now and get it over with? No, he would shoot the German first. Then one of the Germans did start walking toward him. Sam froze, petrified. This was it. Surely this was the end. He closed his eyes and heard the German's steps getting closer, crunching across the stony ground. About fifteen yards from where Sam was lying, the German stopped. At last he shouted, "*Ein toter.*" *He's dead.* And then he walked back.

Sam initially felt elation, then cursed himself for being such a fool. He should have surrendered, of course he should. Watching them go back the way they'd come until they were out of sight once more, he felt another wave of despair, until suddenly from behind he could hear artillery firing once more—British artillery. Shortly after, tank engines began rumbling too, and so he sat up.

"Are you wounded too?" said a voice behind him. Sam turned and saw a ginger-haired lad hobbling toward him with a sub-machinegun. "I was shit-scared," said the soldier, "but I would have shot them."

"You'd never have killed all of them," said Sam.

"No, but I'd have had a good go at them." He'd been wounded in both legs. "Can you walk?" he asked.

"No," Sam told him. The shock was now wearing off and his wound was beginning to cause him pain.

"There's an attack coming in," the lad told him. "Let's wait here and try and attract some attention." The tanks were getting nearer, so with his new companion's help, Sam stood up and waved his beret, until a Crusader rolled up beside them. It was from Sam's own squadron.

Two of the crew jumped down and helped Sam onto a camel-stretcher—a form of hammock made from bamboo and canvas—which they then strapped onto the underside of the tank. Trussed up in this manner, Sam listened as the tank commander—a man he knew well—radioed for permission to take Sam back. It must have been granted, as the tank began to turn around. Soon they were traveling over the German lines of defense that Sam and the rest of the regiment had crossed earlier that morning. There were still Germans in their trenches, and still armed, even though they had been all but overrun. One soldier stood up and pointed his rifle at Sam. Sam stared at him, once more sensing the worst. The German stared back and then slowly lowered his barrel. "Good luck," he said, as the tank rumbled past. "Danke," mumbled Sam.

They crossed the first ridge, ahead of where the German first line of defense had been, and where the 2nd Rifle Brigade had made their attack. The dead lay everywhere. On they trundled until they reached a mustering point away from the battle. One of the men from the regiment—another Scouser like Sam—saw him and said, "Are you bad?"

"I think so," Sam told him. "I can't walk, I can't use my leg."

"Don't worry," he said. "We'll get you on a stretcher. You'll be all right."

But Sam's nightmare was far from over. He was put on a stretcher alongside another wounded tank man, who was clearly in a very bad way indeed: severely burned and covered in bandages. He told Sam his name was Ashbridge and that he'd been with the 7th Hussars fighting the Germans southeast of Sidi Rezegh airfield. The advanced dressing station, just out of the battle area, was heaving with the wounded and dying. Doctors and medical orderlies were rushing from one case to another, applying dressings and injecting morphine. Sam and Ashbridge were taken to a tent, and a man in a white coat came over and asked Sam whether he'd been given any morphine. "No," Sam told him, "but I think the feller next to me needs it more than I do." The doctor looked at Ashbridge and said, "He's gone." Then he called over the padre and said, "This one's for you," and pulled the blanket over Ashbridge's head.

The morphine made Sam pass out. When he came to, he was cold; all he had on was his shirt and blanket. A vast convoy of some eighty ambulances arrived at the dressing station and Sam was picked up and loaded into the back of one of them, along with five others, two stretchers one above the other on one side, two on the other and two sitting wounded in the well. By now, with the morphine wearing off, Sam was in absolute agony, but as soon as the ambulance started off with the rest of the convoy, the pain became unbearable. Had Sam still had his pistol, he was certain he'd have shot himself there and then; the pain was more than he could stand. The man above him was moaning; another had had his nose shot away and had a large pad covering his face; and there was also a blond major, from the 1st Royal Tanks, who had almost severed his arm. It turned out that he, too, was from Liverpool.

All of them were in bad shape and the ambulance began to smell terribly, and not just from the festering wounds: a couple of them had soiled themselves. Sam watched the major wincing with pain; he looked deathly pale. The convoy stopped for food and water, then off it went again, throughout the night, onward and onward, bumping over the rough North African scrub, each jolt bringing with it new agonies.

When first light showed on the morning of 22 November, there were no other ambulances with them. During the night, they'd somehow become detached. Now they were alone in the middle of the desert: six wounded men, writhing in pain, with just a driver and one other. The major went mad. "Do you know what you're doing?" he shouted at the driver. "Do you know where you are? Do you have a map?"

"No sir," the driver told him.

"How the hell did you lose the convoy?" The two men shrugged. What could they say? It was dark, they'd had no lights, the desert was a big place . . .

They drove helplessly around the desert all that day and all the next, the driver and his companion arguing over which way they should be headed. At one point Sam fell asleep. When he woke up the stench was even worse and his body was damp. At first he thought the man above him had pissed himself, then he realized it was blood, and that he was dead. Bled to death, all over Sam.

At last he heard the two up front shouting: they'd seen armored cars ahead. Sam didn't care anymore whether they were Germans; he'd happily turn himself in. He'd had enough. But they weren't Germans, they were members of the Long Range Desert Group and they were well behind enemy lines, the far side of Tobruk. "Come on," said one of the men, "we'll get you out of here."

Following the LRDG armored cars, they at length reached another dressing station. It was too late for another of the men in the ambulance, however. The two bodies were lifted out, but Sam was increasingly aware of his own worsening condition; his wound was beginning to stink. Two orderlies told him to lift his shirt and turn on his side and then they applied a steaming poultice to the open wound. The pain was so intense, he passed out.

Shortly after, Sam and the other three men were heading off in the ambulance again—not along any marked desert track, but over the battle area once more with its slit trenches and sand bars. With every jolt Sam was flung into the air and landed back on his wound. He'd thought he'd already reached unbearable levels of pain, but now discovered there were even greater depths of agony.

Near nightfall they reached an American volunteer field hospital, where Sam was given more morphine and a clean bed for the night. He'd no idea there were Americans in the desert; they weren't even at war. The American doctors removed the shrapnel, but his wound was becoming gangrenous. He needed better help than they could provide, and soon. So back he went into an ambulance and after a further day's driving they came to the railhead, which by now extended some eighty miles west of Mersa Matruh in Egypt. Unfortunately, the day before, German dive-bombers had mistakenly attacked a train full of German prisoners of war. At the dressing station, there was chaos; the medical staff could not cope with the sudden increase in numbers. Sam was put in a tent full of wounded Germans. One of them had gone mad and was jumping on some of the others. The men were all screaming and shouting, but Sam kept quiet, terrified the madman would attack him for being English. Then he heard voices outside and plucked up the courage to call out. An orderly came in and said, "You shouldn't be in here. We've stopped bothering about them."

More doctors examined him. Unsurprisingly, his condition had deteriorated further; in addition to his gangrenous wound, he now had a huge swelling of pus between his legs. But at last, at long, long last, there would be no more ambulance rides across the desert. Sam was placed on a plane and flown to an underground hospital in Mersa Matruh, a place he'd never even realized existed.

The first person he saw there was an English nurse. She was so beautiful and clean, and he so stinking and filthy and unshaven that he felt ashamed.

"How old are you?" she asked.

"Twenty-one," Sam told her.

"I thought you were older," she told him. "We'll put you on a bed and clean you up, and get a barber to shave you and cut your hair." Sam lay back, relief surging through his mind. He'd made it, he'd survived the war! Now he could go home at last—after nearly two whole years of fighting back and forth across the desert.

But in November 1941, there was still three and a half years of war to come, and the British Army was not quite so eager to let go of its men. A smartly dressed tank officer came over to Sam and began asking questions. How had the battle been going when Sam had left? Not so well, Sam admitted. "Your whole brigade has been wiped out," the officer told him flatly.

"I'm not surprised," Sam told him.

"Well," said the officer, "you'll get a few days leave, then we'll have you back at the front."

The British offensive of November and December 1941 brought victory, in the end, albeit a somewhat pyrrhic one. The Battle of Sidi Rezegh, on 21 November, was the most intense fighting the 6 Royal Tank Regiment had experienced in their short history. By nightfall that day they had just one tank left out of fifty-two that was wholly fit for action. Four Victoria Crosses were won by the 7th Armoured Brigade, including one by Brigadier Jock Campbell, who had led the British effort north of the airfield at Sidi Rezegh.

The breakout from Tobruk was also successful—so ending the 242 day-long siege. That alone lifted British spirits. Over the ensuing weeks, Rommel's mixed forces of Germans and Italians were pushed back some three hundred miles, out of the Libyan bulge of Cyrenaica, as far as El Agheila—the very place Rommel had started his campaign on arriving in North Africa the previous February.

For a brief month, the huge effort had seemed worth it. Then, on 21 January, 1942, the German general launched a counterattack. Back went the British, back almost as far as Tobruk, to a small coastal village called Gazala. They were still holding the Gazala Line when, in March, Sam Bradshaw rejoined B Squadron of the 6th Royal Tank Regiment—a mere four months after being severely wounded and a hair's breadth away from death. Eighth Army needed experienced men like Trooper Sam Bradshaw for the next round of the War in North Africa.

TOGETHER WE STAND

PART I

NADIR

"I think a new Higher Command is wanted."
Corporal Bill Eadie, 2nd South Africa Infantry Brigade

CHAPTER 1

Enter America

FOR MANY AMERICANS, it must have seemed odd that the one place where Britain was actually fighting Germany and Italy on the ground was in the Western Desert of North Africa. After all, the three nations involved were European. But although North Africa seemed impossibly far away even to the British, few in the United Kingdom questioned why this tract of sand, strange winds, and Arabic names should be the place to fight a war. Britain's Imperialist past had for some time taken the young men of her cities and shires to the far corners of the world, and even by 1939—despite the colossal cracks appearing in her huge global reach—the map of the world was still liberally covered with British Empire pink. That British men should be fighting in strange-sounding places, so far from home and over terrain that was vastly at odds with their own countryside was in no way unusual. And so names such as Sidi Barrani, Mersa Matruh, and Sidi Rezegh were, by 1942, quite familiar to anyone back in Britain, whether they be from Exeter or Edinburgh, London or Leeds.

But the United States of America had had no such imperial thirst. True, they had interests in the Philippines, but theirs was a comparatively new country—with almost half its states less than a hundred years old—and by nature both introverted and isolationist. Most Americans had enough trouble getting to know their own vast country without bothering themselves with some flea-bitten desert in far-off Africa. Nor did those who volunteered for the army do so because they wanted to "see the world," an incentive for many young British recruits before the war. The large majority of those who joined before August 1940 did so because they were from a poor working-class background and simply wanted something to do. This was certainly true of Tom and Henry Bowles, who, when they volunteered in March 1940, had never left their home state of Alabama—let alone the USA—nor even seen the sea. And if someone had told them then that the first time they ever went into action would be in Algeria, they'd have thought them quite mad. Africa had barely registered on their radar.

Henry and Tom were identical twins, tall, dark-haired and strikingly good-looking, brought up in the cotton-mill town of Russellville in northwest Alabama. Life was incredibly hard during the Depression-hit 1930s. The Bowleses were poor, although they admit they always had enough to eat. When they were twelve, the twins lost a brother and then their mother as well. Soon after, they left school and started working; few in Russellville were pushed to go to school, especially if they could help the family by earning a few bucks here and there. By 1940, however, the cotton mill in Russellville was already in terminal decline, even though the rest of the country was lifting itself out of the Depression. "We wanted to go to work," says Tom, "but there wasn't no work around." They'd tried to get into the Civil Conservation Corps—a scheme set up by Roosevelt to try to combat massive soil erosion and declining timber resources by using the manpower of large numbers of young unemployed—but could not secure a place. Instead, two months after their eighteenth birthday, they decided to enlist in the US Army. Of the two, Tom tended to be the decision maker, so he was the first to hitch a ride to Birmingham, the state capital, in order to find out about joining up. Four days later, on 9 March, Henry followed. "We hadn't heard from Tom," says Henry, "so I told Dad I was going too. He said, 'Son, make good soldiers,' and we always tried to remember that." After being given three meal tickets in Birmingham and a promise of eventual service in Hawaii, Henry was sent to Fort Benning in Georgia, one of the country's largest training camps. He still didn't know where his brother was—or even if he had actually enlisted—until eventually he got a letter from his father with Tom's address. It turned out they were only a quarter of a mile apart—and that both were in the 1st Infantry Division, even though Tom was in the 18th Infantry Regiment and Henry the 26th.

Their initiation into army life was straightforward. On arrival at Fort Benning they were told to read the Articles of War, after which they were given a serial number and told to make sure they never forgot it. After eight weeks' basic training—drill, route marches, and plenty of tough discipline—they were considered soldiers. They were living in pup tents, eating more than enough food and surrounded by young lads of a similar age; as far as the Bowles twins were concerned, life in the regular army seemed pretty good.

Training continued. More marching—three-mile hikes, then ten-mile, then twenty-five-mile hikes with a light pack and eventually thirty-five miles with a heavy pack. A mile from home, they were greeted by the drum and bugle corps, who played them the last stretch back into camp. But while this was doing wonders for their stamina and levels of fitness, they had little opportunity to train with weapons. Admittedly, most in the 1st Division had now been issued the new M-1 rifle, but it wasn't until the Louisiana Maneuvers of August 1941, that the Bowles twins realized how unprepared America was for war. These were the largest military exercises ever undertaken in the US and were designed to test staff and the logistical system to the maximum—but were hardly a thorough examination of the military capabilities of the Army. Henry and Tom Bowles were slightly surprised to see lorries with logs strapped to them that were supposed to simulate tanks, and aircraft dropping bags of flour instead of bombs.

But when Tom and Henry had joined the US Army in early 1940, it had still been only the nineteenth largest in the world—behind Portugal and Paraguay. Incredible though it may seem now, in September 1939, the United States Army had been just 210,000 strong; Germany had marched into Poland with an army of 2.5 million highly trained, highly mechanized men. By May 1940, when the Blitzkreig began, the US Army still struggled with a severe shortage of training facilities and equipment. Many trainee infantrymen were forced to use wooden rifles, and those that were available were largely of a First World War vintage, as were many of the field guns, most of which were still horse drawn. In 1940, the US still had no heavy tanks and only 148 medium tanks in use or on order. There were still mounted cavalry and even in early 1941, Congress authorized the raising of another cavalry division, including the purchase of 20,000 horses. Tom Bowles even has a photograph of massed cavalry horses grazing at Fort Benning. Hadn't America's leaders seen the newsreels of massed German armor and aerial attacks? How could they possibly think, in 1941, that there was still a place for mounted cavalry? While the Axis invaded the Balkans and Rommel launched his first offensive in North Africa, in America the April 1941 front cover of *Life* magazine showed a picture of a US cavalryman, Private Buster Hobbs, standing stiffly at attention next to his horse, Gip.

There had not been enough thought in America during the inter-war years about the future of warfare.[1] Admittedly, times were a-changing, and a-changing fast, but the United States had an awful lot of catching up to do and a long, long way to go before it would be anything like ready to take on the might of the Third Reich. ·

On Sunday, 7 December, 1941, Winston Churchill had been dining at the British prime minister's country retreat, Chequers, with three Americans: Gilbert Winant, the new ambassador; Averell Harriman, the lend-lease expeditor; and Harriman's daughter, Kathleen. At 9 PM, the prime minister switched on the radio to listen to the news. Initially, there were a few updates on the situation in Libya and Russia, then finally there came a brief announcement that the Japanese had attacked the American naval base in Hawaii, in the Pacific. There was a stunned silence, shortly after which Churchill put a call through to the president, Franklin D. Roosevelt. "It's quite true," Roosevelt told Churchill. "They have attacked us at Pearl Harbor. We are all in the same boat now."[2]

Churchill noted that his American guests took the news with "admirable fortitude," while he himself could barely resist jumping for joy. "So we had won after all!" he wrote later. "United we could subdue everybody else in the world. Many disasters, immeasurable cost and tribulations lay ahead, but there was no more doubt about the end."[3] Four days later, Germany and Italy both declared war on the United States, honoring their treaty with Japan. At long last, America was officially in the war too.

The US had been helping Britain before Pearl Harbor, however. As early as 1938, Britain had placed its first substantial munitions contract in America—an order for 450 military planes. The US already had a rapidly growing aircraft industry and, unlike Britain, a huge automobile industry. Throughout 1941, the majority of these immense car factories was converted to producing military aircraft. Britain was also highly dependent on America for shipping, despite a large number of shipyards of her own and a long tradition of shipbuilding. Unfortunately, the demands of the war soon rocketed; furthermore, British shipyards had lost a large proportion of their skilled workforce during the Depression, a loss from which it had never recovered. And then there was the problem of the paucity of British tanks, and so she again turned to the United States to get her out of trouble. America's tank industry was almost nonexistent before 1940, but from the outset US manufacturers managed to achieve what Britain never could: mechanical reliability. With British advice, various models were produced, each better than the one before. Stuarts were the first American tanks to be used by the British in North Africa, followed by the much-improved Grant. America was in a league of her own when it came to mass production—and of pretty much anything: tanks, aircraft, cars, lorries; unlike in Britain, size was not an issue. There were no payload restrictions in America, no shortage of labor, no lack of know-how or steel. Even by the middle of 1941, almost all Eighth Army's tank transporters and heavy lorries had come from the US.

By December 1941, Britain had already ordered a staggering 21 billion dollars' worth of munitions from the United States, both in cash and in the form of the Lend-Lease agreement—although less than 10 percent of these orders had become available by the time of Pearl Harbor. But as Churchill was well aware, the real significance of these orders was that they substantially accelerated American rearmament. Britain simply did not have the resources to achieve ultimate victory herself, but America did, and at an astonishing rate of growth. And once the US was producing thousands of tanks, planes, ships, vehicles, and ordnance—and making herself rich as a result—her own road to war seemed ever more likely.[4] By 7 December, 1941, America was still nothing like ready for all-out war, but thanks to British orders—and money—she was a lot closer than she might have been. For this far-sightedness, Churchill deserves greater recognition.

Five days after Pearl Harbor, and a day after Germany declared war on the United States, the British prime minister set sail for Washington on the battleship HMS *Duke of York* for the first joint wartime conference of military personnel. Now they were in it together, they needed to work out a plan of how their combined forces could be best used, and as far as Churchill was concerned, there was not a moment to lose.

The conference that followed—code-named ARCADIA—set out the joint grand strategy, which was, in a nutshell, a Europe-first policy, i.e., that the Americans should join the British in the defeat of Nazi Germany before they made an all-out attack on Japan. This decision was seen by the apprehensive British as one of the first great hurdles to overcome, but in fact the Americans needed little persuasion. The war would be easier to fight successfully with both Britain and Russia's help, yet in 1942, both her new allies were struggling badly against the Axis, and certainly no concentration of effort in the Pacific would help Russia. If the Axis were defeated first, then Britain would be in a far better position to help the US take on Japan. It was a matter of common sense, and so the broad aim agreed on was for a joint Anglo-American force to invade mainland Europe as soon as possible. This was written up in the form of a Declaration of War Aims by the associated powers: Britain, America, and the Commonwealth countries, henceforth to be known as the United Nations.

By the beginning of 1942, however, America was still far from being the colossal military power it would become by the war's end, and it was, as Churchill had predicted, a good thing that Britain had helped kick-start its rearmament program, or else the situation would have been even worse. The US may have built the tallest buildings in the world and have been market leaders in mass production, but not until war broke out in Europe had this capability been applied to her armed forces.

Mobilization had, however, begun in the autumn of 1940, and did so fairly rapidly largely because of over 100,000 army reserve officers who could be called to active duty and because the numerous regiments and even divisions of the National Guard—the part-time Army—could be mobilized whole as complete units. This meant that by October 1941, the Army had eighteen new divisions mobilized—just under 400,000 men—from the National Guard alone.

At this time there was still no conscription as such. Instead, in August 1940, the Selective Service Act had been passed, commonly known as the draft. By December 1941, all males in the US between eighteen and sixty-five had to compulsorily register, with those aged twenty to forty-five eligible for military service. There were six thousand draft boards across the country; when someone registered, they were given a number. When that number was randomly drawn, every person with that number given from the 6,000 boards was then called up for military service, initially for just one year, and then, in July 1941, extended to thirty months.

Edward "Bucky" Walters had been drafted in early 1941. He'd been in college at the time studying history and English and had been allowed to continue his studies and graduate that June. Almost immediately after, however, he was packed off to do his basic training at Camp Croft in South Carolina. The son of a New Jersey cop, Bucky had, like the Bowles twins, lost his mother as a teenager, but despite this blow, had had an equally happy childhood, growing up in a Jewish neighbourhood in Newark. "My dad was an Irish Catholic, but these people were good friends. It was a great neighborhood." Bucky had been far from overjoyed to receive the draft, and was unhappy to be leaving home. It was bad enough that he was going off to war, but he had another brother, two years younger than he, who would inevitably have to do his bit too; Bucky worried about how his father, whom he adored, would cope with having both sons away fighting.

At Camp Croft, Bucky and the other recruits were given wooden rifles for close drill and World War I-era bolt-action Springfield rifles for use only on the firing ranges. Weapons training was minimal. In the immediate aftermath of Pearl Harbor, mobilization was sped up even more, and Bucky and the other Eastern draftees at Camp Cross were sent to join the 135th Infantry Regiment, part of the 34th "Red Bull" Division, a former National Guard division from the Midwest states of Iowa, South Dakota, and Minnesota.

Despite being "soft citified comfort-seekers" amongst these outdoor farm boys from the Midwest, Bucky and the other Eastern draftees were made to feel a part of the regiment right away. "Even though there was this vast social difference," says Bucky, "we became a 'band of brothers' long before actual combat." He was also impressed by their morale and keen sense of patriotism. "They were eager to meet the enemy and get the job over with," says Bucky. "Just the company we needed to bolster our spirits at the time." Nor did he ever hear them grumble about the reorganizational turmoil they had recently experienced. "They were a wonderful bunch of guys, but," adds Bucky, "I probably knew a little more what to expect than most of them. I'd read a lot of war novels—and things like *All Quiet on the Western Front*—so I wasn't quite so gung-ho."

Although now with a proper regiment, Bucky was still using a wooden rifle more often than a real one. And like everyone in the army at that time, they wore old-fashioned strapped leggings and British Tommy-style tin helmets, rather than the coalscuttle hats that were later introduced. At the time, Bucky accepted this, although he was certainly conscious that most of the cadre and officers who were training them had little or no experience either. This was an army rising from the ground, an army that had little experience on which it could rely. Yes, the United States had made a significant contribution to the First World War, but American troops first went into action only in May 1918, and most not until September, two months before the war's end. President Wilson's decision to enter the war in the first place had been highly divisive and once it was over, those who believed that maintaining a large army was both provocative and unnecessary had their way. So it was that throughout the 1920s and 1930s, America maintained its isolationist policy. There were no colonial spats for them to cut their teeth on, nor an empire to patrol. So, while there were some senior commanders who had seen action in France in 1918, there were no junior officers or NCOs with any combat experience whatsoever.

And with the severe lack of equipment, there was little means of training the new army other than endless marching and occasional rifle practice. The American soldiers who were being trained to take on the formidable Germans would certainly be fit, but tragically deficient in the kind of training needed to compete in modern warfare—namely all-arms—alongside mechanized armor and artillery, training that had been the norm in the German Army for nearly a decade. Most infantrymen like the Bowles twins or Bucky Walters never even saw a tank. In part, this was due to the lack of equipment at the time, but it was also because of a new philosophy that was emerging. The American command had studied the German Blitzkrieg operations of 1939 and 1940, but the conclusions they had drawn were that future war depended on mobility and the machine, not the infantry. This is unsurprising given America's rapid industrialization and absorption with technology, but it meant that prioritization was given to the mechanized and more technological areas of the army, such as the Air Corps and Army Services Forces. Smart weapons were believed to be the key to the future, not the "Poor Bloody Infantryman." As they would discover, in this they were misguided: technology was not enough; well-trained infantry, and plenty of them, are needed to win wars.

Even the bottom rung on the military ladder needed processing however, and so infantry training, by necessity as well as because of any military doctrine, was viewed rather in the same way as one of America's burgeoning factories: recruits arrived at the various camps and were then almost mechanically driven through the assembly line of basic training,

and then regimental and divisional training in the most efficient and eco-
nomical way possible. Once this was completed, they could be boxed up
and shipped out.

This was pretty much the route Bucky Walters took. No sooner had he
joined the 135th Infantry Regiment than the 34th Red Bull Division, to
which the 135th belonged, was alerted for overseas movement. This,
however, was an odd decision, because the 34th was scarcely ready to
leave the factory. The division had been one of the last National Guard
divisions to be federalized into the US Army, and had had less time to
train than almost all the other National Guard divisions or regular divisions. And in January 1942, when the first units of the division set sail
from New York for Northern Ireland, it was not just under-trained but
still under-equipped too.

One of the first being shipped out was Staff Sergeant Warren Evans,
of B Company, 109th Engineers. From Aberdeen, South Dakota, Warren
had had a tough upbringing. Just four when his father had died of can-
cer, his mother was left to raise both him and his younger sister on her
own. She did what she could waiting tables, but they were always broke.
Time and again, unable to pay the rent, they would be kicked out of their
home. Then his mother became ill. Warren got a job selling newspapers.
"I had the best block in town," says Warren, "but the only way you kept
that block was to fight for it." But he was tough and never lost a fight—he
couldn't afford to. It did get him in trouble, though. One time, he put an
opponent in the hospital and found himself before a juvenile court. Fortunately, the judge looked upon him kindly and secured him a job as a
salesman on the understanding that he give up fighting. Warren jumped
at the chance—the $18 a month was enough to keep him and his sister
alive while his mother was in the hospital.

When his mother's health improved, Warren went back to school and
life began to pick up. He excelled at sports, especially football—six foot
three was unusually tall back then—and he won an athletic scholarship to
South Dakota State. He was also a pretty decent baritone—and everyone
knew him as "Bing," after Bing Crosby. The football scholarship gave him
a room, two meals a day, and tuition, but he still had no money, so he
joined the National Guard. A dollar a week for a bit of drill on Thursday
evenings seemed like easy money.

In February 1941, when Bing was in his third year at college, he was
drafted into the Army. His sole motivation for joining the National Guard
had been the dollar a week, but by the time he was called up, he felt sure
war was inevitable. The problem was that he'd fallen madly in love. He'd
met Frances Wheeler at a dance during Thanksgiving weekend the previous November. As Bing puts it, "Sparks flew that night." The feeling was

entirely mutual, and they were both distraught that he had to leave so soon after they'd found each other. She promised to wait for him—active service was for a year only at that time. This soon changed, however, so at the end of the summer, after the army maneuvers were over, she drove all the way to New Orleans, where the two of them were able to spend a weekend together. After dinner and a night of dancing, Bing proposed and was accepted. He'd saved $21 for a diamond ring.

Shortly after Pearl Harbor, the 34th Division was posted to Fort Dix, in New Jersey. This was an embarkation camp. The penny quickly dropped: before long the division would be posted overseas. Bing was distraught. It had been bad enough leaving Frances in South Dakota. Now he would be heading to an unknown destination for an unknown period of time. Possibly for years. God only knew how long the war would last. Perhaps, Bing suggested, they should get married straight away. Frances asked her parents. "If it'll make him a better soldier, then perhaps you should," they told her, and so she packed up her wedding outfit and prepared to travel to Fort Dix while Bing bought a ring and the wedding license. It was fifteen hundred miles from South Dakota, but Frances managed to get a ride in a car with two of the officers' wives who were going to visit their husbands before the battalion set sail. But it was winter, and there was snow on the road, and having driven through the night they had only reached Rockford, Illinois, when they were hit head-on by another car. The driver had been drunk and asleep. Frances' traveling companions were badly hurt, but although Frances was flung from the car, she suffered no more than a cut lip, chin, and broken arm. Far worse was seeing her wedding clothes strewn across the road and struggling to get them back into the suitcase. All three were taken to the hospital. The officers were given leave to visit their wives, but because Bing was as yet unmarried, he had to stay behind at camp. There would be no wedding after all, nor a chance for the two of them to see each other and say good-bye.

Three days later, a heartbroken Frances left the hospital and began the bus journey back to South Dakota. Bing was already on the ship sailing out into the Atlantic. In the black of night, he went out on deck, tore up his wedding license and tossed the ring into the ocean. "I figured it was bad luck," says Bing. He could only hope that Frances would wait for him to return.

The 34th Division had not left as one, but a bit at a time. Bucky Walters was with the last consignment, pulling out of port nearly three months after Bing Evans and the first batch. Although now in H Company—the heavy weapons company—the only "heavy" weapon Bucky got close to was the already obsolete 37mm gun, which they would occasionally fire at makeshift wooden targets. Fort Dix might have been in his home state of

New Jersey, but that was small comfort—the facilities at the camp were below par, to put it mildly. New Jersey in January 1942 was gripped by temperatures reaching nine degrees below zero, yet at Fort Dix the men were expected to sleep in tattered pup tents with neither stoves nor lighting. "Fort Dix will live forever in the memory of those men as a stark example of total inefficiency," wrote Lieutenant-Colonel John H. Hougen in his history of the 34th "and, as an example of what unpreparedness can mean to a nation suddenly confronted by war."[5]

Bucky finally boarded the SS *Acquitania* with the remainder of the division on 27 April, 1942. Like Bing Evans before him, Bucky had felt terrible about leaving. He had a sense of foreboding he couldn't shake as he said his farewells to his father and brother. He was sure he'd never see his father again. "I hugged him and kissed him," says Bucky. "I didn't know whether it would be me that would die or him, but I felt very strongly that this really was good-bye."

The US Air Corps had been equally starved of investment during the twenties and early thirties, but this rapidly changed with the onset of war. By the beginning of 1942, it was faring more successfully than the main body of the Army. Admittedly, it was not so large a machine, but it had certainly benefited from the emerging military philosophy of giving priority to the more sophisticated and mechanized areas of the armed forces. In January 1939, Roosevelt demanded and was granted $300 billion to increase the corps into a force of 6,000 aircraft, and to build a numbr of new airfields. In May the following year, as the Blitzkrieg began in the West, the president proposed, and was again granted, funding for a further 50,000 aircraft.

Unfortunately, there were not enough airfields or facilities to train the quantity of pilots needed for such a sudden increase, so a number of civilian flying schools were roped in to help. One of those given civilian flying training was Edward "Duke" Ellington (so nicknamed after the famous jazz musician). Born on a ranch on the plains of South Dakota, Duke had then moved to a small town in the Black Hills near his grandparents after the combination of a series of droughts and the Depression had forced his father to quit farming. Duke had left school at fourteen, but unlike the Bowles twins, did manage to join the Civilian Conservation Corps. "You were meant to be eighteen," says Duke, "but I was big and they were happy to have me." He stayed with them fifteen months, living on a large camp in the forest, until being invited by the football coach of the college at nearby Spearfish to go back to school; like Bing Evans, Duke was tall, athletic, and a natural sportsman.

The college ran the Civilian Pilot Training Program. Duke signed up, passed the ground school test, and so was given his chance to learn to fly at the nearby airfield—all for free. "I didn't have to pay a nickel," he says.

Having gained his private pilot's license, Duke was sent straight into the newly renamed US Army Air Force when he was drafted in early 1941. New airfields were rapidly being built all across the South, where the weather was better and would allow greater numbers of flying hours for the hordes of new pilots needed. Along with four others from South Dakota and Minnesota, Duke was sent south to Pine Bluff, Arkansas, where he flew a further sixty hours as part of his basic training. After three months, his course was posted to Randy Field in Texas, and three months after that, he was earmarked to become a fighter pilot and sent to a brand-new airfield at Victoria, Texas. There he began flying the T-6 Texan, a highly maneuverable two-seater monoplane developed in the US for training pilots and which had also been eagerly bought in large numbers by the RAF.

Duke loved it. He'd done plenty of aerobatics before, but they'd never let him loose in a modern plane before. "This was freedom," says Duke. "It was just marvelous." They were even visited by an RAF fighter pilot, a veteran of the Battle of Britain. "Boy, did he inject the fighter pilot spirit!" says Duke. "The first time we saw him fly was when he came over the hangars upside down."

Duke graduated with his wings five days after Pearl Harbor, on 12 December, 1941, and was posted to the 56th Pursuit Group in Charleston, South Carolina. The winter weather was appalling, but this was no bad thing: if they were to fly operationally overseas, they needed experience in all types of conditions.

The state of the rapidly evolving Air Force was reflected by the large numbers of new aircraft that kept arriving during the first few months of 1942. Fighter planes were given the prefix P for pursuit; on arrival at the 56th Pursuit Group, Duke found himself flying the same P-40 Kittyhawks that the RAF were now using in North Africa. "We thought we had attained the utmost in life," says Duke. The T-6 Texan—or Harvard as it was called in Britain—had represented a considerable jump in terms of power, but the leap to 1000 horsepower aircraft was rather like stepping out of a Ford saloon and into a Ferrari. During these first few months of 1942, Duke also flew twin-engine P-38 Lockheed Lightnings, P-39 Bell Airacobras, and was also one of the first to try the new P-47 Republic Thunderbolt, which would later prove so successful over the skies of Europe. Few new RAF pilots had a chance to fly so many different aircraft before they went into combat for the first time. Nor were they given as much flying time.

In January, the 56th had moved to Connecticut, to an airfield near New York. As the days grew longer, Duke and Bob Hoske, one of his good friends in the squadron, began taking to the air most evenings to practice their dogfighting. "We would go at it until we were exhausted," says Duke. Then, with the day's work over, they would slip into midtown Manhattan and go and see all the new shows on Broadway—for free. Later, they would visit bars and listen to the bands playing. Duke was a big fan of Helen O'Connell of Jimmy Dorsey's band, who were on at the Pennsylvania Hotel. Most nights, Duke wound up there. The following morning, there'd be more flying. It wasn't a bad way to fight a war.

In July 1941, General H. H. "Hap" Arnold, Commanding Officer of the US Army Air Force, gathered together a four-man team to create a basic plan for the employment of air power should America enter the war. This was known as the Air War Plans Division 1 (AWPD-1). One of those in the team was thirty-five-year-old Major Laurence S. Kuter. He had begun his military career in the artillery, but after a couple of years was accepted for flying training. Although he flew with the Air Corps aerobatic team, it was aerial bombardment that really interested him. Having helped pioneer high-altitude bombing techniques, he was selected to attend the Air Corps Tactical School; he came top of his class and was retained to teach "bombardment aviation and the employment of air power."[6] At the Tactical School, Kuter carried out a number of tests on behalf of the Air Corps. Although he had been convinced by the argument that wars could be won by precision bombing, he was horrified to discover that precision bombing needed to be very precise indeed to have any real effect. The alternative was to use many more bombs and bombers than had been previously estimated.

His work was duly noted in higher Army circles, however, and in July 1939, Kuter was brought into the Operations and Training Division in Washington, DC. A year later, he and three other former Tactical School instructors were brought together to form the AWPD-1 team.

Throughout August, Kuter and his fellow teammates toiled nonstop through the summer heat to produce their paper. Their conclusions were certainly bold. Air power, they agreed, could, indeed, win the war. With 6,800 twin-engine medium and four-engine heavy bombers based in Europe and North Africa, it would take six months' strategic bombing of German industry, the Luftwaffe, submarine, and naval facilities to ensure a land campaign was entirely unnecessary.

The problem was that in the summer of 1941, the US Air Force had just 700 bombers of all types. Even so, the paper still impressed not only Arnold, but General George C. Marshall, the Army Chief of Staff, who were both much taken with the statistics produced by Kuter and his fellows, so much so that they were used to form the basis for levels of air production and training and cemented the notion of a strategic bomber offensive. Furthermore, it also ensured that the US Air Force continued to see its heavy bomber aircraft as playing a critical part in its war plans. When it came to deploying for war, it would be these heavy bombers who would go into action first against the Axis powers.

Texan Willie Chapman was one of those training for the bomber war the US expected to fight. He had joined the Air Force voluntarily. Having registered for the draft, he'd realized that eventually his number would come up, but feared ending up a private in the army. "I'd never joined the OTC [Officer Training College in the National Guard]," he says, "so reckoned my best chance of getting a commission was to join the Air Force." Entering course 42-C in July 1941, he, like Duke Ellington, embarked on a highly thorough training program. Nine months later he was awarded his wings and posted to Barksdale Field in Louisiana to join the 3rd Air Force and to learn how to fly heavy bombers. Training on B-24 Liberators—and briefly B-17 Flying Fortresses—they remained in the sunshine states of the south: Louisiana, and then Florida. Blue skies all day long.

On Monday, 4 May, 1942, Willie was assigned to the 98th Heavy Bombardment Group along with twenty-four other pilots from his course. Like Duke, Willie was enjoying life in the Air Force. As an officer, he had money in his pocket, plenty of good pals, and loved the flying. For the trip to Fort Myers to join the 98th, Willie and his buddies decided to form a "safari" for the transfer. He and a few others had cars, so all twenty-four piled in and set off. Driving down the highway in a tight *V* formation, they moved into line astern every time an oncoming vehicle was spotted. Once they arrived at Fort Myers, they discovered there were no officers' quarters on base, and so, having decided the only hotel in town fell short of expectations, Willie and four others rented a large four-bedroom house complete with two bathrooms and a three-car garage. The house had a phone, radio and gramophone, as well as a fridge. Outside, there was a river and boat dock, and a lawn lined with palm trees with enough room to play football. It was called Shangri-la.

Here the 98th Bombardment Group organized itself and began to prepare for deployment overseas. Squadrons were formed—Willie joined the 415th—but while there was plenty to do for the staff officers, the crews were given few tasks. Duties were posted around seven in the morning, so the men would take it in turns to check, and then phone through to Shangri-la to warn those who needed to get out of bed and report for duty. The rest spent the day at the beach. Much like Duke Ellington, Willie Chapman was discovering that the first months of America's war was a good time to be in the Air Force.

* * *

There was little opportunity for taking it easy in Washington, however, where the US military chiefs and their staff were desperately trying to make up for lost time. The icy winter may have given way to spring, and spring to the long days of early summer, but most of those involved in war planning had little time to notice the passing seasons. Since the Air Force (as it now was) had had its AWPD-1 paper accepted, there was much to be done. Larry Kuter, now a brigadier-general and the youngest general in the US Army, was busier than ever. An assistant secretary to the War Department general staff, Kuter spent much of his time in meetings and presentations—with the Secretary of War, with the Production and Munition Boards, Committees of the Congress and even the White House—in an effort to accelerate the speed with which the Air Force could be deployed on an effective war footing. And as the Air Force increased exponentially in size, so did Kuter's workload.

Kuter's promotion was directly due to US Chief of Staff General Marshall. The chief was well aware that America had far too many senior officers who were, frankly, too old and out of touch. Former Army Reserve officers who had been forced back into service with the onset of mobilization were slowly but surely being sacked and replaced, and Marshall urged General Hap Arnold, the chief of the air staff, to do the same. In Marshall's view, too many of Arnold's "top crust" were World War I pilots and mechanics who had done little but look after airplanes and who "could not handle" the rapid expansion.[7] What both Arnold and Marshall needed were dynamic people with vision, energy, and determination, men who could make key decisions without constant reference to a higher authority; men who could be depended upon to get the job done. In Marshall's—and Arnold's—view, Larry Kuter was one such man.

Another of Marshall's protégés was fifty-one-year-old Brigadier-General Dwight D. Eisenhower. Like Kuter, Eisenhower—or "Ike" as he was known to most—had rarely been so busy, although he really had only himself to blame. On his return from the Philippines in 1939, he'd been given command of a battalion in the 3rd Infantry Division and then, in June 1941, joined the 3rd Army as Chief of Staff. During this time, he'd been partly responsible for the Louisiana Maneuvers of August and September 1941. This massive war game pitted the 3rd Army against the 2nd. It had been up to Ike to draw up plans for the 3rd Army, which had then completely outflanked the 2nd and forced it to retreat. "Had it been a real war," wrote the *New York Times,* "[the 2nd Army] would have been annihilated."[8] With no live rounds and sacks of flour instead of bombs, the only link to real war was the number of troops involved. Yet although to those taking part—bemused young men like the Bowles twins, for example—the maneuvers were the "wooden gun war," it brought Eisenhower to the notice of General Marshall and earned him a promotion to brigadier-general. For those who stood out in these changing times, it was possible to go a long way very quickly.

Even so, Ike had hoped to remain with his troops, so when he received a call five days after Pearl Harbor telling him to get to Washington without delay, his heart sank. During the previous war, every effort he had made to get to the front had been denied—"for reasons which," he wrote later, "had no validity to me except that they all boiled down to 'War Department orders.'"[9] Once there, however, he rather shot himself in the foot. When Marshall asked him directly what the US should do in the Philippines, Ike replied, "Give me a few hours." Handing over his notes, as promised, later that day, Ike waited for the chief's verdict. Marshall read them, then eyed him for a few moments and said, "I agree with you."[10] If Ike had ever hoped to get back to his troops, he could think again; Marshall needed men like him. He was staying in Washington.

Ike was born in 1890 in little more than a shack beside the railroad in Denison, Texas, the third—with his twin—of six boys. Soon after, his family moved to another small railroad town, Abilene, in the heart of Kansas. There his father took a job as a mechanic at the Belle Springs Creamery. They were poor, but from an early age, Ike learned to make the most of his opportunities. He worked hard at school and at home, and excelled at all sports, and later won a place at West Point, the military academy, graduating in 1915. Rather than being given command positions, however, he began his early career with a string of staff postings, in which he soon made a name for himself. He was also fortunate enough to serve under General Pershing and later, in the Philippines, under General Douglas MacArthur, two of the biggest names in the US military.

Now, in May 1942, Eisenhower was busy planning, just like everyone else in Washington. Although he had attended the ARCADIA conference, he had initially been in charge of the Far Eastern Section of the War Plans Division, toiling in vain to save the Philippines from the march of the Imperial Japanese Army. From mid-February, however, General Marshall had broadened his remit by making him head of the entire War Plans Division (WPD), soon to be renamed the Operations Division (OPD). With it came yet another promotion—to temporary major-general—and the task of putting together plans for the Europe-first policy adopted at ARCADIA. The key to this, as far as Ike was concerned, was ensuring that Russia stayed in the war, which, in early 1942, looked increasingly unlikely. Any Anglo-US action that could help Russia, by drawing off German forces from the Eastern Front, needed to happen sooner rather than later. With this in mind, by the end of March, Ike proposed a plan to invade Northern France with forty-eight Anglo-US divisions by no later than 1 April, 1943. The code name for the plan was ROUNDUP. In addition to ROUNDUP, another plan was developed—SLEDGEHAMMER— which, if the Russian position looked particularly desperate, would be a suicide mission to France that year. Meanwhile, troops needed to be hurriedly built up in the United Kingdom, from which ROUNDUP would be launched. The code name for this massing of forces in the UK was BOLERO. These plans were agreed to by General Marshall, then President Roosevelt, and, in turn, by Prime Minister Winston Churchill and the British Chiefs of Staff, albeit with some reservations. Ike was delighted that something concrete had been agreed upon. "I hope that, at long last, and after months of struggle by this division," he noted in his diary, "we are all definitely committed to one concept of fighting. If we can agree on major purposes and objectives, our efforts will begin to fall in line and we won't be just thrashing around in the dark."[11]

Ike was unusual in thinking a lot about the future of war and had been nervous about American isolationism and complacency during the 1930s. He'd still been in the Philippines when the war had begun, and from Manila had listened to the then prime minister of Great Britain, Neville Chamberlain, make his sad and weary declaration of war. Depressing though the news was, Ike had long been expecting it. A number of senior officers had warned of war and Ike had found himself in agreement. After all, the expanding dictatorships in Germany, Italy, and Japan seemed to point to only one conclusion. Nor did Ike believe America could avoid the whirlpool of global war, however woeful the state and size of the US Armed Forces were. "Comparatively few," he noted later, "understood the direct relationship between American prosperity and physical safety on the one hand, and on the other, the existence of a free world beyond our shores."[12] Well, they had certainly woken up to the reality now. All across America, at camps and airfields, at dockyards and ports, in factories and in government offices, millions of men and women were being galvanized into a machine that, before too long, would be pitted not against fellow countrymen with wooden rifles, but a battle-hardened, highly trained and motivated German army and their Italian allies.

CHAPTER 2

Calm Before the Storm: Monday, 4 May, 1942

THE SECOND WORLD WAR affected the lives of almost every man, woman, and child of every country that was involved in this truly global conflict. For many millions, this meant they were uprooted from the tiny corner of the world in which they had lived before the war and flung to far parts of the globe—places that, before it began, they would never, in their wildest dreams, have imagined visiting. Never was this more the case than for those who fought in Egypt and Libya. Apart from a few towns along the Mediterranean coastline, this was a vast tract of largely inhospitable land: stony scrub, home to only the hardiest of living creatures and plants, almost bereft of trees and water, with sizzling daytime temperatures and freezing nights. Whether you were from Nepal or New Zealand, London or Paris—or even California or Calcutta—the Western Desert was an alien place, and certainly seemed like a long, long way from home.

The majority of men—and women—who were there in May 1942 were only temporarily in uniform. Before the war they had been civilians, not professional soldiers or airmen; the war not only uprooted people from their homes, it meant they also ended up doing things they had never imagined they would do. The very fabric of life was utterly and completely turned on its head.

Few people, for example, would have thought the photographer Cecil Beaton would be wearing a uniform, least of all the sandy cloth of the Royal Air Force's tropical desert wear. After all, he belonged to the delicate world of art, fashion, and theater, hardly a breeding ground for soldiering.

By the time war had broken out in September 1939, Beaton was thirty-five and, with recent commissions to photograph the queen, his reputation had never been higher. He had turned to photography as an amateur after dropping out of Cambridge, but had soon risen to prominence through his daring portraits of the young, rich, and fashionable. A certain notoriety from his association with the Bright Young Things—a group of young, aristocratic men and women who had scandalized London society with their camp theatrics and extravagance—did him no harm. More work followed; then trips to Hollywood, contracts with *Vogue* and finally, commissions from the British Royal Family. For someone who worshiped beauty and glamour as much as Beaton, his was a thrilling lifestyle: friendships with artists, movie stars and the richest in the land; and near-constant travel—to New York, Paris, Hollywood, Rome.

It was also a lifestyle that came to a crashing halt with the outbreak of war in September 1939. Hearing the news that Germany had invaded Poland had been "like a death knell,"[13] and affected him profoundly. Rather than mourn the passing of a way of life, however, he discovered he no longer had an "appetite for the sort of things that had been fun. They were remote."[14] Rather, his concern came primarily from his fear for Britain's future. His reaction was entirely typical of most people his age, who could no longer rely on the callowness and naivete they had possessed at nineteen or twenty. To the middle-aged man, war spelled doom. To the younger man, still flushed with youth, thoughts of potential death and destruction rarely registered; many viewed it as a chance for adventure, to see something of the world or to fly fast, modern airplanes.

Cecil Beaton had very quickly begun to feel both frustrated and ashamed. "This war, as far as I can see," he confided to his diary, "is something specifically designed to show up my inadequacy in every possible capacity."[15] He offered his services as a driver, then as a camouflage designer, and finally took work as a telephonist at an Air Raid Precaution unit. It wasn't until July 1940 that he'd started working extensively as a photographer for the Ministry of Information, a job that would soon demonstrate his enormous versatility as a photographer and also provide him with worthwhile employment of lasting value to his country. On one of his first trips around England for the Ministry of Information, he photographed Eileen Dunne, a three-year-old girl from a north of England village who had been slightly injured by a German bomb. With her bandaged head and large wistful eyes, and clutching her stuffed toy, Cecil's photograph of the girl became a front cover for the American magazine *Life* in September 1940—and a British propaganda coup. More followed: St. Paul's Cathedral in London amidst the smoke and ruins of the war-torn city, portraits of the prime minister, of the "Few," the fighter pilots who had saved Britain in the hour of need; even Mrs. Churchill featured on the cover of another magazine, *Picture Post*. Pictures that defined the spirit of Britain during the first, desperate years of war.

Warming to this new role, Cecil was, by the beginning of 1942, hoping to be sent to the only theater in which Britain was actively waging war against the Axis on the ground: the Middle East. In March, his wish was granted. Officially, he was being loaned to the British Air Ministry, and although primarily given the job of photographing the work of the RAF out there, he was also given a free hand to photograph anything else that might be of interest. Reaching Egypt in April, he finally set out for the Western Desert from Alexandria on Saturday, 2 May, accompanied by Derek Adkins from the RAF's Public Relations Directorate.

The men who lived and fought in the desert quickly grew accustomed to its strangeness, but seeing it for the first time was a bewildering experience. Rattling along a rough road in a truck piled high with camp bedding, provisions and fuel, Cecil was surprised to discover that it was not a desert of high dunes or Beau Geste forts, but rather a largely flat, empty, desolation, "a drab mottled succession of dun colour stretching in all directions like an emptied sea." The ground was covered with stones, grit and rock, and the vegetation, such as it was, looked dry and "unsympathetic. One wonders," he wrote, "that even a camel can digest the patches of prickly vetch."[16]

On and on they went, all day, the landscape barely changing over a hundred miles. For those new to the desert, the sheer size and distances involved often took some getting used to. Cecil thought the scale seemed so "incomprehensibly large," he wondered how warfare could be carried out in such an arid world.

They were heading toward the front, some four hundred miles from Alexandria—roughly the same distance as London to Glasgow. Since February, the "front" had been the Gazala Line, a forty-mile stretch running from the tiny coastal village of Gazala in the north to the nondescript watering hole of Bir Hacheim some forty miles slightly east of due south. It was not a continuous network of trenches like the Western Front during the First World War. Rather, the line was made up of a series of defensive "boxes"—areas in the desert marked out by entrenchments and filled with a number of all arms—artillery, infantry, tanks, engineers and so on—and both linked and fronted by deep minefields.

Along this line, and within the rough triangle between Gazala, Bir Hacheim and the port of Tobruk, were the various brigades (and their divisional and corps headquarters to which they officially belonged), that made up Eighth Army, and numerous landing grounds from which the Desert Air Force operated.

Here and elsewhere in the Middle East theater, Britain was largely dependent on the extraordinary reach of its empire, for while the German and Italian forces were, for the most part, exactly that—German and Italian—the men lined against them were an extraordinary hodgepodge of nationalities and cultures, drawn from all corners of the globe.

Although in terminal decline by 1939, the empire had, curiously enough, been given one last breath of life with the onset of war. Plans for the independence of India, for example, were put on hold; this was just as well for Middle East command: of the fourteen divisions serving in the Middle East in May 1942, six were Indian. More than 200,000 Indians, from Mauritius to the Punjab, were currently wearing British uniforms of one kind or another in the Middle East theater. There were also divisions from Australia, New Zealand, and South Africa, as well as other allies, such as the Free French, Poles, and Greeks, and among those serving in the Desert Air Force, there were Canadians, Belgians, and even Americans.

Moreover, many of these men were volunteers rather than conscripts. In South Africa, for example, there was no conscription, yet half the Desert Air Force was made up from South African Air Force squadrons and there were two South African infantry divisions within Eighth Army. This was, in many ways, an extraordinary contribution. Just forty years before, South Africa had been torn apart by the Anglo-Boer War, and it was only in 1912 that the disparate units of the former Boer republics and the British territories had united to form the Union Defence Force. The government of the fledgling Union of South Africa had imposed conscription during the First World War, but there had been a major uproar from a large section of the Afrikaan-speaking population. This was quite understandable; fighting for a king and country who only a few years before had been the sworn enemy was simply not acceptable to many Afrikaaners, especially as most were not just anti-British, but also decidedly pro-German. Many flatly refused to serve at all, and armed rebellion looked likely. It was only thanks to the efforts of two Afrikaans who had fought for the Boers—Generals Louis Botha and Jan Smuts—that a crisis was averted. Even so, conscription had to be abolished, and when South Africa followed Britain and France and declared war against Germany on 6 September, 1939, the Defence Force staff were only too aware that compulsory service was still out of the question; the pro-German and anti-British sections of the population still had a loud voice. Indeed, the very declaration of war had been divisive. Only seven of the thirteen-man cabinet—including General Smuts—had been in favor of war, and when put to the Union Assembly, the decision was passed by only eighty votes to sixty-seven. Despite this, one in three able-bodied men enlisted, including a fair number of Afrikaaners; many more were involved in the various munitions and other war industries that were suddenly needed with the onset of war.

One of those who had been quick to join up was Corporal Bill Eadie. With a Scottish father and New Zealander mother, he still thought of Britain as the "mother country," and it was from a sense of patriotic duty that he signed up to fight. He'd even lied about his age to do so—said he was born in July 1907, rather than two years earlier as was really the case, because at the time the maximum age for those sent on active service was thirty-four. Joining the Prince Alfred's Guard (PAG), he'd then been sent on one course after another, steadily rising through the ranks to sergeant. But despite having a wife and two children back home in Port Elizabeth in the Eastern Cape, Bill had felt frustrated. He felt he would hardly be doing his bit if he sat out the war teaching new recruits parade ground drill, and managed to get himself transferred to the 2 Regimental Tank Depot (Prince Alfred's Guard detachment) and then, in September 1941, was finally posted overseas to Egypt. But hanging about at the tank depot in the Canal Zone was no more his idea of how to spend the war than instructing had been. By now a sergeant, he dropped a rank to corporal in order to transfer again to Brigade Headquarters of the 2nd South African Infantry Brigade, part of the 1st South African Division.

That had been nearly seven months before, in October. Initially, 2nd SA Infantry Brigade had been left out of the 1st SA Division for the Crusader Operation that had begun 18 November. But it was not only Sam Bradshaw's 7th Armoured Brigade that had been annihilated at Sidi Rezegh—the 5th South Africa Brigade had suffered a similar fate. Urgent reinforcements were needed, and so Bill Eadie and the rest of the brigade had been temporarily attached to the 2nd South African Division, and with them had traveled with Eighth Army across Cyrenaica throughout December 1941, and back again to Gazala once Rommel launched his counterattack in January. A year before, there had been the "Benghazi Handicap." This latest race back and forth across the desert was soon christened the "Msus Stakes." In war, a sense of humor helped.

By May, however, and with a lull in the fighting, 2nd South African Infantry Brigade had rejoined the 1st South African Division and was dug in along the northern sector of the Gazala Line next to other brigades from the 1st Division. Their defensive box, behind the front line of minefields, was some five miles south of the Mediterranean coast, with only the 3rd South African Infantry Brigade's box between them and the sea.

On Sunday, 3 May, and throughout much of the night, the *khamseen* had been blowing. Raging sandstorms could bring all activity to a grinding halt, but the winds of the khamseen were also a cause of major irritation, and could make an already uncomfortable existence worse. It had been very hot and dusty all that Sunday, but by the evening the wind was really getting up. Bill Eadie rose the following morning to find everything covered in a fine layer of dust, but not a breath of wind at all. Bill sat on the edge of his dugout in just his shorts, his skin as dark a nut brown as any of the other old-timers. It was a court-martial offense to get oneself sunburned, and when he had first reached the desert he'd had to be careful because, despite dark brown hair, he had a fair complexion. A few months in the sun had sorted that out, however. Now, on that Monday morning, it was so quiet, all he could hear was the faint tick of his wristwatch and the buzz of flies nearby, and, occasionally, the dull boom of artillery fire some four miles away.

Bill was better suited to life in the desert than most. Short, with dark, narrow eyes and an easy smile, he liked the outdoors. Back home in South Africa, he had always enjoyed trekking in the veldt and bird-watching. He was even an accomplished snake handler—a useful skill in the desert. Yet, he was also easy in his own company—another helpful trait during the long periods of boredom.

But even Bill struggled with the vast hordes of flies, the constant companions of the men in the desert. There were millions and millions of them. Attracted to saliva and sweat—not to mention excrement—they never left the men alone for a minute, although they swarmed particularly thickly during hard physical work or at mealtimes. Food had to be eaten one handed, the plate close to the mouth, with the other arm acting as a whisk. Bill Eadie used his tin hat for this task. Even so, it was impossible to eat anything without swallowing a fair number of the insects as well. Although in appearance very similar to the common housefly, desert flies—*musca sorbens*—were smaller and infinitely more aggressive. And unbeatable—you either accepted them or allowed them to drive you mad.

Even getting used to them, however, as Bill had done, didn't mean there wasn't pleasure to be had from exterminating a few. He'd cut down a four-gallon petrol tin and filled it with fly poison, and he reckoned it was pretty effective. That morning there was a good catch of flies in his tin as well as a couple of wasps, a tick and a number of fleas that he was picking out of his shirt and other clothes. A lizard had been a frequent visitor, gobbling up all Bill's victims, but he hadn't seen him for a couple of days.

By the evening, the khamseen had returned and with it came rumors. Most of the men were given few hard facts about what was going on, so the grapevine was the major news telegraph up and down the line. Of course, many of the rumors turned out to be wrong, but it was amazing how often there was some element of truth. The latest that Bill heard was that all leave had been canceled. This meant something was brewing for sure.

* * *

There was more activity that first Monday in May for the men of the 2nd Battalion of the Rifle Brigade, who for the past month had been operating forward of the line in the southernmost sector, ostensibly acting as a mobile antenna watching out for any sudden movement from the enemy. Most of their operations were carried out at night—patrols would creep up toward the enemy lines, maybe take a prisoner and generally observe any signs of an impending offensive or other significant activity. And an offensive was surely not far around the corner: the lull in the fighting had lasted for over two months now. It didn't take much brains to realize both sides were working hard to retrain and reinforce and that once preparations were complete, the fighting would start again.

Corporal Albert Martin, like Sam Bradshaw, was an old hand in North Africa. There were plenty of young men from Britain in the desert, as well as from the dominions. Like most in the 2nd Rifle Brigade, Albert was a Londoner, from Poplar in the East End. He'd been a nineteen-year-old clerk in a Greek shipping firm earning eighteen shillings a week when war had been declared. His father, who had served in the trenches in the last war, was against Britain getting involved. "It's none of our business," he told his son. "Mark my words—we'll rue the day."[17] But Albert couldn't help feeling a frisson of excitement. Perhaps he and his mates weren't quite so gung-ho or patriotic as his father's generation had been in August 1914, but the promise of excitement and derring-do certainly appealed. Thoughts of danger and discomfort simply never entered his head. And while Albert had not rushed to volunteer his services, when his call-up papers dropped onto his doormat he was not particularly upset; rather, he felt a big new adventure was opening up before him. Before the war had come along, he had already begun to feel there was little to look forward to; Britain was governed by a very solid class structure that inhibited any significant advancement. As a working-class lad, there was little to which he could realistically aspire.

The war had changed that, had shown him a world beyond the East End of London. Even during his training he had met people that, in ordinary life, he could never have expected to encounter—men like David Niven, the movie star, who in 1940 was one of the officers at Tidworth Barracks. Niven had been only too happy to entertain the recruits with his tales of Hollywood. Albert had also learned to take great pride in the battalion. The Rifle Brigade had been formed in 1800, during the Napoleonic Wars, to provide a highly mobile skirmishing and reconnaissance force that could also be used to lead the advance, cover movements and guard any withdrawal. This *raison d'etre* was drilled into each rifleman. They considered themselves elite troops, and this pride helped forge not only discipline, but intense camaraderie too.

Albert had reached Egypt in September 1940. Like Sam Bradshaw, he'd been in the thick of the fighting against the Italians, and every subsequent major offensive in between. He'd even attacked the same ridge as the 6 Royal Tank Regiment on the morning of 21 November. Many of his colleagues had fallen that day—but Albert had somehow survived.

His luck had run out in December. On the eleventh, after particularly vicious fighting, he had approached a stationary but seemingly undamaged German Mk III tank. With a Bren gunner covering him, he had gingerly climbed on and peered into the turret. He immediately wished he hadn't. Blood, chunks of flesh, and body parts littered the inside. A swarm of thousands of angry flies whirled in a cloud as Albert recoiled from the sight. He had grown used to scenes of carnage—had taught his mind to shut them out—but this had unbalanced him for the rest of the day.

He was still feeling unsettled when a Messerschmitt 109 strafed the truck he was traveling in. A bullet hit his arm and a piece of shrapnel hit his knee. With so many casualties over the past couple of weeks—the battalion strength had been halved—he had already begun to wonder when the inevitable would happen, so it was with something close to relief to discover his turn had come but that he was not too seriously hurt. Exactly a month after he'd been wounded he was discharged from hospital, and two months after that, having had a spell convalescing and then at the Infantry Base Depot, he was once more back with the battalion.

Albert had returned to the front line with a certain amount of resignation. His first few months in the desert, when they had been fighting what amounted to a colonial war, had been much like the Boy's Own adventure he'd imagined. "Battles were planned and executed rather like a school sports day," says Albert, "with magnificent trophies there for the taking in return for comparatively light casualties." The arrival of the Germans in February 1941 had stopped all that; they were a tough, highly trained opposition. As the 2nd Rifle Brigade had prepared to move back up into the desert at the end of March, they knew ahead of them lay bitter fighting: fighting that would be over ground they had contested several times already, but which was now being fought with increased ferocity and ever-increasing numbers of men and machinery. Those early days in North Africa now felt like a long, long time ago.

The 2nd Rifle Brigade had been out of the line for some time, building up strength and retraining, but it hadn't taken long to get back into the swing of life in the blue, as the Western Desert was known. They were still a part of 7th Armoured Division, but within the division had been attached to the newly-formed 7th Motor Brigade, a mobile but fully supported and armed infantry brigade. And operating in a scouting, reconnaissance manner was exactly what the Rifle Brigade had been born to do.

That night, 4 May, Albert Martin was part of a patrol sent forward to observe the German and Italian positions west of the Gazala Line. He always felt a bit apprehensive before such a patrol—a few butterflies in the stomach—but there was excitement too. Once the patrol was under way, he discovered his senses became very sharp. "It's unbelievable," he says. "When you're walking and it's the middle of the night and you know the enemy's up ahead somewhere but you don't know *exactly* where, you're conscious of every little noise, and the slightest shadow or movement." There was also an overwhelming sense of relief on safely making it back. On this particular occasion, Albert had even greater cause for satisfaction. He and another man had managed to creep right into the middle of an enemy position, observe and get out again, while the rest of the patrol had captured a prisoner who could then be interrogated—and all without a shot being fired. "Quite a successful bit of work all round," Albert noted in his diary.

Not far from Albert Martin and the roving 7th Motor Brigade were the 1st Free French Brigade, holding the southern end of the line at Bir Hacheim. Under the charismatic General Pierre Koenig, the 3,700-strong French contingent had come under the command of Eighth Army in December, having fought tenaciously in Eritrea against the Italians and then again against their countrymen, the Vichy French, in Syria.

They had reached Bir Hacheim on St. Valentine's Day, 14 February. A "bir" was a desert watering hole, an underground cistern where winter rainwater collected, and, because of the shade and depth of the well, evaporated only slowly. Bir Hacheim was such a place, and a crossroads too, of ancient Bedouin tracks. A meeting point for Arab traders and their caravans, but little more. True, there had been an Italian fort there once, but it had crumbled. Apart from the two underground wells, a couple of concrete shacks, and a small hill soon known as the Observatoire, Bir Hacheim was nothing but a spot on a map. A dusty, barren pinprick in the vast openness of the desert.

Captain Pierre Messmer was a company commander of the 13th Foreign Legion Half-Brigade (13th DBLE). A Parisian, he had completed his studies and then almost finished his two years' military service when war had been declared—and so he remained where he was, a junior office in the French Territorial Army.

On 17 June, 1940, Messmer was near Clermont-Ferrand when he heard Marshal Pétain's thin voice coming over the radio and ordering the laying down of French arms. He immediately vowed he would do no such thing. "I decided to continue the war, whatever happened," he wrote later, "simply because I couldn't bear to be conquered and live with the humiliation and lies."[18] In making this decision, he was outlawing himself from the country and people he adored. Vichy rebels were treated as traitors—their properties and possessions dispossessed, their citizen rights stripped from them. If they were caught, they would be shot.

Having made his way to Marseille, he failed to find a ship that would take him to North Africa; instead, along with a friend and a major-general from the French Armée de l'Air, he managed to steal an 8,200-ton Italian steamer and sail it to Liverpool. In England, General Charles de Gaulle had already begun rallying men to his Free French cause. The 13th DBLE were also there, having returned from the failed Allied mission to Narvik in Norway, and having decided to sign an initial six-month contract to fight on behalf of de Gaulle's Free French.

From an early age Pierre had craved adventure, excitement, the thrill of the open sea and the vastness of the desert, so he was an eager recruit to the French Foreign Legion. Less than two years later, when he finally arrived at Bir Hacheim, he had already fought at Dakar, in Gabon and the Cameroon, in Eritrea and Syria. He was now twenty-five and "thrilled" to be in the African desert. "I am proud to have under my leadership a hundred men," he wrote, "who have a taste for freedom but adhere to strict 'legionnaire' discipline, who eagerly accept modern weaponry, but who also respect age-old traditions."[19]

Since their arrival, Pierre and the rest of the 1st Free French Brigade had been kept busy, laying even greater minefields (there were now over half a million along the Gazala Line) and digging through the hard-baked limestone to create a defensive post that was almost entirely below ground level: gun pits, dugouts, sloping pits to garage the Bren-carriers and ammunition dumps. Wiring parties surrounded the area with barbed wire; engineers lay miles of telephone lines. Day in, day out, getting ready for when the fighting began again.

There were also occasional patrols. Pierre found it incredible that one could drive all day and still encounter nothing of any interest. He thought the war seemed sterile out there in the desert. In the Battle of France there had been refugees on the roadside, burning buildings, signs of civilian destruction. "The horrors of war touch only the fighters," he wrote. "That is why the desert war, so hard on the body, does not besmirch the soul."

On one patrol, Pierre had discovered a bir that did not appear on any of his maps. With rations of only a gallon of water a day for drinking, washing, and shaving, he decided to keep the discovery a secret for the use of his men only. This worked well until, returning from another patrol, one of his officers seemed ill at ease.

"Did everything go all right?" Pierre asked

"No, my Captain," came the reply.

"Did you come across a German patrol?"

"Well, not exactly . . . We found two Germans at the bottom of the bir, but they'd been there for a long time." They had been rotting in the water his men had been using for the past three weeks.[20]

Preparations for the renewal of fighting continued all along the line—and behind. The railway was extended almost as far as Tobruk; huge ammunition and supply dumps were strategically set up, including at Belhamed, where Rommel had ordered his guns be turned onto the British 7th Armoured Brigade the previous November. But Eighth Army and the Desert Air Force were only part of Britain's forces in the Middle East. General Ritchie, the Eighth Army commander, in turn came under command of the commander-in-chief Middle East Forces, General Claude Auchinleck, whose brief included the Sudan, East Africa, Palestine, Trans-Jordan, Iraq, and Persia. With Axis forces in Greece and the Balkans, and with their advances in Russia, the threat of German attacks through the Caucasus meant there was still the possibility that Syria would become a new battleground. As a result, divisions and brigades were rotated out of the Eighth Army and dotted around the Middle East theater, albeit principally in Egypt (and Libya) and Syria.

Both the remaining Australian and New Zealand divisions were in Syria at this time. Despite any potential threat in the Eastern Mediterranean, their deployment there did offer them a chance to recuperate, refit, and retrain after what had been a long, hard year. Most of the 9th Australian Division had, for six months, almost single-handedly defended Tobruk, before their daring seaborne breakout the previous October. The 2nd New Zealand Divison had served in Greece, then Crete, and then throughout the Crusader battles of November and December.

By May, the 9th Australian Division was based around Aleppo, a border town in northern Syria. For the men of the 2/13th Battalion, life was fairly quiet—parades, drill, training, border patrols, and keeping the camp clean—but they had perhaps deserved this respite more than any other battalion in the division. During the October breakout, the 2/13th had been the last due to leave, along with 20th Brigade HQ, but they arrived at the wharf only to learn that the convoy due to take them to safety had been attacked by enemy bombers and a U-boat. The convoy, heavily damaged, was forced to return to Alexandria and the 2/13th back into Tobruk for another seven weeks. They were then involved in fierce fighting around El Duda at the end of November and again during the final breakout that ended the siege on 7 December.

Joe Madeley and his mates in A Company were disappointed to still be in the Middle East. Once they had finally been pulled out of the line at Christmas, they had hoped they would be sent back home to Australia as the 6th and 7th Australian Divisions had been. The Japanese were pushing farther and farther south out in the Pacific Theater, and Joe wanted to be there to defend his home if the worst happened. But it was not to be. For the time being they were stuck in the Middle East, and that was that.

Like many who had joined up in Australia and New Zealand, Joe had been brought up a country boy, living on a farm in Weethalle in New South Wales. He'd been educated in a school of just fourteen pupils, then at thirteen had gone to high school. After a year, he'd had enough and had returned to work on the farm. Joe had had few qualms about joining up when war finally came. His dad had come back from the trenches of the Western Front and Joe had always loved hearing his stories of those days. To be a soldier just like his dad seemed a good thing to do, especially since a drought had meant there was less work to do on the farm. Nor did he have any doubts about why Australia had got involved. Britain was the Mother Country, and so as far as most young Australians were concerned—Joe included—if Britain was at war, so were they.

A few of the boys from Weethalle joined up at the same time—friends like Keith Boal, Ken Cruchett, Jack Stuart, Scotty Baxter, and Jack White, mates he'd known all his life. They were all sent off together to a training camp at Wagga Wagga, around a hundred miles north of Joe's farm. Drill, troop marches, and shooting was how they spent most of their time. Joe was good with the rifle—all the country boys were. "A rifle was part of equipment from the time we were about six or seven," says Joe. "A rifle to shoot foxes, dingoes and rabbits." After six months, they were allowed one last week of leave in Weethalle before being shipped overseas. Joe and his mates were given quite a send-off, then they were on their way to Sydney. Joe had been to Sydney once before—when he was little—but couldn't remember it. He'd certainly never been on a ship, and was seasick the moment he boarded the converted liner, the *Queen Elizabeth*. "I could ride a horse better than I could walk," says Joe, "but on a ship—well, that was terrible." Neither Joe nor his mates had any idea where they were headed, although they supposed it would be England. They pulled into port in India, and then on they went again, until finally reaching Port Tewfik in Egypt. After a few weeks, they were taken to Alexandria and put on another boat for Tobruk. As they crept into port, Joe was still leaning over the rails being sick. "I didn't care what or who was there," says Joe. "I couldn't get off that boat quick enough."

Not all the New Zealanders were in Syria. Some, like eighteen-year-old Maiki Parkinson, were stuck, in transit, in the Canal Zone of Egypt—a replacement troop which had yet to replace anyone. Maiki was a Maori, from Opotiki in the North Island. There was conscription in New Zealand, but not for the Maori—all were volunteers. Different Maori tribes were spread throughout New Zealand, but they all had one thing in common: a martial tradition. Maiki Parkinson, just like every Maori, was brought up on the stories of his elders, tales of heroic deeds from the past, and of clashes with other tribes. War was a part of Maori culture and the potential to win honor in battle remained a considerable motivation, even in 1939.

The Maori had lived peaceably alongside the Pakehas—the white men—since the end of the New Zealand Wars in 1869, yet there was still a reluctance on the part of the government to have whites and Maori fighting shoulder to shoulder. A Maori Pioneer Battalion had been raised with reluctance on the part of the government during the First World War and disbanded soon after, but by 1939, and with war approaching, Sir Apirana Ngata, the foremost Maori in New Zealand, had repeatedly lobbied the government for permission to raise a Maori force. Quite apart from any cultural desires the Maori may have had, it was clear to Sir Apirana Ngata that the Maori people could not expect any further political acceptance if they did fight alongside their Pakeha compatriots in the conflict that was surely coming. As soon as war was declared, the four Maori members of Parliament formally requested that Maori be allowed to fight overseas as part of the expeditionary force that was hastily being raised. This was granted a month later, although with one crucial caveat: the government was allowed to appoint its own Pakeha officers and NCOs until such time as they saw fit. The response was swift. Within a month, the newly formed 28 (Maori) Battalion already had 900 recruits.

Maiki Parkinson only managed to join up through much perseverance. South African Bill Eadie had been too old; Maiki, at eighteen, was too young, although at just five foot five inches and with a round, hairless face and dark, wavy hair, he looked even younger. The minimum age for enlistment was twenty-one, and the first time Maiki went into the post office at Opotiki to get the enlistment papers, he was given a talking to by the postmaster and sent packing. Undeterred, he then hitched a ride down the coast to the next town, where he wasn't known. There he managed to get his papers, but thinking he would never get away with saying he was twenty-one when he looked so obviously younger, wrote down his age as nineteen instead. Unsurprisingly, he was rejected. His chance finally came a few weeks later when a letter arrived for his younger brother, Jerry. Unbeknown to Maiki, Jerry had also tried to join and although only sixteen, *had* written down his age as twenty-one. Jerry's letter informed him that he'd been accepted, so Maiki stole the enclosed chit and presented himself on the appointed day to the nearby drill hall. When they called out for Jerome Parkinson, Maiki stepped forward. They put him against a height chart. "You're a bit short," he was told, so Maiki said, "Well, if they can't see me, they can't shoot me." That was good enough for the recruiting officer. Maiki was in at last. "But by that time Jerry had found out I'd tricked him," says Maiki, "he was going berserk."

Nor did Maiki wait to be called into camp. When a number of reinforcements arrived in Opotiki on their way to Papakura, Maiki, his friend Jim Richarson, and two others climbed onto the bus with the rest of the reinforcements. "When we arrived at the railway station, we were quite amazed to see this iron monster steaming and hissing," says Maiki, "as we'd never seen a train before." The others had chits for their travel, but after a whip round, enough was collected to pay for Maiki and his friends' tickets. Not until they were actually inside camp were they rumbled, and although they were told they would be sent back, after a few days they were suddenly called to the orderly room, where they were given their regimental numbers and uniforms, and sent out to the parade ground.

After training at Parakura, Maiki finally left New Zealand on 30 September, 1941. "Jim Richardson and I were among the last reinforcements to leave New Zealand that year," says Maiki. His parents still didn't even know he'd joined up. As one of thirteen children, he'd been left to his own devices and had been living with cousins in Opotiki, rather than his parents who'd inherited a farm seventy miles down the coast a couple of years before. So Maiki had a strong independence of spirit and was excited at the prospect of adventure and the chance to see something of the world. And he'd be with friends: his mate Jim Richardson was on the ship with him, and he knew he'd end up in C Company. The Battalion was divided into companies on a tribal basis. Most of the young men from the northeast of the North Island were from the Ngati Porou tribe that made up much of C company, known as *Nga Kaupoi*—the Cowboys. The journey, however, was tortuous. Like Joe Madeley before him, Maiki had had no idea where they were headed, and also like Joe, he'd been sick as a dog all the way. He was also in for a disappointment on his arrival. Far from joining the battalion, Maiki was sent to Madi Camp, near Cairo, and from there to a number of courses, at which, amongst other things, he learned to dismantle mines. Then, with thirty others, he had been sent to the Canal Zone to guard Italian prisoners of war. One day, Maiki was patrolling the outside perimeter of the prison camp, marching up and down. The prisoners inside were doing the same, saying, "Ah, Bambino!" and cradling their arms and making baby noises, and pointing at Maiki and laughing. His temper rising, he stood for a while and leaned his rifle on the opposite fence, then started saying, "Inglesi bambino," pointing to himself, "boom, boom, boom," motioning to the Italians and covering his head with his hands, looking for somewhere to hide and scratching a hole in the sand. "Then I pointed to my backside," he says, "and looked down at my trousers as though I'd shit myself, and walked about bow-legged." He then began goose-stepping and with an outstretched hand in a mock-fascist salute, said, "Mussolini uno bastardo." Suddenly one of the prisoners spoke up in English, "You black bastard, you think you're a smart-arse." Maiki turned on him and said, "You cock-sucking skunk, wait till your mates get hold of you and your arse will be bigger than your mouth." They left him alone after that. By the beginning of May, he had moved again and was guarding underground ordnance stores in the Trura Caves, along the River Nile near Helwan, sweltering under the heat, and wondering whether he was ever going to join the battalion and see any action.

Middle East Command also extended to the island of Cyprus. In March, the 4th Indian Division had been divided with part of it sent to Palestine, part to Cyprus and one brigade to the Canal Zone. The 1/2 Battalion King Edward VII's Gurkha Rifles was part of 7th Brigade that had been posted to Cyprus to help improve existing defenses and to train in anti-invasion techniques.

The 1/2 Gurkhas were still there in early May when Rifleman Nainabahadur Pun arrived with a group of other reinforcements. Born in the tiny mountain village of Dudawa in the Myagdi District of West Nepal, Nainabahadur Pun had a very different upbringing from the majority of those in Eighth Army. The mountain villages of Nepal are remote to this day, but back then they were even more isolated from the rest of the world. There were only about a dozen houses in his village, and Nainabahadur Pun's home consisted of just one room, where his family lived and slept. Meals were cooked on an open fire in the middle of the room, but because there was no chimney, the smoke simply drifted through the thatch. There was a practical reason for this, however. The smoke helped dry the grain and rice that was stored on planks laid across the top of the roof, and also discouraged the numerous insects and other pests. Nainabahadur Pun slept not on a bed, but on a simple straw mat.

There was no school, and no shop, so they had to grow everything they needed and occasionally barter some of it at markets—a day's walk away—in order to buy clothes. He joined the army as soon as he could. "It is every Gurkha's ambition to join the army and have the chance to earn money for his family," says Nainabahadur Pun, "and also to make a name for himself." Gallas—or hill recruiters—regularly toured the mountain villages, and Nainabahadur Pun joined with twenty-one other potential recruits. One then ran away back to his village, but the others stayed. "We were all nervous about the training and going so far away," says Nainaba-hadur Pun, "but none of us could face the shame of returning home."

He and the other recruits all passed their selection tests and on 21 November, 1941, were enlisted into the Indian Army at Gorakpur, followed by three months' training at Dehra Dun. Discipline was "very, very strict," and conditions tough. They were housed in barrack rooms and given wooden beds—charpoys—on which to sleep, with daily inspections. The training was also extremely tough, not least because they were expected to work long hours; there would be three hours' worth in the morning before they were even given anything to eat or drink. Nainabahadur Pun enjoyed it all the same. He had been looking after himself much of his life and was already very fit with a practical approach to life. The instructors—or "Gurus" as they were known—were regarded more like elder brothers, and respected rather than feared.

Their initial training complete, they were given a short period of battle training then shipped off to the Middle East. Like Joe and Maiki before him, Nainabahadur hated the sea and was constantly sick. Nor had he ever seen the ocean before, so found it very strange and disconcerting to be out of sight of land. It was a great relief to finally reach Cyprus and to join A Company of the 1/2 Gurkha Rifles. They may not have been in the front line, but they were certainly kept busy. New equipment was arriving with which they had to familiarize themselves, and there were also a number of exercises against parachute and seaborne troops. And, of course, there were inspections, one being made by the Duke of Gloucester. Cyprus may have been a very long way from home, but Nainabahadur was proud to be a Gurkha and glad to be doing something he believed was worthwhile.

After only a few days in the desert, Cecil Beaton was beginning to understand what life was like for men like Bill Eadie, Pierre Messmer, and Albert Martin, and the thousands of other troops in the desert. He could see how much digging went on, the defenses continually being improved and deepened. Constant repairs to vehicles and telephone lines were also needed, while the enormous difficulty of transporting equipment and supplies played continual, and frequently debilitating, havoc—even in a static situation such as the one they were in. He saw that just like any office or workplace the world over, there were always incompetent people who conspired to make a difficult situation worse—and the delays and difficulties that could be caused by unnecessary inefficiency. He also saw how many long hours the men had to endure being harassed by flies and dust and a scorching sun. "The chores," he noted, "are as actual a part of war as the excitement."[21] And he also saw the destruction already caused by the see-sawing of the desert war thus far—once-pretty coastal towns like Mersa

Matruh and Sollum now pock-marked and roofless from repeated bombardment. In between were the countless carcasses of airplanes, burned-out tanks and vehicles, some even already half-buried by the ever-moving desert sand. They were, he thought, "grotesque, tortured shapes." At one point, they came across an abandoned Italian aerodrome, with numerous destroyed aircraft left on the ground. "Their skeletons looked like prehistoric animals," Cecil noted.[22]

Once at the front, first port of call was the Air HQ of the Desert Air Force at Gambut, some thirty miles east of the main Gazala Line. On arrival, Cecil was quickly ushered into the immaculate trailer of the air officer commanding the Desert Air Force, Air Vice Marshal Arthur Coningham. Cecil could not detect a single grain of sand that had passed the metal mesh at the trailer's entrance. Inside, not one item was out of place. In leather frames were photographs of Coningham's attractive-looking wife and family. "The atmosphere was peaceful," Cecil later scrawled in his diary, "as if he had everything in control, a most encouraging feeling. There emanated from this confident man an atmosphere of well-being and health."[23]

Coningham had been commanding the Desert Air Force—or DAF to use its acronym—since the previous July, and there were few who had much cause to doubt his ability, tenacity, and leadership qualities. The DAF had fought tirelessly and under his command had contributed greatly to the successes of the Crusader campaign the previous autumn. Now, with this current lull, Coningham had been able to not only build up the strength of his air units, but also give the entire DAF a complete organizational overhaul with plenty of hard training to boot. He was tough on his men, but always fair.

Coningham had been born in Australia—his father had once played test cricket for Australia—but after his parents were exposed for trying to swindle and blackmail a local priest, they fled to New Zealand when Arthur was just five. At the outbreak of war in 1914, he had been a farm worker, but hurried to enlist. After two years in the New Zealand Army serving in Samoa and then the Middle East, his health collapsed and he was discharged and sent back to New Zealand. Undeterred, he decided to sail to England, where he joined the Royal Flying Corps and eventually found himself flying over the Western Front with 32 Squadron. It was during these days that he acquired the nickname that stuck with him evermore: Mary. How he got the name is something of a mystery—it seems to have been in part worn down from "Maori," an obvious nickname for a New Zealander, and in part from his association with a New Zealand nurse called Mary. Whatever the source, he himself, for some strange reason, *liked* the name, and henceforth rarely answered to Arthur ever again. By the end of the war,

Mary Coningham was a major commanding 92 Squadron, with nine confirmed aerial victories to his name, a Military Cross and a Distinguished Service Order, as well as a reputation as a fine and natural leader of men. When the embryonic Royal Air Force was forced to make drastic cuts after the war, Coningham was not one of the officers to be axed. Instead, he enjoyed a highly active career, firstly instructing, then with the RAF display team and then with commands in Iraq and Egypt. Indeed, it was in 1925, during his time in Africa, that he made a pioneering and record-breaking flight across tropical West Africa to Helwan, near Cairo. This journey would later form the basis of the Tokoradi Route, an invaluable means of bringing supplies of aircraft to the Middle East.

The beginning of the war saw Coningham posted to Bomber Command, from which he rose to command 4 Group. For someone who had spent much of his career on fighters, working with bombers gave him valuable experience. By the time he took over as AOC in the desert, he was perfectly placed to deal with the mixed forces of fighters and light, medium, and heavy bombers under his command.

From behind the desk in his caravan, Mary chatted at length to Cecil, explaining patiently the inherent problems of trying to run an air force in such extreme conditions. Cecil was impressed by his size—over six foot and with broad shoulders and strong, well-tanned face, neck, and arms. His eyes sparkled and he was quick to laugh. It was important, he told Cecil, to make sure the men never became too static. If he discovered someone had built themselves a concrete floor, he moved them a mile. Every squadron, whether fighter or bomber, had to be ready to move their aircraft, equipment, tents—the lot—at an hour's notice. Because of the heat and because of the emptiness of the desert, it was hard to keep the men fresh and alert, but he insisted each man work every hour of daylight, to make them "pleased to go to bed." Relaxation was important too, however. "I always send batches of thirty people at a time down to the beaches," Mary told Cecil, "for a holiday to keep them efficient and give them a break of thirty-six hours." Logistics, were, of course, his biggest headache. Provisions, he told Cecil, would win the desert war. "To fight here is like trying to fill a bath without a plug," he continued, "where everything gets washed down the pipe. There are two hundred thousand gallons of petrol used here each week, eighty thousand vehicles of which the life of each is only about six months." Aircraft had to be overhauled constantly. Mary smiled. "It is, as the captured German General von Ravenstein said, the tactician's paradise and the quartermaster's nightmare."[24]

* * *

Cecil was then called to see the Army commander, whose HQ was next to Coningham's. Like Mary, General Neil Ritchie was tall and strong-looking with equally bright eyes, but there, Cecil noted, the similarity ended. Where Mary was informative and even witty, Cecil found the Eighth Army commander earnest, with an air of anxiety and worry. And shy too. Cecil tried to goad him into easy conversation, but failed. "The interview was pleasant, agreeable," noted Cecil, "but unproductive."

But well might Ritchie have been worried. Mary Coningham may have licked his air force into shape, but Eighth Army command was floundering. Across the Mediterranean, Malta had just been pounded to dust: more bombs had rained down on that tiny yet strategically important island since Christmas than during the entire London Blitz. But damaging though the bombardments were, it was the Axis threat to Malta's lifeblood—supply convoys from Gibraltar or Alexandria—that threatened Malta's survival most. Total superiority in the central Mediterranean meant the Axis had enough aircraft, torpedo boats, and submarines to make it almost impossible to resupply the island with anything like the kind of quantities of fuel, armaments, and equipment that were needed to keep Malta afloat. A large convoy had reached the island the previous September, delivering 85,000 tons. The next convoy, in February, had been forced to turn back without delivering a single ounce; the next, in March, had just about made it to Malta but only 5,000 tons had been salvaged after the remaining ships were sunk in the harbor. Best estimates suggested Malta would be able to survive—just—until July, so it was essential a convoy made it through in June.

If Malta should fall, as at the beginning of May 1942 looked quite probable, the knock-on effect in North Africa would be considerable. The reason for this was simple: as Mary Coningham had told Cecil Beaton, whoever won the supply war would ultimately win the war in the desert. As it stood, the Axis already had far shorter supply routes than the British, which dealt them an enormous advantage. Tiny Malta, with its three airfields, harbors, and submarine base, offered the best chance Britain had for attacking those supply lines from Southern Italy.

It was for this reason, as well as the psychological damage that would be caused at a time when Churchill was trying to woo the Americans to his way of thinking, that the prime minister was determined that Malta should not fall. In February, General Auchinleck, Commander-in-Chief Middle East (and Ritchie's boss), informed Churchill that he needed at least four months before he launched any new offensive. Churchill was not happy. With the precariousness of Malta troubling him greatly, he felt the capture of forward airfields in Cyrenaica would greatly help the chances of a convoy reaching the island, and so urged Auchinleck to launch his offensive as soon as possible. Auchinleck promised that he would, but again stressed that he could not do so until June—at the earliest. "To give our offensive a *reasonable* chance of success, we should have a numerical superiority in tanks of 50 percent over the Germans, and equality with the Italians."[25] And achieving this, he reckoned, was still some way off.

The italics have been added, but the message was clear: even with this superiority, Auchinleck was far from certain any offensive would be successful. The prime minister was furious and frustrated in equal measure, but Auchinleck was not to be budged. The C-in-C gave a fuller appreciation on 27 April. "Failure on our part in Libya," he wrote, "is likely to have an immediate and most far-reaching effect not only in the Middle East, but on the whole world situation. Whether the threat to Egypt from the north [through Syria] materialises or not, the threat from the west is constant, and may easily grow."[26]

This paper passed Churchill's eyes on Monday, 4 May, the very day that the South African Bill Eadie had sat on the edge of his dugout catching flies and wondering about the rumors of a new offensive.

CHAPTER 3

Britain's Mistakes:
A Brief Discourse on
Tactics and Equipment

GENERAL AUCHINLECK was certainly stretched. Middle East Command was vast, and, in the first few months of 1942, German successes in Russia meant the threat from the north through the Caucusus was a very real one. Furthermore, in February 1942, Singapore had fallen, the worst defeat ever in British history; the British were also being thrashed by the Japanese. Since the end of the Crusader battles, many of Auchinleck's troops and equipment had been diverted to the Far East, stretching his resources further; the recall of two of his Australian divisions, for example, was part of this redeployment. A time when Japanese and Axis territories stretched from the Middle to the Far East seemed distinctly possible. As far as Auchinleck was concerned, it was hard enough trying to keep the vast swathes of land under his control adequately defended without having to launch a major new offensive.

Yet this only partly explains his anxiety. To demand a ratio of two to one in armor suggests a lack of faith in Eighth Army's abilities—albeit with reason. The command was muddled and equally lacked confidence, the tactics adopted were increasingly suspect and, if anything, demonstrated a regression rather than an advancement in the command's understanding of modern warfare, while in certain rather crucial areas the equipment fell some way short of the German equivalents. America was not the only one tragically behind the times; the difference was that Britain had already been struggling against the Axis for over two years. So why was this? There is no easy answer, but the root of it lay in the years following the bloody attrition of the First World War.

By the time of the armistice in 1918, the British Army had swollen to a fantastical size, not just in terms of sheer manpower, but also in the complexity of its administration and the levels to which it had developed technologically. Of course, such a huge army was no longer needed now that the slaughter had ended and it could return to Empire policing once more. There were also huge financial constraints from a country impoverished by four long years of conflict, coupled with a general revulsion—amongst politicians and the public alike—at the mass destruction caused by a war of such magnitude. It was obvious that the armed forces should be severely reduced in size, and at the time, the "Ten Year Rule," (which ensured plans for the armed forces were based on an assumption that there would be no major conflict for a decade), was a perfectly logical measure.

But just because an army is smaller does not mean the mentality of those within it should shrink too. Defense cuts did not mean that the army should take a step back in time. Rather, there was every reason for the British to continue their traditional position at the edge of technical and industrial development. Warfare had advanced exponentially during the First World War: tanks, aircraft, bigger guns—even the thermionic valve that led to wireless telegraphy and portable radio communication—had changed the nature of warfare forever. Yet instead of embracing this new technology and applying serious thought to how it could be developed and applied, too many hid behind the traditions and mentality of the pre-1914 colonial army. Perhaps the fact that this was primarily the army's role once more did not help; there were spats in Ireland, Afghanistan, Iraq, and along the North West Frontier of India throughout the 1920s.

The culture within the army must take a large share of the blame for this complacent outlook. The British regimental system was such that "talking shop" was simply not done. In the mess, one discussed cricket, polo, or pig-sticking, not how to improve the mobility and firepower of a field howitzer. Anyone who studied the lessons of war was considered eccentric at best. This was certainly the case with Major-General Francis Tuker, who by May 1942 was commander of the 4th Indian Division. Having survived the First World War, he had briefly considered giving up the army to become a painter. However, he stuck with it and saw further action in Iraq, Assam, and northern Iran as well as border operations along the North West Frontier and Waziristan. Tuker was a great student of warfare—both ancient and modern—and like Eisenhower, spent much time thinking about the shape future wars might take. He also despaired that so few appeared to share his outlook; he was appalled, for example, by the low standard of teaching during his year at Staff College in 1925.

During the 1930s in India, he devoted much time to infantry training, and his methods were considered so successful that they were adopted by GHQ India for use throughout the Indian Army; indeed, by 1940, he had been appointed director of training for the Indian Army, much to the annoyance of many of his contemporaries: mavericks and free-thinkers like Tuker were generally regarded with suspicion and were not popular.

A young officer who tried to express his ideas to his superior officer would have been at best ignored and at worst viewed as a dangerous subversive. Journals such as the *Royal United Services Institute Journal* published forward-thinking essays, but again, little notice was taken of these and the authors were usually seen as show-offs, a vice considered to be extremely bad form. Tuker personally got around this problem by publishing many of his articles anonymously under the pseudonym "John Helland" or "Auspex." On one occasion, he submitted an essay on the use of combined air and armored forces—precisely as later used by the Germans during the Blitzkreig—to the *United Services of India* magazine, but it was rejected for being too "controversial and against the settled policy of the day."[27] (It was finally published anonymously in the same magazine in 1941, under the heading FOUND IN A BOTTLE.) Of the big thinkers of the day, none were generals, while of the best known, John Fuller was a colonel and Basil Liddell-Hart a mere captain from the 1914–18 war and a newspaper correspondent.

The most exclusive regiments were the Guards and cavalry regiments, who were largely closed societies where decorum and tradition counted for everything. Lieutenant Nigel Nicolson joined the Grenadier Guards shortly after the outbreak of war. Without exception, all officers were from public schools. In all parts of the army, officers, and other ranks ate, slept, and socialized apart, but in the Guards these barriers were accentuated by strict codes of behavior. When in uniform, Nigel was not allowed to carry any bag, parcel, or even a book. He could smoke Turkish tobacco, but not Virginian. Nor could they ever reverse a waltz. In the mess, women, religion, and politics were forbidden topics of conversation. Gentlemanly conduct that befitted one's position as a Guards officer was of paramount importance. "Asked to define a gentleman," wrote Nigel, "our commanding officer replied, 'A gentleman is a man in whose presence a woman feels herself to be a lady.'"[28] There were, in fact, sound reasons for such levels of exclusivity. It encouraged the best recruits, and its customs and traditions created a great sense of pride among its numbers, which in turn led to greater discipline and higher standards of soldiering. They were, without question, the elite regiments in the British Army. However, tradition could also get in the way of progress, and this was the rub. The Guards and cavalry regiments, for all their positives, were rarely societies in which forward thinking about warfare would flourish.

They were also the most influential within the British Army. In the thirties, most of the cavalry regiments were appalled at the notion that they should give up their horses for anything so vulgar as tanks. The Royal

Scots Dragoon Guards, for example—the Scots Greys of Waterloo fame—
were so disgusted at the idea of mechanization that even in 1938, they
were lobbying Parliament against such a move and taking their grievances to *The Times* newspaper.

Some of the old regular cavalry regiments must have glanced with envy
at their Yeomanry cousins, who were left alone with their horses. The Yeomanry had first been raised during the Napoleonic Wars, volunteer units
whose members each had to own or have access to a horse. This meant that
most were landowners, mad-keen huntsmen, and steeplechasers. In peace-
time, the Yeomanry was often little more than a club for the young gentry of
the shire, their annual two-week camp a grown-up version of Scout camp,
but with horses. It was also important that the camp be held somewhere el-
egant and aesthetically pleasing. For their last camp on the eve of war, the
Nottinghamshire Sherwood Rangers went to Welbeck, the estate of the
Duke of Portland. A photograph taken at the time is revealing: capacious
white bell tents have been pitched between the oaks of lush parkland.
Colonel E. O. "Flash" Kellett, MP, leads a parade of B Squadron. All are
proudly seated on their chargers, swords hanging from their sides, and old
Boer-war-era ammunition bandoliers slung around their necks. A few weeks
after the photograph was taken, the regiment was mobilized under Colonel
the earl of Yarborough, MC, and sent to the Middle East via Marseille—
along with their horses.

This state of affairs with the cavalry—regular and irregular—was
largely due to the inter-war chiefs of the Imperial General Staff (CIGS) not
wishing to rock the boat too much; instead a kind of compromise developed, whereby the Royal Tank Corps supported the infantry in heavily armored tanks, known as I (for infantry) tanks, while the cavalry were given
lighter, faster, less well armed and armored tanks that would be used in a
reconnaissance and forward-screening capacity, much as the cavalry had
always done, and with the Yeomanry regiments largely left to their own devices. But this meant that, in effect, the next war would be fought with tactics dictated by a few highly placed, and well-connected, cavalry officers.

Furthermore, in all parts of the army, pay was low even at the highest
ranks, and so promotion was stripped of one its great incentives. For many
middle-ranking officers, it was easier to keep one's head down and make
the most of the benefits the army offered: sport, good company, and a reasonable standard of living. This descent into complacency and even apathy was unforgivable and should have been stopped before the rot set in.
But it wasn't, and would be paid for in blood when, all too soon, Britain
found herself at war again.

* * *

While British commanders sipped their pink gins, in Germany the war machine had been gathering pace. Even before Hitler came to power, it had resisted the limitations brought by the Treaty of Versailles in 1919, hiding large amounts of weapons and covertly rearming itself throughout the twenties. Although only 100,000 strong and with severe limitations imposed upon it, the German army—the *Reichswehr*—had not been entirely disbanded nor its martial traditions cowed. Rather, the army commanders were determined to learn from defeat, and throughout the 1920s and into the thirties, devoted much energy to exhaustive analysis of the 1914–18 war and how future wars might develop. Unlike in Britain, publishing scholarly articles in military journals was actively encouraged, as was the writing of highly detailed after-action reports by officers who'd served during the First World War. One example of this difference of attitude stands out. In the early 1920s, a young German captain named Heinz Guderian wrote a series of articles about the use of mobile armor in the *Militär-Wochenblatt* (*The Military Weekly*). Ironically, it was having read British books and articles by Colonel Fuller and Liddell-Hart that had prompted Guderian to think further about such matters. Guderian was actively encouraged to develop these ideas during various military maneuvers and exercises, and also to discuss them with both military scholars and leading generals of the time. He was later instrumental in forming and training the first panzer* (armored) divisions and went on to spearhead the Blitzkriegs in Poland and the West.

The close examination undertaken by the German command in the aftermath of the First World War drew three basic conclusions. First, that purpose-built ground-attack aircraft operating in direct support of mobile ground forces was the way forward in aircraft design. While the rest of the world—and Britain included—spent much of the thirties panicking about the mass-destruction capabilities of aerial bombardment, the Germans were envisaging a different use of air power. Second, they realized that the existing highly flexible command ethos was sound and should be continued. This was known as *Auftragstaktik*—or "mission command"—and had originated during the Napoleonic Wars after the Prussians had been defeated at Jena. It was then further developed by Field Marshal Helmut von Moltke, chief of the General Staff of the Prussian army from 1857 to 1888. He realized that independent thinking and action amongst junior officers meant his forces could act more decisively and with greater speed than his enemies. In a nutshell, Auftragstaktik boiled down to this: rather than giving precise and detailed orders, a commander would tell his junior officer what his intention was, and would set clear, achievable objectives. The junior officer would then be given a free rein to carry out that task however he

---

Panzer literally translates as "armor" but is the German word for tank

best saw fit, without requiring his senior officer's approval should the situation change. While British officers would be waiting for new orders or approval for a change of tack, German officers would have made their own decisions and acted upon them—a crucial advantage. It was this flexibility that made them so particularly effective at counterattacking and responding quickly to a rapidly changing situation, a situation that could often bring the British to a standstill. This flexibility also carried through to the ranks, where every soldier, whether private or colonel, was expected to lead if the situation required him to. The British Rifle Brigade had adopted a similar practice since its formation in the Peninsular War; during training, Albert Martin, for example, had been taught to act at least two ranks above his own should the need arise. The flexibility this gave the Rifle Brigade was one of its strengths, yet this was not common practice throughout the British Army.

The third conclusion by the German army command was that it had failed to match the Allies in technology. They therefore determined not only to replicate the technological developments of their enemies—such as the tank—but advance them further, by combining increased firepower with mobility. Large amounts of highly innovative weaponry were developed in the twenties and then, once Hitler came to power, mass produced. And this emphasis on innovation continued. It was to the future that Hitler looked, not the past; he was a modernizer, a man who embraced technology and all that it could do for him and the future of Nazi Germany.

The upshot of British interwar apathy was that by the time the war started in 1939, far too many commanders were way behind the times, as was demonstrated with startling clarity during the Blitzkrieg in the west. A year later, when Rommel turned up in North Africa with two divisions (designed purely to help the Italians in a "holding" capacity), he quickly proved that German tactics, organization, and equipment still hugely outclassed anything the British could offer. Admittedly, Wavell, the Commander-in-Chief Middle East at the time, had been forced to divert a large portion of his forces to Greece and Crete, and had also had to deal with a pro-Nazi uprising in Iraq, but the harsh truth is that whenever the British came up against German forces, they lost: in the Low Countries and France in 1940, in Greece and Crete during April and May 1941, and in North Africa in March and then again in June 1941. During Wavell's June offensive, the British lost 220 tanks in three days to the Deutsche Afrika Korp's (DAK) twenty-five. No one can possibly doubt the bravery and tenacity of the British fighting men—indeed the dogged and determined resistance shown by the largely Australian and New Zealand defenders of Crete, for example, is testimony to that. It was in leadership, tactics, and equipment that they fell behind. And in North Africa, British deficiencies only served to flatter the abilities of Rommel, who, while having undeniable flair, was simply using prescribed German procedures in the use of his forces.

The experiences of the Sherwood Rangers Yeomanry during the first couple of years of war is testimony to the kind of muddle-headed thinking that was rife in the army at this time. By early 1940, they were in Palestine, and at the end of February were sent to Jaffa to help quell riots. Captain Stanley Christopherson, a former barrister and keen huntsman, had, along with the rest of A Squadron, taken part in a mounted charge down the main street with swords drawn. After this excitement, the regiment was encamped at Karkur, where "there was energetic training and shooting practice, enlivened by fine sea-bathing."[29] Only at the beginning of July were they finally told to send home their horses. "It came as a great shock and blow," noted Stanley Christopherson. "I shall miss Bob [his charger] terribly." The whole regiment was devastated at the news. "Major Donny Player, fine horseman and enthusiastic follower of hounds, was in tears as the last horse left," recorded the regimental history.[30]

For a while they became coastal gunners and then began training as motorized infantry. Then in early 1941, they were split up—two batteries were sent to Crete, RHQ and three batteries to Tobruk and one to Benghazi. Stanley Christopherson was part of A Battery sent to Tobruk. Now a major, in early April he was sent out with two lorries and three Bren carriers on a patrol to El Gubi airfield. Although they had no experience with carriers, "horsed cavalry tactics appeared to meet the situation," and although they failed to spot any of the enemy, they did spy and shoot two gazelle.[31]

Enthusiasm and a love of sport—important ingredients to the Sherwood Rangers—was hardly going to defeat the Germans; but matters barely improved when they were finally mechanized in the autumn of 1941. Throughout November and December the entire regiment had just three tanks, and they were still hopelessly under-strength and undertrained when, on 30 March, one Grant tank arrived. The farce continued when one of the regiment's light tanks crashed into it the same day. That these men would soon be expected to take on the highly trained and battle-hardened panzers of the Afrika Korps was, frankly, a desperate proposition.

To those unfamiliar with military jargon and terminology, understanding the complexities of structure and organization can appear confusing. An army of the Second World War—British, American, German, or Italian— was divided into corps, divisions, brigades, regiments, and battalions. A force could be designated an army if it consisted of two or more corps. In the case of Eighth Army, for example, by May 1942, it consisted of two corps: XIII and XXX. A corps—its number always written in Roman numerals—had no great significance but was a contained force within an army, usually comprising at least two divisions, i.e., no less than about 30,000 men. Thus, next down the scale was a division. This was still a major tactical and administrative unit of an army, and within its structure contained all the various forms of arms and services necessary for sustained combat. However, different divisions had different emphases: the fighting core of an Infantry division was an infantry brigade, made up of a group of infantry battalions. These battalions were the basic infantry unit, usually made up of four companies of, in total, around seven hundred to nine hundred men of all ranks. In the British case, these infantry divisions were usually from a particular part of the country (such as the 51st Highland Division from Scotland), or the Empire (Tuker's 4th Indian Division). An armored division, on the other hand, had as its core an armored brigade, comprising a tank regiment (about seventy tanks at full strength), and a motor battalion made up of mortar gun, machine-gun and anti-tank gun teams. A typical British armored division would comprise around 15,000 officers and men, while an infantry division would be slightly larger—nearer 17,000 men, although these figures could fluctuate considerably.

In May 1942, the German Afrika Korps comprised three divisions: the 15th Panzer, 21st Panzer, and 90th Light. Panzer divisions were equally strong in both tanks and infantry, while the Light was essentially infantry, although still fully mobile and motorized. At any rate, all German divisions were fully mobile and were regarded as the key operational unit. And however they were grouped, these divisions moved together, en masse, each unit close to the next and arranged in such a way that tanks, artillery and motorized infantry could all support each other with ease and with the minimum amount of fuss, however the situation changed, boosted by the use of Auftragstaktik, which minimized the need for time-wasting orders.

By December 1941, General Auchinleck, Commander-in-Chief Middle East, was thinking hard about reorganizing his forces, especially those in Eighth Army. Analysis of the winter operations had drawn clear conclusions that tanks, operating alone, could not win battles. This was something the Germans had worked out over a decade before, and had been based on the assumption that the principal role of the tank was to kill infantry and destroy small arms, such as machineguns. In contrast to the confused British way of thinking, the Germans realized that an armored battle of tank versus tank was to be avoided as far as possible. On meeting enemy tanks, the

Germans would withdraw and try and lure them toward their own anti-tank guns.

All too often the British tanks fell for this ruse, believing they had the Germans on the run and rushing toward them and invariably destruction. By the end of 1941, Auchinleck and his staff finally came to the conclusion that their view of how tanks should operate had, indeed, been flawed, and asserted that in future, "tanks must act in the closest co-operation with infantry and artillery in order to defeat the German armored forces." This, of course, was absolutely right. Furthermore, they concluded that the necessary understanding and cooperation needed between all arms could be achieved only if they all lived and trained "in the most intimate association."[32] This was also very sensible, especially since there had been little or no all-arms training up until then, and no common training program or doctrine amongst armored units; cavalry regiments, particularly, tended to do their own thing.

Francis Tuker had drawn the same conclusions about the need for all-arms cooperation and close training many years before, and upon his arrival in the Middle East in December 1941, Auchinleck asked him for his views; after all, the Commander-in-Chief was an Indian Army man too, and was fully aware of Tuker's reputation for training. Glad to be of help, Tuker wasted no time in submitting a paper in which he emphasized the need for a *mobile* corps of two armored divisions supported by a lorried infantry division, whose assault troops would be mounted in armor—in other words, exactly the same setup as the German Afrika Korps. His suggestions, however, were not adopted. In fact, he was never given any feedback at all about his proposals, nor did he ever discover whether his paper was passed onto GHQ Eighth Army; for although Tuker and Auchinleck agreed about the need for mobility and cooperation of all arms, they were thinking along quite different lines about how to achieve this.

The truth was that Eighth Army was quite overawed by the dash and cohesion of the Germans. Even the troops began to regard the "Desert Fox" with barely concealed awe, and this was not healthy. The Italians, by contrast, were viewed with little esteem: they were considered to be poorly trained and their equipment hardly up to much; moreover, before Rommel turned up, Eighth Army had crushed them at every turn. This only exacerbated the British inferiority complex when it came to the Germans, whose smaller numbers seemed all too often to get the better of them.

The trouble was that British troops were not trained like German troops. To begin with, there was no Mission Command. German use of radio was far better too: they took more effort with radio security and in listening to and analyzing the less-secure radio codes of the British. The trickle-down effect was twofold: the Germans had less need to talk over the radio because they already knew what they should do, and they also had a greater understanding before and during an engagement about what the British were doing.

Auchinleck wanted to ape German tactics, but at the same time realized British training and structure did not allow this. Not for a while, at any rate. The answer, he believed, was to follow German principles, but in a way that could be adapted by the existing Eighth Army. First and foremost, he wanted greater flexibility and cooperation of all-arms and the only way to achieve this, he concluded, was to split up his divisions into smaller brigades, either armored, motorized, or infantry. Brigades were traditionally the fighting core of a division, but because he wanted them to now operate independently, he attached a proportion of artillery and other arms to these newly formed brigade groups and even gave them each an administrative headquarters, enabling them to operate independently.

So it was that by May 1942, the brigade group, rather than the division, had become the principal fighting unit. They had developed from "Jock Columns," small task forces of all arms—infantry, tanks, and gunners—initially designed as highly mobile forces for reconnaissance and harassing enemy supply routes. The name "Jock Column" came from their primary proponent, Jock Campbell no less, Sam Bradshaw's commander at Sidi Rezegh. Campbell was a dynamic leader, highly popular among his men and senior officers alike, and with no shortage of personal courage. These columns had performed well during various moments of the Crusader tank battles, but instead of analyzing these successes calmly and sensibly, Eighth Army command had latched onto the notion of small mobile columns as being the panacea with which to combat the mighty German panzer divisions. Jock Columns, it was decided, would continue to be used in their established form, while the main bulk of the fighting would be carried out by brigades—perceived as operating like Jock Columns, only larger and less unwieldy than whole divisions.

Tuker was horrified by this development, and with reason. The reality was that brigade groups were scarcely more maneuverable than whole divisions, and offered considerably *less* in terms of concentrated firepower. This fragmentation of the available forces meant that Rommel could now potentially pick off these smaller forces one by one with his much larger divisions of mobile all-arms. Success in open battle depended on packing a punch with speed, not lightly tapping the opposition on the shoulder.

* * *

The Gazala Line had begun only as a temporary measure covering the construction of defenses along the Egyptian border, a line to which Eighth Army could have retreated had Rommel continued his advance in February and overrun Tobruk. However, once the Axis stopped short of Gazala, and pressure began to mount for a British offensive, the position had taken on greater significance: either it would provide the launchpad for Eighth Army's attack, or the place from which they would make their next stand against Rommel's forces. And despite Auchinleck's quest for greater mobility, it was felt that a strong defensive line with minefields, coils of barbed wire, and properly constructed gun and troop emplacements—rather like the lines of the Western Front in the previous war—should be able to stop anything Rommel threw at them.

But how long should the line be? Ritchie reckoned around forty miles should do the trick—enough to prevent a successful outflanking maneuver. But forty miles was a long way—especially since it was to be manned by around 80,000 men. In other words, a line much the same distance as San Francisco to San Jose was defended by the equivalent of a full house at, say, the Hollywood Bowl. Static infantry brigades were put along the line, with mobile armored and motor brigades waiting to pounce in support behind them. But the size of these brigades meant there was no strength in depth. And because of Auchinleck's need to police the whole of the Middle East command, there were barely enough troops in reserve, should they be required.

As it was, the line was worryingly lopsided. In static positions there were only seven infantry brigades, each formed into defensive "boxes"—a holdover from the eighteenth century and essentially a self-contained defensive position along the line. The size of one of these boxes varied—but typically, they were usually a few miles wide in diameter. All around them were rings of mines, wire, and prepared gun emplacements, slit trenches, while somewhere near the center would be soft-skinned lorries and transport vehicles, small dumps of supplies and the various brigade and battalion HQs, a collection of tents and maybe even a caravan or two. They were entirely self-contained deployments of as many as 10,000 men, although, the Free French Brigade, for example, was less than 4,000 strong. Each brigade had a supply unit—or echelon—that brought ammunition, food, and water and so on from depots and dumps dotted between twenty and forty miles behind the lines.

The boxes were joined together by minefields, and while five of these were bunched fairly close together in the north, the two boxes that covered the latter two-thirds of the line were hopelessly far apart. When Cecil Beaton had first driven into the Western Desert, he had done so with a sense of incredulous awe at the size of the vast openness it presented.

"How any 'lines' of battle can exist," he wrote, "let alone be 'held,' is beyond my comprehension. A regiment is soon reduced to the proportion of
a pinprick in this terrain."[33] Absolutely. Yet Pierre Messmer and the rest of
the Free French at the bottom of the line were a staggering fifteen miles
from 150th Brigade, their nearest neighbors to the north. If they were left
alone by the enemy, they were too far away to be of any help to the rest of
the army. But if they *were* attacked—and they must have seemed too obvious an option to be ignored—they would be quickly isolated from the rest
of Eighth Army, facing Ritchie with a conundrum: either he would have to
leave them to their fate, which was a complete waste, or channel forces and
supplies as quickly as possible, which would be a huge drain on his limited
resources.

Admittedly, the static infantry boxes were supported by armored
brigades hovering behind the lines. They were formed up across a similar
sized tract of land to the infantry brigades—i.e., a few miles in diameter—
and also had several locations where gun emplacements were prepared,
where they hoped they would be able to lie in wait and surprise any enemy
attackers. But if Rommel attacked the line head-on, they could only react
to where the Axis decided to concentrate their assault; until they arrived
on the scene, the enemy would always be able to bring to bear greater,
more concentrated forces than the defenders could offer.

Brigade-strength boxes, then, led to the dispersal of forces in defense,
while the mobile columns led to a dispersal of forces in attack. As Rommel
himself once said to a captured British officer, "What difference does it
make if you have two tanks to my one, when you spread them out and let
me smash them in detail?"[34] It was a good point—not that any of the British
command was taking note.

The faulty strategy didn't stop there. It was also naïve to place the
French, of all people, at the bottom of the line. Should the French be cut
off and abandoned, the political consequences would have been great.
The French had still not recovered from being "abandoned" at Dunkirk,
nor had their anger abated since the sinking of the French Fleet at Oran
in July 1940. De Gaulle, the leader of the Free French, had been considerably upset by the British occupation of Syria, a pre-war French colony, and
the level of mistrust between these uneasy allies was only growing; so
adding fuel to the fire would not be a good idea. It was a ridiculous and totally unnecessary risk, and would have made much more sense to place
them amidst other brigades in the more heavily defended northern sector.

The whole concept of the Gazala Line seems even more cockeyed
when one considers that Tobruk—some sixteen miles behind the northern
sector—had held out against the Axis for nine months with only one division. Surely, with the defenses improved and with minefields laid down,

Tobruk could have been made pretty much impregnable: a semicircle of lines with both flanks closed by the sea. Furthermore, surrounding the port to the south, east, and west, were a number of steep escarpments with only a few openings for wheeled vehicles, and which were thus easier to defend than open scrub. Admittedly, the Royal Navy had had a torrid time trying to resupply Tobruk throughout the siege, but during this current lull enough supplies could have been safely brought in to last six months, if need be. And if Rommel tried to bypass the position, he would soon come unstuck because there was no other port between Tobruk and Alexandria, a distance of four hundred miles. It would be a simple task for Eighth Army to break position and sever the Axis lines of communication. Instead, mines were lifted from the defenses of Tobruk and moved to the Gazala Line.

However obvious these flaws in the plan might seem now, both Auchinleck and Eighth Army command embraced them wholeheartedly. None of them were fools, especially not Auchinleck, but all had convinced themselves that the plan in hand was the best in the circumstances. Francis Tuker was not so easily persuaded, however, and spent much energy trying to talk them out of it.

In February, as the 4th Indian Division was being employed with helping build the Gazala Line defenses, Ritchie paid a visit and Tuker expressed his reservations about such a linear defense, especially one that offered no obvious natural features to recommend it. His concerns were swept aside. Equally unimpressed was Brigadier Harding of XIII Corps Staff, when Tuker spoke to him later in the month about his anxiety for the exposed position of Bir Hacheim. In March, he had a go at Norrie, Commander of XXX Corps, urging him to reconsider Tobruk—but again, his arguments fell on deaf ears.

His final attempt to dissuade the army command from their current line of thinking was on 15 March. Ritchie came to see him and for the best part of twenty-four hours, Tuker urged him to at least ensure Tobruk was properly defended with new minefields and improved anti-tank ditches. But it was no good. The Gazala Line defended Tobruk, Ritchie told him—and that would have to be enough.

Then what about using 4th Indian Division in a similar role to the German 90th Light, Tuker suggested, i.e., as highly mobile lorried infantry? Fat chance. Other plans had been made for 4th Indian. They would not even be given the chance to retrain as a division, for as at the Gazala Line, so throughout the Middle East, divisions were being systematically dismantled. Far from being deployed en masse, the 4th Indian was to be scattered. Part of it was sent to Cyprus, another part to Palestine; 11th Brigade was dispatched to the Canal Zone for training in "combined operations." Two battalions were lost to Tenth Army. For Tuker, it was a bitter blow and left him hopping between Cyprus and Palestine, determinedly training his troops, however dispersed, so that when eventually they were called upon, they might show Eighth Army Command just what they were capable of.

Behind much of Auchinleck's—and Ritchie's—concerns, however, was the problem of equipment, a matter that was linked directly to the Commander-in-Chief's issues over training and organization. While Britain was proving herself to be perfectly capable of building four-engine bombers and ever-larger naval guns that could hurl a shell more than twelve miles, much of the equipment was simply not up to scratch.

Once again, these problems dated back to the 1920s and 1930s, but it meant that by the outbreak of war much of the equipment used by the army was the inferior of its equivalent in Germany. By May 1942, it still hadn't caught up. This disparity related to a multitude of material, from radios and even to petrol cans. The British four-gallon kerosene tin was notoriously flimsy and prone to leak. "It was my estimate that for every two gallons that were shipped to the Middle East," wrote General Tuker, "one gallon actually reached the vehicle. All along the road as one followed the petrol convoys there would be a constant and abundant stream pouring from under the tailboards."[35] This might be a slight exaggeration, but he wasn't far off the mark. The German jerrycan, on the other hand was a shining example of Teutonic efficiency: sturdy, airtight, with a levered fastener, it came in a variety of sizes and was ideally suited for its task. In contrast, the task to which the British four-gallon tin was best suited was as a brew-can for making tea. Both radios and jerrycans were always captured with glee by British troops. Even the Tommy helmet was less efficient than the German—or American equivalent. While its rim offered good protection from shards dropping directly from above, it perched on the top of its wearer's head and gave no close cover around the back or sides.

But for the soldiers, this disparity showed itself more obviously when it came to guns and tanks. It's not quite fair to say that the Road Traffic Act of 1930 was responsible for this, but strange though it may seem, it certainly had some bearing. At the time, the British government wanted freight to move by rail, of which there was a vast network, and not road, and so the act imposed heavy penalties for road haulage with payloads of over 2.5 tons. This had the desired effect of ensuring rail was the only real means of transporting freight, but also meant there was little or no call for heavy road vehicles. Consequently, most commercial vehicle manufacturers built only lightweight lorries that did not require large engines. And with minimal armored vehicle production before 1940, it was hardly worth the while of Britain's vehicle manufacturers to bother investing in the machinery or know-how to build anything as large as tanks. Furthermore, few vehicle factories were large enough to cope with the mass production of tanks. An exception was Vickers-Armstrong, and also Nuffield Mechanisation & Aero, which was the ordnance branch of the Morris Motor Company. Admittedly, Nuffields built a purpose-built tank factory, but most of their design and production staff were drawn from Morris, who had previously built nothing larger than an eight-ton lorry, and so had little experience with building anything as substantial as a tank.

Muddled control at the top did little to help. For much of the 1930s, tank development was run by the War Office and the CIGS, but with the help of the heads of various departments, such as the Directorate of Mechanization and Mechanizational Experimental Department, and even the Master General of Ordnance. Needless to say, too many people were involved and there was little central policy direction or a cohesive plan. By 1938, responsibility for the supply of tanks was handed over to the Ministry of Supply, but by then it was too late. And anyway, there were not enough steel plants and foundries to build the necessary armor plating required for tanks. In 1939, for example, some fourteen-inch armor plate had even been ordered from Bohler & Co in Nazi-occupied Austria—revealing at a throw the current armor standard of British tanks.

The railway also imposed severe limitations. Railways linked every port and major factory, not to mention military establishments. Rail was the only real means of transportation, and so tanks had to fit the railways: it was no good building a tank that could not pass under a bridge or through a platform because it was either too wide or tall. The problem was that if the width of the tank was limited, then so was the width of the turret; and if the size of the turret was limited, then so was the size of the gun on which it operated.

This didn't seem to matter in the 1930s, because the army planners believed tanks would rarely operate at distances of over five hundred yards, in which case the highly reliable and accurate two-pounder gun was just the job and could fit into the smallest of turrets. Unfortunately, as the Germans soon showed very quickly in North Africa, they were only too happy to operate at greater distances, and 1,200 yards, not 500 became the standard field of fire. Not only that, in Germany and elsewhere in continental Europe, the loading gauges of the railways were much wider. Platforms were built lower and bridges and tunnels wider, so freight with a greater width than the wagon on which it was being carried could be transported. Both the German panzers Mark III and IV were over a foot wider than the British Crusader, Matilda, or Valentine tanks—and they had the potential to be fitted with even larger, more powerful guns, which is exactly what happened. The Mark III, for example, was adapted with a longer 50mm gun similar to the successful Pak 38 anti-tank gun—which gave it substantially greater velocity.

By May 1942, however, the Germans only had a few Mark III "specials," and the Italian tanks were significantly worse than those of the British—both in terms of armor and armament. On paper, at least, there wasn't much difference between the majority of panzer Mark IIIs and, say, the British equivalent, the Crusader. Paper statistics, however, can be deceptive. Although the Mark III and the Crusader were both supposed to have 50mm-thick frontal armor, in reality the Crusader's was rarely this strong and certainly never had the confidence of its users—Sam Bradshaw included—who always maintained that pretty much anything could get through it. Both struggled with the sand and dust of the desert, where engines were literally sandpapered to death. German mechanical reliability suffered in North Africa, as did every machine—but not as much as British tanks. Crusaders would usually develop oil or water leaks after a couple of days; the Nuffield engine was one of the worst ever built for a British tank. In contrast, the Daimler-Benz engines of the panzers were first class. A glance at a Mark III or IV standing side-by-side with a Crusader will amply demonstrate their superiority: one looks solid, strong and formidable; the other lightweight and ineffective. Appearance is not everything, but it usually is.

The only advantage Crusaders had was speed. Designed as light "cruisers," they had a maximum speed of nearly 30 mph, far faster than any other tank in North Africa. But while this must have seemed like a good idea to pre-war planners, it was next to useless in the heat of battle, where only two things counted: firepower and ability to withstand firepower—i.e., arms and armor. German tanks, on the other hand, were built for a multitude of roles. All were considered to be "medium tanks"—there were no I tanks or cruisers. Any panzer could be used singly with a small patrol (and often was to great effect), or en masse in an armored division.

As it was, the British I tanks—the Valentines and Matildas—were more or less obsolete by May 1942. Large numbers of American Stuarts—or "Honeys," as the British called them—had begun arriving the previous year, but like the Crusader, these were light cruiser tanks, similarly armed and only fractionally better armored. As one British tank man commented, they were "more like Baby Austins than bloody tanks."[36] The last variety of tank available to Eighth Army was the new American Grant, which was undoubtedly the best in its armory, even if not quite a match for the German panzer Mark IV. A medium tank like the Mark III and IV panzers, this heavily armored machine also possessed a 75mm gun, which, although set in the hull with a small traverse, packed the kind of punch needed to take on the panzers. There were 138 of these available to Eighth Army by the end of May, most of which were still unfamiliar to the men who used them. In contrast, the Germans could call on 320 Mark IIIs and IVs.

The preeminent weapon in the desert was, however, the gun, rather than the wheels it moved on. Again, the terminology can be confusing. The two-pounder, for example, refers to the weight of the shell it fired (2.38 pounds to be precise), while 75mm refers to the muzzle diameter. In terms of millimeters, the two-pounder was a 39mm gun. But size was not everything; velocity was more important—the speed and distance with which a gun fired its shell. The velocity of the two-pounder was as good as anything in terms of feet traveled per second over six hundred yards, and could, in theory penetrate 40mm of armor at 1,000 yards (although the users disputed this), but then its effectiveness tapered dramatically. This still made it useful against the less well-armed Italian tanks at ranges of 1,000 yards or less, but if it struck armor of over 40mm, its shell simply bounced off—which was exactly what happened when it came up against the panzers. The Grant's 75mm gun was better than the short-muzzle panzer Mark IV, and on a par with the longer-barreled 75mm.

Then there were anti-tank guns. Again, Eighth Army was riddled with two-pounders, small, and highly maneuverable, but fairly ineffective in May 1940, let alone May 1942. Warfare had sometimes operated at five hundred yards or less in the wooded and hilly countryside of Northern France, but certainly not so in flat open desert, where guns with open sights—a clear view to the target—could see for over a mile. At any rate, it would have been more sensible to produce guns that operated with decent velocity at 500 yards *and* 1,500 yards. After the disaster at Dunkirk, Britain was faced with a choice: either churn out plenty of two-pounders immediately with the existing infrastructure to do so, or wait for the new equipment with which to mass produce the larger six-pounder. Churchill chose the former on the basis that it was better to have some guns, however useless, than none at all. The new six-pounder anti-tank guns were finally beginning to arrive in North Africa, but by the end of May there were only 112 available—which was not enough.

This meant that Eighth Army had to use the remaining 516 two-pounders and try and adapt the twenty-five-pounder field gun in an anti-tank role instead. These were totally unsuited to the role. Field guns are howitzers, supposed to operate at distance and to lob shells in an arc. Consequently, although capable of firing heavy shells, their velocity was not good. Look at any picture of field artillery firing, and its muzzle will be pointing skyward at an angle; in contrast, the muzzle of a tank or an anti-tank gun will be almost horizontal.

One of the field regiments changing to this role was the South Notts

Hussars of the Royal Horse Artillery. Both Bombardier Ray Ellis of 425 Battery and Lance Sergeant Harold Harper of the newly formed 520 Battery had been in the desert a long time. Both had joined the regiment pre-war, Ray in 1938, and Harold in March 1939. And both had left England for the first time when the regiment was deployed overseas in January 1940. They'd been in the Middle East ever since, including a long stretch supporting the Australians during the Siege of Tobruk.

Both had become used to the vagaries of the desert—the flies, the heat, the cold. Ray had even had sandfly fever and gastroenteritis, the latter during the breakout from Tobruk; Harold had suffered from dysentery, jaundice twice, and countless numbers of camel ticks. Once he'd even had a snake in amongst his blankets, which had reared up and tried to bite him; he'd hit it over the head with a shovel. Like most of those in the South Notts Hussars, they could also sing "Lili Marlene" in three languages. Neither, however, had been expecting the new role that had been prepared for them in the spring of 1942.

After the breakout from Tobruk, the South Notts Hussars had been sent to the Nile Delta to retrain and regroup. Ray Ellis began to realize something was up when he was sent on anti-tank gunnery course. Furthermore, as part of Auchinleck's reorganization of Eighth Army, the South Notts Hussars were attached to the 22nd Armoured Brigade, with each battery assigned to work with a tank regiment. Ray's 425 Battery became attached to the 3rd County of London Yeomanry, while Harold's 520 Battery joined the Royal Gloucester Hussars. This in itself was loopy thinking. By trying to be the equal of German tactics, the British command was forgetting the basics: splitting up an artillery regiment in such a way was fragmenting British firepower even more.

Ray Ellis was certainly not that impressed. Quite apart from its lack of velocity, he felt the twenty-five-pounder was "out of its class when attempting to compete with fast-moving, tracked and armored vehicles equipped with guns of equal caliber plus heavy automatic weapons." Furthermore, as Ray points out, "the twenty-five-pounder was, by comparison, slow to traverse and immobile, which made it an easy target."[37] Even worse for the gun crews was that the shield around the gun offered almost no protection. This was fine if fighting in a static position behind the lines, but when in open battle against tanks meant they would be cruelly exposed.

The various batteries soon began training alongside their new colleagues in the brigade, practicing operating in box formation all the way up to the Gazala area. None of them were particularly proficient at moving like this, so there was confusion at times, especially during night exercises, when everyone started getting mixed up. "It was a little disheartening," says Ray, "because we just hadn't had long enough. There were conferences galore."[38]

When they finally reached the front, they discovered that they were to be operating in a mobile box some ten miles behind 150th Brigade at the center of the Gazala Line. There were also daring new plans for the South Notts Hussars gunners, who were to operate away from the edge of the box. The guns would be put into action in such a position that they would appear to be easy meat for the enemy tanks. As soon as the panzers approached, the British tanks would break cover and attack their flanks. "It was straight from *Alice in Wonderland*," says Ray. "The whole idea filled us with horror and dismay because it depended on split-second timing that is rarely ever achieved in such situations."

Fortunately, this practice was never adopted in battle, but the regiment was still expected to operate on the edge of the box. Clearly, using twenty-five-pounders in an anti-tank role was far from ideal, but with the lack of proper anti-tank guns, what else could their commanders do?

Well, actually, there was something. The German 88mm, by far the best weapon on either side, had been originally designed as an anti-aircraft gun, but in the desert had acquired a highly effective dual role. The mere thought of one of these guns brought British soldiers out in a cold sweat, and with good reason—just four had heavily contributed to the destruction of Sam Bradshaw's 6 Royal Tank Regiment the previous November. While the two-pounder could get through 40mm at 1,000 yards on a good day, the 88mm could penetrate 100mm of armor at the same range and only fractionally less at 1,500 yards. Or, to put it plainly, an 88mm could completely destroy a Crusader with one shot from a distance of one and a half miles. Rommel may not have had hundreds of these guns at his disposal, but then with that kind of effectiveness, he didn't need them in bulk.

The British equivalent was the 3.7-inch anti-aircraft gun, with a slightly larger muzzle diameter, but similar levels of velocity. These guns were designed to send a twenty-eight-pound shell in a straight line some 20,000 feet into the air, which is a long way, especially when one considers that cruising heights for modern-day passenger jets is less than double this height. Like the 88mm, the 3.7-inch gun came in two forms—mobile and static. The 3.7-inch weighed around 7.5 tons on the ground compared with the 88mm's 5.5 tons, but that was no real obstacle to its use, and there were certainly lorries in North Africa capable of towing 3.7-inch guns from A to B. The 88mm also had a good telescopic sight, while the 3.7-inch did not, but again, this was not insurmountable. Levels of British ingenuity could certainly cope with such a challenge, especially as much of the firing occurred over open sights. A pair of binoculars could soon establish range. In fact, 3.7-inch guns around Tobruk had been used with some effect during the siege. Nor were the British short of 3.7-inch guns in May 1942. There were 220 of them in Egypt, many more than the besieged island of Malta could muster, for example. In the Canal Zone—hardly the focus of fierce fighting—there were 106, and 48 around Cairo. Surely some of these could be spared. In Britain there were also a large number of three-inch anti-tank guns now sitting idle, having been replaced by the 3.7-inch. They may not have had quite the same velocity as the 88mm, but they would certainly have been hugely effective in an anti-tank role in the desert.

Another argument against the use of the 3.7-inch was the time it would have taken to train crews, but this simply doesn't stand up. If twenty-five-pounders could suddenly be given radically different roles, then why not an anti-aircraft gun? The principles of firing a gun were much the same whatever the size or shape they took. Swapping of guns and equipment also occurred throughout the desert war as both sides overran previous positions and took on board whatever weaponry was left behind, guns included. Ray Ellis certainly agrees with this. "To say that it would take too long to retrain the gun crews is utter nonsense," he says. "Obviously to change the role of an artillery regiment would take longer than that, but in time of war such a thing would be nothing more than commonplace." Harold Harper agrees. "It wouldn't have been difficult to train us on a 3.7-inch," he says, "especially as we would have been using it as an anti-tank gun and not anti-aircraft. And the principles are the same on most guns." And, of course, the Germans had managed it without much ado.

So why weren't they used? It's hard to say. A lack of imagination. Red tape. Maybe it was simply down to the kind of muddle-headed thinking that was prevalent within the Eighth Army at the time. Yes, there would have been some problems adapting such a gun, but these difficulties were seen as an excuse not to try rather than as obstacles to overcome. The decision was typical of a command that had forgotten some of the fundamental basics of any kind of warfare, let alone a modern one.

Fortunately, however, there was one area of Middle East forces that was in pretty good shape. In the early stages of the war, the RAF had also been behind the times. Bomber strategy had not been successful or in any way developed, while fighter tactics had proved less effective than those of the Luftwaffe. Nor had there been any real concept of the RAF working in tandem with the army, as the Luftwaffe had demonstrated so skillfully during the Blitzkrieg. Indeed, inter-service tensions and rivalries had frequently gotten in the way of the job in hand.

The Battle of Britain had done much for the confidence of the RAF, however. A German invasion had been avoided by the courage of the RAF's fighter pilots and by the skill with which squadrons had been deployed and the good use made of radar and the observer corps. The mighty Luftwaffe, who before the summer of 1940 had swept all before them, had been forced to call off the fight and retire with their reputation for invincibility severely shaken. Furthermore, the RAF now had a hard core of seasoned, battle-hardened fighter pilots who could pass on their experience to the new blood coming through—men like Squadron Leader Billy Drake.

A pre-war pilot, Billy Drake had flown Hurricanes in the Battle of France, where he had destroyed several enemy aircraft before being shot down and wounded himself. He made a good recovery and after a stint of instructing, rejoined a combat squadron for the tail end of the Battle of Britain. By early 1941, he was a squadron leader and being posted to Sierra Leone in West Africa. Someone obviously realized that this was a waste of good talent, and so in March 1942, Billy was sent to North Africa as a supernumerary squadron leader to 280 Squadron and then, on 25 May, he took over command of 112 "Shark" Squadron.

By this time, although still only twenty-four, Billy was an "ace," with double the five confirmed kills needed to be labeled as such. He had learned that to shoot anything down, a pilot needed to get in as close as possible, that he also needed to watch his back at all times and to get maximum performance from any aircraft he was put into. He also knew that pilots had to adapt quickly to any situation, which was just as well because although both 280 and 112 Squadrons were equipped with Kittyhawk fighters, they were no longer being used in the traditional interceptor role. "The first thing I saw," said Billy upon his arrival in North Africa, "was a Kittyhawk with a bloody great bomb strapped underneath it." The new emphasis was on ground-attack—flying in swiftly at low levels, dropping a single bomb and then machine-gunning—strafing—other targets on the ground. "It was ground attack first and foremost and then occasional air-to-air work," says Billy. Billy's huge combat experience would prove invaluable, because this was new work for everyone. "The whole of my air force career in World War II was learning on the job," he says.

This change of role—or emphasis at any rate—was largely due to the efforts of Air Vice Marshal Mary Coningham, AOC Desert Air Force. In sharp contrast to his Eighth Army counterpart, Mary Coningham was an outstanding leader: bold, innovative, and resolute. Although he had led the DAF successfully since his arrival the previous summer, his grasp had tightened considerably since the arrival of new staff. Most significant of these was Air Commodore Tommy Elmhirst. Although the same age as Mary, Tommy Elmhirst was shorter, less imposing, and more quietly spoken; but his large, flamboyant eyebrows and good-humored face leant him an air of sagaciousness that was not unfounded. His background was naval—from ships he had been transferred to airships in the Royal Navy

Air Service, and by the end of the war found himself part of the newly
formed Royal Air Force. And although an experienced pilot, by the Battle of Britain he had become a controller—a ground job—and later a
bomber-station commander.

He was the perfect foil for Mary Coningham, who, while undoubtedly charismatic and inspired, was somewhat haphazard in his methods.
Tommy Elmhirst, on the other hand, was a supremely good organizer,
and it was as Chief Administrator that he joined Mary Coningham at
Air HQ in Gambut, east of Tobruk in February 1942. At the time, the
RAF did not have air superiority—many of their promised replacements had been redirected to help the crisis in the Far East, and as
Tommy reached Gambut he saw columns of smoke rising from the edges
of the airfield—burning aircraft recently shot up on the ground by enemy fighters.

Within a few days, Tommy had a pretty clear idea of what was needed,
and set to work. The lull proved a godsend, and by May, the DAF was
completely reorganized. Gone were small piecemeal units. In their place
came a group of fighters, divided into three wings with their own administrative staff and repair units, and where possible, based on the same
landing ground. This centralization of administration enabled wing and
squadron commanders to get on with the job of leading their men and
also halted the fragmentation of the DAF.

This was the exact opposite of what Auchinleck had done to Eighth
Army. The DAF's new fighting unit was a wing of three squadrons, rather
than just a single squadron. Elmhirst also ensured their mobility was
increased by establishing plenty of reserves of fuel, ammunition, bombs,
vehicles, and aircraft on a number of landing grounds all within easy
reach. Mobile radar units and air controllers were established near the
front line at Gazala and also at El Adem, forty miles behind the line in the
east. This meant that if need be, wings could leapfrog one another, either
forward or back, at a moment's notice.

This, in turn, meant that Mary Coningham now had the infrastructure
with which to bring his air force into shape. Training was intensive. Since
most captured pilots appeared to think little of RAF shooting abilities,
Mary insisted his pilots practice hard at "shadow firing" rather than the
prescribed RAF method of shooting at towed targets. Navigation was also
improved and regular discussions held with bomber crews. Groundcrews
were also brought into line: rapid refueling and rearming was drilled into
each and every man. There were weekly conferences between Mary and his
wing commanders in which tactics, training, and administration were discussed and analyzed in detail, so that each leader knew exactly what was
expected of him.

In fact, what Mary Coningham was developing were ideas about how to win air superiority and how to support the army to the best of his ability. He had seen how devastating Stuka dive-bombers could be—but they were slow and easy pickings for fighter aircraft. So instead, he had started using fighters in a similar role—faster, more agile and potentially far more effective. The American Kittyhawks were not good at high altitude, but at 10,000 feet or below they could more than hold their own. Furthermore, they could outdive both the German Messerschmitt 109 and the Italian Macchi 202 and had a very stable gun platform, so were ideally suited to the ground-attack role. Hurricanes, too, while pretty much obsolete against either Me 109s or Macchi 202s, could be used as night fighters and in a ground-attack role. Some Hurricanes were also armed with high-velocity cannons and used as low-level "tank busters." In addition, he could also call on a number of twin-engined aircraft: light and medium bombers and attack aircraft such as the heavily armed Beaufighter, equally at home attacking shipping or land targets.

The Luftwaffe, on the other had, were losing their cohesion. Fighters were used for strafing, but rarely in a bombing role, and they were also still too dependent on Stukas for low-level bombing. Nor was their administration comparable to that established by Tommy Elmhirst. There was no system by which squadrons could rapidly move from one airfield to another; rather, their units effectively closed down when on the move. Nor did Rommel enjoy the close relationship with General Von Waldau that Mary Coningham did with General Ritchie. Luftwaffe fighter squadrons still revolved around their leading aces, and shooting down enemy fighters—considered to be tougher opponents—was seen as preferable to shooting down bombers, when it should have been the other way around. In North Africa, the Luftwaffe was becoming complacent.

By and large, the aircraft and equipment at Coningham's call was comparatively better than that enjoyed by Eighth Army. In only one area was he really deficient. The Me 109 was supreme at heights over 10,000 feet and so there was no point in trying to take them on at levels above that figure. However, this meant that the German fighters did frequently have the twin advantages of height and speed when attacking RAF fighters. What was needed was an interceptor that could match the Me 109 and which could provide protection, or "top cover," for the Kittyhawks and Hurricanes while they carried out their new ground-attack roles.

The Spitfire Mark V was this aircraft. Unquestionably the finest British military machine to have emerged from the inter-war years, it was every bit as good as the Me 109 and, crucially, had the potential to be even further improved upon. Coningham had been asking for Spitfires ever since his arrival in North Africa, but it was not until May that the first fully equipped

Spitfire squadron arrived. This was entirely the fault of the Air Ministry back in London, who hedged around these requests from the Middle East, using excuses such as the lack of suitable air filters to deal with the sand and dust of the desert and the Spitfire's comparatively narrow undercarriage as a reason for not getting them out there sooner. This was ridiculous: there were plenty of Spitfires being built, but unfortunately the memories of the threat of invasion ensured that Fighter Command in Britain had first call.[39] Still, one squadron was better than nothing, and in the months to come more would arrive.

By the end of May, then, Eighth Army did at least have a much-improved air force to help them in the coming offensive. And there was another cause for optimism too. Britain may not have had the industrial or technical wherewithal to take on the might of the Axis alliance, but the United States of America did. By May, the first new Grant tanks had arrived. An even better tank was also nearly ready for shipping and would be available within months. But the best news of all was that the United States was now in the war too, and building an army that was itching to get amongst the enemy. Britain was no longer alone.

But in terms of manpower, this next battle would have to be a British show. Those in the desert had been waiting many weeks, but in the early hours of Wednesday, 27 May, dust clouds were gathering across the desert. Not the khamseen this time, but Rommel's Afrika Korps. Battle had begun.

CHAPTER 4

Missed Opportunities:
26 May–5 June, 1942

ON THE MORNING of Tuesday, 26 May, 1942, twenty-year-old Pilot Officer Johnnie Fairbairn was flying a brand-new Hurricane from 73 Squadron's rear base at Sidi Haneish, near Mersa Matruh, to their forward landing ground at El Adem, southwest of Tobruk. He'd only been with the squadron a couple of days—not long in which to acclimate to the strange flying conditions of the desert. He hadn't appreciated, for example, the amount of hot thermals that rose up from the ground and buffeted his aircraft about the sky. Nor had he realized how difficult it would be to attune his eyes to a horizon that stretched forever; the heat haze rippled the ground, making objects almost impossible to pick out, while the glare of the sun was so bright, Johnnie found himself permanently squinting. And nor had he considered how hot it could be. The first time he tried to clamber into a Hurricane, he burned his hand on the metal wing. But he *had* learned his first level in navigation: if lost, he simply turned to the north until he hit the coast, then worked his way back from there.

Johnnie and his escort had been flying an hour and forty minutes and he was beginning to feel quite exhausted when his leader started to descend. Johnnie followed, unable to see anything but sand, then gradually picked out a few aircraft and tents dotted about. But just as he was turning in to land, he was shocked to discover dust and smoke billowing up toward him and a landing strip pitted with craters. Vehicles were careering round, kicking up more dust, and as Johnnie touched down, desperately hoping he'd successfully dodged the craters, a cannon tracer whooshed past his nose. He had landed in the middle of an enemy raid. Quickly climbing out of his plane, Johnnie ran for his life. "I thought afterwards," he noted, "that this was a rather unfair and premature baptism of fire for a new fledgling like me."[40]

* * *

That same morning, Sergeant Bill Eadie had overslept and was late for the normal 5:30 AM "Stand To." He was dog tired after a busy few days trying to prepare Battle HQ, and from the increased enemy air activity, both day and night; it was hard to ever get a proper sleep. "Everyone is battle conscious," he'd noted in his diary a few days before. There'd been bets going around about when and where the attack might come.

By lunchtime that Tuesday, the enemy air activities were rapidly increasing, until by the afternoon, waves of Stuka dive-bombers were coming over every quarter of an hour and dropping their bombs on the main 2nd South African Infantry Brigade positions. Bill might have been exhausted, but there was now even more for him to do, and in between taking cover, he was frantically trying to help dig in the brigade's trucks and heavy vehicles in an effort to give them some protection against flying shrapnel. The noise was terrific. Every time the insectlike Stukas approached, the brigade's anti-aircraft guns began firing furiously. Bill was amazed that any of the enemy aircraft managed to get through. Moments later, the ground would shake from the reverberations of the bombs exploding.

The South African guns were also rapidly firing in a duel with the Axis artillery which had begun raining their fire onto the northern sector. At about four o'clock, armored cars from a South African recce battalion scuttled back through the minefields, having earlier in the day seen that huge dust clouds were forming across the desert to the west; yes, the khamseen was once again blowing, but this was not just a capricious desert wind—rather, Rommel's entire force mustering some twenty miles to the southwest at Rotunda Segnali. Midafternoon, the Axis formations split, and a large force of mainly Italians under Rommel's deputy, General Crüwell, began rumbling over the scrub toward the northern sector of the Gazala Line.

Around the same time, Major-General Francis Tuker was flying across the vast expanse of the Western Desert from Cairo. His 4th Indian Division was still spread throughout the Middle East, but Eighth Army Command had decided to make use of him at the front after all, giving him command of the southern desert flank of the line, which included not only the Free French but also the 7th Motor Brigade and the newly arrived 3rd Indian Motor Brigade, which, on the afternoon of the twenty-sixth, were still settling into their position to the south of Bir Hacheim. The irony of being put in charge of a handful of such brigades was not lost on Tuker, who had made it perfectly clear how much he disapproved of the "pernicious" brigade group system.[41] At the time, neither he nor GHQ Cairo had known the Axis attack would come quite so soon, and so his divisional staff, which would help him in this new posting, were sent by road; they would not arrive until the morning.

Tuker landed around six o'clock and headed off toward XXX Corps HQ, ten miles north of El Gubi. It was still quiet in the southern sector, but the bombardment of the north had increased. Throughout the afternoon, Bill Eadie and the rest of 2nd SA Brigade HQ had suffered no direct hits, only occasional shrapnel. But as the sunset cast a golden glow along the horizon, the Stukas returned once more and this time blasted the Battle HQ. Fortunately, everyone—Bill included—was in their slit trenches and no one was hurt. Three five-hundred-pound bombs failed to explode, but one blew up the kitchen and one man was buried alive by the sand. HQ had to be abandoned, but Bill couldn't help feeling awed by the stupendous sight of seeing nine Stukas peeling off, their sirens screeching, and one by one dropping their deadly loads. In their wake, dense black columns of smoke poured into the sky. "The blood-red sunset made a perfect backing," Bill noted. It was the last time the Stukas came over that day, but the guns—of both sides—would be flaming all night.

As daylight slipped away, at XXX Corps HQ General Tuker watched a single searchlight beam up over the sky to the west. Outside the canvas tents and caravans, he spent a tranquil hour, chatting and watching the stars come out. The night was now still—from where he was, not a gun could be heard. Even so, reports from the north suggested the main battle was about to explode and the silence made them feel suspicious and uneasy.

Twenty miles to the west of XXX Corps HQ, it was also calm. At Bir el Harmat, the South Notts Hussars were in position with the 22nd Armoured Brigade. Rather than being ready to move at a moment's notice, as might be expected from a mobile force, they were dug in with their guns pointing westward over the minefields. Sergeant Harold Harper certainly saw no cause for alarm—he for one had not been given word of what was going on in the north or of mass enemy musterings to the west. Of course he'd heard distant explosions, but then there were air attacks and exchanges of fire all the time. So he wandered over to B troop and sat in the back of a 15cwt truck. By the light of a hurricane lamp, he and couple of others played cards. Just after midnight, he decided to try and get some sleep. Walking back across the moonlit desert it seemed so quiet he could have heard a pin drop.

A little way away at 425 Battery, Ray Ellis had a slightly better idea that something was brewing. He'd only just rejoined his battery that evening, having been away in hospital in Tobruk after a small wound in his hand had gone septic. As he'd traveled back with the B echelon lorries, he'd seen the

sky ahead lit up with flashes and heard the rumble of gunfire from the front
and realized this was more intense than usual.

By this time, Ray had already been in the desert for two and a half
years and it was beginning to get him down. During the recent period of
retraining at Beni Yusef, near Cairo, he'd started to feel increasingly dis-
enchanted with war. The thought of heading back to the desert and going
through yet more battles, more discomfort, and more danger filled him
with dread. One afternoon he'd managed to slip away and spend a bit of
quiet time on his own. Sitting thinking under the shade of some palm
trees, he suddenly heard children playing and laughing. It struck him
that this was a universal sound, "almost exactly the same the world over."
And delightful too. "It told me of purity and innocence and trust and
wonderment, and it filled me with contentment," he noted.[42] His spirits
lifted immediately.

After a few weeks back at the front, however, his earlier gloom had returned. "There were so many things to contend with," he wrote, "the
heat, a raging thirst that was never quenched, the weariness, the continual attacks from the air and, very often, the hot, stifling winds of the
khamseen. Such a combination made life unbearable."[43] Now, on this
moonlit night in late May, he was back again, in charge of the twenty-five-
pounder he'd earlier christened "The Saint." He'd even painted the
white stick-figure from the Leslie Charteris novels onto the gun shield.
His was a comparatively new crew—he'd only known them a few weeks
and missed the camaraderie of his old mates, fellows he'd been with right
through the Siege of Tobruk, and right up until the regiment had been
reorganized. With the gun dug in, he wrapped a blanket around himself
and tried to get some sleep.

It had been even quieter to the far south of the line, where the men of the
7th Motor Brigade—part of General Tuker's new command—were also
dug in at the Retma Box, exactly twenty miles southeast of Bir Hacheim,
and waiting for something to happen. 26 May had been an "ordinary
day" for Albert Martin. The only news he'd heard was that the Japanese
had made a fresh attack on China, and so he'd kipped down that night
with no great sense of expectation.

The calm was shattered, however, when he was shaken awake at 5 AM
and told to get to his gun right away as "Jerry was on his way." Minutes
later, he was hurrying to his slit trench, "fully alert and senses tingling."[44]
He only just made it. As he leaped into his trench a massive artillery barrage burst down upon them, ripping apart the quiet and shaking the
hard desert beneath them. Albert couldn't help but be impressed by the
accuracy of their guns. The range was spot on.

The enemy had clearly been busy the previous night getting into their attack positions, and their attack would not have been such a surprise to Albert had those in command passed on the mass of information that had been coming in since the previous evening. At 11:35 PM, Ritchie had reported to Auchinleck in Cairo, "Personally, I feel that [Rommel's] main operation is now starting and as a first phase enemy advanced close to our defences and [made] chief showing in North. It is too early yet to deduce where main thrust will come."[45] It seemed pretty clear to those patrols down in the south, however. Albert Martin and his fellow members of the Rifle Brigade may have been unaware of what was developing, but nighttime recces by his colleagues in the 7th Motor Brigade and the Free French had brought back reports as early as eight o'clock the previous evening suggesting the main attack was heading south around the open southern flank. Later reports seemed only to confirm this, as patrols returned saying they'd heard the telltale chink and clanging of tank tracks rumbling toward them from the west. At 2:15 in the morning, and again at 4 AM—while General Tuker was sleeping—General Norrie, Commander of XXX Corps HQ, was woken and warned that it looked likely the main Axis thrust was heading southward. At 3:30 and 4:20 AM, Eighth Army HQ was also told that everything was pointing to a principal attack in the south, not the north.

Any remaining doubts were dispelled when Brigadier Filose, commander of the newly arrived 3rd Indian Motor Brigade, signaled at 6:30 AM that there was a "a whole bloody German armored division" bearing down upon them,[46] the implication being that his *brigade* was not strong enough to deal with anything so large and powerful as an armored *division*. He was absolutely right, too: within an hour of ear-splitting, dust-filled carnage, the brigade virtually ceased to exist, although the enemy storming down upon them was principally the Italian Ariete Division with a handful of German panzers. The Indians had shown plenty of courage and had managed to put out of action fifty-two Italian tanks in the process, but it was not enough to save them. "One by one the anti-tank guns were knocked out, and their crews died where they stood," read one account. One such who fired to the last was Lance-Daffadur Ali Mahboob Khan, who single-handedly fought until he too was killed—although not before he'd destroyed two tanks within fifty yards of his position.[47]

Rommel had launched Operation "Venezia" the previous evening, having massed some 10,000 vehicles for this purpose. Crüwell's attack in the north had indeed been nothing more than a feint, and in the evening, he'd withdrawn a number of his tanks from the north so they could rejoin the main attack in the south. So it was that in the early hours, the two divisions of the Afrika Korps, along with the German 90th Light and Italian Ariete Divisions, had headed southward, charging round the southern flank with some four hundred tanks. Rommel had originally intended to pivot on Bir Hacheim, but at the last minute changed his mind and decided to pivot five miles farther south; he expected the French to crumble anyway, so felt there was little point in delaying his main aims, which were to get behind the line and then swing north to attack the British armor. Meanwhile, the Italians were to make various attacks along the Gazala Line in order to keep Eighth Army's infantry pinned down in their boxes while the armored divisions sorted out the British tanks.

It was a highly cavalier plan by the Axis commander. His intelligence was faulty, to say the least, which was inexcusable: Rommel had the benefit of the 621st Radio Intercept Company led by Captain Alfred Seebohm, which, as its name implies, listened and analyzed British radio traffic. Eighth Army had no equivalent, but did have Ultra; however, since British radio security was generally pretty lax, the Germans were usually able to get hold of information that in practical terms was every bit as useful to the Axis as Ultra was to the British. Also available to the Axis was what Rommel called the "Good Source." In August 1941, SIM, the Italian military intelligence service, had persuaded a clerk at the American Embassy in Rome to make a copy of the "Black Code," used by the American attaché there for deciphering messages. From the autumn onward, both the Italians and Germans were therefore able to intercept and read any messages using this particular code. Most helpful were the messages relayed to Washington by Colonel Bonner Frank Fellers, the American attaché in Cairo, in which he often described in great detail secret data relating to the British military effort in the Middle East, including exact figures of troop and aircraft movements.

Before the war, Rommel had insisted that an army must be "untiringly active in determining precise information regarding the enemy and the terrain."[48] Prior to this latest attack, however, he had forgotten his own rules. The intercept company's intelligence for this period no longer exists, but it must have been either unusually unsuccessful or incomplete before Rommel launched his attack. Furthermore, relations between the Axis commander and his Luftwaffe chief, Von Waldau, were strained, which led to a lack of proper army/air force cooperation and insufficient aerial reconnaissance. At any rate, by the time he launched Operation Venezia, Rommel was unaware of the true strengths and dispositions of Eighth Army. He had no idea, for instance, that 150th Brigade was where it was or that mine marshes had been laid down either side of it. Nor had he appreciated the number of British tanks or that among their number were new 75mm Grants from the USA.

It seemed like a devastating plan, however, to those bearing the brunt of his armored attack. At the Retma Box, Albert Martin could see hundreds of enemy vehicles spread out in front of him, and the firing from both sides continued without letup. Smoke and dust billowed into the sky as shells screamed and whined and exploded, and guns roared. At least the new six-pounders were doing their stuff—Albert could see they were certainly inflicting casualties on the Germans bearing down on them. But all too quickly it was clear they could not hold their position. "These wonderful defensive positions which had taken us so long to prepare," he noted in his diary, "were broken, smashed to the four winds." They were forced to make a dash for it through the ring the enemy was rapidly enclosing around them, "but not before we managed to get a good smack at him." By 9 AM, the Retma Box had been completely wiped out. They raced across the desert to Bir el Gubi, ten miles to the east, while the Afrika Korps wheeled and thundered north, overrunning 7th Armoured Division's HQ and 4th Armoured Brigades as easily as they had the Indians and 7th Motor. With his concentrated mobile forces, Rommel had systematically dealt with each brigade in turn, precisely as General Tuker had warned.

Tuker, meanwhile, was still at XXX Corps HQ. He'd been dressed and ready to take command for several hours, and was waiting impatiently for the liaison officer (LO) to take him to the Free French in Bir Hacheim. Before the LO arrived, the corps commander turned up and announced that there was little left for him to command. So what should he do instead? Tuker asked. General Norrie wasn't sure, but perhaps it would be best if he stayed where he was for the moment—which is what he did, twiddling his thumbs and wondering how such a dog's dinner could ever have been allowed to occur.

At Bir Hacheim, the French soon found themselves under attack from the Italian armored formations of the Ariete Division. As the Indians and 7th Motor Brigade came under attack, General Pierre Koenig, commander of the Free French Brigade, was warned by 7th Armoured HQ that they should batten the hatches and lay more mines over the established routes in and out of the box. Shortly after, on this clear late May morning, came another message from the British announcing a counterattack. After that the radio went dead.

Koenig immediately sent out some more patrols, only for them to quickly return with alarming news: German formations were to the east, not west, in the direction of the brigade's supply base. Already, they had been outflanked and were cut off from their supply echelon. In other words, they were on their own with no obvious means of getting any more food, water, or ammunition.

At around nine that morning, the first Italian tanks crashed into the southern defenses, with six managing to break through. Pierre Messmer and a number of legionnaires swarmed toward them, jumping onto their hulls and firing furiously through the observation slits until their crews were all killed. A further Italian attack came about an hour later, but was even less successful. Shortly after, the enemy withdrew. The Italians had lost thirty-two tanks and retreated, unwilling to make another assault that day. Rommel had assumed that Bir Hacheim would be overrun within an hour; this was his first disappointment of the day.

The German 90th Light Division had proved what a highly mobilized unit of highly trained troops could achieve in a very short space of time. Having overrun Albert Martin's 7th Motor Brigade, then 7th Armoured Division HQ (capturing its commander, General Messervy, in the process), it had continued its thunderous march northward to reach the El Adem crossroads, a mere fifteen miles south of Tobruk. However, this motorized division would have been somewhat hoist by its own petard had the British acted faster. Now completely separated from the Afrika Korps, the division had been forced to leave some tanks behind because they'd run out of fuel. Fortunately, they discovered one of a number of British supply dumps and with no sign of any counterattack, were able to pause to refuel and rearm. Meanwhile, scouts from 29 Indian Brigade at Bir el Gubi, almost twenty miles due south of El Adem, had spotted the stranded tanks, but instead of launching straight off to attack them as the Germans would have done, went through the normal procedures by seeking permission to do so. Because of the disruption to communications caused by the morning's fighting, there was a considerable delay before they got a reply, by which time most of the German tanks had been successfully refueled and had rejoined the rest of their division.

The pilots of 73 Squadron had also spotted the German column. Johnnie Fairbairn and a number of the other pilots had been straining at the horizon with their binoculars when they'd seen a number of vehicles moving fast to their east, a large column of dust billowing in their wake. "They're Jerries!" one of them shouted. It was quickly decided it was time to move: the airfield was to be evacuated, the squadrons at El Adem moving back to Gambut, some thirty miles farther east. The ground crews, already packed and prepared for just such a scenario, also set off, heading down the Trigh Capuzzo. They'd not gone far when they were stopped by British armored cars. The Germans were blocking the road up ahead, they were told. They stayed put, watched El Adem get heavily bombed overnight, then eventually reached Gambut the following morning.

Meanwhile, Johnnie had wondered how he was ever going to get to Gambut. As the new boy, he was without a Hurricane: the shiny new one he'd brought up the day before had been claimed by one of the squadron stalwarts. Fortunately, he was offered a ride by a Royal Navy pilot, whose Alabacore biplane was a two-seater. They left as El Adem came under attack again. Without waiting to collect their gear, Johnnie and the naval pilot ran for the Albacore, some three hundred yards away. "It seemed like a mile," noted Johnny. With bullets thudding into the ground behind them, they eventually reached the plane, panting and sweating. Johnnie hastily clambered into the back gunner's seat and then promptly lost his peaked cap, which was blown off his head by the slipstream of the whirring propeller. "We headed due east," wrote Johnny, "not bothering to gain much height, and I had a grandstand view of tank battles going on below."[49]

What Johnnie had seen as he'd made his escape was the British armor running straight into the bulk of the Afrika Korps. Fifteen miles southwest of El Adem, 22nd Armoured Brigade been given preplanned battle positions to the south should the enemy burst through around the bottom of the line, but by 8:45 AM, they were only beginning to move. This was also a disgrace, because two hours before, at 6:45 AM, Norrie had phoned General Lumsden, his subordinate and commander of 1st Armoured Division, and ordered him to send 22nd Armoured Brigade south to these positions immediately.

At 520 Battery of the South Notts Hussars, Harold Harper had risen normally and with no sense of urgency, completely unaware that trouble was brewing. When, after breakfast, he'd seen dust clouds on the horizon, he'd assumed it was some of their own troops rather than the enemy. When they did finally start moving south, it was too late and they ran headlong into the 15th and 21st Panzer Divisions well short of their planned—and prepared—positions. So why had Lumsden ignored Norrie's order? Principally because he still didn't believe the southern thrust was the main attack; as commander of 1st Armoured Division, Lumsden had supreme confidence in his own judgment and frequently disagreed with Norrie, his corps commander. Norrie, like Ritchie, was not firm enough with subordinates and let him get away with arguing over decisions. When Norrie told Lumsden to get moving at 6:45 AM, the latter replied that he couldn't possibly for another hour and a half. This was nonsense, a mere excuse because he believed it was the wrong decision. In any battle, decisiveness is essential. Arguing over orders and dithering can lead to only one thing: disaster.

Harold Harper was not part of any gun crew, but rather, an "OP/

AC"—an observation post assistant to the battery commander, Major Gerry Birkin. It was their role to drive ahead of the battery, stop and set up an OP from which by radio they could direct the fire of the guns. At 8:45 AM, Major Birkin decided they should go and see the staff at the Gloucester Hussars' HQ, to whom they were attached. In the two armored cars they used as their mobile OPs, they set off—two radio operators and a driver with Major Birkin in one, and Harold and Birkin's brother, Captain Ivor Birkin, the commander of D troop, and a signaler in the other.

They hadn't gotten very far before they came into range of the advancing panzers. Shells whistled overhead and exploded nearby, and then Harold heard gabbling on Major Gerry Birkin's radio and realized immediately that something was wrong. Captain Birkin immediately jumped out of the car and ran the fifty or sixty yards to his brother's vehicle, Harold following behind. "When we reached the truck," says Harold, "I've never seen anything like it." There were blood and body parts all over the inside of the car. Major Birkin was on the floor, dead, with a hole through his middle. An armor-piercing shell had gone straight through him as he'd been standing in the turret and then neatly sliced off the heads of the two wireless operators, both of whom were still sitting there, their hands clutching the mouthpieces. Their heads lay motionless on the floor. The driver was still gabbling incoherently into the wireless. Harold knew he had to get him out and also persuade Ivor Birkin to leave his brother, but the captain refused, so he rushed back to the other armored car intending to drive over and pick him up. He got in and started the vehicle, but ahead was a cloud of dust and before he knew what was happening, one of the new Grant tanks of the Gloucester Hussars had emerged and crashed right into them. "We hit it head-on and literally bounced back," says Harold. The engine caught fire and so the two of them had to jump out again, along with Ivor Birkin's driver and signaler, and dash back to the first armored car to get the captain. Fortunately, another British tank passed near them and so they were able to clamber onto it—albeit with some difficulty. "The tank commander had no idea we were there," says Harold, "and kept firing," so they had to duck and dodge as best they could as the turret and barrel swung around.[50] One of them fell off, but by shouting continually, Harold and the others eventually made themselves heard and were taken back to 520 Battery supplies. Once there, Harold discovered he had crushed several ribs and suffered a shrapnel wound in his knee, and so was taken off to a field dressing station.

The rest of the regiment had hardly fared better. Ray Ellis had moved off just after 8:45 AM, but like Harold had almost immediately come under heavy fire. He and his crew began hurling as many shells as they could at the tanks and vehicles ahead, but they soon found themselves being fired on in turn—but from behind. It seemed likely that they too were in danger of being encircled, so Ray was not at all sorry when the order came to move. Heading eastward to safety, they heard that D troop had suffered badly and that B troop had been annihilated. Ray could hardly think straight with worry—his older brother was in B troop and many of them were his friends.

Hurrying across the desert, they headed east, then north until they reached a track crossing known as Knightsbridge. There they stopped and swung their guns around again to the south. No sooner had they done so than Ray saw what appeared to be hundreds of tanks ahead of them. Watching them, he felt his adrenaline start to pump. Any moment now, they would be in range. As Number One on the gun, Ray selected their first target and swung The Saint around until it was in line with the target. Then he shouted the range, and the gun layer set his sights on the tank Ray had picked out. As soon as they layer reckoned he'd got it about right, Ray gave the order to fire. No sooner had they done so than Ray was thinking of the next target. They had few misses because the German tanks were coming straight at them—rather than across their sights. Shells were now raining down on them too, and bullets. Ray felt understandably exposed, standing by his gun, shells crashing around him and machine-gun bullets spitting past his head. "It's rather like being near a beehive," he says. "The surprising thing is however anyone ever survived it."[51] Even so, it was not fear he was feeling but excitement as they fired round after round after round. Behind, he was aware of 426 Battery joining them. But to his dismay, "they were facing the other way. We had no idea at all what was going on."[52]

Bill Eadie may not have been in the thick of an armored battle, but in the northern sector, it was certainly a pretty uncomfortable time for the South African brigades dug in behind the minefields. Bill Eadie had heard the guns blazing much of the night, and then they started up again at six—there was no danger of him oversleeping that morning. Like most in the Eighth Army, Bill tended to think of the enemy as Germans, rather than Italians, who were widely regarded as a lesser foe. "Jerry has dug himself in immediately in front of our minefields," he recorded, but in fact it was the Italian Sabratha Division. Shells continued falling all morning, aircraft droned overhead and at noon the Italians put up a huge smoke-screen to hide the advance of their infantry. Machineguns and small arms spat out their rounds. "Several men have lost their nerve," he scribbled, and felt that on the whole they were all feeling a bit "querulous." Who could blame them? Even so, morale was still high, especially with the good news arriving from the tank battle in the south. The word going around was that their armor had lured the enemy into a trap and "shot him up."

Meanwhile, Harold Harper had reached the safety of the field dressing station only for it to be overrun by the Germans. Soon after, British artillery shells began raining down on them. Then a strange thing happened. A German Fiesler Storch suddenly dropped out of the sky and landed close by the dressing station. Harold watched in amazement as a high-ranking German officer got out and clambered into a waiting tank and headed off. Around half an hour later he reappeared and having jumped down from the tank, strode over to the dressing station and began talking—in English—to the doctor, just a few yards from where Harold was lying, apologizing for the lack of food, and assuring him everything possible would be done for the prisoners. It was none other than Rommel himself. Harold had seen numerous pictures of him. "He was unmistakable," he says. "You think to yourself, you can't start admiring the enemy, but I must admit I was very impressed."[53] Shortly after, the German commander stepped into a staff car and drove away.

Ray Ellis was still firing away, and as far as he was concerned it was nothing but chaos. All around him was the crash of shells and roar of guns. Ahead and either side of him angry flames and columns of pitch black smoke leaped into the air where a tank or other vehicle had exploded. Ambulances and recovery vehicles were also weaving crazily across the battlefield desperately trying to pick up the wounded and broken, and adding to the mayhem. Tanks and vehicles littered the desert. Some had ground to a halt, their broken tracks lying flat beside them. Others had been grotesquely twisted and distorted, barrels pointing crazily from mangled and decapitated turrets.

The first German attack had been beaten off, but then came another. Stukas also joined in, their screaming sirens still clearly heard over the din of the guns. In between attacks, Ray and his crew frantically tried to gather rocks and stones together in order to build some kind of protection around the front of the gun. There was certainly no chance of digging any kind of gun pit as the ground was nothing but rock—doubly bad because any nearby shell that exploded then kicked up lethal shards of stone.

But while this was perhaps not a trap in the true sense of the word, the rumors that Bill Eadie had heard of British successes in the armored battle were not so wide off the mark. As the afternoon wore on, the German panzers were beginning to flounder. Even early on, as they had swept aside the southern brigades, they had still lost a number of tanks in the process and many more as the day continued. Rommel's faulty pre-battle intelligence meant he had assumed he'd already disposed of most of the British armor by mid-morning, so the new Grant tanks had been something of a shock. Rather than ploughing on into the static infantry positions as he'd intended, his forces had themselves begun to disperse amidst the dust, smoke and confusion. Rommel later admitted that his divisions had "suffered extremely serious losses. Many of our columns broke into confusion and fled away to the southwest, out of the British artillery fire."[54] In fact, they'd lost a third of their tanks, were desperately short of fuel and hopelessly fractured. Rather than encircling the British as he'd envisaged, it was the panzer army that was almost encircled—*and* with their lines of communication all but severed. After their rout of the southern brigades, the table had turned dramatically; now it was the Axis who were facing annihilation.

* * *

Although Eighth Army had a massive superiority in infantry, the next few days saw them stick rigidly to their boxes along the line, while the armored battle continued behind them. That this enormous advantage over the enemy was not put to better use demonstrated a tragic lack of confidence on the part of Ritchie and his commanders. Opposite the northern sector were the vastly inferior Italian infantry divisions and one German light brigade. Italian divisions were of similar size to a British brigade group, but were woefully equipped and trained. British levels of training and equipment may have fallen short of German standards, but the Italians were no match for the British, as had been demonstrated in 1940–41 before the Germans had turned up and spoiled things. Admittedly, the Italian armored division, the Ariete, and its motorized division, Trieste, had learned a thing or two from the Afrika Korps, but they were tied up with the armored battle. Eighth Army's five brigades in the line and the 32nd Army Tank Brigade a short way behind was overcautious to say the least; half that force should have been able to contain the Italians with ease. But Ritchie kept them where they were.

On 28 May, Eighth Army was once again slow to get started, largely because of the wait to reassemble armor and for reports from patrols trying to work out what was going on. Consequently, there were few serious engagements until the afternoon. Twenty-first Panzer continued forging northward before turning back south the following day; the 90th Light began heading westward again before turning to face the re-formed 4th Armoured Brigade; Ray Ellis and the rest of 22nd Armoured made attacks against 15th Panzer, while the 2nd Armoured Brigade engaged the Italian Ariete, who, having called off their attack against Bir Hacheim, had headed northwards too. All along the front line to the west, the Italians kept up the pressure, firing their artillery relentlessly. The Axis air forces also continued harassing the front line, even though they had completely lost contact with Rommel and so had little idea how they could help his armored formations. Bill Eadie, with the 2nd South African Brigade, was strafed by an Italian fighter plane in the morning—the bullets pinging the ground just a few yards from him. In the afternoon he had to send one of his drivers back out of line because "he was getting the jitters." Later, two shells landed within fifteen feet of the Brigadier's dugout. "Oh yes," he noted ironically, "the fun is developing." To the southwest, away from the fighting, Albert Martin was regrouping with the rest of 7th Motor Brigade and protecting the huge dumps of stores to the rear. Rumors were running riot. "It's said we've knocked out 135 German tanks," he noted, and then, with a wisdom borne of experience, added, "Probably an exaggeration though losses in equipment are mounting for Rommel."

This was true, but rescue was almost at hand for the Axis forces. During the day the Italians managed to drive two narrow gaps through the minefields either side of the British box along the line of the Trigh Capuzzo (the same Trigh Capuzzo Sam Bradshaw had been trying to cross the previous November) and Trigh el Abd. Only 150th Brigade, in between, separated the Italians to the west of the line, and the panzer army now gathering in a hollow area of land between two slight ridges—the Sidra Ridge to the north and the Aslag Ridge to the south. This depression in the ground was known as the Cauldron, and now the only thing preventing the Axis armor from resupply was the 150th Brigade in their way.

Rommel spent the day trying to bring precious supplies in columns around Bir Hacheim and up the eastern side of the minefields, and having insisted on leading the charge himself, had a number of narrow escapes in the process. He also ordered Crüwell to try and break through the northern part of the line. The attack failed. "The enemy pushed last night and this morn," noted Bill Eadie. "We took 460 prisoners and several guns including the big gun which has been giving us hell." And there was another bonus of this failed attack: General Crüwell, desperate to make contact again with the once more incommunicado Rommel, took to his Fiesler Storch reconnaissance plane and was promptly shot down and taken prisoner.

Meanwhile the armored battle continued, even though Norrie was still struggling with the insubordinate Lumsden. "Get a move on," Norrie urged the 1st Armoured Division commander. "Hit them up the backside."[55] Lumsden replied that he would, but only when he felt he had enough forces. This was, once again, not until the afternoon, when fierce fighting continued, with the various British brigades closing in on the panzer army, increasingly encircled in the Cauldron.

* * *

While for the most part the British were able to get prisoners away out of the line, this was hardly top of the agenda for those Axis forces caught east of the Gazala Line. Harold Harper had not been budged from the field dressing station where he'd been deposited on the opening day of the battle. There were a number of Germans about the place, but no guards as such—they quite understandably had their minds on the battle raging around them. Harold had always had an eye for detail and watched the Germans with interest. He noticed, for instance, that German tanks puffed out purple smoke if Axis aircraft flew overhead as a means of identification, and he also mentally noted down the numbers of tanks passing by and their various markings. His ribs were causing him some trouble—he'd had them strapped with four-inch-wide elastoplast, which if anything made him feel more constricted than before—but his knee hurt less. By 30 May, he noticed that the Germans had been pushed back a bit, and so the following night, 1 June, he and a Welsh sergeant decided to make a break for it. Harold's plan was simple: to walk due southeast, away from the current fighting, and hopefully they might bump into some friendly forces. It was certainly bold: both were badly if not seriously injured. They were weak with hunger, and yet could take nothing with them—not even a drop of water—and Harold had no clothes but his boots and shorts. In this state, they were intending to venture out into desert, a desert that was mercilessly freezing cold at night and scorching hot by day.

Waiting until the moon was up, they crept away, soon passing by a German tank. Harold began speaking German so that if they were spotted they would arouse less suspicion. The ruse worked and by morning, having navigated by the stars, they were some way away. They laid up throughout the day, and once the sun had set, began their journey again. They had managed to scrounge some water from the radiators of wrecked British vehicles, but their situation was not looking good. Then tragedy struck: Harold's colleague trod on a mine. "That was the end of him," says Harold. "It was sad. He was from Cardiff—I'd made quite a big friend with him." Harold tried to bury what little remained the best he could, but he was worried the explosion might have alerted someone. Not only that, it was clear he was now in the middle of a minefield. "I suppose it did make me a little wary," he admits.

Harold was now desperate for water. "Eventually I had to drink my own urine," he says. "I swilled it around my mouth and hoped for the best." Miraculously, he at length reached the Guards Brigade HQ, approaching tentatively with his hands in the air and shouting English as loudly as he could. He was, he admits, in a fairly "bedraggled" state by then. "I had a mug of tea," says Harold, "and that went down beautifully." Then he was taken to the cookhouse, where they were having rice pudding. It was one of Harold's favorite dishes, but after two mouthfuls he felt full. "It literally stuck in my throat," he says. After being starved for the best part of a week, he realized that returning to normal eating would take some time. But he was now safe and, unlike the rest of the South Notts Hussars, out of the battle. Having passed on all the information he had accrued in such detail while a prisoner, he was sent to hospital in Tobruk and then put on a ship to the Delta. Harold Harper was one of the lucky ones.

While Harold had been walking his way to safety, events had been unfolding around the Cauldron. By the morning of 30 May, around two hundred of Rommel's tanks were out of action. Wrecked tanks and vehicles littered the battlefield, many still smoking and twisted. However, his efforts to reach his armored divisions with his supply train had been largely successful, and more had trickled in during the night of the thirtieth. Furthermore, his forces, once scattered, were by then together, in some kind of strength, within the Cauldron—collectively contracted in number, but collectively concentrated too.

Even so, Rommel's situation was still precarious, to put it mildly. Strong and decisive British leadership at this point could—and should—have seen the panzer army finished off for good. Instead, there was dithering, hesitation, and far too much conferring. Lumsden announced that the panzer army were "boiled"[56] and decisively trapped with, he felt, little chance of escape. Ritchie and Norrie agreed, unaware of the gaps in the minefield being widened by the Italians to the west. From Cairo, the Auk was trying to piece together the events unfolding as best he could. Hearing that Rommel's armor was now cornered in the Cauldron, he urged Ritchie on 30 May that the "enemy must NOT get away and reorganize."[57] Naturally, the army commander agreed, and with this favorable situation in mind, Ritchie began working on a plan—Operation LIMERICK—in which units from XXX Corps—the Free French included—would swing around Bir Hacheim in a movement that mirrored Rommel's opening attack on the twenty-seventh, and attack the Axis supply lines, while General "Strafer" Gott's XIII Corps attacked from the north and the rest of the British armor hit the panzer army head-on from their current position east of the Cauldron. In no time, Ritchie believed, they would be in Benghazi.

This was a perfectly sensible plan, using all his forces in one big, coordinated punch. His commanders, however, were not happy. It was all well and good, they told him, but couldn't possibly be done right away; such an operation needed time to prepare. Twenty-four hours at *least*, Ritchie was told emphatically by both of his corps commanders, Gott and Norrie. Re-inforcements were needed, and anyway, as Lumsden pointed out, Rom-mel's anti-tank guns were still causing all manner of trouble. Caution was needed, he assured Ritchie, to avoid unnecessary casualties.

At this point, a more forceful character would have told his subordi-nates to get a grip and do as they were ordered, sharpish. Unfortunately, Ritchie was not that man, and swallowing their advice, accepted Lumsden's increasingly gloomy and defensive appreciation. After presenting his thoughts to the Auk, the Commander-in-Chief also added a note of cau-tion, pointing out the the "enemy may yet try to assume the offensive and as we have learned, he has surprising powers of recovery."[58] What was needed, Lumsden then suggested, was a nighttime attack by the infantry to put the panzer army's guns out of action. This, too, he claimed, would take time to prepare, and although Ritchie was initially concerned that Rommel might try to break out west by the morning of 1 June, he was convinced the panzer army was staying put in the Cauldron, with the intention of consol-idating and then attacking later, once he'd built up his strength.

Ritchie's reading of the situation was more-or-less spot on, except for one small omission: he hadn't reckoned on Rommel hurling the bulk of his remaining armor against 150th Brigade, which the German commander had at last discovered. Rommel had his faults, but indecision was not one of them, and realizing 150th Brigade was behind him to the west, recognized that his only real means of bringing his strike force back up to some kind of strength was to destroy it and open clear lines of supply through the British minefields. Having made a reconnaissance of the position himself, and with no attack from the British armor materializing on 31 May, Rommel launched his remaining forces and those of the Italians on the other side of the line against 150th Brigade.

The brigade was made up largely of territorial battalions from York-shire. Like the vast majority of men in the Eighth Army, their bravery and fighting quality was outstanding. Almost entirely surrounded, and with lit-tle help from the large numbers of British forces stretched out along the line, they battled all day along a massive five-mile front against the com-bined, concentrated fire of the panzer army, which, although depleted, could still pack a considerable punch. "The defence was conducted with considerable skill," Rommel admitted, "and, as usual, the British fought to the last round."[59]

While 150th Brigade was heroically fighting toward complete annihi-lation, the rest of Eighth Army—its armor, mobile divisions protecting the supply dumps, and South African brigades in the north—was doing very little. Lumsden ordered his tanks to attack again, but by now had become so obsessed with the invincibility of the German 88mms, that he decreed that further assaults would be pointless until the infantry had sorted out Rommel's anti-tank guns. So as soon as his armor came under fire from a few 88s, he ordered them back. Bill Eadie at 2nd South African Brigade HQ wrote, "Hot day and quiet. Hardly a shot fired until evening."

Had Eighth Army attacked that night, as Ritchie had originally wished, they would have almost certainly succeeded. The Tynesiders had exhausted the panzer army, which, after a day of intense fighting, was desperately short of everything: food, water, fuel, and ammunition. Rommel's senior commanders pleaded with him to call off the attack or surely face surrender—the Axis situation was *that* dire. But while Ritchie acquiesced to the officers under him, Rommel stuck to his guns, literally, and the following morning—having received overnight supplies—continued the attack unmolested. By the afternoon, 150th Brigade was no more, and Rommel had punched a massive hole through the British line from which he could easily now resupply his panzers.

For three whole days his panzer army had lain at the mercy of the British, yet time and time again the chances to go for the kill were passed over.

That Ritchie and his commanders failed to make the most of this enormous opportunity must rank as one of the most inexcusable acts of British generalship in the whole war. "I am distressed over the loss of 150 Brigade after so gallant a fight," Ritchie signaled to Auchinleck in Cairo on 2 June, "but still consider the situation favourable to us and getting better daily."[60] How he could have thought this is utterly baffling. The desert was, in fact, nothing more than an enormous gladiatorial arena—a dust-swept expanse in which two opponents could fight their duel without hindrance. Here the skills and failings of each combatant were starkly exposed into a straight trial of strength. And Ritchie was definitely failing.

In Ritchie's defense, it is true there were periods of sandstorms. The old desert hands could tell when they were coming: hot, strong winds would begin to blow and they would brace themselves. As the wind strengthened, the fine sand loosened by the mass of tire and tank tracks would be whipped into the air. Visibility would soon drop to fifty yards, then an hour or so later, twenty yards. At times it was hard to see anything at all. This, of course, brought everything grinding to a halt, but especially flying. Billy Drake and the other fighter pilots were unable to fly on 2 June, for example, because of such storms. But this was just one day and the storms were also to some degree localized. For the vast majority of the time, the Libyan desert was burned by a fierce and relentless sun, bearing down through cloudless skies of deep blue.

Nor is the fog of war a convincing excuse in Ritchie's case. The various Eighth Army message logs and Ritchie's own analysis of these days show that he was only occasionally in the dark. Although his HQ was at Gambut, hundreds of miles of telephone wires kept him linked to his corps and divisional commanders for much of the time. Any visitor to his HQ would have been impressed by the hum of activity: signalers and telephonists busy at their desks, vehicles pulling up and taking off again, dispatching liaison officers to different parts of the battlefield. Most days, Ritchie himself visited the front line, arriving at the various HQs covered in dust. On 29 May, he left his caravan 4:45 AM, and moved his Tactical HQ forward, visiting both Norrie and Gott. The following day, he was touring again, including a visit to Lumsden. The rest of the time he was receiving near-constant messages and telephone calls. At Gambut, tents and trucks full of radios, maps, typists, and telephonists dealt with the influx, relaying them to the various members of his staff, who hovered with colored pencils waiting to plot the latest information on their maps, black for the Axis, red for the British. Mary Coningham was just round the corner for conferral at any time, and in addition to the high number of ground attacks, the RAF also flew a number of "Tac Rs"—reconnaissance flights that produced reports of enemy movement. On 31 May, messages streamed in with news of developments west of the Cauldron, including a large number from 150th Brigade, yet no one—including Ritchie—seems to have recognized what a desperate situation they were in.

The task of a battlefield commander is an extremely difficult one. Conflicting information arrives all the time, yet it is his job—with the assistance of his staff and commanders—to do his best to make the right decision. Inevitably, mistakes are made, and on the afternoon of 31 May, when Ritchie told Auchinleck that 150th Brigade were "doing wonders,"[61] he made a poor assessment. However, much of Ritchie's analysis during the battle was correct, which is why his indecisiveness and unwillingness to make his commanders act quickly without demur is even more unforgivable. Air Commodore Tommy Elmhirst used to talk regularly with the army commander. One evening, while the two men were taking a brief break, Ritchie said sadly to Tommy, "I have sent out my orders for tomorrow, but I know my corps commanders will hold a tea party on them, and whether they will comply with my exact intentions is questionable." This quibbling over orders appears to have continued further down the chain. Lumsden and Messervy regularly questioned orders from Norrie, while it had become de rigueur for 1st South African divisional commander, General Pienaar, to argue over every order issued by his corps commander, General "Strafer" Gott. Tommy Elmhirst also records an occasion when he was speaking with a tank commander. "I was in action against some German tanks," he told Tommy, "when my brigadier came on the 'blower' and ordered me to withdraw. I said, 'Not a bit, George. I've got some good tank targets and I'm staying.'" By this breach of discipline he then lost all his tanks.[62]

But armies need to be led from the top, and the truth is that such a command was a task too high for one of Ritchie's experience and capabilities, and this was now being ruthlessly exposed. Until he took over in November 1941, he had never commanded anything larger than a division, and in the front line, nothing bigger than a battalion. The job had been thrust upon him during the Crusader Battles after Auchinleck had returned to Cairo with increasingly nagging doubts about the current incumbent in the post, General Sir Alan Cunningham. Believing he had no choice but to sack Cunningham, the Auk was left with a quandary. With both Eighth Army corps commanders busy with the current offensive, there were few obvious candidates to fill the post. Instead, the Auk turned to his able and cool-headed deputy chief of the General Staff in Cairo, Major-General Neil Ritchie. Ritchie, in fact, suggested bringing someone over from England, but the Commander-in-Chief would not hear of it, and promptly promoted him to Acting Lieutenant-General and sent him into Libya to take over. As a result, Ritchie was effectively lower in rank than his new corps commanders. This need not have been an insurmountable problem, but he allowed it to be as he failed to stamp his personal authority sufficiently enough. Being a good staff officer was not the same as being a good general in the field.

Some blame must also be taken by Auchinleck. Admittedly, his responsibilities for the whole of the Middle East were huge, but thinking he could control events from far-off Cairo with Ritchie as his eyes and ears on the ground was a mistake. All too often his interference would make the situation worse. Messages would arrive at Ritchie's caravan that began, "Do not think I am trying to dictate to you in any way, but . . ."[63]—clearly designed to make Ritchie do exactly as he suggested. For example, as soon as it became clear in mid-May that Rommel would attack first, the Auk wrote to Ritchie telling him to keep all Eighth Army's mobile forces in the middle of the line astride the Trigh Capuzzo, which, as events turned out, might have been more sensible; Ritchie disagreed, but by 26 May, both believed each had come around to the other's plan. This was certainly not the case, but such were the distances that missives between the two often passed in the night, resulting in more confusion and crossed wires—precisely what happened over the issue of Eighth Army dispositions before Rommel's attack. The German commander, on the other hand, had much less interference, and when drawing up battle plans was left entirely to his own devices. Nor did anyone within his staff ever question his authority or leadership: the chain of command was clear and undisputed.

Ritchie's grip had hardly been tight before battle was joined, but was rapidly loosening itself completely as his corps and divisional commanders began openly squabbling about what should or what should not be done. Lumsden's proposed infantry night attack had been launched on 1 June— too late to save 150th Brigade—and had been a fiasco. Two separate assaults had been planned: one from the north, which made no impression at all, and one from the south by the re-formed 7th Armoured Division. Albert Martin and the 2nd Rifle Brigade had been moved up as part of this attack, but it was called off at the last minute due to lack of sufficient reconnaissance. Despite this, the army rumor mill was positive the following day. "Reports state that the enemy is bogged down through lack of supplies," noted Albert in his diary. "Everyone is in high spirits and very optimistic." However, they'd been told much the same before Sidi Rezegh, and they'd been all but wiped out there. This time, Albert, for one, was taking such news with a massive pinch of salt.

And he was quite right to. Ritchie temporarily dropped plans for Operation LIMERICK, then briefly adopted them again, partly due to pressure from Auchinleck, then decided on a new plan of attack, Operation ABERDEEN. Incredibly, rather than prepare this himself, he delegated it to Norrie, who in turn delegated it to his two divisional commanders, Briggs and Messervy.[64] It was then discussed and argued over, each commander seemingly finding good reasons not to commit their troops rather than making an effort to overcome any difficulty. In the end, ABERDEEN came down to this: an assault on the panzer army still in the Cauldron, but now much revitalized and strengthened. A nighttime artillery bombardment to clear the enemy anti-tank screens would be followed by an infantry attack from the east of the Cauldron, and then the following morning, the armor would go in, supported by a feint from the north. Yes, at long last the infantry were being used in an all-arms operation, but the forces involved were to be made up of just one armored brigade group (7th), and two infantry brigade groups (10th and 9th Indian), against the combined efforts of a reinforced (albeit far from completely), highly experienced, and dug-in panzer army of four armored divisions.

In the meantime, the minutes, the hours, and then the days ticked by. Yet Ritchie's general appreciation of the situation remained essentially accurate. "By the 2nd of June," he commented later, "it became clear that the enemy, having liquidated 150 Infantry Brigade Group's position on 1st June, obviously intended stabilising himself in the 'Cauldron' under cover of very strong anti-tank gun screens and build up his strength prior to resuming offensive operations."[65] Spot on. So why the delay, especially when Eighth Army had such overwhelming superiority in infantry? Lumsden's fear of Rommel's anti-tank guns is at the root of it. The British had seen the tank as the preeminent piece of equipment on the battlefield, but in this they were wrong. The *anti*-tank gun held the key, and Lumsden had nothing to match the German 88mm and not enough of the new six-pounders. It makes the decision to overlook the 3.7-inch anti-aircraft guns even more inexplicable. But Lumsden was only a divisional commander, and Ritchie—and Norrie for that matter—should have stamped their authority with far greater resolution. Rommel was incredulous at the way the British were keeping so "astonishingly quiet," and, as Ritchie predicted, made the most of the lull. On the 3 June he wrote to his wife, "The battle continues, though we're in such a favorable position that I've got no more serious worries."[66] It's easy to understand why. Ritchie's attack, when it did finally come, would be made up from a force of insufficient size and insufficiently armed, heading into the waiting jaws of an enemy whose strength was increasing every day.

While the British army commanders were losing their heads, Air Vice Marshal Mary Coningham was keeping his. Like Rommel, Mary was unafraid to make bold decisions and on the morning of 28 May, had issued orders that no pilot was to engage enemy fighters or fly above 6,000 feet: attacks of Axis supply columns were the absolute priority. To leave his pilots exposed to attacks from above was a lot to ask, but supporting the army had to be their prime objective, and he had no fighters to spare to act as cover, save a very few Spitfires. In three days, from 29 to 31 May, thirty-nine fighters were lost, but over a thousand enemy vehicles were also destroyed.

Operating from the airfield at Gambut, close to both Ritichie's and Mary Coningham's HQ, were 112 Squadron, part of 239 Wing. Billy Drake had now taken over as commanding officer and it couldn't have been at a busier time. Up before first light, the pilots were expected to be at their dispersal tent ready to take to the skies at a moment's notice. "Usually we knew roughly what we were about to do," says Billy. "On the whole we were carrying out offensive operations. We'd find out what was cooking and then, depending on how many aircraft were required, I'd detail who would fly." The ground crew would already be there waiting with starter batteries, and soon the airfield would be alive with the roar of engines. Swathes of sand and dust would be whipped up by the propellers. It was hard enough for the pilots to see over the huge engine cowling as it was, but the man-made sandstorm hindered vision even more, and so they tended to take off in a long line so as to avoid collisions; after all, there was no shortage of space.

For the ground crews, the work was ceaseless. With minimal amounts of equipment, they performed miracles, not just patching up shot-up aircraft but also in trying to fight an uphill battle against the sand. There were sand filters on the aircraft, but rather like a visit to the beach, the stuff still got everywhere—in the pipes, the oil, the petrol tanks, the guns.

Billy Drake had flown many aircraft in his time, but was rather impressed with the American P-40 Kittyhawks they were now using. Having flown in France and during the Battle of Britain, he was used to watching out for the "Hun in the sun" and soon noticed that under 10,000 feet the Kittyhawk could match the Me 109. Billy's first operational sortie as CO had been on 26 May, when the squadron had raided Tmimi, thirty miles west up the coast. Each of their aircraft had been weighed down with a 250-pound bomb strapped underneath, but Billy had been unable to release his—an embarrassing start. "What a black!" he noted in his logbook.[67]

It was no easy matter dropping a bomb accurately from a 350 mph fighter plane. "You came in at an angle of about sixty degrees," explains Billy. "As leader, it was my job to judge what sixty degrees was. It doesn't sound very steep, but until you got used to it, it felt like you were coming in practically vertical." A dive would usually start from around 8,000 feet. Billy aimed to pull out around 1,500 feet. "You'd get in as close as you possibly could without hitting the ground," he says.

He soon began to master this technique and in the ensuing days was more successful, as the squadron were directed to attack the massed enemy supply columns. The squadron had lost three men by 1 June, and their losses would continue: low-flying ground attacks were lethal because if hit—and there was often plenty of small-arms and light flak whistling about the sky—there was very little room to maneuver. You couldn't bail out at only a few hundred feet or less. "You had no bloody idea what your chances were," says Billy. Through skill and experience a pilot could improve his chances in a dogfight, but anyone could be hit by flak: it was purely a matter of chance. "And that is why the golden rule on any ground attack was to only attack once: you dropped your bomb and got the hell out. You always made sure you strafed a different target on the way back."

Despite the dangers, their attacks were certainly causing considerable damage and disruption. Two British army officers who were captured soon found themselves on the receiving end of the RAF's fighter-bombers. On escaping, they reported they "commended the fighters for the daring and accuracy of their attacks," and confirmed their effectiveness in destroying and disrupting enemy columns. A captured German diary also suggested Coningham's strategy was having some effect. "Low-level machine-gunning," it recorded, "RHQ dispersed. Some MT abandoned and lost. Chaos. Panic."[68]

Limited resources were Coningham's and Tommy Elmhirst's constant headache. In terms of numbers of serviceable aircraft, the Axis had a slight edge, but while Billy Drake confessed himself to be satisfied with the Kittyhawk, a number of squadrons were still equipped with the earlier and less powerful version of the P-40, the Tomahawk Mk II. There were also four squadrons still using the even more obsolete Hurricane. Shortage of aircraft, particularly Kittyhawks and, of course, Spitfires, meant Mary and Tommy were constantly juggling as best they could. On 1 June, Mary wrote to Tedder, "I am sure everything is being done to send a few more Spitfires to us," and urged Cairo to get more bomb racks from America as quickly as possible, so they could convert even more of their fighter aircraft into dual-role "Hurri-" and "Kittybombers."[69]

While the Eighth Army commanders let the days slip by in a blur of indecisiveness, Rommel had turned from his destruction of 150th Brigade to the problem of Bir Hacheim. The French had not been standing idle during the past few days and had busied themselves breaking out in patrol strength and attacking the Axis lines of supply. General Koenig had even ordered a POW cage to be built to house the increasing numbers of prisoners captured during these raids.

Particularly involved in these raids were Pierre Messmer's unit, the 13 DBLE. Promoted to Tactical Group Commander, Messmer had spent much of the first few days of the battle operating from a makeshift camp to the north of Bir Hacheim, and harassing the Axis columns. He had felt a great sense of exhilaration to be finally taking the fight to the Germans, an enemy that had crushed the French Army two years before and conquered his country. Along with all the Free French, Pierre burned to avenge this catastrophe.

Pierre Messmer may have been a true-blooded Frenchman, but many nationalities were drawn to the Foreign Legion's ranks, and at Bir Hacheim there were men from nearly every country in Europe among the 13 DBLE, including Germany. Commanding the battalion was a Georgian—Lieutenant-Colonel Count Dimitri Amilakvari, a White Russian prince who had fled the Russian Revolution at fourteen. Devilishly handsome and square-jawed, and rarely without the tattered green cloak he had acquired during the Norwegian campaign, he was adored by his men and completely forged to the Legion and all it represented. Known for his fearlessness, Amilak—as he was known—never wore a steel helmet even under the most intense fire, preferring the traditional, and more glaring, white kepi instead.

There was also the only woman ever to have joined the Foreign Legion. Susan Travers, was, in fact, English, a former Wimbledon tennis player, although she had spent much of her teenage years in Southern France, spoke the language and felt as wedded to her adopted country as most Frenchmen. She had always had an adventurous spirit. As a teenager she had felt shackled by her aloof patrician father and shy brow-beaten mother, and yearned to escape. Her freedom finally came at six-teen, when she was sent to finishing school in Florence. Tall, with dark hair and piercing gray-blue eyes, she was certainly striking and soon found herself drawing the attention of numerous young Italian men. Her intention had been to be "wicked" and for the next few years she certainly fulfilled that ambition, bed-hopping and partying across continental Europe in a social and sex-filled whirl.[70]

She had been staying with a wealthy American divorcee near Poitiers in France when war had been declared. By now aged thirty, and with neither a career nor husband in sight, she initially joined the French Red Cross, then volunteered to go to Finland as an ambulance driver. She got as far as Sweden, but after eventually returning to England in July, immediately offered her services to De Gaulle. In September, she found herself on a boat sailing toward Dakar in West Africa.

The war had certainly brought the adventure and excitement she'd craved. After a spell as a nurse at Brazzaville in the French Congo, she had then, after much persuasion, joined the Free French as they journeyed to East Africa. On board the ship she had met Amilakvari—and was soon in his bed—and also Pierre Messmer, whom she liked immediately: he was "thoughtful, intelligent and *très gentile.*"[71]

Once in Eritrea, she gave up nursing for good and became a driver for the 13 DBLE, even sustaining a shrapnel wound at the end of the campaign. The men started calling her "La Miss"—which she rightly took as a sign of acceptance. When the Free French moved to Syria, she followed, and became not only General Pierre Koenig's driver, but also his lover. Their affair continued—albeit clandestinely. There would and could be no public displays of affection. Even so, Susan was determined to be with him whenever and wherever she could, even if it meant following him into the desert. "There'll be no dishonour if you want to stay behind, La Miss," he told her. "Life in the desert is no picnic, you know, and there'll be few opportunities for us to be together." But Susan was adamant. "Wherever you go, I will go too," she replied.

The only other women at Bir Hacheim—all nurses—had been evacuated on 26 May, but Susan had returned a few days later as Rommel was breaking 150th Brigade. She had picked up a new staff car in Tobruk and it needed to be delivered. "Here I am at the rear echelon," she signaled to Koenig, "can I come back?"

"Yes you can," came the reply.[72] After all, by 31 May, Bir Hacheim was quiet. In fact, Koenig had been told to prepare to advance up the western side of the line as part of Ritchie's Operation LIMERICK.

This was soon canceled, however, and two days later, there were reports of numerous vehicles massing to the north. As forward patrols and supply vehicles hurried to get inside the perimeter, the Free French held their breath and waited. Nothing happened until two Italian officers appeared bearing the flag of truce. Rommel had offered 150th Brigade a chance to throw down their arms, and he was offering the same to Koenig now. "Gentlemen," replied Koenig, "thank your generals for their pleasant conduct, but tell them that there is no question of surrender."[73]

The French position was now almost as precarious as that of the Yorkshiremen two days before. They were almost completely surrounded and now cut off from their supply echelons. Throughout the afternoon, increasing amounts of enemy shells began to rain down upon their beleaguered position. Susan Travers sat in her dugout, her tin hat on her head and with the rifle Amilak had given her nearby. Every time the bombs stopped, she would creep out, peer around and think, "Well, it's not my turn this time."[74] With von Waldau now back in contact with Rommel, the Axis were also able to provide much better coordinated air attacks. Like most people unfortunate enough to find themselves on the ground at such times, Susan Travers found the Stukas the worst. At first sight she thought they looked like "a plague of silver locusts hovering above us." Her heart would quicken and her legs weaken, fear rising from the pit of her stomach. "I would count the seconds in my mind, one, two, three, four, five . . . And then it would come, that horrible crump and the blinding flash of white light, making me jump every time even though I'd fully anticipated it."[75]

On that first day of June, the shelling and bombing stopped abruptly with the arrival of a sudden sandstorm. In the morning, however, with more enemy forces ringed around the French positions, the attack continued and with mounting ferocity; nor was there any sign that the rest of Eighth Army were about to jump to their defense.

On 3 June, Rommel sent another message: *"To the troops of Bir Hakeim. Further resistance will only lead to pointless loss of life. You will suffer the same fate as the two Brigades which were at Got el Ualeg and which were exterminated the day before yesterday—we will cease fighting as soon as you show the white flag and come towards us unarmed. Rommel, General Oberst."* Koenig refused the offer, responding by opening fire with all his guns.[76] Pierre Messmer had dreamed of a chance to take on the Germans—well, now was the time. The French had lain down their arms all too easily in 1940, but here was an opportunity to show their enemy there were those who were prepared to die for a Free France and who would surrender at nothing. Alone and isolated, the French forces at Bir Hacheim braced themselves.

CHAPTER 5

Into the Cauldron:
4 June to 10 June, 1942

WORD OF THE BATTLE raging over three hundred miles away was filtering through the bars, clubs, and cafes of Cairo. "The news we hear at the moment," Cecil Beaton scrawled in his diary, "is that the two armies are locked in combat—a mêlée of tanks producing, in the heat, an Armageddon." The staff at GHQ were making "tremendous guesses as to the outcome." One of the men there thought it would simply fizzle out, but most felt it was likely to be decisive "one way or the other."[77] Another said he wouldn't be surprised if Rommel soon appeared parading down Solomon Pasha Street.

Beaton had only been back in Cairo a week and had already settled into a daily routine at GHQ. It was often said that there were six thousand too many staff officers in Cairo, but Cecil, for one, was impressed by their long hours—hours spent without the help of clerks, which tripled their paperwork. Like everyone else, he, too, was left to fend for himself, so the task of sorting out all the photographs he'd taken took four times as long. His mood had not been improved by a severe bout of "Egyptian stomach," accompanied by constant headaches and an aversion to the terrible heat, heat that was, for the most part, far more uncomfortable in the fetid confines of the city than it was in the open desert.

By Saturday 30 May, though, he was feeling better and went to photograph Lady Lampson, wife of the British ambassador in Cairo, Sir Miles Lampson. Sitting in the loggia in the embassy gardens, the ambassador's wife fanned herself with a papyrus leaf and told him about the never-ending stream of letters she received from mothers trying to find news of their wounded, missing, or dead sons. Some wrote continuously, although usually there was little she could offer other than soothing letters in return. Cecil found her rather impressive. "She has a great vitality and quickness," he noted, "that makes her very useful in her job."[78]

The following day he was given an even more interesting assignment. An "important person" was being flown into Heliopolis and Cecil was to head over there with Dudley Barker from GHQ right away. It was a bit of a rush to reach the airfield in time, but as they raced through the streets of Cairo as fast as their car would take them, they wondered who it might be—Rommel perhaps? Cecil hoped so. It wasn't—that proved too much to hope for—but it *was* his second-in-command, General Crüwell. "A good name for a German general," Cecil noted. He made an impression at any rate. "Sitting in a car, smoking a cigarette," Cecil observed, with his usual waspish eye for detail, and "wearing dark glasses and a florid uniform like a Tyrolean beater covered with red tabs and buttons, he looked like something stuffed and put in a cage."[79]

The fighting may have been taking place in the desert, but the spiritual home for the British Army in the Middle East was Cairo. "The fly-blown mecca of artifice and noise,"[80] it pullulated with peoples from across the world, jostling their way through the dust-filled streets, past cars, trams and bicycles, mules and oxen. The place hummed with constant noise: car horns, bells, the muezzin from a thousand mosques, and at night the drunken singing of troops making the most of a few precious days' leave; for Cairo was a city still teeming with light, food, and alcohol. For those newly arrived from a Britain of blackouts and rationing, it was a place of shining brightness indeed.

Egypt was, in fact, an entirely independent country, with its own place amongst the League of Nations—officially, at any rate. The reality was somewhat different. Britain had held it as a "veiled protectorate" from 1882 to 1914, then as a formal protectorate until 1922, when it was given "qualified" independence. This meant that there were some caveats to independence—principally the British right to defend Egypt, which included the Suez Canal and the route to India. So British troops remained stationed there throughout the inter-war period, and Sir Miles Lampson—the only ambassador in the country—maintained an influence and preeminence more akin to a governor than a mere diplomat. In other words, Egypt was a vassal state in all but name.

Cairo may have been humming with Egyptians and servicemen, but since the war, it had also become a haven for foreign nationals and asylum seekers. Sophie Tarnowska had made her way there from Poland and had lost her heart to the city. She loved hearing the muezzin calling the people to prayer, she loved the architecture, the bizarre mixture of French town houses and Coptic minarets; and she loved the fact that she felt so welcome there—at last, after so long on the run.

Sophie had led a peripatetic existence since the war began. The war had broken out—without being declared—on 1 September, 1939, when Germany invaded Poland. From the country estate of Gora Ropczycka, where she lived with her husband, Andrew, Sophie had heard planes roaring overhead. Like many people, she had rushed out to wave at them, assuming they must be British or French showing solidarity to their Polish allies. Only when they turned on the radio did they learn to their horror that town after town was being bombed by the Germans.

Over the ensuing days, as more and more refugees began streaming eastward, they began to realize they would have to leave. They moved first to their shooting lodge further east, then set off again—Andrew and Sophie's brother, Stanislaw, wanted to help the Russians in forming a second front. On the night of 8 September, they all piled into a car—Sophie, Andrew, their baby, Stanislaw and his girlfriend, Chouquette, Chouquette's sister, the midwife and the chauffeur, and set off under the cover of darkness for Rudnik, where Sophie's father lived. He refused to come with them—it was the last time Sophie would ever see him—and so on they went. "Going east, one could only travel by night with very dimmed lights," says Sophie, who was far from well at the time. "It was horrific. There were huge potholes, dead horses, burned-out vehicles. Sometimes Andrew or Stas would have to walk ahead to guide us."

By the time the Russians invaded in turn, Sophie and her small party had reached Chouqette's family home in the east. The roads were flooded with refugees, there was no hope of turning back home and so they headed south toward Romania. Sophie had told herself she would never leave Poland and had burned her passport. When she explained this to the border official, he looked at her and said, "You can pass." He gave her a piece of paper and added, "Wherever you go, you'll find love and friendship." "My eyes filled with tears," admits Sophie.

So began the long journey to the Middle East. Both Andrew and Stanislaw applied to join the Polish forces now forming in Britain and France. Stanislaw was accepted, and having married Chouquette, headed to France, while Sophie and Andrew made for Belgrade. After France fell, Stanislaw and Chouquette were lucky enough to make their escape and join Sophie and Andrew once more. By this time, Sophie's baby had died—she had now lost almost everything. Then in March 1941, they received word that Polish forces were being formed in Palestine. Sophie was not keen to move again. "We had already left one country—I didn't want to leave again," but both Andrew and Stanislaw were anxious to join and so, once again, they moved on. With both Andrew and Stanislaw with the Polish forces, Sophie settled in Tel Aviv and Chouquette in Jerusalem.

During their time in Palestine, Sophie's marriage ended. Andrew had been her first cousin—her parents had been against the match for this reason—and indeed, their child died soon after birth as a result of genetic complications. But they had been young, and for Sophie, Andrew had offered a means of escape and independence. In Palestine, however, her husband began having an affair with Chouquette. Matters came to a head one night in a club in Jerusalem. Andrew arrived brandishing a revolver and announced to Stanislaw, "I'm in love with your wife! Shoot me!"

"Don't be stupid," Stanislaw told him, "the war will sort this out." Even so, the breakup put a strain on her relationship with her brother, the only close family she had left. "There were things we could no longer talk about," she says. Soon after, both Andrew and Stanislaw were posted to Egypt and from there to Tobruk, then at the height of the siege.

Before the war, the vast majority of Europeans rarely had cause to leave the town or village of their birth. The war changed this, displacing millions. Sophie Tarnowska was just one of these, but solace of sorts was at hand. Shortly after the breakup of her marriage, she and Chouquette received a letter from Prince Youssouf Khamal. A relation of King Farouk and a member of the Egyptian Royal Family, he had once, before the war, been invited to shoot on her father-in-law's estate. Somehow, he had heard of their plight and so invited both to Cairo, where, he assured them, he would set them up in a villa of their own. Initially, Sophie was reluctant—the thought of living with her husband's lover hardly appealed—and nor did she particularly want to move yet again. But she was not happy in Jerusalem and a fresh start did have some appeal, and so eventually, she was persuaded to accept the offer.

As soon as she reached Cairo, she knew she had made the right decision. Prince Yousef had given them a villa in Quba Gardens, a leafy suburb, complete with furnishings and their own servant, known as a *sufragi*. The vibrancy of the city and the friendliness of the people made her feel immediately welcome, even though there were hardly any other Poles in Cairo at this time. Both soon found jobs: Chouquette as a secretary, while Sophie began working for the International Red Cross.

In October 1941, the leader of the Polish government in exile, General Sikorski, visited Cairo, and because both Sophie and Chouquete were two of only three Polish ladies in Cairo at the time, they were invited to meet the general at the Polish Legation. "And what are you doing?" he asked Sophie as she was introduced to him. When she told him, he said, "Why not the Polish Red Cross?"

"Because there isn't one here," she replied.

"Then perhaps you should set one up." All right, Sophie agreed, but only under certain conditions. In Britain, the Red Cross wore blue uniforms and stockings, but if she was to start the Polish Red Cross in Cairo, there must be no stockings and they should wear khaki. "We want to be able to work," she explained, "not stifle in hot clothes." Sikorski agreed. "And there must be no ranks," she continued.

"Why? Are you a communist?" he asked her.

"Good God, no," she replied. But she knew more Poles would arrive, possible wives of high-ranking officers, and so for her to be in charge of them might make life awkward.

"You know, you're right," the general told her.

But having no formal papers—which had to come from London—to identify her as a Polish Red Cross worker, Sophie turned to Sir Duncan Mackenzie, head of the British Red Cross in Egypt, and placed herself under his wing. "To him I owe the beginning of the Polish Red Cross," she says. Within days he rang her and told her that an anonymous bene-factor was giving her the use of a spacious flat in town in which to set up office. More benefactors offered to pay the electricity and telephone. The only problem was Sophie's lack of papers, which failed to arrive from London. In desperation, she turned to Lady Lampson, who prom-ised to vouch for her.

By June 1942, Sophie had a number of people helping her—not just Poles, but all kinds of people who could spare a bit of time. "It was all done by word of mouth," says Sophie. "Cairo was full of parties and this was the perfect way to spread the word." They prepared food parcels to send to prisoners of war across Europe and also sent bundles of clothes to Tehran, where Poles were congregating after being released from the Russian gu-lags; with the German invasion in June 1941, the Russians and Poles had become allies of sorts. By May, even the Polish HQ was also helping with funding. And in the evening there were always parties going on somewhere. In Cairo, Sophie had no need to ever be alone.

Also in Cairo at this time was the war reporter, Alan Moorehead. An Aus-tralian, he had left his native Melbourne and arrived in England in 1936, hoping to find more to write about than "magistrates courts, bush fires and sport."[81] He had not been disappointed. By 1942, with reporting on the Spanish Civil War and three years of this latest war behind him, he had become one of the best known journalists in Britain, writing for one of its most popular newspapers, Lord Beaverbrook's *Daily Express*.

Short of height, but with dark good looks and clear blue eyes, he had a natural talent for reportage, even though he had shown little aca-demic promise as a schoolboy. An adventurous spirit and natural charm combined with an eye for detail and a talent for writing evocative descrip-tive prose had proved a winning formula—especially with his reports from the desert war, which he had vividly brought to life for readers unfamiliar with such a barren and far-off land. With the Battles of France and Britain long since over, it was to the Middle East that much of the population turned, and Alan Moorehead, along with his great friends Alexander Clifford of the *Daily Mail* and Christopher Buckley of the *Daily Telegraph*, had become the most celebrated correspondents of the war to date.

Moorehead's reputation was beginning to reach across the Atlantic as well with an increasing number of articles for US magazines, most notably *Life*. He had also recently published his first book, *Mediterranean Front*, about the opening year in the Desert War, which had been well received back in Britain. He was lucky in other respects too: unlike most people during the war, he was able to live with his wife, Lucy, and baby son in their own flat in Cairo. Moreover, Lucy, a former *Express* journalist herself, had been working as the Auk's personal private secretary. Although Alan had had misgivings, believing the job might cause a conflict of interests, her closeness to the C-in-C and others in authority had opened doors that might otherwise have remained firmly shut.

Even so, by the beginning of 1942, the catastrophic situation in the Far East meant Alan, like Joe Madeley of the 9th Australian Division, had been itching to get back home to Australia. His editor had had other ideas, however, although with the lull in the desert fighting he had been posted to India to report on the threat from the Japanese and to cover Sir Stafford Cripps's mission to present the Indians with the British proposals for granting independence.

By the time battle had resumed in the desert, Alan had only just returned from his trip to India. His first piece for the *Express* had been a feature entitled simply "The Auk," which had run on the 28 May, but he, like other correspondents, had been caught off-guard by Rommel's attack. Hurrying out to the desert, he only reached the front on Monday 1 June. "As I drove out from Sollum into Libya," he wrote, "a stream of lorries passed me going to the rear. They were carrying Axis guns and German and Italian prisoners." He had also seen General Crüwell being brought into British Headquarters, and had then gone to see General Strafer Gott, commander of XII Corps in the north of the line, whom he had befriended the previous year. "There are only two places where I want to fight the Nazis," Gott had told him defiantly. "Either on our minefields or here." "Here" wrote Alan, "was that undulating patch of desert sown thickly with salt-bush that sweeps up from the sea not far from the old Italian fort at Acroma. In this area is Knightsbridge."[82]

Initially heartened by Gott's confidence, Alan then saw Colonel Desmond Young, the Indian Army public relations officer, loitering at the XII Corps Intelligence unit. "From him," wrote Alan, "I got my first indication that something was wrong." Like everyone else, Colonel Young felt the Germans were on the run. "But," he told Alan, "I don't understand why we aren't following up. Why don't we push in and mop them up? It's a job for the infantry now. We will have to move quick or you can bet your life they will re-form a line." He told Alan he was worried it might already be too late.[83]

That conversation had occurred on 1 June. Two days later he visited Army HQ and noted "the astonishing absence of news." Everyone appeared tense. "It *felt* as though we were on the edge of a considerable victory," he wrote, "Yet there was no real news."[84] Only two days after this visit did the British finally launch their attack.

The Battle of the Cauldron began in the early hours of Friday, 5 June. The infantry of the 10th Indian Brigade easily achieved all their objectives, but intelligence had been tragically inaccurate: the nighttime efforts of the Indians and artillery had taken merely a few Axis outposts; they had certainly not driven a wedge through the Axis anti-tanks screens as they'd thought. So when 22nd Armoured Brigade and the infantry of the 9th Indian Brigade set off at dawn, they were unwittingly advancing into a valley of death every bit as lethal as that at Balaclava ninety years before.

The night before, Sergeant Ray Ellis of the South Notts Hussars had known that at dawn they would be going into battle. He was tired, physically and psychologically: tired of fighting, and battles, and the desert, and killing. His gun crew were new and he could see they were all frightened. "I'd got past that stage," he says. "I was only twenty-two, but as far as warfare went, I was an old man. I felt sorry for these men who were homesick, frightened and cold."[85] He sat on a pile of sandbags, exhausted but wide awake. Taking out his watch, he began counting the minutes. Bad thoughts filled his head. "Someone was going to die very soon," he wrote, "maybe it would be me . . . I could feel the old familiar stiffening of my body as I thought of hot steel tearing through my flesh."[86]

Just before 3:30 AM, Ray ordered his men to "take post." The night was still and quiet until through a megaphone he heard, "Zero, minus five, four, three, two, one . . . fire!" The air ripped apart as each of the guns opened fire with a deafening roar. Working to a prearranged plan, Ray and his crew kept pounding away until the barrage was halted and they began preparing to move forward. The gun was hooked onto its carrier—a truck known as the gun tower—and with the tanks and other vehicles of the brigade they headed the advance to join battle.

Ray was up front in the cab of the lorry, his head poking through the hatch in the roof and peering into the early dawn mist covering the desert. There was no return fire at all from the enemy as they drove up toward the edge of the wide circular depression of the Cauldron. Then, as they cleared the rise, the desert erupted. The anti-tank guns and artillery of the Afrika Korps had been waiting for them. "He must have had it all ranged and ready," says Ray, "because the very first shells landed right among us. It was appalling. The horizon was a sea of flames."[87]

As the sun rose, the sky was filled with arcs of fire. The gun crews of the South Notts Hussars hurriedly unhooked their twenty-five-pounders and desperately tried to bring them to bear—but clearly there could be no further advance. A number of vehicles on either side of him were hit and burst into flames, but all Ray could think of was that he should keep firing and firing. Much to his relief, British tanks soon appeared, clanking through between their guns and toward the enemy over a mile away in front of them. Digging in as best they could, the gunners kept firing shell after shell. Soon the gun barrel was glowing red with the heat.

To the northwest of the Cauldron, around a shallow high point named Eluet el Tamar, the 32nd Army Tank Brigade had also launched an attack aimed at pinning down the 21st Panzer Division along the Sidra Ridge at the northern side of the Cauldron. The 32nd was made up of slow, largely obsolete I tanks, which had been pooled off from the northern sector where they had been supporting the various infantry brigades.

This was, frankly, suicide. The I tanks would have been hard-pushed to so much as scratch the paintwork of the panzers, but to make matters worse they ran into an unexpected minefield. While they were struggling through this, they neatly came into the aim of 21st Panzers' anti-tank guns. In a horribly short period of time, fifty of the seventy tanks that had set off that morning were now out of action, and the attack was called off. Job done, the panzers turned and headed southeast to join the battle developing in the Cauldron.

By early afternoon, the rim of the Cauldron was still being held by the South Notts Hussars and the rest of 22nd Armoured and 9th Indian Brigades, but any advance was now out of the question. Disaster loomed, however. Unbeknown to Eighth Army, the previous day Rommel had cleared a hole in the minefields *south* of the Cauldron. Through this gap, he had been able to surreptitiously retrieve a number of disabled tanks knocked out in the earlier fighting. With the British attack going nowhere, he was now able to spare 15th Panzer, which had been lining the southern edge of the Cauldron, and send them through this gap and out by Bir el Harmat, with a clear line of attack on the left flank of the British position. (See map)

It was a classic example of out-maneuvering, and surging through the minefield gap later that evening, 15th Panzer completely overran 5th Indian and 7th Armoured Division headquarters: for the second time in ten days, General Messervy had lost his HQ. Mayhem ensued. Ritchie—and in turn Norrie and Gott—had not only left the planning, but also the command of the battle to Bragg and Messervy, the divisional commanders. Once they were overrun there was no one commanding the battle until new headquarters could be established some time later. As Messervy noted afterward, "Everything went wrong on this day."[88] Eighth Army HQ was now completely in the dark and could rely only on guesswork. Ritchie knew that some of the Indians had been driven back but hoped 22nd Armoured Brigade would rally. "This done, we should have superiority," he signaled to Auchinleck. "But it takes time and the danger lies in surrendering the initiative."[89] In fact, this had already long since been lost. In contrast, Rommel had been personally commanding the panzer army himself since early afternoon—and from the front.

When night fell, the battle within the Cauldron finally quieted down. The guns stopped so that the only noise was that of the still-burning vehicles scattered all around. Then Ray Ellis heard the rumble and squeaking of tanks—their own tanks, coming back toward them. But instead of stopping and leaguering nearby, the remaining British armor passed through them and slid away like specters into the night. A further shock was in store: rumors began to spread that the army was in retreat, but that they were to stay behind and fight a rearguard. They and three Indian battalions, one reconnaissance battalion and three other artillery regiments. At first Ray could not believe it, but more tanks and then even infantry continued to pass through their positions. Some of the gunners began shouting out into the darkness, asking the tanks to stay. "Gradually it began to dawn on us," wrote Ray, "that there was now nothing but the open desert between the 21st Panzer Division and ourselves."[90]

To the north, the infantry brigades along the Gazala Line had had another quiet day of little activity. "A perfect day, though warm," wrote South African Bill Eadie, unaware of the carnage unfolding ten miles to the south. "Hardly a shot until sunset"—at which time a German plane zoomed over very low. It was clearly in trouble and the South Africans opened fire. The plane crashed a short distance behind them, "causing a hell of an uproar as may be imagined."

In the Cauldron, one of the South Notts Hussars' officers ordered the men to remain fully dressed and alert. Ray Ellis ignored such a pointless order—they were all dead tired—so he got out his blanket and went to sleep. One of the junior officers woke him shortly afterward. He was a "silly little upstart," so Ray told him where to go and went back to sleep again. "I had long since learned the importance of snatching sleep whenever possible," wrote Ray later.[91]

He was up again before dawn and waiting by his gun when Captain Slinn and Lieutenant Timms approached him. During the night, the rumors had been confirmed: General Ritchie had indeed decided that the artillery and infantry still in the Cauldron should remain there, hoping they could hold the line until the armor had yet again regrouped and reorganized itself. This wasn't quite how it was seen by Captain Slinn, however, who told Ray that they had been ordered to fight to the last man and last round of ammunition. "He warned me that it was going to be absolute carnage," recorded Ray, "and he voiced the opinion that few of us would live to see the end of the day."[92]

As dawn broke, the panzer army approached, as the defenders had known they would. Ray watched as they appeared over the lip of the far side of the depression and then rumbled and clattered down the slope. Sensing no opposition, they began to move forward less cautiously. Ray and the other crews loaded their guns with armor-piercing shells and waited for them to get within good effective range. "No one in my gun crew spoke," he noted, "as the tanks came bouncing towards us, each one leaving a huge cloud of dust in its wake."[93]

Having selected a target and estimated the range, Ray gave the order to fire. By chance, nearly every gun sergeant along their line seemed to have chosen the same moment to re-open the battle, and from their first salvo a number of German tanks were hit, belching flames and smoke into the air. In fact, after a few more rounds, the panzers began to retreat. Another attack was launched soon after, but yet again, the gunners managed to send them back.

There was another lull, but as Ray saw puffs of purple smoke rising into the sky, he realized they were calling for reinforcements from the Luftwaffe. They were also bringing forward their own artillery for counterbattery fire and as the enemy guns began pounding the British positions, Ray watched the Stukas wheeling above. Already the situation was desperate. Even so, the crews kept frantically loading and firing, empty shell cases rapidly mounting around them.

At around ten o'clock, Ray's crew had just hit a German tank, when their position erupted. The explosion flung Ray into the air, and he landed heavily. Badly shaken and with his ears ringing, he was trying to get to his feet when another shell crashed down upon their position, hurling him into the air once more, only for him to fall again amidst a thick cloud of smoke and dust. He was not sure how long he stayed there, but eventually he came to, "coughing and retching and at last I got onto my knees. Everything was covered in black smoke and shells were falling in every direction."[94] Looking around, he saw his gun was upside down, his crew draped over it. He thought he must be wounded but couldn't feel a thing. The blast had ripped off his shirt and his body was black and bleeding. For a while he just knelt where he was, shaking his head, until his brain began to clear. It appeared that another attack had been beaten off, so he crawled over to see if any of his gun crew were alive. He soon discovered the worst; he was the only survivor.

Having crawled into a small depression, he then took ahold of himself. There were still two workable guns left—albeit without any crews—so he dragged himself back out of his hole determined to have another go at the enemy. Tanks, guns, vehicles, and bodies littered the landscape. Smoke from the wrecks spiraled into the sky. The stench of cordite and burning rubber and flesh hung heavy in the air. There were now almost none of the original gun crews remaining, but a number of the regiment's support troops—drivers, signalers, and orderlies—began appearing, and by the time of the next attack later that afternoon, Ray and the other remnants of the regiment had managed to get three of their guns firing again. Still the enemy kept attacking—tanks, guns, machine-gun fire, and more dive-bombers. By late afternoon, Ray was still blasting away madly, although now alongside complete strangers. One man beside him was not from the regiment at all, but from the Royal Signals. A spray of machine-gun fire hit him in the lower body and flung him back on the trail of the gun. "I went over to pull his body clear and as I did so he looked up at me with such frightened eyes," wrote Ray. He tried to comfort the signalman with the normal platitudes, telling him he wasn't badly hurt, that soon he'd be in hospital with nice clean sheets; that he'd be home before he knew it. But the man was dying, the constant scream of explosions and bullets ricocheting around them. "It was like being in some corner of hell and talking about heaven," noted Ray.[95] He also watched other friends die: Jim Hardy was sliced in half by a shell; Jim Martin—an old pal from Tobruk days—was burned alive as the petrol tank of a truck poured over him and then caught fire. The second in command then loaded his truck with food and water and fled—the only man to desert his post all day. By now it was late afternoon and they were almost surrounded. Of the three surviving guns, only Ray's was still firing. Machine-gun fire suddenly drummed from behind them and the man beside him was "hurled spinning into the gun shield." Ray turned around to see a German tank only yards away. He waited for the inevitable, but it never came. "Whether he was distracted, or whether it was an act of compassion, I shall never know. I prefer to think it was the latter," he wrote later.[96]

The regiment was finished—utterly destroyed. Tanks began sweeping through the position, while Ray, dazed and numb, wandered aimlessly, not quite aware he was now a prisoner of war. He stumbled over to where Jim Hardy lay and saw his friend's water bottle was still attached to his webbing. Taking out his knife, Ray cut it free. "I drank the tepid water and then as I looked down at my old friend's lifeless face, the tears ran down my face." Then he saw his gun, with his crew still sprawled over and beside it. And there, on the shield, now upside down, was the painting of The Saint. It had fired its last.

It was now six o'clock, and although the British forces that remained in the Cauldron had, like 150th Brigade before them, fought against impossible odds to keep the mass of the panzer army at bay, the day had been a disaster. A German tank drew up beside Ray and the commander beckoned him to climb up. He did as he was bidden, and for a moment, they looked each other in the eye and then turned skyward, in a mutual expression of empathy. "We drove away from the battlefield together, two enemies who felt no hatred for each other, only a shared sense of loss and bitterness."[97]

As the field regiments and other units trapped within the Cauldron were slowly being destroyed on 6 June, confusion continued to reign at Army Headquarters. Throughout the day, the British armor had made only a few half hearted attempts to relieve the Cauldron, but even so, they had taken a pasting and by the morning of 7 June had only 132 tanks left from the 300 with which they had begun the attack.

Only one British general seemed to have some grasp of what was actually happening, and that was Major-General Francis Tuker of the 4th Indian Division. After his command of the southern flank at Gazala had so abruptly evaporated on the opening morning of the battle, Tuker had spent the rest of 26 May at XXX Corps HQ observing Rommel's progress. In the evening he had gone up to Eighth Army HQ to see if there was anything he could do, and the following morning was told he was needed not at the front, but at Sollum to make sure that reinforcements heading from Egypt and Iraq came through without a hitch. It was hardly a taxing task, but fortunately it meant regular visits to Army HQ and even occasional opportunities to drive out to one or other of the divisional, brigade, or corps HQs close to the fighting. He was therefore reasonably in touch with what was going on and, as a spectator, "saw as much as or more of the game than the players."[98] He didn't like what he'd seen. Ritchie, he believed, "had shown the same complete lack of ability to make a plan or to accept a risk. For days Rommel lay at his mercy, badly mauled," but nothing had been done.

When the attack had finally come, Tuker had been at the HQ he had established in a cavern near Sollum. The spot had already been much used—its floor was thick with fleas—but it did save Tuker and his divisional staff from the sandstorms that raged across the desert on 2 June. But on the fifth, having been told about the formations going in and the basic concept of the plan of attack, Tuker realized they were heading for disaster. He immediately rang Eighth Army HQ and pointed out that they had now forwarded the last reinforcing troops through Sollum and could he now rejoin the core of his division in the Delta? Yes, he was told, as soon as he'd handed over to another officer. This occurred the following day, after which he headed as fast as he could to Cairo and GHQ.

On his arrival, he ran upstairs to the chief of the General Staff (CGS), Tom Corbett, whom he knew well. In no uncertain terms, Tuker told him that unless the Auk went out to the desert at once, to take control and concentrate all he could lay his hands on for a single heavy blow in the northern sector to wrench the initiative back from Rommel, they were heading for the most unnecessary disaster of the war. It was clear to Tuker that neither Corbett nor Auchinleck appreciated the seriousness of the situation in the desert. Pointing to the map, he showed Corbett how dispersed the troops were and how these small formations were being left all over the battlefield in an attempt to cover every threat that might come from the Axis forces. "Soon Eighth Army will be sprinkled about with a man to every grain of sand," he told him. It was of tantamount importance that a concentrated striking force should drive a blow within forty-eight hours. There was, Tuker told him, yet time to save Eighth Army, even turn the tables, but this window would soon pass.

Corbett immediately went in to see the Auk, but returned a short while later saying the C-in-C would not go. "He [Corbett] couldn't have put it strongly enough," was Tuker's verdict. "He should have said 'Either Ritchie goes or I go.'"[99] Having pushed the matter as far as he was able, Tuker then made his way to his division near Cairo.[100] The following day, around noon, Ritchie signaled the Auk, "Yesterday was a day of hard fighting in which we suffered considerably, but I am confident that enemy suffered no less." Was Ritchie genuinely in the dark, or was this disingenuous understatement? It is hard to say, but with every day that Ritchie remained in command, the more perilous the British situation became.[101]

Eleven Hurricanes took part in 73 Squadron's morning sweep over Gazala and Acroma. It was Johnnie Fairbairn's first combat sortie since joining the squadron and he was "shit-scared." He had had no training whatsoever for daytime operations. After being called up in September 1940, aged just nineteen, he'd gone through initial and elementary flying training, had gained his wings—in Canada—then been posted to Scotland to train as a night-fighter pilot, and had spent only four months with an operational night-fighter squadron in South Wales when he'd been posted to North Africa. The 73 Squadron had been due to be converted to night-fighter duties; Johnnie had been sent out to them in anticipation of this, but with Rommel's attack, such plans had, for the time being, been put on the back burner.

The squadron had taken off in two flights, line abreast, but Johnnie had been behind his section leader and so had been engulfed in a miniature sandstorm. He'd left the ground completely blind and praying he wasn't about to collide with anyone. Quickly emerging into clear sky he soon found himself lagging behind. "Try pulling your wheels up, Red Three," said the flight leader. Johnnie felt himself smarting with embarrassment.

The patrol leveled out at around 18,000 feet. Below, the desert and the Mediterranean appeared to be little more than smudges of brown and blue. Through his headset, he suddenly heard the ground controller's voice, clear and calm. "Fifteen plus bandits approaching angels twenty, ten o'clock high." This meant there were at least fifteen enemy fighters two thousand feet above them, approaching from ahead and slightly to the left of their current position.

"There they are!" shouted the CO suddenly. "About twenty of the bastards! Watch them carefully." Johnnie craned his neck, scanning the sky for all he was worth but couldn't see a thing, although from the excited yells of his colleagues it was clear they were having no such problem identifying the foe. As Johnnie was discovering, it took a while to attune one's eyesight for aerial combat; it was one of the many reasons new pilots, particularly, were so vulnerable. Then someone shouted, "Here they come!" and the CO ordered them to break. Before he had had time to think, Johnnie discovered the others had disappeared and that he was flying completely alone. "For the first time in my life I experienced sheer terror," he noted. "My mouth went bone dry and my tongue attached itself to the roof of my mouth and stayed there. My breath inside my mask smelled of vomit and my body went ice cold."

His fear caused him momentary paralysis and he began flying straight and level—the biggest single sin in aerial combat. A loud bang brought him to his senses as the control column was nearly knocked out of his hand. A large chunk had been blasted out of his right aileron, the device on his wing that enabled him to rotate his aircraft. Without waiting to see who was attacking him, Johnnie flicked the Hurricane over on its back, pulled the stick hard into his stomach and dived for his life. With the airspeed indicator needle off the clock and hurtling towards the ground, he then struggled to pull out of the dive, and straining and

groaning, the Hurricane gradually did so. Despite flying somewhat lop-
sidedly, Johnnie managed to nurse his plane back to base. "On shaky
legs," he wrote, "I walked back to the mess feeling that I had not exactly
covered myself with glory."[102]

With his overwhelming victory in the Cauldron and with no sign of any
further attack by the remains of the British armor, Rommel turned once
more to Hacheim. Ritchie began by sending forces to the aid of the French
then began to wonder whether perhaps they should evacuate the position.
He was once again in two minds, but from Cairo, the Auk advised him to
keep the French where they were; with the Germans turning their attention there and away from the Cauldron, it would give Eighth Army's armor
time to regroup once more.

The Free French had been under near-constant attack since 1 June,
but despite being completely isolated many miles from the rest of Eighth
Army, they had defiantly held their ground in their hellish corner of the
desert. The French—or Fighting French as they had been renamed—were
proving to be a bothersome thorn in the side for the Axis commander.
Twice more Rommel had appealed to them to surrender. At dawn on
5 June, a German officer had driven up to the French lines and demanded a parley. The legionnaire sentry happened to be a German and
told him he could not possibly wake Koenig to ask him such a question.
Infuriated, the officer drove away again, only to hit a mine. Leaping out,
he was forced to continue on foot, German insults ringing in his ears.

Although surrounded, the French gunners had rarely let up. At night,
however, the defenders were given some respite. Pierre Messmer could
not understand why the Germans never attacked during the hours of
darkness—after all, the desert nights were always clear and cool, the ideal
fighting conditions. Still, he was not complaining. Nighttime gave the beleaguered outpost a chance for a few much-needed supplies to be sneaked
in. The 2nd Rifle Brigade had been operating to the west of the Gazala
Line, attacking enemy supply columns feeding both the attacks on Bir
Hacheim and the Cauldron, and also making forays into the French positions at night. On 7 June, Albert Martin had been told that S Company
would be escorting a supply column into Bir Hacheim. "They are desperately in need of these supplies, poor devils," he noted in his diary. "I'm
willing to risk it." And quite risky it was too. They had to rely on complete
darkness to avoid detection by the Axis troops leaguered around Bir
Hacheim, but this also made it harder to navigate; it was all too easy to
wander into mined areas or even lose one another. Knowing that at any
moment the next step might be their last or that they might be discovered
made such operations particularly tense affairs. That night the resupply

was only partially successful. Although they managed to avoid the mines, they did become dispersed and Albert's company commander along with a few others found themselves trapped within the French box. As it was, they only managed to get a small amount of food and water through. "We're all dead beat," wrote Albert the following day.

The French were also being supported by the RAF. On 3 June, seven Stukas from a flight of twelve were shot down by fighters of the Desert Air Force—amid gleeful cheering from the defenders below. The next day, Billy Drake did well, too. In a letter to his commander-in-chief, Air Marshal Sir Arthur Tedder, Mary Coningham wrote, "highlight of the day, however, was Drake of 112, spotting either a German or Italian party formed up in a square and obviously being addressed. His bomb landed right in the middle, and he claims well over 100 knocked out. His description was that he found one of the enemy colonels giving a pep-talk."[103] Isolated though they were, the defenders took heart from the efforts of the RAF. On the 4th, General Koenig signaled to Mary Coningham, *"Bravo! Merci pour la RAF!"* Mary replied, *"Merci pour la sport!"*[104] Two days later, Billy Drake was leading a flight of 112 Squadron over Bir Hacheim yet again when he spotted four Messerchmitt 109s below them. Making the most of this unusual advantage, Billy led his flight down to attack. In the brief exchange that followed, four 109s were shot down, including one by Billy. Not content with their aerial victories, they then bombed Axis vehicles, leaving one in flames and six others badly shot up. Later on in the day, the squadron destroyed a further five enemy vehicles and damaged another twelve. In all, thirty-eight sorties were flown that day by 112 Squadron, most of the pilots flying at least three sorties each, including an attack over the Cauldron in the afternoon. This was the kind of intensity of flying experienced at the height of the Battle of Britain. "Not a bad result, we felt," Billy Drake noted.[105]

But it wasn't enough. Mary Coningham was struggling to keep abreast of demands. It had been impossible to provide nonstop standing patrols over the Cauldron, for example, because there were simply too few aircraft available, although fighter bombers had destroyed around seventy enemy vehicles in the Cauldron. Coningham's difficulties were also compounded by the lack of radar—he could not afford to lose the one radar unit he had at the front—while the telephone links to his forward fighter wings were frequently cut by enemy air attacks. This meant all too often his pilots were unable to intercept the enemy in the air; even on the day Koenig had signaled his thanks to Mary, the RAF had only managed to intercept six out of the twenty-four enemy air attacks.

For those on the ground at Bir Hacheim, twenty-four Stuka raids in one day meant one every half hour. No sooner had one attack passed than another batch of thirty or forty would scream down upon them, releasing their deadly loads into a mass of dust and smoke, while from the desert the Axis guns continued to fire round after round into the shattered encampment. The ferocity of these repeated attacks was already taking its toll when, on 8 June, Rommel himself had also arrived to take personal command, along with sections of the Afrika Korps, which had been sent south to support the Italians and German 90th Light Division already striving to break the French will.

Although the morning had begun with a mist, Susan Travers had sat alone in her dugout and heard the Stukas screaming overhead as usual. "Sadly, they were just as effective," she noted.[106] As the mists cleared, the barrage began. Then more aerial attacks. Then infantry and tanks, and yet more dive-bombers. By evening, with vehicles still burning amidst the French positions and with the number of dead and wounded mounting, Susan listened with mounting anxiety to the Axis troops clearing mines only a few hundred yards away.

Pierre Messmer and his men had spent the day taking cover from the attacks, but that night, Koenig had ordered him to relieve some of the artillerymen who had faced the brunt of the Axis attacks that day, and were by now demoralized, tired, and thirsty. Before he moved into position, Pierre saw Colonel Amilakvari, who told him, "If it's necessary, you will have to die there."[107] Everyone in Bir Hacheim realized how hopeless their situation was becoming.

At around midnight, Messmer's unit took over his allotted section of the line. The outgoing officer had been wounded earlier that day when the roof of his command post had collapsed on him, and was now in a considerable state of shock. For the past few days they had spent every waking hour under near-constant bombardment. With every shell that had whistled over and every bomb that had been dropped, every man had been forced to pray that none of this massive ordnance would land on their dugout. The strain had been enormous.

The cover of darkness offered some respite, however, and Pierre and his men made the most of it, taking the chance to settle into their new positions. His unit had been reinforced by some African troops, but this had been something of a part exchange: in return for the extra troops, he had been forced to relinquish his Bren carriers, their only source of mobility. As they stowed their pitiful kit and cleaned their weapons, they could hear scraping a few hundred yards away: the Germans were clearing the mines that protected Bir Hacheim.

Pierre noticed one of his men, Mamuric—nicknamed "Mammoth"—sitting apart from the rest of his men and lovingly polishing his heavy machinegun. This worried him somewhat, especially when he heard the big man muttering, "You must be beautiful for tomorrow, my lovely. You're all cleaned up now . . . have a rest." From Croatia, Mammoth had saved Pierre's life in Eritrea and since then, they had, from time to time, talked openly to one another. Mammoth had told him about his childhood in Croatia, where he had been abandoned as a child and had survived by working most of his life as a farm laborer until being sent packing for getting the farmer's daughter pregnant. He'd been a legionnaire almost ever since. Wandering over to him, Pierre said, "Tomorrow is going to be a nightmare. What are you fighting for, Mamuric?"

"For freedom, my captain," Mammoth replied without thinking. Pierre was astounded. "Big ideals rarely spring from the mouths of soldiers," he noted. "If Mamuric invokes freedom it is perhaps because he is going to die."[108]

The following afternoon, after a morning of further heavy bombardment, German infantry appeared through the mist of heat and dust. Advancing to the right of the French position, the Germans severed the legionnaires from the rest of the Brigade, but by bringing to bear a heavy artillery strike of their own, the Fighting French once more repulsed German assault. By nightfall, the French brigade still held their positions. They had not been overrun, but their situation was without hope. Over a hundred aircraft had attacked Bir Hacheim that day. Susan Travers was disgusted that despite being clearly marked, even the hospital and surgical theater had come under attack from the Stukas, and although the RAF had dropped urgently needed supplies of plasma, the bottles had shattered as they'd hit the ground. They were also now down to less than a cupful of water per person per day. Albert Martin and his colleagues in the 2nd Rifle Brigade were once again up all night, hoping to bring in more supplies, but the French guide never appeared.

More and more enemy aircraft arrived the following day, bringing with them a hurricane of fire, metal, and stone. Pierre had been in a foxhole but was half buried as the sides collapsed on him. He emerged momentarily blind and punch-drunk; when his eyesight returned, all he could see was a thick black cloud of smoke covering the landscape like a funeral shroud. A pause, and then the Axis artillery struck, shells from the German 88s exploding before Pierre had even heard the report. Tanks also emerged ahead of them and began advancing towards his section of the line. "Open fire," Pierre told the commander of his three 75mm anti-tank guns. "If I do," the officer replied, "the guns will be detected and destroyed."

"Open fire," Pierre told him again, "because it's now or never." One enemy tank was hit, but within a couple of minutes the Legionnaires' guns were, as predicted, destroyed by the lethal fire of the 88s.[109]

Unbeknown to Pierre Messmer, Koenig had already decided that they would attempt a breakout that night, 10 June, and although Ritchie had spent the previous few days urging him to hold on, he did finally authorize the decision. Koenig had told his lover, Susan Travers, in person the night before, and so she spent the next twenty-four hours preparing herself for what seemed like "nothing less than a suicide mission."[110] Each hour dragged by; there was little she could do but prepare the car as best as she was able, lining it with sandbags, making sure it was filled with fuel and water and placing Tommy guns on the backseat. After that, there was nothing for it but to wait.

Koenig had decided a mass breakout through the southwest was their best chance of success. Sappers would clear a fifty-yard path through their minefields, then battalions of legionnaires would push forward creating a corridor through which the rest would follow. The French commander, with Susan driving, would lead the convoy of vehicles carrying the wounded behind the legionnaires.

H hour was midnight. The mood in the camp was tense, although the senior officers, Pierre Messmer included, did their best to appear outwardly calm. Susan Travers brought the car to the assembly point, sick with nerves. The car had played up badly the last few times it had been out and she feared it would break down on them. "Please don't let me down tonight," she muttered to the car, "don't stall on me."[111]

It was a dark, moonless night, and cold too. Dead on midnight, the general appeared and got into the car beside Susan. "You're to do exactly as I tell you, when I tell you, for both our sakes," he told her. Then, putting the car in gear, Susan crept them forward. More agonized waiting followed, while the path was cleared of mines, then they trundled forward again, in total silence save the low rumble of their engines.[112]

The comparative calm was shattered as a Bren carrier hit a mine. In moments, the sky was lit with Axis flares and then another Bren carrier exploded too. Shortly after, shells began falling, and arcs of tracer cut across the sky. Susan Travers fully expected this to be the end, especially when Amilak's car also hit a mine. The Russian count, was, however, unhurt, and having ordered his troops to move forward, joined Susan and Koenig in their car. "Drive straight ahead, as fast as you can!" the general shouted. "If we go, the rest will follow."[113] Susan did as she was told, but first had to maneuver around the various burning vehicles ahead of her. In doing so, she was forced to venture off the cleared path and into the minefield. But all fear had left her. Instead, she felt only exhilaration as she hurtled the car toward ever-increasing amounts of tracer and gunfire.[114]

* * *

By 7 AM on 11 June, only 1,500 French troops had reached British lines, and it appeared the breakout had been a costly failure. Koenig, Amilak-vari—and Susan Travers—were all missing. But as the morning wore on, the situation improved. At 8 AM, the 7th Motor Brigade signaled that they had 2,000 further troops from Bir Hacheim, including a number of their own who had been trapped during an earlier attempt to resupply the be-sieged brigade. "What a bloody night it was!" noted Albert Martin in his diary. At dawn, he had been sitting in a disused slit trench watching the French emerge through a "solid wall of fire." Albert had helped round up hundreds of wounded, dazed, and exhausted men and led them to wait-ing trucks and ambulances.

Shortly after, with the French safely out of the way, Albert and his sec-tion had seen a huge column of enemy tanks, vehicles, and troops head-ing in their direction.

"What do we do now, Corporal?" asked one of Albert's section.

"What you don't do matey," Albert told him, "is run around like a headless chicken—now keep still, stay in your trench."[115] His experience was showing, but clearly there was little they could do to save themselves. Heroics would achieve nothing, and so Albert resigned himself to being taken prisoner—"put in the bag." He felt completely drained of emotion. He'd been in the desert a long time, and now it was over. They all started collecting their things together—water bottles, spare socks, photographs, and letters—and waited to be rounded up.

To their surprise the Germans then suddenly changed direction. "They clearly saw us," says Albert, "but we were ignored." After a while, the Riflemen got up out of their slit trenches and gingerly moved off in their trucks on a parallel line with the Axis column. "We gave the enemy a wave, which they returned," says Albert, "and then they moved off at a tangent and away." Sometimes collecting prisoners in the desert was more trouble than it was worth.

Koenig and Amilak were still missing—but were safe. Miraculously, the car never let Susan Travers down, even though it had been punctured by a number of bullets. In the early hours before dawn they had even mis-takenly stopped in the midst of a German leaguer. "Drive! *Vite!*" Amilak had urged her as they heard German voices and then rifle fire. "My heart was in my mouth," wrote Susan, "as I flew past the menacing silhouettes and on into the darkness."

As the faint flush of dawn appeared on the horizon, they realized they were now in an empty stretch of desert. Nothing could be seen for miles and miles. Miraculously, they had survived, but Koenig was in de-spair, believing they were the only survivors. In the early afternoon, however, they saw a large convoy. As they approached, they realized to their joy and relief that it was a large part of the brigade that had broken out with them the previous night.[116] Even Pierre Messmer, who had been ordered to stay until the last moment, had made it to safety. At one point he and his men had found themselves in the middle of a German company, with only one armed pistol between them. A number of equally lost French armored vehicles inadvertently rescued them in the nick of time. They later stumbled upon a German command post, which they overran before the startled Germans had time to realize what was happening.

Over 2,500 from a garrison of 3,700 managed to escape that night. On 26 May, Rommel had reckoned Bir Hacheim would be destroyed in less than an hour. Instead, the Free French had held out for two weeks, despite desperate shortages of water, food, ammunition, and equipment. When it seemed that all was lost, they had saved themselves with a breakout of outrageous daring, and in doing so, had done much to restore the pride and reputation of the French. For General Koenig, the leader of this remarkable band, the relief was almost too much. Turning to Susan Travers, tears filling his eyes, he said, "Well done, La Miss. Between us we did it. We got them out."[117]

But with Bir Hacheim no longer in the equation and the southern half of the Gazala Line destroyed, it was time for the armor to once more face each other. And this time, the outcome would conclude the battle once and for all.

CHAPTER 6

Knightsbridge: 11–18 June, 1942

SINCE THE BROAD AGREEMENT on Anglo-US strategy in April, planning had not gone as smoothly as either of the Allies had hoped. A string of disasters in the Pacific Theater had proved understandably distracting. That same month, America had lost the Bataan peninsula to the Japanese; in May, the US garrison at Corregidor surrendered as well. Meanwhile in Burma, General Alexander was retreating back across the Irrawaddy River and toward the Indian frontier; the Japanese threat to both India and Ceylon—the jewels of the British Empire—had never been greater.

The attack on Pearl Harbor, combined with the US losses in the Pacific had, unsurprisingly, made US popular opinion fearful of a Japanese attack on America's western seaboard and favor a Japan-first strategy. Despite these setbacks, however, the American chief of staff, General George Marshall, was still in favor of pursuing the three plans devised for the Europe-first policy, namely, the buildup of troops in the UK, a cross-Channel invasion in 1943, and a limited ground attack in Northern France in 1942. But time was running short. Despite the catastrophes in the Pacific, the Western Allies needed to get a move on.

The British, however, were not quite so enthusiastic for the US proposals as Marshall and his chief planner, Major-General Dwight D. Eisenhower, had first supposed. The few "reservations" they had expressed to Marshall in April were, in fact, the British way of euphemistically saying they did not like the plans at all. Marshall's opposite number, General Sir Alan Brooke, had little enthusiasm for any kind of Channel crossing in 1943, let alone 1942. As he pointed out, "the prospects of success are small and dependent on a mass of unknowns, whilst the chances of disaster are great and dependent on a mass of well established military facts."[118] Meanwhile, the prime minister had been giving Brooke further headaches by talking in terms of invading Norway instead. And while Churchill was still anxious to see a cross-Channel invasion in 1943, by May he too was losing his enthusiasm for SLEDGE-HAMMER, even though it had originally been a British idea.

Matters were forced to the forefront, however, by the arrival of the Soviet foreign minister, Vyacheslav Molotov, in London on 20 May. Although he had ostensibly arrived for discussions about the terms of a new Anglo-Russia treaty, he also wanted to hear about plans for a second front in Europe, which, understandably, he hoped would happen as soon as possible. He was frank with Churchill, telling him that any American and British effort against the Axis needed to draw off at least forty German divisions from Russia. The PM replied with equal candor: that would not be possible. Even if they did make a move in 1942, there was no chance of them launching a big enough operation to draw off that kind of number of Axis troops. The Allies were simply not ready. With this disappointing news, Molotov then journeyed on to Washington. Before he had crossed the Atlantic, however, Churchill had already written several letters to Roosevelt, reporting on his talks with the Russian. It was during this correspondence—on 28 May—that he reminded the American president of a suggestion he had first made the previous October and again during the ARCADIA conference, a suggestion at which Roosevelt's military chiefs had universally balked, even if the president had not. This was a plan for an Allied invasion of French North Africa, which Churchill had code-named GYMNAST.

Molotov arrived in Washington and immediately pressed the Americans hard on their plans for a second front, warning that with the German summer offensive approaching, the Russians may well not be able to hold out. If the Western Allies postponed their decision to take action against Germany in 1942, he warned them, "you will have eventually to bear the brunt of the war."[119] In reply, General Marshall assured Molotov that a second front of some kind *would* be launched that year. He did not, however, specify where.

While these talks were going on in Washington, Eisenhower was making a whirlwind tour of Britain to see for himself how the proposed offensive plans were developing. He had become concerned that little was being achieved by both the American and British general staffs regarding a joint stategy. "Everybody is much engaged with small things of his own," he noted in his diary. "We can't win by giving out stuff in driblets all over the world."[120] Another reason for the trip was to check up on the existing American staff in London, who, Marshall believed, were out of touch with the plans. It was Ike's first visit to Britain and he flew there on the now increasingly used air route via Newfoundland and Iceland to Scotland, arriving in Prestwick on 25 May. After a further long and arduous journey by train, he eventually reached the war-torn capital in the middle of one of its very worst pea-soup fogs. This same fog seemed to have clouded the minds of the US military team in London, who, as Ike had suspected, were completely confused about their role and had little concept of what they should be doing for BOLERO, or ROUNDUP, let alone SLEDGE-HAMMER. As a result, on his return to Washington, Ike recommended to Marshall that a proper US HQ was set up in London with a "punch behind the job"—someone who could act swiftly and decisively and who would make things happen. "We must get going!" he warned.[121]

During this trip, Ike also took the opportunity to meet Brooke and the various British military chiefs, and was also taken to see a large-scale army training exercise in southeast England conducted by Lieutenant-General Bernard Montgomery. Shortly after their arrival at Montgomery's HQ, the British general briskly marched in and lectured them on the development of military maneuvers. Then suddenly, he stopped midsentence.

"Who's smoking?" he demanded.

"I am," Ike admitted.

Montgomery eyed him then said, "I don't permit smoking in my office."[122] Yet, despite this reprimand, Ike had been impressed by the diminutive British general. "General Montgomery," he noted, "is a decisive type who appears to be extremely energetic and professionally able."[123]

Meanwhile, the long battle in the desert was continuing, and the casualty figures mounting. Wounded troops had been arriving thick and fast to the military hospitals in Alexandria and Cairo. A number of volunteers would tour the wards, handing out tea, books, magazines and cigarettes. Sophie Tarnowska may by now have been busy with the Polish Red Cross, but she still found the time to help in the hospitals too, wandering through the wards with her usherette's tray, handing out five cigarettes to any patient who wanted them, along with a small booklet of matches; it was the least she could do. A difficult task, though; it was depressing seeing the lines of beds filled with young men, often with horrendous wounds: stumps where legs or arms had once been. Jagged shrapnel rarely caused neat wounds. Sophie found it so hard to think of anything to say. "'How are you today?' is such a silly thing to say to someone so obviously suffering," she says, "and the gap between each bed was only a few feet, so the next patient could hear what you said before."

Cecil Beaton had also been touring the wards—with Barbara Crichton-Stewart, a friend of his who worked at the 15th Scottish General. One man they stopped to talk to was a captain who had been wounded on the first evening of the battle when his tank had been hit. His driver had been killed, and the observer's arm smashed, while he had been hit in the leg by pieces of shrapnel. Cecil was impressed not only by how well he looked but also by his eagerness to get back to the front. The captain told them that the worst bit about being wounded was the journey in the ambulance—as Sam Bradshaw had discovered before him, each jolt brought new agonies. In the ambulance with them was a German screaming with pain; none of the patients felt they could let the side down by crying out themselves in front of a German, so had borne their wounds in stoic silence.

Later he met a number of patients who were recovering from head wounds. Many had been brain damaged. "How like children they were, learning to walk again," Cecil recorded in his diary. Another man— "Jock"—had had his eye blown out but was wearing a new glass one for the first time. Meanwhile, the doctor had removed the bandage from one man's forehead to reveal nothing but a large red cavity. Despite all this, Cecil was impressed by the men's patience and "zest for life." He didn't see a single man grumbling—unlike himself, who complained constantly about the heat and his unsettled stomach to his diary. The heat, he wrote, was "calamitous." "What can it be like in a tank when your hand is hurt by touching the metal? It's too appalling to contemplate the agonies these men must be going through."[124] He also thought Cairo "a most tatty capital," and was beginning to feel stale and frustrated, and so on 7 June, set off again—not to photograph the battle still raging in the west, but eastward to Tehran and Syria, the other end of Britain's enormous Middle East Command.[125]

One of those sweltering in his tank was Sam Bradshaw, since February recovered from his wound and back with 6 RTR. Once the battle had opened, the 6 Royal Tank Regiment had been hastily dispatched from Mena Camp outside Cairo, to the railhead at Fort Cappuzzo just west of Sollum where General Tuker had been marshalling reinforcements. From there, they were sent forward to El Duda. Sam was surprised to see so much evidence of the recent fighting. From his tank he spotted what at first looked like a concrete pillbox, but as he drew closer, he realized it was the turret of a Grant. "My God," he thought, "what are the Germans using against us now if they can knock a Grant turret off its hull?" Like most who were used to the flimsy Crusader, Sam had been impressed with the few Grants they'd trained with back at Mena. It had been a good day when they'd heard that the whole regiment would be re-equipped with them. The sight of a wrecked turret was sobering indeed.

Sam Bradshaw and the rest of 6 RTR soon found themselves concentrating with the rest of 4th Armoured Division southeast of the Knightsbridge Box, still held by the 201st Guards Brigade. Most of the British armor was now dug in east of the Cauldron, near the Knightsbridge cross-roads. Since Rommel had turned his attention to Bir Hacheim, there had been no full-scale attack, but a number of small skirmishes, as scout and reconnaissance forces probed forward, both sides trying to discern the other's intentions. As at sea, the problem was that armored formations were able to move constantly and with ease across this featureless desert. By the time any reports reached the commanders, the situation had all too often changed.

On 8 June, 6 RTR had engaged a reported formation of around fifty enemy tanks at extreme range, and then had done so again the following morning. Two days later, 6 RTR, together with 1 RTR, moved forward to attack an enemy column reported to be moving north along the Hacheim track toward Kinghtsbridge. As the early morning sun began to burn off the desert mist, they were told to halt and delay their attack for an hour. But no sooner had this order arrived than they came under fire. Shells were now raining down amongst them through the dust and smoke. Yet again, the two tank regiments had moved forward without the support of either troops or artillery, enticed by the firing of far-off German tanks. And yet again, they had lurched forward straight into the trap. The Grant's 75mm gun was certainly an improvement, but it was no match for the 88s and in no position to take on a well dug in screen of armor and anti-tank guns. Within moments, 1 RTR was in chaos, with a number of its Honeys and Grants burning fiercely.

Meanwhile, 6 RTR had also come under attack by the same well-directed 88s. Sam Bradshaw with B Squadron had been on the extreme right of the advance, and approaching from a shallow ridge, his troop had immediately moved into hull-down positions the moment the two regiments came under attack. Having seen two Grants of C Squadron brew up, he frantically surveyed the Axis positions. Flashes were coming from the enemy tank guns and also flashes lower down, which he guessed must be from the 50mm anti-tank guns between the tanks. Believing it was best to try and hit the anti-tank guns first, he ordered the gunner to fire high-explosive rather than armor-piercing shells. Once more, sweat glistened on the faces of Sam and his tank crew, their tank filling with the acrid stench of smoke and cordite, each blast resounding and shaking through the iron hull. With his head sticking out of the turret, Sam strained to see the enemy ahead of them. "Our fire was obviously having some effect," he says, "because eventually the lower gun flashes ceased." But it was all ready too late: his regiment had lost three Grants and two Honeys, while 1 RTR's B Squadron had by now ceased to exist. When were the armored commanders ever going to learn? Bad tactics had caused two regiments to lose tanks, not to mention good crew. They could ill-afford to in a scrap that wasn't even part of a concerted attack on the enemy's position.

Above them, the Desert Air Force never let up. Over Gazala, some of the most intense aerial fighting of the war was taking place. A combat veteran of Billy's caliber might have taken to this strange kind of air combat like a duck to water, but for someone as green and inexperienced as Johnnie Fairbairn, survival was increasingly in the hands of Lady Luck. On 8 June, he returned from a sweep only to find a local sandstorm blowing up over the airfield. He couldn't see a thing, and they were short of petrol so were unable to divert elsewhere. His flight commander ordered them into a tight formation, and with considerable coolness led them safely back down. Had Johnnie returned alone, as he had on several occasions, it might have been a very different story. "He was very old indeed," noted Johnnie, "about 26." Later, though, Johnnie was shocked to walk into the mess and discover the same man sitting in the corner sobbing like a child.

Two days later, Johnnie had another close shave. At around 1:40 PM on the tenth, he had taken off along with eleven other Hurricanes for another sweep over the front line. Some 109s attacked them straight out of the sun. The CO shouted, "Break!" and once again, Johnnie found himself alone in the sky.

Then a strange thing happened. Johnnie suddenly noticed two 109s on either side of him. They were so close he could clearly see the nearest pilot's face and squadron markings along the fuselage. They were flying slightly faster and slowly edged in front of him until they drifted toward one another and straight into his gunsight. Just fifty yards ahead, they were sitting ducks. "It then occurred to me," noted Johnnie, "that I had been trained and sent halfway round the world at vast government expense to kill Germans and that the time had come to make an effort." Pressing his thumb down on the firing button, he heard nothing but a loud hiss of compressed air: all four of his guns had jammed.

Cursing, Johnnie glanced into his mirror and saw it filled by a further 109 sitting right on his tail. "I was stuck right in the middle of an enemy formation with no guns," he noted, but for some strange reason he couldn't fathom, none of them seemed to have realized he was a British plane. Slowly, he peeled away to the right. None of them followed him and he was able to get back in one piece. Almost certainly, however, his guns had saved him. Had he opened fire, the German behind him would have been left in no doubt as to his true identity and would have had just as easy a shot. Johnnie wondered how long his charmed existence was going to last.[126]

* * *

Meanwhile, following some of the tank skirmishes and firefights on the ground was *Daily Express* war correspondent Alan Moorehead, now based in Tobruk but daily venturing onto the battlefield. As he discovered, a "spanking good pace" could be made across the desert on clear, wind-free days—within an hour he was with the front-line brigades around the Knightsbridge area, watching reconnaissance groups and salvage teams retrieving disabled tanks. The versatile desert soon absorbed the carnage as the battle moved this way and that across the scub. Passing over land where fighting had recently taken place, Alan was amazed to see that all was calm once more and that "it was just another summer's day with larks singing in the sky and a few wild flowers growing."[127]

He also spent much time talking to the men on the ground. He had been personally critical of British equipment, so it was a relief to discover that both the Grant and the new six-pounder anti-tank gun were widely praised. A trip to a tank workshop in Tobruk increased his good impression of the new equipment. There he was shown a Grant that had been hit no less than seventeen times. "Look," the Scottish major in charge had said, pointing to a spot where a 50mm German shell had struck the side. Alan was genuinely impressed. "It had pitted the steel with a series of tiny veins radiating from a shallow central crater," he noted, and had only been sent to the workshop because one of its tracks had broken.[128]

Even so, by 10 June, 350 tanks had been completely destroyed since the beginning of the sixteen-day battle. Despite the recent reinforcements, tank strength stood at 185. Seventy-seven of these were were Grants, but a further sixty-three were the all but useless I tanks. Both Auchinleck and Ritchie were now in agreement that rather than attack, they should let Rommel make the first move. In every other regard, however, the command was as muddled and chaotic as ever, and affected the various battalions and regiments not just in the way they engaged the enemy, but in other ways too. When Sam Bradshaw and 6 RTR had arrived near the front, they had initially been told that the regiment would be split up to fill gaps elsewhere. "We considered this an insult," says Sam. The men were proud of their regiment. They had survived some fierce battles, and now, in the middle of another scrap, they were to be disbanded and separated. Then at the last minute, the regiment was suddenly spared and re-equipped with Grants and Honeys. A number of units were not so fortunate, however. Even single tanks and crews were sent from one regiment to another. As it was, 6 RTR was shunted to and fro between divisions. On their arrival, they had spent two days as part of 1st Armoured Division, then been transferred to 4th Armoured Brigade, and so were back with their old parent unit, 7th Armoured Division. Their experience was not uncommon: all armored brigades had changed division at least twice since the battle began. The result was not only unsettling, but led to administrative and communication confusion.

The commanders themselves were also still at loggerheads. In the still-static northern half of the line, General Strafer Gott of XII Corps had been trying to persuade General Dan Pienaar, commander of the three South African Brigades, to attack southwestward into the Axis positions on the other side of the line. Pienaar, however, was not having any of it. There was no way, he told Gott, that he was going to allow his one infantry division to be annihilated by the equivalent of one German and two Italian divisions still lined against him. This was somewhat exaggerating Axis strength at that point in the line and also flattering Italian capabilities, but instead of telling Pienaar to pull his finger out and do what he was told, Ritchie had accepted his objections, suggesting the South Africans make a brigade-group raid instead. But Pienaar then decided he did not have enough time to organize this, and so the end result was a handful of company-sized raids on 7 June. Bill Eadie, at 2 South African Infantry Brigade HQ, was unaware of anything happening at all that day. Only the following morning did he hear the first rumors that things were not going too well. "The CTH [Cape Town Highlanders] column seems to have fallen into enemy hands," he recorded. "News of frantic fighting further south." Pienaar's halfhearted, badly executed raids had achieved absolutely nothing except the loss of 280 of his men.

Meanwhile, ULTRA had produced details of Rommel's intentions after Bir Hacheim, which was, in a nutshell, to destroy as much as possible of the British armor in Knightsbridge, and then cut off the remainder of the Eighth Army and march on Tobruk. There appears to have been little response to this news at Army HQ, except to sit and wait. In the meantime, Ritchie somehow also found time to produce a lengthy document grandly entitled "Notes on the situation in the Western Desert (Eighth Army) on 11/6/42 with a view to determining future policy." This future policy was, he concluded, "the destruction of the enemy forces in Cyrenaica. The enemy must not be left to withdraw and reorganise."[129] In other words, exactly the same policy as at the start of the battle, but with considerably less forces and only half his line still intact with which to enforce this strategy.

Events soon showed that Ritchie's optimism was desperately misplaced. Barely had Bir Hacheim been overrun than Rommel was on the war path once more, sweeping northwards towards Knightsbridge during the afternoon of 11 June. At 6:30 PM, dust clouds were spotted from the south, and the Grants of both 1 and 6 RTR lined up, hull down, on the agreed battle line. A short while after seven o'clock, a few long-range shots whistled through the evening sky.

The battle would not begin that night, however, and after a stand-off for an hour and a half, both sides withdrew to leaguer for the night. Three more Grants reached 1 RTR during the night, all manned by American crews. Although the Americans were supposed to hand them over to British crews, not enough men could be found to man them, and so they stayed with them, becoming among the first American troops on the ground to fight against the Germans in the Second World War.

At dawn the following morning, the Grants of both 6 and 1 RTR were lined up, hull down, along their battle line, having had another long night to contemplate the battle ahead. In the case of 1 RTR, this meant just five Grants (not including the Americans) of C Squadron; after the losses on 10 June, B Squadron had been temporarily disbanded. Still defending the southeast of the Knightsbridge Box, they now faced a formidable opposition: the combined armor and anti-tank guns of the Italian Trieste and 15th Panzer, while behind, after its march toward El Adem to the east the previous day, the 90th Light was also swinging back toward them. In other words, the panzer army was attacking from both sides, squeezing the British armor like a vise.

The Germans nearly captured General Messervy for a second time. Again unhappy with Norrie's plans, Messervy had been travelling to XXX Corps HQ when he had run into the Germans as they thundered west in a cloud of dust and clattering metal. Hiding in a dried-up bir, Messervy had managed to avoid capture, but once again, 7th Armoured—which again included the 4th Armoured Brigade to which 1 and 6 RTRs were attached—began the battle without a commander.

At 6:30 AM, both 1 and 6 RTR came under heavy attack, not only from two 88s, but heavy 105mm field guns and around seventy tanks. Several men of 6 RTR were wounded by the shelling, while one tank was completely destroyed, bursting into a ball of flames. Thick, black smoke belched from the contorted iron hulk. Meanwhile, more enemy tanks were approaching from behind. This was 21st Panzer who had swiftly moved from their position on the east of the Cauldron, slipping through the gap in the minefields to the south, and in no time were attacking the rear of 7th Armoured Division. Rommel now had much of the British armor as well as the 201st Guards Brigade caught at Knightsbridge in much the same way that they had been ensnared in the Cauldron nearly a fortnight before. The difference was that the Axis commander, once more leading from the front, had no intention of letting his quarry off the hook.

Eighth Army, however, did still have 22nd Armoured Brigade to the northwest of Knightsbridge. That morning they had been facing 21st Panzer, but it wasn't until after two o'clock that afternoon that they finally set off in pursuit. By the time they were in a position to engage, the Germans had dug in their anti-tanks once more and so Lumsden's tanks faced another mauling. Meanwhile, Norrie was clutching at straws and issuing nonsensical commands from his headquarters. At noon he had decided to change overall command of the two armored brigades now battling for their lives to the southeast of Knightsbridge, and so in the heat of battle yet again switched 4th Armoured Brigade and 2nd Armoured Brigade under control of Lumsden at 1st Armoured Division HQ. He told Lumsden that these two brigades were still to advance south. With the weight of German armor and artillery a deadly and impregnable wall in front of them, this was an impossible command, proving just how out of touch Norrie was with his forces and how rapidly the situation was worsening.

1 and 6 RTR were now in a highly perilous situation, having come under continuous artillery fire and repeated tank attacks all day from the south, east and west. Like almost everyone else in Eighth Army from the very top to the bottom, Sam had no idea what was going on. Fire seemed to be coming from almost all directions. The heat was intense and all around him was dust and smoke and the sickening stench of burning tanks. Making the most of the heat haze, the Axis moved their 50mm anti-tank guns even closer, raining shells into the British positions. Many of 6 RTR's tanks not entirely destroyed had tracks knocked off or their guns damaged. By late afternoon, the tank brigade was so badly mauled there was no option but to withdraw, and this meant northward, the only way now open to them. Inching their way out of the fray, they hurried toward the high ground of the Rigel Ridge, around five miles southeast of Acroma, a position that was within shouting distance of the perimeter of Tobruk. The entire Gazla Line was beginning to disintegrate.

That night, from the heights of the Rigel escarpment, Sam could see the remnants of the British armor: dotted amidst the dark of the desert night were the twinkling fires of the still-burning tanks.

The Auk had made a visit to the front that day to see General Ritchie. News from the fighting was unclear, but from his desert caravan, Ritchie still appeared calm and optimistic, so the C-in-C signalled to Brooke from Eighth Army HQ, "Atmosphere here good. No undue optimism and realities of situation are being faced resolutely. Morale of troops appears excellent."[130] He returned to Cairo the following morning unaware that around 120 British tanks had been put out of action the previous day, and unaware that Eighth Army was on the point of annihilation.

Rommel continued his attack the following day. At first light, those like Sam on the high ground of the Rigel Ridge could only watch as the German armor began to break leaguer. The panzers led the column, spreading out into a line toward the ridge, followed by a long stream of guns and lorries. For those watching, it was a terrible sight; 1 RTR now had just four Grants and twelve Honeys left.

All day small groups of tanks of 22nd Armoured valiantly tried to hold off the panzer army ranged against them, while the Guards Brigade held on in the Knightsbridge box. 1 and 6 RTRs, now operating side by side and under one command, were ordered to help later in the afternoon when the Scots Guards came under sustained attack by 21st Panzer on the western end of the Rigel Ridge. The tank crews found the Guardsmen both confused and badly shaken. A storm was beginning to swirl up and before long, visibility was less than two hundred yards; there was nothing to be done but to call off the attack. With the sandstorm worsening, the tank regiments struggled to meet up with their supply echelons. Not until eleven o'clock that night were 1 and 6 RTRs finally replenished, and even then they were "uncomfortably close to a minefield."[131]

The sandstorm did allow the Guards Brigade to safely evacuate the Knightsbridge box that night, however. But it was now clear that the Gazala Line could no longer be held. The British armor was all but finished and the panzer army was pressing northward with the gap between them and the sea shortening. If they didn't act fast, the British and South African brigades still holding the northern sector would soon find themselves cut off and stranded.

One can only wonder what must have been going through General Ritchie's mind. Just a few days before, he'd still confidently talked of retaking Cyrenaica; now, with just fifty cruiser tanks and a handful of obsolete I's, there was no longer any chance he could face Rommel again in the open desert. The best option left to him now was to salvage as much of the remains of his army as possible.

Early on 14 June, he warned Strafer Gott to get his brigades in the north ready to withdraw to the Egyptian frontier, where he intended to build up as strong a force as quickly as possible with which to counterattack. He then told Auchinleck of his decision and expressed his intention to stand firm on the southern perimeter of Tobruk, which would keep access to the city open from the ground. He pointed out that "temporary investment" of Tobruk was likely, i.e., that Axis forces may well breech part of the perimeter defenses, but added that he was confident that with the vast buildup of stores and a force of greater size than during the siege the previous year, Tobruk could be held until sufficient forces could be built up on the frontier with which to relieve it once more. The alternative was "to go the whole hog and give up Tobruk."[132] He did not favor this latter course, he told the Auk, so therefore did the C-in-C accept the risk of temporary investment?

Before he received any reply, Ritchie flew in his captured German

Storch reconnaissance plane to see Gott at XIII Corps and then Norrie at XXX Corps. Pienaar's three South African brigades, he told Gott, were to make a dash for it along the coast road into Tobruk and then onto the border, while the two British brigades of 50th Division still in the line were to make a more audacious escape west across the minefields and around the southern end of the old line, rather in the same way that Rommel had sent his panzers on the opening morning of the battle. With the Panzer Army now almost entirely in the north, it was felt this was a risk worth taking, especially if they got on with it. Pienaar, as was his way whenever Gott gave him an order, quibbled about leaving their position during daylight, so it was agreed they would break out that night. As it turned out, this delay in getting going was not fatal: Rommel's panzers were, by the fourteenth, absolutely exhausted, and made little effort to push even further northward and cut off the South African line of withdrawal.

When Ritchie returned to Army HQ at around four o'clock, Auchinleck's reply was waiting for him. Tobruk must be held, he told Ritchie. Tobruk must *not* be invested. Rather, a line using 50th Division and 1st South African Division should be held at all costs in front of the Tobruk perimeter. There was also a message from the PM. "Your decision to fight it out is most cordially endorsed . . . Retreat would be fatal."[133] What Ritchie had failed to mention to the C-in-C in his message earlier that day was that he had already ordered 50th and 1st South African Division back to the border . . .

Ritchie rang Cairo again requesting permission to allow a temporary investment of Tobruk if necessary. The Auk was not there, but replied later that night, saying, no, Eighth Army was still a mobile field army and the line should be held in front of Tobruk. After all, Rommel's forces were exhausted, and there were fresh troops in Tobruk with plenty of supplies.

Meanwhile, XIII Corps were carrying out their plans for escape. These infantry brigades had been given little to do throughout the battle, but Sunday, 14 June, was certainly busy for Bill Eadie at 2nd South African Brigade HQ. He had been told to get himself over to Division HQ first thing, where he was informed about the plan to evacuate and told to collect fifteen trucks. He and his men then drove them back to Brigade HQ and began frantically preparing to leave. They even had to destroy all remaining stocks of petrol—"thousands of gallons went to waste," noted Bill. The day was scorching hot and Bill was so thirsty, he found himself wishing he could drink the orange-tinted petrol that lay in pools in the scrub.

Although the main evacuation was to be that night, Bill and his team got going around half past three. No sooner had they done so than a group of nine Stukas dived and unleashed their bombs. The truck directly in front of Bill immediately burst into a ball of flames. Dressed in only his shorts,

Bill felt a shard of shrapnel whiz over his naked back. Diving for cover, he watched helplessly as another salvo of bombs erupted. Another piece of flying shrapnel pierced the radiator on his truck. Several men were wounded.

This was just the beginning of a hellish journey. Stopping the hole in his radiator with chewing gum, he refilled it with water and tried to carry on. But the gum would not hold, so he pulled off the road, switched off and allowed the engine to cool. His intention was to wait until sunset and so they found a shallow trench and took cover. The few roads were heaving with men and vehicles. Enemy fighter bombers appeared in waves, machine gunning and bombing. They were flying so low, Bill could even see the grim-looking expressions on the pilots' faces; so low, he saw several climb away with telegraph wires stuck to their tail wheels. "It was most unsettling," he noted, "lying out in the open absolutely exposed to the roaring enemy planes belching fire and lead." Black smoke sprang up all around the desert where vehicles had been hit. He heard that two truckloads of men had tumbled over an escarpment and been lost. "Road congestion was unbelievable," he recorded, "like crowds leaving a football match."

As the sun set, he watched fires dotted along the road and either side of him, still burning orange in the night. To make matters worse, the truck had a flat battery, but they pushed it down a slight slope and somehow managed to get it going. In pitch darkness, they eventually pulled off the road again inside the Tobruk perimeter and slept. Despite the noise of constant ack-ack fire and enemy shelling, Bill slept "like a dead thing." At sunrise, they set off again, nose to tail in a long column of vehicles. Bill could not help thinking about their escape. "What did pull at my heart string," he wrote, "was seeing those lads fleeing for their lives before that merciless hail of bullets and bombs. It seemed so unreal and fantastic . . . Now I have some idea of the tragedies in France when the Hun broke through Belgium and drove out the panic-stricken populace—old men, women and children before them. Too ghastly to contemplate." A cockney soldier came up to him and told him to keep going. "Run like bloody 'ell," he told Bill, "cos the Jerries are comin' with tanks the size of bloody battleships."

Despite these images of carnage, the majority of the South Africans did get away successfully. The pilots attacking them had been mostly Italians, less accurate and generally less determined to press home their attacks than the more dogmatic and experienced Luftwaffe pilots. The reason was another Allied convoy bound for Malta, which had drawn off a large number of German aircraft. This was unfortunate for the convoy—which failed to get through—but helped Eighth Army considerably. The irony was that the original reason why Churchill was so anxious for Auchinleck to launch an offensive was to help the beleaguered island; as events turned out, exactly the opposite happened.

The South African rearguard was eventually cut off by Rommel's forces, but the 50th Division broke through the Italian positions with ease, and successfully rounded the old line south of Bir Hacheim. Elsewhere, others were on the move. 6 RTR were kept south of Acroma until nightfall when they passed through Tobruk, and by dawn on the fifteenth, were back at Sidi Rezegh, where, still lying in the early morning sun were the grim and derelict remains of Crusaders and Panzers from the battle the previous November. Sam Bradshaw, however, had set off for Tobruk early the previous day. There were no longer enough Grant tanks to go around, and three of the regiment's Honeys were now in need of urgent overhaul. Sam was given the job of taking the tanks to workshops in Tobruk and picking up replacements. Sam had not been inside the town since the siege the previous year and was impressed by the defenses. "It was like a fortress," he says, "with minefields everywhere and concreted positions, and wired up electronically." Having completed his task, he set off to rejoin the regiment through the eastern gap in the minefields, picking up free chocolate and cigarettes from a NAAFI wagon along the way.

The confusion between Ritchie and Auchinleck was continuing as messages crossed back and forth across the desert. Churchill was also adding his money's worth, insisting that as long as Tobruk was held, then Rommel could not advance on Egypt—which was precisely what General Tuker had advised Ritchie long before the battle had begun. Unfortunately, although the Auk was still insisting Tobruk should not be breeched, Rommel had already begun sweeping along the southern perimeter of the town. With the loss of Acroma, the line that Auchinleck had suggested should be held had already been partially overrun. By the 16 June, an Indian Brigade was still holding firm at El Adem, but the rest of Eighth Army was either streaming back to the border, within Tobruk itself or to the southeast. The only other active force was Albert Martin's 7th Motor Brigade who were still harassing Axis columns south of El Adem.

The Auk sent General Corbett, his chief of staff to see what was happening. On arrival, Corbett soon realized the C-in-C's orders could no longer be fulfilled, so he suggested he must either accept the breeching of Tobruk or order a wholesale evacuation. Auchinleck now had no choice but to agree. Through clenched teeth, the C-in-C told Ritchie, "Although I have made it clear to you that Tobruk must not be invested, I realize that its garrison may be isolated for short periods until our counter-offensive can be launched. With this possibility in mind you are free to organize the garrison as you think best."[134] Armed with his commander's acquiescence at last, Ritchie immediately told Norrie that, if he felt it necessary, all troops in El Adem and to the southeast of Tobruk could be evacuated.

Since he knew perfectly well that Norrie was itching to do so, this meant Tobruk was now virtually on its own and besieged once more.

On the night of 16/17 June, El Adem was evacuated, but the following day the troops to the southeast were not so fortunate. The advancing panzers routed an Indian brigade and inflicted serious damage on 4th Armoured. This included Sam Bradshaw's 6 Royal Tanks, now entirely without artillery support—in retreat, as in attack, there was still little concept of using concentrations of all arms. Now back from the 1st Armoured Division and part of 7th Armoured Division once more, these tanks had been ordered by General Messervy to go south of the Trigh Cappuzzo to attack the flanks of the advancing panzers, but as had so often been the case during the three weeks of battle, they met the Afrika Korps' panzers before they reached their intended positions. With the sun in their eyes, the British tanks battled through the afternoon but they were outgunned and out numbered by the panzers and forced to retire. It was the last action both 6 RTR and 4th Armoured Brigade would fight in Libya. Rommel, leading his panzers personally once more, halted the pursuit and ordered his armor northward toward the all-important coast road, the Via Balbia. In the early hours, the leading tanks of the 21st Panzer Division crossed over it and in doing so, effectively surrounded Tobruk.

The only forces still on the ground outside Tobruk who were not now racing to the frontier were those of the 7th Motor Brigade. Cut off from the rest of the Eighth Army and miles behind enemy lines, they were still operating south of El Adem, harassing enemy leaguers and columns at night. A resupply column arrived on June 19, a much-needed fillip for Albert Martin and the men of the 2nd Rifle Brigade. "The canteen came up," he noted, "which cheered us up no end. Nicer still, I've had a couple of letters." Orders that day were rather vague. They were still to carry on with their harassing activities, but they knew they were now out on a limb. "Everything has been a jumble," scrawled Albert. "Does anyone at the top know what they are doing?"

One person who had a pretty good idea was Air Vice Marshal Arthur "Mary" Coningham. Air Commodore Tommy Elmhirst had always thought highly of the AOC's leadership qualities, but these past few weeks were the first time he'd seen him tested in battle. "Mary's handling of the air battle was superb," Tommy noted later. "He used his smaller and less modern air force with fine judgement which produced its maximum offensive effort."[135] Throughout the battle, Mary's task had been threefold: to try and protect the Eighth Army on the ground; to direct his bombers onto enemy vehicles whenever possible; to attack enemy airfields and, whenever possible, concentrations of aircraft as they were forming up before taking off. He had pushed all his men hard, but Tommy believed the morale and fighting spirit of the Desert Air Force remained at a high level, and there is little reason to doubt this was true. Billy Drake certainly thought Mary was a "bloody good commander." Like Ritchie, Mary spent much of his time visiting and talking with his commanders, both Wing and Squadron leaders, but there the similarities ended, for while he listened carefully to their views, "when the orders went out at night for the next day's fighting, there was never any question of discussion."[136]

The Desert Air Force had shown its mettle during the fighting to date, but once the withdrawal from the Gazala Line began, soon proved to be the difference between the survival and total destruction of Eighth Army. The troops evacuating the Gazala Line had certainly been fortunate that on both 14 and 15 June, the bulk of the Luftwaffe had been distracted with attacking the Malta convoys heading from Gibraltar and Alexandria, but their flexibility and determination in the days to come would prove decisive. It was Tommy Elmhirst, who, in the lull preceding the battles, had made plans that would enable the RAF to move forward or back very quickly should the land battle require a rapid advance or retreat. All of the various fighter and bomber wings were split into two parties so that pilots, aircrew, and aircraft would never be out of action and would be able to operate, at a push, for a couple of days with only half their men and equipment, while the other half was moving forward or back to a new location. Then the two parties would swap roles.

This leapfrogging began on 15 June. Gambut was just thirty miles from El Adem—less than twenty minutes' flying time for his Boston bombers—and while Mary was determined to keep a number of his squadrons there for as long as possible, he did begin the process of moving his forces back to cover the inevitable retreat when it occurred. The workload of Billy Drake's 112 Squadron, for example, was typical of the fighter squadrons during these days. On 15 June, for instance, they carried out thirty-four sorties, attacking the forward columns of 21st Panzer, and scoring "three flamers and 34 severely damaged vehicles." Then in the evening, A Flight moved back to LG (Landing Ground) 75, while B Flight remained at Gambut.[137] On the sixteenth, Mary signaled Tedder, "I have prepared landing grounds all the way back to the frontier and plan is steady withdrawal of squadrons keeping about twenty miles away from the enemy."[138]

It wasn't until the afternoon of 17 June that Mary learned of the evacuation of El Adem. Although Gambut was now effectively untenable, Mary did not pull out just yet, for reconnaissance photos showed the enemy had moved forward to an advanced airfield before any anti-aircraft guns had been emplaced. All available fighters of 239 Wing—including those of 112 Squadron—were then sent to attack. German records suggest that the RAF claim of twenty fighters destroyed on the ground was higher than the reality, but the attack certainly seems to have hindered the operational efficiency of this forward airfield. It was, wrote Tommy, "a masterstroke . . . Accordingly, all our long lines of retreating columns have not been harassed at all by air attacks."[139] This says much about the efforts of the entire Desert Air Force during these crucial days. By the time the last RAF aircraft left Gambut—73 Squadron included—the panzer army was just twelve miles and one hour's distance away.

The Fortress of Tobruk now waited. This time, General Rommel was determind to take it swiftly, and then, with the port in his hands, he would march on Egypt.

CHAPTER 7

Surrender and Retreat: 19 June–1 July, 1942

THE ROYAL NAVY had been undisputed masters of the Mediterranean since Nelson's day, and the early months of the war proved that whatever superiority the Italian Navy held in terms of ships, they were still some way behind the British when it came to training and leadership. Unlike the Army, there was no shortage of extremely able and talented commanders, as exemplified by Admiral Sir Andrew Browne Cunningham (C-in-C in the Mediterranean from the opening salvoes of the war until April 1942), and by men like the exceptional Rear-Admiral Vian, commander of the 15th Cruiser Squadron and victor of the 2nd Battle of Sirte back in March.

But the long years of war were taking their toll. The battle for the Atlantic was showing no signs of letting up and continued to draw upon much of the navy's resources. The Mediterranean Fleet had also been weakened by the diversion of ships and men to the Far East, and sapped particularly by the evacuations of Greece and Crete, and the demands of escorting convoys to the beleaguered Malta. "There is nothing I should like better than to send you a present of twenty or thirty destroyers and a dozen cruisers," the First Sea Lord wrote to Cunningham at the end of 1941. "You know how terribly hard-pressed we are in every direction, and this will account for the smallness of our presents."[140]

By June, operations by the Mediterranean Fleet were being further hampered by the overwhelming amount of Axis aircraft operating from bases in the Mediterranean and by a number of U-boats. On 15 June, a heavily escorted convoy from Alexandria to Malta had been forced to turn back because both the merchant ships and Vian's escort had been so consistently attacked they had become in serious danger of running out of ammunition before they reached their destination. That even Vian was helpless to do anything about it had been a terrible blow, but starkly showed the importance of air power not just over the land, where Mary Coningham's men had numerical parity, but over sea as well, where the RAF were massively outnumbered.

Even so, by June, the Royal Navy in the Mediterranean was still expected to carry out a number of different tasks, including supporting the army by coastal bombardment of enemy positions. It was also its job, along with the Allied air forces, to seek and destroy Axis barges that were ferrying enemy supplies up and down the coast from one port to another. Best equipped to fulfill this role were the fast, highly maneuverable Motor Torpedo Boats of the 10th MTB Flotilla. Based in Alexandria, most of the flotilla, however, had spent much of the previous few months operating from Tobruk, carrying almost nightly excursions up the Libyan coast and attacking anything that came their way.

One of those was MTB 262, commanded by Lieutenant Charles Coles. He too had been in the Mediterranean a while—since April 1941, when the 10th Flotilla had been posted from Home Waters. His association went even further back than that: he'd also been based at Malta before the war in the 1st MTB Flotilla, when called up with all RN Reserves in the summer of 1939. Since his return, Charles had often found himself caught up in the waxing and waning of British fortunes. Shortly after his arrival, for example, the 10th Flotilla had begun operating from Suda Bay in Crete. They were there when German parachutists attacked in May 1941, and during the battle had their boats destroyed by enemy aircraft. Charles and his crew had escaped unscathed, but with his chance knowledge of the little harbor, Sphakia, which became one of the principle evacuation bases, he was hastily temporarily posted to an Australian destroyer as a pilot and beach master, and made two extremely hazardous trips as the navy valiantly tried to evacuate the defeated British troops.

Charles had never had a particular urge to join the armed services as a career. The son of colonial parents based in India, he had spent much of his childhood at boarding school, and after leaving Radley at seventeen had been slightly at a loss as to what to do, so enrolled in various courses until eventually securing a job with the chemicals company ICI. At that time, however, with the possibility of war looming, a number of his friends were joining the Auxiliary Air Force or the Territorial Army, and as he'd always had a fascination with ships, decided to put himself down on the waiting list to become a midshipman in the Royal Naval Volunteer Reserve (RNVR).

The RNVR operated differently from the other reserves in as much as volunteers were not kept together. Charles found himself being sent off to join the battleship HMS *Revenge,* where he was the sole RNVR midshipman amongst thirty-nine RN "snotters"—regulars—all of whom looked down their noses at him and made his life as uncomfortable as possible. "I wouldn't say it was enjoyable," says Charles, "but it was a valuable experience." During the Munich Crisis in 1938, he was called up to his war station, which turned out to be the torpedo school at Portsmouth. It was here that Charles first went aboard an MTB. Charles found the speed and diverse opportunities of the MTBs most appealing. "I didn't want to go back to big ships after that," he says. "I saw myself commanding an MTB and sinking vast numbers of enemy ships!" After the Munich Crisis had passed he returned to his job with ICI, but the die had been cast, and when war finally came, it was to motor torpedo boats that he returned.

Most Royal Navy MTBs were around sixty to seventy-five feet in length—roughly the same as a tennis court—and they were faster than any other service vessel in the navy. While most British submarines had a maximum surface speed of around eleven knots and merchant vessels between twelve and fourteen, MTBs could nip along three to four times that speed, which, on open sea, was pretty swift. "Forty knots on a moonlit night," says Charles, "who'd be in the infantry?" Most of the early British MTBs had been wooden Vospers with aero-engines, not entirely suitable for marine use. In 1942, however, after Crete, the 10th Flotilla was given brand-new American Elco boats with excellent Packard engines. "They were lovely," says Charles, and heftily armed too, for a small boat: the twelve-strong crew could handle two torpedo tubes, two twin five-inch machine guns, a 20mm Oerlikon, two further .303 machine guns and usually two depth charges.

By 19 June, Charles had carried out several nighttime operations westward along the Libyan coast, although the MTBs were now part of a rapidly dwindling naval presence operating from the port. Two days before, all nonessential troops and staff had left for Alexandria, and with them destroyers, hospital ships, and various cargo boats. The few MTBs and a small handful of other vessels, plus the Officer in Charge, Tobruk, and his staff at Navy House were all that remained. That day, however, shells started landing in the harbor with increasing regularity—the battle was drawing closer—and Charles had been glad when, later that evening, MTB 262 and three others left their mooring and headed out along the coast once more.

General Rommel had spent 18 June handing out his orders for the attack on Tobruk, the next day gathering his forces, and then opened his attack at first light on 20 June. The town of Tobruk—or rather, the port—had built up around a narrow inlet, and was no great size. The perimeter, however, extended some five to ten miles from the port and consisted of a complex web of concrete ditches, wire, and minefields that created a thirty-mile front. Within this perimeter were further minefields and defenses as well as natural barriers in the form of a series of steep escarpments that ran east-west. Tobruk the Fortress was, then, mostly open desert, rather than an actual town, and it was this area that the Australians and others had defended so stoutly the previous year.

Seven months on, the latest troops given the task of defending this much-bludgeoned fortress were a mixture of the green and the battle weary. The main fighting contingent was the inexperienced 2nd South African Division under General Klopper, hurriedly reinforced by two infantry brigades and one armored. This latter was the 32nd Army Tank Brigade, which had hardly covered itself with glory during the Gazala battles, and which was still equipped with mostly obsolete I tanks. Artillery and anti-aircraft guns were under strength and there were now no aircraft on the airfields within the perimeter. Nonetheless, the garrison held over 30,000 men and had 3 million rations, 7,000 tons of water and 1.5 million gallons of petrol. In addition, there were about 130,000 rounds of artillery ammunition. On paper, with the other defenses already in place, this should have been enough to save Tobruk, especially since the panzer army had been fighting continuously for over three weeks and were clearly exhausted.

But the difference between armies weary with success and those weary with defeat is marked. Eighth Army was on the run, and Rommel, for one, was not going to be denied his quarry again. For all his weaknesses—his rashness, his cavalier attitude to reconnaissance and intelligence, and his sometimes inexplicable tactical decisions—the German commander could never be accused of lacking decisiveness or an ability to inspire. Sensing that the Panzer army's blood was up, he demanded a concentration of effort that he felt certain would give him his prize. To this end, Field Marshal Kesselring was prepared to help, and sent over from Crete and Greece every Stuka and Junkers 88 dive-bombing formation he had available.

At midnight on 19 June, MTB 262 was still patrolling west along the low desert coastline. The sea had been calm and a warm, scented breeze was blowing from the shore. The moon was high, and Lieutenant Charles Coles could see quite clearly the patches of sandy beach along the shore and even the headlights of a vehicle inland.

Four hours later, having seen nothing all patrol, Charles opened the throttles and they headed full-speed back to Tobruk along with the other MTBs, unaware that it was about to become one of the most eventful days of his life.

Meanwhile, some twenty miles south of Tobruk, the 7th Motor Brigade was still valiantly carrying out its particular brand of guerrilla warfare. Their orders were to raid German leaguers, shoot them up and cause as much destruction and mayhem as possible, then slink away into the darkness of the desert at night. "We were used to our targets being caught napping," recalls Albert, "the enemy being sound asleep with just a token perimeter guard." But that night, the German leaguer they had chosen to attack was wide awake and seemed to be expecting them. As the riflemen opened fire, the Germans responded with equal ferocity. It quickly became clear they could never hope to penetrate the camp and so pulled out, losing two good men in the process. "One of those suicide patrols," Albert noted in his diary, "when all we seem to achieve is annoying the enemy." Worse was to follow. As dawn broke, they heard the distant sound of guns firing, and looking northward they saw the ominous sight of rising plumes of thick black smoke from Tobruk.

Rommel had begun his attack with an artillery barrage, followed by hundreds of dive-bombers, who peeled off and screeched down toward their targets. During the siege, Tobruk had been a hellish place to fly over—Axis pilots had faced a terrifying wall of anti-aircraft fire—but on this June morning the response from the gunners was light by comparison. Certainly, there were fewer guns, and the surprise and sheer weight of the Axis attack played its part too. But principally, the weak reply was because the South Africans did not have their guns as well coordinated and controlled as they had been under the Australians. Their lack of experience and training was proving decisive. And while the Axis artillery and aircraft were pounding away, their sappers were clearing a path through the mines and bridging anti-tank ditches; shortly after 8 AM, the first Panzers breeched the perimeter of Tobruk.

MTB 262 had reached Tobruk to the sound of gunfire to the south, but although they knew the Gazala Line had been evacuated, neither Lieutenant Coles nor his crew had any idea of just how close the Germans were and so arrived believing the situation to be no different from the previous two days.

Getting into the half-dark harbor was always tricky—one had to find the faint blue light at the entrance and then pilot cautiously through the boom and weave around the countless wrecks that littered the port. It was rather like dodging icebergs—all too often the worst was below the surface, and as they inched their way in, they heard a sound of scraping at the back of the boat followed by a sudden decrease in performance; one of the propellers had damaged itself on a piece of wreckage.

This was an occupational hazard in Tobruk, and they would have to get that mended urgently, ready for patrol the following night. But first of all Charles signaled "Nothing to report" to Navy House, then chugged to the petrol jetty waiting to refuel. Refuelling was painfully slow. By now enemy aircraft were almost continually bombing and strafing the harbor.

At least one stick of bombs erupted close by. Standing amidst fumes from the 100-octane petrol was nerve-wracking to say the least. At least one stick of bombs erupted close by. Nonetheless, a sapper officer assured Charles that although the enemy were attacking the garrison, the bulk of the British forces was yet to go into action. Rommel, he told him, had overstepped himself.

The refuelling over, Charles took 262 over to anchor just offshore on the largely deserted and seemingly quieter south side of the harbor, first behind a wreck, and then later, another ship, the *Bankura*. There it seemed to be slightly quieter. Not far from them was a destroyer hurriedly unloading essential supplies and taking away some of the wounded. Hastily, they gave Charles and his crew supplies of bread and topped up 262's water tanks. "One could see they were tense and anxious to leave as soon as possible," says Charles.

The welcome smell of frying bacon drifted up to Charles from the cabin below, but before the crew had a chance to serve it, shells began falling on the waste ground just opposite their mooring. Having been up all night, Charles was now exhausted, but the moment he thought about getting his head down in the cabin, the shelling seemed to increase. Clearly, the Germans were closing in.

So began a long morning. The day was very hot and still, and the sea glassy smooth. A sandy haze hung heavily above the surface. Suddenly, on the shore, trucks started arriving, and South African troops tumbled out looking shaken—"almost as though they were drunk," Charles recalls. One man emptied the contents of his water bottle down his throat and over his face and then threw it away. Another set fire to his jeep—desperate to ensure it would not fall into enemy hands. Others had already jumped into the water and were swimming toward 262. "I was angry and alarmed at what I was seeing," says Charles, who as far as he was concerned was still due to be going out on another patrol that night. Certainly, no word had arrived about a possible evacuation. "It's no bloody good coming out to us," he yelled to the men. "Stay where you are!" But rather than turn around, even more jumped in. One exhausted officer shouted back, "Can you evacuate us, man?"

"Sorry, have to stay here—got a demolition job to do," Charles lied. Sadly, the South African turned away. Three swimmers did make it, however. One, an English signals corporal, calmly told Charles that the Germans had broken through and would, he guessed, be over the escarpment above the harbor in about half an hour. On the cliffs above them, a retreating Bofors anti-aircraft gun began firing furiously until silenced by a direct hit. Both gun and crew were obliterated amidst a cloud of dust and smoke.

Events were clearly beginning to move fast. There was still no word about what the remaining naval forces should do, and just as worryingly, no signal from Navy House as to when Charles could go to the repairs jetty to get new propellers. Charles decided that his three "passengers" probably possessed vital information from the front line and that they should tell this in person to those at HQ. So, taking 262 back across the harbor, he moored them alongside the jetty near the boom, and then commandeered a vehicle from a somewhat surprised army officer, claiming priority. The three soldiers were then sent off to Navy House for debriefing. While Charles waited, he was once again assured that the situation was "completely in hand." It didn't seem that way to him, however, and to make matters worse, his coxswain was now blind drunk. Unbeknown to Charles, he had been given a bottle of rum while drawing water from the destroyer earlier in the morning, and was now a complete liability. Putting him ashore nearby with one of his crew acting as jailor, Charles then tried to find out what on earth had happened to his divers, who, he had been promised earlier, were coming to repair his propellers. Having moved again, this time to the repairs jetty, he was told the divers would not be coming after all; they were now on the sick list, suffering from shell shock.

Fast running out of options, Charles inspected the old and heavy Siebe-Gorman diving suit—complete with brass helmet and weighted—on the jetty. It was far from ideal, but having discovered that none of his crew had ever dived before and with no one rushing to volunteer, there was nothing for it but to try and repair the damage himself. Moving the boat as close inshore as they could, he donned the top half of the suit and waded in, while one of the crew turned the air-pump wheel. The helmet was not exactly watertight, but so long as he barely bent his head the air pressure kept the water level just below his mouth. Spanners and a new propeller were gently lowered on a piece of string, and Charles set to work while the motor mechanic gave him instructions. He soon found himself forgetting about the war; under water the world was once again peaceful and beautiful. Colored fish swam happily around him, oblivious of the carnage and chaos going on above. To his great relief, his efforts were a success. The new propellers were firmly in place.

The shelling had intensified further, however, and back on board his boat, Charles was peering through his binoculars when he saw infantry coming over the ridge across the harbor, carrying rifles and machine guns and in good order. Clearly, these were not men in retreat. Wagstaff then pointed out some tanks that had come into view. Moments later the panzers traversed their guns and were selectively picking off targets in and around the harbor. It was the first time Charles had ever seen a tank in action, and although their deadly shelling was accurate and lethal, he felt as though he were watching a military tattoo rather than war. "It was the clarity of the black cross on the side of the tank, and the figures sticking out of the turret," admits Charles. "We had seen it often enough in war photographs, but it seemed somehow unreal and theatrical."

With such a clear view of the tanks, Charles telephoned Navy HQ, just in case they were unaware that the enemy had broken through. The news was received with complete astonishment. It was now clear that Tobruk had been all but overrun. Soon after, the order came from Navy HQ that the planned MTB that night had at last been canceled. They were then told that all remaining naval forces were to get ready to meet the enemy, and that every vessel was to make to the naval stores where the crews would be issued with rifles, ammunition, and hand grenades. This was then followed by yet another order telling them to be at the first state of readiness to evacuate. One by one, the minesweepers, MTBs, and other craft inched up to the base store, halfway up the harbor to load up with rifles and ammunition, but also engine spares and the remaining maintenance staff.

There was no shortage of supplies at base stores, making standing next to so much ordnance an unnerving experience; Charles couldn't help holding his breath every time a shell screamed by. The other MTBs had all crept back to the shelter of the Italian wreck, the *San Georgio*, but one boat was needed to stay behind by the base store and to sit by the only working telephones still in touch with Navy HQ. This dubious honor fell to 262.

Further scenes of chaos were unfolding. South African Army lorries were now arriving at the harbor's edge, whereupon their drivers set fire to them rather than let them fall into enemy hands. By now the Germans were bringing field guns to bear on the mouth of the harbor—within easy reach of the gap in the boom—making any escape almost impossible. Since there was no point in needlessly risking the lives of the whole crew, Charles set most of them ashore to take shelter in the cave where the coxswain was still being held, while he, Wagstaff and two others stayed on board and manned the guns. One of the volunteers was Leading Stoker Lloyd—the boat's engineer—usually somewhat dour and bolshy; but he now rose to the occasion, bringing some much-needed humor: at one point a shell hit the jetty so close they all felt the hot blast and zing of metal slicing through the air. Jumping for cover, Lloyd muttered, "This is no place for Mrs. Lloyd's little boy!"

Despite the proximity of the shell fire, the enemy gunners had apparently not spotted them, but then Charles had to pass on a message to the other MTBs sheltering behind the *San Georgia*, and the Aldis lamp they used to do so quickly gave away their position. Moments later the jetty received two direct hits. A splinter sliced 262's aerial in half. After another near-miss knocked Charles off balance and completely deafened him, he frantically recalled the rest of the crew from the cave and started the engines; to have stayed any longer would have been suicide. As it was, their survival seemed increasingly unlikely: the next shell tore into the concrete beside them. Miraculously, everyone safely made it on board, and although they still hadn't been given the order to leave, they hurried away again to find a safer place to shelter toward. The other MTBs were sheltering behind the *San Georgio*, but this refuge was full, so 262 eventually found some kind of sanctuary behind another wreck, the *Chantala,* although Charles knew it was still full of ammunition. There were others sheltering there—a schooner, and on the wreck itself a number of Rajputs from the 11th Indian Brigade, a detachment from General Tuker's 4th Indian Division, who had been based in Tobruk since the beginning of the battle.

The situation was clearly hopeless, and on MTB 262, Charles and his crew were watching with mounting apprehension for the signal from Navy House to evacuate. Something rather bizarre then happened. A lone MTB suddenly entered the harbor. They were new arrivals from the UK—the white knees and clean uniforms gave them away, but why no one in Alexandria had stopped them from coming was hard to understand. Despite the bombing and shelling, the skipper obviously thought this was a typical day in Tobruk, because he dropped anchor very casually as though it were the most normal thing in the world. Charles even watched him take out a book to read. They were soon brought to their senses. Within minutes a shell whistled down the harbor and exploded just in front of the boat. Moments later the hapless MTB started engines again, slipped anchor, and was streaking toward the open sea in a cloud of spray, and although he failed to find the boom entrance again, somehow managed to squeeze through some rocks at the end of the steel netting without damage.

At around six o'clock, Captain Smith finally gave the evacuation order and at the same time ordered his Number One, Lieutenant-Commander Harris, to personally oversee the starting of the fuses at the much-prized ammunition caves and fuel dumps.[141] Harris personally broke the time-delay pencils in the ammunition caves and, after dodging a German tank, managed to reach the fuel dumps too. Rommel would not be getting his hands on any of the navy's fuel.

On receiving the Aldis lamp signal from Navy House, the remaining lighters, post-boats, and other vessels began racing toward the harbor boom. "From our shielded viewpoint," says Charles, "we observed this grim race at very close quarters. I remember the expressions on the faces of the escapers: taut, strained, and fearful." A harbor defense motor launch came into view, but as it drew level with 262, it received a direct hit. "One second I was looking at the boat—the number painted on the bow, the officers standing rigidly on the bridge, the crew on the two-pounder," Charles recalls, "and then suddenly she was gone, and there was nothing but a patch of oil spreading out over the water and an officer's cap floating on the surface like a floral tribute after a committal at sea."

Having then seen the other MTBs head off, Charles realized it was—finally—his turn to go too. The Rajputs asked politely if they could take passage on 262—Charles agreed, and then they started the engines and slipped away from the protection of the *Chantala*. They were now completely exposed and at the mercy of the German gunners. Charles felt his stomach tighten, especially when he realized his engines had stopped—and in full view of the panzers. One of the Rajputs had inadvertently knocked the main electrical switch as he fled down the engine-room hatch. But even once this had been resolved, 262 was so laden the throttles hardly responded at all. Charles's hands were shaking and slippery with sweat and his mouth was bone dry as he watched the lethal bottleneck developing at the boom entrance. Then he remembered their chemical smoke apparatus for laying a smoke screen. The breeze was drifting toward the enemy positions, so the conditions were ideal. In no time, a decent fog had separated them from the shore and although they had some difficulty finding the gap in the boom, they eventually spotted the hole and gently nosed their way through, as did most of the other escaping craft, now hidden from the enemy tanks.

Three miles out to sea, Charles turned and surveyed the scene. The shore was almost entirely hidden behind a thick pall of smoke that was rising ever higher into the sky. Here and there, an orange glow would lighten the fog as more explosions erupted. Even out at sea he could feel the deep shudder of one of the demolition charges detonating. They had made it to safety, but the majority of those still in Tobruk were not to be so fortunate. There were warm greetings from their Flotilla SO (Senior Officer), who told them, "I thought you were dead!" At that moment, the now sober coxswain handed Charles a cup of strong tea in a tin mug and a sandwich. "Happy birthday, sir," he told his skipper. Charles was twenty-five.

Tobruk had been sliced in half. The South Africans were stuck in the western side of the garrison, and at 8 PM, Ritchie authorized General Klopper to fight his way out, promising him he would try and help him get out through the southwest face since the panzer army was no longer there, but within Tobruk itself. By dawn, even this plan had been thwarted. With most of his transport already captured, Klopper realized there was little hope of safely escaping and that fighting on would just cause pointless sacrifice. As the first glint of sun appeared over the horizon, on this, the longest day of the year, General Klopper ordered the white flag to be raised over the Fortress of Tobruk.

* * *

The summer heat was also sweltering in Washington, where Prime Minister Winston Churchill, his chief of staff General Sir Hastings Ismay, and the British CIGS, General Sir Alan Brooke, were having further talks with the Americans about the direction of Anglo-US strategy. In a separate meeting, Brooke and his American counterpart, General George Marshall, had established that they were both against any joint operation in either North Africa or Norway and were both strongly in favor of BOLERO, the building up of troops in the UK. They only differed on SLEDGEHAMMER, the plan to fight somewhere in 1942. Meanwhile, Churchill had also been having private talks with Roosevelt at the president's country residence, Hyde Park. However, they were now back in Washington, and although a day off had been scheduled, both agreed that they and their chiefs of staff should meet at the White House for further discussions immediately.

Later that afternoon, they were in the president's Oval Office on the second floor when an aide came in with a pink slip of paper and handed it to Roosevelt. The president read the message, then silently passed it to Churchill. "Tobruk has surrendered," said the note, "with twenty-five thousand men." In fact, it was worse: over 32,000 men had fallen into Rommel's hands. Aghast, Churchill at first could not believe it, and asked for confirmation, which arrived soon after. "This was one of the heaviest blows I can recall during the war," the prime minister wrote later. "I did not attempt to hide from the President the shock I had received. Defeat is one thing; disgrace is another."

In Syria, the 9th Australian Division, part of the heroic defense the previous year, took the news badly. Joe Madeley of the 2/13 Battalion was as disbelieving as the prime minister. "My mate Rex McDonald turned to me," says Joe, "and said, 'To think of all those flaming holes we dug up there and now the Germans and Eyeties are in 'em.'"

Nearby, the photographer Cecil Beaton was watching a military exercise. The smoke screens and artillery fire were certainly impressive, but he was once again suffering from the oppressive heat. "But," he noted later that day, "there was much greater reason why I should feel so miserable—the news was whispered from man to man that Tobruk had fallen." One soldier was severely reprimanded for saying that the Germans would be in Cairo in a week. "I am not ashamed of saying," Cecil admitted, "that I felt absolutely sick with panic." Like Churchill, he believed it was "one of the most crushing disappointments of the war."

The Eighth Army had suffered a devastating defeat after more than three long weeks of battle, and it was still not over. Troops were continuing to pour across the frontier, and the victorious Rommel—appointed field marshal with immediate effect—had every intention of taking not just Cairo, but the whole of Egypt and the Middle East as well. On 21 June, Germany's newest field marshal issued a declaration to his men. "Soldiers of the Panzer Army Afrika! Now for the complete destruction of the enemy. We will not rest until we have shattered the last remnants of the British Eighth Army."[142] After the long weeks of battle, this was only possible because of the "vast booty" of ammunition, petrol, food, and numerous vehicles captured at Tobruk.[143] The British had tried to destroy as much as they could, but there was still much that fell into Axis hands. The surrender of the 32nd Army Tank Brigade, for example, had given Rommel thirty serviceable—albeit largely obsolete—tanks. He was thus sufficiently strengthened to continue the offensive. As far as Rommel was concerned, a great opportunity to completely destroy the Eighth Army now lay in front of him. Speed, however, would be the key. The British could not be allowed the time to regroup and reorganize.

Field Marshal Kesselring flew over on the afternoon of 21 June to confer with Rommel. For months he had been pounding Malta into the dust, and although Operation HERCULES—the plan to invade the island—had been postponed, he was determined it should still take place in July, as agreed by Hitler and the German High Command (OKW). Rommel, however, insisted that he had the Eighth Army on the ropes and had to follow up his victory immediately. For this he needed the full support of the Luftwaffe. The problem was that if Kesselring diverted his air forces in support of Rommel, he would not then be able to invade Malta after all. And if Malta was left alone and given the chance to recover, the panzer army's lines of supply from Italy to North Africa could be placed in serious jeopardy. In other words, Kesslering believed it was essential to capture Malta first, and then attack Egypt and the Middle East.

Unsurprisingly, Rommel strongly disagreed. If they acted now, he argued, straight away and with all available forces, they had a unique opportunity to take the Suez Canal before Malta could possibly make any difference. It was essential, Rommel urged, that the British should not be given even a couple of weeks in which to recover. Furthermore, Rome had given him assurances that adequate supplies could be guaranteed as long as the ports of Tobruk and Mersa Matruh were available.

Neither man could come to an agreement. Kesselring returned to Sicily determined to stick to his guns, while Rommel went over his superior's head by appealing directly to both Hitler and Mussolini—which in the case of Hitler was now his right as a field marshal. Il Duce had suffered his fair share of humiliations since the beginning of the war, so the chance to enter Cairo in triumph was met with delight. He promptly arranged to fly over to Africa, with his favorite white stallion, to lead the procession into Cairo himself. Hitler was also only too happy to go along with the man now being fêted by the German propaganda machine. After the losses suffered in Crete, he never had much enthusiasm for airborne invasions anyway. So the decision was made.

Another struggling through a birthday they would rather forget was the British commander-in-chief. On 21 June, the Auk was fifty-eight, and he spent the day with his fellow chiefs in Cairo—the Middle East Defense Committee—planning a transmission to London with an appreciation of the situation and a list of the various courses open to them. Despite the arguments raging within the Axis command, they were under no illusions that Rommel would press on. Consequently it was clear that reinforcements were urgently needed and so orders were sent to X Corps in Syria—which included the Australians and New Zealanders—to get themselves to Egypt right away.

The Auk then flew to see Ritchie the following day. Never in their worst nightmares had they expected Tobruk to fall in a day, but it was now clear they no longer had time to build up strength at the frontier. Gott, quite reasonably, had pointed out to the army commander that the farther they were away from Rommel, the bigger the Axis logistical headache would be, and so suggested they immediately fall back again to Mersa Matruh, another 120 miles farther east in Egypt across almost waterless, featureless desert. This had also been discussed in Cairo and became the basis for the new plan. The 1st South African Division plus a few other units would hold up the Axis as long as possible at the frontier, then fall back all the way to the Alamein Line, a narrow stretch of land forty miles wide, which unlike the Gazala Line, had its flanks closed at both ends—by the sea in the north and by the impassable Qattara Depression in the south. Meanwhile, at Mersa Matruh, the soon-to-arrive X Corps, along with the 5th Indian Division, would prepare defenses and ready themselves to take on Rommel once more.

Back in Cairo the following day, the Auk wrote to the CIGS offering his resignation and suggesting that General Alexander, who had done well during the fighting retreat in Burma and who would be passing through Cairo shortly, might take over. The offer was refused, but Auchinleck was at last persuaded by both the AOC-in-C, Tedder, and Dick Casey, the minister of state in Cairo, that Ritchie should go and that he should take over himself. On the afternoon of 25 June, the Auk flew to Eighth Army HQ at Bagush. Alone, he walked to Ritchie's caravan. They talked at some length and then Ritchie got into his car and drove back to Cairo.

Alan Moorehead, who had been in Tobruk until almost the last, was also back in Cairo and reported on 22 June that Tobruk had fallen because it had been "outgunned and outnumbered 3 to 1." He tried to end his dispatch with a note of optimism. "Nobody is going to underrate the importance of Tobruk to our supplies," he wrote, "but it is equally essential to realise that the Eighth Army is reassembling on the frontier supported with new armour."[144] There was, however, also a note at the bottom of the front page reporting that civilians in Alexandria were being evacuated from the center of the city. *The Times* was less charitable, pointing out that the capture of Tobruk was not only "a victory of prestige for the enemy, of which the most will be made, but it will also give him clear lines of communication along the coastal road." Such a victory, the paper asserted, proved that Rommel was "in possession of great tactical superiority."[145] Even Alan Moorehead felt he had to make the most of the loosening of censorship restrictions in an analysis piece the following day. To his mind, the reasons for the retreat were more to do with equipment than tactics. "The Germans still have the better all-purpose gun—the 88mm," he wrote, "The better tank—the Mark Four. The better plane—the Messerschmitt 109." Furthermore, Eighth Army had suffered from a lack of experienced senior officers. "Quick-decision men," he concluded, "that's what we lacked most."[146] He was quite right on all counts.

The prime minister was also feeling the heat of this latest defeat. The influence of the press on public and political opinion was considerable, yet up until this point, the British media had stuck resolutely behind their war leaders. The criticisms of Alan Moorehead and his colleagues were felt keenly. Britain had suffered an endless succession of disasters since the year began: the loss of Malaya, then the surrender of Singapore. Soon after, Rangoon fell, then in May, the whole of Burma. And now Tobruk—one humiliation too many. On the same day that Ritchie was sacked, Churchill—still in Washington—faced a motion of no confidence in the House of Commons from MPs whipped up by the media storm. Newspapers on both sides of the Atlantic carried the story as their headline, just to add to the prime minister's discomfort. When he finally left America on the evening of 25 June, he was bracing himself for "a beautiful row" back home.[147]

Just before leaving Washington, however, the prime minister took one his most capable and celebrated commanders to see the president. Admiral Sir Andrew Browne Cunningham had been charmed and impressed by Roosevelt, but he was soon wearying of the unending number of official calls he was expected to make on his arrival as head of the admiralty delegation and the First Sea Lord's representative on the Combined Chiefs of Staff committee. Five feet ten inches tall and with penetrating gray eyes and a lined, weather-beaten face, ABC—as he was known to all—was a man of action more used to standing on the bridge directing his fleet as the sea-spray lashed across the foredeck. He was far from happy to be now stuck with a desk job, however important it may be.

He had also been particularly reluctant to leave the Mediterranean Command at such a critical time. Throughout a long career in the Royal Navy he had served in the Home Waters, the Baltic, West Indies, and the Atlantic, but it was the Mediterranean that he regarded as his spiritual home. It was there that he had spent most of the First World War, there that he had taken part in the attack on the Dardanelles and the evacuation of Gallipoli. It was there that he had served for much of the 1930s as rear-admiral of destroyers, and it was there that he had spent the first three years of the war as commander-in-chief, Mediterranean Fleet.

Those had been difficult times. There had been the early victories: Calabria in July 1940, then the great success of the Fleet Air Arm against the Italian Fleet at Taranto in November the same year, and the Battle of Matapan in March 1941. Victories in which ABC's flair and tenacious leadership had seen the numerically superior Italian Navy bow to the supremacy of the Royal Navy. But then had come the disappointments. The evacuations of Greece and then Crete had cost him precious lives and ships. And there was the problem of Malta. The submarines operating from there had been doing well, but the job of supplying the besieged island was an almost impossible task. At the end of March he had overseen a much-needed convoy to the island, but having ensured that three of the four ships safely made it to port, blunderings had seen the vessels sunk in port with only a fraction of their precious cargoes unloaded.

Furthermore, ABC felt that Admiral Sir Charles Little, who was already in Washington, could fulfill the task far better than he. However, Cunningham had also made a rule of never questioning any appointment; if this was what the First Sea Lord wanted, then he would do as he was asked, and keep his own reservations to himself. Even so, as he lowered his flag in Alexandria, he had not been able to help feeling "poignantly overcome at leaving all my faithful friends and comrades, rather as though I had lost everything."[148]

ABC and his wife Nora had arrived in England on 9 April. He had not been back since before the war; now the country seemed "a very strange place" after such an absence.[149] He remained there for several weeks, having numerous consultations with the admiralty about the tasks facing him once he reached Washington, taking a brief holiday, and staying with the prime minister at Chequers. There they had a long tête-à-téte, and although ABC found himself disagreeing with the PM on several matters, he was "in thorough sympathy with his offensive outlook."

After the enormous responsibilities of the Mediterranean Command, ABC discovered his duties in Washington were "not particularly exacting." He immediately took to Marshall—"one did not need to be long in his company before recognising his sincerity and honesty"—but he could not say the same for his opposite number, Admiral King.[150] On his arrival, ABC had asked King for an interview to discuss joint naval matters, but was told the American admiral was busy and could not see him for six days. Infuriated, Cunningham then called a Combined Chiefs of Staff meeting at which he then apologized for wasting their time but explained that his hand had been forced because he had urgent matters to discuss with King. The ploy worked—he got his interview—but King, who favored a Pacific-first rather than Europe-first strategy, was brittle, "and at times became rude and overbearing." Matters came to a head over the issue of King lending a handful of US submarines for work in the Atlantic. After initially brushing the matter aside, ABC lost patience and snapped back telling him what he thought of "his method of advancing Allied unity and amity." King apologized and the two "parted friends." Perhaps; both certainly respected the fighting qualities of the other, but they would soon find themselves at loggerheads again.

Nor were matters helped by the lack of a specific strategy. The broad aims were in place, but agreement on exactly where, when and how Allied forces would be used in the immediate future was still unresolved. Amongst those now using the increasingly busy air route between Washington and London was Major-General Eisenhower and his team. On his return from the UK at the beginning of June, Ike had submitted to Marshall a draft of a "Directive for the Commanding General, European Theatre of Operations." This was, Ike told his chief, one paper he should read in detail. "I certainly do want to read it," Marshall told him. "You may be the man who executes it. If that's the case, when can you leave?"[151] Three days later Ike's appointment as Commander of the ETO was confirmed.

When he left America on 23 June, his instructions had been simply "to prepare for and carry on military operations in the European Theatre against the Axis Powers and their Allies."[152] Four days before he had been at a meeting between Marshall and his staff, and the British General Sir John Dill, General Brooke, and General Hastings Ismay, in which serious concerns about GYMNAST—the plan to invade northwest Africa—had been aired. Such an operation, it was agreed, would hinder plans to reinforce the Middle East, would cause a very serious drain on Allied shipping in all theaters, and would be of little help to the Russians. Furthermore, success would depend on political conditions, which, with Vichy France, were impossible to predict; and finally, the operation would be detrimental to BOLERO, the buildup of Allied forces in the UK.

It was also agreed that the possibility of launching an attack against mainland Nazi-held Europe at some point in 1942 was, despite certain hazards, preferable to a joint invasion of Africa. With this in mind, Ike set off for London believing he was preparing for such an operation. He was even accompanied by Major-General Mark Clark, already earmarked to lead the US corps in the proposed attack.

Also traveling with him was forty-year-old Lieutenant-Commander Harry S. Butcher, now into only his fourth week as a full-time officer in the US Navy. "Butch" had met Ike back in 1929 through the landlord of Ike's brother Milton, and they had remained friends ever since, although they had seen a lot more of each other (more often than not on the golf course) since Ike's return to the US from the Philippines. Originally from Ames, in the farming state of Iowa, Butch had during his journalistic career been editor of *Fertilizer Review* before heading to Washington, where he had become chief of the Washington Bureau of Columbia Broadcasting System (CBS) and vice president of WJSV Radio. He'd joined the US Naval Reserve back in 1939, but had finally quit his life in media on 1 June, 1942, for permanent military duty.

Butch had been to Britain before. As a young student, he'd spent the summer taking a load of cattle all the way from Iowa to Scotland by rail and then boat. When he'd joined the US Navy full time, he'd hardly been expecting to return to the UK so soon into his new career, but a week before, he'd unexpectedly been summoned to join Ike's staff. He'd been talking things through with his successor at CBS one evening, when the phone had rung. It was his wife, Ruth. She was having dinner with Ike and his wife, Mamie, and Ike had told her he wanted Butch to go with him. "What he wanted," noted Butch, "was an old friend around to whom he could talk eye-to-eye without becoming subservient, and who might know something about public relations."[153] As Ike was to discover, good PR would be critical for the task he had to perform. No army general had ever had a naval "aide" before, but King was happy to grant the new commander of the ETO his request. "Everyone congratulated me on my fortune for being selected aide to General Eisenhower," Butch wrote in his diary. "I even congratulated myself."

Eisenhower and his team faced a monstrous task. Decisions made in the next few weeks would shape the future of the war, and very probably its outcome; in the short term at any rate, it would be up to a small-town boy from Kansas to plan and prepare for the first land operations his countrymen would undertake against Germany. But he was also expected to do this hand in glove with the British. Ike may have impressed Marshall and the chiefs back in Washington, but he was still a comparatively junior general. As Brooke later pointed out, his first meeting during

Eisenhower's visit to the UK in May had hardly made a big impression. "If I had been told then of the future that lay in front of him I should have refused to believe it," he later wrote.[154] Brooke was not alone in this view.

Moreover, Britain and America may have shared a common language, but culturally and ideologically they were poles apart even before the war. In June 1942, Ike and his team were coming to a country already nearly four years into war, a country that had faced invasion, mass bombing, nightly blackouts, rationing, and a shortage of every conceivable luxury, luxuries that were still in abundance the other side of the Atlantic. Planning any military operation was hard enough, but Ike also faced the challenge of winning the hearts and minds of these strange and alien people.

In the Western Desert, the remains of the Eighth Army were struggling across the hot and dusty land. For the exhausted soldiers, the events of the past few days, let alone weeks, seemed utterly baffling. South African Bill Eadie had reached Fort Cappuzzo on the frontier on 16 June. Three days later, he was drinking a "marvelous" bottled beer with some men from the Signals when he heard rumors of another hurried move. The next day he was on five minutes' notice to get going. "Aircraft are zooming overhead," he noted, "and occasional gunfire can be heard. Wish I could have a pukka bath." The following day—21 June—he still hadn't moved, but news of the fall of Tobruk made it seem ever more likely. Then came rumors that the enemy had landed by sea near Mersa Matruh. By the twenty-third, with gunfire getting ever closer, some of his men were beginning to feel twitchy. He gave a cowboy novel to one man he feared was "well on the way to getting the jitters." They eventually would move off that night—toward the Alamein Line, although Bill did not know it yet. At Siwa, they met a load of Tommies moving forward. These were men from the newly-arrived X Corps from Syria. "Things look very black," he noted and then added prophetically, "I think a new Higher Command is wanted."

Albert Martin of 2nd Rifle Brigade was equally disillusioned; he and his mates couldn't believe their generals had allowed the situation to fall apart so quickly. Even the rearguard of the Army, 7th Motor Brigade, was finally ordered east on 21 June. Albert couldn't understand why Eighth Army was not making any effort to stop the marauding Axis forces. "Why?" he wrote in his diary. "What is the strategy?" Like Sam Bradshaw, Harold Harper, and Ray Ellis, Albert had been trekking back and forth across the desert with no appreciable respite for too long. "Personally, I've had enough," he added. "I just want some peace and quiet for a while." The next day, they "crossed the wire," but rather than stop and make a stand at Sollum as they'd initially assumed, they were now told to continue on to Mersa Matruh. He and his colleagues were suffering badly from lack of sleep. Fatigue had been steadily accumulating after four weeks of battle and too many nighttime raids. And as they pushed on across the desert, they were harassed by enemy aircraft, who bombed and strafed their columns with what felt like uncomfortable and alarming regularity. On 23 June, he felt the pain of retreat acutely. "When, for heaven's sake, are we going to stop running?" he complained bitterly in his diary. "Whatever is happening, we have all had enough. No fighting spirit left." He was wrong about that, however. When, on 25 June, they turned to face the advancing Panzers—now only a few hundred yards behind—Albert and the rest of the 2nd Battalion opened fire with their customary determination and courage. After a brief but ferocious exchange, they hurried on again. "I think we came off best in that sortie," he noted later.

One morning during the retreat, they awoke to find themselves next to an Axis leaguer. They immediately got going as quietly and quickly as they could, but Albert's truck had broken down and so they were being towed. As they tried to make their escape, they came under fire from two Italian tanks. Hastily they stopped, grabbed what they could, and jumped onto the tow truck. They'd only gone a few hundred yards when their own truck was hit twice and disintegrated.

Mary Coningham and Tommy Elmhirst's leapfrogging of their squadrons continued. Under Tommy Elmhirst's efficient and organized system, it was drummed into every man that nothing—*absolutely* nothing—could be left behind that could be of material advantage to the enemy. Any aircraft that was unfit for service but was flyable was shoved into the air and taken to the next landing ground. One aircraft, for example, was flown without its instrument panel. Others were towed by salvage trucks, while those that could not be moved were covered with petrol and torched. The ground crews also toiled to save what fuel and ammunition they could. One wing managed to salvage 260,000 gallons of fuel and three hundred bombs, the last trucks hurrying into the desert with shells already falling around them.

The ground crews had been stripped of much of their equipment to enable them to move at a moment's notice, but despite this handicap, they maintained an extraordinary level of serviceability. By working through the night, they ensured the DAF was able to keep around 80 percent of its strength for much of the time. On a visit to the front-line squadrons, Air Marshal Tedder watched in amazement as around a hundred men bodily lifted a Spitfire in order to get an articulator underneath it. "There was no crane available there," reported Tedder to the Chief of the Air Staff (CAS), "but they were determined not to lose this Spitfire and that is the spirit one

has seen throughout." He was also impressed at the doggedness of the pilots. One squadron leader told him "the intensity of operations was far
greater than anything he had seen during the Battle of Britain"[155]

Billy Drake's 112 Squadron would not have disagreed. The entire
squadron had reached Landing Ground 075 by 21 June, but two days later
A Flight was on the move again, followed by B Flight the following day. It
was a similar story for 73 Squadron, who had reached LG 115 on June 18,
only for half the squadron to move farther east the same day to LG 76. On
23 June, they then moved again, this time to an airfield at Qasaba. Now almost entirely out of touch with the army, the RAF had to rely on their own
reconnaissance rather than any reports from the ground for their targets,
and so 112 Squadron were carrying out both reconnaissance and escort
duty for the day bombers, as well as bombing and strafing themselves. The
mass of the panzer army streaming across the desert in a cloud of dust provided a very obvious target from the relentlessly clear blue skies above, and
so on 25 June, Mary Coningham began round-the-clock bombing. Every
hour of the day, the panzer army was pounded by bombers and strafed by
marauding fighters. At night, led by Albacore biplanes armed with flares,
Wellington bombers were sent out to attack not just the Axis columns, but
also their ports and lines of supply as well. During the day, escorted by
bomb-carrying fighter aircraft, twin-engine Boston medium bombers continued the work.

That same day, 112 Squadron made three trips escorting the Boston
and eight sorties of their own bombing missions. The following day, they
broke the record for the number of sorties flown by a fighter squadron—
sixty-nine—the first at 6:25 AM, the last some time after seven o'clock that
evening. This meant each pilot flew an average of between five and six missions, most of just over an hour each. At the height of the Battle of Britain,
few pilots flew more than half this number during a single day.

Flying requires incredible levels of concentration. This is tiring in itself;
but flinging an aircraft around the sky, pulling negative gravity and trying
to avoid flak, small-arms fire, and at the same time keeping an eye out for
enemy aircraft—*superior* enemy aircraft—causes an incredible mental and
physical strain. Six or seven hours' combat flying in one day demonstrates
an astonishing commitment and level of determination on the part of Coningham's pilots. To make matters worse, they were rarely given much
chance to sleep either. As Billy Drake points out, "there was a great deal of
noise when we were on the ground, both by day and night." Much of the
time they could hear firing uncomfortably close and often they had no idea
whether this was coming from their own tanks or the enemy's—"which
could be quite traumatic at times."[156]

This gargantuan human effort was paying off, however. The Luftwaffe, with no similar system in place, were lagging behind the Axis forces on the ground, and despite Albert Martin's experiences, were not seen in any great numbers during these crucial days. But they were also exhausted; huge efforts at Bir Hacheim and then again during the capture of Tobruk, when they flew a staggering 580 bomber sorties in *one day*, had created an overwhelming strain on crews and greatly affected serviceability levels. Even before this achievement, their system of maintenance was nothing as efficient as that established by Tommy Elmhirst. The Luftwaffe could rarely fly more than 50 percent of their aircraft on any given day. Consequently, the panzer army had been forced to advance without the protection of its air force—and it was suffering as a result; Rommel was paying for his desire for speed. One German artillery unit operating at full strength just before the fall of Tobruk could barely move six days later. Another anti-tank battery lost four out of seven guns during this same period as a direct result of air attacks. A captured Italian officer confessed that the attacks gave them "no peace. We found this most demoralizing, particularly after a day's fighting when we badly needed a rest." In a German diary, a soldier described an air attack by the RAF. "It was then that I became really conscious of the horrors of war," he had written. "Tommy fired on us well into the night. We have had many attacks, but these bombs were the worst I have ever experienced."[157] And all the time, the Eighth Army was retreating ever closer to safety.

Joe Madeley and the 9th Australian Division were still in Syria, but by 26 June were on two days' notice to leave. The New Zealanders however—including 28 (Maori) Battalion—had arrived at Mersa as part of General Holmes' X Corps. Their commander, General Freyberg, however, had not been impressed. The paltry defenses at Mersa, were, he felt, an obvious trap, so after making a few withering comments about the chaos and confusion of the current situation refused to allow his men to fight in such circumstances. As a result, they were promptly transferred to XIII Corps and sent to Minqar Qaim, some thirty miles south of Mersa Matruh, on top of the southern escarpment, which, as at Tobruk, was dramatically high and ran east-west. The rest of Eighth Army at Mersa was in a bad state: the two brigades of 50th Division, after their epic breakout from the Gazala Line and trek across the desert, were without most of their equipment, which they had been forced to leave behind. The 10th Indian Division was also in disarray, while the 29th Indian Brigade had lost one battalion during their escape from El Adem and had since been inexplicably whittled down to half a dozen undermanned Jock columns. Farthest south was the 7th Motor Brigade, which included Albert Martin's 2nd Rifle Brigade, and around 160 tanks cobbled together from 4th and 22nd Armoured Brigades. The rest of Eighth Army was already safely behind the Alamein Line some 120 miles away.

The panzer army was lined up in front of them by 25 June, but had been held up by fuel shortages and by the efforts of the Desert Air Force, so did not begin their attack until late on June 26. The previous night, S Company of 2nd Rifle Brigade had been told to hold "until the end" a gap in the minefield through which the enemy had to pass. Albert Martin was incensed. "One company expected to hold up the might of the German armour!" he railed to his diary. All night he lay on the ground with his finger hovering over the trigger, waiting for the end. Flares and Verey lights lit the sky and he could clearly see enemy soldiers lifting the mines in front of him. They made a tempting target, but then if Albert and his section of nine others opened fire, the weight of Axis anger would soon hurl itself down upon them. To his great relief, no attempt was made by the enemy that night to come through the gap. In the morning, a few Messerschmitt 109s managed to make an appearance, shooting up their positions and missing them by as little as twenty feet, but soon after, as the shells began to fall among them, they were given the order to withdraw.

Sam Bradshaw and the 6th Royal Tanks spent much of 26 June waiting to be attacked—reports and rumors suggested by as many as two thousand enemy tanks and vehicles. By evening, a hundred enemy tanks were reported to be approaching their positions, but these did not materialize; the attack had been called off for the night. At dawn on 27 June, twelve enemy tanks were sighted in front of them, at which point they formed a battle line and Sam Bradshaw's B Squadron opened fire. No sooner had they done so than the enemy responded with tanks, artillery, and anti-tank guns, knocking out several Grants in the process. The regiment withdrew slightly to hull-down positions, while Sappers were sent forward to blow up their knocked-out tanks. This was their only major engagement of the day. Some enemy tanks were fired upon just after noon, and the regiment was shelled fairly heavily early in the afternoon, but after that they were withdrawn into a box formation along with 8th and 1st Royal Tanks, and after refueling, simply waited there for something to happen

The Auk saw the mixed bag of Gott's under-strength XIII Corps and General Holmes' newly arrived X Corps as little more than a holding force, with the main defense at the Alamein Line. Once it was clear Rommel was about to attack again at Mersa, he told Gott and Holmes that if necessary they should fall back to Fuka, some forty miles east of Mersa Matruh. The Auk had also made it clear that he did not want any unit to become isolated or pinned down. Unfortunately, communication along this hastily conceived position was not good and neither corps commander knew much about what the other was doing. Once more, confusion reigned. The New

Zealanders were almost surrounded and with their commander, General Freyberg, wounded by a shell splinter, decided they needed to withdraw. The problem was where to—they had not been told about the plan to head for Fuka. Eventually, they received a garbled reply from XIII Corps headquarters, which they took to mean the Alamein Line. Meanwhile, Gott had ordered a general withdrawal of his forces—Sam Bradshaw and 6 RTR, for example, crept away east just after midnight. Not long after, the New Zealanders made their daring break out from their encircled position. With fixed bayonets, they stunned the leaguered German positions with their ferocity; in the fighting, Captain Charles Upham joined the elite few to win a bar to the Victoria Cross won at Crete the previous year. Even so, despite their successful escape, the New Zealanders had suffered over eight hundred casualties since arriving at the front.

Meanwhile, General Holmes was not aware that XIII Corps had withdrawn, so on the morning of 28 June, began mounting totally pointless attacks in order to relieve the pressure from his nonexistent colleagues to the south. They were not particularly successful in any case, and the situation was made worse because the Germans had swept on round Mersa and cut off the coast road—Holmes' obvious means of retreat. That night, once more under cover of darkness, the remains of X Corps were forced to break out southward as 50th Division had done at Gazala. By the time Holmes's forces finally reached the Alamein Line, he reckoned he had only 60 percent of his men left.

Vehicles streamed across the desert on 29 June amid clouds of dust and sand. Fuka was forgotten about as the stragglers of the defeated Eighth Army made a dash for the Alamein Line, the last defense of Egypt. The German 90th Light was hurried forward, spearheading the Axis advance. With so many captured vehicles, it was often hard for the numerous columns and units on both sides to tell one another apart. As usual, it was the indefatigable 7th Motor Brigade who were last across the line. By June 30, Albert Martin and his small band of the 2nd Rifle Brigade were operating south of Daba, some thirty miles west of the Alamein position, and by now, well behind enemy lines. Albert was absolutely exhausted. Three hours' sleep every twenty-four hours if he was lucky. "All of us are fast becoming physical wrecks," he noted, "living on the last reserves of strength dredged up from goodness knows where." They still kept going, however, harassing Axis columns whenever they could. That morning, the entire 7th Motor Brigade attacked the rear of the recently arrived Italian Littorio Division, knocking out two-thirds of its tanks and a number of guns. Along with the RAF, Albert and his colleagues were upsetting Rommel's timetable.

The German commander was still exultant, however. That same day he wrote to his wife, "Mersa Matruh fell yesterday, after which the Army moved on until late in the night. We're already 60 miles to the east. Less than 100 miles to Alexandria!"[158] Since the end of May, Eighth Army had now lost over 50 percent of its fighting force killed, wounded, or captured. Rommel, meanwhile, had made good 50 percent of his material losses with captured British equipment.[159]

The collapse of the Eighth Army, the loss of Tobruk, Sollum, then Mersa Matruh, and the flight back into Egypt, taken hand in glove with the awesome reputation of the seemingly invincible Field Marshal Rommel, had a terrible effect on the civilians and military back in Alexandria and Cairo. As the panzer army reached Alamein, German radio broadcast a message to the women of Alexandria to "Get out your party frocks, we're on our way!"[160] Lord Haw-Haw, during his broadcasts, warned that Cairo would be attacked by two hundred bombers. Rumors abounded that the Egyptian government had already prepared assurances of cooperation to Rommel. Then, at the end of the month, Admiral Harwood, Commander of the Mediterranean Fleet, began moving his ships away from potential enemy air attacks and even capture. Some were sent to Port Said, others Haifa in Palestine and Beirut.

Lieutenant Charles Coles, having escaped from Tobruk and safely made it back to Alexandria, wandered down from his flat one morning to find the harbor almost deserted, except for a few MTBs and the few French Vichy warships that had been moored there since June 1940. He and the other MTB skippers were then each given a sealed brown envelope, ordered to go to different parts of the harbor and told to open the envelopes at midnight. At the appointed hour, when Charles opened his, he discovered orders instructing him to bring his boat to instant torpedo readiness and that on a signal he was to fire them and sink the French vessel in front of him. "We sat up all night waiting," says Charles. "It was horrible having to be ready to kill Frenchmen." Dawn arrived, but no such signal. The following morning, they were stood down, and the French crews were soon going ashore as usual and returning with baskets of watermelons, dates, and other stores.

But with the departure of all but the MTB wing of the Navy, panic ensued, starting what became known as "the Flap." For those following the events in the desert it seemed that only a miracle could stop Rommel now. German radio boasted that Rommel would be in Alexandria on 6 July, and Cairo three days later. In Alexandria, military files were burned and the population began packing up and heading into the Delta, out of harm's way. The Flap soon spread to Cairo. On 1 July, Cecil Beaton went as usual to his office at GHQ, only to be told that they were all under twelve hours' notice to leave. Squadron Leader Houghton showed Cecil a map. "We're lined up here now," he said, pointing to the narrow strip of the Alamein position. "The last line of defense. If that goes, there's nothing left." He told Cecil that he should consider heading south to Khartoum. The news horrified him. He "longed to get shot of this awful sick feeling in the upper stomach," but what could he do? He felt utterly helpless. "Cairo was in a dreadful state of unrest," he noted, "the streets jammed with terrific crowds outside the banks, and at headquarters, everyone was burning secret papers. The effect was horrible."[161] Alan Moorehead's wife, Lucy, now working for General Corbett, the Auk's chief of staff, was also instructed to burn a number of secret papers. The British consulate was besieged by people desperate for visas, while the trains heading east were also packed with fleeing civilians. "A thin mist of smoke hung over the British embassy by the Nile and the sprawling blocks of GHQ," noted Alan Moorehead. He went into one office only to find the floor covered in ashes. "The smell of a burning rag hung over the whole building."[162] He then left Lucy and baby son "with some misgiving" and headed back to the front. As he motored out of Cairo he had scarcely passed the pyramids when he saw the signs of full-scale retreat. "Guns of all sorts, RAF wagons, recovery vehicles, armoured cars and countless lorries crammed with exhausted and sleeping men, were pouring from up the desert road to Cairo." As he neared the front, this procession only thickened.[163]

On what became known as Ash Wednesday, there was one person who had no intention of fleeing. The Polish Legation told Sophie Tarnowska that she should head to Palestine; then her sister-in-law, Chouquette, also tried to persuade her. "But I said no," says Sophie. "I told them 'I've left Poland, I've left Belgrade and I've left Jerusalem. I'm not leaving again.'" But nor did she stay in Cairo. Instead she made her way through the carts and cars piled high with belongings to the railway station, where she bought a ticket on a very empty train to Alexandria. Although she had run in the past, this time she felt sure she would be safe. "Ridiculous really," she says, "but it was how I felt." Booking herself into an otherwise deserted seafront hotel, she was the only person dining that night. The staff were so pleased to have a customer, they gave her one of their best bottles of wine on the house. "The best I have ever tasted," says Sophie. Even so, as she sipped this delicious wine, she could hear the guns, sixty miles away.

A little over a month before, the Eighth Army had been dug into a highly prepared defensive position and had numerical superiority in both armor and infantry, and yet it had been utterly defeated and flung back nearly three hundred miles. Sophie Tarnowska may have maintained an admirable state of sangfroid but there were not many who doubted Rommel would be as good as his word. Egypt and the Middle East appeared to be his for the taking.

PART II

COMING TOGETHER

"Our two nations will march together
in a noble brotherhood of arms."

Winston Churchill

CHAPTER 8

Parry: July, 1942, Part One

YET, IF THE AUK'S FORCES could just keep the panzer army at bay for a while, there was every reason to believe that not all would be lost. On that black Sunday of 21 June, the Americans had immediately rallied to their ally. No sooner had Roosevelt handed the news of Tobruk's fall to Churchill than he asked the prime minister, "What can we do to help?"

Quick as a flash, the prime minister replied, "Give us as many Sherman tanks as you can spare, and ship them to the Middle East as quickly as possible." The president called for General Marshall and told him Churchill's request. The American chief must have nearly choked. "Mr. President," said Marshall, "the Shermans are only just coming into production. The first few hundred have been issued to our own armored divisions, who have hitherto had to be content with obsolete equipment. It is a terrible thing to take the weapons out of a soldier's hand." Neither Roosevelt or Churchill appeared to be moved by this, so he continued, "Nevertheless, if the British need is so great, they must have them," and then he added with great magnanimity, "and we could let them have a hundred 105mm self-propelled guns in addition."[164] As good as their word, three hundred Shermans and the self-propelled guns (SPs) were shortly shipped and heading across the South Atlantic.

The General Sherman M4A3 tank demonstrated the ingenuity and industrial might that Churchill had always known America possessed. They might have been late into the game and desperately behind the times, but when the United States channeled their energies, great things could be achieved. The General Sherman—as the British called it, or simply Sherman as it became universally known—was a progression from the Grant. Physically it had a similar hull, but was more conventional in design with its main gun mounted in a fully rotational turret. The 75mm gun was also an improved version of those used in the Grant, with that most important of factors, greater velocity and armor-piercing potential at distances of over one mile. Its Ford engine—originally designed for aircraft—was reliable too, and with a top speed of around 30 mph, it combined maneuverability and speed to good effect. In short, it was a tank that was the equal of, if not better than, the German Mark IV panzer. A test of the effectiveness of any military equipment is its longevity. The production line on the Sherman began in February 1942—a year after its conception—with the first batch sent for testing in May. It was still in use at the end of the war and for seven years after that.

Unsurprisingly, while the Germans had been only too happy to develop SP guns, the British had not, preferring to think of artillery as a gun mounted between "two wheels and kept simple."[165] Equally unsurprisingly, the Germans *had* used SP guns, and to good effect. Although mounted on tank chassis, the main difference between SP guns and tanks was that the former had thinner armor, no revolving turret and a lack of additional fire-power. They were designed to be used as field guns, i.e., for indirect, rather than direct fire like tanks, but were obviously for more maneuverable than traditional field guns. Needless to say, the promise of these large self-propelled field guns as well as an initial batch of three hundred Shermans was greeted with considerable enthusiasm by the prime minister, who signalled Auchinleck with the good news on 25 June. They were due to sail on 10 July.

And it was not only American equipment that was being sent to the Middle East. Although the plan to send Major-General George S. Patton to Egypt with an armored division had been discarded, American combat personnel *were* operating in the Middle East by mid-June. The Halverson Detachment—or HALPRO as it was also known—was a unit of B-24 Liberator heavy bombers, which had originally trained under Colonel Harry A. Halverson for specific bombing raids on Tokyo from Chinese bases. But when Burma had fallen on 20 May, it became clear that such operations could not be logistically supported. Instead, General Marshall, with Roosevelt's approval, diverted HALPRO to the Middle East. On 12 June, from Fayid airfield in Egypt, thirteen B-24s set off to bomb the Axis-controlled oil refineries at Ploesti in Romania. The results were modest to say the least, but the mission was the first American strategic bombing raid against Germany of the war. Furthermore, the Halverson Detachment stayed put in Egypt, supporting the June convoy to Malta and then, a few days later bombing the Axis-held port of Benghazi in Libya. On 27 June, they chalked up yet another long-range mission, when they were sent to attack Tobruk in an effort to disrupt enemy supplies now coming into the port.

The HALPRO detachment was soon to be joined to further reinforcements from the US, although this had placed General Arnold, Chief of US Army Air Force, in something of a quandary. Like Marshall, he supported the Europe-first policy and was eager to build up his forces in order to attack Nazi-held Europe as soon as possible. But British needs in the Middle East were swallowing many of his aircraft and equipment—and the demands from the RAF were only increasing: even by the end of May, Mary Coningham was worrying about where new replacement aircraft would come from. On the other hand, if the British were pushed out of the Middle East, their task in Western Europe would become significantly harder. Hap Arnold was faced with a stark choice: either he could allow the RAF to continue swallowing many of his resources, or he could send his own units: American aircraft, manned by American pilots and crews. He opted for the latter course, which was later confirmed with Air Marshal Portal, the British chief of the Air Staff, on 21 June. Nine groups* were earmarked for the Middle East, although only one heavy bomber group and two fighter groups would be operating in the theater by October.[166]

The heavy bomb group was to be the 98th. For several weeks before they actually departed, the pilots and crew had guessed something was up, although as new aircraft arrived painted olive green, they assumed they would be heading to the Far East. Texan Willie Chapman admits that they were all beginning to think about being part of the war at last, and he was excited about the prospect of heading overseas. "I'd slipped over the border into Mexico a couple of times, but otherwise I'd never been out of the States," he says. "It felt like a big adventure." They began getting ready to go. Willie wanted to sell his car, but with gasoline rationing looming on the horizon, he was finding it difficult. In the end the problem was solved for him when he crashed it one rainy night en route to a restaurant with some of the other pilots.

First to head off in mid-July was the 344 Squadron, under command of Major "Killer" Kane. Two days later, it was the turn of Willie and the rest of 415 Squadron. After a final phone call to his girlfriend, Dottie, and a last-minute delay of twenty-four hours, Willie eventually took off just after four o'clock in the morning on 15 July from West Palm Beach in Florida. On board were the eight crew plus several other maintenance personnel. First port of call was Trinidad, then two stops in Brazil before finally heading over the Atlantic on what was known as the South Atlantic Supply Route. The fun-loving 98th were used to having drink, girls, and parties more-or-less on tap, but on tiny Ascension Island there was no entertainment, so they were forced to resort to poker. At Kano, the roughly made

---

*A US "group" is the same as an RAF "wing," i.e., three squadrons and accompanying personnel

airfield was not suited to anything so large as a B-24, and Willie's plane sank several feet into the mud. A bulldozer had to drag them off the runway. The men managed to find the only restaurant in town and made the best of things by gambling with bottles of the local beer, but the following morning they discovered there was barely enough fuel there to get them to Khartoum. Moreover, Willie's aircraft had been badly damaged on landing and, with the limited facilities there, could not be repaired. The crew was split up among other Liberators, and on they went, struggling through a vicious thunderstorm to reach Khartoum. There they paused before heading onto Heliopolis just outside Cairo and then to their final destination of Ramid David airfield outside Haifa in Palestine. "And so," noted Willie, "our war began."[167]

The first fighter group to be sent over was the 57th. In June, Duke Ellington and a number of others from the 56th Fighter Group were transferred to the 57th. Most were sent to the 64th and 66th Fighter Squadrons, but Duke and his good friend Bob Hoke joined the 65th, which already had something of a reputation largely thanks to its original commanding officer, Captain Phil Cochran. Not only had Cochran been immortalized in a comic strip called *Terry and the Pirates* as the daredevil pilot Flip Corkin, he had also instilled an aggressive gung-ho attitude amongst his men. The 65th, for example, was one of the few fighter squadrons in June 1942 to have had any kind of gunnery training—arranged by Cochran. As soon as Duke arrived to join them at Mitchell Field, New York, he the other "new sports," as they were called, were told they had better damn well immerse themselves in the spirit of the 65th or else they could look elsewhere for another squadron.

No sooner had Duke arrived than Cochran was promoted and Captain Art Salisbury took over. Duke respected him immediately. "He was smart and a very good pilot," says Duke, "but he was also a people person and always made what we felt were the right decisions." During initial briefings at Mitchell Field they were told they would be going overseas, but not when or where. "But we did know that there were seventy-two brand-new P-40Fs waiting for us, all painted in a camouflage desert pink," says Duke. After practicing short takeoffs for a couple of days, they were warned to say their final farewells to their loved ones and then were ordered to Quansett Point in Rhode Island. The runway ran right alongside the quay, where a large aircraft carrier was waiting. Duke landed, brought his plane to a halt and was just filling out the details of his flight on the Form 1 as normal when he suddenly realized ropes were being placed under his aircraft. Moments later, and still sitting in the cockpit, he was lifted and hoisted onto the USS *Ranger*.

Like Willie Chapman, Duke—"just a kid from South Dakota"—viewed

the prospect of going overseas as a huge adventure. Sure, he was apprehensive, but it was also exciting. They traveled across the South Atlantic
towards the Gold Coast in West Africa, a journey fraught with the risk of
submarine attack, then a hundred miles off shore, began taking off from
the *Ranger*. None of them had ever done this before. Aircraft were brought
up in lifts from the deck hangar and told to fly off in groups of eighteen.
Engines were revved to full throttle, then on the signal, the brakes were
released and each P-40 hurtled down the deck. Duke suffered a few tense
moments before it was his turn, but like the other seventy-one pilots, managed to take off successfully. Some only just, however: several dropped out
of sight off the end of the deck and later the pilots swore their wheels
touched the water.

First stop was Accra, and from then on they were to follow the Takoradi
Route, as pioneered by Mary Coningham and others back in the 1920s.
Duke managed to reach African soil without too much difficulty, but from
then on his journey to the Middle East became something of a nightmare.
In the US, he had been used to mainly cloudless blue skies, but flying from
Accra over alien country and in and out of cloud cover, Duke began to suffer from vertigo. Only by flying almost on the wingtip of the flight leader
was he able to keep going. Much to his relief, he landed safely at Lagos,
but then, as he was taxiing off the landing strip, one of his wheels also
dropped in some soft mud and he broke his propeller.

While the rest of the squadron continued on their way, Duke had to
hang around waiting for a new prop—which arrived with the ground crews
a few days later. Flying with some British fighter pilots, he then made it to
Kano, where some of the 98th Bombardment Group's B-24s were coming
in just after him. There were too many aircraft landing and taxiing, and
when the Hurricane in front of him suddenly stopped, he was forced to
slam on his brakes to avoid slicing into it. "The nose goes down," says Duke,
"and wham, I've got the prop again." There were no more propellers, but
the resourceful ground crew managed to improvise and get him airborne
once more, although not before he saw a twin-engine Lockheed Hudson
stall and crash into a wall of fuel barrels. All the crew and a large number
of African workers were killed. "It was devastating," says Duke, unused to
watching men blown to smithereens and burned to death before his very
eyes. But at long last he got away and managed to reach Khartoum, where
the rest of the squadron were waiting. Like the 98th Bomb Group, the 57th
Fighter Group flew on from Egypt, ("where I got my first glimpse of the
pyramids"), to Palestine. There they were split up, with the 65th Fighter
Squadron posted to Cyprus—where Rifleman Nainabadahur Pun and
much of General Tuker's 4th Indian Division were still training.

On Cyprus, the 65th underwent a period of acclimatization and training. That this was deemed necessary before the Americans were flung against the best of the Luftwaffe was a cause of frustration for Tedder and Mary Coningham. They desperately needed aircraft—and pilots—now, not in a couple of months' time. Nor had the HALPRO detachment particularly impressed either Tedder or Portal. During the June convoy to Malta, seven of the US Liberators, along with a number of RAF bombers and torpedo-carrying aircraft (over forty in all), had attacked the Italian fleet. The sum of their efforts was one torpedo hit on the heavy cruiser *Trento* (which was later sunk by the British submarine HMS/S *Umbro*), and one bomb and one torpedo hit on the battleship *Littorio*. On their return, the elated Americans told reporters they had made no less than thirty-eight hits on two Italian battleships and that the attack was "like shooting fish in a barrel!"[168] Portal immediately told Tedder not to let the Americans say anything about any future operation without consultation first. "Such exaggerations not only provide excellent Axis propaganda and cast doubt on Coral Sea and Midway claims [of US victories in the Pacific]," Portal told him, "but are also likely to cause serious ill feeling between Allied Air Forces."[169]

Most airmen—usually unintentionally—embellished claims. The HALRPO detachment's exaggerations are understandable. A heavy cruiser to an untrained eye looks much like the bigger battleship; fountains of spray would have surged into the sky, smoke would have billowed from the hits that were scored, and no doubt it did seem as though they had been more successful than was really the case. No wonder then, that they chattered so wildly on their return—this was, after all, only their second combat mission. But Portal's concerns are no less understandable; he had a lot more experience of the latest and previous wars than anyone in the American Air Force and was wary of the overconfidence of the new ally. Even so, he was conscious that unity was also essential. "I am sure you will do your best to preserve harmony with the Americans," he wrote to Tedder at the end of June, "and I think that the best way to do so is to give them complete independence on paper, while, in fact, guiding them behind the scenes to do what you want."

At the end of June, Major-General Lewis H. Brereton was sent to Cairo to command the newly established US Army Middle East Air Force, of which both the 98th Bombardment and 57th Fighter Groups would be a part. Brereton was to serve under Major-General Russell Maxwell, who had already arrived to take command of US Forces Middle East. Thus, for the first time in the war, British and American commanders found themselves working together in an active theater of war.

* * *

One of Brereton's first tasks had been to prepare a plan for the US Middle East Air Force should the Battle for Egypt be lost. The Auk had also been readying his forces for the next Axis onslaught from his new HQ fifteen miles southwest of El Alamein railway station, and sent his assessment of the situation to Brooke on 28 June. The RAF was the only *offensive* weapon he had left, he told the CIGS; as a result, defense was the only option for his ground forces until they had been sufficiently rebuilt. His intention was therefore to keep Eighth Army "as a mobile field force and resist by every possible means any further attempt by the enemy to advance eastwards." However, he did concede that this might not be possible at the Alamein Line and that further retreat was a possibility. Plans for the withdrawal of his troops to Alexandria, Cairo, and the Canal Zone were prepared.

Most of his commanders thought this was a necessary precaution, in the circumstances. In fact, Strafer Gott was quite openly defeatist, a view which he revealed in a conversation with Brigadier Kippenberger, who, on 29 June, was acting commander of the New Zealand Division. A general retirement and evacuation of Egypt was being planned, Gott told him. "I protested that we were perfectly fit to fight and that it was criminal to give up Egypt to 25,000 German troops and a hundred tanks (disregarding the Italians)," Kippenberger later recalled. "Strafer replied sadly that NZ division was battle-worthy but very few other people were and he feared the worst."[170] This kind of attitude was not what was needed from one of the Auk's corps commanders. Pienaar also felt a further retreat was necessary and that Eighth Army should fight on the Suez Canal, although in the next breath was urging his troops to stand and fight at Alamein to avenge the 2nd South African Division's defeat at Tobruk.

Admittedly, the Alamein position was not a line of properly prepared defenses as the Gazala Line had been; it was not really a line at all, with few minefields and only a handful of small defensive boxes. But if the British forces were exhausted, then so too were the Axis, especially thanks to the relentless round-the-clock efforts of Mary Coningham's Desert Air Force. The panzer army was severely short of sleep and equipment and still had little air cover of its own. Kippenberger had been absolutely right. And despite plans for further withdrawal, the Auk was determined to fight Rommel at Alamein, and to defeat him. On 30 June, he issued a message to "All Ranks" of the Eighth Army: "The enemy is stretched to the limit and thinks we are a broken army. His tactics against the New Zealanders were poor in the extreme. He hopes to take Egypt by bluff. Show him where he gets off."[171] Fortunately, General Norrie also believed Alamein was the place to make a stand—which was just as well, as it was on XXX Corps in the north of the position that Rommel decided to make his main attack.

El Alamein itself was a tiny railway station—a two-room, one-story building along the coastal railway line, and some two miles inland from the bright turquoise of the Mediterranean Sea. Half a mile north of the station ran a ridge parallel to the coast on which the main coast road was built. From this elevated position one could see for miles the wide-open expanse of desert: soft sandy soil, speckled with mounds of brown desert vetch, a brittle sturdy shrub, giving the desert a dark, mottled color. To an untrained eye the desert looked utterly flat; but this was a deception. One could travel south across it then realize the horizon was gradually shortening; behind, one could see for perhaps five or even ten miles, but then ahead, one's view stretched no farther than a few hundred yards. Suddenly, without really realizing it until on the summit, one might find oneself standing on a long shallow ridge. The first of these along the Alamein position was the Miteirya Ridge, just four hundred yards wide along its summit and running roughly parallel to the coast, and some eight miles inland. Here the sand and vetch were gone: instead, underfoot there was nothing but stones and rock, some tiny, others as much as a foot wide, and very hard to dig into. Although no more than thirty meters above sea level, such was the general flatness of the desert, a ridge like this became a significant landmark from which troop movements could be seen for miles.

Continuing south, the next significant feature was the Ruweisat Ridge, bisecting the line east-west, and then, farther south again, another ridge, Alam Nayil. Approaching both, distances were deceptive and the consistency of color and texture made orientation difficult. Once again, horizons suddenly stretched away and then dramatically shortened, as the desert gently undulated. Farther east was the larger feature of Alam Halfa, another longer and more significant ridge. Here, along the summit, it was pitted with small dips and rises: an ideal place in which to place a gun or tank. Its southern face was more pronounced and from there one could see the southern part of the line, the edge of the gigantic Qattara Depression. The landscape of this southern half of the forty-mile stretch between the coast and the Depression was very different from the northern half. Between Alam Halfa and Alam Nayil—some fifteen miles apart—the desert dropped in strange lunar valleys of sudden sharp escarpments, ranging from just a few to as much as forty feet high. This was a difficult part of the line over which to attack, because the dips and ridges made it almost impossible for mechanized transport of any kind, even tanks. But farther south, the land once again flattened into a broad gravelly plain, before rising gradually towards the enormous horned feature known as the Qaret el Himeimat, a huge rock formation more akin to Arizona's Monument Valley than the featureless Western Desert. West from this ran another high ridge—over a hundred and eighty meters above sea level, across which no machinery could pass, before dropping into the vast expanse of the Qattara Depression, where the land stepped down through huge escarpments, and which were more or less impassable to vehicles.

Eighth Army was dispersed along the line in mostly brigade-strength boxes, which, although now manned by fewer men, were better equipped with transport. In the north, around El Alamein and covering the railway and main coast road, was the principle defensive position, prepared earlier and now manned by 3rd South African Brigade. In the rugged area twenty-five miles to the south, the New Zealanders were also dug into fairly well-prepared positions, known as the Kaponga Box.

Rommel had fewer resources than even Kippenberger had claimed: just fifty-five German tanks (6 RTR—one regiment—had begun the Battle of Sidi Rezegh with fifty-two) and thirty Italian tanks. The 90th Light Division had merely 1,000 motorized troops remaining (little more than a battalion), although he did have over three hundred guns, of which twenty-nine were the feared 88mms. His supply lines were also severely stretched: no use could be made of the railway line, since there was not a single repairable locomotive available to him. The Luftwaffe was still seriously short of transport and his stocks of water, fuel, and ammunition were causing major anxiety. In short, Rommel's panzer army was running out of steam. If his shock and awe tactics were to be successful, he had to smash through the Alamein Line very quickly indeed, and make the most of captured British material to see him through to Cairo and the Suez Canal.

He decided to attack in the north, between the coast and the Ruweisat Ridge and either side of the Miteirya Ridge, in order to capture the coast road in the shortest amount of time and then sweep south to cut off the remains of the British forces. His attack, launched in the early hours of 1 July, was soon pinned down by dogged defense, until a dust storm enabled the panzer army to get going again. Bill Eadie, with 2nd South African Brigade HQ, was outside the Alamein Box southeast of the defenses, and was more buoyant than he had been for several days. He'd been watching the hourly display of bombers sailing overhead and thought they looked "grand." His job was to transport troops about when needed, but he was running short of water, essential not just for the men, but for the lorries' radiators. Dogged humor was resurfacing, and he saw that on one lorry someone had written, GAZALA HANDICAP—4 TO 1 ON VAPOURISING ANN. Later in the afternoon he heard the British "big guns" roaring and heard that "our boys are holding Jerry." In fact, the combined artillery efforts of all three South African Brigades and the 1st Armoured Division were giving the 90th Light the shock of their life. For the first time since the beginning of the Gazala Battles in May, British artillery was pouring concentrated artillery fire onto the Germans, who had been caught out in the open as the dust storm cleared. Panic had set in, and parts of the 90th Light were fleeing in disarray. Even Rommel, who had moved up with the 90th Light to give them renewed impetus, was impressed. "Terrific British artillery fire slammed into our ranks," he wrote. "From north, east, and south, the British shells were screaming. Tracer from the British anti-aircraft guns whizzed through our forces."[172]Although this was as a result of chance rather than any prearranged plan, it proved very clearly what could be achieved if the basic age-old principles of concentrated artillery fire were adhered to—concepts that General Francis Tuker, for one, had been appalled to discover back in May were being flung to one side.

Farther south, on the northern edge of the Ruweisat Ridge, 18th Indian Briagde had also held off the armored units of the Afrika Korps, and although night fell the Indian positions were overrun, Rommel's attack had stalled. His Afrika Korps now had just thirty-seven tanks left. Nor did he get much farther the following day, when it became clear that a battle of attrition rather than a decisive breakthrough was developing. The experience of Sam Bradshaw and the rest of 6 RTR was typical of the kinds of inconclusive actions that were taking place. They saw little action on 1 July, but the next day lost five Grants while inflicting considerable damage themselves on the 90th Light, claiming "many" anti-tank guns damaged and enemy transport destroyed.[173]

Bill Eadie had spent the last twenty-four hours on the go almost non-stop, ferrying troops and supplies as the battle raged. The previous night, he helped a few New Zealanders who were trying to take their new Ford trucks down the line but had become bogged down in sand. He and his driver then took out their Thermos flask and drank some coffee just as the moon came out. The battle had died down, but signal lights and Verey flares sparkled and lit the sky. And overhead, Mary Coningham's round-the-clock bombing continued, with the drone of aero-engines and the odd boom of bombs dropping resounding across the desert, mingling with the faint roar of numerous trucks revving as they tried to free themselves from the sand.

Bill was soon off again, and busy all through the following day—collecting broken-down vehicles, bringing up more fuel and supplies. "Actually, I'm enjoying this rather hectic activity," he confessed. For others, however, the strain of the past few weeks was taking its toll. Bill came across one of his colleagues, Private Slattery, in a bad way. Slattery, Bill noted, "used to sing his Irish songs so well in the PAG [Prince Albert's Guard] concerts;" but was now a changed man. "One glance at his eyes and I knew his nerve had failed him. He seems quite helpless; little spirit left. This is what we call being bomb happy—'shell shock' in the last war."

* * *

While these decisive engagements were raging in the desert, Cecil Beaton had finally left Cairo. "With what tremendous relief had I left this restless, corrupt, unfortunate, suburban town," he wrote as the plane took off from Heliopolis, "with the Germans only ninety miles away, for England, where the Germans are only twenty miles distant."[174] The news that Rommel appeared to have been checked had not reached him. Later, at their hotel in Khartoum, he and his fellow passengers heard the BBC News on the radio. Sebastopol in the Crimea had fallen to the Axis—another disaster for the Allies and another triumph for the seemingly unstoppable Germans. "The news could not have been much worse," Cecil noted, then added, "After being away so long, it seems strange to hear the war in terms of Whitehall again. Their interpretation after one has seen the battlefield and the men fighting is so remote from reality." The debate over the Vote of Censure was also continuing at Westminster, and parts of Churchill's speech were relayed on the radio. Cecil was unimpressed by what he heard. Some of the men he had spoken to in the hospitals in Cairo had been depressed that their shells appeared to bounce off the German tanks, yet now Churchill was extolling the virtues of their armaments and claiming them to be every bit as good as the enemy's. When it came to the vote, the prime minister won with a massive majority: 475 votes to 25—"because there's no alternative leader," Cecil scrawled bitterly in his diary.[175]

There was one string to Auchinleck's bow, however, that was never available to Rommel, and that was the use of special forces. Certainly, Britain had a pre-war advantage in that most of the desert explorers of the 1930s were English. The most notable of these, Ralph Bagnold, Bill Kennedy Shaw, and Pat Clayton, later formed the Long Range Desert Group, who from early on in the desert campaign began traveling far behind enemy lines, carrying out reconnaissance and making occasional sabotage raids. From the summer of 1941, there was also L Detachment, Special Air Service Brigade, otherwise known as the SAS, who by May 1942 had gained quite a reputation for their daring attacks behind the lines. There had been a lull in their activities while they reorganized and trained, but now, in July, this small unit of eccentrics and adventurers was ready to begin operations once more.

Lieutenant Carol Mather had joined the SAS in May, but like a number in the detachment he had, back in February 1940, volunteered for the first British special forces unit to have been formed during the war. He'd been at Sandhurst Military College at the time, and a candidate for the Welsh

Guards when he'd learned that volunteers were being asked to form a special Ski battalion of the Scots Guards to help the Finns in their war against the Russians.

Travel and adventure was in Carol's blood. His father, who ran the family engineering firm in Manchester, had been a friend of the great explorer Ernest Shackleton, and still found time to travel extensively himself. This rubbed off on his son, who, while in his teens, had joined expeditions to Finland, Newfoundland, and even the Yukon and Alaska. "I'd originally intended to be an Arctic explorer," says Carol, "but the war rather stopped all that." Then out of the blue had come the call for volunteers for Finland. As an experienced subarctic explorer, and knowing the country as he did, Carol readily volunteered.

After somewhat haphazard training in the French Alps, the British expedition was heading for the Baltic when the Finns and Russians signed an armistice. The battalion was disbanded, but in October Carol volunteered for and was accepted into the newly formed No. 8 Commando. After training in Scotland, a detachment known as Layforce was then sent to the Middle East. They were an eclectic bunch. Amongst Carol's colleagues were the author Evelyn Waugh, the prime minister's son Randolph Churchill, and a contemporary from Sandhurst and the Ski Battalion, David Stirling. Carol had shared a cabin with Stirling throughout the voyage and was amazed at the enormous amount of time his friend spent asleep. "The sleeping sickness became so endemic," Carol recorded later, "that he became known among fellow officers as 'the great sloth,' and one wondered whether he would last the pace."[176]

Their subsequent arrival in Egypt brought disappointment. Layforce never achieved its potential in the Middle East, largely because the Royal Navy, who was to transport them on raiding missions, was particularly occupied at the time with the evacuations from Greece and then Crete. Underused and losing their sense of purpose, the men became frustrated. Layforce, noted Carol, "was now becoming more and more of a fiasco, with the consequent collapse of purpose, discipline and morale."[177] The writing was on the wall. Like the Ski Battalion before it, No. 8 Commando was disbanded, in July 1941.

David Stirling, however, having overcome his bout of sleeping sickness, was determined their skills should not be wasted. While recovering from a parachuting accident in Alexandria, he drew up a memorandum for the deputy chief of the General Staff, who at the time was still General Neil Ritchie, in which he outlined his ideas for a small specialist raiding force. He had realized that the desert was a vast place, and that airfields, especially, were difficult places to guard. If they could just get close enough, a handful of men should be able to sneak in at night, and with a few guns and lumps of high explosive, cause serious levels of damage and mayhem. Bluffing his way into GHQ, he managed to gain an audience with Ritchie. To Stirling's great surprise, three days later he was called back for an interview with Auchinleck. The Auk thought the proposals worth a shot, and so promoted Stirling to captain and authorized him to recruit six officers and sixty men for what was to become L Detachment of the Special Air Service Brigade.

Early missions were disastrous, but Stirling—and the C-in-C for that matter—persevered, and their achievements began to mount. By May 1942, their exploits behind enemy lines were well known. The key to their success was the use the SAS made of the Long Range Desert Group, who readily worked alongside the SAS, offering a form of desert taxi service. Such was the quality of their desert navigation, they were able to drop Stirling's men at very precise locations from which the SAS could easily make their lightning raids.

Stirling had asked Carol Mather to join his new enterprise shortly after the disbandment of 8 Commando, but at the time, Carol had thought it "harebrained" and "doomed to failure." Instead he'd joined GHQ Liaison Squadron, surviving the Crusader Battles and life in the desert until David Stirling began recruiting again in May. "I had to admit that I had been wrong in doubting that he could bring it off," Carol later confessed. "In effect, I had to eat humble pie in asking to rejoin him."[178] He was not alone, however, and at the SAS camp at Kabrit—just north of Suez on the canal—met a number of old Layforce colleagues, as well as another friend from Sandhurst days, Stephen Hastings.

Tall and lean, with fair hair and a narrow, good-humored face, Lieutenant Hastings had been all too ready to volunteer for the SAS when he heard that David Stirling was looking for more recruits. He'd tried to join the Ski Battalion at the beginning of the war but had been refused admission, and so had subsequently spent eighteen months in the desert with the 2nd Scots Guards fighting the Germans and Italians back and forth across Cyrenaica. At Gazala, he'd begun to feel ready for a change. The Jock Columns on which they were regularly sent seemed to him to be of little value. "We would head out into the desert with a couple of twenty-five-pounders," he recalls, "and sit around as they pelted the Germans having breakfast in their leaguer, and although I'm sure it annoyed them very much, I couldn't say that it served any tactical or strategic purpose." Furthermore, he had had enough of his company commander, a difficult man to please, and whom he'd served under since he'd joined the battalion the previous March. "Charm he had in abundance," wrote Stephen later, "but all too easily it could turn to a morbid sarcasm, and that is hard to live with in the midst of war."[179]

As Stephen quickly discovered, life with the SAS was very different from serving in a Guards' Battalion, where discipline and strict hierarchy still counted for everything. In contrast, the SAS seemed to him to have no discipline at all, with other ranks, NCOs and commissioned officers all treating each other on more-or-less the same footing. The unit was full of larger-than-life characters, of which David Stirling was but one. Another of the "originals" was a large Ulsterman and pre-war rugby international called Paddy Mayne. Like Stirling, he was well over six foot, but was also blessed with extraordinary physical strength. Full of Irish charm and good humor, he was nonetheless also prone to bouts of severe bad temper, usually prompted by one too many drinks. "He was," says Stephen, "a frightening character." During leave in Cairo, Major Mayne once famously had a "difference of opinion" with six Australians and laid them out cold, wrecking a Greek cafe in the process. Even in wartime this was a serious offense, but Stirling managed to persuade the director of military operations (DMO) that however grave a crime, his prizefighter had already destroyed over fifty aircraft and was more use in the desert than in the glasshouse.

Throughout June the newly enlarged L-Detachment SAS—now around one hundred strong—prepared for a new series of operations. Stephen Hasting, Carol Mather, and the other newcomers were put through their parachute training, even though Stirling's men were no longer using air jumps as a means of reaching the enemy. This consisted of hurling themselves off the back of a moving lorry. Those who avoided breaking limbs in the process were then sent up in an aging Bristol Bombay and pushed through a hole "like a large funneled loo" in the center of the plane.[180] The rest of June was spent readying themselves for the next series of raids and operations. New American four-wheel drive jeeps had arrived for the first time in the Middle East and needed to be customized, and much time was spent between the base ordnance depot and the base workshops, overseeing the various modifications.

The SAS left Kabrit on 3 July, and trundled en masse to Cairo for their final briefings. This took place at Peter Stirling's flat. David Stirling's brother was second secretary at the British embassy at the time and his flat had for some time been the SAS's focal point in the city. The entire convoy of some thirty-five vehicles, packed to the hilt with kit and machine guns parked in the side streets around Peter Stirling's flat. Stephen Hastings was amazed. While several of the officers poured over maps with TOP SECRET stamped all over them, a party was going around them, most of whom were going to the Gezira Races later that afternoon.

Previous raids had been carried out during moonless periods only, but Stirling now felt that with their jeeps and increased numbers they should be able to operate in the desert for several weeks at a time without having to return for more supplies. This, he hoped, would greatly help Eighth Army's attempts to counterattack at Alamein.

After final briefings with Eighth Army HQ in Alexandria, they finally set off into the desert, led once again by the LRDG. The only feasible means of avoiding the southern flank of the Axis line was to drop down into the Qattara Depression. It was hard not to be impressed by the massive chasm of the Depression. As they hugged its northern lip, Carol Mather gazed into its hazy expanse. "The bottom of the Depression could not be seen," he noted at the time, "only a descending series of cliffs and boulders dropping sharply until their outline was lost in a shimmer of pink."[181] No wonder it was considered impassable, and the lorries that held much of their supplies soon became bogged down in the soft sand. The only option was to send much of their kit back to Kabrit. Thereafter, their progress was swift. On the third day, they emerged from the Depression and headed north, weaving their way through flat-topped hills until they reached the Qara-Matruh track that ran up to the coast. With evening upon them, they suddenly spotted a lone figure on the crest of a rise, silhouetted against the dying sun. They had made their next appointment with the LRDG.

Carol Mather, for one, was excited to be a part of this latest expedition. It might not have been in the Arctic, but he was discovering the desert was still a fascinating place in which to travel. "There was something very special about the desert," he says. "It was exhilarating, really." And, he thought, rather like being at sea, navigating over such a wide and featureless expanse. "The difference between the battle raging in the north and what we were doing was quite marked because the north had been tremendously traveled over, churned up, there were flies and dead bodies," he says. "It was pretty unpleasant really, but the south was pristine, untouched, in some places never traveled over before."

Elsewhere in the desert, things were continuing to look up. 3 July had been another bad day for Rommel. The 90th Light and Afrika Korps were still held at bay, while in the south, the New Zealanders had fought with the tenacity and energy that Brigadier Kippenberger had promised Gott, completely destroying the Italian Ariete Division's artillery. After three days of flinging his exhausted and overstretched forces at the Alamein positions, Rommel was forced to call off the attack, his dreams in ruins. His divisions were now operating at no more than 1,500 men each, a mere tenth of their full strength. He himself had spent the battle at the front line, as was his way, "living in a car or a hole in the ground." Even he was beginning to feel the strain of nearly six weeks of constant fighting. "Things are not going as I should like them," he wrote to his wife. "Resistance is too great and our strength exhausted. However, I still hope to find a way to achieve our goal. I'm rather tired and fagged out."[182]

Rommel had taken the opportunist's gamble and failed. But in the end, the deciding factor—more than any other—had less to do with the men on the ground than the comparative performances of the Axis and Allied air forces. Rommel, for all his inspirational and daring leadership, had failed to appreciate the importance of air support for such a strike, nor had he realized how effectively the RAF was still operating. He had allowed his ground forces to outrun his air forces: the Eighth Army had been almost unscathed by either the Luftwaffe or Regia Aeronautica (in whom von Waldau had little faith), while the RAF had not only covered their retreat but had continually pounded the advancing panzer army. "The enemy air force is bothering us a lot," a German soldier had noted in his diary on 4 July. "From five until eleven o'clock it was over us more than five or six times—the least of the bombings we had. Night and day it seems to go on without interruption, and there's not a moment's peace. We are becoming like potatoes—always underground."[183]

On 26 June, Rommel had begun to realize his error of judgment when he ordered Italian motor transport and fuel to be handed over to the Luftwaffe, but by then it was too late. Eighth Army, with the umbrella of the RAF, had been able to make good its escape. As Mary explained later, "We learnt that a well-organised retreat enables an air force to fall back upon great strength."[184] Those on the ground were aware of this. As Albert Martin points out, "the RAF's total control of the air lifted morale greatly." Round-the-clock bomber operations continued "with the regularity of seaside excursion trains in August."[185] Bill Eadie also felt his spirits rise every time he saw them fly over. He had been on the receiving end of air attacks countless times: he knew the effect continual bombardment would be having on the enemy. On 3 July, for example, the DAF flew more than 1,000 sorties. In contrast, the Luftwaffe managed just 203, and this was with forward units now based at Fuka, some forty miles west of Alamein. Most of these sorties were by German fighters and dive-bombers. British fighters did occasionally find themselves engaging their German counterparts: Billy Drake shot down another Me 109 on 2 July—it dropped out of the sky with glycol (radiator coolant) streaming its white smoke behind. That day, 112 Squadron had carried out eleven bomber escorts in which they had dropped their own bomb loads as well. On 3 July, they flew another twelve escorts and twenty-one bombing raids of their own. The same day, almost at dusk, No.1 South African Squadron in their Hurricanes attacked what was becoming known as a "Stuka party"—thirteen out of fifteen of these increasingly helpless aircraft were shot down.

On 4 July, Johnnie Fairbairn added to the mounting score of enemy aircraft destroyed when he shot down his first enemy aircraft—a 109, no less, blasting off its tail and watching it plummet to the ground. "I had been blooded at last," he noted, "and experienced a surge of ecstatic joy as I sang my way back to base." He had passed the crucial "three-week" test, after which odds of survival for fighter pilots dramatically increased. And as the shock of the new began to wear off, he noticed a change had come over him. "I was gradually losing the feeling of fear," he noticed. "My self-confidence increased as I gradually mastered the fundamental rules and techniques of combat."[186]

This crucial use of air support, as devised by Mary Coningham and maintained by Tommy Elmhirst's brilliant support system, was one of the very few areas where the British had tactical and strategic advantage over the Germans. Britain had much reason to thank Mary and the men of the Desert Air Force.

Their achievements are all the more impressive considering the equipment and conditions in which they were operating. By mid-July, most of the fighter squadrons were operating at half-strength: 73 Squadron had just six serviceable Hurricanes. Since the opening of the Gazala battle, they had lost 202 fighter aircraft. Nine squadrons existed in name only, having no serviceable aircraft at all. The change of policy over the supply of US aircraft (as agreed by Portal and Arnold in June) was causing Coningham and Tedder considerable anxiety, but not only was there a shortage of aircraft, most of those available were outclassed entirely by those of the Axis. There were still too many obsolete Hurricanes and Tomahawks (an early version of the P-40), but even the Italian Macchi 202 was faster and had greater range than the improved P-40 Kittyhawk.

What was needed, as Mary Coningham and, in turn, Tedder never failed to remind the chief of Air Staff back in London, were Spitfires. In May, these aircraft had soon proved their enormous worth when they secured a major victory above the skies of Malta. Having struggled for survival with obsolete Hurricanes, a large number of Spitfires had arrived, and within a month, the RAF had secured air superiority over the island. They would never lose it again. Clearly, the lessons were there to be learned, but the Air Ministry in London chose to ignore them, demonstrating extraordinary short-sightedness. The Spitfire, in all its variants, was the one piece of British kit that was the equal to anything the Axis had. During the retreat to Alamein, Coningham had just twenty-one Spitfires that were serviceable and only six available on the battlefront. On the one front where British forces were actively fighting the combined forces of Germany and Italy and trying to stave off a major disaster, this paltry number was the best that could be provided for them, while at home, Fighter Command could field over eight hundred on any given day. "The Squadrons, I think, are doing marvellously with their Hurricanes and Kittyhawks," wrote Tedder in a letter to Portal in July, "but the basic fact remains that owing to inferior performance they rarely if ever have the initiative . . . Inferiority in performance is an incessant handicap in every way."[187]

Furthermore, Mary Coningham was getting little help from the Army Command, even though the DAF's efforts were almost entirely in support of the ground forces. The lack of information passed on to Air HQ was understandable during the confusion of the retreat, but Mary's heart sank when he realized the Auk had set up the combined Army and Air HQ half an hour's drive from the nearest airfield. Despite the use of a captured Feisler Storch (a highly agile reconnaissance aircraft), with which he was able to visit his wings and squadrons, it soon became clear that the situation was far from ideal. As Tommy Elmhirst recalled, "Mary decided that we were out on a limb: no close touch with the Army, no airstrip, poor communications with our wings and squadrons and with AHQ in Cairo and, almost worst of all, an unpleasant camp site in the open flat desert with millions of flies."[188] So they moved: close to the sea at Burg el Arab and to the main road with water and telephone links to Cairo, Army HQ and the wings and squadrons. But even now that the line had stabilized, there was little information about enemy dispositions being offered by the army. "We still lack Army co-operation to a quite deplorable extent," Tedder wrote to Portal on 12 July. "Coningham has had to ram air support down their throats and in order to get the necessary information to give to effective support has had to rely almost entirely on his own sources of information."[189] These sources of information meant squadrons such as Billy Drake's carrying out daily reconnaissance flights—"Tac/R's"—in addition to their escort and ground attack duties.

Nevertheless, a great change in fortunes had occurred: with the Axis suddenly on the defensive, British prospects were looking up. Rommel's front line was now 1,400 miles away from Tripoli, his principle logistical base, with the ports in between being pounded daily by the RAF and Americans and with his supply lines across the Mediterranean also under relentless attack. In contrast, the Auk was a mere hop and skip away from his supply base. Cecil Beaton may have been heading home, but it was mostly one-way traffic into Egypt, as more and more troops poured in to the Middle East. Again, the Americans were partly responsible. Because of the arrival of US troops in the UK, more British soldiers could be released from Home Defence. The 8th Armoured and 44th Infantry Divisions were both now on their way from the United Kingdom. From around the world, other imperial troops were answering the call as so many had done already: Men like Petrus Dhlamini, who had reached Egypt in June.

Petrus had not been sent to the front straight away, and so had avoided the fate of many of his fellow South Africans at Tobruk. In fact, since arriving at Port Suez, he had been training at camps in the Delta—not with rifles or machine guns or artillery, but just drill and more drill, because as a black South African, Petrus was allowed to serve in uniform but not to bear arms.

Petrus was a Zulu, born in Petratief in the Transvaal, the son of Chief Nyabela. His father had four wives, although Petrus was the son of the first. As chief, Nyabela also had a number of head men reporting to him; theirs was an agrarian life, so these men acted rather like tenant farmers, tending cattle and growing crops, but under the instructions of the chief. Home was a mud hut, and they still wore traditional Zulu clothes and sandals: by the 1920s, little had changed among the Zulu tribes since the war against the British some fifty years before. Petrus had no schooling as such. Rather, he was given guidance—about how to look after himself, to respect women, and "not to force ourselves on them." And as soon as he was old enough, he was expected to look after the stock, and plough with the oxen. It was a happy childhood. Once a year there would always be a big feast, and in between a number of weddings to celebrate. These were great events: a beast would be slaughtered and the entire community would come together to eat, drink, dance and sing.

But life for Petrus and his community was becoming increasingly hard. "We were being oppressed by the Afrikaan farmers of the bush," says Petrus, "and being told to move on to new lands." Furthermore, with four wives, Nyabela had a lot of children to keep; as Petrus became a man, he was encouraged to leave and find work elsewhere. He went to Amelo and took a job in a coal mine.

Shortly after, war broke out, but it wasn't until November 1941, when he lost his job in the mine, that Petrus decided to join the army. He was one of some 123,000 non-whites who volunteered. Employment was one incentive, "but the main reason," he says, "was because I wanted to fight and defend my country and king." There was certainly little antipathy for the British. "They were different from the cruel Boers," explains Petrus. He was not alone in this view. Despite the comparatively recent Zulu War of 1879, most Zulus had come to accept British authority. Posters were pasted around their communities with a call to arms written by their chiefs. "We are truly wed to our Government under the British Empire," ran Chief Mathole Buthelezi's appeal, "the forces of which subdued our former King Cetshwayo, who was supported by my grandfather, Mnyaman. We do not woo any other." Then at the end came the crux of the matter: "If we now do our best in the work for which we are called perhaps our Government will in future view us from a different angle as regards our welfare in this country."[190]

Only a handful of colored and black troops found themselves serving in the front line. Most blacks—and "coloreds," as South African Asians were labeled—were employed in factories and motor transport companies. A number of blacks also made up the native military corps, designed to guard vital installations around the country. These troops *were* armed, but not with rifles or guns. Extraordinary though it may seem now, they were given assegai—their native spears.

Petrus, however, was sent to North Africa. Like Gurkha Nainabadahur Pun, or Maori Maike Parkinson, Petrus had never seen the sea before sailing away to war on 1 June, 1942. But unlike Maike or Nainabadahur, Petrus did not view the war in terms of adventure or excitement. "I was frightened," he says simply. To begin with, even the waves scared him. "They made me nervous," he says. "I couldn't stop vomiting and it was very hot."

But he survived the journey and by the beginning of July, the training and endless drill was over. Back in South Africa, he'd been taught to drive a truck, so Petrus was posted to join the prestigious Regiment President Steyn as a much-needed driver.

General Tuker's 4th Indian Division was still scattered between the Delta and Cyprus, but the 5th Indian Division was brought up to strength, and General Morshead's 9th Australian Division was also finally brought down from Syria. On 4 July, Joe Madeley and 2/13th Battalion reached Alexandria. Their arrival was supposed to be a secret, but a number of Egyptian kids ran up to them shouting, "Hello Aussie." "I think they recognized our ruddy brown boots," says Joe. They remained near Alexandria for a week, until rumors started circulating that they were about to move. "Rumors came from the lavatory seat," says Joe. "You'd be sitting side by side doing your business and would pick up all sorts of information." Some would start false rumors, but in this case, it was true. The following day, Sunday, 12 July, they moved up to within ten miles of the front. That night, Joe heard the naval guns off shore, pounding enemy positions, and saw flashes and flares streak across the sky. He was also impressed by the numbers of bombers and fighters flying over all day. "It gave us a great lift," he says, echoing the feelings of Albert Martin and Bill Eadie. "We'd all shout, 'You beauty!' at them." His battalion were now digging as best they could into the hard, rocky ground. He'd forgotten how hot it could be in the summer in the desert. Swarms of flies hindered everything they did, attracted by their sweat and their rations. It was dusty too, but at least the rumors from the front were good.

In fact, Eighth Army had gone on the offensive almost as soon as Rommel had called off his own. The Auk initially hoped to swing XIII Corps in the south around onto the Axis rear, but Gott showed little enthusiasm for this and the outcome was a number of raids by mobile columns with little result, although the 7th Motor Brigade did manage to reach the Luftwaffe airfields at Fuka on 7 July and bombarded them for half an hour before slipping away again. This they did without Albert Martin: two companies of the 2nd Rifle Brigade, including his own S Company, had been sent back to Mena Camp outside Cairo for refit. "Cheers!" noted Albert in his diary. "Everyone is smiling." The trip back across the desert was laborious—Albert's truck broke down several times—but eventually they made it. After six long weeks of battle, they looked dreadful: socks rolled down, boots scuffed and covered in dust, bandages around their knees covering up the ever-present desert sores, and shirts bleached and sweat-stained. Most had several days' stubble and red watery eyes, and "rounded off by a mop of hair that no comb ever devised could penetrate."[191] They were told they would only be there a few days and that Cairo was out of bounds, but the order was treated with complete indifference. Albert, along with his mates Ernie, John, and Pat, soon made their way into town. Newly promoted to sergeant, Albert had his photo taken with his three stripes, and then went to see his Lebanese girlfriend, Rosemary, whom he had met during his leave in the city, way back in March. His friends had given him a ribbing, assuring him she would no longer be interested, but to his relief she was overjoyed at seeing him again and agreed to meet him and his friends later at the Americano Bar. They were still doubting her existence when she duly arrived. "I must say, I plied on the kiss and hug," admitted Albert, "just to rub it in with my audience." Later, as they walked alone in Ezbekia Gardens he couldn't believe that just a few days before, he'd been in the desert fighting a bloody battle. "Neither could I accept that in another week this evening could belong to a fantasy world."[192]

David Stirling's men of the L Detachment SAS were now 150 miles behind enemy lines, and some 60 miles south of the coast. From their position, the desert climbed gradually westward to a series of ridges, behind which they would be able to conceal their vehicles. This area was to be their base in the desert for the next month.

On 6 July, Stirling gathered his men around him and explained the plan. They would be carrying out a series of raids in support of the Eighth

Army's counter-offensive at Alamein. These were to be coordinated, with their bombs set to explode around 1 AM on the morning of 8 July. Four patrols would travel together toward the Fuka-Bagush area, then two would attack Fuka, another landing on the ground nearby; and the fourth would raid Bagush. The remaining two patrols would raid Sidi Barrani and El Daba airfields.

Both Stephen and Carol were part of this latter patrol, under Captain George Jellicoe, son of the First World War admiral and another former member of the Ski Battalion and Layforce. Just as they were about to leave, a radio message from Eighth Army HQ told them the counterattack had begun and that under no circumstances were the El Daba airfields to be attacked; instead they were told to attack any enemy traffic traveling along the coast road between Fuka and Galal. They finally got going at around noon on 7 July, their patrol setting off in three jeeps. The aim was to reach the great escarpment that dropped down to the coast at sunset. During the afternoon they were astonished to see a column trundling across the desert ahead of them. Straining through binoculars they identified several twenty-five-pounders, but knowing the Germans were using captured British equipment decided it would be unwise to approach. It was, in fact, a Jock Column of the 7th Motor Brigade—but no one at Eighth Army HQ had thought to warn them. Although now delayed, they still managed to cross the railway and reach the coast road under cover of darkness. But no vehicles came their way. The road was quiet, revealing only one stationary lorry and capturing a handful of German prisoners. Even so, it was a disappointing night's work.

Some of the other patrols had fared better, however. Around thirty or forty vehicles and over thirty enemy aircraft had been destroyed, but Stirling was furious to discover from the captured Germans that El Daba was still the Luftwaffe's main base. The mixup of intelligence is hard to understand. Admittedly, confusion had been caused by the retreat, but by the end of the first week of July, the order not to attack El Daba seems extraordinary. No wonder David Stirling felt a major opportunity to help Eighth Army had been missed.

CHAPTER 9

And Thrust:
July 1942, Part II

IN WASHINGTON, ABC had moved out of the hotel assigned to him. "Instead, we took a flat, or I should say an 'apartment.'"[193] In London, Eisenhower had been given VIP rooms at Claridges, one of London's smartest hotels. He felt uncomfortable there, as ABC had been in his hotel, and wanted a place out of town where they would not be distracted from the job in hand. "In the meantime," wrote his naval aide, Harry Butch, "we are operating in the old apartment building, called 'flats,' at 20 Grosvenor Square."[194]

Differing uses of the English language was the least of Ike's worries during those first weeks in London. He was unused to the formality and rigors of British etiquette. At Admiral Lord Louis Mountbatten's country estate "somewhere south of London," he was sneered at by a servant for the simplicity of his overnight bag; at a formal welcome to the Washington Club, Butch could tell that "under [Ike's] outward pleasantness the 'la-de-dah' of the occasion was getting under his skin." There were other dinners with the ambassador, meetings with the king and overnight visits to Chequers, discussions with Brooke and the other chiefs of staff, trips to watch field exercises. When invited to a dinner given by the Lord Mayor of London, Ike made his excuses: from then on, he told Butch, he would only go to engagements that were strictly necessary, and then added, "I sure want to get the hell out of London."[195]

The task of planning had to fit around the essential engagements. He himself expected to work seven days a week, and demanded the same of his staff. He also tended to work late and did not like any of his staff to leave before him. "We're here to fight," he told them, "not to be wined and dined."[196] Like Marshall, Ike wanted his men to solve their own problems rather than pass the buck, and warned them that defeatism and pessimism of any kind would not be tolerated. He encouraged informality, was friendly and easygoing; but he was also tough and unafraid to act with ruthlessness if he felt it necessary.

At the Washington Club reception, Ike had been filmed, and Butch had wondered how he would come across when the footage was shown on newsreels. Very well, was the answer. As Butch was all too aware, the Eisenhower PR machine had to be faultless in this new media age. Robert Capa was brought in to photograph him in color and Butch encouraged the commanding general to hold regular press conferences. It quickly paid off. Ike may have been unused to the public glare, but his wide grin and charm were definitely scoring points with the British and Americans alike. Butch ended his diary entry on 9 July with two points: "Let this go down as a note," he wrote. "'Singleness of purpose'—this is the phrase I have heard about Ike on many sides during my first week in London." The second point was just as valid: "General Eisenhower has reached these isles at a moment when the morale of the British is at its extreme low. Their sons and husbands and brothers and fathers were at Tobruk. How or whether they have come through, these proud wives, mothers, and sisters do not know."[197] Building up that morale once more and maintaining Anglo-US unity was to be essential.

On 8 July, however, Ike received his first major blow. Conversations with Brooke, Ismay, and Portal made it clear that they no longer supported SLEDGEHAMMER. During a formal conference two days later—the day he was promoted to a three-star Lieutenant-General—this was confirmed. The diversion of Allied shipping and the lack of suitable landing craft were cited, the latter making it impossible to establish a footing on European soil. Failure would have disastrous knock-on effects for the proposed invasion of Europe the following year. Instead, they suggested keeping up the bombing raids and mounting a series of commando-style raids. Ike explained all of this in a letter to Marshall. He also made it clear that he still believed SLEDGEHAMMER was preferable to an invasion of Africa. "I do not, repeat, *not* believe that British rejection of SLEDGE-HAMMER arises from any lack of desire to take the offensive," he concluded, "but from deep conviction that it is not feasible as a permanent invasion."[198]

Back in the desert, Auchinleck was still hoping to break the Axis line. Joe Madeley's 2/13th Battalion may not have been in the front line, but most of the 9th Australian Division were, and so another attack, this time by XXX Corps in the north, was planned for 10 July. Meanwhile Rommel, also now reinforced with the German 164th Light Division and with more on the way, was preparing to attack through the New Zealand positions. An Ultra decrypt warned Auchinleck of this and so the Kaponga Box was abandoned and the New Zealanders moved north toward the Ruweisat Ridge.

In contrast, Rommel's intelligence had been dealt a blow when, in June, Colonel Fellers' leaks were discovered and he was hastily sent back to the US. Unaware that the New Zealanders had moved, Rommel attacked the empty box on 9 July and then tried to push on eastward in an effort to get around Eighth Army's southern flank.

The guns from the north heralding the start of the Auk's new attack ensured Rommel called off this drive and hurriedly sent his forces northward too. The Aussies and South Africans had completely overrun the Italian Sabratha Division and only a scratch force of panzers and the newly arrived 164th Light managed to stop the entire Axis northern front from collapsing. Even so, this was a particular blow for Rommel because among the prisoners taken by the Aussies was Captain Alfred Seebohm and his 621st Radio Intercept Company. Rommel was furious; he had now lost another vital source of intelligence. When no radio intercepts arrived, he asked to be shown on the map where Seebohm's company was situated. As soon as he saw that it was near Tel El Eisa, where the Aussies had attacked, he said angrily, "Then it is *futsch*—lost!"[199]

The SAS had been planning more raids. David Stirling was particularly anxious to make up for the missed chance at El Daba, although he wanted to have another go at the landing grounds at Fuka as well. On 11 July, Paddy Mayne's party headed for Fuka and managed to destroy around twenty aircraft at one of the landing grounds there, but El Daba was to prove something of a jinx. Late afternoon on 12 July, George Jellicoe's detachment was once again approaching the great escarpment, and although the desert plateau was uncomfortably exposed, they were just heading for the cover of a patch of camel scrub, when Stephen Hastings spotted the menacing shapes of three fighter aircraft dropping toward the edge of the escarpment. "We stopped," noted Stephen, "hoping against hope. Hope failed. The planes roared over us in triumph, wheeled and came in to attack." They had time to run a few yards but by the time the planes had used all their ammunition and had sped off again, both Stephen and Carol's jeeps were burning fiercely. George Jellicoe had hidden his vehicle in a small crevice, and although hit, it still appeared to be functioning. "His foresight ensured our escape if not our lives," says Stephen. Predictably, more aircraft soon appeared, but by this time they had hidden themselves in the camel thorn and with the light now fading, the aircraft were left circling without ever spotting their quarry.

Despite their escape, their situation was deeply perilous. Enemy patrols would almost certainly be sent out the following morning and the surviving jeep was in a bad state. There were several bullet holes in the radiator, and the tires were slashed. Plugging the hole in the radiator was essential if they were to get anywhere at all. They soon agreed that their best chance of doing so was to use a lump of plastic explosive. This was hardly ideal, however, and there were a few anxious moments when they started the engine.

Having decided the jeep seemed unlikely to explode, nine of them crammed into the limping vehicle and set off. There was no water in the radiator, so they were forced to take turns to urinate into it to keep it going. Each man's effort lasted only about fifteen minutes, so they would then have to stop, turn it to the wind to cool it down, and another person would step forward to do the honors. "It worked," wrote Carol, "but it smelled like a chicken coop!"[200] The rendezvous was seventy miles away, but they managed to get within a few miles before the jeep finally died on them. Ingenuity and a good dose of luck had saved them.

The raiders had been away from Kabrit for over two weeks and since they'd sent back much of their supplies on the journey out, food and ammunition were now growing low. Furthermore, eight vehicles had been destroyed or put out of action. With this in mind, Stirling decided they would have to temporarily halt operations. A small holding force would remain at their base under the escarpment while he and most of the men went back to get more equipment. Time, though, was of the essence: should Eighth Army break through and advance west, they would also need to be up and running without delay.

Left behind in charge of the British contingent were Stephen Hastings and Carol Mather, and the SAS doctor, Malcolm Pleydell, although there was also a party of Free French attached to the SAS and an LRDG patrol, who were camping a couple of miles to the north. For Carol and Stephen, waiting in their caves was an eerie experience. "We'd already been shot up," explains Stephen, "and had been lucky to get away with it." Neither ever discussed the possibility of their being left stranded there forever, but it certainly crossed their minds. Enemy aircraft also flew over quite regularly, and they worried they would be spotted even though they had hidden themselves well. Netting had been stretched out over the entrance like a canopy and sprinkled with vetch and camel thorn, while the remaining vehicles had been driven down the crevices made from dry water courses that ran off the flat plateau above the escarpment, and carefully netted and camouflaged.

They agreed that movement during the day should be avoided, although a sentry was always on watch on the top of the escarpment from where it was possible to get a good all-round view of the surrounding desert. "We would search round and round with our glasses over the barren landscape," wrote Carol, "staring for minutes on end at dust clouds and vehicles which seemed to be making our way, only to disperse in mirages."[201] Various warning sounds were devised, although they soon gave up the alarm whistle—"we found it had too shattering an effect on our nerves"—and so instead the sentry would quietly make his way down and inform them about what he had seen. Then, wrote Carol, "we would consider the matter placidly and take whatever steps we considered necessary, which usually involved killing a few more flies and telling the sentry not to disturb us again unless he could prove the camp was being attacked by Germans."[202]

In their cave, there was nothing to do but sit and wait, and then wait some more. The flies were terrible, so was the heat. They were now burned black, filthy, and bearded. "We were a wild-looking lot," Stephen admitted.[203] Food and water were of limited supply, although the shortage of water was the major concern. On any expedition, water had to be brought with them—even if they came across a bir with local water, it was often brackish and undrinkable. Consequently, each man was always rationed to one bottle per person per day for all purposes. Carol Mather found this quite manageable. "You got used to it, actually," he says. "There's an old army saying, 'never drink on a march,' and in fact, if you were on your feet, you didn't think about it too much. Disciplining oneself was much harder, however, when twiddling thumbs all day with nothing to do."

Dawn and dusk were eagerly awaited: at these two moments it was neither too hot nor cold and there were no flies. Meals were then prepared over petrol tins filled with fuel-soaked sand. There was not much, but enough to get by. They had also learned to bury their water bottles at night. "The water was near iced in the morning," noted Stephen, "and as one always woke up thirsty this was a good moment."[204]

Both Carol and Stephen were glad of each other's company. They barely knew each other beforehand, but during those ten long days became lifelong friends. They shared the tattered books they'd brought with them, endlessly discussed why so many of the rocks in their cave contained the fossils of seashells, and talked about how they would spend their first day back in Cairo. This "comfort day" was refined many times, but included a shave and a Turkish bath, plenty of long iced drinks, exotic meals, and a film in an air-cooled cinema. They also agreed that it should be rounded off with a visit to a club where they would be entranced by beautiful belly dancers.

Around four o'clock in the afternoon on the eighth day, the sentry came down to their cave and reported vehicles approaching from the east. Stephen and Carol scrambled to the top of the escarpment and peered through their binoculars. A constantly changing mirage appeared to be coming toward them, but then seemed to shrink and stop. "Then suddenly they emerged from the mirage," wrote Stephen, "quite close and recognizable—jeeps and several 30 cwt trucks." David Stirling and the rest of L Detachment were back.

Up near the coast, Bill Eadie was busier than ever, bringing supplies up to the various units of the 2nd South African Infantry Brigade. Masses of tanks were moving up through their lines, heading for the battle. At Alamein station he came across large number of Aussies as well as several different South African regiments, but later could not find the Natal Mounted Rifles, who had moved twice during the night. Aircraft continued to zoom overhead, even two Me109s, who streaked over his head "no higher than twenty feet—did not fire a shot, thank heavens." He also heard that Rommel was "right in front of us"—which was true. "I am told that he always keeps tanks and an aeroplane at his HQ," noted Bill. "Really, he must be a grand leader right up with his men in the line."

Fifteen miles behind the British Lines, the Auk was planning yet another battering ram at the enemy. Realizing that most of Rommel's forces were in the north, he decided to launch a strike at the Italians in the center of the Axis line. The plan was for the 5th Indian and the New Zealanders to launch a silent night attack, but with coordinated artillery and 2nd and 22nd Armoured Brigades in support. This included Sam Bradshaw's 6 RTR, which had now merged with 1 RTR as both had become so depleted that neither could make even half a regiment on their own. They were some six miles farther south on Alam Nayil.

Watching this activity was journalist Alan Moorehead. "It was hot and there was no shade," he wrote. "Sitting there in the sun, smoking and drinking a mug of tea and occasionally looking through binoculars, you felt as though you were sitting in a grandstand waiting for a cup-tie to begin."[205] In the event, the First Battle of Ruweisat, as it became known, opened under cover of darkness on the night of 14 July, and began well with the Indian and New Zealand infantry overrunning two Italian Divisions. But this early success was short-lived. In the dark, the New Zealanders bypassed a leaguer of German panzers as well as a few German infantry positions. As daylight spread over the gentle stony slopes of the Ruweisat Ridge, the German tanks attacked the unprotected New Zealanders in the rear, capturing 350 men in the process. 2nd Armoured Brigade tried to help, but got bogged down in a minefield. 22nd Armoured also moved up during the day, but likewise stumbled into Italian minefields; and in any case, they were too late to help the New Zealanders. It didn't stop Sam Bradshaw and the rest of B Squadron making vain efforts to find gaps through the mines, even if it was to little avail.

Meanwhile, Rommel was responding with his usual élan, scraping together detachments of 21st Panzer, 90th Light, and several other units and ordering them to counterattack along with 15th Panzer. This they did that same afternoon, emerging through the dust and smoke with the sun behind them, and straight into the New Zealanders. By now short of ammunition and with no artillery support, the Kiwis' position was hopeless. Another 380 were captured, including Captain Charles Upham, winner of two Victorian Crosses. The panzers stormed onward, but were eventually stopped by the combined efforts of 22nd Armoured. At the end of the day, 6 RTR had knocked out one Italian tank and captured two lorries, but had lost or damaged several of their own tanks while trying to get through the mines. Although Rommel made two more attacks the following day, these were held off. By the evening, the battle had run its course.

The New Zealanders had 1,400 casualties during the battle, but for little gain. Replacements were arriving, however, including the thirty Maori who had been on guard duty in the Delta since their arrival the previous winter. They were posted to 28th Battalion's C Company—or Ngati Porou, mostly men from the northeast of the North Island; one of these was little Maiki Parkinson.

They joined the battalion as the Battle of Ruweisat was raging, but the Maori had been placed in reserve a couple of days before, after their battalion commander, Colonel Love, and another senior officer, had been killed by an enemy airburst. The Maori had seen this as a terrible omen for the forthcoming battle—so it was just as well they were kept out of the thick of it. Even so, the Maori were not entirely out of the firing line. As Maiki and the other replacements bumped across the desert in a brand-new truck, they could hear the noise of battle getting ever closer. "We couldn't believe it," says Maiki. "These big bastards were firing away, shells whistling over our heads. Jesus, you never forget that sound once you've heard it. Such a strange whistling, whining noise. It was terrible."

As they arrived late in the afternoon, the Maori were coming under fire from the advancing enemy. No sooner had Maiki and the other replacements stepped down from their new truck than it was obliterated by a direct hit. Everyone was trying to take cover as the enemy shells began falling, and then British tanks started to rumble through. Maiki was frantically trying to dig in as ordered, but the rock was so hard his spade was bending. It had been quite an introduction to the front line, but the following morning they came under attack again, and this time by Stukas. This was another first for Maiki, as was the sight of a number of dead bodies later in the day. He and a couple of others had been picked to form a makeshift burial party. The dead were Italians, casualties of earlier fighting. "It was a shock," admits Maiki. "They were bloated from lying in the sun and the smell—Jesus, it was awful. I'd smelled dead cows and sheep, but this . . . you've never smelled anything like it." They began by shoveling sand over them, but it just ran off their chests. Then Maiki noticed a small lee, so they got a ground sheet, and trying to hold their breath, put the dead onto it and carried them over to the lee and then covered them in sand—hardly the best grave in the world but it would have to do.

On 20 July, three weeks after arriving in expectation of a triumphant march into Cairo, Mussolini returned to Italy. The following day, the panzer army reported to the OKW that since the beginning of July, the Italians had lost the equivalent of four divisions, while the Afrika Korps had forty-two tanks left and the Italians around fifty. Furthermore, the RAF still had the upper hand and were destroying, on average, around thirty vehicles a day. Even so, there was a heavy price to pay for this sustained air assault. Mary Coningham was losing plenty of aircraft, especially fighters. Joe Madeley watched one Hurricane shot out of the sky by a Me 109 on 20 July. "Plane smashed to bits, also pilot," he noted in his diary. The 2/13th Battalion were by now readying themselves to go up to the front. After a few days' lull, the Auk was preparing his third attack of the month, again along the Ruweisat Ridge, but this time aiming at the German armor, still the backbone of the panzer army. And once again, it was the 5th Indian Division and the New Zealanders who were to take the brunt of the attack.

The idea was for another nighttime infantry assault, supported by artillery. Once gaps had been made in the minefields, the newly arrived 23rd Armoured Brigade would follow through at dawn. As darkness fell on 21 July, the Australians of 2/13 Battalion were taken in lorries up to their start point. Clambering out, they waited for the artillery to open up, then began their advance. Their attack looked at first to be entirely successful as they gained all their objectives. But the minefield gaps were neither wide nor clear enough; by first light, the armor was struggling to make much headway and without their support, the Aussie infantry was unable to hold off an enemy counterattack and was pushed back. Auchinleck may have been a far more experienced battlefield commander than Ritchie, but basic tactical mistakes were still being made. There was still no proper, coordinated use of all-arms. As had been shown time and again during the preceding fortnight, infantry could not defeat armor single-handedly. Later, 23rd Armored Brigade made an old-fashioned cavalry charge without either artillery or infantry support and were, true to form, blown to pieces by enemy mines and the panzer army's defensive screen. They lost eighty-seven tanks. Armoured tactics had not progressed one inch, either in North Africa or back home in Britain.

In the north, the Australians were also attacking, trying to exploit the lack of German armor in the area. The 20th Australian Infantry Brigade—which included Joe Madeley's 2/13th Battalion—had been detached and placed behind the Indians on the Ruweisat Ridge during the First Battle of Ruweisat, but was now being sent into action behind the 24th Aussie Brigade, six miles west of Alamein Station. By afternoon, the Aussies had gained the upper hand, but for Joe and his mates it was a "pretty warm reception" after a four-mile hike to their positions, and after seven months out of battle. Holding defensive positions in support of the main attack, they found themselves under heavy shell fire and with shrapnel zipping all around them. At seven o'clock, the Australians attacked again. "All hell broke loose," noted Joe, as the Aussies, along with British tanks of 50 RTR, made their attack. Yet again, armor and infantry failed to work together as planned; as night fell, the tanks withdrew, but minus twenty-three of their Valentines, which lay charred and smouldering on the battlefield.

That night, Joe and his platoon were sent out wiring. He saw several of 50 RTR's tank blow up on mines as they continued to struggle to get back to their lines. When he returned to his slit trench just after two in the morning, the wounded from the day's fighting were also still crawling back to their positions. By the following day, the fighting had once again petered out. Some of the men in Joe's platoon went scrounging in the Germans' old positions. "We liked their tins of stew," Joe explains. They were also looking for ammunition for their captured Spandau, a rapid-firing German light machine gun that was much envied by the Eighth Army men.

Joe and his mates were fortunate not to come under fire from German snipers as they scavenged. Alan Moorehead, trying to follow events from behind the line, met a wounded Australian captain who told him, "They lurk behind stones and lie absolutely still. Then as soon as one of our men pokes up his head, dash, whack."[206]

Perhaps overconfidently, Alan had been taking himself closer and closer to the action. During the Second Ruweisat he drove up and inspected a burned-out German tank on the most western high point of the ridge, dangerously close to the action. "Its crew is dead," he wrote. "The turret and gun were lifted bodily from the chassis by a British shell and dumped in the sand." But at least for Alan and the other journalists, there was the daily respite of their camp, fifteen miles behind the lines and close to the sea. A camp bed, food, and enough water to shave every morning without worry eased the strain of battle. And on their arrival back at camp after a day dodging shells and traveling the length of the front line, they unfailingly stripped naked and dived "straight off the world's most perfect beach into the world's most perfect sea." For the men at the front, however, there could be no such relaxation. Not yet, at any rate. The Auk was determined to break Rommel. Next time, he was sure he could do it.

* * *

Less than a week after Eisenhower had warned Marshall of the British stand against SLEDGEHAMMER, the American chief of staff and a party that included Admiral King and Harry Hopkins, arrived in London. The Americans had taken the news about SLEDGEHAMMER stoically; after all, since the British were to have supplied the bulk of the men and material, so there was little they could do. But it was now imperative a specific strategy was agreed upon once and for all for 1942. Of no small importance were the views of the British and American public, both of whom were clamoring for a second front. On 16 July, Harry Butcher read three American editorials, all of which urged such a move, to help the Russians as much as anything. After the fall of Sevastopol, the destruction of the Soviet Union was expected any moment.

It was this threat that ensured Ike stuck belligerently to SLEDGE-HAMMER. When Marshall asked him to prepare a survey of the existing situation, he turned back to the possible attack on mainland Europe, although in order to make it seem more palatable to the British, he suggested a landing in Normandy rather than the more obvious Pas de Calais, where the Channel was narrowest. "GYMNAST," he stated bluntly, "would have no effect on the 1942 campaign in Russia," and while the chances of establishing up to six divisions somewhere in northern France were no more than "1 in 5," he pointed out that "we should not forget that the prize is to keep 8,000,000 Russians in the war."[207] Moreover, as he told Harry Butcher, it was important that the British and American people believed that something positive was being attempted. "We must not degenerate into a passive and mental attitude," he told his friend.[208]

But SLEDGHAMMER was finished. On 20 July, Churchill had persuaded his chiefs of staff—even Brooke—that an invasion in North Africa was the only viable option in 1942. Two days later, at talks between both parties, a deadlock was reached. The British stuck to their guns: a cross-Channel landing was suicidal and could not be sufficiently large or protracted enough to bring any real help to the Russians. Marshall confessed that he needed to talk to the president for instructions. Roosevelt told them there was no longer any point pressing for a cross-Channel landing and urged his delegation to reach an agreement whereby American troops could be used in land operation against the Axis powers some time that year. Furthermore, Roosevelt had been warming to the North Africa idea since Churchill's talks with him in June; in his brief to Marshall before the London conference, he warned the American team to consider the effects of losing the Middle East and suggested an operation in Morocco and Algeria should be worth their consideration.

At breakfast the following day, Ike was depressed. "Well, I hardly know where to start the day," he told Butch. "I'm right back to December 15." Wednesday 22 July, he added, could well go down as the "blackest in history," especially if Russia was defeated during this latest drive by the Germans.[209]

By now, the die was cast, however. On 24 July, GYMNAST—or Operation TORCH, as Churchill had renamed it—was agreed on in principle, the British contingent refusing to share the view that it would rule out an Allied invasion of mainland Europe the following year. The next morning, the Joint Chiefs thrashed out the basic form such an operation should take. A supreme commander was needed, which Brooke suggested should be American. It was also suggested the operation should be led by US troops. Partly this was a sop to their ally, but principally was because French antipathy to the British was now considerable; they would probably be more amenable to the Americans. This was agreed. Two simultaneous operations were envisaged—one on the west coast of Africa, the other on the northwest coast. Planning would be conducted from London, with the US team of a joint planning staff to hurry to London as soon as possible, because the date suggested for the landings was October—a mere twelve weeks away.

Ike had not been at this final session, but was briefed by Marshall that afternoon while the American chief of staff scrubbed himself in his bath. A detailed plan for TORCH was needed as soon as possible, which would then be presented to the Joint Chiefs for approval. He was backing Ike to command the whole operation, and imagined this would soon be confirmed. In the meantime, Ike was to be given the new title of deputy allied commander in charge of planning for TORCH. He was to get cracking right away.

Spruced and cleaned up, Marshall and the rest of the American party left by plane for Washington, leaving Ike to ponder the prospect of even greater responsibility and the task of preparing a plan for an operation that a few days before Churchill had strenuously opposed. But at least the Prime Minister was happy. He had brushed aside the dissenters at Westminster, Rommel had been halted, and he'd maneuvered not only his own military chiefs, but also the Americans into his way of thinking. The United States might be rich and increasingly powerful, but there was no question of Churchill playing lapdog to the American president in this war. "All was therefore agreed and settled in accordance with my long-conceived ideas," he wrote with satisfaction. "I had enough to be thankful for."[210]

David Stirling had arrived back at the SAS escarpment armed with gifts of rum, cigars, Turkish delight, and tobacco, and twenty brand-new jeeps. As soon as they had been camouflaged and ample rations consumed, their commander outlined his latest plans. During his trip back, he had learned that one of the landing grounds in the Fuka area, Sidi Haneish, or LG12, was in constant use and bursting with enemy aircraft, including a large number of troops carrying Junkers 52s. He wanted to try and destroy every single enemy aircraft there by a massed jeep attack in full moonlight. Sensing that the Axis were getting wise to their small hit-and-run raids, he felt that a large-scale operation at a time when they would not expecting them would ensure complete surprise, and thus success. Eighteen jeeps would be used, two columns of seven led by George Jellicoe and Paddy Mayne, forty yards apart and firing outwards, with Stirling and four other jeeps navigating in the middle. Their task was to identify targets and signal to the two columns by using Very lights. This obviously required practice, so the night before—25 July—they drove into the darkness above the escarpment and carried out a dress rehearsal. Carol Mather, driving at the end of the left-hand column, felt particularly vulnerable as they all opened fire. "My front gun fired across my face and rear gun behind my head," he says, adding, "so it was important to sit very still and not to lean forward or backward."[211]

They were back at camp by three in the morning, but were up again at dawn. There was still much to do. New trucks arrived with more ammunition and supplies. Stephen Hastings watched a group of men busily making up explosive charges "amongst a litter of black adhesive tape, time pencils, fuses, primer cord and heaps of strong-smelling sticks of plastic." Every vehicle had to move from dump to dump collecting loads of ammunition, water and fuel, extra rations, and escape kits. Guns were stripped, cleaned, and tested. Stephen couldn't help wondering what it would be like. He worried about whether the Germans would be well dug in and surrounded by wire, and that before they ever reached the airfield, enemy aircraft would have spotted them. He could remember that last attack all too clearly: the aircraft banking and preparing to attack, and the moments of fear as they roared ever closer. Then the machine guns would open fire, kicking spurts of sand, and followed by a longer burst that slammed into the ground with terrifying proximity.

The party set off at sundown, traveling in no particular formation. After about an hour, the moon was up and they paused to take a bearing. The men stopped to talk in low tones and light cigarettes. Stephen felt the dust settle on him and looked at the surreal desert landscape, and the dark horizon that might have been mountains many miles away or a low ridge just yards ahead. Such was the fickleness of the desert.

There were more stops along the way—they suffered numerous punctures—but after four and a half hours' driving they were drawing close to the airfield, and approaching the final escarpment that overlooked the coastal plain. As they descended, they realized they were crossing a recent battlefield. Stephen noticed the smell first—"the sweet-sour smell of rotting flesh"—then a British truck was spotted and two corpses, "one on his back, arms and legs spread, the other just a hump."[212] Carol Mather saw them too—they all did—and took another swig of rum.

Shortly after, the desert leveled and Stirling stopped again to get everyone in formation and to check their position once more. He was badgering the navigator, saying, "Where the hell are we?" They watched as two Very lights rose ahead of them to their left, briefly glowed, then sank. "We knew we were close," says Stephen, "but we didn't know exactly where it was. And then luckily a German aircraft came in to land and they switched on all the landing lights. We were up on a slight ridge a mile or so away, so were in no doubt about where we had to get to from then on."

They set off, the pace quickening as they approached. Stephen drove into a small trench, but the jeep easily pulled out the other side, although he now had to accelerate hard to catch up. "Then it happened, the flash and crack of a rifle." Moments later, they all opened fire, "First, one tentative burst, then the full ear-splitting cacophony roaring and spitting." Streams of tracer crazily crisscrossed into the darkness. Stephen was aware of figures running ahead of them, some falling, others fading away, then their guns were curiously silent once more. The green Very light from Stirling's jeep shot into the sky and they were through the defenses—there had been no wire as Stephen had feared—and onto the flat, smooth airfield itself, only their engines and the rattle of empty cartridge cases breaking the silence of the night. It was only a brief moment of quiet. A minute later, fire poured from the jeeps once more, a deafening and lethal roar. Stephen was crouching over his steering wheel, desperately trying to concentrate, and then noticed the large shape of a Junkers 52 troop carrier loom up to his right. "The bullets were ripping through the fuselage with a curious swishing sound audible at the same time as the detonation of the guns," he recorded. "The interior of the aircraft glowed red for a second; there was a dull explosion and the whole body burst into flames."[213]

The landing lights had long since been turned off, but the burning Junkers served to dimly light the forms of other aircraft. The smell of cordite and aviation fuel filled the air. Two more Junkers blew as the columns of jeeps continued firing their broadsides.

Stephen's rear gunner spotted two figures lying on their fronts, heads and shoulders slightly raised.

"There's two Jerries," he shouted.

"Well, shoot at them, go on, shoot at them," yelled Stephen.

The machine gun rattled again.

"Did you get them?" Stephen shouted.

"Don't know, sir," came the reply.

They were now abreast of a line of Stukas, with planes bursting into fireballs on both sides. Stephen was particularly pleased to see the stream of tracers zipping through these particularly hated aircraft. He could feel the blast of hot air—many of the men suffered singed hair and eyebrows—but while the flames meant they could now spot aircraft all around the airfield, it also meant the enemy could see them as well. The line of jeeps suddenly halted, and Stephen watched as a man hurriedly leaped out of one and stuck a stick of explosives onto the wing of a large Dornier bomber. They moved forward again and as Stephen's jeep drew alongside the Dornier, it exploded, a wing dropping to the ground and momentarily stunning them in the process. Other aircraft were now exploding as well, but they were beginning to come under fire themselves as an anti-aircraft gun had been turned around and was firing cannon shells toward them. The raiders returned fire, but Stirling's jeep had been hit. Carol Mather halted with the others, but then heard the order, "Switch off!" yelled out. "We were still in the middle of the aerodrome," he wrote, "but there was dead silence." Then Stirling called out again to check how much ammo everyone had left—not much, came the answer.

Stephen's jeep had also been hit. "I felt something hot pass most uncomfortably close beneath my seat," he recorded. "Clang!" Both he and his gunner were covered in oil, and as he tried to wipe his eyes, the jeep swerved and hit a bump, but somehow kept going. The brief delay meant they'd lost the others and they faced an anxious few moments until they caught up.

Meanwhile, Stirling's driver, Johnny Cooper, had jumped out and was assessing the damage: a splinter in the engine block. The jeep was finished, and their rear gunner lay dead in the back. Another jeep picked them up and they set off again for one last drive past of shooting and mayhem. Then they sped off, melting into the night in twos and threes, as planned.

Behind them, the glow of thirty-seven burning aircraft littered the airfield. Many of these were transporters, of vital importance to Rommel in bringing up supplies. The SAS had lost just one man and two jeeps. It was their last operation that month, a month in which this strengthened band of raiders had claimed at least eighty-six aircraft destroyed and around forty vehicles. "Quite apart from the airplane score," adds Carol Mather, "I think creating uncertainty in the mind of the enemy was an important factor." This was certainly true. Moreover, at a time when British successes were few and far between, David Stirling and his men had given the Allies something to cheer about.

* * *

Although the four attacks already launched by Auchinleck at Alamein that July had achieved very little, on the night of 26 July, the C-in-C ordered one last push, again by XXX Corps in the north, reinforced by 1st Armoured Division. The South Africans were to make a gap in the rapidly increasing minefields southeast of the Miteirya Ridge, and then at 1 AM, the 24th Aussies were to seize the eastern end of the ridge, while 69th Brigade from 50th Division would pass through the gap created by the South Africans and then gap any further minefields they might encounter. Then the armor would follow.

Nighttime attacks such as these depended on fairly tight adherence to the timetable, finding and creating large-enough gaps in the minefields and good communications between various units and brigades. This was a tall order, especially since they were all scrabbling about in the dark in stony desert scrub where it was all too easy to lose a sense of direction, even in middle of the day. In addition, as Joe Madeley points out, there was "artillery pounding all night." Tracer and flares would have been crisscrossing the sky. Small arms and shell fire, dust, and terrific noise would have been the companion of the men trying to clear the mines, a highly hazardous task at the best of times. With this in mind, it is perhaps unsurprising that the attack soon floundered. The Australians captured their objective, but not until 3 AM. Word came back by 1:30 AM that the gaps had been partly cleared. There was confusion as they passed through the minefields, but two battalions were clear by 8 AM, by which time it was clear daylight. More confusion followed, about what gaps had been made by whom and where, which meant the armor was greatly delayed.

Joe Madeley recorded that it was "a hell of scrap all day. Dive-bombed, shelled, bullets everywhere." And he was dug in behind the leading formations. With the armor lagging behind, the forward infantry were once again critically exposed. 6 RTR was one of the first armored units to try and come to the rescue as the panzer army counterattacked. They soon found themselves under intense fire. Sam Bradshaw's B Squadron also found their path blocked by another minefield, but still managed to fire on targets of enemy vehicles and infantry. In the evening, by which time the 6th Durham Light Infantry, 5th East Yorkshires and the 2/28th Australian Battalion had all been overrun, the enemy brought up a number of tanks and a large SP gun, which soon forced 6 RTR back through a minefield gap, with two of B Squadron's Grants pitching smoke into the sky. At last light the regiment managed to knock out two enemy tanks and silence the SP gun, but a further Grant was lost in the exchange of fire. Thus, when they withdrew away from the dust and carnage to the comparative safety of reserve positions well behind the front line, they did so with three more of their Grants gone, and with a number of others badly damaged. Over a thousand men had been lost during the day with absolutely no material gain to show for it. The First Battle of Alamein, as the month-long fighting came to be called, was over.

CHAPTER 10

New Faces:
1–12 August, 1942

ON SUNDAY, 2 AUGUST, the Bowles twins, Henry and Tom, along with the entire 1st US Infantry Division—the Big Red One—found themselves steaming out of New York harbor, en route to Britain. Like most young men heading off to war, it was the first time they had ever left home shores. It had been a somewhat bewildering past couple of days. After the long months of field exercises, mock landings, drill and more drill, they had suddenly been warned they would be shipping out before dawn the following day. It was still dark on the morning of 31 July when they were put on trains and began chugging across Pennsylvania to New York, unaware of their ultimate destination or how long they would be away.

The following morning they had finally reached New York docks. Tied up there were the two great rivals of pre-war transatlantic shipping, the *Normandie* and the *Queen Mary*, as well as the *Queen Elizabeth*, all of which had long since been painted gray and converted to troop-carrying. Henry and Tom had heard about these great ocean-going ships—who hadn't?—but it was quite something to see them lined up in such a way, and so Henry hastily took out his camera. In the years before the war, these ships had carried the rich and famous and had been a byword for glamour and decadence. The *Queen Mary*, once a favorite of Hollywood film stars, was now about to transport the entire Big Red One to war.

As Tom and Henry discovered, there was little that was luxurious about the great ship now. Built to carry just under two thousand passengers, it had managed 2,552 (plus $44 million in gold bullion) during its final peacetime crossing; conversion to a troop carrier in Australia had raised this capacity to 5,500. But on 2 August, 1942, the *Queen Mary* was carrying 15,125 troops and 863 mostly British crew. "It sure was crowded," admits Tom. They were given hammocks, four bunked on top of each other along each wall of a cabin. Although in different regiments and in different cabins, they still managed to see plenty of each other, and despite being packed like sardines, they both rather enjoyed it. "Well, to us it was rather like being on a vacation," says Henry. They were given plenty of hot meals, each eaten at a table and served by waiters. The threat of U-boats was ever present, and there were nothing like enough lifeboats for the number on board, but it didn't worry the Bowles twins too much: the ship was fast, and it continually zigzagged all the way to avoid the German submarines. As they approached the British Isles, aircraft arrived to escort them over the final part of the journey into Gourock in Scotland.

They docked on the morning of 7 August, beneath the dull gray barrage balloons that floated above the harbor. The division was quickly ushered off the ship past a line of women handing out cups of tea and then led straight onto waiting trains. The Bowles twins, separated once more into their respective regiments, had no idea where they were heading, but it soon became clear the final leg of their journey was not a short ride. British officers appeared, demonstrating in each compartment how to pull down the blinds; the blackout was something new to the American troops. The train chugged on through the night, past nameless towns and villages, until at around seven the following morning they finally reached their destination. Tidworth Barracks, some ten miles north of Salisbury in southern England, was shrouded in early-morning mist as the soldiers stepped down onto English soil for the first time. On Salisbury Plain, one of the British Army's largest training areas, the Bowles twins and the rest of the division would begin training for the largest seaborne invasion the world had ever known.

But not for a bit. The men of the 1st Division might have safely arrived in Tidworth, but not their equipment. A week after their arrival it still hadn't turned up, so many of the men were given leave to have a look around their new surroundings. Many took this to mean a trip to London, but because most had had the same idea, it caused mayhem on the railways. The creaking British infrastructure barely managed as it was; now, there were suddenly 16,000 Americans to contend with, most of whom wanted to go to the same place at the same time.

Meanwhile, the 34th Infantry Division was, for the most part, still in Northern Ireland, and, along with the 1st Armored Division, part of US V Corps. Sergeant Bucky Walters of the 135th Infantry Regiment had been based at Omagh since his arrival, bivouacked in the local poor house, which was cold and damp. "The people were wonderful, though," says Bucky, although the men at the British Army Transport Service (ATS) refused to have anything at all to do with the newcomers. Nonetheless, with his Irish background, Bucky was still happy to have been posted there. The locals were amazed by this sudden influx of glowing young men. "Most the girls we spoke to fully expected us to be wearing spurs and six guns! They really did!" says Bucky.

The 34th had their equipment, but it was largely out of date. New uniforms had yet to arrive—they still wore the World War I Tommy helmets—and were using old Springfield rifles. Bucky, in H Company, the heavy weapons company, was training as an anti-tank gunner with a totally obsolete "pop gun"—a 37mm, even less effective than the cursed British two-pounder. Since there was neither a comprehensive program of all-arms training or any tanks on which to practice, much of their time was spent carrying out physical exercises over obstacle courses and speed marches. Furthermore, Northern Ireland, with its rolling hills, small fields, and numerous towns and villages, was not best-suited for large-scale maneuvers. Consequently, most of the division had been split up into battalion-size units. "We had no inkling of the importance of infantry-tank coordination," admits Bucky. A few obsolete British tanks were given to the 34th, but Bucky, for one, swears he never came into contact with a tank the whole time he was there. Most of their instructors were British combat veterans, however. "This made all the difference," says Bucky. "For the first time we learned about actual combat." This was just as well, because actual combat was not far away: the planned invasion of Northwest Africa, provisionally set for 7 October, was now just eight weeks away.

Staff Sergeant Bing Evans, however, was now in Scotland, having voluntarily left the 34th Division to join a brand new elite force of troops called the 1st Ranger Battalion, based on the same principles as the British Commandos. The commandos came under the charge of Admiral Mountbatten, who was head of Combined Operations, a single headquarters combining ground, naval and air forces to plan hit-and-run raiding parties. During General Marshall's trip to the UK back in April, he and Mountbatten agreed that a number of American officers should be sent to Combined Operations Headquarters. It was also agreed that a number of American troops of all ranks should be attached to the commandos from which a nucleus American commando unit could be formed. The man sent by Marshall to lead the American delegation at Combined Operations HQ was Colonel Lucian Truscott, who, on his arrival in London in May (and now a brigadier-general) suggested that with the number of US troops in Northern Ireland a force of some four or five hundred American commandos should be formed from the best volunteers from V Corps.

With Marshall's authority behind him, Truscott got his wish, and Captain William Darby, aide to General Hartle, the commander of V Corps, was given the task of forming and commanding this new unit. The US

Army was beginning to prove how fast it could raise fully formed units at lightning speed, and the formation of the Rangers was no exception. On 1 June, the directive was announced, calling for volunteers: officers and noncommissioned officers should possess high leadership qualities with initiative and common sense being of particular importance. All ranks were to have extremely good athletic ability, stamina, and be without any kind of physical defects. Bing Evans saw this notice and decided to volunteer right away. "I thought it seemed like a challenge," he explains. He was interviewed by Darby himself, now a lieutenant-colonel. Bing was impressed by the new commanding officer of the Commando Organization. "He had charisma," says Bing. "He led from the front—he was a soldier's leader, and if the going got tough, he was part of it." Bing also impressed Darby: he was among the first three hundred selected on 11 June.

General Eisenhower had told Truscott back in Washington that he hoped some other name than "commandos" could be used for this new force, "for the glamour of that name will always remain—and properly so—British."[214] Truscott came up with the name "Ranger," and on 19 June, the 1st Ranger Battalion was activated. As for Bing Evans, he became first sergeant for E Company.

Bing and the new battalion were soon sent to Scotland, basing themselves at Achnacarry Castle, in the shadow of Ben Nevis near Fort William. A commando training depot had already been established there—"Castle Commando, we called it"—and although the Americans were trying to distance themselves from the commandos, they were initially trained much the same way and for similar purposes. They were even instructed by commandos. It was tough, both physically and mentally. As well as learning hand-to-hand combat, the Rangers were expected to climb mountains, carry out speed marches and river crossings and swim in ice-cold water, in addition to developing scouting and small-unit tactics. Amphibious training was also extensively carried out, usually with live ammunition. "At this time the only difference between us and the commandos was our pay," says Bing, "which used to irritate our British friends." He thought very highly of his instructors, however. "They had their hearts set on discouraging us and didn't think we could take it," says Bing, "but, of course, we were just as intent on showing them we were up to anything they could do."

It was not just front-line troops that were arriving in Britain, but the support teams as well, including doctors and nurses, much needed once the fighting finally began. The US 48th Surgical Hospital had left New York aboard the USS *Wakefield* on 6 August, part of a massive transatlantic convoy. One of the forty-seven nurses speeding across the Atlantic was thirty-one-year-old Margaret Hornback. At five foot seven, and with a petite frame and warm, pretty face, Margaret looked much younger. Fiercely intelligent but kind and warm hearted, Margaret had left school with good grades and had decided to become a nurse. "I liked people," she explained, "and I felt I had something to contribute."[215] After completing her training in Louisville, she returned to her hometown of Shelbyville and began nursing at the King's Daughters Hospital. She was still there when the Japanese struck at Pearl Harbor. Like most Americans, Margaret felt outraged and wanted to do something to help. She and two other nurses from the hospital—Gladys Martin and Ora White—decided there and then that they would volunteer to work for the army. Traveling down to Fort Knox, the nearest military base, they began their army careers on 14 January, 1942.

They were still at Fort Knox in July but rumors of a call-up for overseas duty were rife and when volunteers were called for, Margaret, Gladys, and Ora all offered their services. Promptly commissioned as 2nd lieutenants, they were also given olive drab army uniforms to replace the all-white they had previously worn, and after ten days' leave were told to report to Indiantown Gap. "Were it not for leaving you all," Margaret wrote to her family just before her departure, "I would be most glad to go and do my small part, and woe betide Hitler if I ever get a crack at him."

The 48th Surgical Hospital safely reached Greenock on 16 August, and like the 1st Infantry Division before them, were soon put on a train and taken the length of England to a camp on the edge of a village called Shipton Bellinger, close to Tidworth Barracks. This was something of a relief to Margaret, because on the trip over she met a young army officer, now stationed at Tidworth. "He's a real Yankee from Michigan," she wrote, "but he doesn't smoke, drink or gamble—most unusual in an army officer. You know me, though. I'm not falling in love so don't be alarmed!"

In August 1942, Operation TORCH appeared to be a gargantuan undertaking. In its most basic form, the joint Allied invasion of Northwest Africa would include many thousands of men, and precise inter-service, let alone international coordination, followed by the establishment of a battlefront hundreds of miles in depth. In addition to the organization of the fighting troops, sailors, and airmen, thought had to be given to hospitals, lines of communication and supply, repair and maintenance units, as well as the subduing of the Vichy French. The British in the Middle East, to a large extent, had already had the basic infrastructure in place in Cairo and in other cities and ports within the theater before the war, and over the past three years of war had been able to build up the machinery with which to maintain large forces. Ike had just eight weeks.

Such was the dire shortage of time, Ike decided to get cracking right away, even though most of the US planners had yet to arrive, and even though his exact position had still not been confirmed. On the last day of July he fixed a meeting at the new Allied Force Headquarters (AFHQ) at Norfolk House, in St James's Square, London. The broad plan agreed for TORCH had envisaged a largely American force landing at Casablanca on the Atlantic coast and a largely British force landing at ports within the Mediterranean, although it soon became clear that the British had a "more expanded view of the mission" and told the Americans quite categorically that the taking of Tunisia was the key to the whole operation. With Tunisia in Allied hands, they would be able to sever Rommel's supply lines and make his life very difficult, if not impossible. The Axis reaction to the Allied landings was likely to be rapid, however, so in order to secure Tunisia before sufficient Axis reinforcements arrived, they would need to capture Tunis within a month. The biggest problem, the British planners told Ike, was a shortage of shipping, especially landing craft, and so they suggested the landings inside the Mediterranean should take precedence over any landings further west.

This alarmed Ike considerably. "I urge the most serious thought be given to the mission of the entire force as conceived by the two governments," he wrote in a cable to Marshall the following day. "To seize control of the north coast of Africa is an entirely different operation from denying the west coast to the enemy," as had been devised in the old GYMNAST plan.[216] Harry Butcher, who had sat in on the meeting, began to realize just what a difficult position his chief was in and the enormity of the task facing him. The actual *planning* was only the half of it; equally difficult would be the task of making two nations work together and see eye to eye to a level of unity that had never been attempted before. "Ike will have to exert vigorous leadership to direct the coordination of planning by both British and Americans," Butch noted with some understatement.[217]

At least it seemed as though his ground commanders had been chosen. On 4 August, Ike lunched alone at his apartment with General Alexander, recently back from leading the British retreat from Burma, and designated the British ground force commander; General Patton had also been penciled in to lead the US forces. Harry Butcher believed this was an important lunch for Ike. Alexander had about as much battlefield experience as any soldier in the British Army, while Ike was not only junior in rank, but had no combat experience at all, let alone any battlefield command. "There was," commented Butch, "the touchy question of how accessible Ike might be to Alexander." He needn't have worried; the two got on well and as the British general left, he told Ike that he thought he had got off to a "good start."[218]

Later that evening, Ike sat with Butch in the flat—a welcome night off from formal engagements. Sprawled in a big chair, Ike ruminated on the responsibility that lay ahead of him. It was one he was determined to see through. "The imperative need of our people as well as the British," he continued, "is for victory and I'm going to do my goddamndest to get it for them."

In Egypt, there may have been a lull in the fighting, but the Allied air forces continued to pound Axis positions, ports, and shipping. The RAF could now call on the embryonic US Army Middle East Air Force, which under General Lewis Brereton was beginning to take shape. Despite Tedder's earlier worries, he was now beginning to think "they were shaping up well," although he felt there was much progress still to be made.[219]

That was only natural—they had little experience, after all—but Tedder could not have faulted either their commitment, or, most crucially, their willingness to learn. Furthermore, conditions were quite different than anything they had been used to back in the States. At Ramid Dravid in Palestine, for example, the 98th Bombardment Group was still without most of its ground crew and facilities—who were yet to catch up—and so were using unfamiliar British ground staff, living off British rations and hurrying to get their aircraft combat ready for their first ever combat mission on 2 August.

One of those flying on that day was Lieutenant Willie Chapman, 2nd pilot of one of the seven B-24s to take part. Flying initially to Fayid, they joined the RAF bombers and found themselves being briefed by Tedder himself, before heading off to bomb Mersa Matruh. Willie Chapman admits feeling particularly nervous about his first trip. "We were lucky, though," he says. "We had a real easy target—shipping isn't surrounded by the kind of anti-aircraft fire you can get over other targets." Two days later, Willie flew again when 415 Squadron was ordered to try and find and bomb an Axis tanker and freighter heading for Tobruk. They soon located them not far from the port and recorded hits on the tanker and sank the freighter.

With these first missions under his belt, the commanding officer of the 98th, Colonel Hugo Rush, arranged a meeting between his bomber crews and the British anti-aircraft gunners in the Haifa area. "The British had been in the war for quite a while and were obviously expert in their profession," says Willie, "and we listened." The gunners advised them about the power and velocity of the various Axis ack-ack guns, and the tricks they used themselves in trying to bring their own firepower to bear. They also advised them that flak exploding above a plane usually caused little damage; it was when it burst underneath that they needed to worry about it. "No one bothered to ask about damage should the shell explode inside the plane," noted Willie.[220]

A few days later, on 9 August, they were sent out again, this time to bomb Benghazi. This was some distance—around 800 miles—and further than even the B-24 could manage, so they had to lower the bomb load to accommodate an extra fuel tank. Even with this, there was going to be little margin for error. Their course led them within range of enemy aircraft from Crete and along the North African coast, so they flew as low as they could, almost skimming the white caps of the Mediterranean, in an effort to avoid being seen on radar. After several hours, they turned south for Benghazi, their leader, Major "Killer" Kane, taking them back up to 22,000 feet.

All was going well. The leading B-24s in the formation dropped their bombs and Willie was pleased to note that anti-aircraft fire was late and inaccurate—they'd clearly achieved total surprise. Bombs were released according to a red light indicator that blinked every time a bomb was dropped; but as Willie's aircraft flew over the target the indicator blinked red only once and not one of the bombs left the bay. "We've come this far—let's try again," said Paul Francis, the skipper, so they dropped out of formation, banked, and turned for another run. "Bombs away," said the bombardier, but again, only one light blinked and they still had their bomb load.

By the time they were coming in for their third bomb run, the flak was thickening considerably and since they were now the only plane above the port, all the guns of Tobruk seemed to be aiming in their direction. Black puffs were exploding all around them, and the aircraft was shaking and rattling, but at least this time, with the help of a manual lever, they finally managed to get rid of their bomb load.

The route back had always been to head southeast over Cyrenaica, then turn east toward Egypt, and although they made good their escape from the target area, it soon became clear that they were in some trouble. First they came under attack from some Italian fighters, but managed to see them off. "Our gunners felt our .50 calibers did enough damage to hasten their departure," noted Willie.[221] But then they became aware of a more serious problem. The engines were set at 2,500 rpm for the bomb runs, which gave them a speed of around 280 mph, some 100 mph faster than they normally cruised, but when Willie pressed the switches to reduce rpm, nothing happened. Dropping height to around 12,000 feet, they took off their oxygen masks and tried to assess the damage. None of them were injured, but it was clear flak had caused some damage— quite a few holes, but worse, a load of wiring under the right-hand side of the instrument panel had been severely damaged. The throttles still worked, but the controls for engine rpm adjustment, as well as the flaps on the wings, and all the aircraft's lights and communication systems both inside and out, were all dead.

They leveled out at a low altitude, but it was obvious that they were burning far more fuel per mile than they could afford. They soon caught up with the rest of the formation, then flew on past. Bud Cook, the radio operator tried to let them know what was wrong with a morse signal using his flashlight, but it wasn't very effective. As they flew on, Willie and Bob Greenrod, the flight engineer, got on their knees and tried to do what they could with the damaged nerve center, but there was nothing to be done.

It was getting dark by the time they began flying over the Qattara Depression. "Big Stoop" Harris, the navigator, and Pascoe, the bombardier, had now joined Willie, Paul, and Bob on the flight deck and were trying to decide where to go and what to do. They were still well west of the Alamein Line by the time it was completely dark. With flickering flashlights they reckoned their best bet was to aim for a British landing ground just east of the Alamein Line.

Having decided it would be best to try and get a bit of height, they were still gently climbing when one of the engines packed up. Paul suggested he attempt to set them down in the desert, but with absolutely no lights other than electric torches, Willie felt this was too risky. But if they did not reach the British landing ground, the only alternative was to bail out. Meanwhile, temperatures were rising on the other engines, so by flashlight they manually cranked open the bomb bay, while the gunners at the back hovered by the open camera hatch. Holding his torch over the instrument panel so that Paul could see, Willie glanced across at the revolver by his seat, then decided he would leave it where it was. After all, he could hardly hold off Rommel's army with it and it might only get in the way during his first-ever parachute jump.

The other engines began to splutter. "OK. Let's jump," Paul told him. Willie relayed the message and fired a red flare into the sky. He saw Big Stoop wave and jump through the bomb bay doors. Pascoe, the bombardier, froze with fear and Willie had to slap him a couple of times and push him out. Then, patting Paul on the shoulder, Willie jumped too, and pulled the ripcord. "There was an anxious moment or two when I thought my chute was not going to open," he says, but suddenly it ballooned open and he felt himself drift down. Almost immediately, he hit the ground, "followed by my back and head and I stopped thinking for a short period."

When he came to, he realized he was fine, apart from a very sore ankle. Big Stoop was standing over him, telling him he'd only seen four chutes. "Paul didn't have a chance," Willie told him, but miraculously, Paul then appeared. The dark desert night was suddenly lit up as their aircraft crashed and exploded. Bullets from their machine guns began firing and pinging all around them, so they dropped to the ground until the firing subsided. Shortly after, Bud Cook appeared, but the others had not been so lucky. They had jumped from as little as 200 feet; it was incredible that any of them had made it.

The survivors soon noticed some figures moving cautiously toward them—this was the moment of truth; they still had no idea on which side of the lines they'd landed. A challenge was called—in a decidedly British accent. The Americans, greatly relieved, immediately called back. It turned out they were between one and a half and two miles over the right side of the line. "We were very lucky," admits Willie. "A minute before, and we'd have been in enemy territory." They were taken to the British positions and given something to eat and drink. "After being in the air for over ten hours, anything was welcome," noted Willie. They were also given blankets and a tent and told they would look for their colleagues in the morning. The officer in charge offered them a glass of whiskey. "While this was scotch with no ice," says Willie, "no one was impolite enough to refuse."[222]

The following morning, Willie was taken back to Alexandria for X-rays on his ankle. There were no breaks, but he'd badly sprained it. He would not be flying again for a while. The others went with the British to find the rest of the crew. It turned out all of them had bailed out, but although everyone had jumped before Willie and Paul, they had been slower to open their chutes. "I felt terrible about it," admits Willie. "But you just had to try and put it out of mind." The halcyon days of Shangri-la seemed a lifetime ago.

The efforts of the American bombers were part of the continued and relentless pressure being applied by the RAF in the Middle East. Night after night, the coastal ports were bombed. 205 Group's Wellingtons were bombing Benghazi so regularly, it became dubbed the "mail run." 70 Squadron even rewrote "Darling Clementine":

> Down the flight, each ruddy morning
> Sitting waiting for a clue
> Same old notice, on the Flight board
> Maximum effort: guess where to.
>
> Seventy Squadron, Seventy Squadron,
> Though we say it with a sigh
> We must do the ruddy Mail Run
> Every night until we die.

Allied anti-shipping strikes were also increasing. Since the Spitfire victory over the skies in May, Malta had been increasingly used once more as a base for offensive operations, with Egypt-based squadrons sending detachments to operate from the island. All this was taking its toll, however, on both aircraft and crew. From the Desert Air Force alone, Mary Coning-ham had lost around 600 fighters and 140 bombers since the end of May. That he was able to keep these strikes going was largely due to the extraordinary efforts of the Middle East Maintenance and Supply Organization, run by Air Vice-Marshal George Dawson. Only sixty-one new aircraft had arrived and been released during June, but by 1 July, a further 1,369 were held at the various depots and undergoing repair. By the end of the first week of July, 268 of these were serviceable. Working closely with Tommy Elmhirst, George Dawson and his men ensured that aircraft continued to arrive at the front.

More pilots were arriving too. South African Jack Weinronk joined 24 Squadron, South African Air Force (SAAF) on 19 July, three days after his twenty-seventh birthday. He was very excited to finally be attached to an operational squadron—the wait had sometimes seemed inexorable. He had first discovered his passion for flying as a teenager in Port Elizabeth, then in 1936, when he was twenty-one, begun taking flying lessons, heading off to the airfield early each morning before going to work in his father's furniture business. He gained his civil pilot's licence the following year, and when war was declared, immediately volunteered to join the Air Force. However, he was told that at twenty-four he was too old to be a pilot. Deciding that if he couldn't handle his own plane he'd handle his own truck, he joined the Mechanical Transport Corps instead.

By September 1940, the Air Force had raised the pilot age to thirty and on discovering this, Jack applied again and was immediately accepted. Almost a year later, he was awarded his wings, and a couple of weeks before Christmas 1941 was sent "up north" to Egypt. While there he was given a week's leave and traveled to Jerusalem to see his father. Bernard Weinronk was a staunch Zionist who had left his native Ireland after the local Catholic priest had started giving anti-Semitic sermons. He had settled happily in South Africa, raising a large family—Jack was the youngest of eight—and establishing a successful business. But by the outbreak of war, Jack's father was not a well man. It had always been his wish to visit the Holy Land and to be buried there, and so had managed to make his way to Jerusalem. When Jack found him, his father was close to death. He managed to extend his leave, and was with his father when he died. The following day, Jack buried him on the Mount of Olives.

He was not to remain in the Middle East, however, and was soon after sent to an operational training unit outside Nairobi, in Kenya, where he converted to Blenheims and then twin-engine Boston bombers. He had only just completed his OTU when the news arrived that Tobruk had fallen, and with it the loss of so many South Africans. "I wonder how many of my pals have taken the one-way road, and how many are prisoners," he confided in his diary. "South Africa has taken a terrible blow." One of his good friends on the course received a telegram telling him that both his father and brother had been killed at Tobruk; a week before, his friend's mother had also died. "Poor Tommy," noted Jack. "What a tragedy it is."

Sent back to Egypt, Jack spent a couple of weeks kicking his heels in Cairo then finally got word he would be joining 24 Squadron, flying Bostons. He was now part of 3 Wing along with 12 Squadron SAAF, based at Amorea, south of Alexandria. "Met a number of chaps on the squadron," he noted, "and they seem to be a damn fine bunch. I'm certain I am going to be very happy."[223]

Jack—always known as "Cobber"—was a cheerful person, always able to see the best in other people and in any situation he found himself in. On his first raid—or "stooge"—he was amazed to discover he didn't feel a bit scared. The Bostons flew in tight formation, mainly in an effort to pack a greater punch when they reached their target, and Cobber found this took a great deal of concentration. In fact, he was concentrating so hard on keeping formation that he didn't see much of the raid. Almost before he realized what was going on, they'd dropped their bombs and were heading back. Later, once they'd landed, his flight leader told him, "Cobber, you did very well, but we're not on a Cook's Tour, and formatting ten to fifteen feet away is not good enough. I want you to sit right up my arse until we get to the target." The following day, Cobber took part in two more "stooges," this time over the German positions around Sidi Abd el Rahman. Again, he was concentrating so hard he hardly noticed the target, although he was conscious of a massive fire as they turned for home on the second. On landing, his mechanics pointed out flak damage to his undercarriage—Cobber was surprised. He'd not felt a thing. "On thinking it over," he noted in his diary, "I find I actually enjoyed my first three raids."[224]

Rommel may have been halted, but the Auk had failed to break back. While it had been sensible to retreat as far as the Alamein position, Eighth Army had managed to stem the panzer army's advance largely due to the efforts of the RAF and Rommel's worsening supply situation, rather than because of any sudden new improvement in tactics. Furthermore, the Auk had failed to really gel his subordinate commanders, most of whom were tired, disappointed, and lacking in confidence after the shattering experiences of June, or in the case of the newly arrived New Zealanders and Australians, frustrated at the way their troops were expected to be deployed. The Auk had argued with Morshead, for example, commander of the 9th Australian Division. Morshead disagreed with the Auk's insistence on continuing to use brigade groups, and refused to let the C-in-C split up his division. They would fight as one or not at all, Morshead told him, and threatened to use his right to refer back to his national government if the Auk insisted. The Aussie commander had become even more disgruntled when he'd been passed over as commander of XXX Corps after Norrie had finally been sacked. Instead, Ramsden had been chosen. He was also prone to quibbling over orders and had, like Gott, repeatedly argued with Pienaar. Meanwhile, Strafer Gott, despite outwardly giving his all, was in low spirits and after two years of command in the desert, desperately hoping to be given a rest. Nor were these personnel problems smoothed over by the force of Auchinleck's personality during the ensuing weeks. By the second battle of Ruweisat, Morshead and Ramsden had begun a full-scale row—again over troop deployment—while Kippenberger and Pienaar continued to feel bitter and slighted by the way in which their troops were being used.

Always niggling at the back of Auchinleck's mind was the enemy threat from the north. The fear of an Axis victory in Russia and a subsequent push south through the Caucasus, however unlikely in reality, certainly seemed possible to the British, not least the Auk—after all, the Germans had already proven themselves to be past masters of the rapid, lightning advance. It was for this reason, and because of pressure from the prime Minister in particular, that the Auk felt compelled to keep trying to destroy the panzer army, even though his own army was as much in need of a break from offensive operations as Rommel's. Most of his corps and divisional commanders, however, did not share the C-in-C's view of the wider strategic picture, nor did he make much effort to explain it to them. Had he communicated with them better, explaining his reasons for his four bloody, yet unsuccessful, attempts to beat Rommel he might have found them more cooperative and less dissenting.

The prime minister, on the other hand, understood the overall strategic situation all right, but failed to appreciate the state of Eighth Army or the difficulties facing the battlefield commander. As far as he was concerned, statistics were everything, and these showed three quarters of a million men in uniform in the Middle East and more on the way. That only a fraction of this figure were front-line troops and had to be spread over the entire theater, was something he would and could not grasp. Like Auchinleck and Brooke, the PM read the regular reports from Ultra, and they showed that Rommel was short of everything; so why, he wanted to know, couldn't the panzer army be thrashed once and for all?

When the Auk's final July push failed to bring victory, Churchill was distraught, and railed at Brooke, "pouring out questions as to why Auk could not have done this or that and never giving him the least credit for doing the right thing."[225] The trouble was, Brooke was beginning to have doubts of his own. For a while now he had been conscious that all was not well with the Middle East Command, but he was also aware that it was hard to give a proper prognosis from three thousand miles away. He needed to go there himself, talk with the Auk, see the troops and other commanders and then work out the best way forward.

He had wanted to go alone, but the prime minister had insisted on coming too, believing it was essential to be able to make decisions on the spot without having to wait for Brooke to report back. By the time they safely reached Cairo on 3 August, Churchill had already decided that changes were needed. A new Eighth Army commander was essential, but on that first day he was still inclined to keep the Auk as C-in-C. Brooke's own doubts about the Auk grew as soon as he met Corbett soon after his arrival in Cairo. He thought him unfit for his job of chief of staff and felt his selection reflected poorly on the Auk's ability to choose the right men for important jobs. The Auk's fate was sealed, however, when Churchill and Brooke went up to the front two days later. The PM went alone for a briefing from Auchinleck and his Eighth Army chief of staff, Major-General "Chink" Dorman-Smith, and demanded an immediate offensive against Rommel. "Attack, attack!" he demanded, stamping fingers on the map laid out before him. He was in a foul mood. Quietly but firmly, the Auk explained that fresh troops, untrained and unacclimatized to desert conditions, were simply not ready to be thrown against the skill and experience of the Germans straightaway. Mid-September was the earliest for a new offensive.

Churchill walked out of the Auk's caravan and stood alone, glowering at the desert, before eventually departing with Strafer Gott, whom he had already decided should command Eighth Army. Gott was by this stage completely exhausted and still struggling to control the South Africans. He told the PM frankly that he wanted nothing more than three months' leave in England.

Churchill's black mood was improved by his lunch with the RAF boys, however. Tedder and Mary Coningham took him to Air HQ at Burg El Arab, where he was introduced to Tommy Elmhirst, among others. "He arrived in an Air Commodore's rig, to our delight and honour," wrote Tommy in a letter to his wife. Their party then flew to the Fighter Group HQ, where lunch had been especially sent out all the way from Alexandria and set up in one of their tents. Fifteen of the most senior airmen were seated at the table, while a number more were invited to attend a buffet. Churchill was seated between Mary and Group Captain Guy Carter, commander of 211 Fighter Group, while Tommy was thrilled to have been placed opposite. "A most intriguing lunch," wrote Tommy, "he cross-examined us and allowed us to do likewise. He was on excellent form and obviously enjoyed himself." And well he might: after their successes of the previous two months, Mary and his team exuded nothing but unity of purpose and glowing confidence.

The food cleared, Tedder asked Churchill to say a few words. Tommy was quite unabashedly won over. "A most inspiring talk," he told his wife, Katherine, "which quite definitely brought tears to my eyes. He had great praise for us all and by no means left out any department. He said, 'The country at home knows what you have done in this battle and retreat, and has taken note of you all. The Air Force's work in the Battle of Britain saved civilisation. You have done as well and you will all look back on this battle and feel that you were privileged to serve in such a force and at such a time.'" Tommy only wished he'd been able to take down the whole speech in full. "His oratory is marvelous," he added, "and it was not down to brandy, but on two glasses of beer in a hot tent on a hot August day in the desert!"[226]

While Churchill had been meeting with the Auk and lunching with the RAF, Brooke had been making his tour of the various commanders, and caught up with Gott later in the afternoon. The XIII Corps commander also told Brooke that he needed a rest, and added, "I think what is required here is some new blood. I have tried most of my ideas on the Boche. We want someone with new ideas and plenty of confidence in them."[227] On this occasion, Gott's assessment was bang on the mark.

The following day, Churchill and Brooke thrashed out a series of drastic and immediate changes. The PM had decided that Middle East Command was too big and so decided to split it in two: Near East would include Africa up to the Suez Canal, while Middle East covered Syria, Palestine, Iraq and Persia. He asked Brooke to take over Near East Command, but the CIGS refused immediately; and by the end of the day, it had been agreed that General Alexander should take the post, with the Auk being offered the job of C-in-C of the new Middle East Command, which kept the same title but was much less in scope. Although the PM was a politician and not a military man, and despite Gott having virtually begged to be sent home, Churchill was insistent that he should take over Eighth Army, brushing aside Brooke's arguments that Montgomery would be a better bet. Montgomery, the PM insisted, should take over from Alexander as British commander of Operation TORCH. Corbett, Dorman-Smith, and Ramsden were also to be fired.

The following day, the War Cabinet back in London approved the changes, but fate had other ideas. General Gott, on hearing of his promotion, gave one last briefing to XIII Corps. This prevented him from leaving promptly for a few days' leave in Cairo, so he decided to take passage on a plane rather than drive. Gott also held up the departure of the plane, an aging Bristol Bombay transport, loaded mostly with wounded men. After apologizing to the pilot, the sprightly looking new Eighth Army commander finally set off from the desert at about 4:15 PM. Soon after taking off, six Messerschmitt 109s attacked the aircraft, knocking out both engines and forcing the young pilot to make an extraordinarily skilled landing back down on the desert. Although it must have been blatantly apparent to the German fighter pilots that the aircraft would never ever fly again, they made three strafing passes over the stricken machine, and in doing so killed nineteen of the twenty-three on board, Gott included, as the plane was riddled with bullets and cannon shells and soon erupted into a ball of flames. On returning to their landing ground, the German pilots were greeted by a very senior officer who congratulated them on successfully killing "the new commander of the Eighth Army." At the time, the British were still unaware of the tragedy—they were not to learn the truth until some time later, when the wounded and badly burned pilot of Gott's plane eventually stumbled into a British truck that just happened to be in the desert on test. Clearly, German intelligence had learned that Gott would be on the plane and they had subsequently assassinated him.*

So died one of the most popular commanders in the Desert War. Churchill, on hearing the news, wept openly. It also left a sudden vacuum, albeit one that was quickly filled. At Brooke's urgings, and with Smuts's support, the prime minister finally agreed that Montgomery should take over Eighth Army after all. Thus, only by a strange twist of fate was the most famous British general of the war given his chance for glory.

The Auk took the news of his sacking calmly, but refused the Middle East job. Churchill hoped he would come around, but such a demotion was a humiliation too far: the Auk remained adamant. He stayed a few days in Cairo and then flew home, not to England, but to India.

In Cairo, the journalists were briefed about the new changes. Alan Moorehead realized that an era of the war was now over. Although he had witnessed a number of purges, this time the changes were deeper than a mere exchange of personnel. "A new army of the Middle East was given birth," he wrote, "an army that for the first time was going to include Americans as well as British. A tide of reinforcement such as the Middle East had never known before was going to come in, and from it a better army was going to

---

*In April 2005, the pilot of Gott's plane, Squadron Leader Jimmy James AFC, DFM, finally met the German formation leader, Herr Emil Clade. Herr Clade confirmed that two additional planes had been added to his more usual formation of four aircraft "at the last minute." He confirmed every aspect of the incident, but claimed to have been unaware that their attack had been an assassination. He had also been unaware that so many had been killed as a result, and on hearing the news, was deeply distraught.

be built." He also believed it was time for him to move on too. Over two years he'd spent reporting this seemingly endless desert war. He felt tired, and stale too. "I had been too close to it for too long," he wrote and now wished "to see the war from some other point of view than the desert—even a break for just a few months would be enough." His editor in London, Arthur Christiansen, saw his point but asked him where he wanted to go instead. America, Alan told him, and then anywhere his editor liked—England, Russia, the Far east, even back to Africa. Christiansen agreed.

Alan was about to leave when he heard the shocking news about Gott, news that at once clarified his feelings that an era was over and that the timing of his departure was right. It turned out the pilot had even managed to get the aircraft down, but then the Germans had strafed the stricken aircraft and it had caught fire, killing all but one of the fifteen passengers. "He was the last of the old desert rats to go," wrote Alan.[228]

On 10 August, 1942, from the British embassy in Cairo, Churchill scribbled a handwritten directive to the new commander-in-chief, General the Honorable Sir Harold Alexander:

1. Your prime and main duty will be to take or destroy at the earliest opportunity the German-Italian army commanded by Field Marshal Rommel together with all its supplies and establishments in Egypt and Libya.
2. You will discharge or cause to be discharged such other duties as pertain to your command without prejudice to the task described in paragraph 1, which must be considered paramount in His Majesty's interests.

Alexander read this with a sense of exhilaration. He'd spent the war retreating from one defeat after another, but couldn't help feeling that fortunes were about to change. This, he knew, was quite irrational. "To put it mildly," he noted, "the situation did not look good." Eighth Army, it appeared, had lost the winning formula; and Rommel, although stalled, still maintained his aura of invincibility. British confidence was low, and the army now found itself in a period of desperate upheaval, and at a time when it was increasingly obvious Rommel was preparing another offensive. Nonetheless, the new C-in-C's feelings "were tinged with a new confidence."[229]

This was neither arrogance nor false bravado. No one who met Alexander ever had cause to doubt his integrity; moreover, there were few people more prone to self-deprecation and less likely to blow their own trumpet.[230] Such unassuming modesty had been drummed into him as a child, a childhood in which he had been brought up to respect notions of honor, duty, and impeccable manners in all things and at all times.

Born the third son of the Earl of Caledon, Alexander's background was distinctly aristocratic. His childhood was spent shooting, fishing, and painting on the large Caledon estate in County Tyrone in Northern Ireland. At fifteen he was sent to Harrow, where he excelled at sports,* and from there went straight to Sandhurst, graduating in July 1911, aged nineteen. As a fiercely proud Ulsterman, he was determined to join the Irish Guards. The "Micks" were a young regiment, created by Queen Victoria in only 1900; nearly all its number were Irish. "They were my bosom friends," he later said. "In the Micks there is a great feeling of matiness between officers and men. The Irish love their leaders, as I had found as a boy, and they have natural good manners."[231] He was yet to excel as a soldier, but was certainly developing into a handsome, highly athletic young man, and the perfect gentleman. Between duties, he found plenty of time to go to dances and the theater, to hunt, shoot, box, and play polo, as well as cricket and golf. He even went motor racing at Brooklands, and in Easter 1914, entered—and won quite effortlessly—Ireland's most famous sprint, the Irish Mile.

The four long years of the First World War developed him as a soldier. He quite openly enjoyed it, despite—or rather, because of—spending almost the entire war with fighting troops. At the First Battle of Ypres in November 1914, he was seriously wounded in the thigh and hand and invalided home. He recovered well and, determined to get back to the front as soon as possible, walked sixty-four miles in one day to prove to a cautious doctor that he was fit enough. Sure enough, by February 1915, he was back, and later that summer led his company at the Battle of Loos. His reputation was growing rapidly, notably for his exceptional personal courage, but also for his extraordinary imperturbability and the gift of quick decision. Always leading from the front and with no regard to his own personal safety, he soon had the complete devotion and respect of all those who served under him.

He was wounded twice more, survived the Somme, Cambrai, and Passchendaele, and in 1917, aged just twenty-five, became acting lieutenant-colonel commanding the 2nd Battalion. By the armistice, he had earned a DSO and bar, an MC, the French Legion of Honour, and had been mentioned in dispatches five times. Nor did his combat record stop with the end of the war. In 1919, he was sent to command the Baltic Landwehr, part of

---

*In his final year of school, Alexander played in Fowler's Match at Lord's, the most famous Eton-Harrow cricket match ever to have been played. Harrow made 232 in the first innings then bowled out Eton for 67. Eton followed on scoring 219, leaving Harrow just 55 to win. Alexander was last man in when Harrow was 32–9. He scored 8 in a 13-run partnership before edging to slip, and so Harrow lost by 10 runs.

the Latvian Army, in the war against North Russia. Since most of the men under his command were of German origin, he was unique among British commanders of the Second World War in having commanded German troops in battle. Staff college and staff appointments were followed by stints of further action along the Northwest Frontier, where his superior at the time, Brigadier Claude Auchinleck, took note of his cool efficiency and began a lasting friendship.

By the outbreak of war in 1939, this gilded officer was one of the army's youngest major-generals and commanding 1st Division. He went with them to France, and after the British retreat in May 1940, was left behind to supervise the final withdrawal of British troops, only leaving on 3 June, the penultimate day of evacuation.

Remaining in England for the next two years of war, Alexander realized that the vast majority of infantry troops under his command were simply not ready for battle. He subsequently began to develop battle schools in which men were taught simple forms of battle drill to which they would react automatically in times of stress—simple orders such as, "Down, crawl, observe, fire." He also recognized that some kind of battle inoculation was needed before submitting green troops to the terrors of German dive-bombing, shelling, and machine-gunning. This could only be done with live ammunition. Thirdly, he realized that it was essential that all troops were battle fit. However obvious this may seem now, the battle-school system was considered quite innovative at the time and became the basis of future infantry training.

It was particularly during his time commanding Southern Command that Alexander came to Churchill's notice. The PM was certainly influenced by Alexander's aristocratic background, but also by his calm control and a military record that was second to none. Even in Burma, yet another retreat from defeat, Alexander had impressed with his unflappability and ability to make the best of a bad situation.

And he looked the part, too. Modest though he was, Alexander had a streak of the dandy about him; he always dressed immaculately. On leave during the First World War, he spotted a Russian officer wearing a high-peaked cap, with its visor dropping over his eyes. Alexander liked the design so much he went straight to his hatter in St. James and had him make an exact copy. It was a style he kept throughout his career simply because it *had* style.

There was also plenty of charm. He never swore: describing something as "tiresome" was the closest he got to cursing, and only once was he ever seen to lose his temper, and that was when some of his men refused to give two dying Germans a drink of water during the Battle of Passchendaele. He drank but was never drunk; he would sketch and paint whenever he had the chance; spoke a number of languages including German, French, and Russian, and was one of a very few British (rather than Indian) Army officers who bothered to learn Urdu while in Burma.

With these credentials it is perhaps no wonder that Churchill and Brooke had high hopes for him as the new C-in-C in Egypt. He was not a devastatingly brilliant tactician. Neither was he an intellectual, nor a keen student of warfare like General Tuker, for example. But he had developed a very sound sense of judgment, and perhaps even more importantly, understood the men under his command. He understood how much men could endure and what could be expected of them. He understood that armies need confidence and experience in combat, and that the approach to battle—the preparation and the closing-down of potential stumbling blocks—was the key to victory. That, at the very least, was something Tuker could appreciate.

His immediate subordinate and the new commander of Eighth Army was a different kettle of fish altogether. He, like Alex, was born an Ulsterman, but there the similarities ended. Four years older than his new boss, Monty was fifty-four when he arrived in Cairo on 12 August. At five foot seven (compared with Alex's five foot ten), he was unimposing physically, had thinning hair, a beaky expression and a rather shrill voice that was incapable of pronouncing its R's properly. Alex, on the other hand, spoke with the laid-back but clipped tones expected from one of his standing. But however unprepossessing Monty's appearance may have been, he did have piercing gray eyes, as keen as hawk's eyes, that bore into whoever he was talking to without ever appearing to blink.

The son of a vicar—his father was absent in Tasmania for much of his childhood—Monty went to Sandhurst in 1907, where he disgraced himself by setting fire to one of the other cadet's shirttails. He was allowed to continue but performed only averagely, and when he graduated did not do so high enough to gain a commission in the Indian Army, which had been his intention. Instead he became a subaltern with the Royal Warwickshires. By August 1914, he had become a platoon commander and led them in a courageous attack in the First Battle of Yres, for which he was promoted and awarded a DSO. He was also badly wounded, but unlike Alex, this ensured he spent the rest of the war behind a desk.

Monty may have been out of the action, but he did prove himself to be excellent at planning and ended the war as GSO1—head of planning—of an entire division. His operations in 1918 demonstrated what training, careful preparation, and an understanding of all-arms could achieve. It was this background that led him to a succession of staff appointments, most notably as an instructor at the Camberley Staff College between 1926 and 1929. The post-war apathy in the Army distressed him greatly. Like Tuker, he took the study of past, present, and future warfare very seriously, and was unimpressed by the rapidity with which the army returned to its obsessions with sport and horses. At Camberley he met Brooke, at the time one of the senior instructors, and taught both Tuker and Alex. Although he did not endear himself to the staff there—they considered him a "bloody menace"[232]—he impressed enough to be given the task of rewriting the infantry training manual. Through the 1930s, he continued to excel as an instructor, both in England and as senior instructor at the Qetta Staff College in India, and although he was not popular, he *was* respected.

If anyone was destined to be a confirmed bachelor, it was Monty, but in 1926, he defied those who knew him by falling in love with Betty Carver, a widow whose husband had been killed at Gallipoli. They married the following year, and there is no doubt she had a calming influence on him, smoothing some of the most disagreeable aspects of his difficult and opinionated character and injecting a healthy dose of humor into his life. Tragically, she died ten years later of septicemia, leaving Monty with a nine-year-old boy and two stepsons, then in their twenties and both in the army. Her death changed him: from that moment on, he dedicated his life entirely to soldiering.

Commands in Palestine and then France followed as war broke out. By July 1940, he had been given V Corps under General Auchinleck, then commander of Southern Command; the two clashed, but Monty's reputation for training grew and it became clear that a battlefield command was not far away. Sure enough, by July 1942, he had been earmarked to lead the British forces in Operation TORCH.

Field Marshal Lord Gort, commander of the BEF in France in 1940 and by the summer of 1942 governor of Malta, once remarked that in dealing with Monty, "one must remember that he is not quite a gentleman."[233] This was not an insult anyone could throw at Alex, but the fact that Monty *was* such an outsider in the boys' club that was the British Army and yet had still made it to lieutenant-general says much about his determination and utter belief in his abilities and destiny. General Tuker, another maverick, had struggled since war began; he was still only a divisional commander.

They made an unlikely couple, Alex and Monty, yet their backgrounds, experience, and differing skills complemented one another perfectly. Together they made a team, as solid as Mary Coningham and Tommy Elmhirst, a team which, both Churchill and Brooke desperately hoped, would bring them victory and the prestige to give them a lasting equal partnership with the Americans.

CHAPTER 11

A Victory At Last:
13 August–4 September 1942

SLEDGEHAMMER MAY HAVE been discarded by the British, but an Allied cross-Channel raid had been planned for July by Mountbatten's Combined Operations Headquarters, with much of the training prepared by Montgomery before he had been sent to Egypt. Six thousand men would be used—less than half a division—but the assault would also include tanks and massive air cover. On paper, the idea was to force the Luftwaffe into the skies and to capture the port of Dieppe, with the aim of learning some valuable lessons for future raids and amphibious landings, and to also draw German troops away from Russia. Unlike SLEDGEHAMMER, there was never any intention of maintaining a bridgehead; rather it was to be a "butcher-and-run" attack only. Political motivations were also considerable: the need to be seen doing something to help the Russians, both in the east and to the impatient public in America and Britain, played a significant part in the acceptance of the plan. The majority of the ground troops involved were to be Canadian, 200,000 of whom had been based in the UK since 1940, but special forces were to be included too: 4 Commando under Lord Lovat and a detachment of the 1st Ranger Battalion, despite the fact that the Americans had barely started their training.

It was clearly a scheme fraught with danger, and Brooke, for one, was against it: he was quite happy to support Mountbatten's plans for specific Commando actions—their raid on the docks at St. Nazaire on 26 March had been a great success—but the proposed Dieppe Raid was a different matter. All decisions in war are like gambling—the level of risk has to be weighed up. But to land and then extract so many men and machines was very different from lightning cut-and-dash operations the commandos had carried out before. The odds on the Dieppe Raid being successful were not high.

Sergeant Bing Evans was one of seven officers and eleven enlisted men earmarked to take part in the raid. On Independence Day, 4 July, Bing had been on board ship off the Isle of Wight on the south coast of England. "The weather was not at all decent," says Bing. In fact it was terrible, and the operation was promptly postponed until 8 July. On 7 July, however, their cover was blown when four German aircraft attacked the concentrations of shipping. The crucial element of surprise had gone and so the raid was called off again. The Rangers were sent straight back to Scotland, where Bing was promoted to battalion sergeant-major, and although the raid on Dieppe was rescheduled, with fifty Rangers now involved, Bing was not one of them—Colonel Darby refused to risk losing his most trusted NCO.

That it was remounted was extraordinary. All the troops involved had been told of their destination, so there was a huge security risk in continuing with the same plan. Furthermore, the Germans had now been alerted to its possibility; coastal forces were expecting some kind of attack. The odds for success had been dramatically slashed further.

"Trying to follow the evolution of TORCH is like trying to find the pea in a three-shell game," noted Harry Butcher in his diary on 12 August.[234] Two days earlier, Ike had submitted his latest plan to the Chiefs of Staff Committee, which, in a nutshell, suggested there should be four landings, at Bône, Algiers, Oran, and Casablanca, "with a view to the earliest possible occupation of Tunisia, and the establishment in French Morocco of a striking force which can ensure control of the Straits of Gibraltar."[235] The landings inside the Mediterranean, which would include the US 1st Infantry Division, would come directly from Britain; those along the Atlantic coast would come straight from the USA.

This was agreed in principle, but there were still all manner of stumbling blocks that needed to be overcome, from the issue of timing, through to the continued problem of shipping, even to the swell and surf conditions on the Atlantic coast, and the thornier issues of how the Vichy French and even the Spanish would react.

The British also seemed to be having great difficulty in letting the Americans know their exact shipping capabilities—again, this depended on a number of factors, including whether they suspended any further Russian convoys and whether the Americans could help out in protecting British home waters. The two navies did agree, however, that they could not jointly provide escort for simultaneous attacks on Casablanca and inside the Mediterranean. Matters were not helped by the sinking of the carrier HMS *Eagle*—earmarked for TORCH—during a convoy to Malta on 11 August. Another carrier, HMS *Indomitable*, was also badly damaged on the same operation. Moreover, the losses on this convoy further underlined the danger for any Allied shipping venturing into the U-boat infested waters of the Western Mediterranean. Nor were there enough assault craft, either for the operation itself or with which the troops could immediately train. And the US Big Red One's equipment had still not arrived from the US. This alone did not augur well. On August 12, Ike was told that there were only nine combat loaders (vessels of all kinds for unloading troops) available—hardly enough for training the twelve divisions needed for the landings. "Ike said he would be glad if someone would give him some good news," noted Harry Butcher, "as every step in planning disclosed further obstacles."[236]

That same day, General Marshall informed Ike that in Washington the view was that TORCH appeared to be increasingly hazardous. "As the British might say," said Harry Butcher, having noted their penchant for understatement, "the prospect for success is somewhat less than consoling."[237]

At least Ike was surrounded by men he both liked and trusted. His deputy for TORCH now that Alexander was out was General Mark Clark, whom he had also placed in charge of plans. General Patton was also in town to discuss planning—he was still to lead the US invasion force. Like Ike, Patton had been one of the few members of the US Army to think progressively during the twenties and thirties. "Patton is a good fellow," noted Butch, "curses like a trooper and boasts that while he is stupid in many particulars (his own description) there is one quality he knows he has—the ability to exercise mass hypnotism."[238] In these difficult times, Ike needed people with this kind of self-belief around him.

Together with Clark and Patton, Ike drew up an assessment of the situation for Marshall on 15 August. Success or failure depended on a huge range of "ifs." Vichy French forces in North Africa stood at fourteen divisions—mostly poorly equipped, moderately trained, and reasonably ably commanded—and five hundred aircraft, albeit mostly obsolete. If these forces resisted strongly, it would make life very difficult for the Allies indeed. Gibraltar was also a cause for concern, because of its vulnerability due to its proximity to Spain. Sure, Spain was neutral at the moment, but it *was* fascist, and might allow Germany to use their airfields, or worse, enter the war on the side of the Axis. It was recognized that any unusual activity in Gibraltar was known in Berlin within twenty-four hours—so deception plans were also needed. Weather could also potentially become a critical factor. Having taken a copy of Ike's cable to Marshall, Harry Butcher summarized the situation for his diary: "The chances of making successful initial landings look better than even. The chances of capturing Tunis before Axis reinforcements arrive look considerably less than fifty percent. Building up a land-based air force presents great difficulties. Poor port facilities will delay heavy concentration of ground troops. Communications between Oran and Casablanca are long and uncertain. The attitude of the French remains problematical. Any sign of failure or hesitancy might lead the Axis to occupy Spain at once, with serious results to the whole course of the war."[239]

There was about a week between General Alexander's arrival and his actual taking over of the reins as C-in-C Middle East. Initially put up in the British embassy in Cairo, he spent his first few days there looking around and taking in the atmosphere. He wasn't altogether impressed with what he saw. There seemed to be too many troops in Cairo for starters, and although they looked fit and tough, it struck him that they lacked the usual air of confidence that he had come to associate with British soldiers. Talking to a number of officers, this impression was confirmed. "They were bewildered, frustrated, fed up," he noted; Churchill may have found the Eighth Army in good spirits, "but who wouldn't cheer up at the sight of Winston and his cigar?"[240] And he was also troubled to hear that most believed there would be another withdrawal next time the Axis attacked in strength. The awe with which Rommel was regarded had been endemic for some time, but Alex was appalled. "That legend contributed a lot to the Eighth Army's widespread belief in the invincibility of the Afrika Korps," he observed, and while he accepted that the German commander clearly had his strong points, "it was hardly necessary to attribute to him preternatural gifts in order to explains his successes."

Another thing that struck Alex was that the whole of Middle East Command operated from within the city—a city where there were restaurants, clubs, and a thousand other distractions. While troops on leave needed these welcome delights, Alex considered GHQ to be far too divorced from the battlefield. He remembered that during the First World War, their superior commanders had been housed in luxurious chateaux, with little understanding of the conditions of the front-line soldier. He was determined not to make the same mistake, and so as soon as he took over, set up his own HQ with key members of both his operational and administrative staff into a series of bell tents and caravans—"simplicity itself"—just west of the pyramids near Mena. There, he and his staff could get a feel for the desert; moreover, it marked the beginning of the desert road that led to the front. Alex christened his new HQ "Caledon Camp," after his family home back in Ireland.

Although it had been agreed that neither Alex nor Monty would take over until 15 August, Monty had hurried straight down to Eighth Army HQ on the thirteenth, the day after his arrival. He had arranged to meet Brigadier

Freddie de Guingand, the Auk's chief of staff in the field, outside Alexandria. The two had known each other for years, although had not run into each other since the beginning of the war. De Guigand had been in the Middle East since the beginning of the year as director of military intelligence (DMI); he had only been a few weeks as the Auk's COS and was completely new to staff work in the field.[241] Even so, Monty liked the cut of his jib and as the car sped on through the desert, turned to him and said, "Well, Freddie my lad, you chaps seem to have got things into a bit of a mess here. Tell me all about it."[242]

De Guingand did so, frankly and in detail. Morale, he admitted, was not good. What the Eighth Army wanted—and this was undoubtedly true— was direction and "a firm grip from the top." When they finally reached Eighth Army HQ, Monty was appalled. It was Spartan to say the least, with flies everywhere and little shade from the oppressive sun. While these were quite normal conditions for most of those in the desert, it was, as Mary Coningham had concluded, a needlessly robust place for the Army HQ. And where was the RAF HQ? Monty wanted to know. Many miles back, came the reply, by the sea. "The army and the air forces appeared to be fighting two separate battles, without the close personal relationship which is so essential," he noted. "The whole atmosphere of the Army Headquarters was dismal and dreary."[243]

After a brief conversation with General Ramsden, who was temporarily in charge, Monty told him he was now taking over immediately—despite orders to the contrary. Over lunch with the flies, he did some "savage" thinking and then issued the order, as already agreed with Alex, that there would be no withdrawal to the delta under any circumstances. While no one in Eighth Army had had any intention of retreating further—the Auk included—it was true that contingency plans had been made and a number of troops had been deployed further back to prepare defenses there. Both Alex and Monty were in total agreement that this was pointless. There was no better defensive position than the one they were in at present. If they could not repulse Rommel when he next attacked, they would certainly not be able to hold him off in the delta. Further defenses there were irrelevant. Psychologically, it also was important for Eighth Army that there would be no more retreating. As Alex pointed out, "Anyone can be forgiven for 'looking over his shoulder' if he is aware that preparations have been made for a possible retreat."[244]

Over the course of the following days, the new team certainly imposed a clarity of purpose and the "firm grip" that de Guingand had hoped for. On 19 August, Alex gave Monty his formal directive, reiterating the decision to stand firm with no thought of further withdrawal. "I ordered that this decision should be made known to all troops," noted

Alex.[245] This Monty was already doing, in a series of addresses, first to his staff at HQ, where he made it clear that things were going to change and that the rot had to stop. If they were to fight where they stood, they needed defenses in depth; troops in the delta were required at the front; ammunition, water, and rations all needed to be stored in forward areas. More troops were arriving, he told them, and they would be brought up quickly too. New equipment also was due soon, including the three hundred Shermans promised by Marshall back in June. De Guingand, for one, was impressed. "The effect of the address was electric—it was terrific!" he wrote. "And we all went to bed that night with a new hope in our hearts, and a great confidence in the future of our Army."[246]

When Air Commodore Tommy Elmhirst first saw the new army commander, he thought he looked rather unprepossessing and wondered whether he would be able to stand up to conditions in the desert. He soon realized, however, that he had "tremendous drive" and that he was "a veritable little tiger." Both Tommy and Mary were also impressed by Monty's talk, which Tommy recounted almost verbatim in a letter to his wife. "There is no discipline in this Army! None!" Monty had begun. "And from today anyone in Eighth Army who bellyaches about orders received from his superior, whether colonels to brigadiers, brigadiers to divisional commanders, divisional commanders to corps commanders, or corps commanders to me, will go very quickly to the worst place I can think of, the very worst—the verandah of Shepheard's Hotel in Cairo!" Since "bellyaching" had been a source of many of Eighth Army's problems, this was an absolutely crucial change in Eighth Army culture. If Ritchie had been the teacher every pupil talks over, Monty was the schoolmaster whose discipline was unquestioned. As if to prove the point, when General Lumsden raised a question, he was cut off immediately with, "I am talking here. You can see me in my caravan afterwards if you want to raise a point."

"He gave an excellent talk on leadership and organisation," wrote Tommy, "with every word of which I silently agreed." Even better, close cooperation with the RAF seemed to be at the heart of his military philosophy. Tommy was also encouraged to hear him outlining his plans "as though nothing could prevent their accomplishment. 'Rommel will attack in two or three weeks' time,' Monty had continued, 'and we shall dig in and defeat him. Then we shall do some hard training for two months. Every unit will go out of the line one by one to train, and on the beach, if it is possible, to bathe and get clear of flies. Then I shall attack with two corps in the line, a mobile one in reserve to come through the break, which we shall make in his line, and chase the remnants of his army out of Africa.'" "It was," noted Tommy, "quite clear as to who was now commanding Eighth Army."[247]

The low morale that Alex had noticed, and that de Guingand had mentioned, was felt more keenly by the commanders than it was the men, although there were obvious exceptions, particularly among men whose units had been decimated by the recent fighting. The 6th Royal Tank Regiment now had just twelve tanks left—less than the full compliment of a single squadron. Sam Bradshaw and several of the crews from B Squadron were transferred to C Squadron—now comprising six Grants and six Honeys. "We did feel low," admits Sam. "The regiment had almost ceased to exist, although I think we'd also lost a lot of confidence in the commanders. Gazala had a been a mess."

Harold Harper was another who felt morale was low. After his extraordinary escape at Gazala he'd been taken to hospital in Tobruk and then to the 42nd Military Hospital at Ismailia, between Cairo and Port Suez. After a week or so, he'd then been transferred to a convalescent hospital nearby. One day he spotted a vehicle with the South Notts Hussars markings on the side, and realizing it was a regimental HQ truck, called over to the driver and asked him for news. It was then that he had heard the regiment had been annihilated. "I felt terrible, terrible," says Harold. By chance, earlier that same day he'd been told by an orderly that Captain Ivor Birkin, who'd been in the truck with him the day he'd been captured, was in another hospital nearby, so he immediately asked the driver to take him to see the captain.

Like Harold, Birkin had not been told the fate of the regiment. "He took it reasonably cheerfully, I suppose," says Harold, "but this was probably the worst moment of the war as far as I was concerned." Having discharged himself, Harold then hitched a lift with the same driver back to Cairo where the remnants of the regiment—mainly men from regimental HQ—were being reformed into the 7th Medium Regiment. Far from being physically fit, he was also mentally feeling the strain. "To say that one was war weary was putting it very mildly indeed," he admits. For the next month the new unit trained together at Mena Camp. "The battery was formed from a lot of rag-tags," says Harold. "Cooks, clerks, stores blokes—all sorts of people were flung together."[248] Even former convicts, released early in return for active service. They were also given the new 5.5-inch heavy guns, the biggest field howitzer ever to reach Eighth Army. At seven and a half tons, they were as heavy as the 3.7-inch anti-aircraft guns, but this weight did not prevent them training as a mobile formation, with an also impressively sized gun tower known as a Matador. Harold, now a sergeant and in charge of his own gun, was still at Mena when the change of command took place, and still far from happy. "We were very dispirited," he says, "no doubt about it."

But other units, such as the 2nd Rifle Brigade, were still more or less intact. Albert Martin may have been frustrated by the army's retreat, but that was not the same as suffering from low morale. Similarly, while Bill Eadie might have recognized that new commanders were needed, he had been fairly cheerful of late. Certainly neither was particularly excited by the change of command. On the day that Monty took over, Bill Eadie was having a quiet day, and although he was aware that Churchill and other "big wigs" had been in town, nothing had been mentioned of their visit. A number of the men were suffering from dysentery—"gyppo guts we call it"—while those that were fit were carrying out raids in order to capture prisoners for questioning. The previous night they'd taken some Indian soldiers by mistake. Albert Martin was also aware that Churchill was around, "but no VIP ever visited my slit trench." He had little time for the PM, the man who'd ordered half the Eighth Army's troops to Greece the previous year. As far as Albert was concerned, they would have wrapped up the desert campaign there and then had Churchill left those troops where they were.

Since then, there had been so many changes of command, this latest seemed little different. New commanders had to be sized up; respect had to be earned, not given automatically. He'd heard of Alexander, who was known and respected, but he and his mates were all wondering who Montgomery was, and were only sorry that Gott had been killed. Maybe Monty would turn out all right, but Albert was certainly not going to get too excited just yet; as far as he was concerned, the new army commander's pep talks were a source of irritation more than anything else.

Frustration rather than loss of morale was also the principal gripe of the 4th Indian Division. "All they wanted," noted their commander, General Francis Tuker, "was to be given an opportunity and the order to stand and fight."[249] Well, they would soon have that chance. Even before Monty had arrived, Tuker's HQ had been recalled to Cairo and orders had been given for the gradual reassembly of his division at long last. Tuker was also less impressed than most by Monty's pronouncements on his arrival. Since his arrival in the Middle East the previous December, Tuker had been dismayed at the "gross incompetence, military ignorance and lack of any sort of grasp" by the army commanders. What Monty was saying about bellyaching and the need for training went without saying as far as he was concerned, and like Albert Martin, he wanted to see how the new command shaped up before he passed judgment.

Tuker was quite right, and as Alex was the first to admit, the changes they were introducing were largely common sense. That they had not been established before proved only how low command of Eighth Army had sunk. First and foremost, it was perfectly obvious that brigade groups as an operational unit were not working, and it was equally obvious that armor and infantry were not working well together. The Auk had even begun to realize this, and by the end of July had begun planning a complete reorganization of his armored forces. He wanted to do away with the distinction between armored and infantry divisions, terming them "mobile" instead, and made up from one armored and two infantry brigades. This was all well and good, but making such drastic changes in the middle of a campaign was well nigh impossible—complete retraining was required.

The Auk's expert on armored forces, Major-General Dick McCreery had strongly disagreed with the Auk and found himself out of a job as a result. When Alex arrived, McCreery was waiting for a passage home. He had been Alex's chief staff officer when he'd commanded 1st Division and Alex rated him highly as a staff officer and field commander, and so promptly made him his chief of staff. Another to survive the cull was Major-General John Harding, the Auk's director of military training (DMT). Harding had been summoned to see "the C-in-C" on 12 August and had hurried to the Auk's office only to discover Monty sitting behind his desk and Alex sitting on it, drumming his heels against it. He'd had no idea they would be taking over, nor who was doing which job. Monty wanted to form a *corps d'elite*—or *corps de chasse* as he called it—which he planned should be both highly mobile and strongly armored and which he envisaged would act as a spearhead. He had supposed that Rommel's Afrika Korps was such a force. He was partly mistaken—the DAK was supposed to be used for any role given to it, although in reality, Rommel did generally use it as the spearhead of his attacks. At any rate, having grilled Harding about the make-up of Eighth Army, he turned to him and said, "From all this muckage, can you organize for me two desert-trained armoured divisions and a mobile infantry division?" This was exactly the plan Tuker had suggested to the Auk the previous December. Harding told him yes, he thought he could, and returned later that evening with his plans for doing so. X Corps, the most recent addition to Eighth Army, would form the basis of this new strike force.[250]

There was absolutely nothing of tactical genius about this, nor was there anything startlingly original in Monty's plan to meet Rommel's new offensive. Since the July fighting, Eighth Army could no longer rely on the natural barrier of the Qattara Depression; the line had shrunk by fifteen miles. It was Gott who had predicted that Rommel would make a thrust around the south of the line, as he had done at Gazala, and so had drawn up plans to meet this attack by placing a series of defensive positions along the Alam Halfa Ridge. As Alex pointed out, "It was obvious to any well-trained military mind that with the area between Ruweisat and the sea strongly held, an enemy advance could only be attempted between Alam Halfa and the Depression; any such advance could not be sustained without extreme peril while the defending forces on and below the ridge remained intact."

The main difference between Gott's plan and Monty's was that Monty gave the strictest orders that the armor was not to be let loose against the Axis armor, as they had in the past. They were to fire from hull-down positions and hold their ground. There would no more heroic cavalry charges. From now on, Eighth Army would play it Monty's way, not Rommel's.

On 19 August, Churchill paid another visit to the front, having stopped over in Egypt on his return from Moscow. As he drove with Alex along the desert road he saw troops and equipment heading forward, and was cheered by all that his new C-in-C told him about the changes that had already been made. The prime minister, always impatient for offensive action, had chastised the Auk countless times for his refusal to bow to his demands. This was not why Churchill had sacked him, but it was a contributing factor. But as they motored west, Alex told him that the new offensive would not be ready until the end of September, and that was without taking into account the effect of the blow they could imminently expect from Rommel. Even this news was absorbed by the PM with equanimity.

The party was to stay the night at Burg el Arab, where Eighth Army and the Desert Air Force now both had their HQs. Churchill was delighted to be taken down to the sea for a "delicious" bath; a few hundred yards down the coast, many more troops were also splashing about in the cool turquoise water. Later, in Monty's map wagon, the army commander gave his now well-rehearsed seminar on the changes he'd made and how he was going to beat Rommel, and this cheered the PM even more.

Nearly three thousand miles away, however, the ill-fated Dieppe Raid was finally taking place, and was every bit the fiasco both Monty and Brooke had feared. The attack never got off the beaches, and over half the force of 6,000 were killed or taken prisoner, and 106 RAF aircraft were shot down. Thirteen US Rangers were also lost. Nothing had been achieved except to underline the great difficulty of making a seaborne landing successful, especially when carried out without sufficient firepower and against a determined and well dug in opposition.

The following day, 20 August, Churchill was given a tour of the next battlefield. Everything seemed to be in order. All the troops he saw greeted him with cheers and smiling faces. "Everybody said what a change there was since Montgomery had taken command," he wrote. "I could feel the truth of this with joy and comfort."[251]

* * *

Lieutenant-General Eisenhower had never been particularly keen on the TORCH plan in the first place, but felt that orders were orders and he was determined to carry them out to the very best of his ability. But he felt as though he was taking one step forward and two back. Recent reports increasingly suggested that a large number of the Vichy French would fight, and fight hard. The combined chiefs were still determined that the landings should take place by 10 October, but Ike felt strongly that this rigid time frame was seriously jeopardizing the whole operation. Nonetheless, it was now suggested that the landing at Casablanca should definitely be scrapped, partly because the two US divisions required would not be ready until November, partly because of the ongoing concern about the Atlantic swell and partly because of the old problem of shipping.

On 23 August he submitted another appraisal of the current situation and prospects of success to the Combined Chiefs of Staff, warning that as things stood, he did not have the forces to carry out the job. "As an expression of personal opinion," he wrote, "I believe that if the two governments could find the naval, air and ground forces, with the shipping, to carry out, simultaneously with the attack planned inside the Mediterranean, a strong assault at Casablanca, the chances for success would be greatly increased." This, he believed, would reduce the potential risk of a Spanish or French hostile reaction and would enable them to establish a firmer footing with greater port facilities in North Africa. But, he warned them, such an attack could not be carried out before 7 November, a month after the Combined Chiefs had desired.

In the northern section of the Alamein Line, Joe Madeley and his mates watched as a German plane swept over dropping leaflets. Slowly they floated to the ground and the Australians all tried to grab them for souvenirs. "Diggers!" it was written on some, "You are defending the Alamein Box! What about Port Darwin?" On others it said, "Aussies! The Yankees are having a jolly good time in your country. And you?" They were hardly the most invective morale breakers. "We thought them a great joke," says Joe. Much more damaging was the increased shelling. By the last week in August, the amount of ordnance whistling over their positions was increasing daily. "Jerry attack expected," noted Joe in his diary.

Elsewhere, there were telltale signs that the panzer army was about to launch an attack. One morning toward the end of August, Maiki and his section were waiting for their breakfast and were talking to an anti-tank gun crew sitting in a hollow below them. From across the desert ahead of them, an American Dodge truck hove into view, so one of the officers went forward down to the fence line of their minefield to show them where the entrance gate was.

"Christ!" he shouted, "they're Germans!" Then, swinging up his Tommy gun, he shot one of the Germans who'd been standing on the running board. The truck immediately swung and the pakeha officer fired another burst that killed two more in the back. "Christ, he saved us," says Maiki. "Those two jokers in the back had a Spandau." As the truck careered off back toward enemy lines, the machine gun battalion behind the Maori opened fire. "There were tracers going over it and under it, but they never hit," says Maiki.

The enemy returned later that night. "One of our blokes was out having a crap," says Maiki, "when he heard this clink, clink. So he crawled back to the company and told them there were Jerries lifting mines." The company was immediately told to stand to, and then flares were sent up. It was the first time Maiki had ever seen star shells—the desert was lit up like day, and as the flares gently floated down on their parachutes, the Maori opened fire. "I skittled three of them," says Maiki. It was the first time he'd ever killed anyone. It wasn't a good feeling.

Increased enemy reconnaissance activity in the south further suggested that Rommel was intending to send his attack that way. In the mess at RAF HQ, they were laying bets as to when it would come. "Last night," wrote Tommy Elmhirst on 26 August, "the betting was 6–4 on that it started that night. No attack came and Mary lost a bob."[252] In fact Mary had sneakily been trying to cheat. Ultra (to which he was privy) had warned that an Axis attack was likely that day. During the past week or so, Tommy had been working hard bringing their squadrons to maximum strength in readiness for the attack, while Mary had wound down aerial activity considerably. Two South African bomber wing commanders had visited Air HQ asking for more work to do, but Mary had been adamant. "I will give them and their squadron plenty to do when the time comes," he explained to Tommy. "But at the moment there aren't enough targets showing and I am not going to have them wasting their engines and bombs, and possibly the odd crew when there is nothing worthwhile to hit."[253]

But every effort was still being made to attack Rommel's supply lines. As Ultra had been revealing, the panzer army and Axis air forces were still desperately short of supplies, especially fuel. Rommel had gambled on taking Egypt during the first week of July. Now he was about to stake everything on one last effort to achieve his goal. If this failed there would be no more opportunities; with Eighth Army's shorter supply lines and the vast amounts of men, fuel, and equipment arriving daily, he realized he was fast running out of time. As Mary Coningham had wisely told Cecil Beaton back in May, the war in the desert was ultimately about who had the better lines of supply.

The major problem for Rommel was that his panzer army needed around 100,000 tons of supplies every month if it was to function to capacity, but there was simply not the means of getting it to him. The principal ports under his control along the North African coast were Tripoli (around 1,300 miles from Alamein), Benghazi (around 800 miles), Tobruk (300 miles) and Mersa Matruh (109 miles). Between May and August, Axis shipping was able to reach Tripoli and Benghazi almost unscathed because these routes were too far away to be affected by Allied air attacks from the Middle East and because Malta had virtually ceased to operate as an offensive platform after the terrible aerial blitz it received during the first four months of the year, while efforts to resupply the island with fuel, especially, had largely failed.

Before Rommel had continued his advance to Egypt in June, Rome had assured him "several times" that so long as the ports of Tobruk and Mersa Matruh were in Axis hands, adequate supplies could be guaranteed.[254] These assurances had proved false, however. First, Tobruk and Mersa Matruh were well within range of the Allied air forces in the Middle East, and were attacked almost continuously. Again, the actual numbers of ships that were sunk in port were not great, but the level of disruption and damage caused to two already heavily damaged ports was considerable. Rommel liked to blame the Italians for much of his woes and complained that the unloading of shipping in Tobruk, where little more than six hundred tons a day were ever successfully disembarked, was "a terribly leisurely affair," made worse by "lack of initiative and a total absence of any sort of technical ingenuity," but this was unfair. If Charles Coles could easily damage his propellers navigating at the entrance to Tobruk harbor in his shallow-bottomed MTB, then the hazards for incoming supply ships were clearly far, far worse. Furthermore, frequent aerial attacks brought more damage to the port as well as time delays: while bombs were being dropped, all work stopped, and then, once the bombers disappeared, more time had to be spent clearing up the rubble and wreckage. This was now even the case with Benghazi, which was frequently attacked at night and by the American long-range bombers during the day. At any rate, the 20,000 tons a month Tobruk was handling was, in fact, quite an achievement.

Certainly, Rommel did not have direct control over the logisticians in Italy. Supplying the panzer army was principally the job of the Italian high command, the *Commando Supremo*. So it was that in July—despite Rommel's angry protestations—the Italians insisted on sending nearly all their monthly supplies through Tripoli and Benghazi. Only 5 percent of shipping was lost and 91,000 tons were successfully docked, but at such huge distances from the front, this was of little use to the panzer army. Half the precious fuel landed was used just getting it across the huge distances to the front. It took a week, for example, just to bring supplies from Benghazi. In August, Rommel put his foot down and insisted the Italians dock at Tobruk and Mersa Matruh. The result was that although the route to the front shortened dramatically, losses rose and only half the required monthly supplies ever made it onto dry land.

But the second reason why the Italians failed to deliver at Tobruk and Mersa was due to the size and scale of Axis shipping. While shipping remained high enough to supply North Africa in terms of tonnage, the number of large vessels had dropped dramatically.* Consequently, greater numbers of ships were required, which took longer to load and unload, and a bottleneck ensued. More significantly, despite the damage inflicted, five from a fourteen-ship convoy managed to reach Malta by 15 August, including the tanker *Ohio,* and with these arrivals, Malta's capabilities as an offensive platform rose considerably. Working in conjunction with the Allied air forces of the Middle East, they made Rommel's urgent need for fuel one of his biggest nightmares of the entire campaign in North Africa.

"Unless I get two thousand cubic meters of fuel, five hundred tons of ammunition by the twenty-fifth [August] and a further two thousand cubic meters of fuel by the twenty-seventh and two thousand tons of ammunition by the thirtieth, I cannot proceed," he told General von Rintelen, the German military attaché in Rome.[255] The Commando Supremo hurriedly put together a plan to send more fuel-carrying ships. Nine vessels were to leave Italy over a period of six days starting on 28 August. Rommel had to pray they would all safely arrive, for as Kesselring pointed out, "Petrol was already scarce, and the loss of a 4,000 to 6,000-ton tanker meant an almost irreparable gap."[256]

This supply headache did not affect Alexander to anything like the same degree. Just 60 miles from Alexandria and only 150 from the Suez Canal, Britain was unloading around 100,000 tons of fuel a month. Britain would not be defeated because of lack of supplies.

* * *

*In June 1940, the Italians possessed 1,748,941 tons of shipping, but had lost 1,259,061 by the end of 1942. However, in the meantime, they had gained around 300,000 tons of new shipping, as well as 582,302 tons of German shipping. In other words, they now had 77 percent of the shipping with which they began the war.

Ike tended to dine or lunch with the PM in London at least once a week, and on 25 August, he and General Clark were summoned to dinner at Number 10. The prime minister had recently returned from his trip to the Middle East and Russia, and he was in good form—his talks with Stalin had gone well and he was pleased with the new team in place in the desert. But he was insistent TORCH should go ahead, despite Ike's concerns and the impasse over plans during the previous week. If necessary, he told Ike, he would hop on a plane and go to Washington to discuss the issue with the president.

It was impossible to leave the prime minister until well past midnight. Knowing this, Ike had told Butch that he would "sleep in" the following morning. As usual, though, he was up at seven and, along with Clark, was telling Harry Butcher some good anecdotes about the PM. At one point Churchill had knocked a tall glass off a side table, but carried on talking as though it had never happened. He also suddenly asked for a change of socks and without any hint of embarrassment took his old pair off and put on the new. Later, the PM stood up and started scratching his back against the edge of a door. "Guess I picked 'em up in Egypt," was his explanation.[257]

However amusing this may have been to the two American generals, Butch was conscious of the heavy weight bearing down on his boss's shoulders. "The harassed Ike," noted Butch, "mulling over his troubles as Allied commander dealing with America and Britain, not to mention the land, sea and air services of each, nor the variety of high political problems involved with Spain and France, has always to consider not only the purely military matters, but international politics and personalities."

This was all too true. Furthermore, living in central London, there were few opportunities for light relief from the grueling pace required of him. Ike would occasionally insist on stepping out for an hour, and one Sunday they had even taken a long, leisurely drive into the country, and had then stopped to watch a game of cricket—"but couldn't get very excited about it."[258] But such trips did little to recharge the batteries. What was needed, as Ike had suggested soon after their arrival, was a cottage out of town—a "hideout to escape the four forbidding walls of the Dorchester."[259] Butch eventually found what he thought was just the place at the end of August. "It is called Telegraph Cottage," he noted. "Small, unpretentious, remotely situated on a ten-acre wooded tract, with a lawn at the back and a rose garden." Even better, it also sat between two golf courses. Butch took it on the spot.

General Tuker's dream of having his entire 4th Indian Division back together again and ready for action was not to be entirely realized. In the third week of August, the 7th Indian Brigade was released from Cyprus, but one of his field artillery regiments remained on that island. Tuker was a particular student of artillery, and had spent much time in Cyprus training his infantry to work alongside his gunners; so it was extremely galling for him to now find these two halves separated. Furthermore, another of his field regiments was still in Amariya, while his 11 Infantry Brigade had been entirely lost at Tobruk. No wonder he felt frustrated. However, 1/2 Gurkhas, the battalion he had originally joined as a young lieutenant, was now in fine shape. They had been training intensively—not just with artillery, but also practicing nighttime attacks and how to disable anti-tank screens. "Frankly," wrote Tuker, "I built the infantry of the division round that battalion, for it had been mine and I had put into it the whole of my knowledge of training and war."[260] When they were finally given a chance to fight, he had high hopes his Indians would show the rest of Eighth Army what they could achieve.

Rifleman Nainabadahur Pun reached Egypt with the rest of 1/2 Gurkha Rifles on 25 August, but three days later, tragedy struck. A number of mines accidentally exploded in the midst of a large number of men during an instruction course. Out of 153 casualties, sixty-eight were fatalities, ripping out the heart of HQ Company. Many of those killed were among the best trained in the battalion. "It can never be the same again," wrote Tuker, who must have been wondering when his fortunes would finally take a turn for the better. It was also a great blow to Nainabadahur Pun. "I lost a lot of my new friends," he says.

But a number of new units were already at the front, including the 44th Infantry Division, which had recently arrived and was now holding Alam Halfa Ridge itself. Also back in the front line was gunner Harold Harper, whose new battery was going into action for the first time. He was already keenly aware of the changes in equipment now taking place within Eighth Army. Not only was he firing a huge new gun, but after a couple of days spent digging themselves in as best as they could, a bulldozer had arrived and scooped out four gun pits in what seemed like no time at all. "We'd never seen one of those before," says Harold, "we thought we'd reached Mecca."[261]

There was an air of tense expectation hanging over the British lines. Harold was supporting the Australians, still holding the northernmost part of the line. With the increase in enemy shelling, Joe Madeley and his mates had even been ordered to dig crawl trenches between their dugouts. A few miles to the south, Bill Eadie and the men of the 2nd South African Brigade were also coming under greater enemy bombardment. On 27 August, a shell landed just behind him, but miraculously did not explode. "We are just waiting, waiting," he wrote two days later. So too was the prime minister. Alex had agreed with him that he would signal the word "Zip" when Rommel's attack began. "What do you think of the probabilities of 'Zip' coming this moon?" asked Churchill on 28 August. "Zip now equal money every day," Alex replied.[262]

In London, Harry Butcher discovered that their new home, Telegraph Cottage, lay only half a mile from an important decoy for enemy aircraft. But as August drew to a close and September began, Eisenhower was only too grateful for this bolt-hole away from the rigors of preparing TORCH. There was still no firm decision on the form Operation TORCH should take. General Kenneth Anderson had been appointed commander of the British Task Force in the absence of Alexander and then Montgomery, and after a lengthy briefing with Clark on 27 August, had added his two cents' worth by expressing his doubts about the feasibility of forestalling an Axis occupation of Tunisia, regardless of the date. Clark told Anderson that the operation was still definitely on "and that ways and means to make it successful would have to be found."

On 29 August, Roosevelt stepped into the ring and suggested that all British land forces be dropped from the calculations and that landings be made only at Casablanca and Oran, making it an entirely American operation except for supporting naval forces and shipping. The president felt certain that an all-American operation was far less likely to be resisted by the French, and that once the French did lay down their arms, Algiers would quickly follow anyway. The British appeared to be warming to this idea, but were still insisting Algiers should be included in the landings.

Whatever final form TORCH took, Eisenhower still believed they were undertaking "something of a quite desperate nature." He felt rather as he imagined Napoleon must have done on his return from Elba. "If the guess as to the psychological reaction is correct, we may gain a tremendous advantage in this war; if the guess is wrong, it would be almost as certain that we will gain nothing and will lose a lot."[263]

The Battle of Alam Halfa opened on the night of 30 August. The first three Axis tankers that had set sail from Italy two days before had already been sunk by a combination of Malta-based aircraft and submarines, and by Wellington bombers from the Middle East, but despite this blow, Rommel had decided to go ahead with his attack as planned, trusting that the next tanker due in, the *San Andreas,* would successfully reach Tobruk with her cargo of over 3,000 tons of fuel. By the time the Axis barrage opened, however, the *San Andreas* was already at the bottom of the Mediterranean. Once more, the Malta Beauforts and Beaufighters had hit their mark.

As shells rained down on the British positions, Joe Madeley and the men of the Australian 20th Brigade sat crouched in their dug-outs with their rifles and Tommy guns, listening to the barrage screeching over and around them. After two hours the shelling stopped and at three in the morning the men of the German 164th Light Division advanced toward the Australian wire. As had so often happened during the trench warfare of the previous war, the defenders were ready and waiting, and, as Joe noted, they "gave them hell." But it made for an extremely uncomfortable few hours, all the same. "Lord there was some stuff flying about," he admitted. The fighting continued until daylight. This was the most hard-pressed attack along the northern half of the front, but the barrage was followed by attacks all along this stretch of the line. Bill Eadie also sat tight while the barrage fell about them, but the South Africans, having stood to just after two in the morning were every bit as ready for the attackers as their Australian neighbors.

Nonetheless, this was not the main attack and deceived no one. In addition to information from Ultra, Mary Coningham's reconnaissance squadrons had been working hard during the previous ten days and immediately picked up the Axis concentrations of armor on the move in the south. In a carbon copy of his attack on the Gazala Line, Rommel had sent in holding attacks in the north while the Afrika Korps and the bulk of the panzer army's armor thrust through the minefields to the south and then turned north. This had been tactically suspect at Gazala and so it was again now, because without a simultaneous punch through the British line further north, the panzer army would once again find itself looping behind enemy lines without an easy means of resupply. Had he gone for a two-punch strategy, it would have been easier for him to encircle and cut off part of the British line and draw the rest of Eighth Army away from its prepared defensive positions. [See Map]

Through British ineptitude Rommel had gotten away with it at Gazala, but to assume that Monty was cut from the same cloth was an error. This time there were no crossed wires between the British C-in-C and army commander, no disputed orders and no surprises.

As at Gazala, Rommel had underestimated how long it would take to achieve his goals. His armor reached the first of the minefields at around two in the morning, right opposite the positions of the 2nd Rifle Brigade, who were once again operating in the south with the rest of the 7th Motor Brigade. Immediately, the riflemen opened fire with their six-pounders, making the most of the easy targets that were slowly making their way through the mines. By dawn, though, it was clear they could hold on no longer and so at first light were ordered back through their own minefields with the intention of retreating back past the British armor dug in and lying in wait at the base of Alam Halfa Ridge. But they had done the task asked of them: held up the advancing panzer army and given the impression that the southern sector was more heavily garrisoned than it really was. On the signal, Albert and his five other crew members jumped into their truck and set off, but soon found themselves isolated from the rest of their company. However, this had been agreed, for when they had finally left, there had been no time to form up and leave in an orderly column. Rather, it was a case of each crew and section being left to their own devices, and making the most of the open desert to create as small a target as possible.

The panzer army had also come under attack from Wellington night-bombers, who left thirty fires burning in the desert by the time the Axis armor was emerging through the minefields and beginning its wide sweep north. General Nehring, the commander of the Afrika Korps, was wounded during one of these attacks. It had not been the ideal start for Rommel, who had expected his armor to be ready to attack together by 6 AM along a wide front. At 9 AM, three hours behind schedule, he even considered calling off the entire attack. After some discussion with his commanders, he decided they would try at noon instead. The capricious desert winds then began to swirl, and while the dust storms that followed undoubtedly saved the panzer army from further attacks by the RAF, it also caused problems as they tried to form up, and meant different units set off at different times, most well after one o'clock. When they did finally get going, 15th then 21st Panzer came under heavy attack, the latter eventually lured onto the British armor of 22nd Armoured Brigade.

A fierce armored battle followed, with the County of London Yeomanry and 1st Rifle Brigade (2 RB's sister battalion), taking on the brunt of the panzers, but heroically resisting. When, at dusk, the panzers were forced to retire to leaguer for the night, Alam Halfa was still barring their route north.

No sooner had darkness fallen and the dust settled than the RAF returned in strength. The Axis leaguers were lit up by flares as wave after wave of night bombers caused havoc. By morning, a pall of smoke hung over their positions from numerous burning vehicles. These attacks had also affected the panzers' efforts to resupply. Through lack of petrol, 21st Panzer could not move at all, but 15th Panzer got going and soon created problems for the newly arrived 8th Armoured Brigade as it tried to close the gap between its positions on the eastern foot of Alam Halfa and 22nd Armoured, five miles to its west on Bare Ridge.

This was the first battle for the Sherwood Rangers Yeomanry. They had been eagerly waiting their chance since the previous evening, with Colonel "Flash" Kellett "longing to get at the enemy."[264] Their attack finally began around 11 o'clock in the morning and demonstrated just how pitifully ill-prepared they were. The Sherwood Rangers had no idea of the enemy's strength, nor had they formulated any kind of plan with the regiment supporting them on the left, the equally inexperienced Staffordshire Yeomanry; and although the artillery fired a fifteen-minute barrage beforehand, there was only one battery and they had not had time to register any targets and so were firing blind. The Sherwood Rangers first sight of enemy tanks was from 2,000 yards—mere black dots on the horizon. Although the Rangers opened fire, there was no reply, so they surged forward and in a long line cruised to within 150 yards of the enemy positions, at which point the enemy anti-tank guns opened fire. "The enemy had cunningly held his fire until we were right on top of him."[265] Hardly very sporting, although this was not a mistake they would make again in a hurry.

Seven tanks were soon blazing, four more were disabled, and the Rangers' attack stalled. They were hopelessly underprepared to meet the slick professionalism of the Germans. The whole culture of the regiment was to treat the war as little more than a glorious adventure, or a kind of highly dangerous extreme sport. Nearly every aspect of their existence was given some kind of sporting reference. This even went as far as their radio communication, and was hardly the most taxing code in the world to break, even to non-cricket-playing Germans and Italians. "The Yeomanry found the official [code] vocabulary unenterprising and a nuisance to learn," noted Keith Douglas, an officer who was to rejoin the regiment in October, "and supplemented it with 'veiled talk' of their own." The two main sources of allusion they used were horses and cricket:

> "Uncle Tom, what's the going like over this next bit? Can we bring the, er, unshod horses over it?" "Uncle Tom, I'm just going over Beecher's myself, you want to hold 'em in a bit and go carefully, but after that it's good going for the whole field." "King 2 Ack," says someone who has broken a track. "I shall need the farrier, I've cast a shoe." Someone else is "having trouble with my horse's insides. Could I have the Vet?" Metaphor changes . . . "King 2, now that that chap has retired to the pavilion, how many short of a full team are you?"[266]

With their horses rapidly losing shoes, and with too many already having been put down, they were ordered to return to the paddock under cover of smoke bombs fired over their heads. Fortunately for them, 15th Panzer did not follow up their success—they too had fallen short of fuel, but when, the following day, Colonel Kellett went to inspect the battlefield, he saw that all but one of their burned-out tanks had been completely shattered. The turret of one had even been blown some thirty yards by the explosion. This engagement was the Sherwood Rangers' first major step on their journey from part-time amateurs to becoming battle-hardened professionals. But they still had some way to go yet.

Meanwhile, throughout 1 September, the RAF poured bombs and cannon fire over the hapless Axis forces, now caught in the wide, open expanse of the desert that lay to the south of the long ridges of Alam Halfa and Alam Nayil. The bombers tended to fly over in formations of eighteen aircraft—the "Eighteen Imperturbables" gave great pleasure and comfort to the British soldiers below. Cobber Weinronk missed the first stooge of the day, but flew later along with three American Mitchell bombers and their crews. The flak was heavy and Cobber saw one of the Bostons lose its tail while one of the Mitchells had a wing shot off. "Initially, they rose above the squadron and it looked as though they collided overhead," he noted, but he was later told they hadn't and that some of the crew had managed to safely bail out.[267] But in this bare and featureless country, the bomb bursts from the Allied bombers were made even more vicious by spraying out jagged shards of rock. Seven German officers were killed at Afrika Korps HQ that day.

There were victories to be had in the air, too. Having already flown two missions that morning, Billy Drake was then scrambled at 2 o'clock and ordered to lead the entire wing of three squadrons, which included a number of Americans from Duke Ellington's 57th Fighter Group. When the wing spotted six Me 109s, an American, Captain Saville, shot one of them down. Billy Drake's fighters then spotted a large formation of around fifty Stukas and thirty Me 109s. Turning toward them, they swooped straight into the dive-bombers, forcing them to jettison their bombs. Stukas may still have brought fear to the bravest of men on the ground, but to the British fighters they were meat and drink, all menace gone. Billy sent two plummeting to the ground, while among the rest of the wing, another thirteen other enemy aircraft were claimed. The entire wing then made it safely back to their landing ground.

That night, 2 September, the Wellingtons returned once more, pasting the panzer army until dawn. Fires from these raids were still burning when, shortly after first light, the day bombers took over. By this time, Rommel had already had enough, and gave the order to go on the defensive, his dream of taking Egypt smashed for good. That morning, the Axis commander drove through the area still occupied by the Afrika Korps. Between ten and twelve o'clock, they came under attack six times. At one point he had a very narrow escape himself—he only just had enough time to fling himself into a slit trench before the bombs began falling around him. A spade lying next to the trench was pierced by a red-hot shard of shrapnel that then landed beside him. "Swarms of low-flying fighter-bombers were coming back to the attack again and again," he wrote, "and my troops suffered tremendous casualties. Vast numbers of vehicles stood burning in the desert."[268] Cobber Weinronk flew four separate raids that day: at 7 AM, then again at ten. The third was at one o'clock and the last at four in the afternoon. "The target was armoured vehicles," he noted, "and there was so much of it that one could not miss."[269] These attacks continued all day and on into the night. A steady succession of parachute flares swamped the desert with light. Magnesium incendiaries, impossible to extinguish, crackled on the ground, flooding their vicinity in a bright glow. With their targets lit up like a floodlit sports ground, the bombers droned over, pouring fragmentation and high-explosive bombs onto the men and vehicles below.

Meanwhile, rather than leave all his infantry brigades static in the north, Monty began bringing troops down and ordering up some of his reserves to shore up their defensive line along the two ridges. The 2nd South African Brigade was one of those units moved south. At sunset on 1 September, they moved onto the Ruweisat Ridge, a sensible precaution that gave Eighth Army added defense in depth. Bill Eadie was with the column of trucks taking the brigade to their new positions, and they soon found themselves under air attack. The enemy hit several vehicles, but fortunately, not Bill's. The following day he went to Amariya, some forty miles up the coast towards Alexandria to pick up some new replacement trucks and on the way saw plenty of air activity, witnessing several planes being shot down. But the rumors were all good: "We have smashed about ninety enemy tanks," he noted, then added, "This is a preliminary to the big battle for Egypt." This was exactly what Monty had told his men before the battle on a flier handed out to all the troops. Unlike previous desert generals, Monty wanted to keep his men informed, from the top to the bottom; Monty's different command style was reaching everyone in Eighth Army.

By this stage in the battle, there was clearly a great opportunity to take the attack to the panzer army, the bulk of which now lay shell-shocked and crippled by lack of fuel in the desert south of Alam Halfa. But Monty refused to be drawn. He had only been in the desert a fortnight and was conscious that many in the front line were still green with little experience of the desert. His aim had been to stop Rommel's offensive; this had been achieved, and so however tempting the situation appeared, the risk of suffering at the hands of a German counterattack did not strike him as one worth taking.

Nonetheless, he did allow the Australians to carry out a long-prepared attack in the north, to the west of Tell el Eisa, on 1 September. A bridgehead was made but not maintained. Joe Madeley was not directly involved in the raid, but during the day his company fired 36,000 rounds as the enemy tried to press home a counterattack. Monty also ordered one staged offensive operation, the aim being to close the minefield gaps through which the panzer army had crossed on the opening night of the battle. This was planned for the night of 3 September, and involved both New Zealand brigades and the 132nd Infantry Brigade, plus two squadrons of I tanks. On the right, silent raids by the 6th New Zealanders were to create a diversion, but were also intended to secure the right flank of their attack through which the 132nd Brigade would then pass. Unfortunately, these raids merely stirred up a hornet's nest. In time-honored fashion, the operation failed to be properly coordinated and so 132nd Brigade were an hour late getting going. When they eventually came into contact with the enemy, they walked straight into a wall of machine-gun and mortar fire.

Meanwhile, on the left flank of the attack were the 5th New Zealanders, which included the Maori. Maiki Parkinson, in C Company, was among the leading troops along the battalion's front. Setting off at 10:30 PM as planned, they walked a couple of miles before the darkness was suddenly ripped apart by a machine-gun tracer. Shortly after, the RAF, which had once again arrived to bomb enemy positions, started dropping flares, bathing the battlefield in bright light. Although this caught the Maori in the open, it also showed them where the enemy positions were. With bayonets fixed and yelling their war cries, they charged down upon the Germans. "Kamerad!" one terrified German cried. "Kamerad be buggered," yelled a Maori in return and killed him.[270] As a platoon from D Company charged a machine-gun nest, one man had his arm blown off by a burst of fire. As he hit the ground, he was so worked up that he picked up his arm and in his fury threw it at the machine-gun post. Another Maori from A Company single-handedly charged an 88mm gun, killing all the crew.

Confusion reigned. Maiki watched his section leader, Lance-Corporal "Nugget" Tukaki, shoot one of their own men. "The joker somehow got in front of us," says Maiki, "then the dunes were lit up and there was this figure and Nugget went bang with the Bren. When we got to him . . . well, Christ, we saw it was one of our blokes. That was the first of our blokes I saw killed in action." It would not be the last. As they surged forward, Maiki and a party of C Company found themselves fighting alongside some men from A Company. They had reached a depression where there were a large number of parked vehicles, and so immediately opened fire, killing the drivers and shooting up every truck and wagon they could. "It broke your heart," says Maiki, "because they were mostly our captured trucks."

As first light began to creep over the desert, word reached the Maori that 132nd Brigade had been shot to pieces. Moreover because the battalion had gone beyond their objectives, they were now dangerously stranded and in danger of being encircled and annihilated. Digging themselves into the soft sand, the Maori soon came under heavy shellfire, although fortunately the sandy ground lessened the effect of each explosion. During the morning a lull occurred, and then a lone figure appeared with a white flag. This turned out to be a soldier from the Buffs, captured during the night and sent over to ask for surrender. The Maori refused, which was just as well because rescue was at hand. Smoke shells had been fired over them and runners sent out to recall them. The isolated Maori, Maiki included, then hurried back to safety as the smoke drifted across their positions.

Despite the success of the Maori, the attack had failed. The sappers had been unable to close the minefield gaps and the 132nd Brigade—in its first battle—had lost 697 killed, missing, and wounded, while the New Zealanders suffered 275 casualties. Monty's decision not to launch a major counterattack in force had been vindicated.

The battle was now all but over, and during the next few days, Rommel withdrew his forces back through the minefields. The RAF continued to harass the enemy, but with less intensity than during the previous days; sandstorms and their own losses saw to that. Albert Martin, having now rejoined the rest of S Company, was also involved with 7th Motor Brigade's "usual harassing tactics."

The panzer army had unquestionably suffered from its desperate shortage of fuel. Of the nine tankers sent from Italy during this period, only four made it to Tobruk, and one of those was no help at all: the fuel it carried had been contaminated and was useless. The architects of the British victory, however, had been the gunners and especially the RAF, who had been almost entirely responsible for the British offensive operations in the battle. The Desert Air Force had begun the battle with slightly fewer aircraft than the Axis, but with much more fuel and so had been able to maintain almost total air superiority. As Rommel himself admitted, "nonstop and very heavy air attacks by the RAF, whose command of the air had been virtually complete, had pinned my army to the ground and rendered any smooth deployment or any advance by time schedule completely impossible."[271]

At the RAF HQ, Mary Coningham had reason to be pleased. Sixty-eight aircraft had been lost, but it had been a great victory; once again, their efforts had helped the army to an incalculable degree. Mary, Tommy, and the other senior air staff had taken to dining with the army commander every night, but on 4 September, before wandering over for supper, Mary brought out a bottle of champagne, which he had been keeping for a special occasion. Raising their glasses, Mary gave a toast: "To the further confusion of the Hun!"[272]

Bill Eadie also sensed that a significant victory had been achieved. "Today is the third anniversary of war's declaration," he recorded on 3 September, "a day of prayer in Great Britain. I hope it is going to be a turning point in the vicious war that has resulted. Somehow I think it is and we are going to move victoriously from now on." His hunches had so far proved right.

Monty and Alex could also pat themselves on the back. Their brief tenure had so far followed the path they had prescribed, and Eighth Army was once more buoyant. Both men had warned there could be no more retreat. Nor would there be, for by the end of the Battle of Alam Halfa, the Middle East had been saved.

CHAPTER 12

Getting Ready Part I—
September, 1942

FROM THE MOMENT HE ARRIVED in Britain, Ike had
been determined to maintain Allied unity, and his resolution became only
stronger once he became Allied commander-in-chief. Time and again he
reiterated to his staff the need to work together. It was often an uphill battle but whatever the problems, he told his subordinates, they must be
overcome. "Ike is insistent that his idea of complete integration of both
nationalities will work," noted Harry Butcher, and when Clark expressed
the difficulties of getting British and American personnel on his planning
team to work well together, the chief told him to make changes until the
right personalities were found.[273]

Eisenhower also recognized that as the senior American in Britain, he
needed to lead by example, yet by the same token was "constitutionally
disinclined to personal publicity." This was where Harry Butcher, with his
media and PR background, was so helpful, and did much to nudge, push
and coerce the chief into becoming the publicity dream that did so much
to forge Anglo-US relations. Putting the right spin on Ike's public appearance and perception went as far as trying to influence Ike's waxwork
model at Madame Tussaud's. Butch knew perfectly well that almost every
US soldier and sailor who visited London would pass through the waxwork museum, and so tried to persuade them to take their pose from a
photograph of Ike saluting. "It shows him in a proper military salute, with
bronzed face, overseas cap, and his jutting chin," he noted. But Madame
Tussaud's felt this looked too formal. "T'hell with artistry!" Butch added in
his diary. "We want morale and leadership!"[274]

British public perception of not only Eisenhower but all Americans
was also recognized by the chief to be of vital importance in his quest for
strong and lasting military alliance. The advice of an American Oxford ac-
ademic was even sought. Professor Goodhart echoed Ike's thoughts ex-

actly when he said, "The relations between the American army and the English people is a problem of outstanding importance because it will affect not only the immediate conduct of the war but also Anglo-American cooperation in the future."[275] There were two simple things to consider, he said: first, that American soldiers should be happy in Britain, and second, that the British like them.

But achieving this was no easy matter. The British War Office outlined the difficulties in a "Memorandum on Good Relations Between the People of Great Britain and the USA," a memo of lasting good sense. "We have the war to win," it began, "and when that is done, there will be the peace to win. Last time, we won the war, but lost the peace. We shall not easily win the war unless we achieve harmony and unity between our armed forces and those of the USA. We cannot possibly win the peace unless we can create real friendship and understanding between our people and the people of the USA." The problem, it continued, was that "The average Englishman, in his own heart, views with alarm the prospect of having his country swamped with Americans . . . He has been taught to think of them as noisy, boasting people, without our traditional regard for other people's feelings, rights and property." The average American, on the other hand, "knows us chiefly as a nation suffering from a slow decay, a nation of superior, unfriendly, discourteous people, set in the old ways of inefficiency, clinging to old dreams of a greatness which we cannot perpetuate."

Overcoming these ingrained perceptions could not be done by orders. Rather, time, skill, and unobtrusiveness were the keys. "You need a creative imagination that has been tempered by a knowledge of what works and what does not. You need men trained in advertising and propaganda on the job."[276] This was all sound advice and such people were soon put on the case. Eric Knight, an American writer and author of a best-selling war novel, wrote *A Short Guide to Great Britain,* issued to all American troops now arriving in the UK. "You will find right away that England is a small country, smaller than North Carolina or Iowa," it warned. "England's largest river, the Thames (pronounced "Tems") is not even as big as the Mississippi when it leaves Minnesota," but, he added, it was a place of pretty and varied scenery. "Britain may look a little shop-worn and grimy to you. The British people are anxious to have you know that you are not seeing their country at its best." It might look like it needed a lick of paint, it continued, but this was because the paint factories were making aircraft rather than paint.

Under such headings as "Age Instead of Size," and "British Reserved Not Unfriendly," the guide offered practical advice about how GIs should best come to terms with this strange and peculiar land with its even stranger people. A map was included, as well as a translation of British currency and a glossary of terms. The guide rounded off with some important do's and don'ts. "You are higher paid than the British 'Tommy.' Don't rub it in. Play fair with him. He can be a pal in need." It was also important not to show off—"'swank' as the British say . . . Don't try to tell the British that America won the last war or make wisecracks about the war debts or about British defeats in war." And most important of all, "NEVER criticize the King or Queen."[277]

On the whole, however, American troops were proving to be popular in Britain. US troops were felt to be "well mannered." Henry Bowles certainly believes most US troops were courteous and behaved themselves at that time. "And we *were* there for a purpose," adds Tom. They were also generous with their liberal allowances of sweets and cigarettes. "Oh yes," says Henry, "you could go and get cigarettes and different kinds of candy bars," luxuries that were scarce and expensive in Britain. This bargaining power made a number of American troops very popular with young women and children. When the 1st Infantry Division were sent back to Scotland in October, Henry Bowles became very friendly with a Scottish girl. "She was singing down the street," says Henry, "and we got talking. We never got up to much—we'd just ride a tram up to the park and talk and so on." It was true, however, that discrepancies in pay, especially, did cause a certain amount of resentment from the British troops. "We had more money to spend than British soldiers, I guess," admits Henry, "although we personally weren't making as much as others because we were sending some home. But we still had more than the British." An American report of September noted that British soldiers complained that US troops were "too soft" on account of their pay and so didn't see how they could be any good at actual fighting. And despite the guide's warning, American troops were also reported to "throw their money about" and "rub it in" about their higher levels of pay.[278]

While jealousy and resentment were at the root of such complaints, General Eisenhower was determined to stamp down hard on anyone caught ruffling Anglo-US feathers. "You can call a man a son of a bitch," he told his staff, "but if you call him a *Limey* son of a bitch, you're out!"[279] Harry Butcher recorded a story of an American officer who had sauntered into a London hotel dining room juggling two grapefruit. The officer had then sat down, had his fruit ostentatiously cut and then proceeded to bring out a bag of sugar and sprinkle them liberally. Since both the grapefruit and sugar were almost nonexistent in Britain, Ike, when he heard about the episode, condemned it as ungentlemanly and said that had he been present he would have had the officer sent home immediately "by slow boat, preferably unescorted."[280]

One person who was doing much to foster a sense of solidarity between the British and Americans was American "human interest" journalist, Ernie Pyle, now on his second visit to England. In America, he was already something of a national treasure, a master columnist whose record of everyday American life had made him seem like a personal friend to millions who followed his travels and musings across the United States. Despite the warmth, humor and sensitivity with which he wrote, the man himself was somewhat different from his brand. Funny, yes, and intelligent certainly; but also prone to depression and neurotic with the fear of failure.

His columns were syndicated throughout the Scripps-Howard chain of newspapers, although most prominently ran in the *Washington Daily News*. His first regular column for them was as aviation correspondent, but in 1935, he became a roving reporter with the brief to travel the US writing a story every day about what he'd seen. He was still doing this as the RAF were fighting for the defense of Britain in the summer of 1940, but his thoughts were with what was going on the other side of the Atlantic. By October, with the Blitz already under way, he had made his mind up to try and get posted to London and to continue his column from there, recording the daily life of the British instead. "It seemed to me that in London there was occurring a spiritual holocaust—a trial of souls—that never again in our day will be reenacted," he wrote. "It seemed to me somehow that anyone who went through the immersion into fear and horror of the London bombings, could not help but be made fuller by it."[281]

He reached England in December 1940, and immediately fell in love with the place. His intention was not to produce propaganda, but to once again make his readers see what he saw. But it *was* brilliant propaganda all the same. His descriptions of "London stabbed with great fires, shaken by explosions, its dark regions along the Thames sparkling with the pinpoints of white-hot bombs," were amongst the most vivid ever written, and awoke America to the reality of living in a city under fire.[282] Americans had already been told many times that Britain could "take it," but when Ernie Pyle confirmed this, he sounded convincing. "So far," he wrote at the end of December, "the blitz on London is a failure. London is no more knocked out than the man who smashes his finger is dead." His amazing eye for detail and human observation shone through. As he told his readers, his hotel maid had told him, "I'll never forgive that old Hitler if he gives us a blitz on Christmas Day."[283] Back in America, his pieces were proving the most popular of his career. In the rapidly developing media age, a nonpolitical newspaperman from New Mexico was having a greater impact on the American public than the best efforts of the politicians.

In September 1942, Ernie Pyle was forty-two, but looked older. Short, with a slight, unprepossessing frame, his face was lined and his head balding badly. Physically, he had a weak constitution and was forever nursing colds, sinusitis, and an array of other aches and pains; and he drank too much. So did his wife, Jerry, who back home in Albuquerque, was suffering from alcoholism and mental illness; this too, had a devastating effect on Ernie, causing him further bouts of agonizing and depression.

His second trip to England had come at one of the lowest points in his life. Several affairs had done little for his self-esteem, and Jerry's mental health was deteriorating. They divorced in April, then a few days later he proposed again. In June she finally entered a sanatorium, while he wondered how he was ever going to find the will to write again. Nonetheless, off to England he went, this time to write about the US troops over there as they readied themselves to go into battle against the Axis.

It took him a couple of weeks to summon up the effort to start writing again, but as soon as he did, he once again became Ernie Pyle the American Everyman, writing from "Somewhere in England" with tales of how US boys—and girls for that matter—were finding their feet in strange little old England. He wrote about soldiers from all over the United States—one day it was hill people from eastern Tennessee, "probably the purest strain of Anglo-Saxon blood in America." "Today many of these straight-back English Tennesseans are back here in the land of their ancestors," he wrote, "ready to fight for the country they came from, and the country they went to."[284] Another time his subject was Patricia Hartnett, from Washington, DC, one of the Red Cross girls who were coming over to England to work as "entertainers and general all-around pals to the American troops who live at Red Cross clubs while on leave." Ernie followed her around as she spent her first few days in England, comparing the differences and similarities between America and Britain. "Well, I like it here," she concluded in Ernie's third column about her. "It's different to be sure, and so are the people, but there is no doubting their warmth and sincerity. I like their ways—they are gracious and courteous and too much can't be said for their spirit and humor."[285] This was precisely the kind of message the new Allies in Arms were anxious to get across.

Lieutenant Margaret Hornback of the 48th Surgical Hospital was also rather taken with England. "We had one swell weekend in London," she wrote to her aunt in September. "We got to visit Westminster Abbey, Windsor Castle, Tower of London, and many of the places we've always read about and never expected to see." But while sightseeing was all well and good, most were itching for something more positive to happen. TORCH was a complete secret to anyone but the planners. "London is full of second front rumors," wrote Ernie Pyle to a friend back in the

States, "third front, fourth front, middle front, air front, no front, and of course nobody knows a damn bit more about it than I do."[286] Back home, Americans were equally impatient for that second front to begin, as fellow journalist Alan Moorehead soon discovered. After a long voyage on a boat full of German prisoners of war, Alan finally reached Halifax toward the end of September. Even on the train to New York he heard a man in the next compartment complaining, "Why don't they DO something? What's wrong with them? What can't they start a second front?"[287]

Americans in New York, were, he discovered, all too aware of the lack of progress. There seemed to be little to cheer about. Even in Guadalcanal, things were going badly for the marines. A U-boat had penetrated far up the St. Lawrence River; another had sunk an Allied ship just off Long Island; the Dieppe Raid had also been a bitter blow. As Alan was aware, "morale during bad times is nearly always lowest at the base and highest at the front," but it was still something of a shock to discover that almost everyone he spoke to was feeling the same sense of frustration, even anger, that what little was happening was going badly. What was needed, he was told time and time again, was a second front, and soon. This was also picked up on by Wing Commander Forbes who had been sent out to the United States in May to find out about American attitudes to Britain and the war. "The American people are becoming weary of no Allied success," he reported. "They feel that the war is being incompetently conducted by the British." He also discovered that most Americans felt they were propping up the British to a detrimental degree. "It is generally believed that all the war material in [the] Middle East is American, and that all the fighting is done by Australian and other Dominion troops," he continued.[288] Alan noticed that many blamed the politicians and the big businesses profiting from war work. "The cynicism about Washington was so intense it was bewildering," wrote Alan, although he suspected that once the Americans were actively involved, a lot of this discontent would vanish. "They say there is no moment for the soldier which is worse than the short period of nervous tension before he goes over the top," he wrote, "To a stranger, America appeared to have reached that difficult moment just before going over the top."[289]

This would happen soon enough, however, for TORCH was finally beginning to take shape. On the third anniversary of Britain's entry into the war, Harry Butcher recorded in his diary that both parties had found a way forward. Recommended by the US Joint Chiefs were simultaneous landings at Casablanca and Oran but also Algiers, with US troops leading the way at Casablanca and Oran and supporting the British at Algiers. This was agreed by Churchill two days later, albeit with some caveats about the number of troops to be deployed at each of the landings. "We agree to the military lay-out as you propose it," he wrote to the president. The Casablanca task force was to come directly from the US, while the troops for Algiers and Oran would come from Britain. All three landings were to be simultaneous, if at all possible. After securing the beaches, ports were to be seized for follow-up forces and for supplies, while beachheads were to be expanded rapidly with a view to securing French Morocco and western Algeria. Ground bases and airfields could then be quickly established to support the push toward Tunisia. "Hurrah!" came the one-word reply from the president. A day later, Churchill told him, "OK, full blast."[290] What Harry Butcher called "the transatlantic essay contest" was finally drawing to a close.[291]

There was still much to be done, however, and General Eisenhower's mind was swimming with the enormous number of imponderables that faced them, not least the weather for D-Day. "I am searching the Army to find the most capable chaplain to assure a fairly decent break in the weather when the big day comes," he wrote to Patton.[292] But despite such anxieties, the broad plan of TORCH had now been agreed upon, and with that box safely ticked, the rest of the planning could gather pace.

The numerous staff and command appointments were also being finalized. Soon to arrive in London was Brigadier-General Walter Bedell-Smith to take up his position as Ike's chief of staff. An American veteran of the First World War, Bedell-Smith was another who had caught Marshall's eye and since February had been secretary to the US Chiefs of Staff. Intimately familiar with the machinations over TORCH within the US War Department and in the White House, he was also well-acquainted with all the key players in Washington, both British and American, and was a good friend of Ike's. His good humor, flair for getting on with people and sound judgment would be invaluable to the Allied C-in-C in the weeks and months to come.

Bedell-Smith had also become firm friends with Admiral Cunningham, and at one point had called on ABC for a "heart-to-heart" about TORCH and its prospects. He told ABC that personally he felt enthusiastic about the plan, but was getting little encouragement from the US Navy Department. What did ABC think the effect of the Allied occupation of North Africa would have on the naval and shipping situation as a whole? The American Admiral King, who saw little benefit to possessing the Mediterranean, had told Bedell-Smith it would have little or no consequence. Unsurprisingly, ABC vehemently disagreed and told his friend that in his opinion the gain from complete success in Africa would be "incalculable from every point of view." It would lay Italy open to invasion, would give them dominance in the air throughout the Mediterranean, and allow them to run convoys to Malta and the Middle East without looping all around the Cape.

This appeared to be the assurance Bedell-Smith wanted, but he then told ABC he thought it was important that the naval commander was someone who was wholeheartedly in favor of the operation and so asked him whether he would be prepared to take on the role. Not wanting to tread on the toes of the First Sea Lord, ABC replied guardedly, although in reality he was keen as mustard, and itching to escape his desk job and the "detached atmosphere" of Washington, and get back to sea and some proper action.

It had been Ike's idea to have one single Allied naval commander directly responsible to himself, and despite some skepticism in both Washington and London, his wish was granted; it was another personal goal in his development of united Allied command. Admiral Sir Bertram Ramsay, the architect of the relief of Dunkirk, had been appointed naval C-in-C, but at the end of August, just before Bedell-Smith set off for London, the Americans (Admiral King included) appeared to have second thoughts, pointing out that the obvious man to command the naval forces for TORCH was none other than ABC, the hero of Matapan and former C-in-C of the Mediterranean. To Cunningham's great relief, the prime minister agreed. The American Admiral Hewitt would command the Western Task Force from the USA, and ABC the Eastern Task Force from Britain, but from the moment the Americans passed the latitude 40 degrees west, command of the entire naval operation would be turned over to Cunningham.

But while Ike may have gotten his way over the naval commander, his demand for a single Allied air C-in-C fell on deaf ears. For some bizarre reason, no one thought to consult Tedder or Mary Coningham, or even Tommy Elmhirst for that matter, the architects of army/air cooperation and who, along with the American General Brereton, had already so successfully brought US air forces to work alongside the RAF. Instead, control of the air was split into two quite separate commands: Western Air Command, covering Morocco and West Algeria, would be an American affair commanded by Brigadier-General Jimmy Doolittle, and the Eastern Air Command, covering Eastern Algeria, would be left to the RAF and commanded by Air Marshal Sir William Welsh. Quite apart from the fact that there are no demarcation lines in the sky, this division meant that the two air commands planned almost entirely in isolation of each other.

But at least Ike now had his commanders in place and with Bedell-Smith on his way, and with TORCH finally taking shape, he felt able to slip away from the office early on Sunday, 6 September, and head for the golf course next to Telegraph Cottage. He and Butch played two holes twice for a bob each. A little rusty, Butch only managed two sevens and a nine before taking par on the last hole, largely thanks to a 30-foot putt that curled in from the edge of the green. It was enough to win a bob off Ike, who, after hitting the green "in the orthodox two," then took three more putts.

Far away in the desert, the rapidly evolving Eighth Army was making the most of a lull in hostilities. General Alexander spent much of his time visiting the men and various units of his new command. On 7 September, he went to the Base Ordnance workshops at Tel el Kebir to see the new Sherman tanks that had finally arrived from the USA. For the most part, they had traveled well, although seawater had caused corrosion to some of the electrical fittings. These repairs plus certain desert fittings meant the 317 new tanks were only being released from the workshops at a rate of twenty a day.

General Tuker's 4th Indian Division was finally back at the front and on active operations, albeit still deprived of its full compliment. They were to take the role of a static infantry division, shorn of their transport, which was much to Tuker's chagrin as he had been training his men as motorized infantry. Even so, fiercely proud of his division and their place in the Indian Army, he issued a stirring order of the day to all his troops as they moved into the line. "The eyes of the Army are upon us," he told them. "Dominion and American troops are closely watching us. Let us show the Italians that it is of no avail to struggle against us; the Germans that they can never hope to stand against our fury in battle."[293]

On the Ruweisat Ridge, Nainabadahur Pun and 1/2 Gurkhas finally took over from the 3/14 Punjabs on 9 September. Despite the lull, the days were still long for Nainabadahur. Defensive positions needed to be strengthened, gun pits and slit trenches dug, and at night there were regular patrols to find out enemy dispositions. Almost every day around teatime they were raided by Stukas, but the attackers caused little damage and not one casualty all month.

Tuker himself now had his own HQ in the desert with the divisional support units nearby. These included a mobile workshop company, units of the Indian Army Ordnance and Royal Indian Army Service Corps, as well as field ambulances, and a unit of the Royal Army Medical Corps. There was also the Divisional Signals Regiment, split into different companies and sections, each with differing roles. Corporal Mangal Singh was in C Section—the Communication Section—of 1 Company.

Mangal Singh had been in the Middle East a long time—almost three years. The division had been formed in 1939, as part of the Indian government's agreement to help Britain's Imperial commitments should war break out. The first troops had reached Egypt in August that year, a few weeks before war was declared, but divisional headquarters had not set sail

until 23 September, arriving in Egypt eleven days later. Almost immediately
they had mustered under the shadows of the pyramids at Mena Camp, and
there they had remained in a sea of tents amidst the sand and dust until the
war finally came to the Middle East in June the following year.

Mangal Singh came from Raniwala Nawan, a small village in the Fer-
ozepur District of the Punjab in northern India. His family, like most in
the village, were farmers, producing cotton and keeping a few buffalo and
goats. They lived in a one-room mud house, with neither electricity nor
running water. "We were poor," he says, "but everyone was poor." Even so,
he still went to school—in the nearby village, some three miles away, to
which he would daily walk there and back.

At seventeen he was married and then shortly after, he decided to join
the army, although it was almost on a whim. Some friends told him the recruiting officer was going to be in Moga, the nearest town, the following
day. His future as a farmer did not look particularly bright, especially since
the farm would eventually be divided between him and two other brothers.
The army, on the other hand, promised regular income and some kinds of
prospects. After a night sleeping on the decision, he awoke, his mind
made up, and without telling anyone his intentions, set out on the six-mile
walk to town.

When he reached Moga, he discovered he was a day too soon, but
rather than go back home and risk the wrath of his father, he stayed put,
and the following day, signed up, along with around a hundred others.
"The recruiting officer asked, 'All right, who's educated? Hands up,'" recalls Mangal Singh. "Three of us put our hands up, and he said, 'Right,
you three are going into the signals.'" He was given five rupees and
made to swear an oath, and then put on a train to Jabalpur, nearly 1,500
miles away—and without going home first. Instead, he simply wrote to
his wife and family telling them what he'd done.

At the signal training center, he learned to be a lineman, laying telephone cables. He enjoyed it very much, and in turn became an instructor
himself. He missed his family, but realized there was little he could do
about it. At least this way, he was able to send money home regularly.

It wasn't until two years had passed that he finally went home for two
months' leave, and it was then that he saw his son for the first time. He
later applied for permission to take his wife and son to Karachi where he
was now stationed, and this was approved, although their time together
was to be comparatively short-lived. Less than two years later he joined
the embryonic 4th Indian Division, which was readying itself for deployment overseas, and so Mangal Singh found himself putting his family
onto a train and sending them back to the Punjab. He had not seen them
since. In eight years of marriage, he had lived with his wife for just two.

Since the opening phase of the desert war, Mangal Singh had been following 4th Indian Division up and down the coast, and of late across the Middle East, laying cables, mending broken lines, and ensuring the division's signals network functioned efficiently. He was not a fighting man, but he still faced moments of danger, particularly when laying lines up at the front. This was usually done at night, so in his truck he and his team would creep forward in the dark, hoping the enemy did not spot what they were doing. Other times, they were attacked by enemy aircraft. He learned to tell the difference between Italian and German planes and to spot them from several miles away. And he learned to lie down flat and hope for the best that nothing would land on top of him.

Now, with the division back in the line, there was plenty to do. It was up to Corporal Mangal Singh and his section of line layers to link the forward brigades with the division HQ, and despite the intermittent shelling and teatime Stuka raids, make sure they remained linked as well.

For the weary desert veterans, it was a time to recuperate and gather strength. For the newcomers, the lull offered a chance to acclimate to desert life. Some arrived as part of a newly deployed battalion or division, but the majority of new boys were replacements and had to fit in with the old hands. When Albert Martin had been sent up to the "blue" in October 1940, he had joined a section of regulars who'd been in the army for some time. To begin with, it seemed to Albert as though they were from a different world. Their chatter was laced with Urdu, Hindu, Arabic, and unfamiliar soldiers' jargon and Albert struggled to understand what they were saying half the time. There were also a staggering number of acronyms—almost any army phrase or name of more than one word was truncated into letters. Naturally one could not ask what any of this meant—one simply had to pick it up, but like all newcomers, he soon got the hang of it.

He also discovered that the old hands *looked* very different too. Their skin was as dark as could be, but covered in round scars, permanent reminders of countless desert sores. Uniforms were often filthy, and hardly uniform at all. Many adapted their standard issue KD—khaki drill—with variations bought on leave in Cairo. As soon as Albert was given his first leave, he immediately got himself a white watchstrap. "A black or brown strap gave the game away," he says, "it identified you as a new boy."[294] Having made this adjustment, he tried to make it look aged by rubbing it with sweat.

Some people took to life in the desert better than others. Carol Mather found it an exhilarating place; so too did Charles Coles. Often on patrols up the coast, Charles and the other MTBs would stop for the night and sleep ashore, hidden under camouflage nets, then continue their operations the next day. He loved the smell of the land after a shower, and, depending on the time of year, the sudden appearance of the many and varied blooms that sprang up almost overnight. The desert landscape could be dramatic, particularly on the bright starlit nights. Always a keen shot, he also welcomed the opportunity of shooting the occasional gazelle, which offered a welcome change from bully beef. His experience was different from those who were in the front line, but as Albert points out, "if you fight the desert, you're certainly on to a loser. You've got to go along with it and then life suddenly becomes a lot easier." The heat could certainly be devastating, but so could the cold. Each man had a groundsheet—a rubberized piece of canvas with holes along each side. For the troops on the ground there were no tents to creep into at night; Albert used to simply dig a shallow hole for his hip next to his truck and then wrap his groundsheet around himself and lace it up tightly, so that no scorpions and scarab beetles could get in. He would then use his rug for a pillow. Most were lucky to get even five hours' sleep a night—often it was much less. The tank regiments had to carry out prowler guard to protect their leaguer, but night guards were needed for the infantry units too. There were also frequent patrols to be carried out, and these were always at nighttime. Albert says that however uncomfortable sleeping in the desert might sound, he was always so exhausted by the time he did get his head down that he never had any trouble dropping off. Sam Bradshaw agrees. "At the end of the day you were very, very tired indeed," he says. If they'd been in action, once they'd leaguered, he would simply look for a place with the least amount of stones. "But sometimes you were so knackered you wouldn't even scrape the stones away." He used to simply throw his groundsheet down and drop onto it. On the other hand, if they were static for a while, then he would dig a slit trench and sleep in that.

Desert survival was about being practical and making the most of what they had. Uniforms could be washed in petrol, and then laid out in the sun, which gave them a battered, bleached appearance. Gas goggles were used to good effect in sandstorms. Beetles and scorpions could not be eaten, but desert snails fried up quite nicely. Most pretty quickly learned how to take a fix on a star and to change it every twenty minutes, or how to find north by looking at the sun and using a watch. It was all too easy to get lost in the desert—a basic knowledge of astral navigation could mean the difference between life and death. The huge distances of the desert also took some getting used to; and the light played tricks, so that a truck a mile away could appear in the shimmering haze to be an animal only a couple of hundred yards distant.

Although the desert was a clean and healthy environment, the tide of war rampaging across its sands soon changed that. Principally this was thanks to the vast hordes of flies, gorging on rotting flesh, poorly disposed of feces, sweat, and bully beef, and multiplying in their millions. "Flies bad," noted Joe Madeley on 30 July, after a month of hard fighting in much the same place, "worse I've ever seen them." When eating, there would be so many flies it was impossible not to swallow quite a few. "I suppose we ate oodles of flies," he says, "a bit of protein." He was lucky never to get seriously ill, but many people suffered from stomach upsets and diarrhea, and a few days' gut rot was not uncommon. On 16 September, for example, Joe recorded feeling, "Pretty sick in stomach all day." On 10 July, Bill Eadie also noted that he had "Gyppo guts," and even saw signs of blood in his vomit. Maiki Parkinson was laid low with full-blown dysentery shortly after his arrival in Egypt. "Christ, it was awful," he says. "I wasn't sure which was worse, seasickness or the dysentery."

Maiki professes to having never suffered from sores, but they were a regular feature of desert life for most. Albert Martin still has the scars, along with those of his shrapnel wounds. What started as the slightest of abrasions soon festered into something much worse. "In no time the flies would be out and they'd cluster around it in a great heap," he says. "You'd be driven to distraction by it." There were few men who did not wear bandages around some minor sore that had gone septic. Joe Madeley's friend, Ken Crutchett suffered particularly badly. "He was always covered in sores," says Joe. Although the men were given limes, a lack of sufficient vitamins did aggravate desert sores and also led to many people suffering from scabies and other skin diseases. Other hazards were snakes and scorpions. Scorpion stings were unpleasant rather than serious, however. When Albert Martin was stung, he simply walked to the medical officer, who put a dressing on him and sent him away. Later he started sweating and came down with a headache, but after half a day or so, the effect had worn off. Being young and fit helped enormously. And most were—despite the sores, the flies and occasional bouts of sickness. The majority of young men living in the desert had never been fitter.

As motorized infantry, Albert Martin's section of six men operated from their 15 cwt truck. It was a rather stripped-down version of the original: anything that might reflect the sun had been removed, such as the windscreen and mirrors. It was treated very much as a mobile home, where they stored their kit and food, and where they even sometimes slept, ate, or crawled underneath for shade.

As with any small group of people living so closely together, habits and rituals soon developed. Brewing tea was certainly an important part of daily life. It was generally the first thing that happened when they got up in the morning and occurred throughout the day whenever there was the chance. Each section had a Primus stove, but a faster, more efficient way of brewing up was to take an old four-gallon petrol tin, half fill it with sand, and then pour petrol over it. Another petrol can filled with a couple of inches of water was then placed on top. When the petrol-soaked sand was lit, it would burn for a few minutes, just long enough to boil the water. The contents were then poured into another "brew can"—usually an old food tin—in which a handful of tea leaves, plenty of sugar and condensed milk had already been poured. Once stewed, it was ready to drink. The taste varied according to the source of the water. Depending on the tins it arrived in, water would be flavored by chlorine or petrol or even rust. "You seldom got good-tasting tea," says Albert. "It tended to be contaminated in one form or another but that made not a scrap of difference. I think if the tea rations hadn't come up we'd have packed up and gone home."

Meals when not in action were three a day: breakfast, lunch (or tiffin), and supper. Food was delivered by the supply echelon and handed out in daily rations to a representative from each section: half a large mug of tea leaves, then an assortment of tins of corned beef (known as bully beef), condensed milk, cheese, limes, and perhaps pilchards. Mugs of sugar were poured out, as well as rice and hardtack biscuits. There were other variations: dried egg, jam, bacon, margarine, M and V (meat and vegetables), and occasionally tinned fruit or tinned vegetables. Each man was supposed to eat 3,700 calories a day, but the problem was the monotony of the food, and much depended on the ingenuity of the men to make it as interesting and varied as possible. "Corned beef can be a very versatile dish if I may say so," says Albert. It was regularly made into a kind of hash or stew along with crushed biscuits, although rather like the water for their tea, the quality of bully beef depended on where it came from. Argentinean corned beef was considered the best, anything with Arabic on the tin, the worst.

The system was slightly different for those in the line and for the airmen, however. The Maori Battalion, like every other infantry battalion now building defenses along the Alamein position, were fed by their battalion cooks. "Chow wagons would pitch up," says Maiki, "and you'd stand in the queue and wait your turn to get your tucker. Usually bloody bully beef." Maiki spent much of his time feeling hungry. "I never got enough." Nor was he able to drink as much as Albert Martin and those with transport. "We couldn't carry water," he says, "so while we brewed tea when we could, you'd never get more than a couple of mugs a day."

Indian troops were also addicted to tea, but were given completely different food rations, which meant Eighth Army needed a two-line supply system. Nainabadahur Pun, as a Hindu, never had the chance to taste the versatility of bully beef, but certainly ate enough goat to last a lifetime. They were also given plenty of rice, and most meals would be a curry of some kind, vegetable or goat, with dhal. Instead of biscuits, they ate chapatis. "It was very basic," he says, "but there was always plenty of it." As a Sikh, Mangal Singh ate no meat at all. At divisional HQ there were two cookhouses, one for the Muslims and one for the Sikhs. "We ate separately," says Mangal Singh, who was more often than not back at base for his meals, "but it was no problem." The Maori might have gone hungry, but not the Indians. And on the whole, nor did Bill Eadie. With his job he was constantly ferrying vehicles and equipment from base back to brigade HQ and then on to the various units attached to the brigade, and was often able to pick up extra food and especially drink along the way. Bill wasn't a big drinker, but he certainly liked a drop if he could get his hands on it.

Sometimes NAAFI supplies would be sent up—especially if they were static for a while. This was really the only time outside of leave that the men had a chance to drink beer or eat luxuries like chocolate. "Sometimes you'd get two or three bottles of beer per man sent up," says Albert, "and you'd sit and talk all night. They were good occasions."

Eating and brewing tea provided focal points to the day because it often broke up the monotony of life in the desert. As in any war, there were often periods of extreme boredom and little activity. Maiki Parkinson frequently found himself feeling fidgety. The flies bothered him so much, he couldn't bear to sit still and so used to wander around, talking to people and trying to keep himself on the go. Joe Madeley, like the American Willie Chapman, spent much of his spare time gambling. His diary is littered with references to the money he won and lost. On 4 September, for example, he played cards "most of the day" and won about a pound, although he frequently ended up out of pocket too. Mangal Singh, on the other hand, used spare time to carry out his own maintenance work on his truck. Albert Martin says he never saw anyone doing anything particularly demanding. "You'd think chess would be a popular game, but I never saw anyone playing it," he says. He used to read battered paperbacks occasionally—he had a much-thumbed book of Kipling's poems—but otherwise spent his spare time chatting with his mates, cleaning his weapons, and writing up his diary and letters home. "But if it was dark," he says, "and I couldn't do any of these things, we'd sometimes go over to the wireless van and after a lot of delicate maneuvering, the bloke would pick up the BBC and you'd hear the English voice telling us all about what we'd been doing and where we'd been. And that was nice."

Writing and receiving letters provided an essential link with home. Maiki Parkinson never felt pangs of homesickness ("I was with my mates and I was enjoying myself,") but most did. Albert Martin wrote hundreds of letters—they were necessarily anodyne affairs due to strict censorship—but loved receiving letters in return with news from home. "What a lot of people don't realize," says Sam Bradshaw, "is just how long some of us spent out there. It was *years*." There were no tours of duty for the troops, and inevitably the length of separation placed enormous pressures on relationships with wives and girlfriends back home. As Sam points out, it was undoubtedly easier for young men like himself who went out to the Middle East with no ties except to his parents and immediate family. Sam noticed that one after another, each of the men in his troop who had left a wife or girlfriend behind in England received a "Dear John" letter ending their relationship. "You can only imagine what it must have been like for those at home," he says, "particularly in places like Liverpool, where they were being bombed all the time. It must have seemed as though the war was never ending, so what was the point in keeping a relationship going?" Harold Harper was the unfortunate recipient of such a letter—it reached him while he was convalescing after the Gazala Battles.

But one man in Sam's troop, Ronnie Dowie, was lucky. He was engaged and his fiancée continued to send out reams of letters. "He would read out parts of them," says Sam, "She had a peculiar name—Bryn—but we all felt we were part of his life and that she was somehow our girl too." Not only Ronnie, but all of them began eagerly awaiting her letters, full as they were with gossip and inconsequential news from home. "Dowie would say, 'Oh, she's had her hair changed,' and we'd say, 'I'm not sure about that.' And you'd realize how important the little things are." Her letters became the nearest thing to a soap opera they could get in the desert. "We were hoping and praying that their relationship would survive and it did. We used to say, 'You lucky bloke!'"

One day, Sam was out with the sappers learning how to lay mines and when he got back it was getting dark and most of the men were already bedding down. Someone told him that Dowie had had a Dear John.

"Are you sure?" Sam asked.

"I think so," came the reply, "because after the mail came he disappeared on his own and didn't say anything."

The following morning, Sam noticed Dowie was very quiet and so asked him whether he was all right. At first he said yes, he was fine, but when Sam said, "Are you sure?" he replied, "Well, no, not really. I've had some bad news. I'll talk to you about it later."

Sam arranged to do a prowler guard with him that night, and Dowie then told him all. "I've had a letter from Bryn," he said, "and she's finished with me."

"Perhaps she's just a bit fed up," Sam suggested. "They're going through what we're going through, you know. Give it a while—she'll come round."

"No," he said, "she means it. And now I've nothing to live for."

He began twisting the ring she'd given him on his finger. "Don't be stupid, Dowie," Sam told him. "You're only a kid. You've got the rest of your life. Give it time—it's just a phase. Don't give up. All this talk of ending it—you forget about that. You're a good tank driver and you've got a crew who depend on you." Sam made him swear he wouldn't do anything foolish. "I want your word," Sam told him—and Dowie gave it to him.

The following day they were in action and in the evening Sam went back to the assembly area and learned that Dowie was missing. The radio operator had survived so Sam asked him what had happened. "We were hit and there was a terrible smell of petrol," the radio man told him. "The tank commander told us all to bail out, but Dowie stayed and drove straight at the German guns."

"That was a terrible thing," says Sam, "and who knows, a few days later, another letter might have arrived telling him it was all a mistake. Poor Ronnie, he was such a nice lad."

Fortunately, Bill Eadie suffered no such tragedy. He spent a large part of his time writing his diary or copious amounts of letters, and received hundreds in return, including a number of parcels filled with various goodies from home, including cigarettes, photographs, and even swimming trunks. Letters from his wife, Joan, arrived at least once a week, but often in batches of several at once. These were all a source of great comfort to him, because he missed his family dreadfully and succumbed to frequent bouts of homesickness. "HOMESICKNESS IS A SICKNESS," he noted in his diary in August. In early July, while the battle for Egypt raged about him, he still found time to worry about his dad's health. Three days later, he confessed to "feeling morbid." By 23 July, he had heard that his dad was much better and was feeling "very happy" again. Certainly he worried about his family far more than he did himself.

So too did nurse Margaret Hornback. She might have been in England, where comforts were plentiful compared to life in the desert, but she was still a long way from home. She wrote vast numbers of letters—to her parents and younger brother, to her aunt, and also to one of her oldest friends, Lillian Stout, who was still back home in Shelbyville, Kentucky.

But while Margaret was able to sightsee or visit a number of American clubs that had been established to make US servicemen and women "feel right at home," there was little entertainment on offer in the desert. Light relief was sometimes offered by ENSA concert parties, who would bring their shows up to the front and entertain the troops. "Concert at Brigade," noted Joe Madeley on 29 August. "Pretty good. Two girls in it, couple of shells during show." In September, Bill Eadie went to one—this time three men and two girls in a show called "Just Between." It was, he thought, "a very stout effort." Afterward Bill went to a party with the field force boys and got steaming drunk. The highlight of the night was when one of the men passed out and was then dragged out by his heels, ploughing deep furrows in the sand. One of his draggers slapped him and said, "Say good night to the gentlemen, you silly bastard." "He was quite incapable of speech," noted Bill. "It was very funny."

But what everyone looked forward to was leave in Cairo. Drawing on some of their saved-up pay, they tumbled into the many restaurants and bars, bought souvenirs to send back home, watched films and dancing girls and let their hair down for a few days. How many days given and how often depended entirely on the situation in hand, but certainly there were more troops heading into town during September and October than there had been during the previous few months. "WHOOPEEE—Cairo!" noted Bill Eadie on being told he had six days' leave. After withdrawing £20, he waited ages for a train, and eventually made it into the city by 6 PM. Linking up with some mates, he went to a hotel and had a long bath, followed by a grill and plenty of beers. The next day they went for a wander round the city's bazaars, "where all the thieves in the world prey," and followed this with tea at the Springbok Club. Later, they headed off to a restaurant for a meal and more beers and then went to see a film. Their evening did not end there—from the cinema they went to a bar, where they had a "binge with the Kiwis." The next few days he did more of the same, but also took time out to do some sightseeing around the pyramids and to go on a boat trip down the Nile.

But while Eighth Army was making the most of the lull that followed the Battle of Alam Halfa, General Alexander was keen to keep harrying the enemy's lines of communication. The work of the RAF and Navy, both from the Middle East and Malta, was hurting the Axis supply lines, but Alex felt that if they could destroy or even temporarily disable the oil installations and port facilities at Tobruk, and even Benghazi for that matter, the results could significantly help Eighth Army in the coming offensive.

Such an idea had been initially presented to Auchinleck by the LRDG, which had been intending to mount several raids, including an attack on the airfields at Barce in either July or August. Neither had been possible then, but to Alex such an enterprise, on paper at least, seemed like a good idea. He was, however, aware that such an operation was likely to be extremely hazardous, and so the possible advantages had to be weighed against chances of success and failure.

A plan had been drawn up and given the provisional go-ahead just a few days after Alex took over. Monty had nothing to do with it all, although he wondered whether it might be carried out so as to coincide with his planned offensive. It was certainly a bold idea, and relied on the coordination of several different forces: the SAS and LRDG arriving over land, and reinforced by commandos dropped by MTBs. The MTBs were also to attack shipping at the harbor's mouth, while the two destroyers would then drop in demolition teams. Meanwhile, farther up the coast, an entirely separate force of SAS and LRDG were to travel from Kufra to attack Benghazi. They would then creep back into the desert and capture the old fort of Jalo, from where they would continue to carry out raids for the next three weeks. The distances involved were too great for any kind of proper air cover, but the RAF was to bomb Benghazi and create a feint by dropping dummy parachutists on Siwa Oasis.

On 3 September, with Alam Halfa not yet over, Alex reviewed the plan with his C-in-Cs, Admiral Harwood and Tedder. It was clearly a highly risky proposition but it was nonetheless felt, by Alex especially, that the benefits of potential success outweighed the cost of potential failure. Operation AGREEMENT was given the green light.

After the mass raid on Sidi Haneish airfield, the SAS had once again returned to Kabrit in the delta, although during the long journey back, Stephen Hastings had developed a high fever and so had been sent for protracted leave in Beirut in order to properly recuperate. He was still there in late August when he suddenly received a signal to fly straight to Kufra Oasis, a Beau Geste fort surrounded by palm trees more than seven hundred miles, as the crow flies, southwest of Cairo. There he was to join a raiding party of more than two hundred special service men—SAS, SBS (the Special Boat Service), Free French, LRDG and various others.

Carol Mather was already there, having had a hair-raising journey leading a column to the oasis. Their route had taken them through the Gilf Kebir, an enormous rock plateau the size of Switzerland. With its caves and crevices and promises of hidden cities, this extraordinary area had mesmerized the desert explorers in the 1930s; indeed, it was here that the Hungarian Count Almasy had discovered the Cave of Swimmers. Although used since the beginning of the war by the LRDG, it was still a formidable stretch of land to cross, but nonetheless, after countless breakdowns and a severe petrol crisis, Carol and his column had finally made Kufra after a nine-day journey.

The following approach march was even more hazardous, and took them across the Great Sand Sea and around the Italian fort of Jalo, where enemy aircraft lurked. If they managed this without being spotted, they then had to feel their way along an old slaver's route that the RAF had sown with "thermos bombs," anti-personnel mines that blew up on touch.

Stephen and Carol traveled together in the same jeep at the rearguard of their convoy and took it in turns to drive while the other read, first every word of a copy of the *Illustrated London News,* then a book of Stephen's about rough shooting, and next a Somerset Maugham novel. Officially, they were not supposed to know what their mission was, but gossip was rife and everyone had been discussing it since leaving Cairo. The lack of secrecy was worrying. Even as they'd left the city, Carol had been worried at the number of Egyptians who'd watched their huge column heading off. Axis spies were known to be rife in Cairo.

They had been given eight days to travel eight hundred miles to the rendezvous, and this was no small task, especially when vehicles could only cross the enormous dunes of the Great Sand Sea by using sand mats and steel channels and a huge amount of heaving and shoving. This narrow stretch of the journey took them two days, and although they successfully skirted Jalo and managed to avoid the thermos bombs, they had seen a Fieseler Storch patrolling above them on several occasions. At the rendezvous, the news was even worse: their Arab spy warned them that Benghazi had been reinforced and that all approaches had been set up with roadblocks and minefields. The spy told them that all the cafes were full of talk of an expected attack.

The plan was to attack Benghazi and destroy any ships and blow up the port installations on the night of 13–14 September, at the same time as the attack was being made on Tobruk. Leading "X Force"—as they had been designated—was David Stirling, who had been feeling uneasy about the wisdom of attacking in such large numbers. The word from the Arab spy had confirmed all his worst fears, so he signaled to GHQ for advice. Carry on, came the reply. They were not to listen to bazaar gossip.

Cutting a swathe through the deep blue waters of the Mediterranean was Lieutenant Charles Coles and a number of other 10th Flotilla MTBs, returning to Tobruk once more. Charles felt every bit as uneasy about the plan as the SAS men waiting, now readying themselves in the Jebel Mountains. "Arab barbers in Alexandria were telling us all about it," says Charles. "It was an absolute joke." The operation seemed too dependent on too many different things all going to plan: firstly, the LRDG, with the help of uniformed German Jew, (who had fled the Nazi regime before the war), had to infiltrate into Tobruk and somehow spike all the guns defending the harbor. The MTBs also had to actually get their platoons of men ashore. These men then had to wreak havoc before the MTBs and the two destroyers could begin their work of sinking enemy shipping. Any one of these things could go wrong, which in turn could scupper the entire operation.

Charles's confidence was hardly improved when an immaculate-looking subaltern and his platoon of marines turned up, all with shiny kit and polished boots.

"You look a bit puzzled," the subaltern said.

"I thought we were taking commandos on this raid," Charles explained, "camouflaged with blackened faces."

The subaltern smiled. "No, you're taking proper soldiers!"

When they reached Tobruk they tried to get the men ashore but came under heavy fire. The guns had not been spiked, although the small inlet of Mersa Sciausc at the mouth of Tobruk had in fact been successfully captured. Charles certainly never received the signal telling them this. Only two MTBs managed to get their platoons ashore, and 262 was not one of them. By two in the morning, all the MTBs were ordered to retire and return to Alexandria.

The marines being landed by the destroyers north of the harbor also struggled—by five in the morning, only around seventy were ashore and although they fought their way toward the port, they were soon overwhelmed. In the meantime, the two destroyers, *Zulu* and *Sikh*, came under heavy and accurate fire and were repeatedly hit. Hurrying to their rescue was the cruiser *Coventry* and half a dozen destroyers, but they soon came under heavy attack too. *Coventry* was hit by a bomb, caught fire and had to be abandoned. The *Zulu* was also sunk, along with a number of the MTBs: two had been lost while attempting the landings, and a further four were destroyed by enemy aircraft during the return to Alexandria; 262 made it safely back to base, however, but as Charles points out, the Tobruk Raid "was an absolute disaster."

Stirling's men were not faring much better, and although they had gone in as planned—and as ordered—and captured a small Italian outpost, as they crossed the first roadblock they were ambushed. The SAS men fired back furiously and the attack quieted down, but with the crucial element of surprise gone, Stirling was left with no choice but to pull back. They were lucky to lose only a couple of jeeps and a handful of casualties.

But they were followed back into the desert, and although they tried to hide themselves as best they could, the following day they were bombed and strafed until dark. They lost fifteen jeeps and twenty-five trucks, and four men had been killed and a number wounded. Stirling decided they should load up as best they could onto the surviving vehicles and head for a wadi twenty-five miles away. Left behind were four of the most heavily wounded; although they were subsequently picked up by the Italians, they all later died. "I can never forget our having to leave them lying wounded there," noted Stephen Hastings later. "'Death Valley' the lads called the place."[295]

The survivors only had enough petrol to reach Jalo, which during the intervening days was supposed to have been already taken by the Sudan Defense Forces. In fact, the battle for the fort was still raging, but enough fuel was found to get them on their way again and safely back to Kufra. "No romantic fiction of the desert could ever equal the relief we felt when the palms and mud huts of Kufra finally hove into view," wrote Stephen. "Haggard, bearded, filthy, many of us in rags, at last we could wash and swim, eat fresh eggs as well as army rations and above all, drink—and drink."[296]

The LRDG attack on Barce airfield was more successful—sixteen Italian aircraft destroyed—but the combined raids cost 740 killed, wounded, or captured. "From the material point of view," wrote Alex, "the raids had been a failure and our losses had been heavy, but it is possible that they had had the psychological effects we had hoped for."[297] Certainly the Axis desert outposts were reinforced and extra troops kept at Sollum and Mersa Matruh. Carol Mather believes they were worthwhile. "It made Rommel very jittery about his flanks," he says. "All along his lines of communications they were vulnerable. I think creating uncertainty in the mind of the enemy was an important factor."

Even so, although these raids were a good idea in principle, the planning had been suspect from the start—far too ambitious and carried out with insufficient security. Operation AGREEMENT was one of the very few mistakes Alex made during his time in Africa. Nonetheless, it is impossible not to admire those who vainly tried to carry it out. They had performed their duty without question, whatever personal reservations many had felt. The huge distances covered, the dangers and risks that had to be overcome just to get within striking distance of their supposed targets were truly extraordinary. And yet these raids remain, like so many bloody and costly operations carried out during the Second World War, a forgotten episode.

CHAPTER 13

Getting Ready Part 2— October 1942

ON 8 SEPTEMBER, after their now regular Tuesday night dinner with the prime minister, Generals Eisenhower and Clark managed to leave before midnight, something of a first. Ike reckoned his attempt to stifle a yawn, which Churchill spotted, had something to do with it. Also, Anthony Eden, the foreign minister, turned up just after eleven and needed to talk, so soon after, Ike and Clark were released. Even so, Clark still strode down the corridor as fast as he could—past experience had taught him that the PM would all too often stop as he ushered his guests to the door, struck by some afterthought which then had to be discussed there and then in the corridor until thoroughly exhausted.

Ike arrived back at the Dorchester around midnight and immediately woke up Harry Butcher to give him the "dope." Although the PM and president were now as one on the plans, Churchill had been pressing him for a date. The planners were working toward 4 November, but Ike had told the PM, "November 8—sixty days from now." The men needed to be properly equipped and trained, Ike told him—US forces were being formed into regimental combat teams, similar to British brigades, and so the infantry regiments needed to train alongside their attached units of artillery and engineers. Then why not put British commandos, at a more advanced state of training, in US uniforms? the PM suggested. "I would be proud to have them where 'em," Churchill assured him. But Ike wasn't budging. The sham would soon be discovered, he told Churchill, and that could only work against them.[298]

"This is a tragedy," noted Churchill to the chiefs of staff, "and every effort must be made to save at least ten days. Time is our chief enemy now."[299] But the ever-impatient PM was in for another disappointment. Back in August, Alex had warned Churchill that the earliest date for Eighth Army's offensive would be the end of September, not taking into account the effect of an attack by Rommel. Monty then rather put his foot in it by telling Churchill the first week of October was more realistic and that they could expect the battle to last a week. But there was no full moon until the third week of the month, and one was needed so that the sappers could see clearly enough to make a sufficient gap through the minefields—and without open flanks at either end, blowing a hole through the enemy lines was the only means of attack. The necessary equipment needed for this operation would not be in Egypt before 1 October, Alex told him, so it could not occur in September. Moreover, once it arrived the Mobile Striking Force— X Corps—would have to be trained in its use. But Churchill was insistent that the panzer army should be defeated *before* Operation TORCH in order to encourage the French to jump ship to the Allies and the Spanish to remain neutral. "I have carefully considered the timing in relation to TORCH," wrote Alex, "and have come to the conclusion that not only complies with military reasons but also to provide cover for TORCH, the best date for us to start would be minus 13 of TORCH."[300] In other words, around 24 October.

Churchill was not happy. Alex was discovering just how difficult it was to derail the PM once he had got an idea or notion into his head. The new C-in-C had to write two long, carefully reasoned cables to Churchill—in which he essentially repeated his arguments—as to why the third week in October was the only practicable date for launching the new offensive, now ironically code-named LIGHTFOOT on account of the vast numbers of mines now separating the two opposing forces.

Monty knew little of these discussions. Alex rightly believed that his army commander needed to be shielded and protected from any prime ministerial interference. As it happened, Brooke was of the same mind, and when the PM interrupted a rare day's grouse shooting, the CIGS became very terse with him, giving Churchill short shrift over his melodramatic blustering. "It is a regular disease that he suffers from," Brooke noted in his diary, "this frightful impatience to get an attack launched!"[301]

But Alex also entirely agreed with Monty's prognosis about the state of his army. Alam Halfa, Alex pointed out to Churchill, demonstrated the "urgent need of intensive training especially for the Mobile Striking Force."[302] During the battle, Eighth Army had still lost more men and even more tanks than the panzer army. As the Sherwood Rangers had shown, there were sections of the army that were more akin with Kitchener's men at Omdurman than the kind of forces needed to win modern warfare, and the only offensive action of the battle—the New Zealand-led nighttime attack—had been a fiasco and demonstrated how difficult it was to fight across heavily defended minefields. As the Afrika Korps had proved time and again, quality—in training and equipment—counted for more than quantity.

As a whole, Monty did not think much of the British Army and was well aware of the effect of the interwar years of neglect. Despite the growing superiority in tanks and firepower, it was, he noted, "a regrettable fact that our troops are not, in all cases, highly trained," and he accepted that they could easily blow this massive material advantage. But he was wrong to tar the whole of Eighth Army with the same brush. There was little wrong with much of the infantry: the Australians, New Zealanders, 7th Motor Brigade, and Tuker's Indians, for example, were generally quality troops with a collective mass of experience. The problems lay first with the commanders and the faulty military doctrine that had been passed down; and second with the armor. The problem of the commanders could in part be solved by Monty's zero tolerance of bellyaching. He also changed his corps commanders: Lieutenant-General Sir Oliver Leese was brought over from England to take over XXX Corps, and Lieutenant-General Brian Horrocks had also arrived to take command of XIII Corps. Monty had taught Leese at Staff College, and both had served under him in the UK. Both were fairly unimaginative and had so far had steady rather than exceptional careers—Tuker was appalled by their lack of tactical knowledge—but crucially, neither would quibble with the boss. In the future there would be a far smoother dissemination of orders. Moreover, as Alex pointed out to Churchill, both Leese and Horrocks not only had experience of leading men in battle but also of training them.

The thorny issue of the armor was more problematic. By mid-October, Eighth Army would have more than a thousand tanks of which more than four hundred would be Shermans and Grants—but the difficulty was going to be getting the various units of cavalry, tank regiments and yeomanry to work to the same prescribed tactics and hand in glove with anti-tank screens. This required a wholesale change in doctrine, something that could not be done in an instant, especially since the moment battle began, confusion would inevitably reign and bad habits almost certainly come flooding back.

It was a quandary, but Monty believed that the best way around it was to make a simple plan, then stick to it. That way every man, from the top to the bottom of the chain, would know exactly what was expected of them. Then they would rehearse it over and over until the lines had been learned. This did not only mean the troops involved, but the logistics teams too. Supply systems had to be perfected, organizational weaknesses uncovered.

The Sherwood Rangers Yeomanry were sent back thirty miles along with the rest of 8th Armoured Division. A dummy minefield was constructed with lanes marked out by perforated petrol cans with lights inside. Over and over, the regiment practiced going through these lanes at night. To add a sense of realism, flares were shot up into the sky and explosions set off by the sappers. The infantry were also sent back out of the line, partly to train and partly to get fit and refreshed. Monty had decided that the Australians would provide much of the infantry muscle, and since they would be among the first crossing the minefield gaps, it was felt it would be a good idea for them to know something about mines. Shortly after Alam Halfa, for example, Joe Madeley found himself being sent to "Mine School." The whole battalion was then taken out of the line toward the end of the month and sent some twenty-six miles back. Camped next to the sea for nearly two weeks, they underwent training, physical exercise, and swam. At the end of this period, Joe was given five days' leave in Cairo. Apart from suffering a terrible hangover on the train back ("because we'd spent the previous night with the Kiwis"), he was otherwise refreshed and in good shape for the enormous task ahead.

Only the New Zealanders were taken out of the line as a complete division. After ten days' rest at Burg el Arab—where Maiki Parkinson spent the time swimming and watching the Kiwi Concert Parties—they were sent south to a training area. Initially, the battalions trained separately. After a few days' range firing and toughening up with bayonet and physical exercises, the Maori began carrying out mock attacks by dawn, day, dusk, and at night, both on foot and in trucks. Finally came a three-day divisional exercise with live ammunition fired by the artillery as the New Zealanders moved forward under a creeping barrage; the sappers also made paths through real minefields and blew holes in real wire.

Albert Martin and 2 Rifle Brigade were also taken out of their forward positions and moved to Burg el Arab for training, PT, and swimming. Monty paid a visit while they were there, and Albert, for one, was beginning to be impressed by the new army commander. "The impact of Monty's visit stayed with us," noted Albert. "We also liked his scathing comments about Rommel and his repetitive and unenterprising battle strategy. It sounds heresy, I know, but by the time Monty had finished with us we were almost looking forward to the coming showdown."[303] Albert was also cheered by the good military sense that Monty spoke: there would be no more defended boxes with their inflexibility and negative concept; no more penny packet forces and cavalier tank charges, but troops operating on strength. On the other hand, Albert and his mates were sorely disappointed to learn that they were being transferred from the 7th Armoured Division to the 1st Armoured Division, now part of Monty's new *corps d'elite*, X Corps. The 7th Armoured, with their jerboa logo, were the Desert Rats, the original core of Eighth Army; 1st Armoured's logo was "a silly, meaningless figure of a rhinoceros." For several days, feelings ran very high, threatening to undo all the positive things that had been achieved under Monty's command. "The poor fellow who came round to paint a new logo on the trucks was subjected to violent abuse," noted Albert.[304]

"We in the Air Force were ready at any time we might be called on," noted Tommy Elmhirst, "nevertheless, we were able to make good use of any respite for blooding our new-entry American pilots." These were, in Tommy's opinion, "first class material" with a mass of flying experience.[305] Duke Ellington, for example, had around three hundred hours by the time he reached the Middle East, way more than any pilot in the RAF going operational for the first time. But they lacked any combat experience, and so Mary Coningham devised a system of integrating the Americans with RAF units, believing, quite sensibly, that was the best way to teach them the ropes of desert flying.

US Mitchell bomber crews had joined 3 Wing in time for the start of Alam Halfa. Cobber Weinronk liked them well enough, but was surprised by a number of differences. For example, the Americans had copilots, a luxury not afforded by the RAF or SAAF. He also thought their strange "lingo" was "quaint." "Where we say, 'opening the throttle,' they say, 'heaping on the coal,'" he noted. "Where we use the phrase, 'flying speed to takeoff,' they say, 'hearing the blue line.'"[306]

Experiencing front-line duty for the first time at Alam Halfa was quite some initiation, but the 57th Fighter Group were given a slightly less frenetic start. Now collected together once more after their stint acclimatizing, they were sent to Egypt in mid-September. Duke Ellington had enjoyed his brief time on Cyprus. In between the flying, there had also been plenty of time to swim in the sea and visit the various nightclubs on the island. All their ground support had been with the rest of the 57th Fighter Group, and so the 65th Fighter Squadron had been looked after entirely by the RAF. This had meant living off British food as well. Duke had come to terms with the monotony of eating bully beef day after day, but "the weevil-infested bread took a little bit longer to get used to," and he was looking forward to becoming an all-American outfit once again.

In this he was to be kept waiting a while longer, for the bad luck that had dogged his trip to the Middle East had not deserted him. Just before the squadron had been due to join the rest of the group back in Palestine, Duke had damaged his plane while practicing landing from a tight turn—a gust of wind had caught him and he'd knocked the edge of his wing. So once again the squadron went on ahead without him. After a couple of days' morosely hanging around, Duke was told his aircraft was ready again. "So I got my little bird cranked up," he says, "and I was just pass-

ing the coast of Cyprus when my engine quit . . ." He reckoned he had
enough power to get himself landed, and although the island was quite
mountainous, he managed to spot a relatively flat area and safely got
himself down. He'd just got his baggage out when he saw lots of Cypriots
running towards him with pitchforks. "They thought I was the bad guy!"
he says. He was saved by the arrival of a British Bren carrier.

When he finally reached the rest of the group in Palestine, Duke was
feeling a little embarrassed, but his CO, Art Salisbury, immediately said to
him, "Duke, I hope you get the first 109—you've had tough luck." "I can't
tell you how much that meant to me at the time," admits Duke, "and how
much it has stuck with me over the years."

The group was in Palestine for only a few days after Duke's arrival before being posted to their first combat base in Egypt—LG 174 on 16 September. The 65th were attached to a South African fighter squadron and
over the next few weeks they were taught some of the basics of combat flying. "They were so experienced, those guys," says Duke. "They taught us
how to survive."

Until joining the South Africans, Duke had spent much time practicing dog-fighting and aerobatics, but as he discovered, there was less call
for that in the aerial combat of the Western Desert. "The RAF way was to
get to the target area and then get the hell out. It was all ground-strafing
and dropping bombs." But as Johnnie Fairbairn had discovered, it also
took time to adjust to the strangeness of flying in the desert and for those
unused to spotting enemy aircraft, often just pinpricks in the sky until it
was too late, the guiding hand of those more experienced made all the
difference. Not only had Billy Drake, for example, honed his ground-
attack technique, he had also taught his men how to deal with attacks by
enemy fighters who nearly always had the advantage of height. For
starters, the three-plane vic—or "V"—as prescribed by the RAF in the
first years of the war and which was still used by the USAAF, had long
ago been discarded by Billy and most of the other fighter units. "The basic formation was the finger-four," he says, "well spaced apart and working in pairs, leader and wingman." If the whole squadron were flying
there would be three such flights of four—red, blue, and green sections.
"This way everyone had a bloody good sight of what was happening.
Whoever saw the enemy first would inform the leader. He'd say, 'Thanks,
chum—I've seen them,' and then would make up his mind how to deal
with them—whether to detail part or all of his force against them." The
key was the timing of the break, the moment at which the pilots suddenly
turned their aircraft onto its side and pulled them into a tight turn. This
was always the leader's decision. "The trick was to leave it to the last
minute so the 109s would overshoot us," says Billy.

Like Tommy Elmhirst, however, Billy Drake was not only impressed by the very high standard of flying amongst the Americans, but also by their willingness to learn. Mostly, it was men from the 64th and 66th FS who were flying with Billy's 112 Squadron, and it soon became clear that they were catching on fast. "They were a great bunch," he noted, "and I think they respected us. Certainly the feeling was mutual."[307]

Training continued in Britain too. The Bowles twins, Tom and Henry, were now together in the same 2nd Battalion of the 18th Regimental Combat Team. Henry had managed to get himself transferred so that he could be closer to his brother—although not to the same company. He was now in Battalion HQ Company, while Tom was part of a mortar team in Company G. The 18 RCT was still a part of the Big Red One, the First Infantry Division, which as the US Army's most experienced infantry outfit was due to spearhead one of the TORCH landings. Also now attached to the division in preparation for TORCH was Bing Evans's 1st Ranger Battalion.

On 18 October, Ike and Harry Butcher left Telegraph Cottage early and took a sixteen-hour train ride to Kentallen in Western Scotland to watch the Big Red One carry out some training exercises in landing craft. Arriving at midnight, they were taken straight away to see a nighttime exercise. The troops—Tom and Henry Bowles included—were already in combat loaders, some as far as six miles from the coast, others only a mile away. Under the cover of darkness, they were to approach the shore, land, and then take a number of dummy "enemy" positions.

In a caravan of ten cars led by Ike, Butch, and a British officer, they drove from point to point where the various landings were being made. At each place they would get out of the cars and slosh through the mud to talk to the officers and men and observe their operations. Between 1 AM and 9 AM, they drove some ninety miles. For much of the time it was raining, and since their driver looked exhausted, Butch took over the wheel, even though he had never driven in the UK before and was unused to the blackout and right-hand configuration.

When they were stopped by Brigadier-General Ted Roosevelt, son of the first President Roosevelt, they were given a glowing report about the success of the exercises and assured that they had "all but choked Hitler."[308] Ike, however, felt disinclined to agree, and when, after breakfast in Inverary, they watched some more maneuvers, they did so with a growing sense of unease. The troops looked good—healthy, fit, and agile—but Ike was worried by the lack of direction and leadership given by the officers, who all appeared unsure about what they were supposed to be doing. "It is in this level of command that we have our most glaring weakness," he told General Marshall, "and it is one that only time and eternal effort can cure. We

are short on experience and trained leadership below battalion commander, and it is beyond the capacity of any division commander or any
colonel to cure these difficulties hurriedly. Time is essential."[309] They didn't
have much experience above battalion commander, either, not in terms of
battlefield command at any rate. This was the single biggest problem facing
a US Army that was unused to war and growing at an exponential rate.

Unfortunately, time was not a luxury they had. In just a few weeks,
these same US troops would be landing in North Africa. As if to rub it in,
while in Scotland Ike received a cable from Marshall, relaying the message the president was intending to send the Vichy leader, Marshal
Petain, as the landings were being made. "I am sending *an invincible American army*," FDR had written, "to co-operate with your African government in arming your compatriots and repelling Axis invasion."[310]

They returned to London feeling pretty low. Ike was getting a cold
from stomping about in the wet and dark, but back in his office in London,
he confessed to Butch that he was struggling with a "state of the jitters."[311]
This was principally because of the disappointing showing in Scotland, but
also preying on his mind was the fate of Mark Clark, currently on a secret
and highly risky mission to Algiers.

The roots of this mission had begun a month before, in the middle of
September, and had come at the suggestion of the president's man in Algiers, Robert D. Murphy. Instrumental in trying to gauge French reaction
to any Allied landings, Murphy had long-established relations with the
French, having served in Paris for some years before the war and as chargé
d'affaires in the Vichy embassy after the French surrender in June 1940. Recalled to Washington by Roosevelt, in December 1940 he was sent to North
Africa, officially as consul general, but in reality as the president's personal
intelligence agent in Algeria.

Affable and politically shrewd, Murphy had achieved much, having
created strong relations with a number of Vichy French military and political leaders. He had even negotiated an aid pact with Vichy France, all
of which enabled Murphy to continue his extremely useful good relations
with these Nazi subjects, and which gave him an entrée to some of the key
players in Vichy France, most notably Admiral Darlan and General Giraud. Giraud had dramatically escaped from a German prison but on his
return to France had sworn his loyalty to Petain. Darlan had been a mod-
ernizing and popular head of the French Navy before the war, but had
been convinced that the Allies had no chance of beating the Axis powers
and so had tied his colors firmly to the Vichy mast. Although briefly
Petain's deputy, he was still officially head of all France's armed forces. His
dislike of the British ran deep (his great-grandfather had been killed at

Trafalgar), and had intensified after the British sank the French Fleet at Oran in July 1940.

With TORCH given the green light, Murphy was summoned home in September for talks with the president, and then, disguised as Lieutenant-Colonel McGowan, had headed on to London for top-secret talks with Ike and his team. He arrived in London somewhat earlier than expected on the morning of 16 September. Harry Butcher had been having lunch with the broadcaster Ed Murrow when he received an urgent call from Ike telling him to get over to Telegraph Cottage right away. Ignoring jokes about it being the start of the second front, Butch hurriedly left. When he reached the cottage, "Colonel McGowan," in an ill-fitting uniform, was chatting earnestly with Ike in the garden.

These were to prove invaluable discussions for both parties. For Ike, it was a chance to have a frank conversation about many of his concerns over the French situation in North Africa with someone who knew the situation and people there as well as anyone. Murphy was able to brief him about the size, state, and political temperature of the French forces there, of the mood of the civilian population: French Morocco, Murphy confirmed, was the area of greatest danger, and although there were plenty in Algiers who were pro the Allies, his best guess was that the landings would be met with resistance in some areas and swift submission in others.

Ike was then able to give Murphy a comprehensive briefing in turn, and the plan certainly gave him cause for confidence. The proposed scale of the landings, Murphy told him, was exactly what his co-conspirators in Algiers had been hoping for. He also reported on his dealings with General Giraud, who, in August had sent word that the Allies could count on the French Army siding with them as long as landings could take place in France as well. Giraud was suggesting Spring 1943. Perhaps on his return to Algiers, Murphy suggested, he should let Giraud know that the US was now in a position to take action on a substantial scale and should ask whether he was willing to act decisively alongside them. There would be no trouble smuggling him out of France, he assured Ike; but how the French general would react to such an approach, Murphy was not prepared to guess.

And if Giraud did come in from the cold, they would then have to address the question of French command in North Africa. Giraud's circle of friends had made it clear to Murphy that were there to be Allied control in Northwest Africa, it would have to be commanded by a Frenchman. This was out of the question, although Ike was prepared to concede that French troops might be able to remain under French command. On the other hand, General de Gaulle, Ike explained, was going to be kept out of the operation, and Murphy felt this was a good idea: they needed to win over the Vichy French *in situ*; de Gaulle would only throw a wrench in the works.

They talked all afternoon and continued well into the night, long after others privy to the discussions had departed, and then resumed again during and after breakfast the following morning. Butch was there throughout, listening and trying to absorb the implications of this increasingly complicated operation. It was a very thin political tightrope that they now had to cross; bar a few exceptions, most senior Frenchmen had decided to back the horse they felt would win. But who did they think was most likely to win in North Africa? Ike had been charged with planning the biggest seaborne operation ever attempted. Working out logistics and preparing training programmes was a black and white affair, but political intrigue was a different matter altogether. No wonder Murphy confessed that he felt quite humbled by the burden of responsibility.

However, there was one other thing Ike might like to consider, Murphy suggested, something that might make all the difference. If he were to send a senior US military figure over to Algeria for discussions with French Allied collaborators, it would demonstrate serious intent. This person could then also brief their French friends about activities that might help the landings, such as silencing coastal guns, seizing radio stations, and providing signals to the approaching Allied armada.

The risks of such a mission becoming compromised were huge—the entire operation would undoubtedly be blown—and so Ike refused to give Murphy an immediate answer. But after some discussion it was agreed it was a risk worth taking. From many volunteers, Ike chose his deputy, General Mark Clark.

The troops, of course, knew none of this, although in the Western Desert everyone was keenly aware that the offensive was coming. One person in a good position to watch the comings and goings of Army HQ was Sam Bradshaw. The 6 Royal Tanks had never recovered from their efforts during two long months of battle. C Squadron—down to just a dozen tanks—had been attached to 1 RTR at Alam Halfa, while the rest of the regiment became part of an armored column held in reserve. At the end of September, what was left of the regiment was briefly reunited, but was then split again. While most of the men were finally taken out of the line and sent back to Khatatba Camp, B Squadron, including Sam, was sent to Eighth Army Tactical Headquarters at Burg el Arab, where they were to protect the Army Commander and his staff.

"We were supposed to be very proud about this," says Sam, "but to be honest, it didn't seem that great an honor." One of the squadron, Jock

Fraser, had the responsibility of driving Monty around any time he needed a tank. It was Jock who suggested Monty try a tank beret rather than the Aussie broad-brimmed hat he had taken to wearing—an idea the army commander accepted. From then on, he was rarely seen without it.

Even better placed was Lieutenant Carol Mather. He had known Monty before the war—his mother had been great friends with Monty's wife, Betty, and both families had been skiing together. Even then, in the late twenties, Monty had seemed to Carol to be everything a soldier should be, right down to the clipped moustache. The boy and the soldier struck up an unlikely rapport, and when Monty's wife died, Carol, then aged seventeen, was sent to spend a few days with him to keep him company.

In early October Monty suddenly called for him. "I need a personal liaison officer to go around the battlefield to tell me what's happening," he told Carol. It was an offer he could hardly refuse; nor did he have any trouble securing a leave of absence from David Stirling, who was only too happy to have one of his men in the pocket of the army commander. So it was that in the middle of the month, Carol reported to Tac HQ, where he was handed a new jeep and driver and given the task of thoroughly familiarizing himself with the various commanders, dispositions, and minefields of the battle area. He even began driving Monty around himself, as the army commander visited the troops and gave them his regular pep talks. "He was a good person to work for," says Carol. "He wasn't the completely austere person that everybody makes out. He actually had a very good sense of humour, and once he accepted you and trusted you, you had no more worries."

Allied success in North Africa still had much to do with the war of supply. Disrupting Axis shipping throughout the Central Mediterranean remained as critical as ever. This task was made easier now that Malta was again able to make a more positive contribution. In addition to the torpedo-bombers that were now operating between Malta and Egypt, and relentlessly attacking Axis shipping, the submarines of the 10th Flotilla were now back operating from the island and making their presence felt once more. Crippling losses and a base in ruins had forced them to join the 1st Flotilla in Beirut back in April. With the 8th Flotilla operating from Gibraltar, it had meant that any Allied submarines had to steam around 900 miles before they could make any assault on the Axis supply lines. Just two enemy ships had been sunk by submarines in June, and only one in July.

With the Axis aerial blitzes over, however, Captain George "Shrimp" Simpson had begun to move his submarines and crews back to the beleaguered island. In August, his men had accounted for seven enemy merchant ships, some 31,000 tons and nearly a third of the tonnage Rommel reckoned he needed per month. Simpson's force was still severely under strength, however, and so several larger submarines were seconded to bolster his numbers. One of those was the S-Class submarine HMS/S *Safari*, on loan from Gibraltar.* Simpson was delighted to see her pull into Malta on 19 September: her skipper, Commander Ben Bryant, was, as Shrimp put it, "the most experienced and competent submarine commander afloat." A pre-war legend in the submarine fraternity, Bryant was, at nearly forty, old to be still commanding a boat, yet in the opening years of the war, when he had commanded HMS/S *Sealion* in home waters, he had shown that he was as sharp and capable as he'd always been, while his performance since arriving in the Mediterranean earlier in the summer had only heightened his formidable reputation.

Recently joining *Safari* as fourth hand had been twenty-one-year-old Lieutenant Ronnie Ward. The son of a Yorkshire GP, Ronnie had entered Dartmouth Naval College at thirteen. His family had always loved the sea, spending weekends and holidays at Bridlington and Scarborough, and although there was no naval history in the family, Ronnie was certain from an early age that his future lay with the Royal Navy. He loved his four years at Dartmouth. "A lot of people hated it," he says, "but I basically obeyed the rules and had a marvelous time."

After serving as a midshipman on a destroyer—and seeing action in Norway and Dakar among other places—he was sent on his sub-lieutenant's course and then posted to submarines. Although given the option of moving back to surface vessels, he'd enjoyed his time training on submarines so much he decided to stay and was eventually posted to *P.43*, a submarine operating in home waters. Unfortunately, Ronnie's blissful naval career to date suddenly took a nosedive. "I couldn't stand the captain," he explains. Matters came to a head during a patrol off Norway. The CO had ordered the periscope to go up every three minutes, but the seas were particularly rough, the boat** was lurching all over the place and water was sloshing over the lens, so Ronnie had cut back the frequency with which he put up the periscope. Unbeknown to Ronnie, however, the CO had been timing him, and severely reprimanded Ronnie in front of the rest of the crew. Absolutely furious at being so humiliated, Ronnie angrily stormed out of the control room. On their return to the Clyde, he was promptly taken off board and packed off to Gibraltar as spare crew.

---

*HMS/S *Safari* was, at that time, still known as *P.211*. It received its name in February 1943, but will be referred to here as *Safari*.
**Submariners always refer to their vessels as boats, not ships.

There he was taken aside by Ben Bryant, who'd heard about his dismissal from *P.43*. "I don't think you'll do anything like that ever again, will you?" Ben had said.

"No, sir, I won't," Ronnie had replied.

"Good, I think you'll be all right. I'll take you on, but you've got to behave yourself." Since then, Ronnie hadn't looked back. "Ben was marvelous," he says. "Made me feel at home right away." And he was also someone from whom a junior officer like Ronnie could learn a great deal.

Safari set off on her first patrol for the 10th Flotilla on 26 September, heading for the Dalmation coast: British submarines had not been operating there recently and Simpson was anxious to shake up Axis supply roads heading from Yugoslavia and down through the Straits of Otranto. They spent a frustrating couple of days tracking a steamer that eluded them as it went into port between a number of islands, but as darkness fell on 1 October, Ben felt sure he would be able to catch it the following morning as it set out from port.

As submarines were incredibly slow, successfully second-guessing the movements of the enemy was an essential skill for a submarine commander. The S-class, for example, had a maximum underwater speed of nine knots—around ten miles an hour—although this could not be kept up for long: the batteries that powered the diesel engines would soon run low at that speed. For the most part, their underwater operating speed was little more than jogging pace. Conseqeuntly, getting in position to sink enemy ships was about playing a long, and often stealthy, game of cat and mouse.

Under a bright moon, *Safari* pushed out to sea on the night of 1 October to recharge her batteries, a task that could be done only when surfaced. They had begun the process when suddenly the watch standing out on the conning tower smelled a slight whiff of funnel smoke in the air. Immediately the recharging was broken off, action stations were called, and *Safari* slipped beneath the waves. In this case, it turned out to be a small torpedo boat, and although they easily avoided it, they had to give it a wide berth. As a result, the following morning, they reached their position to catch the steamer later than Ben had originally intended.

Working close to the shore meant there was invariably the added risk of mines, particularly in the approaches to any port. *Safari* was equipped with a mine detector unit (MDU), an application of the Asdic—in turn a form of sonar—but the problem with using these instruments was that they could be picked up by other vessels, and so had to be operated sparingly. Nonetheless, they had taken a chance and MDU had shown them a clear path between the islands. In fact, the area was heaving with mines, but either their MDU was particularly efficient, or more likely, they had simply been very fortunate. At any rate, at 9:45 AM on 2 October, as they slipped through a narrow and shallow channel between two islands, they finally caught up with the steamer. The delay meant it was now some 3,000 yards away—some two and a half miles. This was quite a distance for a torpedo strike, especially since Ben reckoned the steamer must be doing at least thirteen knots, and so he decided to risk surfacing and to try and hit it with the 3-inch gun mounted on the bridge instead.

Ben was well-known for his use of the gun. Although equipped with six torpedo tubes, the high-velocity 3-inch gun was, he reckoned, often more effective, especially if a target was not surrounded by large numbers of aerial and destroyer escorts. Opening fire, they appeared to have taken the steamer completely unawares, and although only fifteen of the thirty-six shells they fired hit home, the steamer was soon in flames. Before they could sink her, however, she'd run herself aground on the nearest beach. She was evidently being used as a troop carrier and through his binoculars Ronnie watched men leaping overboard. Ben immediately ordered them to dive, and closing in, they fired a torpedo at 1,000 yards. As it hit home, the steamer erupted into flames again; they could still see the smoke the following day, by which time they had withdrawn safely back out to sea. Even so, after their attack, torpedo boats and enemy aircraft hunted them all morning and afternoon, and on into the night. They eventually escaped only by following the wake of the E-boats as they patrolled further out to sea.

Conditions on the submarines were cramped to say the least. *Safari* had a crew of forty-eight, and everyone, apart from the skipper and the chief engineer, operated on a system of two hours on and four off. In the off-duty period, each man had to do all his eating and sleeping; any kind of normal daily routine went by the wayside, although they did try to have a cooked meal when they surfaced at night. Quite often this was interrupted by having to dive straight down again, however. "Conditions were very primitive," says Ronnie. "How the poor crew survived, I've no idea. We five officers at least had a loo for our own exclusive use and so did the engineers, but the rest of the crew had to share one between them—not much fun." The entire boat reeked of diesel, and toward the end of a voyage, rotting food. Enough provisions had to be taken to last them the entire patrol, and this could be between two and three weeks. Washing was minimal, and old and battered uniforms and sweaters were worn, their smart kit left behind at base. Most returned from patrols with beards. Ronnie had grown one, and then decided not to bother shaving it off; it was easier to keep it grown.

Having hunted along the Yugoslav coast, they crossed to the other side of the Adriatic, spotting and attacking another merchant vessel. Three torpedoes missed, and a fourth failed, so once again they surfaced and turned to the gun. Hits were scored but not enough to sink her, and so then they headed back to the Dalmatian coast once more. On 8 October, they spotted a four-ship convoy. Despite a sea mist and an escort of MTBs, they still managed to sink a heavily laden 1,500-ton vessel. Two days later, they found another three-ship convoy. At a range of 2,000 yards—a mile and a half—they fired three torpedoes and hit two of the ships. This was no mean feat: although they had a primitive computer on board, known as a "fruit machine," much of the calculations were done by eye and rapid mental arithmetic. This required a very cool head, for there were many calculations to make. Speed and range of the target had to be hastily assessed then the Director Angel (DA) calculated, or, in plain terms, the "aim-off" needed in order to hit a moving target. Hitting a ship, unless dead in the water at point-blank range, was very difficult indeed, and made more so by the submarine's delicate trim—or balance. Torpedoes were necessarily fired just below the surface, where the sea's swell could rock the boat, but trim could also be affected by a number of other factors, including sudden changes in depth or even salinity. This was why 80 percent of all successes were achieved by just 20 percent of the commanding officers. Some had the "knack", but most didn't.

This particular attack was followed by heavy depth-charging as torpedo boats swept above them hunting furiously. "This could be pretty hairy," admits Ronnie. Some depth charges came agonizingly close. Corking fell off the ceiling, a few lightbulbs went and the sub was rocked from side to side. Ben ordered them to dive deeper. The needle on the altimeter clicked around the gauge: two hundred feet, two hundred and fifty, three hundred. They were now at the boat's maximum diving limit, but Ben told them to keep going. Three hundred and twenty feet, then three hundred and fifty. By now the boat was creaking and groaning with the intense pressure. No one spoke a word. "You had to be absolutely quiet," says Ronnie. "If you had to open a valve or something, you wrapped a piece of wool around the spanner so it wouldn't clang against another piece of metal." If a depth charge blew within twenty-five feet of them, they would be split apart. Then three hundred and ninety feet.

Ben stopped them there. The attack lasted three quarters of an hour, and in that time they were depth-charged twenty-six times. After three hours of appalling tension, they finally resurfaced and set sail for home.

It was a tradition among the submariners to enter their home port flying a Jolly Roger if they had been successful during their patrol. White bars were stitched on next to the skull and crossbones to denote each ship sunk. As *Safari* entered Malta's Marsamxett Harbor, their Jolly Roger already had four new bars sewn on. Furthermore, they arrived home with much information about the busy Adriatic shipping channels. No wonder Shrimp Simpson was so glad to have Ben Bryant and his crew join the 10th Flotilla.

In Egypt, new troops continued to arrive, fresh from Britain. The 51st Highland Division, at last reconstituted after its almost complete annihilation in France in 1940, had reached Egypt in August. Among them was twenty-year-old Johnny Bain, a private in the 5/7 Gordon Highlanders, part of the 153rd Infantry Brigade. He was not, as it happened, from Scotland, but from Aylesbury in Buckinghamshire. His grandfather had been Scottish and his father had fought in a Scottish regiment in the First World War, but Johnny and his brother Kenneth ended up with the Highlanders purely because they joined up in Glasgow. Both of them hated their father, who was violent and a bully. He once punched Johnny so hard that he knocked him out. When Johnny discovered his father had been fiddling his income tax and stashing money in a box in his wardrobe, they decided to pinch it and flee home. After a week's drinking spree, and by now running short of money, they tried to join the RAF and then the Merchant Navy before finally ending up in Glasgow and taking the King's shilling there, joining the Argyle and Sutherland Highlanders.

Johnny had little idea about what he was letting himself in for. Growing up, the First World War had made a great impression on him—his father talked about it endlessly—but he understood little about the current war. "I was ignorant and uninterested," he admits, and although to begin with the war had seemed quite exciting, he soon discovered he wasn't really cut out for soldiering. He and his brother were also soon separated; Kenneth was sent on an engineering course. Johnny was a talented boxer, however, and won the Highland Area Army Championships, which got him noticed. Given a couple of stripes, he became a PT instructor for a short while, but on returning to ordinary duty decided he was no good at taking drill and organizing guard duties, so one day simply walked out and hitched a lift to London. "I had some idea I could live there," he says, "but of course I never could." He was picked up and brought back, but to avoid a court-martial agreed to revert to rank and to be transferred to the London Scottish. Shortly after, he was transferred again, this time to the 5/7 Gordon Highlanders who were about to leave for the Middle East.

Having won the ship's boxing competition on the journey out, Johnny reached Port Tewfik at Suez and was sent straight to a training camp at Geneifa. In a short time, he would be among those leading the assault when the battle was launched. Having never been in any kind of combat before he had no idea what to expect, but despite his checkered army career to date and a certain amount of apprehension, he couldn't help feeling rather excited by the prospect.

Back in their positions at the front, the 2/13 Australian Infantry Battalion were frequently given the task of slipping over the wire at night in an effort to discover enemy dispositions and, if possible, to capture a few prisoners who could then be grilled for information. Joe Madeley and his section were out on patrol on the night of 6 September. Because it was pitch dark, they had worked out their route beforehand—so many yards in one direction, then turn and head another predetermined distance in another direction. They didn't spot anything, however, and so had just turned to head back when they realized they'd wandered straight into the rear of a machine-gun post. Somewhere along the way, they'd made a miscalculation. "There was barbed wire all round the front," says Joe, "but we walked in through the back. We didn't even know it until we heard a German voice. They thought we'd be coming from the other direction so started firing and lobbing grenades in front of their position." It only took a moment for both parties to realize what had happened. Knowing they were surrounded, Joe and his mates ran for their lives, diving into a shallow gully as bullets whistled over their heads. Joe's heart was racing, but luckily no one had been hit. He fired a few bursts of his Thompson machine gun and between them they lobbed a number of grenades, then, after waiting a short while, silently crept back towards their lines. As they stumbled into company HQ, Joe and the rest of the patrol began laughing so much they couldn't stop. At headquarters they'd heard all the noise and seen the tracers and asked what on earth the hysterics were all about. "We couldn't explain," says Joe. "Nerves I suppose."

The pilots also had been given some time at rest camp and for Johnnie Fairbairn that had included a bit of leave in Cairo. It soon passed, however, and after a few days' "drunkenness and debauchery,"[312] he returned to active duty with 73 Squadron, which, by the beginning of September, had finally changed from day to night figher duties. The task of the night fighter was quite different from that of his daytime counterpart. For one thing, it was a solitary business. Pilots would take off alone, "intrude" far behind enemy lines and then circle around enemy landing grounds waiting for unsuspecting bombers to return home from a raid. Extra auxiliary petrol tanks were fitted so that, if necessary, flights could last up to three hours or more. Johnnie found it a "skulking lonely" business, sitting in a cramped cockpit "eerily lit by the luminosity of the dashboard instruments" and with the constant throb of the Merlin engine the only company. "Like a vulture suddenly appearing from nowhere," noted Johnnie, "the art was to lie low a short distance away from the target and remain unobtrusive until the time came to move in for the kill."

It took him time to adjust back to the role for which he'd originally been trained, but Johnnie eventually grew used to the sudden arrival of a corporal creeping through his tent flap in the middle of the night and telling him it was time to get going. From his warm and snug camp bed, he would wearily put on several layers of clothes and step out into the freezing desert night, then stumble toward the silhouette of his black-painted Hurricane, which for some reason always seemed at least twice its normal size at night.

With the flare path lit, he would then taxi and take off. As soon as his undercarriage was up, the flare path would be turned off and Johnnie would head off into the inky blackness. During the flight to the target, he couldn't help imagining the eyes of the enemy all glaring up at him as they heard the sound of his engine hum overhead. Generally, he flew at around 7,000 feet, too high for light ack-ack, but even so the first time he was caught in the cross-beams of searchlights he had the fright of his life. "I was lit up, naked and ashamed," he wrote, although soon learned that the trick was to push the control column forward and dive out of the way.

Before reaching the target, he would turn out to sea, lower his height to about 4,000 feet and then head inland again. Many nights nothing happened at all, but on others the wait was rewarded. His heart would leap as the flare path suddenly came on and wingtip lights showed the presence of tired enemy bomber crews coming back in to land. That was his chance to pounce.

One night, he was intruding over Sidi Haneish airfield, the same place where he had joined 73 Squadron back in May. Suddenly the flare path shone brightly and Johnnie spotted the enemy bomber coming in to land with all lights on. Following the enemy aircraft as it turned into its approach, Johnnie crept up to within 250 yards of its tail, and then, as the bomber touched down, pressed the firing button, holding it down for a full eight of its maximum fifteen-second capacity. All hell let loose. Johnnie slammed open the throttle, pulled up the nose, and desperately strained for height. But having lowered his speed to little over a hundred miles an hour, his Hurricane was now "floppy as a pregnant duck," and as he climbed away all too slowly, the feared searchlights caught him and tracer began streaming all around him.

Diving down again to avoid the beam, there was suddenly a huge flash of light and the Hurricane lurched violently. It wasn't his aircraft that had been hit, however, but the bomber exploding beneath him. "Looking back over my shoulder," he noted, "I saw the whole drome lit up by a huge conflagration which remained in my rear-view mirror for some time as I headed full bore for home. I was quite proud of that victory."[313]

Around the same time, toward the end of September, the Squadron gained a new flight commander. Flight Lieutenant Tommy Thompson was a veteran not only of the Battle of Britain but had also spent a long stint on Malta, flying at a time when there were no Spitfires, and the RAF fighter pilots on the island were struggling against massive enemy air superiority. Those had been hard times indeed—little food, appalling conditions, and worst of all, almost no drink.

During his time on the island, Tommy had become a founding member of the Malta Night Fighter Unit—word had gone out that volunteers were wanted for night fighting and that the new CO wanted men who liked their drink and knew how to have a good time when off duty. Tommy had been all for that, and so had signed up right away. Somehow, he'd managed to survive ten long months on the island, and so had initially been relieved when he'd been posted to Khartoum as an instructor. However, he soon discovered it was more dangerous than operational flying. On one occasion, a student had braked too hard, flipping them both onto their backs. Another time, he was teaching formation flying and one of his pupils almost flew into the back of him. "I'd told him to catch up," says Tommy, "and the next thing I know there's this bloody great roar, and I looked up and saw him slide straight over me. He took the radio mast off, the tip of the fin and the starboard wing tip." Tommy's aircraft almost immediately dropped a thousand feet, but somehow he managed to get it back down safely. "The first one paid my bar bill for a week and the second for a fortnight!" says Tommy. Consequently, it was with some relief that he was posted back to operational flying.

By the time he joined 73 Squadron, the nature of their night intruders had changed. With the offensive now just a few weeks away, the emphasis was on disrupting Rommel's supply lines to the front. On one of his first intruders, Tommy attacked transport on the Daba-Fuka road, hitting several vehicles. The ack-ack at strafing levels tended to be a bit more intense and Tommy's Hurricane was damaged on the underside by a piece of flak, although he made it back to base in one piece. This was the pattern right up to the third week of October. "The aim was to annoy them, play on their nerves," says Tommy, "and make them feel as though they could never feel safe, even at night."

Meanwhile, Duke Ellington was discovering that combat flying was quite a different proposition than flying when there was no enemy about. One of his first missions was to attack the enemy airfields at El Daba. Mary Coningham had learned that the landing grounds at both el Daba and Fuka were waterlogged from rain, and so on 9 October, he decided to mount a number of large raids while the Axis aircraft were stuck on the ground.

As they flew toward their target, Duke certainly discovered his adrenaline pumping. They were part of a four-squadron escort—including Billy Drake's 112 Squadron—that was to cover twenty-four bombers to the enemy airfields. They were then to follow up with their own ground attack. Maintaining total radio silence, they flew low out to sea and then turned back in to hit the landing grounds. As they reached their target, they shot up everything they could in one pass, then turned back east in a wild scramble to avoid interception.

Unfortunately, the airfields hadn't been as waterlogged as Mary had been led to believe, and a number of 109s were already airborne. They were flying low and fast across the desert when Duke suddenly heard a voice over his radio shouting, "Ship flying straight ahead, turn, turn, turn!" Duke glanced up and saw a 109 diving straight for him. Panicking somewhat, Duke flung his Kittyhawk into a tight turn, and frantically turning his head, saw cannon shells burst into the sand on the desert floor. Around and around he went, the 109 glued to his tail. Only by dropping into the Qattara Depression did he finally shake off his pursuer. "It gave me quite a wake-up call, I can tell you," says Duke.

There is no question that in the Western Desert, life was more dangerous for the Allied fighter pilots than it was the bomber crews. Axis fighter claims were nearly all against other fighters rather than bombers. In part this was because they used their better altitude performance to give them height superiority, an important advantage when attacking other aircraft. But this meant they were rarely able to break through the fighter escorts and get at the bombers. There was also an entirely different culture between German and Allied fighter pilots. The RAF, for example, promoted the success of the squadron and the air force as a whole; who shot down what was not particularly important, and anyone seen to be bragging or "shooting a line" was soon put in his place. The Luftwaffe, however, encouraged the cult of the individual, and all efforts were made to ensure that a unit's ace continued scoring—and against fighters; bombers were perceived to be less worthy adversaries.

In the Western Desert, Hans-Joachim Marseille, the "Star of Afrika," was by some mile the leading German ace, with a staggering 151 aerial victories in North Africa alone. In his entire career he shot down 158 aircraft, of which just four were bombers. He had incredible eyesight, a natural gift for flying, and crucially, had mastered the art of deflection shooting, which meant aiming fire at a point where the target and bullets met. Moreover,

Marseille developed a technique of hitting aircraft turning in a tighter circle than his own, the usual defense adopted by the Allies against superior speed and height.

By September 1942, Marseille had become a one-man killing machine, with the rest of his squadron protecting him while he got on with the business of shooting down RAF fighters. On 1 September, he shot down *seventeen* in one day; on 15 September—Battle of Britain Day—he destroyed seven in seven separate dogfights in just eleven minutes and a further seven just over a week later.

Fêted in Germany, Marseille, with his fair hair, blue eyes, and Aryan good looks, was a publicity dream, and the Nazis milked it for all it was worth. He was awarded the Knight's Cross with Oak Leaves, Swords, and then Diamonds—the highest honors available to a fighter pilot. His brilliant career finally came to an end on 30 September—and appropriately enough, he was not vanquished by a foe, but suffered from engine failure. Although he bailed out, he struck the tail as he did so, gashing his hip. Whether this killed him is not known, but certainly his parachute never opened. His unit JG 27, and indeed the entire Luftwaffe, were distraught, but for the Allied airmen, the skies above the Western Desert were certainly a safer place with his passing.

Planning, planning, planning: in Washington, London and at a dusty camp in the desert called Burg el Arab. Monty produced his plan for Operation LIGHTFOOT in September. The idea was to punch two holes through the Axis defenses, one in the north and one in the south, although it would be through the northern one that Monty would make his main breach. This was also the strongest part of the enemy line, but the army commander believed that any attack in the south would still have to wheel north at some point, and so therefore concluded it was better to hit the strongest point head-on first.

The northern punch would initially be made by Leese's XXX Corps using the 9th Australian, the recently arrived 51st Highland, the New Zealand, and 1st South African divisions attacking on a ten-mile front, and aiming to reach an imaginary objective, a line to be known as Oxalic. This was drawn along the rear side of the principal Axis defenses, some three to five miles from the British front line. Within this ten-mile stretch, two more thoroughly cleared channels were to be made, through which the armor of the *corps d'elite*—Lumsden's X Corps—would pass. They would then break out wide and establish themselves on defensible land beyond the Oxalic line, to be known as Skinflint. Horrocks's XIII Corps would simultaneously punch a hole in the south of the line, through which 7th Armoured Division would pass for what would be no more than a diversionary attack. At the same time, the Fighting French, also now returned to the front line, would attack the Italian-held feature at Himeimet at the extreme south of the line.

Monty was convinced that by making his main attack where Rommel least expected, he would achieve the vital element of surprise. Enormous deception plans were made to make the enemy believe the south was where the main thrust would be. Major Jasper Maskelyne had already proved himself very useful during the Flap, when he had managed to "move" the harbor at Alexandria. Known before the war as Maskelyne the Magnificent, he was an illusionist of considerable repute. The secrets of precisely how he did it have never been revealed, but as with all illusionists, mirrors, smoke, and clever lighting were key ingredients. Monty now wanted Major Maske-lyne to help trick Rommel again. Large numbers of dummy vehicles, guns, and tanks were made and placed in the south where they were constantly shuffled around. Bogus recordings of radio traffic were devised to mislead German radio units; and a dummy water pipeline was laid at such a rate as to make it seem as though the offensive would start in November, not Oc-tober. Albert Martin, who in early October had been sent on a six-pounder gun course, returned to his company to discover "great concentrations of dummy this and dummy that." He reckoned they looked pretty realistic from two hundred yards away on the ground, so must have been even more convincing from the air. The riflemen joined in the game of bluff by driv-ing lorries with chain attached to them, to stir up the dust, up and down the line. "Whether we fooled anyone, I couldn't say," noted Albert, "but it added novelty to our preparations."[314]

This was all well and good, but as September made way for October, Monty began to have doubts about the emphasis of his battle plan. Having watched many of the training sessions and exercises now under way, he was not sure that his forces were capable of what was being demanded of them. "The plan was simple," he wrote later, "but it was too ambitious. If I was not careful, divisions and units would be given tasks which might end in failure because of the inadequate standard of training."[315] Once again, these nag-ging doubts were prompted by the state of the British armor rather than the infantry. On 6 October, he made his decision. X Corps' armor would be set a more modest target, a line only a mile or two in front of Oxalic, to be called Pierson. Originally, Monty had aimed to destroy Rommel's armor and then turn on the infantry. In his new plan, the British armor was only to contain and hold off the panzers while the rest of his forces carried out a methodical destruction of the enemy infantry. This was to happen by a process he called crumbling, whereby unarmored infantry divisions would be attacked and cut off from their supplies. If the enemy armor then coun-terattacked, that was fine by Monty—enticing the enemy forward as they had enticed so many British tanks in the past was exactly what he wanted.

They would then be drawn onto fixed positions of anti-tank screens and blown to pieces.

Clearing the huge numbers of mines was a difficult process. Most were anti-tank rather than anti-personnel, which was why the infantry were able to move forward with, it was hoped, comparative ease. But the Axis had laid at least half a million mines of all kinds, and unfortunately the only effective way to clear them was by the laborious process of tentatively prodding with a bayonet or steel probe. Alternatives, such as the electronic detector and the specially designed flail tanks were few and far between and notoriously unreliable. Clearing them by hand took time, however, especially at night, even though a large number of mine clearers had been allocated for the task.

But no matter how many times they practiced simulated nighttime mine clearing, no one could say for sure how the real thing would go. Nothing on this scale had been attempted before. Nonetheless, by dawn on the opening night of the battle, Monty aimed to have cleared three narrow lanes of just eight yards wide each, through both of the two corridors planned for the northern sector. Through these impossibly narrow lanes, the weight of British armor—hundreds of tanks, trucks, and guns— would travel, and then burst out into the wide open desert beyond the minefields. It was ambitious, to say the least.

Much yet again depended on Mary Coningham's Desert Air Force and the other air forces in the Middle East. They had certainly maintained their air superiority since Alam Halfa, but Tedder was still worried about shortages of aircraft, especially fighters. "I am gravely worried over my fighter position and prospects," he wrote to Portal in September. "Facts are that we are at only 50 percent strength with three Spitfire squadrons and lower with the Kittyhawk squadrons."[316] More Kittyhawks did arrive, but these squadrons were still under strength by the third week of October. Nor had the number of Spitfire squadrons been increased. The Luftwaffe, on the other hand, were being sent a number of the new improved Me 109Gs, which in terms of performance knocked the socks off anything the Allies could offer, even the Spitfire V. In fact, by 20 October, in all of Egypt, the Allies could call on 506 twin- and single-engine fighters, while the Luftwaffe had 595 at their disposal. The difference—and it was a crucial one—was that the Allies had plenty of fuel, and the Axis did not. Even so, Mary Coningham would have to handle his forces well.

And much also depended on the artillery. On the eve of battle, Monty had 908 field guns, of which 824 were twenty-five-pounders and twenty-five were the new 5.5-inch howitzers, as used by Sergeant Harold Harper and the 7th Medium Artillery. In contrast, the panzer army could call on only

200 field guns. The opening bombardment by the British gunners was to signal the start of the battle. For twenty minutes, they were to concentrate on counter-battery fire—i.e., they would aim to neutralize the enemy gun batteries, most of which they knew about thanks to extensive aerial photography by the RAF. They would then provide a creeping barrage, lobbing shells over the advancing infantry, moving their range forward at a rate of 100 yards every three minutes. The differences between the start of this offensive and those of the Western Front during the First World War were negligible. Tactically, Monty was offering nothing new at all.

What he *was* offering was firm leadership, with careful handling of troops and reserves and a plan that everyone could understand. There would be three distinct phases he told his men: the "break-in"—the initial moves; the "dogfight"—in which the infantry would "crumble" the enemy's defenses and which he envisaged would last a week; and the "breakout"— by the armor, when the battle would be wrapped up. "This battle will involve hard and prolonged fighting," he told his commanders on 6 October. "Our troops must not think that because we have a good tank and very powerful artillery support, the enemy will all surrender. The enemy will NOT surrender and there will be bitter fighting."[317]

Rommel's situation was not good—he was short of everything (see Appendix I for comparative strengths)—but experience had proved how effective the Germans were in defense, and anyway, there was no other better place in which to defend than the one they were in. Rommel had stayed put for precisely the same reason that the Auk had stopped along the Alamein line in the first place. As Alam Halfa had shown, making an effective attack across defended minefields was no easy matter. Rommel's sappers had also sown what he called Devil's Gardens—random and particularly unpleasant patches of anti-tank and anti-personnel mines crisscrossed with trip wires and booby traps.

The German field marshal was, however, no longer in Africa. Suffering from fatigue, low blood pressure, and stomach ulcers, he had finally left Egypt on 23 September, a month after requesting a temporary replacement; he had not been well throughout the Battle of Alam Halfa. Nonetheless, his replacement, General Georg Stumme, was a highly competent tank man who had served with distinction in Russia; furthermore, before leaving for Germany, Rommel had thoroughly outlined his defensive plans for the forthcoming British offensive.

Monty was fully aware that his battle would not be easy, despite his massive material advantage, but was his plan the right one? Only time would tell.

*   *   *

"To Ike, the principle of unity of command is almost holy," noted Harry Butcher, yet throughout that summer and autumn of 1942, General Eisenhower was repeatedly told that this vision of togetherness was doomed to fail.[318] But Ike didn't see why, and was pleased to observe that at TORCH headquarters the initial feelings of mutual suspicion and distrust were being replaced by cooperation, comradeship and a common sense of purpose. Even so, the differences between the two allies did on occasion threaten to prove his detractors right. One such stumbling block was over the British War Office's directive to Lieutenant-General Anderson, due to command the British First Army in North Africa. In drawing up this directive, the War Office essentially copied the one given to Field Marshal Haig during the First World War, when he had been subordinated to the French Marshal Foch. By these terms, Anderson was ordered to serve Ike loyally, but if he felt he was being given an order that appeared to "imperil" any British troops, then he had a right to appeal to the War Office before carrying out that order.

Understandably, Ike felt things had moved on since then—and even since Lord Gort had been subordinated to General Gamelin in France in 1939—and strongly believed that the Allies should be viewed as one in the field, and that there should be no doubt about the responsibility and authority of the allied commander. By this time, however, Ike had begun to get a grip on the British way of doing things, so rather than complain to the British chiefs of staff, appealed instead directly to General Sir Hastings Ismay, the PM's chief of staff and a paragon of common sense and discretion. In a carefully worded note, Ike pointed out that there would be many times when both US and British forces were likely to be "imperiled," and although he was sure Anderson would be unlikely to use this right of appeal, he did feel very strongly that the proposed directive would only "weaken rather than support the spirit that should be developed and sustained among all ranks participating in this great enterprise."[319]

Quietly and efficiently, Ismay took this matter to the chiefs of staff, and it was dealt with swiftly. Ike had suggested that Anderson keep his right of appeal but only if, in his view, an order gave rise to a grave or exceptional situation, and even then he had to inform the allied commander of his intention to appeal first, and give the reasons for doing so. In what was a considerable breakthrough on the part of Eisenhower, the British chiefs of staff agreed entirely with his suggestions. In doing so, they enabled Ike to lay down the basis for the strongest military alliance in history.

Ike also formed an immediate and mutual rapport with Admiral Cunningham. The two had first met during ABC's twelve-day visit to England in September. "I liked him at once," wrote Cunningham. "He struck me as being completely sincere, straightforward and very modest . . . We soon became fast friends." ABC had also been impressed by the way Ike had gotten British and US staffs working together and was of precisely the same mind as the commanding general—determined to ensure nothing stood in the way of this crucial unity of thought and purpose. At times his patience was tried, however. "To our way of thinking the Americans are more given than ourselves to calling a spade a spade without troubling to wrap it up in polite verbiage," he noted.[320]

He finally left America for good on 11 October, delighted to be able to get away from the "hothouse" atmosphere of Washington and back to an active part in the war. Even better, he would soon be returning to the Mediterranean. Throughout his time in Washington, thoughts of his old hunting ground had never been far from ABC's mind. He had heard with dismay about the retreat back into Egypt, had mourned the sinking of the *Eagle* and the other losses suffered during Operation PEDESTAL, and his anxiety about Malta had only grown. With this in mind, he and his staff entered into the preparations for TORCH with considerable zest and energy, sure in the knowledge that success would mean the end of the Siege of Malta and Allied victory in the Mediterranean. For ABC, there could be no greater spur.

Keeping TORCH a secret was of paramount importance, yet there were scares along the way. Harry Butcher was beside himself when he discovered that a crucial page of his diary was missing. He could not think of any conceivable way in which it could have gotten out of the office, where it was always written, typed, and then put onto microfilm, but despite looking high and low, there was simply no sign of it anywhere. He hated having to add to Ike's worries, but although Eisenhower was upset, he was "so considerate I could have wept," and told Butch not to tell anyone and to keep looking. "After all," noted Butch, "I'm responsible and probably should be sent home on a slow boat, unescorted, to use one of Ike's favorite expressions."[321]

A more serious scare came in mid-September, when the War Department in Washington intercepted a message for the United Press from their news editor in London warning UP to prepare for coverage at Casablanca and elsewhere in French Morocco, where the US would soon be striking. Whether this had been sent by secure cable or insecure radio was not known, but it was certainly a cause for worry that journalists were prepared to risk so serious a breach of security.

The third and potentially most dangerous scare came a week later. General Clark had written a letter to the Governor General of Gibraltar, which had been taken by hand by a naval officer. Unfortunately, his plane had been shot down and the dead officer had later been washed up near Cadiz in southern Spain, the letter still on him. Amazingly, the letter was then sent to Madrid and then passed on to the British, apparently without being opened. At any rate, one outcome of this episode was that the final date for TORCH was moved from 4 November to 8 November, the last day it was considered feasible to land troops on the beaches near Casablanca.

Worries that the details of TORCH would be blown were never far away. With the clock ticking faster, news arrived that the Vichy government had learned from both German and Japanese sources that the US were planning operations soon against Dakar and Casablanca. Vichy was convinced that Axis aggression in North Africa was imminent. Murphy also warned that German spies were flooding into North Africa—there were rumors that 500 blank French passports had been handed out to Germans.

Meanwhile, Admiral Darlan had expressed his willingness to "play ball" and to bring with him the French Fleet, providing he would be made C-in-C of French Armed Forces in North Africa, and that the US assured him of economic aid on a large scale. On the other hand, Murphy reported that his most senior collaborator in Algeria, General Mast, was still in favor of General Giraud rather than Darlan, and was suggesting the Allies send a submarine to pick him up from southern France. Murphy's personal take on the matter was that they should encourage Darlan with a view to securing his cooperation with Giraud.

Murphy also announced that it was finally time for General Clark and his team of four staff officers to head to Algeria for their covert meeting with Mast and other leading Allied collaborators. "Clark was as happy as a boy with a new knife," noted Butch, but added, "Ike won't breathe easily until Clark is back, for he is a close friend of 25 years' standing and if anything happens to him, Ike would be desperate."[322] Clark finally took his leave from the cottage just before midnight on 17 October. He was to fly to Gibraltar, where he would wait for the signal to proceed by submarine to an ultra-secret rendezvous some miles west of Algiers.

Much still hung in the balance.

In Egypt, the air battle had already begun with an intensification of bombing and strafing on enemy landing grounds, lines of communication, and positions along the front line. On the twentieth, Cobber Weinronk took part in a stooge on LG 21. He spotted a number of dispersed aircraft, and watched their bombs start several fires including one particularly large conflagration. They'd encountered little flak; really, he noted, it was "a milk run." There'd been greater danger when he'd tried to land.

He was only three hundred feet off the ground when his gunner shouted that there was another plane coming in below. Cobber opened the throttle, did another circuit and this time landed OK. "On another drome," he noted, "the Commanding Officer had just landed when a plane landed on top of him, and he was decapitated."[323]

The following day, Mary Coningham paid a call, giving the South African wing "the lowdown on the situation." Like Monty, he had spent the last few days roaming round talking to his men. But the time for talking was almost over. "If there is anything I have not yet done, it is now too late," Tommy Elmhirst had written to his wife on 21 October.[324] Monty must have been feeling the same; that day he'd given his commanders and officers their final briefing. Now he had to just sit back and wait.

Nonetheless, that night both Monty and Mary appeared to be confident and in good spirits. The commanders and their principal staffs had taken to having dinner together—it was another way of harmonizing the army and air force together. Tommy enjoyed them and had recently begun introducing some general, though specific, topic of conversation at the table each night "to take all our minds, including Montgomery's and Mary's, off our responsibilities for a short time." Monty was apparently always in good form at such discussions, and Tommy was able to draw his views on subjects like "the benefits, or otherwise, of a Staff College education," or "a balanced life: so much time for wife and family, so much time for work and play." "A very great deal of sense was talked around our supper table," noted Tommy, "more than the layman might credit the serviceman with possessing."

Supper together on 21 October, was, Tommy observed, quite cheerful. He'd started a conversation going on the subject of "the young married officer is the curse of the services." The conversation soon evolved into what things were likely to make a successful marriage. "It was the first time any of us had seen Montgomery REALLY unbend and be very human," noted Tommy. "Supper overran by twenty minutes."

The next day, Monty told his army that the battle would start the following night, 23 October. He wanted every man to be in no doubt as to exactly what their task was. Throughout the day, up and down the line, briefings were given about the battle and what each unit's role would be. "Nearly all day looking over maps and plans," noted Joe Madeley. "Issued with grenades and extra rounds." Then he went to Battalion HQ to look at a giant twenty-foot-square sand model of the area they were to go over.

Back in London, the prime minister was also waiting anxiously for news of when battle would begin. "Let me have the word ZIP when you start," he wrote to Alex on 20 October, once again adopting the code word from the launch of Alam Halfa. "Events are moving in our favour, both in North Africa and Vichy France, and TORCH goes forward steadily and punctually." Then he added, "But all our hopes are centred upon the battle you and Montgomery are going to fight. It may well be the key to the future."[325]

PART III

ADVANCE & RETREAT

"We are engaged together in a great adventure
which, if all goes well, should alter the whole
course of the war."

Lieutenant-General Kenneth Anderson

CHAPTER 14

Into Battle—
23–26 October, 1942

AT 4:30 AM, on Friday, 23 October, Cobber Weinronk was airborne and flying with a formation of Bostons to bomb LG 21 once again. He made it safely back and was told by their intelligence officer that the "big show" was due to start that night. At midday, he took part in his second stooge of the day, another enemy airfield—this time LG104. Mary Coningham was determined to do everything in his power to maintain absolute air superiority. It seemed to be working too: Ultra intercepts revealed that the Luftwaffe were blaming RAF attacks on their low aircraft serviceability. Crucially, the parity of aircraft numbers between the Axis and Allies was now tipping heavily in favor of the Allies. Later that evening, Mary planned to drop flares over enemy positions as well as bombs, dummy parachutists, and smoke screens, attack with low-flying night fighters, and also to jam the enemy's radio system with specially equipped Wellington bombers. No army commander could have possibly asked for more.

Up and down the line, the men on the ground were tense with anticipation. "Tonight's the night," wrote Joe Madeley on Friday, 23 October. "Feel confident I'll get through OK." After cleaning weapons and loading himself up with extra magazines, he collected a pick and shovel and forty-eight hours' rations, and then listened one more time to a briefing about the task ahead.

Albert Martin spent the day feeling nervous and edgy. As they waited with the massed formations of X Corps behind the main start line, he and his mates whiled away the hours brewing endless cups of tea and smoking incessantly. Around them, activity was constant. Albert watched jeeps tearing back and forth and the clusters of tanks and trucks with a sense of unease. This assembly area, jammed as it was with troops and vehicles made him feel claustrophobic. It wasn't the rifleman's way.

Nor was the task for which they had been chosen. Albert had gotten used to the mobility and maneuverability provided by their truck, but that night they were to operate on foot. The 1st Armoured Division was to pass through the northerly of the two principal minefield gaps once the Australians to their north and the Scots of the 51st Highland to the south had begun their advance. Teams of sappers from the Royal Engineers were then to clear the three eight-yard-wide tracks in their sector, called Sun, Moon, and Star. "There was no point wasting time making them any wider," says Albert. "The key was to get a move on as quickly as possible." The job for the riflemen was to organize and protect the sappers as they gapped each of the enemy minefields—for this task, they had become the Minefield Task Force.

At 7:30 PM, away across the gravel flats to the east of the southern end of the line, Captain Pierre Messmer began leading his company of the 13 DBLE away from the French Base Camp and toward the monstrous two hundred-foot-high feature of Qaret el Himeimat, some nine miles to their west. Since the July battles, this strange desert mesa had been held by the Italians, preventing any outflanking maneuver between it and the short two-mile plateau to the edge of the Qattara Depression. Italian machine gunners were dug in along its summit and lower slopes while dense minefields barred the gentle slopes that led up to the rock outcrop. The Fighting French had been given the task of capturing this formidable outpost.

Earlier that afternoon, Messmer had gathered his company together, section by section, and explained to them the plan of attack. Since Bir Hacheim they had undergone a period of training and refitting, but although they now had new equipment they were short of armor and artillery. General Koenig had managed to scrounge a few extra tanks and guns, but was relying on surprise and stealth, opting to launch his attack from the south, as though from the Depression. His men were not used to being briefed in such detail before an attack, but Messmer could tell it had given them confidence. And as they continued marching across the desert, the stars and slowly rising moon guiding their way, Messmer sensed that his men were calm and resolute—and ready for the task ahead.

Sergeant Harold Harper was counting down the minutes. A week before, they'd buried a lot of extra shells, and then two days ago had finally prepared their gun pit, ten yards wide and six deep—not by bulldozer this time but by hand. "We didn't want to give the game away with a lot of extra noise," says Harold. He'd finally been given his orders at eight o'clock that night. The barrage would begin at exactly twenty minutes to ten.

A few miles directly in front of him was Joe Madeley and the infantry of the 2/13 Battalion. As soon as it had become dark, Joe had eaten a hurried hot meal and then set off on foot with his section and the rest of the battalion along "Square route," a channel that had already been cleared and taped through the British minefields to the start line.

The rumble of traffic that had been incessant throughout much of the day gradually died away. Joe Madeley gripped his rifle tightly and then was suddenly aware that the battlefield had become shrouded in a strange and eerie silence. Some ten miles farther south, General Francis Tuker noticed it too, as he took a moment to wander from his caravan and look at the white moonlight that now bathed the desert. The strange silence seemed quite shocking. Not a gun or rifle fired. He had never known the front so perfectly still. At Tac HQ, Lieutenant Carol Mather was also aware of the sudden stillness. "Full moon, quietness, silvery sea and peace," he noted in his diary.

As gently as the noise had disappeared, so it returned. Shortly after eight o'clock, a low throbbing could be heard that grew louder and louder until over the front line flew the first wave of Wellington bombers, escorted by night fighters, on their way to pound the enemy positions once again.

At 9:30 PM, Pilot Officer John Fairbairn reached his patrol line along the Alamein position. He was to keep a lookout for Axis bombers who over the past few nights had been dropping flares in an effort to find out what the British were up to. But there was nothing moving. The entire front seemed eerily quiet.

Ten minutes later, at exactly twenty minutes to ten, the ground beneath him erupted. "I got such a fright," wrote John, "I nearly bailed out automatically." Also flying over the line at that same moment was John's new squadron colleague, Flight Lieutenant Tommy Thompson, on his way back from a night intruder mission. He'd been strafing enemy transport that had been lit up by flares dropped by the Royal Navy's Albacores and had once again left a number of lorries burning. Suddenly the world below seemed to split apart. As one, a massive flash of fire erupted from the sea down as far as the Depression. The Battle of Alamein had begun.

John Fairbairn hurried back to base, but not Tommy—he wanted a better look at this extraordinary spectacle. Pulling back the stick, he gunned the throttle and climbed into the sky, out of harm's way, then at around 3,000 feet, leveled off and circled for a few minutes watching the massive barrage below. From out at sea he could see the naval guns joining the long line of flickering orange spewing from the British artillery. He could see waves of bombers pounding the enemy positions and occasionally explosions burst skyward. "A magnificent sight," he noted. "What an artillery battle."

Like sheet lightning before a roll of thunder, the flash came before the sudden eruption of noise. On the ground below, Albert Martin had never heard anything like it. The blast of nine hundred guns sent shockwaves pulsing through the ground. As the gunners' loading rhythm changed, the sky became a kaleidoscope of flickering color. To his south, in the South African sector, Bill Eadie had spent all day in his tunnel on the edge of no-man's-land feeling very excited. Just before 9:40 PM, he lit his red beacon lights that marked out their front line and then eagerly took the tot of rum on offer. "On the dot, hell broke loose," he noted. A few miles north, Maiki Parkinson was lying on the ground waiting to start the advance when the barrage began. He had been in position for a while, some hundred yards from the next man. "I thought, my Christ," he says, "what the hell am I doing here on my own?" and had the strange sensation of lying on his back watching the extraordinary spectacle of the biggest single artillery attack of the war.

Near Maiki in the Highlanders' sector was Johnny Bain, also readying himself for the advance across no-man's-land. "The barrage was enough to send you mad with—sort of punch-drunk, really—with terror," he says.[326] This was to be his first ever combat action. He'd not even been on a night-time patrol since he'd arrived.

Now making his way through the minefields south of Himeimat, Pierre Messmer was also impressed by the barrage; it was certainly the most powerful artillery fire he'd ever experienced. Looking up, he could see the dark jagged shape of Himeimat silhouetted against the flickering light of the guns.

From his caravan at Air HQ, Tommy Elmhirst started writing to his wife. "The battle started five minutes ago," he scribbled, "and even here, up wind, there is no mistaking the thunder of the guns."[327] The air battle had been going well, apart from problems caused by bad weather on the twenty-first. On the twenty-second, the Allied fighters had cruised back and forth over the Luftwaffe airfields at Daba, challenging the 109s to come up and fight. The tactic worked, as German fighter pilots were scrambled to take on the intruders. Billy Drake was leading a fighter sweep of 112 Squadron and the US 66th Fighter Squadron over Daba when they spotted four 109s below them. Diving down, they hit all four, Billy claiming one of them. "I think we have definitely set Rommel back," Tommy continued in his letter. "His Air Force was hardly seen in the air today."[328]

Fifteen minutes after the guns began firing, they stopped as suddenly as they had begun, and in Cairo General Alexander signaled the prime minister, "ZIP 2200 hours local time today."[329] The intense counter-battery fire, ranged onto known enemy gun positions, was over. For five minutes the gunners reset their guns, then opened up the barrage, which, as in the First World War, was designed to protect the infantry as they advanced. With the pipes playing, the Highlanders set off. In Johnny Bain's section, men soon started falling around him. "That first night was something that was almost unbelievably terrifying and awful," he says. Above the din of the barrage and of bullets sputtering around them, Johnny heard the sound of a man screaming and yelling. "That was a most blood-chilling and frightening thing to hear," he says. Onward he stumbled and then his sergeant was hit. In the few weeks since Johnny's arrival, the sarge had seemed like something of a father figure: resolute and tough, but kindly too. "He probably wasn't that old," he admits, "perhaps thirty, but he seemed a lot older to me." But now the sergeant was writhing on the ground, crying in a strange parody of his normal voice. "Oh mother!" he was calling, "Mother! Please! Oh Jesus Christ! Oh ma!"[330] Johnny was shocked—this older man on whom he had pinned so much trust was now crying like a child. It was, he says, "a sort of wrench in the universe that shouldn't happen."

A few miles north, Joe Madeley began walking with his section spaced out at the practiced seventy-five yards per minute. They were all laden with kit: extra ammo, grenades, a pick or shovel, four sandbags, personal gear, first aid, and two days' rations. Joe was expected to walk over two miles with all this and fight. Smoke and the stench of cordite was already wafting across the desert. Behind, he could hear the bark of rapidly firing guns and the drone of aircraft. Ahead, bombs and shells exploded with a dull crunch. He'd never heard anything like it and couldn't imagine there'd be many enemy left alive. "When we started off just after ten, we thought it would be a walk-over," he says.

But as on the Western Front in the last war, it didn't take the enemy long to pull themselves together. Suddenly the air in front of Joe was livid with tracer and anti-tank shells, known as flaming onions by the men for the way in which they lit up and skidded across the desert. Machine guns stammered, bullets began to whistle nearby and the sharp clang of mortar fire rang out. As Joe resolutely continued forward, it seemed as though each shell and bullet was heading straight for him.

A machine-gun post chattered angrily in front of them and they hit the deck. Joe could see Tom Duncan and his section just ahead, firing madly. Turning to Jackie Lowe, who was carrying the extra ammunition, Joe said, "Jack, race over to Tommy. He's out of ammo." But no sooner had Jackie stood up than he was hit. Joe rushed over and yelled for stretcher bearers. "He was crying for his mother," says Joe. Their lieutenant then got up to

give them an order and was hit too. Joe then watched the company commander, Captain Sanderson, spin to the ground as well. "They were falling
everywhere," he says.

Joe crawled over to Tom Duncan. A man was lying dead next to him,
his face spattered with blood. "Who the hell is that?" Joe asked him.

"That's Lockie," Tom told him. "They killed old Lockie." Joe was
stunned. "Sergeant Lockie didn't drink, he didn't smoke and he didn't
swear," says Joe. "But everyone loved Lockie. He was fearless and we never
thought anything could happen to him."

A runner suddenly hurried over and told them to pull back two hundred yards, where they were going to form up again. There they found
some cover in some old trenches, but it wasn't long before they were told to
get going again. This time, large numbers of Germans appeared with their
hands in the air and running for their lives. Keith Boal, a mate of Joe's from
back home in Wheethalle, was beside him and said, "This is more like it.
This is the way to fight a bloody war—look at them, bloody running."

A few miles to the south were the Maori of the New Zealand Division.
When the initial counter-battery fire stopped, and the pipes of the neighboring Highland Division began, Maiki Parkinson couldn't believe his
ears. "Those fellows were either the bravest in the world or the most fool-
hardy bastards I ever heard," he says. As far as he was concerned, they
could keep playing because as the enemy guns began firing and blasting
across the desert, they were drawn more to the Scots than they were the
New Zealanders.

The Maori had been given the role of "mopping up" any isolated
enemy positions missed by the initial advance and to support the sappers as they cleared channels for the divisional armor and guns. When
Maiki stood up and began walking forward he was still wondering where
everyone else was. This was not as strange as it might sound. After all,
only six New Zealand battalions were leading the infantry advance—less
than five thousand men. These were spread over their sector, in parts
several miles wide. When one considers that most football stadiums
hold around forty thousand people, it is easier to understand how at
night, across the very wide expanse of desert, Maiki had felt quite alone
despite taking part in the opening moves of the biggest British land
battle of the war to date.

Before long however, he saw one of his mates. The moon, flares, muzzle flashes and explosions, all created plenty of light. "Am I pleased to see
you," said his friend, "I was beginning to think I was the only bloke in this
war." Shortly after, they bumped into another man from their section, then
a moment later a flail tank rumbled forward right past them. Together they

stumbled on until they reached three thick coils of wire stacked one on top of the other two. The flail tank stopped and then moments later was hit by a shell that took the tracks clean off one side. Maiki and his mates didn't stop. They were all wearing their greatcoats, so they jumped on top of the wire and scrambled over, only to find another row of coils.

Eventually they managed to get past it and then noticed shapes moving in the gloaming ahead of them, and soon realized it was about fifteen others from C Company. None of them were officers but they decided to keep going anyway. Suddenly the now familiar sound of Spandaus began firing in front of them and bullets spat overhead. Rather than lie flat, Maiki and the others all started yelling and charging with fixed bayonets toward the enemy position, but before they reached the strong point, the German firing stopped. The Maori couldn't understand it. Approaching the dugout, they saw the guns but there was no sign of any enemy soldiers. Puzzled, they continued on their way.

Meanwhile, at the start line for the northern half of X Corps' corridor there was already a hitch. The Minefield Task Force was forbidden to get going until after 11 PM. The task of gapping the minefields was a tall order as it was without any delay. Then news arrived that they could not even use Star route on the way to the start line, so the columns designated for Star had to go down Moon and then cross over, causing congestion and further delay. This last-minute confusion was apparently due to poor liaison between X and XXX Corps HQs—some things hadn't changed.

When Albert Martin finally set off, the situation seemed to him to be incredibly confused. For all the vast space of the forty miles of the Alamein line, the British armor was desperately trying to channel itself into the six narrow passages. Maiki Parkinson could march into battle feeling he was the only person in the Eighth Army, but the tanks, gun towers, guns, and carriers had to squeeze themselves into a passage that was narrower than a singles tennis court. White guide tape had been laid along the ground marking the route, and then posts had been thrust into the ground at regular intervals. On these were placed empty four-gallon petrol tins, each holding an oil lamp and with either a moon, star, or sun cut out of metal depending on the track. Amid the noise and mayhem, Albert couldn't help wondering who had prepared all these cans and how they had miraculously appeared there.

But the lanterns were only of limited use. The air was thick with dust and smoke, but especially fine, cloying dust. The sand had been crushed as fine as powder and even by walking on it, let alone driving a tank, clouds were thrust swirling into the air. The nostrils, mouth, eyes, and lungs of the men were soon clogged with powder. A thick fog had developed and vehicles began ramming into one another. The enemy was also now adding to the discomfort. "We were getting a bashing from his shelling," noted Albert.[331] And this was also severing telephone wires and making communication difficult.

Also covered in dust were the men of the Nottingham Sherwood Rangers, farther south at the start of the southern corridor. On the way to the start line, Major Stanley Christopherson had had to send one of his A Squadron Crusaders back with a bad water leak, while another had been held up with sprocket trouble. They had not even started through their own minefield gaps when they were ordered to stop. Stanley ordered his men to get their tanks refueled then they drank a cup of coffee made from water carried in tins above the engine. "When the engine runs for any length," Stanley explained, "the water invariably gets heated up, from which you can make excellent coffee."

They eventually got moving again, rumbling through the dust toward the three tracks already cleared through the British minefields—in this sector called Boat, Hat, and Bottle. Three Crusaders led the regiment, but Stanley's nine-strong squadron were following close behind. Congestion once more hindered their progress. Stanley was receiving urgent messages to push on, but he couldn't move an inch until the New Zealand light armor had moved out of the way. It wasn't until 4 AM that they finally reached the first enemy minefield.

By about 1:30 AM, Harold Harper noticed his gun was slowing down on the recoil. For the next half hour, the crew had to push the barrel back into its firing position by hand—a dangerous practice. At 2:30 AM, Harold reluctantly had to report the gun out of action. But they were not held up for long. Thanks to the expert guidance of the battery gun artificer, the breech was dismantled, refilled with buffer oil, and refitted back into action just an hour later. "All this was going on with pandemonium raging around us," says Harold. It was a tense situation and he was very conscious of the need to keep his crew as cheerful as possible. "I tried to keep the banter lighthearted," he says, "while at the same time maintaining a strict discipline to ensure no one cracked under the stress."

In the south, the battle had not been going too well for the Fighting French. The few tanks they had been given had become bogged down, and with the confusion caused in trying to navigate through the minefields, their attack was late. Furthermore, there was no sign of the British artillery they had been expecting to support them. Colonel Amilakvari eventually decided to attack with his two infantry battalions, one after the other. The 1st Battalion's attack failed—coming under heavy attack, their commander ordered them to retreat.

Some time after, Amilakvari ordered the 2nd Battalion to attack. "Take hold of the cliff to the north, straight ahead of you," Bablon, Messmer's battalion commander told him. "As soon as you get there, set off a red and green flare. I'll meet you there with the rest of the battalion."

Messmer was incredulous. He had only a hundred men and was being asked to capture Himeimat and its mortar and machine-gun nests without any artillery support. Bablon hesitated for a moment and then agreed to send in two fusilier companies with him to bolster their numbers. This was better than nothing, but the task still seemed suicidal. Ordering his men to advance in a line, shoulder to shoulder, they set off quickly and quietly toward the huge rock ahead of them. Messmer felt anguish seize his heart.

At the base of the cliff they surprised the Italian outpost, but with the warning now given, the night was cut apart by bullets, grenades, and mortars. Messmer and his men hit the ground. "Forward march!" he yelled. An anonymous voice replied, "Go to it then, idiot!"[332] He was right, Messmer realized, and so jumping up surged forward toward the side of the cliff, his men following in a frenzy of grenades and gunfire. When Messmer reached a dugout cut into the cliff, he saw three men cowering in a huddle; but his blood was up. Pulling the pin on a grenade he hurled it toward them all then continued his scrabble upward.

The summit was taken five minutes later, but although buoyed by the success of their assault, Messmer could see that without artillery, their situation would soon become hopeless: the Italian infantry positions may have been overrun, but slowly advancing toward them were a number of enemy tanks, their growling engines and the clatter of their tracks becoming ever more distinct. Gazing northward, Messmer could still see the flashes of light flickering in the sky, but in the east, the first faint line of approaching dawn was spreading across the horizon. He felt overwhelmed by the sense of powerlessness and hopelessness.

As the tanks drew closer, the now beleaguered legionnaires had nothing with which to fight the enemy armor other than a single and completely hopeless Boyes anti-tank rifle. Then an officer from the Fusiliers approached Messmer and said, "Order from the battalion: disengage immediately and go back to base camp." With the tanks now just a few hundred yards away, the legionnaires were quick to scramble back down the craggy slopes. "Jumping from rock to rock," Messmer noted, "sliding along the sand when I could, I got to the desert plain and without looking behind me, I rejoined my company at full speed." Brief victory had ended in retreat. "The failure at Himeimat stayed with me a long time," he noted later.[333]

The Australians had been advancing with two of their infantry brigades, the 20th and 26th. Joe Madeley and the 2/13 Battalion were to lead the second phase of the 20th Brigade's effort to reach Oxalic. At 2 AM, they set off, by this time with the support of 40 Royal Tank Regiment, on a front of over one and a half miles. All seemed to be going well where Joe was until one of the tanks hit a mine. The explosion caught Joe and his men in a silhouette. "Well, didn't the Jerries turn around and rip into us then," says Joe. Once more they flung themselves flat on the ground, but they were being picked off one by one. "They hit 'Whiz' Nicholls, then Ronnie Bladwell, then 'King' Cole, Chris Davidson, then Keith Boal." Joe was keeping himself as flat as he could, but when he heard Keith cry out, he jumped to his feet. Before they'd left home, Keith's mother had said to him, "Joe, look after Keith—he's only a baby." In fact, he was only four months younger than Joe was, but as soon as he heard Keith, he thought, "My God, what will Mrs. Boal say?"

He went to Chris's aid first, however. Blood was pouring out of his shoulder, so Joe bandaged him as best he could, then turned to Keith, who'd been hit in the foot from behind. Joe tried to get him in a fireman's lift, but he was a big man, and Joe lost his balance and the two of them toppled over, landing on some barbed wire. Keith was screaming and panicking and Joe was suddenly at a loss as to what to do. There was still a lot of noise, but the explosion of the tank had died down and with it so did the enemy machine-gun fire. Then he remembered that his dad had once told him never to panic. "He said, 'If you panic, you're dead.'" Slapping Keith around the face he said, "For Christ's sake shut up—you'll get us both killed." It seemed to do the trick—Keith stopped flailing and allowed Joe to untangle him. Then another tank appeared and Joe jumped up onto it and yelled at them to take them both back two hundred yards to safety. To begin with, the tank commander refused but then Joe threatened to throw a grenade down the turret. "I was far from normal at that stage," says Joe. "I'm not sure whether I would have actually done it, but it did the trick."

Bullets were pinging off the tank as they clambered on and then began rumbling back. They'd only gone a hundred yards when Joe decided it was time to get off. Keith landed on his foot and began screaming again, but a truck suddenly pulled up and Joe knew one of the men sitting up front, an engineer named Merv Linnegar. "Where he came from, I don't know," admits Joe. "It was a bit of a miracle." Together they got Keith into the back of the truck and then sped back to where Merv said the company was now reforming. Dropping Joe off, Merv then continued back toward the British lines to get Keith some medical attention.

But at the mustering point, Joe found himself all alone. "There was nothing," says Joe. "Just dust churned up and the smell—Christ, you could hardly breathe for the smell of gunsmoke." And shells were still raining across the sky, and gunfire whistling over their heads. Constant, ear-shattering din. By now, dawn was almost breaking, and then Joe saw a figure emerge through the fog of dust toward him.

It was Tom Duncan. They realized they were the only two left from their sections. Finding a bit of a hollow in the ground, Joe took off his haversack to get some food only to discover a bullet had gone through it, then on through a tin of bully beef and into his spare pair of socks. They'd been there about ten minutes when they saw some American planes approaching. They began cheering as they began dropping their bombs, and then with a sickening feeling Joe said, "Tom, these aren't going to miss us by much."

"They aren't going to miss us at all!" said Tom. They tried to scramble to safety but moments later were flung into the air from the blast as one of the bombs landed nearby. "I bounced up and down like a rubber ball," says Joe. When they eventually got to their feet again, they were both covered in dust, completely gray but for lines of blood trickling from their mouths, noses and ears. Tom was cursing so much Joe began to laugh. "He certainly told them what he thought of them," says Joe. "He really went to town."

The Sherwood Rangers finally trundled onto a cleared lane through the enemy minefields at around 4 AM, passing through the New Zealanders' sector of the corridor. Halfway through, as they passed by the northern end of the Miteiriya Ridge, they were stopped. Jumping down from his tank, Stanley Christopherson walked up to the front of their column, which had halted by a hastily assembled control post. There he learned that they could move no farther for the moment because the lane ahead still hadn't been properly cleared after all. Up ahead he could see the muzzle flash of enemy guns and tracer reaching out across the desert.

They'd only been there a short time when a message came through from Major-General Alec Gatehouse, 10th Armoured Division commander, to push on regardless. With a fair amount of apprehension Stanley and the leading Crusaders set off once more, expecting to hit a mine at any moment. To his relief, they were all still intact when a sapper told them they'd made it through. Anti-tank and machine-gun fire soon poured toward them. Stanley had no alternative but to keep moving forward, because a dangerous bottleneck was forming behind them at the mouth of the route through the minefields. Turning southward, they had gone about two hundred yards when they ran straight into German anti-tank positions, some as close as fifty yards. All hell broke out. Armour-piercing shells screamed across the narrow gap and in a matter of moments, five of Stanley's Crusaders had been knocked out and were burning brightly in the last darkness of the night. "EDWARD," radioed Sam Garratt in the lead tank, using what he thought was Stanley's code name, "I have been hit twice. Tank on fire—am evacuating." But before Stanley could reply, Colonel Kellett came on the air and shouted, "Get off the bloody air and your name is KING, not EDWARD." As Garratt's crew left their tank they were machinegunned, although despite being wounded, three of them made it to safety. "It was quite one of the worst moments of my life," Stanley noted. "I couldn't go forward, but all the heavy tanks were behind me so I couldn't go back on account of them and the minefield . . . We just had to sit there." But at least they were firing back, and two enemy tanks were soon burning. However bad their situation might seem, the battle of attrition that Monty had envisaged was beginning to take place.

As light crept over the desert, so the enemy fire intensified. Four Grants from B Squadron brewed up, then another four and a further three Crusaders. The Sherwood Rangers were being decimated. Ahead of them, German, Italian, and British corpses littered the ground, some dark with blood and thick with flies. While the remains of A and B stayed where they were, the rest of the column withdrew back through the minefield gaps. Daylight, however, revealed the enemy's own gaps through their minefields and so on the order from the CO, Stanley successfully led them back over the Miteiriya Ridge without any further losses. With its gentle slopes offering some protection, the regiment began reforming.

Maiki Parkinson had been called back to the start line as dawn began to break. The battalion as a whole and C Company in particular had suffered few casualties. Maiki had also solved the mystery of the abandoned German strongpoint. As they'd walked back, they'd come across the same position and this time they could see a whole lot better. What they hadn't realized several hours before was that the position contained a deep underground concrete bunker. "How the hell they ever made it out there in the desert I have no idea," admits Maiki, but clearly the Germans had left their positions and hidden in the bunker—the Maori had a bad reputation amongst the Axis troops—and then had later moved out. Maiki was looking for loot when he heard someone cry out "Germans!" Bringing his Tommy gun to the ready, Maiki waited, but it turned out to be a single German with a Red Cross armband who'd been hiding under a bunk. They cuffed him around the ear and got him out. Then Maiki spotted a radio set—a new model—

and so he lifted it up and carried it back with him. "Yeah, they were pleased about the radio," he says. "It was a new model from Germany."

Monty had gone to bed shortly after the barrage had begun the previous evening. After all, there was little else he could now do. So too did Carol Mather, grabbing his sleeping bag and napping underneath Monty's caravan to avoid the worst of the dew. Both were up at dawn and Carol was soon speeding his way across the desert to get reports from General Freyberg about how the New Zealanders were doing and from General Gatehouse about what was happening to 10th Armoured Division.

"A tense day here awaiting developments," wrote Tommy Elmhirst at Air HQ. "Good and indifferent news coming in, but the Army have not achieved the hundred percent success they planned."[334] The infantry had, in fact, reached to within one to two thousand yards of the Oxalic objective. The problems had really arisen with the advance of X Corps. The experience of the Sherwood Rangers had been repeated along the mouths of both corridors. There had not been enough time to get enough armor clear by dawn and those that had had suffered a mauling and been unable to reach the Oxalic infantry objective, let alone the Pierson line.

With daylight something of a lull occurred. After a night of living on adrenaline and being shot at and shelled, most of the men were exhausted and units spent the day regrouping, while the RAF continued their huge effort by flying more than 1,000 sorties over the enemy positions. Joe Madeley and Tom Duncan had eventually found the rest of their company now dug into positions some half a mile short of Oxalic. Apart from himself, there were now only three men left in his section. A large number of the officers had also been either killed or wounded, including the Battalion CO, Colonel Turner. In the New Zealand sector, the forward battalions stayed where they were, just short of Oxalic, while the Maori returned to the start line to regroup and reorganize. In the South African sector, Bill Eadie had survived the night. He'd not been part of the main infantry advance, but had remained at forward Brigade HQ, which had come under attack by mortars and shell fire. Like most of the army, he'd not slept a wink. One of his fellow NCOs had been badly wounded, another killed. Enemy shelling continued throughout the day. Bill saw one land amongst a group of five black soldiers. "Dead galore," he noted.

In the south, the dejected Fighting French returned to their base camp. Once again, Susan Travers had managed to get herself to the front, despite Monty's orders that there should be absolutely no women on the battlefield. She had spent the opening night of the battle sitting in her car some miles from the front line; the sand there was too soft for ordinary cars and trucks, and so American jeeps had been brought up to ferry the commanders around. For the time being, she and a number of other drivers were redundant; there was little they could do but wait with their vehicles at their tented encampment. Through the next day Susan and the other drivers chain-smoked as they endlessly speculated about what was happening.

Around noon, the column appeared, slowly inching its way toward them. As they came into view, Susan saw that the leading vehicle was an ambulance, flanked by two command jeeps. These three then hurried past them and on toward the hospital tent. Susan didn't dare move. The escorting jeeps and the expressions on the drivers' faces made her fear the worst. She prayed that it wasn't her lover, General Koenig, but the news was almost as bad. It was Amilakvari who was dead. "We struggled to take this in," wrote Susan. "It seemed impossible that he could be killed. He had always seemed immortal."[335] The Georgian prince had been supervising the retreat when a shell fragment had flown straight into his eye and out through the back of his head.

The loss of such a charismatic talisman hit the Fighting French hard. Pierre Messmer was devastated and his mood was worsened when Koenig, in front of other officers, openly criticized the legionnaires' attack. "I dryly replied that we were conscious of having done our duty and that our failure was due to poor management of the operation," wrote Messmer. "The general knew that I was right. He said nothing. But from then on, I was seen as a difficult officer and was made to feel it. I couldn't care less what he thought. I didn't fight the war to score brownie points."[336]

Scraps of news reached Albert Martin and the other riflemen, still in the thick of the German minefields with the Minefield Task Force. They were used to an enemy they could see and short, sharp engagements, but this was most frustrating. "We were surrounded by all the trappings of a major battle," Albert noted, "it had all the tension, stuff was exploding onto our patch, casualties were occurring, but there was no target for us to have a go at."[337] They couldn't understand why there had been no counterattack and assumed that all the deception work during the buildup had paid off.

He was only partly right. For all Monty's half-finished water pipes, none of the Axis commanders were fooled into thinking the attack would come in November. Rommel had even told his replacement, General Stumme, back in September that he should expect the British offensive during the October full moon. Moreover, panzer army intelligence had provided fairly accurate appreciations of British dispositions, and this did not include an extra mystery armored division in the south.

However, Stumme was still uncertain about which was the main thrust, the north or the south, and there was certainly no attempt to bring the 21st Panzer and Ariete Divisions north. Deception also helped keep the 90th

Light and Italian Trieste Divisions well behind the front line. On the opening night of the battle, Major Japser Maskeleyne and his Magic Gang had also pulled off another feat of deception off the coast near Fuka, treating the Axis forces there to an extraordinary sound and light show. With smokescreens, amplified sound effects and fireworks, the magicians managed to simulate a highly convincing phoney landing. In fact there were only three destroyers, eight MTBs—Charles Coles's MTB 262 among them—and a couple of landing craft, but the Axis coastal gunners began shelling furiously and a number of enemy aircraft took to the skies, and so wasted precious ammunition and fuel on attacking this grand illusion.

But the efforts of the Magic Men only partly explain the lack of Axis counterattack. In the morning, Stumme left panzer army HQ to have a look at the front line and the level of enemy minefield penetration in the Australian sector. He was just getting out of his car when he was fired upon and his driver panicked and sped away with the Axis commander still clinging to the side. Stumme then suffered a heart attack, fell off the car and died, although his body wasn't found until the following day. In the meantime, General Ritter von Thoma, commander of the Deutsche Afrika Korps, took over, but for a while the panzer army had been rudderless. He soon grabbed the helm, but as a tank man, von Thoma was all too aware of the shortage of fuel, too much of which was still at Benghazi. A tanker was due in to Tobruk on 26 October, but if that failed, the situation would be critical once again. In consequence, von Thoma decided that it was pointless wasting fuel on a major counterattack when they could stay put on their containing line—roughly the same as Monty's proposed Pierson line—and blast any oncoming attack from fixed positions. It also proved what had been suggested by the comparatively small numbers of prisoners captured so far: that Axis dispositions were far deeper than Monty had hoped.

Cobber Weinronk did not fly until three o'clock that afternoon, although the Wing had been active all day; two Bostons from 24 Squadron had flown up and down the front line at three that morning dropping smoke canisters. Flying on the deck, both planes were full of holes, not from flak, but from small arms. He delivered his bombs all right, but on the way back discovered his intercom was broken and so had no means of speaking to his navigator. This would not have mattered too much had there not been a thick sandstorm, caused principally by the huge amount of dust stirred up by the battle. Visibility was less than a mile and every portion of the desert he flew over looked exactly the same. He began to worry—fuel was getting low—but managed to try and relax and by thinking clearly, worked out how to reach the coast. He then flew on to Alexandria, though itself a no-fly zone, did at least provide him with some familiar markers, most notably the cheese factory on the outskirts, which was on the road to their base at Amorea. He and the other pilots always used to complain about the appalling smell, but now it was giving him a lifeline. Sure enough, by following the road, he eventually found their landing ground. Cobber was safe, but they'd lost a lot of men that day, including two planes, and nearly all the aircraft had come back with some kind of damage. One of the pilots counted seventy-six holes in his Boston. That night Cobber went to a Church of England service. "Any port in a storm," he noted, "and the Almighty will receive thanks via whichever way it comes."[338]

Monty spent the morning trying to gather as much information as he could. He was "reasonably pleased" with the attacks in the north. In the south, the French attack had failed, while the 7th Armoured Division had also been unable to breach the minefields, but had managed to do enough to keep the 21st Panzer and Italian Ariete Divisions pinned down. In the evening, Carol Mather reported back, telling Monty that there had been fairly heavy casualties in the infantry and that the armor appeared to be stuck.

Monty issued new orders. The Aussies were to carry out a "crumbling" operation that night and to exploit their gains, and the New Zealanders were to push southward from the Miteiriya Ridge. X Corps was to continue its efforts to clear the corridors through the minefields and get out into the open desert beyond. In the south, 7th Armoured Division were to make another attempt to push through the minefields there.

Joe Madeley couldn't believe they were going to have to attack a second night. The three men left in his section were now asleep in their hastily constructed dugouts, some with shovels still in their hands. With a heavy heart, he began shaking them awake. "The hardest part was having to empty the sandbags that had been such hard work to fill," he says, "but we had to take them with us."

The Highlanders were to help the 1st Armoured Division open the northern corridor as far as a shallow feature called Kidney Ridge. The Scots were to the south of the Australians, on Joe's left, and he watched them set off in daylight, with bayonets fixed, some hours before the Australians were due to launch their attack. "The bagpipes were playing and people were falling," he recalls, "but they just kept going. I've never seen anything like it. As brave as you can get." Albert Martin also watched this extraordinary spectacle, the steadfast Scots seemingly oblivious to machine-gun and shell-fire, as they disappeared like specters amid the smoke and dust. One of those marching toward the guns was Johnny

Bain, who had survived the first night of battle and was stumbling forward once more. He had absolutely no idea where they were going or what he was supposed to be doing; he still hadn't even fired his rifle. Like Maiki, Johnny thought the pipes were "ridiculous," but Albert Martin thought the whole spectacle of this advance one of the most incredible things he'd ever seen and found the sound of the pipes incredibly stirring. After the last man had faded and disappeared from view, he could still hear the reedy, eerie sound of the pipes above the din of battle.[339]

10th Armoured Division was also to try and break through the southern corridor. Just after 5 PM, a number of German tanks moved forward for a localized counterattack and opened fire on the armor huddled on the northern lee of the Miteiriya Ridge. Major Stanley Christopherson was slightly alarmed when he noticed a lone Mark IV panzer suddenly appear three hundred yards in front and traverse its gun directly toward them. With only a two-pounder in his turret and one that had a jammed breech mechanism to boot, Stanley hastily moved out of the way.

Shortly after, Stanley clambered out of his tank to talk to a squadron commander from the neighboring 3 RTR, and was told curtly that two officers had been lost that morning by unnecessarily leaving their tanks and wandering about. Getting the message, Stanley went back to his Crusader. He was just climbing back in when a shell burst overhead, the blast of which closed his left eye, gave him a nosebleed and concussion, and some splinter wounds. "I had a very lucky escape," he noted. Even so, he was in no fit state to lead the four remaining tanks of his squadron and was taken back to the New Zealand Regimental Aid Post (RAP) and then on to Alexandria to check for splinters in his eye.

Later, the remains of the Sherwood Rangers were formed up again to try and break through the minefield after the sappers had prepared another passage. They set off at nine, but were soon told they could go no further. Colonel Kellett was furious, but they were still stuck where they were, head-to-tail, when they were attacked by enemy dive-bombers. Much of the Regiment's B Echelon, then full of fuel and ammunition, was desroyed. Some twenty lorries were soon blazing fiercely in the night, beacons for enemy ground fire. This was one of the few successes the Luftwaffe had and it caused pandemonium. Two tank regiments had to be hurriedly dispersed and caused severe delays, not to mention the material loss. It also starkly demonstrated the value of the RAF's air superiority; without it, the task facing Eighth Army would have been considerably stiffer, if not impossible— and it was already proving hard enough. Meanwhile, the sappers were finding the minefields were denser and deeper than they had expected. The 10th Armoured Division didn't get very far. It was another disappointing night.

Throughout the day, Carol Mather had sensed a whiff of trouble brewing; Freyberg in particular had once again expressed his great scepticism as to the mettle of the armor in general. But when Gatehouse suggested to Lumsden that 10th Armoured's attack should be abandoned for the night, the pot boiled over. Before Lumsden agreed to Gatehouse's request, he called De Guigand at Monty's HQ. With the reports that had been coming in all day from liaison officers like Carol Mather, De Guingand decided it was time to wake the army commander. The result was a conference at Burg el Arab at 3:30 in the morning with Monty, Lumsden, and Leese of XXX Corps. During this crisis talk, Monty, predictably, stuck to his guns. He spoke calmly to Lumsden and by telephone to Gatehouse, reaffirming his original orders to push on, whatever the casualties. Carol Mather, watching these discussions, noticed there was a certain "atmosphere" and that Lumsden did not look happy; but Monty wanted greater resolve from his armored commanders. He had warned everyone the going would be tough—what did they expect? If they were not up to the task, he would replace them with people who were.

While all this was going on, the forward brigades in the southern corridor had been waiting long hours for some orders. Just after midnight they'd asked whether they should retire but still had no answer and so had carried on regardless. Some armor did eventually emerge through the minefields but although they claimed they had reached the Pierson Line, they were in fact some thousand yards short. And despite causing some damage to German tanks and guns, they could find no cover for hull-down positions and no real means of resupply and so they too were finally forced to withdraw during the afternoon of 25 October.

In the south, XIII Corps had also failed to breach the second of the old British minefields. Monty may have taken no truck with Lumsden and Gatehouse's quibbling, but the "break-in" had not gone at all as he'd envisaged. The armor was supposed to have moved *through* the infantry along the Oxalic line and on ahead to Pierson, but by the twenty-fifth, some of the armor was still behind Oxalic and none any further forward. In other words, the "dogfight"—the next stage—would be fought *alongside* the infantry, rather than in front of it, as he'd planned.

On the night of 24–25 October, the Australian attack had gone well; by first light Joe Madeley and the 2/13 Battalion were dug in once more, this time along the Oxalic line, but after the confusion and mayhem along the southern corridor, the Miteiriya area was now horribly congested. The 10th Armoured Division and a large number of New Zealanders were caught up there. Exhausted and frustrated, their confidence was not at its highest. Monty had wanted the New Zealanders to start crumbling southwest from this position, but during the morning of the twenty-fifth, Freyberg pointed out that it might be better to make the next thrust in the north, where the Australians were doing well and where the crumbling had already begun. It was also considerably less congested and there was an opportunity for them to push northward and capture a strategic spur, Point 29, recognized during the planning stage as the key feature in the coastal sector. Moreover, this area appeared to be far less mined than elsewhere. Monty agreed to this change of tack, and that night an Australian "composite" force of motorized infantry of 26th Brigade with the support of tanks and artillery surged northward across the virtually mine-free desert and was completely successful. By dawn, Point 29 had been taken and consolidated.

It was around midnight on Saturday, 24 October, that General Eisenhower heard the news that his good friend Mark Clark had made it back safely to Gibraltar. The following afternoon the man himself was walking through the door of Telegraph Cottage looking fit and well, apart from slightly reddened eyes due to lack of sleep.

Sitting down, Clark then told his tale. He and his party of four other US officers had flown by B-17 to Gibraltar and from there, a British submarine had taken them to the rendezvous point off the coast of Algiers. They waited there for thirty-six hours, constantly watching through the periscope for a white light signal from the secret house on the shore. Eventually it came and Clark and his team set off to the beach in collapsible canvas canoes, known as folbots.

The leading French collaborator, General Mast and several of his staff officers were there waiting for them, as was Robert Murphy. Clark had opened the discussion by telling Mast that they had to trust one another and that it was essential they were frank and honest with one another. "After that, Clark said he had lied like hell," added Harry Butcher. Mast had prepared detailed plans for landings and the capture of ports and airfields—these were cannily similar to the real plans the Allies had been preparing. He also gave Clark exact details about the location of troops and batteries along the coast. The problems, Mast suggested, would come from the French Navy—they did not trust Darlan and advised against the Allies dealing with him. Clark made it clear that Giraud could never be overall Allied commander—but put forward Ike's suggestion that he be made governor of French North Africa and Mast Deputy Chief of Staff of the Allied Expeditionary Force instead. Mast seemed happy with this and also accepted that British troops could land at Algiers on their way to Tunisia.

Clark and his party had landed around 10 PM, and were still talking at seven the following morning. Clark then excused himself and went to the lavatory, but as he did so, word arrived that local police had become suspicious that something was up and were on their way to the house. The Americans and the three British commandos were hastily bundled into the cellar and soon after, the police duly arrived. While the owner was assuring them nothing was wrong, one of the commandos was seized with a coughing fit. Clark offered him some chewing gum, but the commando had never had any before and looked slightly perplexed. Taking his own wad from his mouth, Clark gave it to the commando, who began chewing nervously. It did the trick. "Have you another piece?" the commando asked soon after.

"Why?" whispered Clark.

"Because this one has no flavor," the commando replied.

As soon as the police had gone, Clark and his team crept down to the shore. A swell had developed, so Clark stripped off except for his overseas cap and getting back into one of the folbots, sat on his clothes. The waves were strong, however, and they were all overturned and flung into the sea, Clark included. Managing to swim back to shore, Clark was now without any clothes and so went back to the house, naked but for his cap. The owner was reluctant to let him back in, but eventually Clark persuaded him to give him some ill-fitting clothes. He and the rest of the party then hid in the nearby woods until the surf calmed down. They were nearly spotted by some Arabs, but eventually managed to get back into their folbots and head back out to the submarine, which had been maneuvered to just half a mile from shore. From there, they safely made it to Gib.

Mast, Clark believed, had committed himself so far that there was now no chance that he was double-crossing the Allies, and so Ike agreed that he should be told on 4 November that the landings would take place four days later. The only issue now still up in the air was whether Darlan would, in fact, play ball.

When Clark finally finished telling his tale, Ike suggested he write it up. "It could be printed in a month," he told Clark, "and I bet you someone would pay you a thousand dollars for it."

Had the mission been worth it? As Butch pointed out, at that point in time it was hard to say. "The proof of the pudding is in the eating," he noted, "and we will know on or about November 8."

The point of no return had now almost been reached. Out in the Atlantic, hundreds of ships were surging toward North Africa. By 26 October, the Bowles twins, Bing Evans, and Margaret Hornback were among the many thousands plunging through the gray autumnal seas. Somehow, some way, an armada of 370 merchant vessels and 300 warships from both Britain and the US had been assembled. The biggest seaborne invasion in the history of the world was underway.

* * *

By the morning of the third day of the battle, Rommel was back at the front and once again in charge.* He was not a well man, but immediately took a firm grip of the situation. Despite the failure of the British armor, aerial attacks and artillery fire had once again made life a misery for the panzer army and losses were mounting. 15th Panzer had just 31 tanks left from the 119 with which they began the battle.

Recognizing the strategic importance of Point 29, he immediately launched an attack with what he had in an effort to regain the feature. Stiff resistance from the Aussies and another concerted effort by the RAF and artillery ensured his attack failed. There was now only one option: he had to bring all his forces together. That evening, he decided the time had come to bring the 21st Panzer Division north so that an effective counterattack could be launched. The German 90th Light and Italian Trieste Divisions were also ordered forward from their reserve positions at Daba. The following night he would launch his counterattack and regain the land that had been lost during the previous long three days and nights. With the front stabilized once more, then perhaps there would be a chance to take stock and get some precious supplies to the front.

But then more bad news reached Rommel's HQ. The tanker, on which he had been so depending, had been sunk outside Tobruk, as had another ship carrying further fuel and much-needed ammunition. The panzer army now had enough fuel to last just a few more days. Much depended on the success of his counterattack the following day.

---

*By agreement between the German and Italian High Commands, the previous day the *Panzer Army Afrika* was renamed the *Deutsch-Italienische Panzer Army*.

CHAPTER 15

Attrition—
26 October–3 November, 1942

AT FIRST LIGHT on Monday, 26 October, Lieutenant Carol Mather had taken the army commander's Humber and driven over to the Aussie HQ. The news had been good, and as he'd driven back he'd seen a long line of mostly German prisoners tramping back along the road. On his return it was still early so he sat outside Monty's caravan and looked out over the icy-still waters of the Mediterranean. Suddenly two Messerschmitt 109s sped past, chased by a Spitfire almost skimming the sea and firing furiously. In moments they had disappeared into the desert. "Shortly after," noted Carol, "a large flight of duck flew past."[340]

Inside the caravan, Monty had much to think about, and like his counterpart, spent much of the day reappraising the situation and planning his next moves. So far, around three hundred of his tanks had been knocked out, although it was reckoned that many of these were recoverable, and even so, he was still left with nine hundred that were serviceable and ready for action. If the British armor didn't have the necessary skill—and he believed it did not—then it would win by sheer force of numbers. This was why he was telling Lumsden and Gatehouse to show "resolve," even if that meant high casualties. Major battles were not for the faint-hearted.

But had his plan been the right one? General Tuker, for one, thought Monty had got it quite wrong. Despite Monty's efforts to fool Rommel and Stumme into believing the main thrust would come in the south, the Axis's main strength had always been in the north, along the main supply routes, suggesting that this was the area the panzer army commanders were most concerned about. With this in mind, Tuker's idea was to create a heavy blow with artillery in support on a narrow front in the north, around a feature at which Rommel *had* to counterattack—such as

Point 29. This would be a limited but devastating operation. Whether the minefields were successfully breached was irrelevant.

While the bulk of Rommel's armor and artillery were bogged down with this attack in the north, Tuker suggested a second thrust be simultaneously launched in the middle of the line, along the Ruweisat feature. Once through the minefields, the panzer army would be split in two. With most of the enemy forces distracted in the north the British armor could deal with the panzer army's forces in the south before turning in a sweeping maneuver toward the enemy flanks in the upper half of the line. Tuker believed that whatever the training levels of the British armor, once out in the open and free of the minefields, the sheer weight of their numbers, combined with the support of motorized infantry, would ensure a decisive and fairly speedy victory.

There is something to be said for this approach. First, the ground along the Ruweisat Ridge and just below is much more stony than in the northern stretch of the desert, where the ground is almost entirely sand and vetch. Dust would still be churned up by the mass of vehicles but not as badly as in the north, where it added considerably to the confusion and mayhem of X Corps' advance. Second, extending across the middle of the enemy positions was a lengthy fingerlike Axis minefield, which would have helped protect the British armor as it broke in to the enemy positions and dealt with the southern half of the Axis forces.

While this is obviously debatable, Monty's misuse of his artillery is less open to conjecture. Of the nine hundred field guns available to him, only four hundred were lined up in support of the main thrust—in other words, less than 50 percent.* Or, to put it another way, over five hundred guns were *not* being used in support of the main attack, while over three hundred were available to XIII Corps for their *feint* attack in the south, an unnecessarily disproportionate number. The four hundred available admittedly made quite an impact, and sounded very impressive, but, as the First World War had proved, lots of bang and earth thrown into the air does not necessarily equate to mass destruction. A figure of, say, 750 guns would have definitely been more effective. As it was, Monty had insufficient guns at the decisive point.

And they would have been even more effective on a narrower front. As it was, there were only a hundred guns to cover each of the four divisions, which equated to one every forty-five yards of the ten-mile front. There was no need for the front to be this wide—ten miles is a

---

*Exact figures vary, but at most there were 408 and at least 385; four hundred seems a safe bet for the purpose of this argument.

long way, after all. Half that length, with almost twice the number of guns firing greater concentrations, and taking out one target after another, would have had a far better chance of creating the devastating knockout blow that Monty's material advantage should have given him.

After Alam Halfa, Monty correctly acknowledged the part played by the partnership of the RAF and artillery working in tandem and the devastating effect it had had, and yet by October, he appears to have been so preoccupied with his deception plans in the south and his concerns over the standards of his forces that he overlooked some of the basic principles of concentration of fire. Ironically, the overall standard of the British artillery was high. British gunners were superbly trained—as men like Harold Harper ably demonstrated—and their skill was second to none. And like his predecessors, he completely overlooked the potential of the 3.7-inch ack-ack gun. Axis bombers had not seriously threatened airfields or installations in the Delta and these guns had sat there largely unused. Even if just half had been brought to bear in the battle, they could have made a huge impact. For all Monty's leadership skills, he was certainly no innovator.

But there were no 3.7-inch guns at the front, and there was still enough Axis artillery and armor to foil Monty's original plan for the battle. So on 26 October, he decided the crumbling process would continue, but at a lower key. Instead, while the Axis armor and artillery was contained, he would withdraw some of the troops now at the front and prepare them for a new knockout blow in a few days' time.

Like Rommel, he decided to bring up his armor from the south too. The southern battle, was, for the moment, over. The 7th Armoured Division was taken out of the line, as was the entire New Zealand Division, and over half X Corps' armor. While the battle continued to rage, Maiki Parkinson and his mates in the Maori Battalion went swimming in the Mediterranean.

The Australians were doing well and so Monty ordered them to continue their drive northward. This would leave something of a gap, however, so the Highland Division was to move up and cover the old Australian sector, while the South Africans were to move into the New Zealand and Highlanders' sector and Tuker's 4th Indian Division, with only three brigades, was to be stretched along an even wider front of some fifteen miles. The Fighting French were also to be brought into the line on the right of Tuker's Indians. Bill Eadie and the rest of 2nd South African Infantry Brigade were withdrawn for a rest, although it was hardly restful for Bill: he spent much of his time over the next few days driving prisoners to the POW cage, and this while struggling with another bout of stomachache and diarrhea.

The moves were completed by the morning of 28 October. The South

Africans had been short of motor transport and so it had been a particularly busy time for Petrus Dlhamini. Although as a black soldier he was not allowed to carry arms, he had picked up an Italian rifle and now carried it in his truck wherever he went. "I never used it," he says, "but it was nice to have it." Not that it would have been much use against an enemy shell or air attack, the two main threats to his safety. He'd already had a number of close shaves, and had found himself desperately running for cover. One of his colleagues had had his clothes ripped from him by the blast of a bomb.

In the meantime, while this shuffling along the line was taking place, 1st Armoured Division had been ordered to keep going through the northern corridor and toward the tiny feature known as Hill 28 to the Germans but Kidney Ridge to the British. Playing a key part in this thrust were the men of 2 Rifle Brigade.

On the afternoon of 26 October, Albert Martin heard the news that 2 Rifle Brigade's role as part of the Minefield Task Force was over; instead, the battalion was to take part in a night attack to capture and then consolidate one of two enemy strong points near Kidney Ridge. The following morning, the plan was for two armored brigades to move up, using these captured outposts as a firm base from which to launch an attack west to sever the Sidi Abd el Rahman track. 2 Rifle Brigade's target was an area known as Snipe, a mile southwest of the Kidney Ridge, while the 2nd King's Royal Rifle Corps (KRRC) would take "Woodcock," a mile northwest of the ridge. But however simple the plan may have seemed on paper, it was obvious to those about to take part that they were going to have one hell of a fight on their hands. Briefing his officers, Colonel Turner, the commander of 2 Rifle Brigade, warned his men that this was likely to be a "last man, last round" sort of action; a rather chilling proposition.[341]

Colonel Turner received his orders at around four o'clock in the afternoon. The battalion then had to assemble and get to the start line of the attack, nearly a mile beyond the mouth of the Star lane in the minefield corridor. Joining the battalion under Turner's command were 239 Anti-tank Battery with eleven six-pounders, and a detachment of sappers. The battalion itself already had sixteen six-pounders, making twenty-seven guns in all, and a total battalion group strength of around three hundred men.

Just getting to the start line was hard enough: the men had been given little time to prepare and with the moon not yet up, the desert was dark and the dust stifling. Even once they reached the start line, there was some confusion not only over whether they were in the right place to begin with, but also about the precise location of Snipe. This was a common problem: throughout the battle, few had much idea of where they were half the time, even experienced campaigners like the Rifle Brigade.

To make matters worse, they were already being shelled by enemy artillery fire. Even so, a column of infantry and Bren carriers set off as planned just after 11 PM, a barrage thundering away ahead of them. In one of the carriers, Albert was relieved to get going. The first thousand yards went well, but then the column came to a halt at some wire, thought to be possibly the edge of a minefield. After five minutes, the sappers declared it to be a dummy, but from then on the enemy fire became noticeably heavier. Moreover, the going was terrible—the ground badly rutted and the air filled with cloying, powdered sand. A few prisoners were captured and ahead of the infantry leading the column, scattered groups were seen fleeing westward into the desert night.

The forward column of the battalion reached Snipe—or rather, a position just south of the real Snipe—shortly after midnight. The success signal—two green Very lights—was fired into the dark desert sky and then the anti-tank guns and soft-skinned vehicles with their supplies of ammunition, fuel, food, and water, began rumbling up through the increasingly soft desert sand. The Bren carriers had struggled, but the heavier gun towers soon became bogged down. Only nineteen of the twenty-six anti-tank guns managed to reach what they assumed to be Snipe, whereupon they began setting themselves up in an oval-shaped shallow bowl with the guns facing outward, although most were lined up along the western and northern slopes of the ridge.

Meanwhile, Albert and a number of the Bren carriers pushed forward to reconnoiter. The moon was now up and they saw a large leaguer of German and Italian tanks to the southwest, but immediately in front of them was a group of about 150 enemy troops and their vehicles. The riflemen opened fire and set alight one of the vehicles. The men—most of whom were German sappers—then looked as though they were about to surrender, but the fire had silhouetted the carriers. The Axis tank leaguer beyond, stirred by this unexpected conflagration, opened fire, catching the enemy troops in between. Albert watched the unfolding massacre with sickness in his stomach. The men started fleeing, but in the crossfire over a hundred were hit. It was, noted Albert, "one of war's tragedies."[342]

The carriers retreated, but the enemy tank leaguer was by now broken up and began to move off. One disoriented Panzer Mk IV strayed into the battalion position and was blasted by one of the six-pounders at only a hundred yards' range. Meanwhile, under the cover of darkness, the battalion's supply trucks finally reached the rest of the riflemen and unloaded their supplies, moving off again just before dawn.

First light began to glimmer across the desert at about 6 AM, and the riflemen could finally see the lay of the land. Albert and his section had found a patch of scrub on the western edge of the hollow, but as they'd moved up in the darkness, he'd little realized just how far they'd pushed into the Axis positions. In fact, they'd moved into the heart of the enemy armor's assembly area, which was massing for Rommel's intended counterattack later that day. Their little depression was a horribly exposed outpost. Digging in was out of the question: there was no time for that. Instead, Albert and his men moved their carrier into the lee of the rise in front of them and hoped for the best.

However, the battalion was offered a gift in the first exchange of the day. Two large enemy leaguers were on the move, and still oblivious of the riflemen, began moving westward, offering an irresistible target. The battalion's six-pounders were quick to take advantage, and in no time sixteen enemy tanks and self-propelled guns had been knocked out. Albert watched with a certain amount of glee. "How often in the past had I seen our armor crucified by well-positioned enemy anti-tank guns!" he noted. "Now, Rommel had failed to heed the lesson he had taught us and was paying the price."[343]

The enemy were in no doubt about the riflemen's positions now, and began shelling them heavily. Three six-pounders were soon out of action and to make matters worse, when the British armor moved up at around 7:30 AM, the tanks stopped on a ridge 2,000 yards behind and opened fire on them as well. They only stopped when one of the battalion officers made a highly dangerous dash over to the leading British tanks and told them to hold their fire at once.

The British tanks then began moving forward as planned, but soon came under attack from high-velocity Mk IV "Specials" and 88s. In just a quarter of an hour, seven Shermans were burning fiercely. Shortly after, the British tanks withdrew. One problem with the Sherman was that its ammunition was stored in lightly armored sections of the turret, and could easily explode, especially if the turret received a direct hit. Before long, they gained a reputation for flaming as easily as a cigarette lighter—not for nothing were they to become known as "Ronsons."

The beleaguered outpost of Snipe was now once again completely isolated. Nor did they have an observation post to help them direct their fire—the OP officer, detached from the Royal Horse Artillery specifically for this task, had managed to get lost during the night and was nowhere to be seen. At nine o'clock, Battalion HQ sent a message saying "our crying need is a gunner OP."[344] One was on its way, came the reply from 7 Motor Brigade HQ. But he never appeared.

And nor did they have a medical officer—their own MO had been unable to reach Snipe during the night because he'd been too busy tending casualties incurred on the journey out. A small party of carriers was sent off to try and find him and also to collect more ammunition. One of the carriers was hit en route and, although a party of vehicles loaded with ammunition was waiting to resupply, every time they tried to make a dash for it, they were forced back by the weight of fire.

It had become clear that the Rifle Brigade were now being subjected to a major trial of strength. Shells screamed down unceasingly on the riflemen's position, their own guns answering furiously. Burning hulks of tanks, often with their mangled and charred crew nearby, already littered the ground; black, angry smoke billowed upward and mixed with the grey fog from the smoke canisters laid by both sides. Small arms chattered viciously and constantly, while choking dust and the acrid stench of cordite and burning oil and rubber fouled the air and made it hard to breathe easily. "From the squaddies point of view," says Albert, "the scene was one of utter confusion and mayhem." He had little idea of what was going on, although it seemed as though every Axis tank and gun in the panzer army was directed toward them.

In fact, the enemy armor was now moving forward, across the southern flank of the battalion's position in an effort to engage the British tanks that had fallen back. The riflemen's guns poured fire into them, and in doing so drew some of the panzers toward them. Eight more panzers were hit, but by midmorning, only thirteen of the six-pounders were still in action, while six carriers had also been set on fire. The Bren carrier, while good at transporting men across the desert swiftly, was hopeless in a battle of this nature. Like most British equipment, it had a number of serious flaws. "It was a slow, hot noisy vehicle," noted Albert, "that would shed a track for no reason, had paper-thin armour, particularly underneath, making it highly vulnerable to mines, and was armed with a Boyes and Bren of limited use." In this armored battle, there was little Albert and his section could do to help, but sit tight and fire at any "soft" target that showed itself.

At Woodcock, the KRRC had been having a comparatively quiet time, and was to continue that way throughout the day. Not so at Snipe. The riflemen had survived the morning's onslaught, but when Italian tanks attacked again at around one o'clock, their ammunition situation was so low along the southwest side of the position, that only one gun could be used against them—and this was now manned by a sergeant, the CO, and Lieutenant Toms, the troop commander. Six tanks had been knocked out when Toms made a dash for a jeep about a hundred yards away, and with machine-gun bullets pinging all around him, sped over to one of the knocked-out guns, loaded up their unused ammunition and scuttled back. Ten yards short, the jeep was set on fire, but together Toms and Colonel Turner unloaded the precious shells and the sergeant knocked out the remaining Italian tanks still advancing toward them. "Good work—a hat trick!" exclaimed the CO.[345] It was an extraordinary action, but one that symbolized the heroic stand made by the riflemen that day. The CO had suffered a head wound; later Toms was also wounded, and there came a moment when there were no officers left at all on the southwest side of the hollow where Albert and his section were positioned.

For a couple of hours, something of a lull occurred, but then Snipe came under intense attack once more. Shells whistled down among their positions, although once again, some of these were from the British armor that was now moving forward again. "During an unpleasant day," noted Colonel Turner later, "this was the most unpleasant thing that happened."[346] Soon after, around forty tanks, mostly German, clanked into view along the mile stretch between Woodcock and Snipe. This was 21st Panzer, also now moving up for Rommel's planned counterattack.

As they continued rumbling forward, Albert couldn't believe their luck when the panzers once again began moving across their front, some only two hundred yards from the guns along the northern side of the position. In the following exchange, two more guns were destroyed, but nine panzers were knocked out. By half-past five, the attack had been halted and the enemy tanks began to withdraw. Fifteen panzers, however, were sent to attack from the southeast, toward Albert's position. There were now three guns left to take on these tanks, each with no more than ten rounds left. Although word had reached them that they would be withdrawing under cover of darkness, Albert was keenly aware that they could not hold out much longer, and began to doubt whether they would be able to make their escape before they were overrun.

The riflemen were not finished yet, however. The remaining six-pounders facing this latest onslaught waited until the leading panzers rumbled to within two hundred yards and only then let fly. Three were hit and trundled to a standstill, amidst thick smoke and flames. Albert and the other carrier crews fired at the enemy tank crews as they bailed out of the burning hulks. Another tank was hit, which then backed away before bursting into flames. When two more brewed up, the remainder finally withdrew, settling down into hull-down positions and firing without letup.

But dusk was now falling and soon enough darkness followed. The riflemen were due to be relieved at 9 PM, but the relief did not show up, nor did the promised transport. These were supposed to have been the men of the 5th Royal Sussex, while the 4th Royal Sussex was to relieve Woodcock. Both battalions were new to the desert and both had moved up as planned, but to the wrong positions. As a result, by 10:30 PM, there was still no sign of them, so the remaining officers decided they should move out anyway. Leaving all but one of the guns and supporting the walking wounded, the column trudged back toward the same Star gap they had set out from thirty hours before.

"Is it possible, I wonder," noted Albert, "to put into words the emotions of soldiers who have now reached safety after long hours when death or a crippling wound could happen in a second, any second, during those interminable hours? The usual words of pleasure, relief, happiness, thankfulness, are totally inappropriate. Substitute bewilderment, incomprehension, drained, numbed or disbelief."[347] Behind them, in that rather unremarkable stretch of uninteresting desert, wreckage lay strewn and twisted and smouldering. These were the remains of seventy tanks and self-propelled guns, along with many of their crew, now charred and blackened. Just seven of these were British. At Snipe itself, the dead were comparatively slight: fourteen and one missing. A miracle, really. They lay where they had died, next to the smashed guns and discarded ammunition boxes, the piles of spent shell cases and contorted remnants of Bren carriers. Through the night, the Axis worked hard to recover what they could, but when the war moved eastward and the British armies peacefully crossed what had been such a devastating killing ground, there were still the remains of no less than thirty-two tanks, twenty-two of which were German—losses the panzer army could not afford. The Snipe action proved what could be achieved by experienced troops full of resolve and determination. And it also showed once again that the most important weapon in the desert was not the tank, but the anti-tank gun.

As ever, the RAF had played their part, bombing enemy positions throughout the day. As 21st Panzer had formed up prior to their attack, they had suffered seven successive pattern-bombing attacks during a two-and-a-half hour period. "Our best effort yet," noted Tommy Elmhirst that day, "with our two light bomber wings putting in 200 sorties and hitting enemy panzer divisions while they were trying to concentrate for an attack."[348] Cobber Weinronk had flown a stooge with seventeen other Bostons and Mitchells at ten that morning. Billy Drake provided cover for bombers heading to attack the airfields at Daba in the morning, shooting down a Macchi 202 in the process and bringing his desert tally to ten confirmed kills in the air along with a shared kill and several "probables," and an even larger number destroyed on the ground. LG 104 was reported to be "black with bomb craters, as are most of the other LGs in the vicinity."[349] In the afternoon, Billy sent one of his flight commanders and eleven other Kittyhawks to escort the bombers making one of their attacks on the Axis armor. Their air superiority was total, their attacks relentless and the effect they were having was devastating and demoralizing. As Rommel admitted, these round-the-clock attacks were exhausting his men and causing a serious sense of inferiority among his troops.

Rommel had launched his counterattack, not just against Snipe and the British armor behind this outpost, but also against the Australians. Joe Madeley, now in an amalgamated A and D Company, had faced a tank attack in the morning but with the assistance of the RAF, it had been beaten off. Rommel, his fuel situation perilous, now went back on the defensive, hoping that if he could withstand Eighth Army's next attack he could have every chance of maintaining his position and gain valuable time with which to bring up more supplies. It was the only real choice now facing him. Retreat would mean a return to mobile warfare. With his lack of fuel, this was out of the question.

Operations around Kidney Ridge had not gone so well on 28 October. Around Woodcock, the entire battalion of the 4th Royal Sussex Regiment had been overrun and 342 men taken prisoner, but Rommel's counterattack had not broken through the forward positions. Then that night, the Australians continued their efforts to drive a wedge northward between the railway stop at Tel el Eisa and the village of Sidi Abd el Rahman. The attack was only partially successful, but Joe Madeley's 2/13th Battalion took its objective, an area called the Fig Garden, after struggling through some particularly vicious sections of Devil's Garden. Even so, by the following morning, Joe's platoon had just twelve men left, his company—normally around two hundred strong—had only thirty-one. Having attacked three nights out of five and faced counterattacks of some kind on the other two, the battalion had been steadily decimated. The survivors were absolutely exhausted. The Fig Orchard brought trouble too. "We stopped just where the Jerries had gone from," says Joe, "and, of course, they knew exactly where that was, so they shelled us, plus they'd left a lot of booby traps." On 30 October, a number of others were lost to shelling. "A shell came over and boom, this chap came in on top of us," recalls Joe. "It was Bill Rattenbury, one of the stretcher bearers. Someone said, 'For Christ's sake get this guy off my back,' and another said, 'Jesus, he's dead.' He didn't have a mark on him." By the nightfall on 30 October, there were seven men left in Joe's platoon and twenty-seven in the entire company.

It was the foreign minister, Anthony Eden, who managed to stir up Churchill's worst fears. The PM had been feeling twitchy about the outcome of the battle ever since it began, so when Eden turned up at Number 10 late on the evening of 28 October and told him that Monty was withdrawing troops, and that the battle was petering out, Churchill was left feeling quite shaken. And then he recalled that Montgomery had assured him the battle would take seven days—well, a week had almost gone by and now he was pulling his troops back!

General Brooke had barely woken up the following morning before being presented with a telegram that Churchill wanted to send to Alex. "Not a pleasant one," noted Brooke.[350] When he later saw the PM, he told him that Eden was hardly the best person to judge the tactical situation, especially since he was in London. The CIGS managed to dissuade the PM from sending the telegram, but at Eden's insistence, Dick Casey, the minister for State in Cairo was ordered to go straight up to the front and to report back on what exactly was going on at Eighth Army Tactical Headquarters.

Casey reached Tactical HQ that morning, along with Alex and his COS, Dick McCreery. Casey took Freddie de Guingand to one side and asked if he was happy with the way things were going. Yes, de Guingand told him, and they were completely confident of success. Meanwhile, Alex went to have a chat with Monty, who was now in the final stages of preparing the next assault with his newly formed reserves, and which, he hoped, would bring about the end of the battle. This operation he had named SUPERCHARGE. The plan was very similar to LIGHTFOOT, with a nighttime infantry attack, and the armor following close behind and then passing through the infantry's objective. The line was not as wide—only 4,000 yards, under three miles—nor were there now so many mines to clear. With a more narrow front, more guns could also be brought to bear. On the other hand, the moon had reached its last quarter and was not rising until one in the morning, so the attack would have to be launched later in the night, leaving them less time until daybreak.

No one doubted this was the right idea, but Alex was concerned that Monty intended to send SUPERCHARGE through the Australian position at the very north of the line. Ultra, however, had warned them that the German 90th Light Division had now finally arrived fresh from being held in reserve and was protecting Axis coastal supply routes in this part of the line. Both Alex and Dick McCreery felt very strongly that a much more sensible point of attack would be a few miles farther south, slightly north of the existing northern corridor cleared during LIGHTFOOT, in the direction of Tel el Aqqaqir. Alex had made a point of not interfering with Monty's plans, but he felt he could not sit back and allow the army commander to go ahead with SUPERCHARGE as planned. Instead, he told McCreery to talk to de Guingand and to try and persuade Monty to change his mind. De Guingand agreed, but insisted he alone should talk to Monty. By now, he had worked out how to put an idea into Monty's mind in such a way that the army commander believed that he had thought of it himself. The ploy worked: "I decided," wrote Monty later, "that I would blow a deep hole in the enemy front just to the north of the original corridor."[351] Alex was much relieved. To his mind, this was the key decision of the Alamein battle.* The following day he wrote to Churchill, assuring him that both he and Monty were agreed that the greatest pressure needed to be maintained. "We are now, however, about to put in a large-scale attack with infantry and tanks to break a way through for the Tenth Corps. If this is successful, it will have far-reaching results."[352]

With the Allied armada steaming toward North Africa, the planners were left to anxiously bite their nails and do their damndest to make sure that surprise and secrecy were maintained right up to the wire. Admiral Cunningham left London on 28 October, his part in TORCH still a "dead secret" to all but a very few.[353] Traveling incognito in his civvies, he took the train to Plymouth and then boarded the cruiser HMS *Scylla*, bound for Gibraltar.

Plans had also been put in place to keep Eisenhower's movements a secret. On 30 October, a story ran in Washington that Ike was about to return to the US for a "consultation." No sooner had this news broken than a colonel from the PR office hurried over to Harry Butcher asking him what he should tell journalists. Butch told him to speak to Bedell-Smith, who pretended to be horrified that the story was out. As far as AFHQ was concerned, Bedell-Smith told the PR team, the response to any newspapermen was "no comment." Ike's recall to the US became front-page news in Washington.

A few days later, Butch was delighted when Drew Middleton, a journalist on the *New York Times,* claimed that he had absolutely reliable information that the second front would soon occur in Norway; another claimed that Ike was already back in Washington and that Marshal was now in London. The false rumor mills appeared to be working.

Messages continued to arrive from Robert Murphy in Algiers. He had still not spoken with Admiral Darlan's agent, but, he reported, Darlan had told Vichy officials that there was little chance North Africa was about to be attacked. Meanwhile, a US submarine had been dispatched to Gibraltar to await final instructions about where and when to pick up the French General Giraud . . .

In the desert, a yellowish fog now hung over the battlefield—dust and smoke stirred up so fine that it no longer settled properly. Like everyone, Carol Mather found it quite suffocating as he wound his way along a net-

---

*There is some debate over who actually suggested this change to the line of attack. It has variously been claimed as being De Guingand's and McCreery's idea, but Alex's ADC, Rupert Clarke is adamant that it was Alex who suggested that McCreery and De Guingand should try and dissuade Monty from attacking in the very north. This seems the most likely to me.

work of tracks up and down the front. His travels around the battlefield had taken him by one track crossing in particular during the past couple of days—a crossing where, in the middle of a tangle of wire, there lay a dead Highlander. Every time he passed, the dead man was still there. Carol could not understand why he had been left unburied. But every day, the body became more and more covered in dust until it looked as though he'd been turned to stone. "In my mind," wrote Carol, "he became a monument to the unknown soldier of Alamein."[354]

While Carol gathered information for the army commander, Monty was at his tactical headquarters making final preparations for the breakout phase of the battle. SUPERCHARGE was to be spearheaded by the New Zealanders, reinforced with 151st Infantry Brigade from 50 Division and 152nd Infantry Brigade from the 51 Highland Division, and supported by I tanks of the 23rd Armoured Brigade, and all under the command of the New Zealander General Freyberg. Monty had originally intended to launch SUPERCHARGE on the night of 31 October–1 November, but Freyberg felt this did not give him enough time to get ready and so asked for a postponement of twenty-four hours. Such was Monty's faith in Freyberg, he agreed without demur.

In the meantime, the Aussies were to launch their third attack in the north. They had now created something of a salient, and while this latest drive was to push them north across the railway and road to the coast, its prime objective was to pin down Axis troops, especially the 90th Light.

The Australian attack had begun well enough. They moved northward, behind the enemy minefields and captured a long, low gray building on the north side of the railway, known as the "Blockhouse." This was an old railway store, but was now being used as an Axis medical post. Captured along with the building were three German doctors. Two Aussie battalions then turned east from the Blockhouse, but met with fierce resistance and were forced back. Meanwhile, 21st Panzer had arrived from the northwest as well, so that by dawn, the Australians were completely hemmed in around the Blockhouse and the foot of Barrel Hill, a ridge to the northwest, in an area that became known as the Saucer. Throughout 31 October, the Australians matched the courage and resolution of the riflemen at Snipe, holding their ground and refusing to give way to the relentless Axis onslaught. During the night, the exhausted and depleted troops were relieved with two fresh battalions. Below Barrel Hill, the new arrivals were horrified to discover that one of their markers was a severed arm attached to a haversack but no body.

2/13 Battalion had not taken part in the main attack, but just under two miles south of the Saucer came under heavy bombardment from the Axis gunners. About one in the morning, Joe Madeley and his good friend Tom Duncan had left their slit trench to go and fetch some water and were walking back with it when a shell whistled over and landed nearby. A shard of shrapnel hit Joe in the leg. He tried to get up but then realized he was in trouble. "Christ, I'm hit," he said out loud, although it didn't hurt much—rather, his leg felt numb. Another man was shouting beside him. "Where are you hit?" Joe asked. "In the arse," came the reply. "He pulled up his shirt," says Joe, "and my God, how he was still alive, I just don't know."

Joe was bundled into an ambulance only to find Tom Duncan already there, wounded by the same shell. At the casualty clearing station, the shrapnel, along with a piece of his trousers, was cut out of his leg. There was no anaesthetic, but it still didn't hurt all that much. Even so, his wound was bad enough for him to be sent on to hospital. There, along with his mates Keith Boal, Tom Duncan, and others from the platoon, he remained for six weeks. Just four hours after he got there, he was scrubbed clean, wearing pajamas, lying on clean white sheets and clean white pillowcases and surrounded by beautiful nurses. "I felt an unbelievable sense of peace," he says. For Joe, the war in the desert was over. "I was the last one to get hit," he says. "The whole section had been cleaned out."

Operation SUPERCHARGE was launched with another blistering attack by the RAF over the Axis positions around Tel el Aqqaqir. For seven hours, they bombed the enemy to hell. Their efforts produced six massive explosions and a number of fires. They also struck the Afrika Korps Advanced HQ, wrecking their telephone communications system. Meanwhile, behind the enemy lines along the coast near Daba, a number of Royal Navy MTBs, including Charles Coles's 262, simulated another landing—a simple diversionary tactic intended to annoy the enemy.

When the barrage opened at 1:05 AM on 2 November, it was not the New Zealanders leading the way but 150 and 151 Brigades, with the I tanks following behind. The exception were the Maori, who had been attached to 151 Brigade and were told to take out an enemy strongpoint that threatened the northern flank of the main advance.

The Maori had moved up to their start line once dusk had fallen, moving through 20 Australian Brigade's positions.

"What the hell do you think you guys are going to do?" the Aussies taunted.

"We're going to take the tanks through," Maiki Parkinson told them.

"You'll never bloody get them through here, mate," one of them told him. This was exactly the kind of comment that wound Maiki up a treat, and he was determined to prove them wrong. C Company, the Ngati Morou, was to lead their assault. Maiki was company runner that night, largely because he was also the company commander's batman, a post he'd been given a few weeks before. "They'd always use the young fellows," explains Maiki. But he loathed Captain Awarau. "He was a dead loss," says Maiki, "a bloody drunkard. Where the hell he got his rum from I've no idea, but his water bottle was always full of the stuff. I was his batman so I bloody well knew." Once, when Awarau had drunk too much he'd grabbed a hand grenade and threatened to pull the pin and blow himself up. He hadn't, but from then on everyone knew him as "Pull the Pin."

After the company had gone about a quarter of a mile, they began to come under fire. Suddenly there was mayhem. Mortars began exploding and Spandaus chattered. Yelling, the Maori charged with their bayonets, hurtling toward the enemy positions and lobbing grenades, firing and stabbing their way through the enemy positions. Maiki could see a line of tracer from a small mound ahead of him, but spotting a shallow gully, ran down it only to find himself emerging at the side of the machine-gun nest just as the three-man team were putting in a new belt of ammunition.

"*Kamerad!*" Maiki shouted, but instead of putting their hands in the air, all three dived into their slit trench.

"Shoot the bastards!" said a voice behind him. It was Pull the Pin. "Shoot the bastards!" he said again, then began wildly firing his revolver. "Shoot the bastards, Parkie, or I'll shoot you!" For a moment Maiki thought about turning around and killing his tormentor there and then. He could feel his anger rising. Why hadn't the Germans put their hands up? "Shoot them, Parky," said Pull the Pin again.

"They were crouched in this trench," says Maiki, "and I shot them with my Tommy gun." It is an action he has regretted ever since.

"Now go and get the rest of the platoon," Pull the Pin told him; cohesion had been lost during the fighting and the company was spread about. Maiki hurried off and soon found Nugget Tukaki and several of the platoon lying down taking cover. Maiki lay down beside Nugget and told him they were to move, but no sooner had he done so than a figure emerged through the smoke and dust. "Hey, over here!" one of the Maori called out. But he was German, not Maori, and opened fire on them with his submachine gun. "How he never hit any of us, I'm buggered if I know," says Maiki, who with his Tommy gun fired back and cut him down.

They began moving forward again, but there was no sign of Pull the Pin. In fact, he'd been wounded just after Maiki had left him. Without him, they still charged another part of the strongpoint, capturing seventeen men and one officer. Maiki went up to the officer. "He was well over six foot," he says, "and I'm just this little fellow. He looked down his nose at me, but he couldn't do nothing."

* * *

The Maori had had a stiff fight, but had captured the enemy outpost. Elsewhere, the forward infantry had also achieved their objectives and with comparatively few losses. At first light, the tanks of 9th Armoured Brigade passed through and out into the open desert in front of Tel el Aqqaqir. But Tel el Aqqaqir was where the vast majority of Rommel's remaining 88mms were situated. The ground around there was ideal for placing artillery: generally flat, but with plenty of small, local humps and depressions—a patch of the desert that offered clear views of the land ahead, but also protection for a gun emplacement.

The 9th Armoured fought with great courage and early on managed to destroy a number of enemy guns and tanks. But as the sun rose and visibility improved, the dreaded 88s made mincemeat of them. Seventy of the ninety-four tanks that began the attack were knocked out. Two yeomanry and one Hussars regiment were almost completely destroyed—but these were precisely the kinds of sacrifices Monty knew would have to be made if victory was to be theirs.

Meanwhile, 1st Armoured Division was slowly inching out of the minefield. Once more fulfilling their duties in the Minefield Task Force were the 2nd Rifle Brigade. Albert Martin and his mates had not been at all happy to learn they were to take part in another major assault so soon after Snipe. They'd all felt they'd had a very lucky escape—to attack again so soon was tempting fate too far. Still, there'd been little they could do about it, and once again Albert had spent the previous day checking, cleaning, and stocking up with rations and water, and wondering what lay in store.

They had emerged through the chaos, dust, and congestion, just after half past nine in the morning, the din of battle shrieking overhead and booming in front of them. The Minefield Task Force was then dissolved and the riflemen took up position with their carriers and six-pounders just north of the Tel el Aqqaqir trig point.

Just after ten, the Sherwood Rangers and the rest of 8th Armoured Brigade also emerged from the minefield, although with the amount of dust and smoke from burning tanks and vehicles, they had some difficulty working out exactly where they were. Major Stanley Christopherson, back from hospital and commanding A Squadron once more, paused to ask some gunners where they were. They couldn't help, but did offer them "a most acceptable" mug of tea instead.

They then set off again, past bodies of dead British and Italian soldiers, already covered in talcum-powder dust. Having made contact with the Staffordshire Yeomanry, they halted once more. Shells whistled overhead. In front, a scout car with a red cross scurried then stopped, scurried then stopped, picking up the wounded and dying. Knocked-out tanks belched dark smoke into the sky. Once more a strange fog had settled over the battlefield. Stanley sent one of his troops forward. Enemy tanks rumbled into view and the troop opened fire claiming two destroyed.

The Sherwood Rangers stood their ground until afternoon, when they were ordered back to their start line to refuel. They arrived safely, but found themselves coming under fire from Axis artillery, an uncomfortable experience for all. In the lee of Stanley's tank, the officers of A Squadron, which now included the poet Keith Douglas, held a hasty conference. As a shell hurtled over them, they ducked, and then, once it had exploded, continued their discussion. Their Crusaders were already springing leaks—two would have to be taken back to the Light Aid Detachment workshops (LADs). Two men had also been killed earlier in the day when a shell exploded above their heads. Their tank was all right, but the turret was splattered thickly with blood; someone would have to clean it up before it could be used again—hardly the most pleasant of tasks. However, there would be no more battle for them that day. With dusk falling, they leaguered for the night.

The attack had finally brought relief for the Australians holed up in the Saucer. The previous day they had held out against attack after attack. The Blockhouse had become something of an international medical center, with the medical teams—both German and Australian—treating the wounded from both sides. But the Aussies' efforts had paid off. Only on the morning of 2 November, with the British armor breaking out into the open, did Rommel finally realize that the decisive British attack was not in the Australian sector. Calling off his assault against the shattered Australians, von Thoma's Afrika Korps were hurriedly brought south. They launched two attacks—one at 11 AM and another around two o'clock that afternoon: a last, desperate bid to wrench the battle back into a stalemate. Both attacks failed. One hundred seventeen German and Italian tanks were knocked out, seventy of which were German. The RAF had found few concentrations in the morning, but as the Afrika Korps had massed for their assaults later in the day, the Bostons and Mitchells had bombed them mercilessly. In the afternoon, Cobber Weinronk led a formation against the panzers. "Not much ack-ack," noted Cobber in his diary. "Reckon Jerry must have been having a gutful of raids by this time as all our squadrons have been giving him a hell of a workout. Wonder how long it's going to be before he breaks back. Can't see him holding out much longer."[355]

Late in the day, the Highlanders made a successful attack to the southwest, pushing back the Italian Trieste Division and capturing 160 prisoners. Since the launch of SUPERCHARGE, the front had taken a huge leap forward. The Maori, for example, had for once been able to stay put, dug into their new captured positions, and now held a stretch of the front line that linked up with the Australians.

"Monty now has Rommel by the pants," noted General Tuker in his battle diary that night, even though he despaired to hear that Eighth Army had lost ninety tanks during the day. But he was right, SUPER-CHARGE had done the trick. By nightfall, Rommel was left with just thirty-five serviceable tanks. "The enemy with his superior strength, is slowly levering us out of our position," he wrote to his wife that night. "That will mean the end. You can imagine how I feel. Air raid after air raid after air raid!"[356] He then gave orders for the withdrawal to Fuka, informing the OKW of his plans. During the night, the Italians at the southern end of the line were ordered back behind the old front line they had held before August; they were then to be taken to Fuka on whatever transport was available, while the Afrika Korps and remaining mobile troops would hold on in the north until as many infantry as possible had safely gotten away.

The previous night, Tommy Elmhirst's head of administration in Cairo, George Pirie, had rung and asked whether they needed anything. Only a bottle of gin and whisky, Tommy told him. That evening, Pirie flew himself to Burg el Arab armed with a bottle of both, which Tommy immediately took around to Mary Coningham's caravan.

He was a bit worried about the one Greek fighter squadron that had joined the Desert Air Force. They had thought they'd shot down their first enemy plane the previous day and had later celebrated in style. But then, earlier that morning, their wing HQ told them their kill had been credited to an Australian Spitfire pilot instead. As a result, the Greeks had been flung into a state of despair. On hearing this, Mary immediately rang up Fighter Control and told them the victory was definitely not the Spitfire's but the Greeks. Later, during supper, the Chief Intelligence Officer arrived and happily announced that the Greeks had finally opened their score. "All at supper were delighted," noted Tommy. "Neither Mary nor I said a word, nor even glanced at each other."[357]

The panzer army's fire had not gone out entirely, however. That night, 2 Rifle Brigade, along with the 7th Battalion and the King's Royal Rifle Corps, were ordered to make another night attack on the Axis defenses around Tel el Aqqaqir. The operation was hastily put together—the riflemen were unable to assemble properly and finally moved forward without sufficient transport, supplies, or guns and soon ran into trouble. There would be no repeat performance of Snipe, and at first light, when an order came to pull back, Albert Martin, for one, obeyed with great alacrity. As they hurried back across the Rahman Track, shelled and harried all the way, they saw over twenty Stukas approaching. So too, however, did a dozen Hurricanes, who immediately swooped in to attack. "The RAF, as ever, was equal to the task," wrote Albert, "and quickly saw them off." In the resulting mêlée, several of the Stukas were shot down, but more important, they jettisoned their bombs, not over the riflemen, but over the Axis positions.

The fortunes of the Sherwood Rangers were typical of the patchy and confused fighting that day. Moving out of their leaguer at two o'clock in the morning, they rumbled back to the front. After nine days of battle, mechanical problems were beginning to seriously affect their capabilities. Stanley Christopherson's A Squadron now had only three Crusaders left, although operating alongside them as a forward observation post was an artilleryman in a Honey. Stanley's own tank had broken down, so he had to catch a ride on another. Nonetheless, by first light, the regiment had put two Italian gun batteries out of action, and pushing forward over another shallow ridge, came upon a further battery of five 74mm anti-tank guns. This time, the Italians manning it immediately showed the white flag. "John Fox then rather rushed the next ridge," noted Stanley, "and immediately had his tank knocked out by another battery behind." A Squadron now had only two Crusaders left, but while Stanley had gone back to talk to the CO, his remaining Crusader had hurried to rescue John Fox and his wounded crew, and captured a further four Germans. By this time, they needed to refuel once more, which meant turning around and trundling back to their supply echelon. In the meantime, Keith Douglas had arrived with a new tank. Having refueled, back they went to the front. They sensed the battle was nearly over, but none of them had much idea of what was going on or when the final breakthrough might occur. It was now afternoon, and spotting two 88s, they opened fire, destroying one while the other was hastily hitched to a lorry and hurried off into the desert.

The German front was now crumbling fast, with Rommel's withdrawal proceeding as planned. Then, to his amazement, at around half past one in the afternoon, he received a personal message from Hitler ordering them to stand firm. There must be "no other road than that to victory or death." Rommel knew he was being asked the impossible, but obeyed, making an effort to reform up on a line some miles to the west of the Rahman Track. But his retreat had already begun; it was too late to halt it now.

At Air Headquarters, Tommy Elmhirst recognized on 3 November that victory was theirs. Since the opening salvoes of the battle he had written up a daily "Evening News," which he sent to all the squadrons in order to keep them informed with the progress of the battle. That night, he added the word *victory*, although there were some at Air HQ who thought he was being somewhat premature. Then during the weekly open-air movie he stopped it halfway through and announced that the enemy was in full retreat the length of the front. "The Hun must have heard the cheers," he noted. "I don't think he can ever recover in Africa . . . let's hope it's the beginning of the end."[358] Certainly, the air forces had had a phenomenal day. All morning, the weight of the air effort had been concentrated on targets on the ground, mainly to the west of Tel el Aqqaqir. But from around noon it became clear that enemy troops were withdrawing, so they were directed onto moving enemy targets heading west. Around five hundred sorties were flown that afternoon alone.

As the endgame of the battle began to be played out, there was at last a role for General Tuker's Indians. He had been champing at the bit throughout the battle, deeply frustrated to have been given no real active role to play other than a series of dummy attacks, but when Monty heard news that the Italians were pulling out from their positions in the south, he called upon Tuker's crack 5th Brigade to join the Highland Division and to cut a lane through the minefields southwest of Tel el Aqqaqir, so that the following morning the armor could pour through.

The operation was a success. In the early hours of 4 November, the Indians and Highlanders set off behind another relentless barrage. Just after seven in the morning they were through and the barrage lifted. For a moment, the desert was quiet but for the crackle of small-arms fire. Then from the east a low thunder could be heard, a rumble that grew louder and louder. Suddenly British tanks emerged through the dust, and plunging out of the gap, began wheeling north.

Further north, the Sherwood Rangers and the tanks of the 1st Armoured Division pushed on across the Rahman Track only to find that Tel el Aqqaqir had been abandoned. As the British armor nosed forward, so the cohesion of the panzer army finally fell apart. Von Thoma was captured fighting a rearguard action northwest of Tel el Aqqaqir, and at 5:30 PM Rommel finally issued the order to withdraw—an order he should have stuck to the day before.

The Battle of Alamein was over. Churchill had his victory at last. Now it was time to put the second part of the grand plan into action.

CHAPTER 16

Lighting the Torch—
5–11 November, 1942

LIEUTENANT RANDOLPH PAULSEN was having a miserable time crossing the Atlantic, not because he was seasick or nervous about what lay ahead, but because his leg was in constant agony and he wondered how he was ever going to make it off the ship. The accident had happened just a few days before they'd departed, while he'd been taking his platoon—3 platoon, L Company of the 15th Infantry Regiment—on a speed march. Jumping into a sand pit, he'd landed on a stone and twisted his ankle. Randy was furious with himself. The entire 3rd Infantry Division had been practicing assault landings during the past couple of weeks, and so although he had no idea where they would be heading, had sussed out that they were about to be sent overseas and he had wanted to make sure he went with them.

Taking himself off to the battalion dispensary that night, Randy had his swollen ankle strapped up, but later, when he went to the bathroom, he noticed he had several lumps as big as hen eggs on his groin and red streaks running down his legs. Randy limped off to the dispensary once more, only to be told that he had blood poisoning. He'd snapped his Achilles tendon and the straps had been put on so tightly they'd cut off the blood flow and his legs had become infected. "You'll miss the invasion," the doctor, Captain Cunningham told him. "You're not leaving like this." In fact, Captain Cunningham wanted him to get to a hospital bed. But having been given permission to go and collect some things, Randy went back to his platoon and didn't return to the aid station. That same night the regiment boarded a train that was to take them to Hampton Roads Port of Embarkation on Chesapeake Bay, Virginia, and although Randy couldn't even get his shoe on, he made sure he was on that train with them.

He'd heard that once boarded on an outbound ship, it was impossible to get off again as it was considered too much of a security risk. "I had a hell of a job getting up the gangplank," says Randy, but just about managed it and then hobbled into the sick bay. There were two navy doctors and also Captain Cunningham, who was somewhat surprised to see Randy again so soon. The naval doctors were all for amputating his leg, but fortunately for Randy, Captain Cunningham managed to dissuade them and instead they simply pumped him full of sulphanilamide. "For three days I didn't know where I was or what was happening," says Randy. "I woke up somewhere out at sea with my leg in a sling."

Lieutenant Paulsen was from the Bronx, New York City, where he'd worked on the advertisement desk of the *New York Daily News*. He hadn't thought too much about the war before Pearl Harbor. On that fateful day, he'd been at home with his parents and two younger brothers listening to a football game on the radio when it was interrupted with the news of the Japanese attack. Randy didn't even know where Pearl Harbor was. He'd already registered for service, as demanded of him, but after the US joined the war, he did call up the draft board and try and hurry things up a bit. It worked: a few days later he was called up. On his father's advice he tried to join the cavalry, but was sent off for infantry training at Camp Croft, where he was soon singled out to become an NCO. Before the war, he'd gone through Marine ROTC (Reserve Officer Training Corps) but had gotten out because he'd been expected to pay for his own uniform, and at the time couldn't afford it; but his time with the ROTC was on his record. So he spent six weeks at a training school for NCOs and then one day was told he'd been selected to go to OCS (Officer Candidates School). He passed the boards and was packed off to Fort Benning, where the officer cadets were trained in map reading, tactics, terrain appreciation, and vast amounts of physical exercise.

Randy was only commissioned on 4 September, 1942. The 3rd Division had been training on the West Coast, but rather than hack over to Washington, Randy was given leave until the division was moved over to the East Coast for assault training before being shipped overseas. Then he took over 3rd Platoon of L Company of the 15th Infantry Regiment. Just six weeks later he was being shipped across the Atlantic.

After about a week at sea, Randy began to feel a bit better, so he managed to get himself up on deck. "Everywhere you could look there were ships," he says. "I'd never seen so many in my life." In fact, over a hundred had now assembled to make up the Western Task Force, although not until several days after the first ships had slipped their moorings did the convoy finally come together, and even then strict radio silence had been maintained.

The naval operation from Britain was even more complicated. Admiral Cunningham's brief had been to arrange six advance-supply convoys and their escorts totaling over a hundred ships, as well as four assault convoys and escorts of more than two hundred ships. These would carry 38,500 British and American troops and equipment, stores, and supplies for the invasion. In addition, orders had to be drawn up for purely naval forces, separate from the destroyer escorts, which, in addition to the hundred vessels already based at Gibraltar, meant another 176 of varying types, from battleships and aircraft carriers to submarines and MTBs. "The whole large-scale movement was extremely complicated," noted Admiral Cunningham, "and success depended upon rigid adherence to a timetable." Simply working out and writing all the various orders was a feat in itself, taking four days of near-continuous dictation to two teams of stenographers. A major headache was the problem of congestion at Gibraltar. The advance supply convoys left Britain through the course of October. At Gib, ammunition, equipment, crated aircraft, and numerous stores had to be hastily unloaded and quickly moved on again.

ABC had arrived at Gibraltar on 1 November and immediately hoisted his flag as naval commander Allied Expeditionary Force (NCXF). He soon installed himself in the recently built tunnel under the Rock, home to naval, army, and air force staffs and the operation's command and control center. Although well protected, these rooms were damp and unpleasant places in which to work, and Cunningham took another office at the dockyard, where he could watch the various ships assembling. Nonetheless, despite these discomforts, he was thrilled to be amongst the seagoing navy once again.

In the tunnel were communications systems and huge wall charts on which ABC and his staff could anxiously watch the progress of the convoys. German U-boats had been very active in both the Atlantic and inside the Mediterranean. As ABC was all too aware, if just one of the troop ships were to be picked off by the wolf packs, the result might have been disastrous. To counter this potential menace, U-boat bases had been targeted by US and RAF bombers flying from Britain, the RAF's Coastal Command had been particularly active, and extra anti-submarine ships patrolled the Bay of Biscay. Yet despite these measures, and despite the hefty escorts laid on for the convoys, they remained vulnerable to attack at all times. On 30 October, for example, eight merchant vessels—fortunately nothing to do with TORCH—were sunk as their convoy passed west of the Canary Islands en route to Britain, only a hundred-odd miles south from where the Western Task Force would shortly be passing.

For the Western Task Force the other major worry was the weather. Storms and even choppy seas could wreak havoc, and potentially ruin the Casablanca landings, but at least they did not have to pass through the eight-mile wide straits that led into the mouth of the Mediterranean. ABC was extremely aware of the dangers lurking there: it was only three months since the aircraft carrier HMS *Eagle* had been sunk by U-boats. Cunningham had spent much of his time as naval C-in-C of the Mediterranean trying to secure the safe passage of ships through the Med. All too often his greatest efforts had been unsuccessful.

The US 33rd Fighter Group was originally due to be sent to the Middle East, but at the last minute, with their aircraft already crated up and ready for shipping, it was decided they were needed for TORCH instead, and so seventy-seven P-40 Warhawks and their pilots found themselves on board the carrier USS *Chenango,* a converted Great Lakes oil tanker, heading across the Atlantic.

For the first few days there wasn't much to do. Twenty-two-year-old Lieutenant James E. Reed whiled away the hours taking the guns out of his plane then painting "Renee" on the engine cowling, the nickname of his girlfriend, Irene Frey. There was occasional guard duty and the cleaning of his six machine guns, but the rest of the time he and the other pilots made the most of the plentiful meals they were given and played cards. Like most American pilots, Jim was never one to pass on a game of poker or blackjack. "We still haven't found out where we're headed for," he noted in his diary after a day at sea, although over the ship's general announcing system the captain did reveal that their ultimate goal was "control of the entire Mediterranean area."[359]

Jim was from Memphis, Tennessee, one of three brothers. Most people had suffered during the Great Depression, and Jim's family was no exception. When he was six, his father had to sell their farm and they all moved to Memphis. There his father took a job as a trolley car driver, while Jim and his brothers made their own contribution by caddying at the nearby golf course whenever they could. In 1935, when Jim was fifteen, his father managed to buy a farm seventy-five miles outside Memphis, although Jim's Uncle Sim took it on to begin with. The three brothers spent two summers there, before moving in for good.

Jim became interested in flying as a boy in Memphis, where he used to see formations of P-26 fighter planes fly over. Later, when he was at college, he, like Duke Ellington, was accepted into one of the civilian flying schools. He enjoyed flying every bit as much as he thought he would and so on graduating from college in the spring of 1941, signed up for the US Air Corps, and after one last summer in Tennessee, was finally called up in September. Just over a year later, he was on his way to war. Like Duke, he was now an experienced pilot with over three hundred hours' flying time under his belt, but he was pitifully ignorant of what lay ahead. No RAF combat veterans had been sent their way, nor had there been lectures on the capabilities of the various German aircraft, such as the Me 109. He knew little about fighter tactics—mostly they just practiced formation flying. Occasionally there'd be a bit of gunnery practice, shooting at a towed target. And unlike Duke and the fighter boys from the 57th, Jim and his fellows in the 33rd were to be going into combat with no time to acclimate, nor with any experienced pilots flying alongside them, or battle-hardened allies to show them the ropes; there had been no attempt by the air force commanders planning TORCH to try and adopt the levels of close cooperation that existed between American and British air forces in the Middle East.

On 2 November, the weather over the Atlantic began to roughen; the following day it was worse. By the fourth, they were sailing through a full-blooded Atlantic storm. It was precisely the kind of weather the planners had most feared. That night, Jim was on watch from midnight to four in the morning and the ship was rolling so much he worried that the planes stacked on deck might come loose. "The next morning," he noted, "I found out that the carrier nearly capsized. It only missed its maximum roll angle by three degrees."[360] If it were still like this on 8 November, it would make the landings around Casablanca impossible.

"Now we have to turn retreat into rout," noted Tommy Elmhirst on 3 November, "and the Hun will not get back along the road to Tobruk as scotfree as we got back in June." Unbeknownst to Mary Coningham, Tommy had earlier arranged for a supply column to be brought up to the front specifically to help with a rapid advance to Daba should the opportunity arise. That night, at 6:40 PM, Mary told his forces that Operation BUSTER, the pursuit plan, was about to be set in motion. This had been prepared over a month before. Tommy had arranged for their air forces to be split into two groups. Force A would provide direct support for the Eighth Army, while Force B would act as a reserve and backup for Force A, and would also protect the Eighth Army's lines of supply. Once again, the system of leap-frogging, particularly of ground support, was to be put into action. Entire fighter wings were ready to move in fifteen minutes, with ground crews and detachments of sappers (ready to deal with potential mines and booby traps) poised well forward to get going at a moment's notice.

On the evening of 3 November, however, the RAF suffered its worst losses since the opening days of the Gazala Battles: fifteen fighters were shot down, of which eleven were Hurricanes, making a total of twenty-four for the whole day. This goes some way to explaining Mary's unusual caution the next day. Tommy Elmhirst urged him to send forward a fighter-bomber wing to Daba, ahead of the advancing Eighth Army and ahead of the retreating panzer army armor, but Mary could not be swayed; he could remember only too well the last time the Germans were on the retreat a year before, when their fighter force had acted most effectively as a rearguard. Nor would he allow a Hurricane "tank-busting" squadron armed with heavy cannons to join in the attacks along the coast. Tommy was disappointed. "This is a pity, I think," he noted, "as we are as strong in squadrons as we were when we began the battle . . . It may mean the Hun has a day on the road out of reach of air attack."

He wasn't far wrong, and certainly air operations on 4 November lacked the intensity of the previous day. Billy Drake's 112 Squadron did not take to the air at all until just after four in the afternoon, when the entire squadron took off on a single bombing raid on the landing grounds at Daba. Cobber Weinronk flew once, in the morning, but noted there wasn't much of a target. "Jerry seems to thinning out," he wrote, although a number of Messerschmitt 109s did try to intercept them.[361] Tommy Thompson and Johnnie Fairbairn did not fly at all.

On the ground, Eighth Army also struggled to get very far. Desultory fighting continued during the first half of the morning, but the only way for the British to make inroads west was either to break through the enemy's delaying positions six miles beyond Tel el Aqqaqir, or outflank them to the south through the channels cut by the Highlanders and the 5th Indian Brigade. The enemy, on the other hand, had the clear, unbroken coast road along which they could make their escape and their lines of supply now ahead of them, rather than behind. In contrast, Eighth Army's supply echelons and other support units still had to pass through the corridors cut through the minefields, where congestion was a serious problem. At Gazala, Rommel already had his panzer army clear of the British minefields before the main pursuit took place; but Montgomery now had no such advantage.

Even so, General Tuker had worked out exactly how to catch up, overtake, and then cut off the retreating panzer army. His leading troops had reached their objectives three miles south of Tel el Aqqaqir at 7:10 AM that morning, and soon after, the rest of the 5th Indian Brigade caught up with them. After a few hours' rest and a drink and a meal, Tuker fully expected them to be off again. He had also prepared the rest of the division for rapid advance, organizing them so that they could take up the pursuit the moment the break came. "We knew we were the only fresh, desert-worthy troops now left in Eighth Army," noted Tuker.[362] He reckoned they could cross straight over the desert and reach the all-important Halfaya Pass—a bottleneck which was the most obvious place to cut off the enemy—by the morning of 6 November, in just two days' time. Tuker was looking forward to it, and for a chance to show what his Indians could do.

But yet again, Tuker was to be disappointed. With mounting frustration, he watched as the armor ponderously crawled through the congested corridors at the front. He could not detect any sense of urgency at all—and even worse, 4th Indian was ordered to hand over its transport to the Greek Brigade and to stay behind to help clear up the battlefield. Why the 4th Indian was not used in the chase is not clear. Tuker was convinced he knew the reason: Monty had been rejected by the Indian Army after passing out of Sandhurst and had been prejudiced against the Indian Army ever since. Whether this was true is debatable, but certainly no plan of pursuit had been properly prepared. Petrol originally earmarked for the chase had been used up and not replaced, while little consideration had been given to having a task force of motorized infantry and guns fit and ready as Tuker had prepared. Clearly such a spearhead would have been more effective than mechanically unreliable, fuel-guzzling tanks.

Certainly this was borne out in the movement of the Sherwood Rangers, who only began to move at about six o'clock in the evening on 4 November. In the early hours of 5 November, they tried a night march along with the rest of the brigade, but as Stanley Christopherson noted, this was hardly a success. "The brigade had not formed up properly before starting; anyhow, the regiment was badly out of formation—and as a result we got lost for a while." By morning, they had managed to sort themselves out, and having now cleared the Axis rearguard position, set off in a north-westerly direction towards Galal Station, a distance of over thirty miles. En route, they started "swanning"—picking up prisoners and capturing loot, which, of course, further held up their pursuit. By afternoon they had reached the station and had shot up a column of enemy trucks and Italian tanks. When a further formation of Italian tanks approached they blasted those as well. "It's quite a debateable point whether they were coming in to surrender," wrote Stanley, "as we found a white flag afterward, but we made a horrible mess of them." The regiment's medical officer was kept busy patching up Italian and German wounded. Stanley came across one man who had managed to tie a tourniquet around his leg even though the lower part had been horrifically shattered. "It made us think how illogical war was," he noted, "first of all we do our best to kill these Germans and Italians, shelling and machinegunning them, and afterwards we do all that we can to save their lives."

Two Rifle Brigade had moved forward about eight miles on 4 November, but only finally set off in pursuit the following day after leaguering with the rest of 7th Motor Brigade. First port of call was Daba, which they reached by 10:30 in the morning—only to find it already clean of enemy, bar a handful of stragglers. Time was then badly wasted by repeated changes to orders, and certainly there was a feeling within the battalion that had they been sent straight away to a point west of Mersa Matruh, they would have had a far greater chance of overtaking and then cutting off the enemy. Much to the delight of Albert Martin, they were eventually sent deep into the desert, having been ordered to make for Bir Khalda, some forty miles due south of Mersa, but the panzer army now had a massive head start. Albert was confident they could catch up and cut them off, but the odds were looking less likely with every passing hour.

On the evening of 4 November, Monty invited the captured General von Thoma to dinner. Carol Mather watched on with great interest, noting that the German was "very polite and not at all surly or arrogant." His English wasn't too good, so an interpreter was brought in. "Now tell the general," said Monty, "that I have enjoyed the battle very much." When this was repeated, Carol watched von Thoma give "a sort of sickly smile."

"Tell the general that I met Rommel once in August and I beat him; and I have met him again now, and shall do the same thing!" said a crowing Montgomery, who had just received a message at the dinner table reporting the capture of Fuka. "Von Thoma was astonished," jotted Carol in his diary that night. "Monty was visibly enjoying himself."[363]

Monty could be allowed his moment of triumph, but for all his boasting, he was aware that the panzer army was slipping away. Earlier in the day, Carol Mather had taken Monty to see Gatehouse of 10th Armoured Division. The army commander had told him to "apply ginger" and to get a move on, but tanks were hardly the fastest most reliable machines in the world.[364] As General Tuker commented in his diary at 11 that night, "Boche is on the run but our armor hasn't yet broken through. Result is that we'll miss half his army." Once more, Tuker's prediction was spot on.

Although Monty was already beginning to shroud the victory in terms of his own single-handed achievement, he was well aware of the role the RAF had played. "They are winning this battle for me," he'd told Horrocks on 2 November.[365] Their contribution had been immense, and as big a factor as any in the victory. Von Thoma, when interrogated, also made great play of the enormous effect the ceaseless air assault had made on the panzer army. Rommel too blamed defeat firstly on his own insubstantial supply of material, and secondly on Allied air superiority. "If the enemy has air supremacy and makes full use of it, then one's own command is forced to suffer."[366] Mary Coningham certainly had made good use of it. His air forces had even been instrumental in ensuring the artillery had been given accurate targets. "The value of vertical air photos prior to and throughout the battle was immense," it was recorded in the

Royal Artillery's official report on the battle. "Practically all CB [counter-battery] locations and the exact whereabouts of enemy defended localities were based on air photos."[367]

Moreover, the way the US forces had been absorbed was exemplary, and a benchmark for future Anglo-US cooperation. By 5 November, Duke Ellington's 57th Fighter Group had accounted for thirty-seven confirmed enemy aircraft shot down, including sixteen 109s, for the loss of only three of their own. "These results can be attributed to both the excellent training our men have had at home along with the training they received from the RAF after arriving at the theater," reported General Brereton.[368] Meanwhile, the two heavy bomber units—Willie Chapman's 98th and the 376th Bomb Groups—had continued to pound Tobruk and Benghazi, furthering hampering Axis efforts to resupply.

The Allied air forces still had a crucial role to play in the pursuit. Mary Coningham may have shown unusual caution on 4 November, but the next day, the Desert Air Force was on the move once more. Air HQ—and Army Headquarters—finally left Burg el Arab, moving eighty miles to Daba, although Tommy Elmhirst was already preparing supplies to go forward for at least two moves ahead to Bagush and then Gambut, their old base during the Gazala Battles. Bombers attacked the coast road relentlessly, but most fighters were now required—at Monty's behest—to provide air cover for his pursuers on the ground. Bombing was further inhibited by the problems of correctly identifying targets on the ground. Tedder, who had come up the front to see what was going on, was horrified to discover that Eighth Army's mobile operations room was nowhere to be seen, even though it was due to be reporting to the RAF the progress of the pursuit on an hour-by-hour basis. They had gone forward and had been enveloped by the fog of war. Meanwhile, the New Zealanders, for example, were reportedly operating in an area of seventy square miles around Fuka—a large area in which the RAF dared not attack for fear of causing a major incident of friendly fire.

For the most part, Eighth Army was now advancing in four distinct columns across different parts of the desert and at different rates, and it was almost impossible to keep track of where they all were. On the afternoon of 6 November, Carol Mather was sent off along the coastal road to try and find out how far he could get without meeting the enemy, and to try and discover where the main Axis concentrations were. The road was nose to tail with traffic, no one seemed to know where the enemy was, and it soon got dark. On the drive back, he was bombed, so that by the time he finally reached Army HQ again, he was hardly the wiser for his efforts.

The same day, Mary Coningham and Tommy Elmhirst found themselves a wisp away from being taken prisoner. Also suffering from the mixed reports about the reach of Eighth Army's advance, Mary decided they should take the Storch up for a recce of their own. "I can land any-where in this," he told Tommy, "so we will see how far forward we can get."[369] Rain had begun to fall and by the time they reached Bagush, roughly half way to Mersa, it was getting dark so they landed. Finding Tommy's transport staff officer already there, they jumped into his jeep and continued by road. After a couple of hours' driving, they saw the lights of a camp, but as they approached, two officers hailed them in Ger-man. Mary and Tommy leaped out of the jeep and plunged into the dark, but fortunately their driver kept his head and turned the car around, switched off the lights, and soon picked them up, heading out of harm's way as fast as they could. "We breathed again," noted Tommy. "The idea of the commander of the Desert Air Force and his second man being put in the bag as prisoners for the rest of the war was not a happy thought."

"Ring out the bells!" General Alexander signaled to Churchill on 6 No-vember. "Prisoners now 20,000, tanks 350, guns 400, MT *several thousand*. Our advanced mobile forces are south of Mersa Matruh. 8th Army is ad-vancing."[370] But the rain had begun to fall—earlier in winter than was usual. Air operations were brought almost to a standstill. In the desert, the mobile forces south of Mersa also became bogged down by the tor-rential downpours. "We got soaked to the skin," says Albert, "and were freezing cold. We were bogged down in mashed, gritty sand and had to stop." They were also short of fuel—the supply echelons had not been able to keep up. Along the coast, the Sherwood Rangers also ground to a halt—their B Echelon, rather than going along the coast road, had tried to follow their tanks across the desert and also became stuck. "The rain continued practically throughout the night," noted Stanley Christopher-son. "We slept in our tanks. Not a very comfortable night."

The panzer army had already given itself a head start on 4 November, and along the metaled coast road, the rain scarcely held them up at all. Now the complete annihilation Monty had hoped for was slipping even further out of reach.

As Harry Butcher prepared to leave London for Gibraltar, he put his di-ary in order and then left it to be put onto microfilm. He hoped that one day, he and Ike might have "fun" going back over the pages recording these trying but absorbing days. "Maybe in retrospect," he noted, "they will seem less trying than at the time we lived through them."[371]

The storms that were afflicting the ships at sea in the Atlantic were also buffeting southern England. Ike had to make a tough call as to whether they should even fly—rain, fog, and ten-tenths cloud cover were hardly the best flying conditions for taking the allied commander and his team off to war. But he decided to take the risk, and he and his staff finally left England early morning on Thursday, 5 November, part of a flight of five B-17s. A sixth, with the US air commander, General Doolittle, on board, was left on the ground with a mechanical problem; they followed a day later. Cross currents around the Rock and congestion on the runway brought further anxiety to a deeply unpleasant journey, but at 4:20 PM the same day, Ike safely touched down at Gibraltar.

That same night, the Eastern Task Force began passing through the Straits of Gibraltar, still in complete silence and completely blacked out. Many of the escorting warships had to call in at Gibraltar to refuel. It was a nail-biting period, but between 7:30 PM on 5 November and 4 AM on 7 November, the entire Eastern and Central Task Forces successfully passed into the Mediterranean. Only shortly after, at 5:35 AM on 7 November, did Allied headquarters receive word that a ship in the Western Task Force, the USS *Thomas Stone*, had been torpedoed. She was carrying 1,400 men, but soon after, another signal arrived saying she was now being safely towed and would still make the landings, albeit a bit late.

There was still much over which Ike and his commanders had little control. The Spanish were causing him much worry, as was the whereabouts of General Giraud. Only on 1 November, Murphy had signaled saying it was impossible to get Kingpin—Giraud's code name—until 20 November, and therefore the invasion should be delayed. This was clearly little more than nervous jitters on Murphy's part, and sure enough, before they left England, word arrived that Giraud would be on board the submarine as planned. The sub had since been sent to southern France to pick him up, but only a single, confusing message had come from them since: "Task gone, radio failing." At Allied HQ, they hoped that they'd meant "task done," but were left wondering. At the Rock, Ike had called together a meeting of his top officers and commanders to discuss how they should handle Giraud should he balk at their plans. ABC tried to assure them all would be well. "He's thrown his coat over the fence," he smiled. "He will do what he's told."[372]

Later, sitting in Ike's room at Government House, Butch listened to Ike and Mark Clark "opining" about their current situation. Ike wished he could be leading an invasion directly into France—he still hadn't come around to the North Africa idea. Both men were conscious that before long they would be either "lions or lice," and both lamented the political role they had been forced to play and wished they could have been commanding divisions instead. "But," said Ike, "we should be thankful for the chance to make a mark in history, an opportunity given to few men." It had already been agreed that Clark was to fly to Algiers as soon as possible to set up the advanced Allied headquarters, but he was only half joking when he suggested he might just keep on going and fly straight to Central Africa, using the gold he would be carrying for bribing natives and putting the whole TORCH operation behind him.[373]

On Saturday, 7 November—D-Day minus one—Ultra revealed that the Germans had sighted the convoys; indeed, later that day enemy reconnaissance planes were spotted shadowing the Eastern Task Force. But the message also revealed that, incredibly, they still did not suspect an invasion of Northwest Africa, even though Berlin was also now aware of the massive increase in traffic at Gibraltar. Rather, they seemed to believe the armadas were either an extra-large convoy to Malta, or possibly even a landing force aimed at somewhere between Tripoli and Benghazi or Sardinia, or even Sicily. The elaborately deceptive course taken from Britain and the ruse of using wireless telegraphy traffic normally adopted for Malta convoys had clearly done the trick.

The weather in the Atlantic also seemed to have died down. An American submarine stationed off the coast of Casablanca reported that the sea had calmed considerably and that conditions at the landings were now much improved. "The text of the weather report," noted Butch, "indicates that Providence or one of Ike's lucky charms is effective."[374] And further good news arrived: Giraud had been safely picked up and was on his way. A Catalina flying boat was sent out to meet the submarine, and it brought Giraud to Gibraltar around four that afternoon. At 5:20 PM, Ike gave the operation the final go-ahead. "Warning order," he signaled, "H-Hour confirmed November 8. For East and Center, 1 AM. For West, about 4:30 AM."

As soon as Giraud arrived, dressed in a shabby civilian suit, he was whisked away into a private conference with Ike and Clark. ABC was not a part of the discussions, but when Ike reappeared at 7:30 pm looking tired and worried, he guessed correctly that not all was well. Over dinner with the allied commander, Cunningham heard that Giraud was being more than difficult. In the meeting room, Clark had told the French general, "We would like the honorable general to know that the time of his usefulness to the Americans and for the restoration of the glory that once was France is *now*."

"But what would the French people think of me?" Giraud asked, if he were to take a subordinate role. "What about the prestige of Giraud; what about my family?"[375] This was of absolutely no concern to either Ike or Clark. "We had hoped that Giraud's influence would unite the many divergent factors in French North Africa," wrote ABC, "and end any opposition to the Anglo-American landing."[376] Instead, it seemed all the effort and anxiety caused by bringing Giraud to Gibraltar had been for noth-

ing; even more insanely, he was also demanding the convoys to be diverted to southern France. After dinner, the discussions continued, but
Giraud would not budge. Some time after eleven that night, Clark finally
walked out. "Old gentleman," Clark told him, "I hope you know that
from now on your ass is out in the snow."[377]

As darkness fell, the Central Task Force carrying the US 1st Infantry Division and Army Rangers melted into the night, still steaming eastward as
though headed for Malta. Sixty miles due south, the towns of Oran and
Arzew were settling down for just another Saturday night, their lights
twinkling across the sea. There was no blackout here. Lying further north
than Sicily or Malta, the Algerian coast was very like southern Europe;
certainly, the fertile strip that lay between the sea and the mountains behind had little in common with the desert coastline of Egypt and Libya.
Nor were their towns and cities particularly Arabic or African in feel: in
Oran, three quarters of its population were European and its boulevards
and houses owed more to the French than its Moorish origins.

Now in darkness, the convoy dramatically turned from its eastward
course, separated, then headed toward the coast, one force toward the
port of Arzew, twenty-five miles east of Oran and code-named Z, while the
rest went toward two landing sites farther west of Oran, X and Y. Having
made their rendezvous with the beacon submarine just before 10 PM, the
ships for X and Y then split, and headed for their anchorage points, some
five miles off the coast. Out of the darkness a French convoy suddenly appeared, directly in front of the approaching ships for X, and so they were
forced to slow down; the French convoy turned tail and fled, but its passage also delayed the minesweepers set to clear the passage to the shore.

Despite this, all transport ships in the three sectors had dropped anchor before midnight and landing craft were being lowered into the water.
Of the three sectors, Z had by far the most men assigned to it: here the
Rangers had been designated with capturing two gun batteries and the
port itself, while on the beaches south of the town, the 16th and 18th Regimental Combat Teams would land, secure the southern end of Arzew including the naval barracks, then head inland. Oran would be taken in a
pincer movement. US paratroopers were also due to land and take the two
crucial airfields at Tafaraoui and La Senia, south of Oran.

Off the coast, troops huddled together in the cold night air, their
packs on their backs and rifles slung over their shoulders as they prepared to clamber onto the nets and down into the shallow-bottomed boats
swaying on the sea below. From the coast, lights flickered, but not a shot
had been fired. Their arrival was still a secret.

* * *

At 12:40 AM, on Sunday, 8 November, Harry Butcher was at Government House with the radio on waiting for the president's and Ike's broadcasts to the people of France. "I don't want to miss my favorite radio hour," he noted. At the same time, twenty-four landing craft carrying the 39th US Infantry Division left the crippled USS *Thomas Stone*, heading for the beaches around Casablanca.

The broadcasts were transmitted later—at 1:20 AM—along with a spokesman for Eisenhower giving instructions to the French and other citizens of North Africa. "Ought to be a good story for the Sunday A.M.s back home," noted Butch, as ever, his mind thinking in terms of media coverage. Overhead, he heard Spitfires, testing their guns with short bursts. Searchlights swept the sky around Gib.

First to land at Arzew were the Rangers, spearheading the attack. Capturing the port was seen as essential—landing heavy equipment would be impossible without it. But to achieve this task, taking out the two batteries was the first priority. The first, at Fort du Nord, was on top of the hill that dominated the harbor, while the other, Forte de la Pointe, was at the foot of the hill on the northeast corner of the port. Colonel Darby decided to split his force into two. Two companies, under Major Dammer, were to take the fort and the harbor, while the rest, including Colonel Darby and Battalion Sergeant-Major Bing Evans, would land on a tiny beach around the headland from the harbor and then travel up the hill and take Fort du Nord from the rear.

Major Dammer's force were in their LCAs [landing craft assault] by 12:15 AM, and at 1:30 AM, guided by the lighthouse and entrance lights, entered the harbor unchallenged and with the boom, thankfully, still down. Scrambling onto the quay, they swept past one sentry and then opened fire on another as he tried to flee—these were the first shots fired. Soon after, sirens began wailing, but the Rangers were already at the fort gate. With shouts of "Hi ho, Silver!" they charged the gun positions without a further shot being fired. Inside the fort, they caught the garrison sleeping, and after a few bursts of their machine guns and having lobbed a few grenades, captured forty-two Frenchmen, including the commandant, who had been in bed with his mistress.

Meanwhile, Colonel Darby and the other Rangers had set off in two LCAs toward their landing point. Bing Evans had studied the sand table models on the long trip out, and memorized them too, and now, as they sped across the inky sea he felt a great sense of exhilaration and anticipation. "This is what we had trained for," he explains, "and I felt anxious to get on with it." The marker for the beach was a buoy, but they had trouble finding it in the dark. "Colonel, I think we've missed our landmark," Bing told Colonel Darby. Darby realized he was right, and after turning back soon found the buoy and the beach. "That was the only hitch we had," says Bing.

They were ashore by 1:30 AM, and an hour and a half later reached Fort du Nord, where they silently set up their heavy mortars. Three companies then approached the wire and when they began to draw fire from the fort, the Rangers opened up with their mortars and rushed the battery. "We were in amongst them before they knew what hit them," says Bing. After preparing the guns for demolition, they sent up a green flare, which informed those watching at sea—including General Terry Allen, commander of the 1st Infantry Division—that the battery had been captured. Shortly after, the two Ranger forces made contact. The port had fallen.

At 3 AM on board HMS *Orbita,* Margaret Hornback and a number of other nurses from the 48th Surgical Hospital were called to battle stations. They looked much like GIs, dressed in olive belted army coveralls and even coal-scuttle tin helmets; the white uniforms they'd worn back in the States and the blue dresses provided in England had been put to one side. Practicality was what was important now. Through the darkness she could hear artillery fire and watched tracer bullets spitting brightly for the first time. "It was a terrible feeling not to be able to know what was happening," she wrote. Later, as the first glimmer of dawn spread over the sea, she spotted small flags at intervals breaking the water, which with her inexperienced eye she assumed must be submarines; only later did someone explain that they were markers signifying channels cleared of mines. She couldn't understand how the Royal Navy had managed it without being seen.

Meanwhile, the other landings in the X and Y sector had met with no opposition, and along the Z sector beaches, resistance was light to say the least. The Bowles twins landed with the 2nd Battalion of the 18th Infantry Regiment as part of the second wave, around 8:30 AM, and immediately followed behind the 1st Battalion, who'd already moved on toward the village of St. Cloud, some seven miles southwest of the town. Like Bing Evans, they felt they were well trained and ready for action. And any slight feelings of nerves were soon swept aside as they stepped quite casually from their LCA and onto African sand for the first time. It would not always be so easy.

In fact, around Oran itself, opposition had been quite stiff. Separate to the landings was an operation to take the harbor at Oran, code-named RESERVIST, specifically with the aim of preventing the French destroying their ships and the port installations. The time of the attack was discretionary and its commander had a free hand to cancel it altogether should the French be found to be both alert and hostile; it had been realized that the operation could not succeed in the face of serious opposition. If even so much as a single gun fired at them, they were to retire.

Similar plans had been made for Safi and Algiers, and in each case, just two ships were to be used, which would storm through the harbor entrance and off-load troops tasked with capturing any guns and taking the port. This was one thing against a small port such as Safi, and when backed by plenty of naval support, but at Oran, which was heavily defended not only with onshore batteries but warships as well, the plan was somewhat overoptimistic, especially since the two ships to be used, HMS *Walney* and *Hartland,* were aging former Great Lakes cutters that had been handed over to the Royal Navy in 1940 as part of the lend lease agreement, and hardly suited to the job in hand. On board were nearly four hundred US infantry, and although the Stars and Stripes was flown from the two ships, the British crews insisted on flying the white ensign as well. This was not sensible, as Oran had been the site of the British attack on the French Navy in July 1940, the cause of the greatest animosity between the two nations ever since. Anti-British feelings ran high; in the town, General Mast's underground resistance network had already largely failed.

The cutters had been just offshore from the harbor at 2:45 AM, when the lights in Oran went out and air-raid sirens rang out. A warning from the task force command ship then arrived telling them not to start a fight unless they had to. Despite all this, the force's commander, Captain Peters, ordered the two ships in. *Walney* crashed through the boom amid calls of *"Ne tirer pas: nous sommes votre amis,"* blaring from its loudspeakers. This was soon drowned out by the blast of guns from both shore batteries and French destroyers inside the port firing at almost point-blank range. Trapped under the glare of searchlights, both ships were sunk amidst scenes of appalling carnage. French civilians watched, horrified, as men were catapulted into the air and then flung back into the flaming water. Many of the men who escaped the cutters were then machinegunned as they floundered in the water. One lady confessed that the screams of the dying would stay with her for the rest of her life.[378] Three hundred forty-six US troops were either killed or wounded, along with nearly two hundred British sailors.

Meanwhile, in the Rock at Gibraltar, Butch was still anxiously listening for reports alongside the other commanders. ABC, standing in a turtleneck sweater and braces ("suspenders," as the Americans say), was also pensively charting his forces' progress. At 2:40 AM, they heard the news that the landings had been successful on A, B, and C beaches, Eastern Task

Force at Algiers. Here, a mixed force of American and British troops had
landed. The US 34th Infantry Division had come ashore east of Algiers,
minus the 135th Regiment—Bucky Walters and his fellows were held in reserve back in the UK, while west of the city, the British 78th Division had
landed. "Trouble in Algiers harbor," Harry Butcher recorded around 7 AM.
An attack on the port similar to that at Oran had also failed, although fortunately less dramatically—this time troops were landed and the ships involved managed to retire, albeit badly damaged. However, General Mast
did manage to bring about a coup in the city. The French Emergency Defense Plan allowed citizen authorities to take over key installations such as
communication centers in order to release the military for more active defense tasks. Making the most of this, Mast and his supporters took control
of the city, locking up a number of officials and placing a guard on the
house of General Juin, the French C-in-C in North Africa.

But nervous pacing continued inside the Rock. "What's holding up
Patton's report?" Butch scribbled. "And what about the paratroopers due
at dawn at the Oran airdrome?"[379] The parachute assault had been another
fiasco. Of the thirty-nine aircraft that had set out from Cornwall, in southwest England, seven never even reached Algeria. One landed at Gib, two
in French Morocco, and four in Spanish Morocco. Twelve aircraft dropped
their men at least a day's march away, while sixteen landed in the Sebkra
Salt Lake; they eventually joined forces with troops that had landed at X
and Y beaches. Another four aircraft dropped their men too far away on
the Salt Lake and they were promptly captured, including the force commander. Fog, rain, and faulty radio communication all played their part.
The beacon signal from a ship off Oran was also never received.

It was an agonizing morning for the allied commander, who in his
dripping cave office in the Rock was beginning to appreciate the terrible,
inescapable strain of being the commander now that his part in the landings was over. Fate and the resolve of his fighting men were what now lay
between success and failure. Jotting his anxieties on a scrap of paper, he
later handed them to Harry Butcher:

Worries of a Commander.
1. Spain is ominously quiet that Gov. of Gib reports himself uneasy.
   No word from any agent of Ambassador.
2. No news from Task Forces. Reports few and unsatisfactory.
3. Defensive fighting, which seemed half-hearted and spiritless
   this morning, has blazed up, and in many places resistance is
   stubborn.
4. No Frenchman immediately available, no matter how friendly
   toward us, seems able to stop the fighting. (Mast, et al.)

5. Giraud is in Gibraltar, manifestly unwilling to enter the theatre so long as fighting is going on.
6. Giraud is difficult to deal with—wants much in power, equipment, etc, but seems little disposed to do his part to stop fighting.
7. Giraud wants plants, radios.
8. We are slowed up in eastern sector when we should be getting toward Bone-Bizerte at once.
9. We don't know whereabouts or conditions of airborne force.
10. We cannot find out anything.[380]

Some time after 7 AM, however, word reached those in the Rock that the Western Task Force landings operations were proceeding according to plan. The armada had split up the day before: the 2nd Armored Division was to lead the assault on Safi, 140 miles southwest of Casablanca and the only other port in French Morocco that could handle heavy equipment such as Sherman tanks. They left the main convoy at 6 AM on 7 November, while ships carrying the 9th Infantry Division split around three that afternoon; they were headed toward Mehida, eighty miles north of Casablanca, with the aim of capturing Port Lyautey airfield a few miles inland. The third force was spearheaded by the 3rd Infantry Division and was tasked with landing at Fedala, a small fishing port and major petroleum storage and distribution point, nearly twenty miles north of Casablanca.

At 2 AM on the eighth, General George S. Patton was up, dressed—immaculately as ever—and out on deck of the USS *Augusta*, Admiral Hewitt's flag, off the coast of Fedala. Patton had waited all his life for this moment, and believed absolutely in his destiny to achieve greatness. Already one of America's best-known generals, his first taste of fame had come in 1916, when he led a raid that killed three of Pancho Villa's Mexican bandits. A year later he was in France, where he became the first officer assigned to the US Tank Corps and where he was badly wounded in the groin; he was still recovering from this close brush with death when the armistice was signed. Like Eisenhower, he thought deeply about the army and the future of warfare. And like Tuker, he wrote a number of far-reaching papers throughout the twenties and thirties, including a prophetic work on the possibility of a Japanese attack on Pearl Harbor. While the US army stagnated—and the development of armored warfare in particular—Patton was one man who desperately tried to buck the trend. For him, these had been long, frustrating years.

A man of many parts—and contradictions—Patton was tall and imposing, with fierce eyes, but a high, squeaky voice totally at odds with his demeanor. A noted horseman and champion swordsman, he had also come fifth in the pentathlon at the 1912 Olympic Games in Stockholm. An amateur poet and utterly devoted to his wife and family, he was, for all his bravado and flamboyance, prone to occasional bouts of self-doubt and introspection. Yet he possessed bucketloads of charisma and the inspiration of a born leader.

Now, as he stood and watched the lights from both Casablanca and Fedala, he sensed the great crusade was about to begin. "The eyes of the world are watching us," he'd written to his son from *Augusta,* "the heart of America beats for us; God is with us. On our victory depends the freedom or slavery of the human race. We shall surely win." It was the kind of rhetoric Churchill used; in some ways, the two were not dissimilar.

Below him, the sea was calm and with almost no swell at all. A few days before, while still at sea, the messages he received seemed to suggest that the French would join them. "I hope not," he noted in his diary, "for it would sort of pull the cork out of the men—all steamed up to fight and not have to—also it would be better for me to have a battle. Well, in six days we will know."[381]

He was not to be disappointed. Word reached him that at Safi, French guns had opened fire at 4:55 AM, while from Mehida, General Lucian Truscott signaled "Play ball"—the code for "am fighting"—just after 7 AM. Meanwhile, at Fedala, the third of the three landing sites, the first troops were having a bad time getting ashore. In the dark, moonless sea, and despite the very obvious lights from the shore, a number of the transport ships lost their bearings and ended up as much as six miles from their drop-anchor positions. As a result, at 4 AM—H-Hour—only eighteen of the forty-two landing craft had been successfully lowered, filled with troops, and were ready to be guided to the shore.

Lieutenant Randy Paulsen was on one of the ships that wound up in completely the wrong position. He was still in a terrible way—the skin hadn't healed properly on his leg and his torn Achilles tendon was yet to mend. Earlier that night, the battalion commander had told him he was not going to be able to go ashore. Later, Randy's platoon sergeant came in to see him. "Don't give me any talk about how lucky I am to be going home," Randy told him. "Get my gear and stow it under the bunk." When the order finally came to get into the LSA, Randy put on all his gear and just managed to clamber down the net and into the landing craft. "My leg was killing me," he admits. The landing craft was swaying up and down from the now increasing swell. Suddenly the sea wasn't so calm after all. "When you came down from the nets you had to time it because otherwise there'd be a pretty good shock when you hit it," he says. When they set off, they were some twelve miles out at sea. "No one's ever explained why that made any sense," says Randy. It didn't, but having crossed the vast Atlantic without ever losing its place in the convoy, their ship had managed to get itself lost within sight of land. So instead of having only five miles to reach the shore with an escort of piloting destroyers, they were left to head toward the beaches all on their own.

In the LCA it was dark, "and kinda rainy," and after an hour, Randy began to wonder what the hell was going on. Manning the boat was a coxswain whom Randy thought looked no more than fifteen or sixteen. He asked him where all the other LCAs were. "I don't know," said the coxswain.

"What d'you mean, you don't know?" said Randy.

"I'm lost."

"Which way is shore?" Randy asked him.

"I'm not too sure," came the reply, "but I think it's that way."

"Well, head for it then!"

Finally they spotted a small light and made toward it, coming to ground on a sand bar a short way off shore. Half the men dropped into the water, but all twenty-four of them safely managed to crawl onto land, even Randy with his bad leg. He hadn't the faintest idea where they were, however. It was still dark, so he gathered his men around him. One man, however, kept crowding in front of him. "Goddammit, get away from me!" Randy shouted in irritation, then realized it wasn't even one of his men, but from a black French colonial troop. "He couldn't speak English and I couldn't speak French," says Randy, "so I kept saying, 'Je suis American.'" Eventually, they persuaded him to stay on the beach while they set off in the direction of Casablanca, which Randy knew was their ultimate objective.

Meanwhile, offshore, the USS *Massachusetts* had been shelling the *Jean Bart*. Although immobilized and still in dock, there was little wrong with the French battleship's four 15-inch guns, and so the US Navy was anxious to silence them as soon as possible. Around 7:15 AM, seven enemy destroyers suddenly emerged from Casablanca and headed toward the landings. There was little they could do against the combined power of the US warships lying offshore, and they soon turned around and hurried back to port, although they tried again around eight o'clock, when a cruiser and two large destroyers appeared. General Patton had just placed his kit into the landing boat—including his pearl-handled pistols—and it was still swinging out on its davits when the *Augusta* surged forward and fired. The blast rocked the landing boat and the general's landing party lost all their kit, except—thankfully—his six-shooters. Shortly after, enemy bombers appeared and *Augusta* rushed to protect the landing ships, before returning to the fight with the French navy. Patton, still aboard, was drenched by the blast of one French shell. Several American ships were hit, but none critically. Shortly after eleven, the French moved back into Casablanca. Coastal batteries had also been busy, but a bridgehead had been established and with the help of navy aircraft from the *Ranger*, the battle for Fedala was soon over.

General Patton stepped ashore around 1:20 PM, his pistols strapped to his waist. The surf was now quite choppy and he got soaked again. Fedala was in US hands, but the landings had suffered their fair share of tragedy. Two thirds of the landing craft were completely wrecked and a number of American troops had drowned. At Mehida, the French garrison had been alerted, and troops also struggled with the coastal surf. Inaccurate navigation, as at Fedala, did not help matters either. Safi had fallen fairly quickly, however. This was the one occasion where charging two ships into the port had worked.

At Gibraltar, news—sometimes conflicting but generally positive—was arriving thick and fast. ABC was anxious that there should be plenty of Spitfires at Blida and Maison Blanche, the two airfields nearest Algiers, later that day to protect against the inevitable Axis air attacks that would surely come. They had been due to be taken by 7:30 AM, but as the commanders were discovering, nearly all the landings were behind schedule. At 8:30 AM, Air Marshal Welsh sent off the first squadron of Hurricanes, then at nine, good news arrived. "Maison Blanche airdrome captured. Hooray," noted Butch. Four squadrons, three of Spitfires, were there by the afternoon, as were the headquarters of two wings. Blida had also been taken.

Further east, around Oran, there had also been fighting. Although Arzew itself had been captured, French batteries inland began opening fire at first light, as did the coastal battery at Mers el Kebir, directing their fire toward ships unloading in the Algiers area and also along Y beach west of Oran. Both batteries were silenced by the guns of the British battleship, HMS *Rodney*, lying some miles off shore in support of the landing operations. Meanwhile, aircraft from the carrier HMS *Furious* attacked the airfields at La Senia and Tafaraoui, managing to damage or destroy around seventy French planes at La Senia, which had been armed and ready to attack at short notice. Two armored columns, whose tanks and heavy equipment had landed by pontoon early in the morning, hurried to capture the airfields; La Senia fell just after eleven, Tafaraoui at 12:15 PM. Just over four hours later, the first two US Spitfire squadrons from Gibraltar landed there.

Margaret Hornback finally came ashore around three that afternoon, having spent the day watching the sea fill with landing craft of various kinds and sizes; they reminded her of ducks swimming on a pond. Their own LCA couldn't reach the beach, so soldiers carried her and the other nurses the last short stretch to dry land. Just off the beach were a few boarded-up summer cottages, so ignoring warnings about booby traps, they opened them up and spent the night there. After nibbling on some chocolate, they all lay down close to one another for warmth and tried to sleep.

That morning, Commander Ben Bryant was holding his regular Sunday morning service on board HMS/S *Safari*, the men crowded around the control room and galleys, when a signal suddenly arrived from Shrimp Simpson back in Malta. "Damaged enemy cruiser NE of Cape ST VITO in tow with 8 destroyers, 6 E-boats and aircraft in company," the message ran. "P.44 close immediately. P.211 [*Safari*] proceed to Cape GALLO to intercept."[382]

Safari had been part of ABC's naval forces amassed for the invasion and, along with five other submarines from the 10th Flotilla, had been patrolling a line off southern Italy ready to pounce should the Italian battle fleet emerge to upset the apple cart. They'd seen nothing, however, and all the crew were getting fidgety and bored. This new directive certainly promised action, but was an extremely hazardous undertaking, to put it mildly: an almost impregnable screen surrounded the cruiser. Even if they did manage to get into a position from which they could attack, the chances of making good their escape afterward would be slim.

They always finished their service with a prayer that Ben had discovered some time before, but which they had now come to look upon as their own. A little more fervor went into its recital on this occasion, and then it was time to get back to business. Ronnie Ward was now Number One, after the previous second-in-command had been sent home to do his Perisher—or CO's—course. It was an enormous responsibility for a twenty-one-year-old, but Ronnie had a cool head and was rarely phased by the tasks expected of *Safari*; he'd certainly proved worthy of the faith Ben had placed in him when taking him on back in Gibraltar. Nor was he especially apprehensive now, as they surfaced and set off at full power toward Cape Gallo off the coast of Sicily. "There were times when I was very frightened," he admits. "You knew there was always a danger of being sunk, but you couldn't let it prey on your mind. It was just part of the game and you hoped it wouldn't happen."

They reached Cape Gallo by nightfall, cutting down their speed so as not to show their wake. It was a very dark night and hard to see; even by straining from the conning tower with binoculars, visibility was less than a mile. The destroyers were weaving about, covering a large area of around seventy-five square miles; somewhere amongst them was the cruiser, but precisely where was anyone's guess. As it was, they were very nearly spotted by the first destroyer they saw, and had to hastily dive out of the way. They were now in among the destroyer screen, an extremely vulnerable position, especially as they were operating mostly on the surface to ensure maximum speed, and only diving whenever a destroyer came too close. "You couldn't hear much on the surface, though," says Ronnie, "because the diesels made such a noise. You just had to keep your eyes open and hope for the best."

After a very tense and strenuous five hours, however, it was clear the cruiser had safely gotten away and made it into port at Palermo. Had any one of the destroyers seen them, they would most likely have not survived to see dawn. Exhausted after the mental and physical strain of peering into the dark so intently for so long, they dived and slunk back out to sea.

Meanwhile, there were further negotiations to be carried out. At Gibraltar, Ike and Clark were once more tackling Giraud, and this time, the French general was more compliant, and finally agreed to be governor of French North Africa and C-in-C of all French forces, but to work under Eisehower. "Ike was tired but happy," noted Butch, and then came even better news: Darlan wanted to negotiate. Earlier that morning, Robert Murphy had talked with General Juin, warning him of the Allies' overwhelming strength and urging him to call a ceasefire. Juin had replied that Murphy must ask Admiral Darlan, C-in-C of all Vichy French armed forces and therefore his senior, and who "happened" to be in Algiers visiting his sick son. Soon after, the French admiral was duly brought to Juin's villa, but played for time, and with no sign of the advancing hordes of Allied troops that Murphy had assured them were inches away, arrested Murphy instead, and together with Juin drove off toward the military HQ at Fort L'Empereur. However, when they realized the extent of the naval forces currently blasting away a few miles out to sea, and discovered that not only had the airfields fallen, but that there were, indeed, many thousands of troops already ashore, Juin persuaded Darlan to have a change of heart. In what was becoming a strange, topsy-turvy day, Darlan and Major-General "Doc" Ryder of the US 34th Division negotiated a ceasefire in Algiers. By evening, American troops had occupied the city.

But Darlan wanted to meet Ike, although Ike made it quite clear that he would not deal with any other Frenchman. "Kiss Darlan's stern if you have to," ABC advised Eisenhower, "but get the French navy." Suddenly, Ike was faced with a dilemma. What should he do about Giraud?

Despite the fall of Algiers, fighting continued. Southwest of Arzew, the 18th Infantry were held up at St. Cloud. Tom Bowles spent the night in a cemetery; he'd also now seen his first dead American soldier. "I saw him lying there," he says, "and that made a big impression on me. I thought, this is for real now." The casualties were beginning to mount. At around two in the morning, Margaret Hornback and the other nurses were told to get up out of their beach house and go to the Arzew city hospital, a one-story roughly built affair on the edge of town. She was appalled by the filth and squalor, not to mention the enormous rats. The electricity and water supply had been cut in the course of the battle for the town, so the wounded were lined up on stretchers side by side while Margaret and the other medical staff went from one to another with their flashlights. They only had the most basic of supplies—fuel and ammunition had been the priority for unloading so far—and as Margaret admitted in a letter home, they were performing operations with equipment she would never before have thought possible. "Throughout all this and since, too, our boys have been the best of sports," she wrote. "They never whimper or complain. They hold on to your hand tightly during painful procedures if you've time to stand there. If not they just take it alone."

The following morning all three battalions of the 18th Infantry launched an attack, but the defenders offered stiff opposition, and the Americans couldn't break through. But by afternoon, the 2nd and 3rd Battalions were able to bypass the town and advance, as had originally been planned, to Oran.

Clark and Giraud flew heavily escorted and low over the Mediterranean to Algiers on the ninth, although Clark, delayed by bad weather, didn't arrive until around 5 PM. Just as he landed, several Junkers 88s arrived to bomb the harbor, but were almost immediately engaged by Spitfires. "Everywhere around us," noted Clark, "Americans and Britons ran out on to the field, yelling and cheering the Spits on." After watching one of the German bombers being shot down, he hurried into the city. Despite the ceasefire, there was still uncertainty as to whether it would hold. American troops were still fighting heavily around Port Lyautey and Patton's advance toward Casablanca had been slow. The political atmosphere in Algiers could not have been more tense. At the Hotel St. George, he met a grim-faced Major-General Ryder, who said, "I'm glad you're here. I've stalled them off about as long as I can." Neither Darlan nor Juin, or a number of other French commanders would see Giraud; clearly, his influence was far less than had been anticipated. Clark realized that the preeminent Frenchman now in North Africa was not Giraud at all, but Admiral Darlan.

He finally met Darlan and Juin the following morning, 10 November. The meeting was long and protracted. Clark thought Darlan seemed nervous and uncertain, anxious over which peg to hang his coat on and about taking responsibility for the inevitable German occupation of southern France, which up to that point had been run by the Vichy government. But eventually, late in the morning, he agreed to issue an order for all French troops in North Africa to observe a ceasefire immediately.

Soon after came word from Vichy that Darlan had been sacked as C-in-C of the French Armed Forces, an announcement that caused the admiral to try and revoke his earlier order. "You will do nothing of the kind," Clark told him firmly, and to make certain, placed him effectively under house arrest, guarded by a platoon of US troops. But while an uneasy peace now reigned in Algeria, around Casablanca the fighting continued, where General Noguès, the Governor of French Morocco, had been named by Petain as Darlan's successor. "The only tough nut left is in your hands," Ike signaled to Patton. "Crack it open quickly and ask for what you want."[383]

Lieutenant Randy Paulsen and his twenty-four men had finally reached the outskirts of Casablanca. They'd been blown so badly off course, it had taken them two and a half days. The going had been slow, thanks to Randy's perilous condition. At the end of each day, he'd literally poured the blood out of his boot. The salt and sand didn't help either. "It chafed my foot raw," he says. They found the rest of Company L bivouacked in a cemetery. "It's about time you showed up," said the company commander. They were the last of the stragglers to rejoin the battalion. Randy got bellowed at by the battalion commander for jumping ship, but having said his piece added, "Even though you shouldn't have done it, I admire your spirit."

It had been an exhausting few days for all the Americans of the Western Task Force, not least General Patton, so that when the *Jean Bart* once more opened fire, he decided it was time to take bold and drastic action. Now armed with Ike's signal, he had Shermans from Safi approaching the southern outskirts of the city, his infantry to the north, and off shore, US warships and carriers waited. At 7:30 AM, the following morning, he would reduce Casablanca to rubble. "God favors the bold, victory is to the audacious," he scribbled in his diary.[384]

At around 2 AM, as news arrived that Port Lyautey had finally fallen, Patton was in his headquarters at the Hotel Miramar in Fedala, when a dispatch arrived from General Noguès announcing that a general ceasefire had been ordered all across French North Africa. Patton's staff wanted him to call off his planned attack of Casablanca, but he wouldn't—not until the French Navy made it clear that it was bound by the ceasefire order. "Beside," noted Patton, "it is bad to change plans."

The French took it to the wire. US Navy dive-bombers had already taken off from their carriers, and the American warships' guns were primed and ready, when, at 6:40 AM, the French Navy surrendered. Soon after, US troops marched into Casablanca. "A nice birthday present," noted Patton. He was fifty-seven.[385]

The Second World War would see larger seaborne invasions than TORCH, but none, not even OVERLORD, just under two years later, surpassed it for the distances covered or for its sheer daring. On 6 June, 1944, the invasion force traveled no more than a hundred miles. For TORCH, the armada journeyed over three-and-a-half *thousand* miles from the US and nearly one-and-a-half thousand miles from Great Britain. Nothing like it had ever been attempted before and yet in a little over three months, an embryonic plan had evolved into an operation involving nearly seven hundred ships, 70,000 troops and more than 1,000 aircraft. Plenty had gone wrong, and there were many lessons to be learned. But it was nonetheless a monumental achievement by new allies working together in a way that two independent nations had never ever attempted before.

CHAPTER 17

The Race For Tunis: November 1942

AXIS REACTION to the Allied landings was swift. On the day of the invasion, Field Marshal Kesselring, German C-in-C South, sent a Luftwaffe liaison officer to Tunisia to pave the way for Axis occupation of French airfields there. The following morning, he then spoke to Hitler in person, who gave him a free hand to build up a bridgehead in Tunisia. Wasting not a moment, Kesselring ordered more bomber units to move to Sicily and Sardinia, from where they could attack the newly captured ports in Algeria. In addition, he sent a further two-man team to negotiate with the French authorities in Tunis, along with a parachute regiment, his own HQ battalion and a number of Me109s and Stukas. These landed at El Aouina airfield just outside Tunis, and although the French commander there hastily flew off to Algiers—where he reported that over forty enemy aircraft had now landed unopposed—the French forces there simply sat back and watched. Two days later, German paratroopers took over Bizerte airfield as well.

From his mountain retreat at Berchtesgarden, Hitler hastily summoned Laval, the Vichy French prime minister, and Count Ciano, the Italian foreign minister, for talks. The Italians were especially concerned about the threat to North Africa, and had, in fact, been urging Hitler to build up troops in Tunisia for several months. But until now, the Fuhrer had shown little interest in the North African campaign; he regarded it as a distraction from the main focus of his energies, the campaign against Russia. He could no longer view Africa as a colonial sideshow, however: the significance of an Allied conquest of North Africa was glaringly obvious; after all, Sicily was a stone's throw from northern Tunisia. "Italy will become the center of attack by the Allies," noted Ciano glumly on 8 November.[386] Only a few days later, Churchill echoed the Italian minister by claiming the Mediterranean was the "underbelly of the Axis" from which they could attack in future. Hitler was already anxious about the sticking power of the Italians. Now fully committed in the East to a tougher campaign than he'd originally envisaged, he was aware that the collapse of his principal Axis partner would be a disaster for Germany. With this in mind, he was determined to keep Italy in the fight and safeguard his continental empire, and so immediately ordered the Axis occupation of Vichy-controlled southern France and Corsica, and for the greater establishment of a bridgehead in Tunisia. This was presented as a *fait accompli* to Laval. There were other advantages for Hitler in establishing a strong bridgehead in Tunisia. Not only would it offer an alternative supply route for Rommel, but by keeping a grasp of the central Mediterranean, the Allies were forced to continue supplying the Middle and Far East via the Cape. So while the war against Russia was still top of the Fuhrer's agenda, Tunisia—"that cornerstone of our conduct of the war on the southern flank of Europe"—remained a key area of his war effort and he issued orders for it to be held at all costs.[387]

In achieving this task, Kesselring was to focus all his efforts. The Mediterranean had already been reinforced during the past couple of weeks in response to the buildup of Allied activity, but further air units were transferred from every front—even Russia—including large numbers of transport aircraft. Within two weeks of the TORCH landings, there were nearly 11,000 Axis troops in Tunisia, hastily drawn from Sicily and from reserve units in France, and which included German paratrooper and Panzer Grenadier units as well as the Italian 50th Special Brigade from Tripoli, partially made up from remnants of the battle-hardened Ariete Division. On 16 November, General Nehring, the former commander of the Afrika Korps until wounded at Alam Halfa, arrived to take charge; by 24 November, the 10 Panzer Division had also landed, along with a number of the new Tiger tanks. This enormous sixty-ton beast, hot from the German factories, was an awesome machine. Although slow, it mounted an 88mm gun in its turret and had body armor that was so thick there was nothing in the US and British armament that could penetrate it.

It was an astonishingly fast buildup and proved what German and Italian logisticians could achieve when there was proper commitment and shortened lines of communication. It also made life very difficult for the French governor, Admiral Esteva, who was receiving conflicting orders from Algiers and Vichy, but who was also increasingly surrounded by Axis forces. Esteva opted for neutrality, although the commander of the French Tunisian Division, General Barré, quickly retreated with his troops away from the plains around Tunis and into the hills between Medjez el Bab and Beja, hoping the Allies would hurry to his rescue.

However, Allied efforts to persuade the French to resist the Axis forces rushing to Tunisia had not been helped by disunity and shilly-shallying on the part of the French leaders in Algiers. Although the French had followed Darlan's, rather than Petain's, orders and laid down their guns in much of French North Africa, the French admiral was continuing to blow hot and cold. Mark Clark, still valiantly leading the negotiations, felt Darlan had "a disappointing reverence" for Petain; the French admiral seemed utterly miserable at his rejection by the Marshal.

As ABC had pointed out, it was imperative that the Germans did not get their hands on the French fleet, but when Clark asked Darlan to summon the French Navy in Toulon and Tunis to come over and join the Allies, the admiral told him he did not have the authority. When Clark insisted, Darlan refused. "This," Clark told him angrily, "merely verifies the statement I made when I came here. There is no indication of any desire on your part to assist the Allied cause."[388] Later in the day, Darlan changed his mind, and issued the orders as Clark had requested, while General Juin also ordered French forces in Tunisia to fight the Germans. Incredibly, Darlan then changed his mind *again*, and revoked the order, claiming he wanted to wait for General Noguès to arrive from French Morocco. Both he and Juin claimed it was a matter of military honor and discipline; they weren't revoking the order, they assured Clark, merely suspending it until Noguès arrived. But the clock was ticking, and the German stranglehold in Tunisia was tightening.

By the following day, 13 November, Noguès had reached Algiers, and in the afternoon so did the Allied C-in-C. Ike, along with ABC and Harry Butcher, safely reached Maison Blanche around noon. ABC had been looking forward to meeting the French admiral. "Darlan is a snake," he wrote to a friend, "but a useful viper if we can use him."[389] Like Ike and Clark, he had no compunction about dealing with Darlan if it ensured peace in French North Africa. Clark still had his doubts that the French would ever reach agreement, but word finally arrived that a solution had been made between them. In an atmosphere that ABC thought was electric, Darlan announced that he would head the civil and political government of all French North Africa, Noguès would remain governor of French Morocco; and Giraud would become the C-in-C of all French forces, which he would mobilize to help fight the Axis. Having agreed on what was to become known as the "Darlan Deal," Ike returned with ABC and Butch to Gibraltar, while Clark held a press conference. "The past four days have been difficult," he told reporters. "We have had to keep looking back over our shoulder instead of to the front in Tunisia. Now we can proceed in a businesslike way."[390]

* * *

But while the resolution of the Darlan Deal may have cleared the way politically, the Allies were discovering that nothing was happening quite as fast as they would have liked. A number of basic mistakes had been made during the initial landings, which had created crucial delays in unloading. At Y Beach in the Oran sector, for example, an unexpected sandbar off the beach had caused a number of vehicles to sink into the sea. Elsewhere, flat batteries, missing ignition keys and even missing drivers had also held up disembarkation of trucks and other vehicles. On British ships, ignition keys had been wired to the steering wheels, but incredibly, this had led to pilfering of toolboxes in the vehicles. The problems this caused would be felt for months.

Moreover, the Allied armed forces were entirely dependent on what was brought from overseas; nothing was available locally and this included, crucially, oil and fuel. Even coal for the single railway running east had to be supplied from across the sea. From Algiers to Tunis the distance was 560 miles of extremely mountainous country. From Casablanca, it was 1,500. There were only two main roads—one that weaved its way along the coast, and another around forty miles inland that twisted and turned up and down all the way. Both routes were built along highly mountainous terrain, while the existing French railway was barely functioning. In other words, it was far easier to get troops from Sicily into Tunisia than it was from Algiers. This was what ABC, for one, had feared from the outset, and the protracted settlement with Darlan, which had wasted precious time, had only confirmed his fears. "Once more," he wrote, "I bitterly regretted that bolder measures had not been taken in Operation TORCH, and that we had not landed at Bizerte, as I had suggested."[391]

The weather also hindered operations, as Lieutenant Jim Reed discovered when he finally landed at Port Lyautey. Air cover for the landings in French Morocco had been provided by planes of the US Navy, as they were the only aircraft able to rearm and refuel on an aircraft carrier. This was why the 33rd Fighter Group on board the USS *Chenango* did not fly off until the airfield at Port Lyautey had been secured. The first P-40s were catapulted off the deck on 10 November. Jim Reed had been sitting strapped into his plane, "Renee," when suddenly the launching stopped. He couldn't understand it and began to think the worst until word got through that the halt was because one of the pilots had crashed on landing.

The next day, the aircraft began taking off again. Like Duke Ellington before him, launching his P-40 Warhawk from a carrier was a new experience for Jim. The day before he'd noted how nearly every aircraft had initially dipped beneath the end of the *Chenango*. Lieutenant Jones, the pilot five ahead of him took off and never reappeared—unable to get out in time, he sank with his plane. When it was his turn, Jim gunned the throttle and with full flaps down, surged forward, hoping for the best. Clearing the deck, he dropped until he was just off the water, but with his engine still racing, he slowly but surely began to inch higher into the air.

Flying over the shimmering white city of Casablanca, Jim and several others headed up the coast to Port Lyautey, where they were met by scenes of carnage. Wrecked aircraft and bomb craters littered the field. Realizing he was not going to clear the craters, Jim flew around again, but as he touched down noticed another bomb crater. Breaking hard, he swerved around it but the force caused his plane to tilt to one side, damaging his wing. Jim was feeling bad enough when the group commander, Colonel Momyer, gave him an earful. "Don't feel too bad," another pilot told him soon after, "that SOB tore his all to pieces."[392]

The 33rd FG lost seventeen out of seventy-seven aircraft, thanks to the craters, thick mud, and because they'd been told to keep strict radio silence. As a result, none of the incoming pilots had been warned of what to expect at Port Lyautey. It was hardly an auspicious start.

With the airfields now in Allied hands, the mass of pilots and aircraft clogging up the narrow confines of Gibraltar could start heading over to Algeria. Squadron Leader Tony Bartley had arrived at Gib with his 111 Squadron on 4 November, with speculation still rife about their ultimate destination. Tony was praying it wouldn't be Malta, which everyone knew was a brutal posting. With several days to idle away, he and a number of other pilots had spent much of their time in the officers' mess, which was decorated with oak beams like an English country pub and even had "The Victory Inn" painted above the door. He was there when news finally arrived on 8 November of the Allied landings in North Africa. "As a score of British and American fighter pilots sat around the Victory Inn bar," he wrote, "we raised our tankards, and drank to the best-kept secret of the war."[393]

On the eleventh, Tony led twelve Spitfires to Maison Blanche. He had been worried about having enough fuel for the journey and sure enough, within sight of Algiers, two of his pilots called up on the R/T and told him they had run out of petrol. "Can you make land?" Tony asked them; they would try, they replied. As he flew over the massed ships in Algiers harbor, another of his pilots called up to say his engine had died; so only nine made it to Maison Blanche. As Tony taxied off the runway, came to a halt and clambered out of his Spitfire, he felt tired, hungry, and depressed. A highly experienced fighter pilot, and veteran of Dunkirk and the Battle of Britain, he had flown operationally almost constantly since the beginning of the war, save for a brief period of test flying, and was frankly exhausted before he had even reached Gibraltar. Now in North Africa, he was filled with bleak forebodings. The airfield itself, like Port

Lyautey, was littered with aircraft. Across the far side were some bombed-out hangars. Food was scarce and there was no accommodation. "Just scrounge what you can," the wing commander told him. Tony's other pilots had gathered around and heard this news but said nothing, smoking in silence instead. By nightfall, the three missing pilots turned up; thankfully, only one was hurt, arriving with a bandaged foot.

Arriving a day later at Maison Blanche was twenty-one-year-old Flying Officer Bryan Colston—one of the few pilots to be taken all the way to Algiers by ship. Two-twenty-five Squadron had sailed together from Gourock, in Scotland, but on safely reaching Gibraltar, the pilots had all disembarked—all except Bryan and Squadron Leader Scott, who were to accompany all non-flying officers and the ground crews—some 120 men in all—for the rest of the journey across the Mediterranean. Meanwhile, the other pilots were to fly their brand-new Hurricane IIs to Maison Blanche as soon as they were able.

Like many young men of his age, Bryan had understood little about the war before he joined up. His father had served on the Western Front, but afterward had rarely talked about it, and his experiences certainly made little difference to his son's attitude to the current conflict. By the autumn of 1940, when still only nineteen, Bryan had been working as a pupil surveyor on the construction of an army camp in Devon, when one of his colleagues had told him he was planning to become a pilot. It sounded like a good idea to Bryan, so the pair took a train to Exeter and signed up for, and were accepted into, the RAF.

During his training he proved to be an above-average pilot and particularly strong on navigation, so while he was kept on single-seaters, he was eventually sent to 225 Squadron, an army cooperation unit. He had been there nearly a year, mainly flying up and down the south coast of England, when rumors started abounding that they would soon be sent overseas. The prospect rather excited him, and now that they had finally reached Algeria, he felt considerably more chipper about what lay in store than Tony Bartley, although his good humor had certainly been tested by the six-hour, fifteen-mile march to Maison Blanche from the harbor in what had become hot sunshine. When they finally got there, it was dark, and Bryan, too, was exhausted. The following day, the pilots began arriving from Gibraltar. "Thus we became a whole squadron again," he noted, "and ready to do our duty in a far-off land."

That duty was initially to get as close to Tunisia as possible and in the case of 225 Squadron, begin carrying out tactical reconnaissance sorties to see what the enemy was up to and just how extensively the Axis bridgehead was developing, but before they could do that, key airfields and ports in

Eastern Algeria, close to Tunisia, needed to be taken. This was the first task of Lieutenant-General Kenneth Anderson, as directed by Ike. Although the landings had been almost entirely an American effort, overall command on the land had now reverted to Anderson, who had flown to Algiers on 9 November along with Mark Clark. General Patton's forces were mostly to remain in French Morocco, but the rest, the US 1st Infantry Division and Army Rangers included, were part of US II Corps, now attached to the British First Army. Bryan Colston had first heard of the existence of this new army on the voyage out, when they had been given a booklet called "First Army Information Bulletin." To begin with, he thought it was a printing error, and that they'd meant the *Eighth* Army. "We, officers and men of the First Army," wrote General Anderson in the pamphlet, "are, (with our American allies, and under an American Commander-in-Chief, General Dwight D. Eisenhower), engaged together in a great adventure which, if all goes well, should alter the whole course of the war."

But as Anderson was the first to point out, the First Army did not spring from the sea "fully formed like Aphrodite," but rather grew steadily as fortnightly convoys arrived, and so the initial thrust had to be made by a somewhat cobbled together combined force made up of airborne troops, commandos, and a seriously under-strength 78th Division, led by Major-General Evelegh.[394] As a result, when Anderson gave the order to advance eastward on 11 November, he did so with very few troops indeed.

As it was, the only resistance came from the weather and the Germans. Storms had caused a two-day delay on the assault on Bougie, however, which was not taken until 11 November. Djidjelli airfield was taken by British paratroopers, but due to rough seas, the assault convoy could not get into the port with their supplies and fuel for the air forces. The result was that for nearly two days, the ships at Bougie had no air cover and were bombed and attacked mercilessly. U-boats that had headed too far east for the main landing convoys were now perfectly placed to attack and did so without impunity: four ships were sunk and another severely damaged. Tony Bartley led the first patrol over the port on 13 November and was shocked by what he saw. "The sea was streaked with large patches of oil stretching out like the tentacles of an octopus," he wrote. "The bay resembled Dante's inferno, and bombed merchant ships lay abandoned at the entrance of the harbor, flames pouring from their hulls."[395] Thick, black smoke spiraled hundreds of feet into the air. He saw no sign of the enemy and eventually turned back to Maison Blanche. No sooner had they gone than the Axis bombers returned again.

Tony's 111 Squadron was moved forward to Bone the following day, 14 November. Conditions were worse than at Maison Blanche, with the airfield under near-constant attack and with no radar and other kind of early-warning system yet in place. For digs, the pilots slept in a ramshackle building near the airfield. It was musty with rotting floorboards and there were no beds, only rough straw mattresses. Since there was no fuel for the cook's fire, they simply broke up whatever furniture they could find.

The next day, Tony spent much of his time either flying or trying to organize his squadron, fixing up petrol dumps and a decent dispersal point, and laying telephone lines to the control tower. At one point he looked up and saw one of his pilots trying to land after attacking a Junkers 88. He had clearly been hit and just before touching down stalled and crashed, his plane bursting into flames. Tony and several others rushed to free him and managed to get him out only to discover he'd already been shot through the top of his skull. It was their first death in North Africa.

Two-twenty-five Squadron had also suffered their first casualty when one of their pilots was accidentally shot down and killed by the airfield's ack-ack gunners. They, too, were soon being moved up to Bone, the first aircraft arriving on 17 November. Bryan Colston landed there two days later, then flew on immediately for a tactical reconnaissance sortie (Tac/R) over Gabes and Sfax, ports on the east coast of Tunisia. The weather had once again turned, however, and he could see almost nothing through the thick cloud and rain.

Further airfields were taken: British paratroopers took Souk el Arba, northwest of Tunisia, on the sixteenth, while American airborne forces were also sent to the front: after the fiasco of the invasion at Oran, they successfully captured Youks les Bains airfield, farther south on the Algerian border, and then two days later, on 17 November, occupied the landing ground at Gafsa as well. But even with these in Allied hands, Bone remained the only all-weather airfield and with the rain continuing, conditions were almost impossible for the fighter squadrons. Moreover, Bone was 120 miles from the edge of the Axis bridgehead, while even Souk el Arba was 60; in contrast the Axis had all-weather airfields that were only ten miles away from the front. It was a decisive advantage.

Major-General Evelegh's forces were split into three. Along the north Tunisian coast road went 36 Infantry Brigade, aiming for Bizerte, while farther south, the 11th Infantry Brigade hurried along the road that led to Beja and Medjez el Bab. Following close behind 11 Brigade were Blade Force, an armored column of useless Crusaders and Valentines, as well as anti-tank guns and a company of motorized infantry. The first clash with Nehring's forces occurred in the north on 17 November, when 36 Brigade repulsed German paratroopers at Djebel Abiod,* some twenty-

---

*A djebel—pronounced with a silent 'd'—is a hill or small mountain

five miles inside Tunisia, with heavy losses on both sides. British paratroopers then destroyed a German armored reconnaissance force near Sidi Nsir the following day. Further fighting took place the following day, when General Barré's French forces withstood a concerted German attack on their positions west of Medjez el Bab. Reinforced by the British 1st Parachute Battalion, they held out all day, but withdrew west during the night. An ominous feature of the fighting at Medjez had been the heavy enemy aerial attacks and the almost complete lack of any Allied air support. In Tunisia, the tables had been dramatically turned.

The difficult terrain did not help. Tunisia was not a big country. While its southern half dipped into the edge of the Sahara, the north was hilly and very Mediterranean, rather like Sicily, or southern Spain. Along the northwest coast ran dense cork forests, while farther inland, rolling ranges of hilly grassland took over. Between these rows of hills ran fertile valleys, which in summer were full of orange and olive groves, wheat fields and vineyards. Nearly two thousand years before, the Medjerda Valley and the plain surrounding Tunis supplied most of the wheat for Ancient Rome. Like Algeria, the coastal cities were mostly filled with French, but inland, Arabs made up the majority of the population, their villages a far cry from the cosmopolitan palm-lined boulevards of Tunis, Sfax, and Bizerte. As the war swept their way, the Arabs became bystanders, uncomprehending yet eager to make the most of rich pickings that accompanied any battle.

From the rolling north sprang two ranges of mountains. The largest, the Grande Dorsale, was Tunisia's backbone, running diagonally northeast to southwest, while to the east, another range, the Eastern Dorsale, barred the way to the coast, running from the north all the way to Maknassy, and then joining another set of jagged peaks that ran east-west from Gafsa. The farther south, the harsher the landscape became; the lush vegetation of the north gave way to increasingly unforgiving, craggy mountains, towering pink and orange, and dominating the arid plains beneath them, until, south of Gafsa, the terrain gave way to a series of *chotts*, extensive and largely non-traversable salt marshes. Farther south from these lay the edge of the Sahara.

Along the seaborne side of the Eastern Dorsale, the land was flat and relentless, from the curve of the Libyan coast right up to Hammamet, just thirty miles south of Tunis. But to reach the hospitable plains, the Allies had to take the hills and mountains first, ranges from which a lone gun, well placed, could wreak havoc. This made Tunisia a difficult country in which to maneuver at the best of times, but in winter, when the weather could be cold and wet, it was torturous, as the Allies were already discovering. In the race for Tunis, there was much that was already stacked against them.

* * *

Across the sea in Gibraltar, Ike was facing up to the disappointment that the Darlan Deal was being very coolly received back in Britain, where, as Harry Butcher put it, Admiral Darlan was seen as a "stinking skunk."[396] Even Churchill was hardly thrilled, although he was sorely grieved that the success at Alamein and of the TORCH Landings had become over-shadowed by what many of his friends and colleagues—Foreign Minister Anthony Eden included—viewed as a "base and squalid deal" with one of Britain's bitterest enemies.[397] Ike patiently explained that the most im-portant thing had been to establish a cooperative regime that would save further Allied bloodshed and enable them to get on with the job in hand as quickly as possible; ABC also made clear his support of the deal, and felt rather sorry for Ike, reassuring him that politicians always wanted it both ways. "In my view," he wrote later, "it was the only possible course, and absolutely right. Darlan was the only man in North Africa who could have stopped the fighting."[398]

But although ABC's staunch defense of Ike certainly helped convince the prime minister, the outrage only gathered pace in Britain, while there were even rumblings in the US: Butch's old friend, the veteran broad-caster Ed Murrow demanded to know, in a highly charged broadcast, why the Allies were now playing with traitors. The president stepped in, hold-ing a press conference in which he explained and endorsed Ike's decision with Darlan, although he also suggested the appointment of Darlan was only a temporary measure born of political and military necessity.

While this did much to quell fears in the US, Darlan was not so happy, likening himself to "a lemon which the Americans will drop after they have squeezed it dry."[399] Nonetheless, on 22 November, the Clark-Darlan deal was finally signed, and the next day, Darlan managed to deliver the crucial port of Dakar in French West Africa into the hands of the Allies.

At Bone, the pilots now had radar of sorts. Tony Bartley had discovered a radar station nearby that had belonged to the French civil airways and where the operators were still tracking aircraft movements for their own amusement. In a matter of hours, he had laid a telephone line between the RDF (radio direction finding) station and Bone and installed their own operators.

It didn't stop the enemy bombers attacking them, however. On the twenty-second, Tony had been struggling with a stomach upset and had been taking a brief nap at dispersal when the alarm sounded. He ran to his Spitfire, but as he was strapping on his parachute harness, a number of fighter-bombers were already circling toward them, and so he dashed for cover under a nearby truck. As explosions began erupting around him, he looked up and saw a Spitfire racing down the runway and take to the air as another bomb exploded just in front of it. The blast knocked the aircraft and it crashed to the ground again, skidding straight toward Tony and with flames pouring from its punctured petrol tanks. He could only watch in horror as the pilot desperately struggled but failed to get out of the inferno.

When the attackers had gone, Tony scrambled out again, saw a charred "scarecrow arm" of his incinerated comrade and then realized the truck he'd been hiding under had been repeatedly hit by bullets and cannon fire. His own Spitfire was completely destroyed. He could only marvel at his escape. Later, his two flight commanders, having lost their aircraft trying to land in Algiers, finally arrived with the rearguard of the squadron and a number of spares and supplies. Until then, Tony had been flying every mission asked of the squadron; the past few days had been amongst the most testing of his entire life. Not only had he been leading the squadron in the air, he had also been looking after all his men and taking care of all the squadron administration. Admittedly, they had only just arrived and Bone was three hundred miles from Algiers, but the ten day-fighter squadrons that were near the front by the end of November were not even placed together in their own wings. For example, 225 Squadron was part 322 Wing, but two of its squadrons were based at Djidjelli; 324 Wing, of which Tony Bartley's 111 Squadron was a part, was now at Souk el Arba with two other Spitfire squadrons, while 111 and 72 Squadrons were kept at Bone. It is no wonder Tony Bartley felt overloaded with the responsibility expected of him. Tommy Elmhirst would have been horrified to see such haphazard organization, but the truth was that the brilliant systems put in place by Mary and Tommy had not been sufficiently noted in Britain and were not adopted in Northwest Africa either. Air Marshal Tedder made a brief visit at the end of the month and was appalled by what he discovered—not only were the conditions and supply situation terrible, but the headquarters of the US Twelfth Air Force and RAF Eastern Air Command were miles apart and hardly cooperating at all.

Mary and Tommy were having their own frustrations, however. Over a thousand miles away, the advance of the Eighth Army was not happening as fast as either they or Air Marshal Tedder would have liked.

The remains of Rommel's panzer army escaped through the Halfaya Pass and into Libya on 10 November. Monty blamed the rain for the holdup, but while that undoubtedly played its part, the truth was that the slow reaction on 4 November had given the Axis a crucial head start. Nonetheless, a great deal had been achieved: Eighth Army had advanced 250 miles, and the Axis pushed back out of Egypt. The key was now to finish them off entirely before Rommel had a chance to regroup and build up his forces once more.

By 15 November, Air HQ had reached Gambut once more, but they had outrun their water, food, transport, and petrol supplies, for which the army was responsible. Only by the great efforts of Tommy's rear head-quarters, which were still working like clockwork, was it possible to supply the forward units at all. Motor columns hurried back and forth, while air-lifts from Egypt brought just enough supplies to enable Force A to operate from the Maturba airfields in Cyrenaica and harry the panzer army's re-treat. But while they could just about keep the Force A fighters in the air, there were nothing like enough supplies to bring the bombers forward. "At the moment we are really out of a job," noted Cobber Weinronk on 19 No-vember. "No raids have been laid on for any of our air force units and we sit around playing cards, talking, eating and watching the bombline. Not even any rumors as to when we'll be changing 'dromes.' "[400] Later, the RAF would be criticized for letting the panzer army get through the Halfaya Pass in particular. But a handful of fighter-bombers were not enough to do the job—bombers were needed too, and in strength.

However, having beaten the panzer army twice, Monty was deter-mined to maintain his 100 percent winning record, and was not going to be drawn into making the same mistake as previous army commanders, and charge after the Axis forces only to find his forces viciously counter-attacked. Deciding to blame the weather for the failure to rout the panzer army rather than the slow pursuit on 4 November, he called off the chase, arguing that he needed time to bring his entire army forward in strength—and this could only happen once his lines of supply had short-ened, with Tobruk and Benghazi once more operating to capacity. This might have been a highly reasonable approach had the panzer army been anything like the size of its previous retreats, but Monty was aware of the intelligence reports about the state of Rommel's forces, and despite the exhaustion of the army, there were still plenty of troops who were raring to go—Tuker's Indians for starters. As it was, total German troops amounted to well under 10,000 men. Twenty-first Panzer had just eleven tanks left, 15th Panzer none at all. The Luftwaffe had also left much be-hind—they had destroyed sixty-three of their planes themselves, aircraft that had been grounded by fuel. No matter how brilliantly well trained they were, not even the Germans could offer much opposition without tanks, fuel, or guns. And unlike the Eighth Army when they retreated to Alamein in June, the panzer army had virtually no air forces.

But Montgomery did not have enough confidence in his troops to take the risk of surging across the bulge of Cyrenaica; and it was a risk, al-beit a small one. What particularly frustrated Mary and Tommy, however, was the army's refusal to help them in their efforts to keep at the enemy. "Mary and I had just one idea," noted Tommy. "To go forward quickly so that the Germans should never be out of striking distance. I know the army supply position was difficult, but so was ours. But, whereas we were stretching ourselves to the limit and making our lorries and their drivers do double their normal stint, the army was holding themselves to a normal seven-hour day."[401] Eventually, Mary turned to the Americans for help. General Brereton could not have been more obliging. Now commanding what had become the 9th Air Force, Brereton arranged a "flying pipeline" to the front. On just one day alone, forty-nine Dakotas carried no less than 48,510 gallons of fuel from El Adem to Agedabia, a distance of 425 miles by lorry and 250 by aircraft. What would have been a minimum three-day journey was completed in under two hours.

This lack of wholehearted cooperation from the army, when the Desert Air Force had given it such unceasing support ever since Gazala, infuriated Mary intensely. Monty aimed to attack the enemy at El Agheila in mid-December, but when Mary saw an appreciation by Freddie de Guingand, in which he suggested the First rather than Eighth Army should be the one to try and capture Tripoli (now Rommel's principal lifeline), he took it as further evidence of the army commander's overly defensive attitude, and immediately sent a copy to Tedder. Clearly, Mary told his C-in-C, Monty had no intention of pushing beyond El Agheila at all, and mentioned that even before Alamein, the army commander had been muttering about the TORCH operation taking care of Tripoli. "The whole tone of past weeks has borne this out," he wrote. "Any competent general with overwhelming force can win a positional battle, but it requires the spark of greatness to do well in pursuit or in retirement."[402] Tedder was of much the same mind, and complained bitterly to Portal. He even urged Alex to persuade Monty to get a move on. However, Alex, quite rightly, was not going to start telling his army commander how to fight his battles, even though he, too, suspected Monty was being overly cautious. If Montgomery did not have the confidence enough to forge ahead with what he had now, then Alex was not about to force his hand.*

Billy Drake's 112 Squadron had been leapfrogging forward as fast as they had fallen back a few months before, moving through five landing grounds in ten days, before stopping at Maturba, where they were attached to the US 57th Fighter Group. And Billy was personally adding to

---

*After the war, Alex admitted that one of Monty's weaknesses was his unwillingness to take a risk. "At times a commander should take calculated risks and not wait for 100 percent assurance of success before he undertakes an operation."

his already impressive record: On 5 November, he shot down one Me 109 and damaged another, destroyed two more on the ground a week later, a Heinkel bomber on the 15th and one Me 110 destroyed and one damaged on 19 November. Already he was one of the top-scoring Allied aces of the Desert War.

However frenetic the pace, morale within the Desert Air Force was still sky high. Cobber Weinronk was itching to be flying again, while John Fairbairn of 73 Squadron was finding the chase back across the desert exhilarating. Often they were operating alone and entirely independently. "In the flush of victory," wrote John, "the morale of the whole unit was high as a kite and from the CO down to the humble cookhouse wallah, we worked as a single team."[403] He had never before known such unity of purpose or intense comradeship.

The Americans now alongside 112 Squadron at Maturba had been learning more than just how to take on the enemy from their RAF colleagues. "Initially we really didn't have the kind of clothing that was suitable for desert conditions," admits Duke Ellington. "The British, having been there for years, mastered all of this, so we adopted their style, clothing, footwear and especially their desert tents." They also learned to put up with the flies and how to create a makeshift shower from a tin barrel. Soon, they, like their colleagues in the RAF, looked a pretty rough bunch, hardly a slick military outfit at all. "But respect for rank and mission were never compromised," says Duke. "Mission integrity was foremost."

Another thing they learned from the RAF flyers was how to drink whisky. "We were all bourbon guys," says Duke, "but in Alex and Cairo there was unlimited scotch." He didn't like it first, but soon acquired a taste for it. And when they drank, they liked to sing. "We learned a lot of songs from the RAF boys," he says. Soon after their arrival in the desert, Gil Wymond—"a mover-shaker amongst us"—decided they needed a focal point in their mess tent. Although they had few maintenance facilities out there, Gil commandeered a large six-by-eight foot strip of aluminum normally used for patching up damaged aircraft and turned it into a bar. The name of every pilot was painted on, as was the squadron emblem, the "Fighting Cock," always known as "Uncle Bud." At first, Duke was horrified. "Gil, you yardbird," he told his friend, "we got airplanes with holes in and you're building a bar!" But he soon realized he'd been wrong. "That bar became our rallying point," he says, "our morale center." After missions the pilots would immediately head straight for it, and from then on, when they moved to a new landing ground, the bar came too.

Mary Coningham might not have been able to call on any of his bombers, but Tedder and General Brereton had agreed that long-range bombers could now operate from Gambut, just south of Tobruk. The 98th Bomb Group had moved from Palestine to Fayid in the Canal Zone on 11 November, but the idea was for them now to occasionally fly two and a half hours to Gambut where an advance party with fuel and maintenance equipment had already been sent, and from where they could reach Tripoli. Lieutenant Willie Chapman and his crew touched down there on the eighteenth. He had returned to the squadron at the end of September, having made a full recovery from his sprained ankle, and once more joined Paul Francis as copilot. Since their crash over the Alamein line, Paul had taken new crew members on board and also a new B-24, christened the "Daisy Mae."

Willie was not that impressed with Gambut, where facilities were considerably more Spartan than at either Haifa or Fayid. He was often hungry and at night struggled to keep warm in his tent as temperatures dropped dramatically. After three long nights and two twelve-hour missions to Tripoli, he was only too glad when the squadron was sent back to Fayid once more.

Despite the growing spat between Mary Coningham and Monty, they were still messing together, and over dinner on 17 November, began discussing the chances of the First Army reaching Tunis. Tommy Elmhirst reckoned Bizerte would be captured in eight days' time. "And my bet," he added, "is a pukka champagne dinner in the first civilized hotel!"

"Eight days—nonsense!" Mary snorted. "With the Americans completely untrained." Either the Germans had realized the whole of Africa was now under threat or they had not. "If they have," he continued, "you can be sure that they will shove everything into it—absolutely everything."

Monty agreed. "Either the Germans will decide to cut their losses, or they will put up a damn good show."

Tommy was still not convinced. After three years of fighting the Germans, he felt sure the planners would have accurately assessed what the Axis could put into the field in Tunisia. "If we haven't done that," he added, "then we don't deserve to win."

"But we *don't* deserve to win the war!" said Monty. It was a telling comment from the army commander.[404]

Carol Mather had listened with fascination to this conversation, but his time on Monty's staff was nearly over. A week before, he had seen David Stirling, who had told him he was planning another large expedition, this time into the heart of Tripolitania, in order to cut Rommel's supply lines. He wanted Carol to come too. Carol spent several days agonizing over the decision, but in the end decided to rejoin the SAS. On 20 November, the day the Eighth Army took Benghazi, Carol left Monty's

HQ and flew back to Cairo, and then went straight to David Stirling's flat. Most of the old crowd were there, but one face was missing. On their return from the Benghazi raid, Stephen Hastings had suffered a recurrence of his earlier illness. Diagnosed with chronic bronchitis, he had been taken off active service for six months, becoming ADC to Dick Casey, minister of State in the Middle East. After two long years of war, Stephen wasn't complaining.

Carol might have been on the go again, but for most of the troops in Eighth Army, this latest lull in the action was most welcome. For some, it even meant the North African campaign was now drawing to a close. Both the Australians and the 1st South African Division were due to be heading home. Bill Eadie had celebrated the end of the Battle of Alamein with an impromptu fireworks display on 5 November using tracer bullets, Very lights, and star shells—"a real Guy Fawkes display"—And the very next day heard rumors that they would all be going home as soon as they had buried the dead and cleared up the battlefield. This had been one of the tasks for Petrus Dhlamini, who had been horrified to see the carnage and vast numbers of dead that littered the battlefield. On Friday, 13 November, they moved out of their Alamein positions; the next day, they passed through Cairo to a great reception and then went on toward the Suez Canal. Shortly after encamping on the far side of the canal, they were visited and addressed by General Smuts, who also intimated that they would soon be shipped back to South Africa. "Everyone's prepared to move at a moment's notice," noted Bill, "but there is some delay I think because of enemy subs in the Indian Ocean. We won't be home by Xmas."

The Fighting French had also been pulled out of the line, as had B Squadron of the 6th Royal Tank Regiment after their stint guarding Monty at Burg el Arab. On 17 November, they reached the rest of the regiment already at Khatatba, in the Delta. Sam Bradshaw, for one, was absolutely exhausted after two years of war and too many battles. "Eventually the message got through that things were falling apart," he says. "There are reserves, but there's always a limit." He stayed with the regiment and in the Middle East too, but for Sam, the war in North Africa was over.

Not for others, however, although Monty's decision to build up his forces enabled even the forward units to pause and regroup. The Maori were pulled out of the line at Bardia. For a month they swam, marched, played rugby and football, mended roads, and occasionally began intertribal fights. The Sherwood Rangers were also resting. After being among the first tanks into Mersa Matruh, they then stayed put for a fortnight, living off scrounged German ham, Danish butter, and Italian tinned fruit.

Meanwhile, the 2nd Rifle Brigade had pushed forward as far as Maturba, back across familiar battlegrounds. Albert Martin found the experience brought vivid memories back again, most far from pleasant. At Sidi Rezegh, El Adem and then Knightsbridge, the debris of war was all too evident: burned-out lorries and tanks, steel helmets and bits of equipment were everywhere, but now half covered with sand.

And while Eighth Army paused, news of awards arrived. For Monty, there was promotion to full general and a knighthood; there was a knighthood too for Mary Coningham. Stanley Christopherson received a Military Cross for his role in the battle, while Colonel Turner, commander of 2 Rifle Brigade at Snipe, was awarded the highest accolade of all, the Victoria Cross.

In Tunisia, the race was still on, although during the last week of November, things hardly went according to plan. Evelegh was now attempting a three-pronged attack with insufficient forces and committing the old British mistake of trying to advance on far too wide a front without proper equipment. His two infantry brigades had now been reinforced with detachments of American artillery and tanks, but because they had not trained together in Britain, it was the first time these troops had ever operated shoulder to shoulder, and so there was understandable confusion over the differing ways in which British and American troops approached matters.

In the north, 36th Brigade were due to press on towards Bizerte but were halted at Djebels Azzaq and Ajred, soon nicknamed Green Hill Baldy and Hill. Fighting continued for three days, after which 36th Brigade were forced to give up. The 11th Brigade also failed to take Medjez el Bab. The only success was Blade Force, which was pushing forward through the Tine Valley to the north. After overrunning a number of German outposts, an advanced guard of Honeys from the US 1st Armored Regiment reached Djedeida airfield, only twelve miles from Tunis. The American tanks surged forward just as several flights of Stukas were being loaded with bombs. Surprise was total and they managed to destroy twenty aircraft as well as blow up a number of fuel and ammunition dumps before safely withdrawing. Nehring was extremely alarmed by this sudden attack, and believing the Allied armored forces were much greater than they really were, ordered the evacuation of Medjez so that his troops could be better concentrated to defend Tunis.

This enabled 11th Brigade to move forward again. Leaving Barré's French forces in Medjez, they advanced and took Tebourba, but with Blade Force now alongside them they were simply unable to get any further. Axis resistance was fierce, but it was the enemy aerial attacks that really did the damage. Reaching a crescendo during the last days of November, their relentless pounding of the Allied positions proved once again that it was almost impossible in modern war to succeed in the face of overwhelming air superiority. On 30 November, Evelegh recommended to Anderson that he should now pause his attack until sufficient reinforcements had arrived. There was little Anderson could do but agree.

"Where are the RAF?" was a common complaint that filtered its way to Squadron Leader Tony Bartley. He remembered the last time he'd heard that, when they'd flown their hearts out above the cloud over Dunkirk and received only bitter resentment for their efforts. When word arrived that Evelegh was about to begin his all-out attempt to capture Tunis, Tony started mounting standing patrols all day, but with only around a quarter of his squadron serviceable and with a severe shortage of spares and equipment—added to the greater distances they had to travel than their Axis counterparts—it was hard to make much of an impression. Moreover, the Axis had early-warning radar, which, along with their all-weather airfields on the flat plain around Tunis, enabled them to attack with impunity.

On 25 November, Tony watched columns of Allied troops trundling forward beneath him on the road to Medjez el Bab. Late in the afternoon, they spotted a formation of Stukas. As soon as the German pilots saw the Spitfires, they began frantic evasive action, but they were easy meat for someone as experienced as Tony. "I picked on one of them," he noted, "who practically turned himself inside out with contortions before I blew his wing off." He shot down another, then headed for home. On the way, he saw a number of Junker 88s, and although now out of ammunition, ordered the other pilots to follow him as he dived into the enemy bombers. His ruse worked: the Junker 88s jettisoned their bombs in panic.

The next day, he watched a number of American B-17s many thousands of feet above him, their white contrails streaming behind them, vivid against the deep blue sky, as they headed for Bizerte. American flying fortresses of the 97th and 301st Bomb Groups had been withdrawn from the US Eighth Air Force based in England and sent over to North Africa instead. Twenty-two-year-old Lieutenant Ralph Burbridge was bombardier of the *All American,* a B-17 of the 414th Squadron and part of the 97th BG. It had been fortresses of the 97th that had flown Ike and his staff out to Gibraltar a few weeks before, but the 414th had left Grafton Underwood in England later, not arriving at Maison Blanche until 18 November.

From Missouri, in the Midwest, Ralph had joined the air force just before Pearl Harbor. He'd been disappointed not to become a pilot but reckoned so were a lot of other people, so quickly knuckled down to the task assigned to him—one that carried no small amount of responsibility. And when he wasn't aiming their bomb load, he was expected to man one of the guns, the noise of which would reverberate deafeningly around the belly of the aircraft. Ralph had taken part in the 97th's first mission over France—a raid on Rouen on 17 August—a nerve-wracking experience. They nonetheless made it back in one piece, although Ralph soon realized just how underprepared they were for war. "We had a cover of Spitfires," he says, "but otherwise I reckon we'd all have been dead." They learned fast, however, and by the time Ralph and his crew left England, they'd chalked up no less than sixteen combat missions. He and his colleagues in the 97th were just about the only American airmen in the theater with any combat experience at all.

This lack of experience among most of Doolittle's 12th Air Force was painfully obvious to Tony Bartley. Doolittle had sent a fighter group of P-38 Lightnings to Youk les Bains, and on 30 November, 111 Squadron were sharing their patrol line with a number of these twin-engine, twin-fuselage fighters, aircraft that had far greater range than the Spitfires but not the maneuverability to take on highly experienced Luftwaffe pilots in the latest 109s and new Focke-Wulf 190s. Watching them flying in such close formation reminded him of the air displays he'd seen at Hendon as a child—the kind of flying the RAF had long since given up. Had he been on their radio wavelength he'd have called them up and told them to go home. Then he spotted two 109s circling, watching their prey, and selecting their targets. Fortunately for the Lightnings, the German pilots had been so seduced by their easy target that they forgot the most basic rule of all. From above them and out of the sun, Tony led his Spitfires onto them just as they began their dive onto the Americans, and the Messerschmitts were both shot down. Turning for home, Tony glanced back at the Lightnings, sailing on in close formation, completely unaware of the fighting behind them or that they had been moments away from death. "I made a note to get in touch with their group commander as soon as I'd landed and tell him the facts of life," noted Tony, then added, "but it was comforting to see some American support at last."[405]

But even Tony Bartley—for all his experience—was unfamiliar with the kind of close army support flying at which Mary Coningham's fighter squadrons were now so adept. Instead of carrying out a multitude of tasks like the fighters of the Desert Air Force, different squadrons stuck to their traditional roles. One-eleven Squadron were not given bombs or ground-strafing targets; instead they patrolled at high altitude looking for enemy aircraft. Meanwhile, 225 Squadron also stuck rigidly to their tactical reconnaissance duties. This involved flying "along the deck" at very low levels, which, as in the desert, was incredibly dangerous. But unlike the desert, the weather was generally appalling, and the ground extremely hilly and mountainous, making flying even more hazardous. Tac/Rs tended to be carried out in pairs with the leading aircraft doing the reconnaissance while the Number Two weaved behind watching the leader's back, but both were extremely susceptible to flak and small-arms fire from the ground as well as enemy fighters swooping down upon them.

Bryan Colston carried his first low-level Tac/R on 22 November, with Pilot Officer Giles as his Number Two. It was a typically hair-raising mission. Having successfully spotted plenty of enemy movement around Medjez el Bab, Bryan was hit by flak—fortunately not seriously—and then later chased by a 109. He managed to evade it and safely made it back to Bone, but a few days later, P/O Giles was on another Tac/R and both he and his pairing were shot down and killed. The following day, so was another of their pilots. Meanwhile, most of the squadron had been moved forward to Souk el Arba. Because of the shortage of aircraft, Bryan set off with the army air liaison officer and two of the other pilots, Ian Ingram from Australia, and Ken Neill from New Zealand. Overnight, they stopped at a primitive hotel high in the Atlas Mountains. It was freezing cold, so to keep warm they resorted to drinking too much Algerian wine.

The following morning, they got going again, but ten miles from Souk el Arba, their truck broke down. Eventually they had to be towed the rest of the way by an army tank transporter. When they finally reached Souk el Arba, the conditions were appalling. It was pouring rain, and although they managed to scrounge a tent, the ground was sodden. With their penknives, Bryan and Ken Neill unsuccessfully tried to dig a drainage ditch around it. In the end, the two of them resorted to sleeping on a wooden table, but because they were both over six feet tall and the table was only five feet long, they kept falling off. To make matters worse, the airfield was bombed and strafed repeatedly throughout the night and the next morning. After this deeply uncomfortable night, Bryan and Ken were off early on another Tac/R. The rain had gone, but now the sun was dazzlingly bright in their eyes. Bryan did spot some enemy tanks, however, and so opened fire on them. To his dismay, his cannon shells simply pinged off them. He later discovered these had been the new German Tigers. Meanwhile, Ian Ingram, on another sortie, was also shot down and killed—the fifth pilot since their arrival in Africa. Two days later, once again flying over the battle area, Bryan mistakenly opened fire on some British troops—men from the 2nd Hampshires, he discovered later. "I was practically in tears over that," he admits. "I just prayed I hadn't killed any of them."

But no wonder the air operations—and in turn the land operations—were not going to plan. During those early days in Tunisia, the lack of equipment and facilities, the relentless bombing and strafing, and the awful weather meant the pilots were suffering conditions as bad as at any time and in any theater of the entire war.

Harry Butcher slipped over to Algiers from Gibraltar on 17 November on a house-hunting mission for Ike and Mark Clark. Together with Clark's aide, they set off in a jeep and before long, Butch noticed two large white villas perched on a hillside that were not on his rental list. Later, they discovered they were both owned by a wealthy pro-German wine merchant—and that they hadn't already been requisitioned. "So without further ado," noted Butch, "Headquarters Command filed appropriate papers with the French, we having come as liberators, not as conquerors."[406] Job done, he returned to Gibraltar.

Five days later, Ike and his staff finally moved to North Africa. The Allied C-in-C had been itching to get over there for some days, but on his arrival at Tafaraouia, south of Oran, Ike came up against the kind of weather that had been giving his armed forces such trouble. A tail wheel burst on landing and then, having taxied off the landing strip, they promptly got stuck in mud. After a half day delay while the wheel was fixed and their plane towed out of trouble, they flew on to Algiers. There, Ike soon discovered there were other problems. The initial advance into Tunisia had been carried out by troops from the Algiers area—the closest to the front—but a few days before, Ike had given orders for more US units to be sent up to Tunisia from around Oran. This had simply not happened. At his office in the St. George Hotel, he met Brigadier-General Lunsford Oliver, commander of Combat Command B, a section of 1st Armored Division and rather similar to a British brigade group. Oliver had returned from a reconnaissance trip to the front and realized the railway network was insufficient to take his troops to the battle area quickly enough, and so had asked permission to take part of his command on the seven hundred-mile trip by road, in half-track troop carriers. His request had been refused, however, on the grounds that half the life expectancy of the half-tracks would be used in just getting them there.

Ike soon overruled such objections, although he could not blame the staff officer in question. "He had been trained assiduously, through years of peace, in the eternal need for economy," wrote Ike. "He had not yet accepted the essential harshness of war; he did not realize that the word is synonymous with waste, nor did he understand that every positive action requires expenditure."[407] These staff officers would soon catch on later to such a degree that enormous equipment wastage would be looked on with mounting envy by their British allies. But as the first weeks of the great adventure came and went, the huge inexperience of both American and British forces was seriously counting against them. And there would be a few more knocks before the harsh lessons of war began to take effect.

CHAPTER 18

Harsh Realities:
December 1942

ADMIRAL CUNNINGHAM moved to Algiers with his staff a day after Eisenhower. Like Ike, ABC had also sent an advance party to prepare offices and a place to stay, and like both Clark and Eisenhower, set up his HQ in the St. George Hotel. But it also turned out that one of his staff had earmarked the very same villas that had been spotted by Harry Butcher. During the intervening days, the staffs of the respective commanders had been having quite a tussle on behalf of their bosses. Fortunately, there was an easy resolution: Ike took one, ABC the other, while Clark remained in town, an arrangement that was to benefit both commanders in the weeks and months to come. Commanding magnificent views of Algiers and its harbor, the villas were also luxuriously equipped inside—"too velvet-arsed and Rolls Royce," as ABC would say; the owner might have been pro-Nazi, but his taste was exemplary.

But as Cunningham quickly discovered, Algiers was no bed of roses. Enemy bombers arrived daily, and the Allies continued to be short of much equipment and many basic facilities; unloading from the harbor continued to be slow due to a lack of transport. At Oran, the inner harbor was still blocked with sunken ships, as ABC had seen for himself during a visit in the middle of November. The French Fleet had remained stuck in Toulon, much to his annoyance, but when the Germans tried to seize it on 27 November, the French Navy reacted quickly. Most ships were promptly scuttled, including a battleship, two battle cruisers, four heavy and three light cruisers, and although the only warships to finally reach Allied ports were three submarines, the Germans were only able to lay their hands on six undamaged destroyers and a submarine.

At least the news from Malta was good. A complete convoy had reached Grand Harbor. The siege of his beloved island was over. He had also reconstituted a fast anti-shipping force. Force K had been most effec-

Cecil Beaton's photograph of Air Vice-Marshal Arthur Coningham in May 1942. Known to all as 'Mary,' he was an inspirational and brilliant leader, with a masterful understanding of modern air warfare.

LEFT Sam Bradshaw. He was already a veteran of the Desert War when he was horrifically wounded at Sidi Rezegh in November 1941. The Eighth Army was not going to send a good tank man home in a hurry, however, and three months later he was back with the regiment.

RIGHT Left to right: Norrie, Ritchie and 'Strafer' Gott. Well might Ritchie scratch his head. A highly capable staff officer, he was out of his depth as a battlefield commander. His inability to control his senior officers was to prove disastrous.

BELOW The South African, Bill Eadie. Bill may have only been an NCO, but his assessments of what was going on around him were usually uncannily accurate.

ABOVE The difference between British and German equipment. The Tommy here is using a battered standard four-gallon petrol tin to fill up a captured German jerrican. General Tuker reckoned the British lost nearly 50 per cent of their fuel using inadequate fuel cans.

ABOVE They look as though they are ready to head off to the Boer War, but incredibly this picture of the Sherwood Ranger Yeomanry was taken during their summer camp of 1939. They later took their steeds off to war as well, and in Palestine, their sabres drawn, took part in a cavalry charge. Although fully mechanised by the summer of 1942, it took them a while to treat their tanks like machines rather than thoroughbreds.

LEFT The US Army had a lot of catching up to do. Cavalry horses are tethered at Fort Benning, Georgia in 1940. Even in 1941, the US government was still buying more horses for the cavalry.

RIGHT Henry Bowles taking aim at Fort Benning, not long after joining the First Infantry Division. Here, he is using the new M1 Garand Rifle, but many recruits used wooden imitation rifles for much of their training.

RIGHT Gazala. A British Tommy crouches as yet another shell explodes.

(Imperial War Museum, London)

(courtesy of Frances Evans)

ABOVE Bing Evans with his fiancée, Frances Wheeler. After being sent overseas, Bing would not see her again for three-and-a-half years.

(Halton Archive/Getty Images)

ABOVE The Desert Fox. The fact that Rommel was so revered by the men of the Eighth Army says more about British generalship than it does about the German commander's abilities. Charismatic and certainly an inspirational leader of men, he was not, however, the tactical genius of legend and failed to understand fully the relationship between the army and air forces – a failure that was to cost him dear.

LEFT A Grant tank of Sam Bradshaw's 6 RTR. The low-mounted 75mm gun can be clearly seen, yet despite its limitations, this US-built machine was a vast improvement on anything the British had produced at that time.

(Imperial War Museum, London)

(Imperial War Museum, London)

(Imperial War Museum, London)

ABOVE LEFT A British infantry-carrying truck of the 7 Motor Brigade. Very similar to that used by Albert Martin and his section of Riflemen, it has been stripped down to its most basic form. Here, British troops try and get some well-earned rest.

ABOVE RIGHT A legionnaire proudly holds the flag of the 13 DBLE. The Free French Brigade's heroic stand at Bir Hacheim won them much-deserved respect from their reluctant Eighth Army allies, and because of it they were soon re-named the Fighting French.

RIGHT Susan Travers at Bir Hacheim. This extraordinary woman and lover of General Koenig was the only female member of the French Foreign Legion. Wounded in Eritrea, she later drove Koenig and the brilliant Colonel Amilakvari to safety during the break-out from the French outpost.

(courtesy of Wendy Holden)

Kittyhawks of
Billy Drake's 112
'Shark' Squadron
lined up ready at
a landing ground
in the Western
Desert.

(ww2images.com)

(Imperial War Museum, London)

(courtesy of Harold Harper)

ABOVE The much-feared German 88mm gun.
Originally designed as an anti-aircraft gun, it soon
proved its worth as a high-velocity anti-tank gun.
It was the anti-tank gun, not the tank, that was the
decisive weapon in the Desert War – and the 88mm
was the best on both sides. The British could have
used their 3.7 inch AA-gun in the same role, but
inexcusably failed to do so.

ABOVE Harold Harper. Another
long-serving veteran of the
North African campaign. Harold
survived the Siege of Tobruk of
1941, only to be wounded and
taken prisoner at Gazala. He
escaped, made it to safety, and
after a spell in hospital, returned
to front-line duties once more.

(Imperial War Museum, London)

ABOVE US-built Elco MTBs surge across the Mediterranean. Fast and highly manoeuvrable, they were also surprisingly well-armed, and a potentially very effective coastal vessel.

(Imperial War Museum, London)

ABOVE Tobruk suffered some of the most intense bombardments of the North Africa campaign. This picture was taken by Cecil Beaton in May 1942, some weeks before its surrender. Buildings are barely standing, while ships lie sunken in the harbour.

RIGHT TOP Charles Coles, commander of MTB 262. His twenty-fifth birthday was to become the most memorable of his life, spent fighting for his life during the Fall of Tobruk.

RIGHT Sophie Tarnowska. Sophie managed to escape from Poland in 1940, and eventually made her way to the Middle East. There, at the suggestion of General Sikorski, she set up the Polish Red Cross.

(courtesy of Charles Coles)

(courtesy of Sophie Moss)

ABOVE LEFT Mary Coningham's deputy and chief of administration, Air-Commodore Tommy Elmhirst. The two were chalk and cheese, but together, made a great team. An unsung hero of the North Africa campaign, it was Tommy's brilliant organisational skills that enabled the Desert Air Force to function at such high levels of serviceability, while his system of 'leap-frogging' enabled them to advance and retreat at speeds that completely out-foxed the Axis.

ABOVE RIGHT John Fairbairn, second from the left with the pipe. Joining 73 Squadron on the eve of the Gazala battles, he certainly had a baptism of fire. Fortunately, he survived his first few sorties and learned quickly. Many were not so lucky.

LEFT Billy Drake. A veteran of the Battle for France and the Battle of Britain, Billy was a tough, highly experienced fighter-pilot by the time he took over 112 Squadron in May 1942.

(Imperial War Museum, London)

Determined, resolute, and a brilliant administrator, General Eisenhower
reached England in June 1942 as a comparative unknown junior American general.
He soon impressed, not least because of his fervent belief in Anglo-US unity and a
singleness of purpose between the new Allies.

ABOVE General Auchinleck. Highly regarded by his men and an experienced and firm battlefield commander, he was less suited to the role of C-in-C and far less successful at choosing the right men to command Eighth Army. The Auk, as he was known, also became too wrapped up in trying to ape, without the necessary training, the superior German battlefield tactics.

ABOVE Eisenhower's Naval 'Aide'. Harry Butcher, a public relations and media expert, was Ike's friend and sidekick – as well as diary keeper – throughout the planning of TORCH and the subsequent campaign in North Africa.

ABOVE Bostons carpet bomb Axis targets.

LEFT The four-crew members of this South African Boston bomber prepare for another mission. 'The Eighteen Imperturbables,' as their formations were known, were instrumental in grinding down the effectiveness of Rommel's war machine.

(courtesy of Sarah Weinronk)

(courtesy of Maiki Parkinson)

ABOVE LEFT The South African, Jack 'Cobber' Weinronk. Always cheerful and positive, Cobber was one pilot who actively enjoyed his experiences of flying over the Western Desert.

ABOVE RIGHT Maiki Parkinson. Just eighteen in 1942, Maiki went to extraordinary lengths to join the 28th Maori Battalion. He finally joined them shortly after the retreat to the Alamein Line.

(Alexander Turnball Library)

LEFT No wonder the Axis troops came to fear the Maori. Although there was conscription in New Zealand for the whites – or 'pakehas' – the Maori who made up the 28th Battalion were all volunteers.

ABOVE Alex and Monty. British forces in the Middle East were in dire need of a change at the top by August 1942, and in Generals Alexander and Montgomery they found a team that offered resolute and firm leadership, and clear-headed military thinking.

RIGHT In May 1942, the SAS increased in size and then throughout the summer, with help from the Long Range Desert Group, carried a number of increasingly outrageous and daring raids behind enemy lines. The distances they travelled, over extremely difficult terrain, were phenomenal. Here, they pause by the Gilf Kebir, some five hundred miles south of Alamein.

(courtesy of Edward Ellington)

(Imperial War Museum, London)

ABOVE LEFT Duke Ellington. As part of the US 57th Fighter Group, Duke was one of the first American fighter pilots to reach the Middle East.

ABOVE RIGHT A night fighter Hurricane of 73 Squadron prepares to take off.

(Imperial War Museum, London)

(courtesy of Albert Martin)

ABOVE A Crusader tank, like those used by Stanley Christopherson's 'A' Squadron of the Sherwood Rangers. Huge clouds of dust follow in the wake of this single tank. An entire armoured division on the move could create a vast and choking fog of finely ground sand that made visibility almost impossible.

LEFT This photograph of Albert Martin was taken during leave in Cairo, shortly after receiving his sergeant's stripes. Like Sam Bradshaw, he was wounded at Sidi Rezegh, but also soon returned to front-line duty. At the Battle of Alamein, Albert took part in the Snipe action, the 2nd Rifle Brigade's finest hour and a turning point in the ten-day battle.

RIGHT AND BELOW RIGHT The Battle of Alamein. Tommies shelter behind a knocked-out Mk III Panzer . . . then leave their shelter to continue the advance. One of their men has been wounded and is being tended by a medic.

(Imperial War Museum, London)

BELOW Johnny Bain. A reluctant combatant, he had already run away from the army once before being posted overseas. The Battle of Alamein, where he was part of the first wave with the 51st Highland Division, was his first experience of combat.

(Imperial War Museum, London)

(courtesy of Vernon Scannell)

(courtesy of Joe Madeley)

ABOVE Bronzed Aussies on the beach on 20 October 1942, just four days before they would be going into battle. Joe Madeley is on the right, middle row, while his childhood friend from Wheethalle, Keith Boal is standing second from the right and wearing the captured German Luftwaffe field cap. Few here made it through the battle unscathed.

(Imperial War Museum, London)

The majority of Italians in North Africa were also reluctant combatants. The last thing on this man's mind was clearly his home and family – he is clutching a photograph of what appears to be his baby daughter.

A B O V E Part of the TORCH invasion force on its way to North Africa.

R I G H T GIs aboard their landing craft *en route* to the North African beaches. Many of these men were barely men at all, but teenagers with no comprehension at all of what lay in store.

LEFT The Bowles twins from Alabama – Tom (left) and Henry (right). This shot was taken in England in 1944, a week before D-Day, by which time they were veterans not only of North Africa, but the Sicily campaign as well.

BELOW Lieutenant Randolph Paulsen. This resilient New Yorker was determined not to miss out when his unit set sail for North Africa, despite suffering from a torn Achilles tendon and blood poisoning. Although marginally better by the time he reached French Morocco, his landing craft found itself miles off course. He and his men finally managed to rejoin their unit just before Casablanca fell to the Americans.

BELOW Pilots from the 33rd Fighter Group take off from the USS *Chenango,* bound for Port Lyautey in French Morocco, on 11 November 1942. None of the pilots had ever taken off from an aircraft carrier before, and not all made it.

LEFT Carol Mather setting off for the final large-scale SAS operation in North Africa, November 1942.

BELOW There was not enough planning or preparation for the Allied air forces in Northwest Africa, and for both pilots and groundcrew, the first few months were deeply frustrating. Here at Maison Blanche, supplies are littered all over the airfield, lacking any kind of order or organisation.

RIGHT Ships being unloaded at Algiers. In Northwest Africa, the tables were suddenly turned. Now it was the Allies, not the Axis, who had the long lines of communication. In the race for Tunis, this was to be decisive.

LEFT An American artillery crew firing. They are using a World War I-designed howitzer, like those used by Joe Furayter and the 5th Field Artillery Battalion.

BELOW Paras from the 2nd Battalion Parachute Brigade. With their red berets and lightweight jackets, these elite troops looked quite different from the regular infantry.

BELOW For the first few months, the Tunisian campaign was characterised by freezing temperatures, rain and mud. Here, men of the Royal Inniskilling Fusiliers tramp across the northern Tunisian countryside.

RIGHT An American GI's muddy boots. Everything ground to a halt in the mud. For the 'Poor Bloody Infantry', trench foot soon became a problem.

ABOVE Squadron Leader Tony Bartley with his pilots. He looks happy enough here in this posed publicity shot, but for Tony, after more than two years of near continuous combat flying, Tunisia was to be one campaign too many.

LEFT Ike and ABC. Admiral Cunningham was a firm supporter – and friend – of Eisenhower's, and was of the same mind over the matter of Anglo-US unity of purpose.

LEFT The crew of HMS *Safari*. Under their brilliant CO, Commander Ben Bryant, they sunk more Axis shipping than any other Allied submarine in the war. Bryant is to the right of centre, his hands in his pockets, with a bearded Ronnie Ward to his right.

RIGHT Ike visits Eighth Army in January 1943. To his right is Major-General Francis Tuker of the 4th Indian Division. A master tactician, Tuker's talents were sorely wasted. Had Britain had more commanders of his calibre, the campaign in North Africa might have been over a lot earlier.

LEFT Roosevelt and Churchill address journalists at the Casablanca Conference. 'The scene was irresistibly like a Sunday-school treat, with the children gathered at the feet of their two schoolmistresses,' noted Alan Moorehead.

RIGHT Bryan Colston, right, with the New Zealander Ken Neill, left. The pilots of 225 Squadron suffered like everyone else from the lack of facilities and appalling weather, although they were given a boost with the arrival of their first Spitfires early in the new year.

LEFT Jim Reed of the 33rd Fighter Group, holding up his damaged thumb, which prevented him from flying for a month.

ABOVE Shortly before this photograph was taken, a Messerschmitt 109 had hit the B-17 *All American*, severing through three-quarters of the fuselage and knocking off the portside stabiliser. Part of the 109's wing was left in the wreckage. Incredibly, the *All American* continued to lead the formation back to base and landed with the crew – Ralph Burbridge included – in one piece.

ABOVE LEFT Ernie Pyle. More than any other journalist, he conveyed the soldier's view of the war. An acute observer with an unerring understanding of human nature, he became an American national treasure, beloved as much by those at the front line as the millions back home.

ABOVE RIGHT Bucky Walters. Severely under-trained by the time they reached the front line in February 1943, Bucky and the men of the 34th Infantry Division had a demoralising time in Tunisia until their redemption on Hill 609.

ABOVE US troops from the 1st Armored Division hurry towards Sidi Bou Zid on 14 February. The following day, appalling generalship, woeful lack of training, and inexperience in battle would lead them to a valley of death every bit as lethal as that at Balaclava ninety years before.

Alex at the HQ he shared with Mary Coningham in the hills at Ain Beida. He quickly took hold of the situation in Tunisia and Allied fortunes soon began to turn for the better.

(courtesy of Celia Elmhirst)

ABOVE Morning Prayers. Mary Coningham holds his normal morning meeting outside his caravan at Ain Beida. Left to right: Mary, Larry Kuter, George Pirie and Tommy Elmhirst.

(National Archives & Records Administration, College Park, MD)

ABOVE GIs travel back through the Kasserine Pass. Poor generalship and insufficient training was behind the shock defeat, but the Americans learnt fast and soon had their revenge.

(courtesy of Peter Moore)

ABOVE Peter Moore. Arriving fresh from England, Peter and the 2/4 Leicesters soon found themselves in the thick of the fighting, helping to stem two major Axis advances. Theirs was a brutal baptism of fire.

RIGHT General Patton. An inspiring leader and brim-full of charisma, he was already something of a legend before he reached North Africa. But he was also temperamental and pig-headed, and was sensibly kept on a tight reign by Alexander during his command of US II Corps. Patton also failed to understand the use of air power, something that led a major ideological disagreement with Mary Coningham.

BELOW Captain Nigel Nicolson. Nigel reached Tunisia in January 1943 as an intelligence officer with the 3rd Grenadier Guards, but was soon promoted to IO of the entire Guards Brigade, a job he found both rewarding and exciting.

ABOVE Ray Saidel. Originally earmarked as officer material, Ray's left-wing political views ensured he arrived in Tunisia as a private and in a pool of replacement troops. After a stint as a truck driver, he was posted to the depleted 1st Armored Division.

ABOVE Men of the Big Red One in their foxholes at El Guettar. With very little soil, the hard rock was a nightmare to dig into, whilst shellfire often created lethal splinters and shards.

BELOW The crew of an American half-track camp down for the night. Ray Saidel found himself operating in such a vehicle on his arrival in the 1st Armored Regiment.

LEFT Margaret Hornback and her officer boyfriend, Andy. Margaret volunteered to serve overseas and worked throughout the campaign – often in difficult conditions and with limited supplies – as a nurse with the US 48th Surgical (later 128th Evacuation) Hospital.

LEFT A Valentine lies bogged down and useless in the Wadi Zigzaou. The assault on the Mareth Line was badly managed by General Leese. Ordering poorly armed and obsolete Valentine tanks across the Wadi Zigzaou, instead of lighter and more effective anti-tank guns proved a tactical blunder, especially once the rain came.

RIGHT Four Spitfire Mk Vs of Bryan Colston's 225 Squadron fly over Tunisia.

ABOVE Gurkhas in action. General Tuker was rightly proud of his Gurkha battalions and at Mareth, and then spectacularly at Wadi Akarit, they proved how effective they could be.

LEFT The Allied armies finally meet. Tension between American and British troops has often been exaggerated. On the whole, the Eighth Army had a massive superiority complex, but looked down their noses at the British First Army more than they did the US II Corps.

(Imperial War Museum, London)

LEFT A British 25-pounder in action in Tunisia, as used by David Brown's 17th Field Regiment, RA.

(Alexander Turnball Library)

RIGHT Takrouna. A shell explodes during the battle. In the foreground is the dense cactus through which the Maori had to advance.

(National Archives & Records Administration, College Park, MD)

ABOVE B-17s over Tunisia. For the most part, General Doolittle's Flying Fortresses concentrated on attacking ports, shipping and other targets in Tunisia, while the Liberators of the 98th and 376th Bomb Groups concentrated on bombing Italian ports across the Mediterranean. The Axis had no such heavy bomber force to support their efforts on the ground.

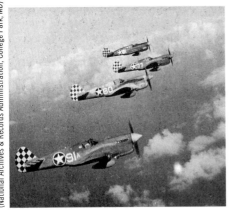

(National Archives & Records Administration, College Park, MD)

LEFT American Curtiss Warhawks, long-range auxiliary fuel tanks slung between the undercarriage, on another sortie. These four are from the 325th Fighter Group.

BELOW Colonel Art Salisbury reads a telegram of congratulations to his pilots of the 57th FG after the April 18 'Palm Sunday Turkey Shoot', when they were largely responsible for shooting down over seventy enemy transport planes off Cap Bon.

(57th Fighter Group Association)

RIGHT Alex strides purposefully with Monty at a meeting south of Enfidaville. Following behind are AVM Harry Broadhurst, Brigadier-General Larry Kuter, Mary Coningham and Air Chief Marshal Sir Arthur Tedder.

(courtesy of Celia Elmhirst)

LEFT An American Sherman speeds by during the final phases of the campaign. All tanks had their faults, but with its 75mm gun, mechanical reliability, and comparative speed, it was the best Allied tank available at the time, and gave British and American tank crews something that was on a par with most Panzer Mk IIIs and IVs.

RIGHT Hill 609. 'Get me that hill,' General Omar Bradley told General 'Doc' Ryder, 'and no one will ever again doubt the toughness of your division.' The 34th 'Red Bull' Division did exactly as Bradley asked, showing extraordinary courage and determination in a five-day battle of repeated assaults and counter-attacks on one of the toughest pieces of terrain in Northern Tunisia.

ABOVE British 3.7 inch anti-aircraft guns being used as artillery during the final push through the Medjerda Valley. Such use of these guns was something that should have happened far more often and a great deal earlier in the campaign.

RIGHT Ray Saidel's picture of his half-track passing through the liberated French colonial town of Ferryville during the last week of the war. He made many sketches during his time in North Africa – he did this one using gasoline and oil.

ABOVE US II Corps proved how much they had learned during the final phase of the campaign. Here, GIs move forward in Bizerte.

ABOVE The end in Africa. Over a quarter of a million were captured between March and the surrender in May – a staggering amount, and at the time, one of the biggest defeats of the war for the Axis.

tive during the autumn of 1941, and now a similar cruiser force—Force Q—was put into action against an enemy convoy that had been reported heading to Tunisia via Ultra. Steaming towards their quarry, Force Q intercepted the convoy shortly after midnight on 2 December. "For the enemy it was a holocaust," wrote ABC. Engaged at point-blank range, four supply ships and three destroyers were sunk. "It was a ghastly scene of ships exploding and bursting into flame amidst clouds of steam and smoke," he added.[408] The following morning, British submarines reported that the sea was littered with debris, thick oil and corpses.

ABC might have favored initial landings at Bizerte, but now that the Axis were in Tunisia in such force and with so many enemy aircraft operating from Sicily and Sardinia, he realized that any attempts to sail reinforcements further east than Bone was out of the question. As it was, Bone was receiving a daily beating, although none so severe as that of 4 December, when at dawn, the port came under especially heavy attack. Unfortunately, the quays and jetties were congested with petrol, ammunition, and other supplies, and the place turned into something of an inferno, with heavy casualties and loss of ordnance. Nonetheless, because the roads were so bad and the railway so poor, a shuttle service of small boats had to continue ferrying up and down the Algerian coast. The bulk of this work was given to four requisitioned cross-channel steamers, who valiantly managed to carry no less than 16,000 troops into Bone by 5 December. Sailing by night, and under constant threat of attack from air and submarine, their regular voyages were always eventful, but crucially, always successful too. Their efforts were, ABC noted proudly, "an outstanding achievement."[409]

His submariners were doing less well, however. For some reason, they'd hit a bad patch, yet the need to disrupt the Axis supply routes from Italy was as great now as ever. Far too much was reaching both Tunisia and Rommel's retreating panzer army. One notable exception, however, was HMS/S *Safari*, which was almost single-handedly accounting for the 10th Flotilla's scoreboard. During November, she was on patrol for three whole weeks, and when she and her crew crept back to Malta on 24 November, they did so with a further four more bars stitched on to her Jolly Roger. This included a 3,000-ton tanker, which they had been ordered to intercept in the Gulf of Sirte. After covering five hundred miles in fifty-one hours, they eventually caught up and chased it back into the tiny Libyan harbor of Ras Ali. The water had been so shallow, they'd been unable to dive, but at night, and in a difficult and rising swell, they had fired a torpedo from over two miles' distance. The tanker had erupted in a sheet of flames. Over the next few days they visited Ras Ali again, finding it packed with landing craft. As well as sinking and damaging a number of lighters, they also hit a panzer that had been down by the pier. *Safari* claimed to be the only submarine to torpedo a tank on dry land. And their extraordinary success continued. On their next patrol, in December, they arrived back in Malta with a further five bars on the Jolly Roger. During the three months that *Safari* had been attached to the 10th Submarine Flotilla, her crew had sunk a staggering 15 vessels. She was the most successful submarine operating in the Mediterranean by a considerable margin.

Although Brigadier-General Lunsford Oliver's Combat Command B was now up at the Tunisian front, most of the American troops that had landed at Oran were encamped in row upon row of pup tents, waiting in reserve for their orders to move forward, and trying to make the best of things through the mud and rain. Bing Evans and the other Rangers were still at Arzew, guarding gun positions and providing town security, while the Big Red One was similarly given the job of keeping order in Oran. All too often, however, it was the troops that needed the policing. The 18th Infantry had the reputation for being the worst-disciplined outfit in the whole division, and when not on duty most of the GIs would make a beeline for Oran on the hunt for wine. "Our commanding officer said he didn't care what we did as long as we fought," says Tom Bowles; he meant on the battlefield, however, not in bars, but drunken GIs frequently ended up brawling. On one occasion, Henry Bowles and his buddy Blake C. Owens had gone into Oran looking for a good time, and having had a few drinks stumbled into a bar full of Legionnaires. As Blake began to get drunk, he started arguing with some of them; and then fists started flying. It was all Henry could do to get Blake out of there. "There were only us two GIs," says Henry, "but that place was full of the French Foreign Legion."

Not all the 1st Infantry Division was stuck in Algiers, however. On 20 November, the US 5th Field Battalion had been one of the artillery units hurriedly sent to the front to bolster the British forces in their attempted final surge toward Tunis. "The British needed the heavy stuff," says Joe Furayter, a gunner in A Battery, "and so orders came to pack up and head for Tunis. They said we'd be under British command."

The 5th Field Artillery were equipped with 155mm howitzers, although it had taken a few days after the landings for them to be reunited with their guns. Landing at Arzew, they had been waiting for their howitzers when they'd come under French fire. The first guns to arrive were four 105mm—from an entirely different unit—but their crews didn't seem to be around, so the 5th were told to take them and to start firing at the French right away. Only after the fall of Oran were they finally given their 155s.

It was Joe's second time in the army. Born in 1917, he had grown up in Uniontown, a mining settlement fifty miles southeast of Pittsburgh. Life was tough; the Depression affected the mining towns of Pennsylvania just as it did most places in the US, but his family was blighted by tragedy when, in 1934, his father and nineteen-year-old brother were killed in a mining accident. Joe tried to find work and to help his mother, but there was little on offer, and so in 1938, he joined the army.

Back then the artillery still used horse-drawn gun carriages—such was the backwardness of the US Army. He left after two years, became a miner like his father, but then in 1942 was drafted and joined the 5th Field Artillery. The horses had gone, but they were still using First World War 1918 howitzers, guns that went with them to North Africa. "They were good, though," says Joe. But big—Joe was a loader, one of two men needed just to lift the ninety-five-pound shell into the breech. There were seven men on each gun: two loaders, two to ram the shell into the breech, the powder man and the fuse man; and the gunner corporal, whose job it was to receive the gun program and to set the sights, elevation and quadrant.

The British Eighth Army might have been made up of people from around the dominions, but in many ways the US Army was just as polyglot. Joe's parents were from Slovakia—they had immigrated to America just before the First World War, and indeed there were large numbers of first- and second-generation Europeans—even Germans—in the US forces in North Africa. In Joe's gun crew there were also two Spaniards, one of whom could barely speak English. It didn't bother Joe one jot that they would be serving under British command. "We were all one," says Joe. "No one paid any attention to whether we were British or American."

In trucks with the guns towed behind, they hurried through the rain along the tortuous road to Tunisia, reporting to General Evelegh at the mountain town of Souk Ahras four days later. How Evelegh expected to command his forces from a mountain HQ some 120 miles behind the front and with poor access and communications to his forward units is unclear, but the Americans were told to head on to Beja, where they would find the headquarters of 11th Infantry Brigade. Even this was fifty miles from the forward troops, a fact that no doubt added to the sense of confusion and almost breathtaking number of different and muddled orders issued to the 5th Field Battalion.

In Beja, they were told to head for positions southwest of Medjez el Bab. Reconnaissance parties then went forward, but soon after, the orders changed; they were to go to a different position east of Beja instead. By the time a messenger caught up with the reconnaissance party, they were sixty miles from where they should have been. The following day, the battalion managed to get themselves together again, and on reporting to

78th Division's command post were told they would be taking over positions vacated by the British 132nd Field Regiment; then they were told the 132nd would not be leaving after all. The battalion had to hastily reconnoitre new positions, but by now it was dark. The following day, 27 November, they were given yet another position, this time northeast of Tebourba. On the twenty-eighth, they were told to reconnoiter a further area north of Djedeida, seven miles beyond Tebourba. En route to this latest location, the battalion reconnaissance party reached Tebourba. It was the middle of the night and the town was coming under heavy aerial bombardment. Furthermore, the Americans were told that the enemy now held the road east-west between Tebourba and Djedeida. Not unnaturally, the Americans wondered whether they were still expected to go forward. Yes, they were told, and right away. Taking this news on the chin, the battalion reconnaissance party set out once more. It was now 11 PM; the rest of the battalion was to follow two hours later.

Just as the main party of the battalion was about to set out, an officer arrived saying the CRA (Commander Royal Artillery) had now canceled the move north of Djedeida after all. Urgent messages were then sent by radio recalling the reconnaissance party, but it was already too late. Although a few men made it back by 4:30 AM, the majority of the forward party—including the battalion commander, Colonel Stout, and commanders of HQ, B and D Batteries—had run into a heavy enemy formation just west of Djedeida and had been killed, with a number of others taken prisoner. With the battalion's command ripped from them before they'd fired a single shell at the Germans, the battalion executive, Major Robert Tyson, hastily took over and reorganized his men, promoting several officers to take over the affected batteries. By 5 PM that day, 29 November, the American gunners were finally given orders to position themselves in support of 11th Brigade, around Tebourba. Before dawn the following morning, A and B Batteries pulled into an olive orchard near El Bathan, southeast of Tebourba and near to where a bridge crossed the River Medjerda. There they began digging furiously—foxholes for the men and ammunitions pits for their shells. The British were struggling: on unfamiliar terrain, and with a chronic shortage of supplies, their lack of experience was showing itself all too clearly.

Muddled planning and confusion had also threatened the 2nd Parachute Battalion's first operation in North Africa. On the morning of 28 November, Lieutenant-Colonel Frost was briefed to take the battalion and capture an enemy airfield at Pont du Fahs, some forty miles south of Tunis the following day. Having destroyed any enemy aircraft they could find, they were then to move to another airstrip at Depienne, twelve miles away; having knocked out all the aircraft there, they were then to cover another twelve miles and repeat the performance at Oudna. Mission accomplished, they were then to link up with the forward units of 78th Division as they advanced towards Tunis. Frost was keen as mustard to get into action, but this seemed like quite a big task one way or another. They were not going in with any transport, so would have to rely entirely on their legs or capturing vehicles, and they would have to carry enough ammunition, food, radios, batteries, and other supplies for at least five days. There was little information on offer about the local inhabitants or the likely opposition, but nonetheless, Frost felt sure they were equal to the task—there was talk of a combined thrust toward Tunis and he had visions of him and his troops arriving *primus in Carthago,* glorious heroes all.

Over six hundred of them, including a troop of Para sappers were to be flown by American Dakotas the following day. The Dakotas normally lived at Blida and so were going to fly to Maison Blanche first thing in the morning. Frost was told the number of aircraft available and how and where they would line up ready for loading, and so made loading plans accordingly, but when, early the next day, the battalion moved up to the airfield, he discovered that not only were the aircraft lined up completely differently from how he'd been told, their numbering system was also totally at odds with what they'd been expecting, so it was impossible to know which lot of men and supply containers was supposed to go where. It was also raining, so the trucks that had taken the troops to the aircraft were now getting stuck in mud. To make matters worse, Frost was then informed that there were no enemy aircraft at either Pont du Fahs or Depienne, which meant a last-minute change of plan. He decided they should now make the drop over Depienne, proceed to Oudna, then make their way to St. Cyprien to link up with the First Army. Time was now running short and it was not possible to either brief all the pilots or his men properly, or sufficiently study a new drop zone.

Despite this, they took off as planned in forty-four Dakotas. The sky was clear and cloudless as they flew over the mountains, but it was an uncomfortable journey. Through the windows, Frost watched other planes lurching up and down from the turbulence. Ever since arriving two weeks before, Frost had been itching for him and his men to be given something worthwhile to do. A week before he'd gone on a reconnaissance flight over Sousse—there'd been talk of an Allied landing there using troops from Malta and with the Paras in support—and although there had been a great risk from enemy fighters, it had been Americans who'd shot at them as they'd tried to land to refuel. Nothing had come of the plan, however, doubly frustrating for Frost because the 1st and 3rd Battalions had already had plenty to do, as had the American paratroopers.

Few men relished soldiering as much as Colonel Frost. Of stocky build and sporting a dark moustache, Frost was just thirty years old, and had only taken over as battalion commander en route to Africa, when the existing CO had become too ill to carry on. He had, however, already shown himself to be an exceptional commander of men, and was one of the very few in the parachute brigade who had proved himself in combat before reaching North Africa.

In November 1942, parachuting was still in its infancy. The Germans had used airborne troops to great effect during the Blitzkreig, but at the time, Britain, typically, had no equivalent. It was left largely to Churchill to ensure that the army embraced the use of airborne forces, demanding a corps of at least 5,000 men. The commandos began the process, but by the time of the first British airborne operation—an attack on an aqueduct in Southern Italy in February 1941–42 (Parachute) Commando was still only five hundred men strong. Frost joined in September that year, when the 1st Parachute Brigade was being formed, and took part in its first operation, leading C Company of the 2nd Battalion into France to capture a vital radar installation at Bruneval, a mission that was highly successful. North Africa, however, was the first major deployment of the brigade and there was much still to be learned.

The Americans, as with all aspects of their armed forces, were also slow starters. They had begun testing the viability of parachute infantry units in 1940, although it took the success of the German airborne invasion of Crete in May 1941 to really kick-start their development. By the end of the year, there were four parachute battalions, of which the 503rd, so disastrously scattered over North Africa on 8 November, was one. Now, however, the molding of parachute units into highly specialized fighting troops was under way: spurred on by the success of the Bruneval Raid, the US Army had, in August, formed, and was now training two brand-new divisions, the 82nd and 101st Airborne.

After flying over the mountains, the Dakotas taking the 2nd Parachute Battalion deep into Tunisia dropped low over the plains. Frost stood by the door as they swept over Pont du Fahs, their original drop zone, then shortly after, over Depienne, he jumped, landing safely on the smooth, flat ground. Having gathered his parachute, he made for a small mound at the edge of the drop zone and sounded a few notes of his hunting horn. A keen huntsman, it had been a parting gift at the end of his time commanding the Iraqi Levies; Frost had been Master of the Royal Exodus Hunt. There they chased after jackals rather than foxes, but in every other respect, the Royal Exodus was like any hunt in England, right down to the hounds and hunting pink.

Slowly his men began to assemble. They and their containers had been scattered over a wide area of around one and a half miles and there was a large watercourse bisecting the drop zone, so it took awhile. Six men had been injured and one killed. A number of Tunisian Arabs had also appeared and had begun trying to loot the containers, although after a few shots were fired nearby they soon scuttled off again. The paras were still gathering themselves together when a troop of British reconnaissance cars suddenly appeared—auguring well for their planned link with the First Army the following day. The injured could not go on, nor could they be left in the hands of the Arabs, who were known to act like piranhas given the opportunity, and so Frost left a platoon of C Company to try and get them to safety.

Just after midnight, the rest set off for Oudna, traveling by foot on rough tracks over hilly country. There was no question of a supply drop during the operation, so they had to take everything with them, and although they had failed to find any vehicles, they had managed to buy a few carts. Even so, each man was carrying around nine stone—or 126 pounds—of kit. Despite this and despite the rough and frequently steep going, they covered twelve miles by around 4:30 AM, at which point Frost called the battalion to rest. Although it had been warm the previous day, at night the temperature dropped alarmingly and under a clear sky it was now freezing cold. The paras wore different clothing from the rest of the army: cotton "airborne smocks" and jumping trousers, less heavy than the thick serge of the regulars—good for jumping and moving in, but not so brilliant when trying to sleep in sub-zero temperatures. Frost lay huddled next to his second in command, Philip Teichman, and covered with maps for extra warmth.

They set off again at around eight in the morning, their progress watched by Arabs all the way. More carts were bought and by eleven they were overlooking Oudna airfield, with Tunis glimmering in the distance. Of the aircraft they were to destroy there was little sign, and it soon became clear the enemy was not using the airstrip at all. About a mile away they saw some armored cars, and assuming they must be advance units of Allies, began waving the yellow silk triangles they had been given as recognition symbols. Getting no response, Frost sent his men down onto the airfield. A few Germans were manning the place but they were quickly killed or captured, and by four the airfield and its immediate vicinity was in the paras' hands. Shortly after, however, Frost heard the distinct and ominous rumble of heavy engines being revved up and the telltale squeaking of tank tracks, followed by the sharp report of high-velocity guns, and the angry ripping of unfamiliar machine guns. With the arrival of five panzers, a number of Me 109s appeared, weaving and diving and strafing the paras' positions at will. Frost watched them swoop past, machine guns peppering the ground, and then climb up and bank, ready for another run, only for more aircraft to zoom over them from a different direction. Now hidden among the scrub surrounding the airfield, the paras used their hard-learned concealment training to good effect, and not one man was hit by enemy aircraft, even when Stukas arrived a couple of hours later.

"Now as the whole object of the mission had been to destroy aircraft etc. on Oudna," noted Frost, "and as there were no aircraft to destroy, I made plans for moving westward to link up with the 1st Army."[410] At dusk, and with the panzers having now retired and the Stukas flown off, they began withdrawing to the higher ground where they'd paused earlier that morning. Frost was worried, however. In addition to those left at Depienne, he'd lost a few more men in the fighting that afternoon. The rest were exhausted, morale had taken a serious dip, and much of their ammunition had been used up. Moreover, they now faced another freezing-cold night in which it was difficult, if not impossible, to sleep. He had to hope that the following morning they would be able to beat off the inevitable counterattack, and then safely and quickly link up with the rest of First Army.

Field–Marshal Kesselring had arrived in Tunisia with Hitler's latest directive to throw the Allies back into Algeria. Critical of Nehring's earlier caution, Kesselring now ordered him to counterattack with the 10th Panzer Division and retake Medjez el Bab. Joe Furaytor and A Battery of the 5th Field Artillery Battalion were covering the East Surreys to the southeast of Tebourba, when at dawn on 1 December, German tanks appeared west of Djedeida, in front of the ridge where the Hampshires were dug in. Although about three miles to the southwest, A Battery soon began throwing volley after volley of indirect fire toward the advancing panzers. The attack was repulsed, but shortly after, the men below heard an increasingly loud drone. In moments, tiny dark shapes in the sky had grown until they were peeling off and screaming down toward the Allied positions. It was the first of many Stuka raids that day.

Before he reached North Africa, Joe had had little idea of what to expect. Fighting the French had given him a taste of what it was like being under fire, but coming under attack from the Germans was something else altogether. As the Stukas started diving, one after another, Joe and his crew ran for the cover of their foxholes. "It was very frightening," admits Joe. "That bomb looked like a little black object, but you'd swear it was going to come down on your head." Once the Stukas had gone, they crept back to man their guns, only to find themselves coming under heavy counter-battery fire. Shells whistled loudly overhead and then exploded, sending fountains of mud and stone high into the sky. Mortar shells also began dropping around them. Shards of shrapnel burst the gun's tires and clanged against the gun shield. Both A and B Batteries took several casualties. When Joe saw his first dead comrade, he thought to himself, "You're a soldier, this is what happens in war." He tried to be practical. "I accepted the fact," he says, "and I accepted that it could happen to me too."

It was becoming horribly clear that they were being attacked from all sides. The Germans had advanced that morning in four different groups in a clinical encircling operation. Blade Force to the northeast of Tebourba had taken the brunt of two of these armored groups and retreated in some disorder. Panzers pushed on, some almost to within reach of the Tebourba Gap, the narrows between two long ridges of hills through which the River Medjerda and the main road to Medjez ran. From the southeast, another German group moved toward the Surreys and the guns of A and B Batteries. Joe and his crew fired volley after volley, empty shell cases building up around them, the big gun thundering then jolting backward with every recoil.

By midmorning they were already running low on ammunition. They had a number of .50 caliber machine guns, however—powerful enough to force the dive-bombers to fly higher and effective against the Germans now advancing directly in front of them, most of whom appeared to be infantry. With this in mind, orders were given for gun crews to be split and the machine guns set up on the flanks of their positions. Joe hurried off with one of the .50 calibers and found he was only twenty yards away from a British machine gun team of the 1st East Surreys. "We talked to each other and exchanged rations," he says. "They had field glasses and as soon as they saw any of the enemy coming in my direction, they'd motion to me and I'd cock my gun ready to fire."

Stuka attacks arrived almost hourly, while fighters sped over and strafed their positions with relentless ease. By evening the 5th Field Battalion had knocked out a number of enemy tanks, and together with the East Surreys, had seen off three companies of German paratroopers and destroyed several mortars. But despite their efforts, the enemy was closing its net around Tebourba. Then news arrived that another German force had bypassed them and had now cut off the Medjez-Tebourba road from the south. They had not heard from the British CRA for forty-eight hours and were now almost out of ammunition; despite sending urgent radio messages for more, they had received no reply.

After consulting with the Surreys, it was decided that they should try and make a break for it and withdraw along the Medjerda River towards Medjez. Captain Rawie, the commander of A Battery, called his men together. "I'm speaking to you like men, not boys," he told them. "You're soldiers and we're at war. We are surrounded. We can't get out." Then turning to Joe's gun corporal, he said, "How many rounds have you got left?"

"One round," came the reply.

"OK," said Rawie, "save it. Spike the gun and then tonight when I give the order, blow it up and torch the trucks and then everyone take off on your own. If you make it out, one day we might meet up again. God bless and God speed."

A nerve-wracking wait followed. All the while, the Germans continued to shell their positions, so Joe and a number of others took cover at a nearby farm. The rain was pouring down and their woolen greatcoats were soaked and weighed a ton. Thick mud covered the ground. Finding some haystacks, they tried to keep dry by hiding in the straw, but were bitten to pieces by bugs and ants, and so emerged looking like they'd caught measles. "You can't believe how horrible it was," says Joe.

They were finally given orders to move out at around two in the morning. Despite Captain Rawie's dramatic speech, it was decided to try and take the guns and trucks after all. Creeping away toward the Tebourba Gap, past burning tanks and with the rain falling once again, they drove within a couple of hundred yards of a German leaguer, but by moving as slowly as possible and not changing gear, the enemy never heard them. For the 5th Field Battalion, the Battle of Tebourba was over.

Meanwhile, things had gone from bad to worse for the 2nd Parachute Battalion. On the morning of 1 December, Colonel John Frost had received the bad news via radio that the First Army's advance on Tunis had been postponed. In a moment, all hopes of a quick link with the First Army were dashed. His situation was now dire. As the previous day's excitements had demonstrated, they were deep in enemy territory, which was swarming with panzers and troops, while above them the skies were owned by Messerschmitts and Stukas. Tunis, that glittering prize, might only have been a few miles away, but Tebourba or Medjez—which, as far as he knew, were still held by Allied troops—were between thirty and forty.

He'd prepared a small ambush at the bottom of the slopes where they had lain up for the night. Unfortunately, an armored column appeared just as a number of the men had slipped out from their positions to fill up water bottles from a nearby well. An Italian armored car drove up to them, and although the paras shot an officer and lobbed a Gammon bomb at the vehicle, it missed, and the car was able to get away. Hastily bringing their mortars to bear, the paras drove off the column, but an hour later, another larger force began approaching their positions. The leading armored car was showing two yellow triangles, and thinking it must be friendly, one of the Para NCOs walked toward it waving his own silk triangle and was promptly taken prisoner. Shortly after, he was sent back again with a warning that they were now surrounded and demanding they all come out with their hands up. "This was a terrible shock," Frost admitted,[411] but he refused to throw in the towel, instead ordering his men to climb further into the hills; if they could just hold on until nightfall, he thought they might be able to take a chance and dash through the enemy lines. The wounded, however, had to stay where they were. It was a horrible decision to make, but with a heavy heart, Frost ordered one of the battalion doctors to stay behind, in the knowledge that, at best, he and the wounded would be captured.

As they began to move, the Germans shelled them without mercy, the blast flinging lethal splinters from the rocky ground. Frost saw one man have his face almost completely sliced from his head. He also watched a terrified donkey scuttle off, carrying the battalion bagpipes. Yet, despite mounting losses, by early afternoon they were in better positions with clear views all around them and able to watch as lorries rumbled up to the lower slopes and reams of infantry jumped out. As these troops began climbing up toward the besieged paras, the panzers and artillery continued to hurtle up shell after shell. Frost watched the enemy troops with horrified awe. The speed with which they set up mortars and machine guns and began spitting out accurate bursts of deadly fire was high class—and better than anything his own men could achieve. As the afternoon wore on, he began to seriously wonder how much longer they could hold out. Nearby, Ronald Gordon, the medical officer, was covered in blood from tending the injured, but had nothing left with which to staunch the wounds. And just when Frost thought things could not possibly get worse, the 109s showed up. Pressing himself to the ground, he waited for the inevitable roar of airplane engines and cannon fire, but to his enormous relief, the Messerschmitts opened up on their own troops instead, presumably the only men they could see. Once again, skilled use of camouflage and concealment had saved the paras' bacon; and with dusk now falling, the attacks finally began to die out.

Frost knew they had to get away that night, and decided their best chance of success would be if he split the battalion into company groups and for them then to rendezvous in the morning on a hill overlooking Massicault, where they could lie up during the day should the town be in enemy hands. He reckoned he had already lost about 150 men, but once again, was not prepared to leave the wounded to fend for themselves and at the mercy of marauding Arabs. In what was another agonizing decision, he ordered a platoon to stay behind, with orders to try and take the wounded to some nearby farms. They were then to attempt to link up with the reconnaissance party they'd seen on the first day. This, however, was a vain hope, as they were all aware. For the fit, prison camps were the best they could realistically hope for. For the wounded—without medical aid and with temperatures dropping fast—just surviving the night was a lot to expect.

With their radio batteries now dead, Frost blew his horn to give the signal for the companies to start moving off. The march was terrible, over heavily churned up ground, and they were soon walking with enormous clods of mud on their boots. They rested ten minutes every hour. Many of the men, now at the limits of exhaustion, would then drop to the ground and could only be roused again by using force. Some were lost in the darkness and never seen again, including Philip Teichman, a trusted friend of Frost's, as well as his second in command.

Before dawn, with a high moon lighting their way, Frost realized they were not going to make Massicault, so paused to take stock. It was essential they found somewhere to lie up for the day, and fortunately they soon discovered the ideal place: an Arab settlement corralled by thick cactus bushes as effective as any roll of wire. The Arabs were found to be friendly and helpful, and HQ and B Companies moved in. Later that morning one of the Arabs brought word that there were some other British in another farm half a mile away—this was the remainder of A Company, who were told to quickly join the rest at Cactus Farm. Of C Company, there was no sign.

By late morning, the first enemy troops had caught up with them, and as the day wore on, the enemy continued to bring up more and more reinforcements until the farm was entirely surrounded. They began desultory mortar firing, but for some reason seemed reluctant to launch an all-out attack. Frost again hoped they might be able to slip away once night fell; they no longer had enough ammunition to fight another battle. Then, as mortar shells exploded nearby, Ronald Gordon suddenly said, "Good heavens, it's my birthday. What a hell of a day to have as a birthday."

"If you survive this one you should have many happy returns," Frost told him. After a quick whip around, they were able to give him three sticky pieces of chocolate for a present.[412] As daylight began to slip away, and as the Germans finally looked as though they were about to mount an assault, Frost blew his hunting horn and the paras made their escape charge, firing their last rounds of ammunition as they went. They were almost completely successful. Darkness and the confusion caused by their nighttime dash had saved them, and once in the hills, the paras were able to rally to their commander's horn.

The plan to reach Massicault was abandoned. At dawn, as they reached some high ground, they could see Medjez in the far distance. Frost decided to lead them straight there instead. On they marched all day, and in the early afternoon met an American armored car not far from the town. After five days, they had finally linked up with the First Army.

The courage and fortitude of the paras was extraordinary. With almost no sleep, and with sub-zero temperatures and insufficient supplies, they had fought their way through three days of battle, traveling over sixty miles of frequently rough and arduous terrain; that any had made it to safety was something of a miracle, and also says much about Frost's leadership. As it was, 266 men were lost, and all for nothing. The entire operation had been doomed from the start. "My main reaction to having my battalion cut to pieces on such a useless venture was astonishment," wrote Frost later. It had been mounted on extremely flimsy information, intelligence that should and could have been sought beforehand. Nor had any effort of any kind been made to try and rescue them. "It was," says Frost, "perhaps the most disgracefully mounted operation of the war."[413]

Another fifty men would reach Allied lines by 11 December—small comfort. But the operation demonstrated once again that while individual men and units could, and did, operate with enormous skill and resilience, at the higher levels, the Allied commanders were seriously found wanting.

Meanwhile, things had not been going well on the main front either. As the 5th Field Artillery Battalion had been escaping southward toward Medjez, Brigadier-General Oliver's Combat Command B was squeaking and rumbling hurriedly in the opposite direction. During the morning they were due to take over from the battered remnants of Blade Force. The infantry of 11 Brigade were still holding on to Tebourba despite heavy losses the previous day, and despite the premature exit of the American gunners. Although they had retreated to a hill closer to Tebourba, the heroic Hampshires managed to keep the German thrust from the west at bay for a second day. Several Allied counterattacks failed miserably, however. It was the same story of old: both British and American tanks, advancing into the open and without coordinated artillery support, were cut to pieces by the concealed German tanks and anti-tank guns. The lessons learned in the Desert War had not filtered through. Had the Allied guns and armor dug in and stood their ground, they might have saved many lives and much equipment, but by the end of 2 December, there was no longer any real chance of maintaining their current positions around the town. Overnight, the enemy was reinforced by a crack panzer-grenadier regiment that had arrived at Tunis the previous day, and on the morning of 3 December, the Surreys and Hampshires finally began withdrawing to the Tebourba Gap. The Hampshires were down to about 200 men, the Surreys

340, and although they tried to save their heavier equipment, were forced to abandon most of it. While the remnants of 11th Brigade plugged the Tebourba Gap, Brigadier-General Oliver was left to pool all the remaining armor and organize the defense of the hills overlooking the Medjerda Valley and the all-important road to Medjez el Bab. But by retreating, Tunis—a goal so tantalizingly near—now seemed impossibly far away.

Ike was faced with a difficult bit of explaining to the combined chiefs. The success of the landings now seemed an age away, and instead the campaign was stuck knee deep in Tunisian mud, the race for Tunis all but over. The conditions and the problems with the lines of supply meant there could be no renewed attack on Tunis until they had had a chance to regroup—he and Anderson had set a tentative date of 9 December, although he warned the chiefs that much depended on the weather. In the six days' pause, he hoped to build up greater reserves at the front, straighten out the congested condition of the railway and secure two further landing strips as close to the front as possible.

"In [the] pell mell race for Tunisia," Ike told the combined chiefs on 3 December, "we have gone beyond the sustainable limit of air capabilities in support of ground forces. Result is that although air forces have been working at maximum pace, without even minimum repair and supply and maintenance facilities, the scale of possible air support is not sufficient to keep down the hostile strafing and dive-bombing that is largely responsible for breaking up all attempted advances by air."[414] He was right to emphasize the importance of air power, but might have added that suspect tactics and insufficient communications systems had also played their part. The Allied commander was finding himself in almost precisely the same predicament as Rommel at Alam Halfa. It was the Allies' turn to have overextended lines of supply and little air cover, and like Rommel, Ike also blamed the overwhelming superiority of the enemy air forces as the key to their failure.

"A dismal beginning to the Christmas month," wrote Tony Bartley in his diary. Bone looked like a scrapyard. Contorted, burned-out wrecks of aircraft were everywhere, including that of a Wellington bomber that had been unable to find the runway and had crashed. They were vivid reminders of the danger and violence of their current situation.

On 3 December, the serviceable planes of 111 Squadron were patrolling over the battlefield, when two 109s dived down through a gap in the cloud base and then zoomed up again. Smelling a trap, Tony told the other pilots to stay where they were while he climbed to have a look. Sure enough, above the cloud Tony spotted around twenty enemy fighters poised to pounce, and so quickly shot back into the cloud again.

The following day, they were told to move forward to Souk el Arba, where 225 Squadron was now based. Set on a low, flat oval plateau and surrounded by mountains, the airfield was even more miserable than when Bryan Colston and his colleagues had turned up—what Tony Bartley called "nothing more than a cultivated field." Bomb craters and wrecked aircraft gave the place an air of unwelcome familiarity. Apart from one battered square white house and 225 Squadron's tents, there were no other facilities. It had stopped raining, so they ate their evening meal sitting on sandbags around a packing case for a table. As the stars began to come out, so the temperature dropped. Over a final cigarette before turning in, Tony asked the CO of 225 Squadron how they'd been doing. "He did not answer for quite a while," noted Tony, but when he did, confessed they'd been having a pretty rough time. They'd lost a lot of pilots—two more that day.[415]

But everyone was struggling, the bombers included. Before the campaign, the Allies had thought it unlikely that they would ever come up against the new Focke-Wulf 190 in Tunisia, but sadly for them, this was not the case. Vastly superior in every respect to anything the Allies could offer—even the Spitfire Mk V—in the hands of combat-hardened pilots, it was lethal. And many of the Axis pilots *were* extremely experienced. Veterans of the Eastern Front, Malta, and the Western Desert had all been rushed to Tunisia. On 4 December, twelve twin-engine Bisley bombers took off from Souk el Arba—without a fighter escort—to bomb an Axis airfield near Tunis. One returned home with engine trouble and crash-landed, but as the rest approached the target they were attacked by between fifty and sixty Me 109s and FW 190s. Not one of the bombers made it home.

The day before, Ralph Burbridge and the crew of the *All American* had flown with the rest of the group over Bizerte. Although flying at 20,000 feet, they had come under heavy attack by German fighters. Their escorts, P-38 Lightnings, had taken the brunt of the attack and nine were shot down. The following day, General Doolittle visited Ike and complained to him about the problems he faced: the Axis had radar, while his airfields did not; levels of maintenance were still poor; and the distances to the targets were too great.

"Those are your troubles?" snapped Ike. "Go and cure them. Don't you think I've got a lot of troubles too?"[416]

To make matters worse, the Germans launched another attack against the American and British forces along the hills over the Medjerda Valley. Instead of trying to force their way through the Tebourba Gap, the Axis

came around the back. By the time the Americans realized what was happening it was too late and the opportunity to pour fire into the Axis
flanks had gone. When General Oliver's tanks did finally go forward,
they once again did so without artillery support and the enemy anti-tank
guns had their usual field day. "The day's lessons were deeply disturbing," noted the division's battle history. "The enemy's armament and tactics had been extremely effective. American armament and tactics had
failed."[417]

Ike had been thinking about further retreat even before this latest
blow, and had said as much to Harry Butcher while they'd shaved earlier
that morning. Meanwhile, arriving at the front was Lieutenant-General
Charles Allfrey and his headquarters staff of V Corps, into which
Evelegh's 78 Division was now being absorbed. Although the Allies still
held the Medjerda Valley, after taking one look at the situation, he realized that to attack again in three days' time was out of the question. He
also advised withdrawing to a more defensible line and abandoning
Medjez. This appreciation was relayed to Ike later that day via Anderson,
but after French protests, it was agreed that the Allies should withdraw to
positions around Djebel el Almara, soon to be renamed "Longstop Hill."

The withdrawal to Longstop, due to take place over two nights on the
10–11 and 11–12 December, was another fiasco. Rains began falling heavily again on the seventh, and the Medjerda Valley turned into a quagmire
of thick, glutinous yellow-gray mud. Before the retreat had begun, the Germans attacked once more. Enemy panzers to the south of the hills had tried
to outflank the French guarding the bridge into Medjez, but had become
bogged down. Seeing this, Oliver had sent some light tanks to try and pick
them off, but although the panzers' maneuverability had been affected,
their firepower had not. Nineteen Honeys were knocked out.

That night, Oliver decided to try and complete his withdrawal in one,
rather than two, nights. They were to drop from their high positions into
the Medjerda Valley and cross a bridge. British troops were to cover them
as they did so. The first tanks reached the bridge only to discover no sign
of any troops there at all. For some reason, they then turned northeast
and ran into several German outposts. Sporadic firing helped start a rumor amongst the rest of CCB that the bridge was now in enemy hands,
and so instead of waiting for confirmation, the American armor turned
south along a track on the banks of the Medjerda. Wheels and tracks soon
began spinning deeper and deeper into the mud. They were digging
their own graves. Stuck fast, most had to be abandoned, and the men and
crews were forced to walk the remaining ten miles or so to Medjez on foot.

* * *

While the US Rangers and 1st Infantry Division continued to camp out near Oran and Arzew, British arrivals in Algiers were hastily sent up to the front. The Guards Brigade had reached North Africa on 22 November, and after getting soaked for several days and then taking part in a wreath-laying parade at the city's War Memorial—attended by Ike, ABC, Darlan, and Giraud—they began the arduous road trip to Tunisia, reaching Beja on 6 December. Four days later, they moved up to positions in the hills southeast of Medjez el Bab.

Battalion liaison officer for the 3rd Grenadier Guards was Lieutenant Nigel Nicolson, just six weeks short of his twenty-sixth birthday and rather excited to be finally taking an active part in the war. It had been a long time coming. He had joined up in 1939, and after graduating from Sandhurst, one of his first tasks had been to take a half company of reinforcements to France, but he'd been sent straight back again and had remained at Wellington Barracks in London throughout the Blitzkrieg. In over three years of war, the closest he'd come to any fighting was watching the aerial battles from his parents' house at Sissinghurst, in Kent, during the Battle of Britain. For much of the rest of the time he'd been stuck in Scotland, training. This had often struck him as odd: he knew troops were always needed in the Middle East, particularly the better units like the Guards Brigade. There'd often been talk of action—raids on Norway, the Azores, even Alderney, but, much to his frustration, nothing had ever come of such plans.

He'd found the prospect of war exhilarating. It promised to give him a sense of worth and purpose that had been missing in his life. After Eton and Oxford, Nigel had spent a year doing volunteer work for Social Services in Newcastle, but he'd never had a job as such, never been really needed. With the war, there was at last something useful for him to do. Just by wearing a uniform and being in the guards, he'd felt a little heroic. This had bolstered his confidence and, he believed, made him more attractive to girls. But as the war progressed, the stakes became higher: with everyone in uniform, it was seeing some action that counted, not being stuck in an icy Scottish glen. The fact that he might get himself killed never really crossed his mind.

His motivations had thus been entirely self-interested. "The idea that I might be fighting for king and country, or to overcome an evil system, hardly occurred to me," he admits. And he felt this way despite having a writer for a mother and a father who was a junior minister in Churchill's government. A few years before, he'd even found himself quite admiring the dictators. When he was eighteen, he'd visited Rome and had seen Mussolini address the crowds. He had thought him impressive. He'd also seen something of the Nazis, having spent two summers in succession there in 1936–37, learning German. On one occasion, he had even joined a torchlight Nazi procession, and on another heard Goebbels address a party rally. At the end of the speech, the crowd rose, arms extended. Encouraged by his host, Nigel did the same, shouting "Sieg heil!" with the rest of them.

Communist friends at Oxford went some way to changing his views, and after the Munich Crisis he recanted entirely. He'd originally wanted to join the RAF, but in early 1939, there had been no great demand for pilots, and he was turned down. Instead, he joined the Officers Cadet Reserve, which bound him to apply for a commission in the Grenadier Guards should war break out.

The Guards regiments were among the most elite infantry units in the British Army, and it had taken Nigel some time to get used to the rarefied and polished standards expected of an officer. On his first day with the regiment, he dressed for dinner in his blues, a formal and traditional uniform which had to be made especially for him by a Saville Row tailor. No one paid him any attention and when dinner was announced, he wondered where he was supposed to sit. There was a long table, so he decided it would be best to sit at the foot, out of the way. To his horror, the commanding officer sat down beside him, eyeing him with surprise; the foot was, in fact, the head. As a consequence, when the mess waiter came to take drink orders, he asked Nigel first. The table was dazzling with regimental silver, so Nigel assumed that nothing less than champagne would be acceptable. Everyone else asked for beer or cider. Still no one said a word to him, not even when the mess waiter opened the bottle loudly behind him. His humiliation did not stop there. Opposite him was a man dressed differently, so Nigel thought he must be a guest. "Are you staying with us long?" Nigel asked.

"I'm the medical officer," he replied. "I've been here eight years."

He never made such mistakes again, however, and soon developed a certain pride in the regiment, bolstered by the camaraderie he felt with his fellow officers, all of whom came from similar backgrounds and had shared interests. With his men, however, there remained a gulf that was impossible to cross. He had spent a privileged, sheltered life, was inexperienced in the ways of the world and how to deal with men from a different class. "They were streetwise, brought up in a much rougher, tougher life," explains Nigel. "I made the mistake of wanting them to like me, but I should have wanted them to respect me."

This was a problem common to many of the young officers who suddenly found themselves charged with leading men about whom they knew or understood little. By virtue of class, many were given commissions without demonstrating any kind of natural leadership skills, and found themselves completely out of their depth. Very early in his career with the Guards, Nigel suffered minor mockery from his men, but nothing worse. In the Gordon Highlanders, however, Johnny Bain witnessed outright dissent. He and one of his colleagues, a man named Private Fenton, had been digging a slit trench when a young lieutenant who had only recently joined the battalion ordered them both to move forward. They were coming under quite heavy fire at the time, and to Johnny's amazement, Fenton simply said, "Not on your life!" The officer accused him of cowardice, to which Fenton said, "Fuck off, you stupid little prick!" The officer left them, humiliated, but later the same day, Johnny saw him talking to Fenton again.

"What did he say?" Johnny asked afterward.

"He was apologizing," Fenton told him. The officer had realized he'd asked them to do something he shouldn't and told Fenton he'd been wrong to call him a coward. "Which I think was very admirable," says Johnny. "Rare too, that kind of humility."[418]

Most officers, however, were given a certain respect purely because they were of a different class. This deference lessened as the war progressed, partly because war inevitably broke down social barriers and partly because more and more men were promoted through the ranks. But while officers ultimately either succeeded or failed because of the example they showed, class offered no head start for American officers, who were not singled out because of where they went to school. Rather—in the case of the army at any rate—they were selected because they'd been in the Reserve Officers Training Corps before the war, or because they'd shown particular aptitude during training. In other words, they'd already shown some inkling of having leadership qualities before they were put before the board. Nor were they necessarily better educated than their charges: only around 51 percent of officers commissioned during the war had gone through one or more years of college. It wasn't a foolproof system by any means, but certainly the social barriers that played such a part in many British regiments were almost nonexistent within the US Army.

For much of his time training in Scotland, Nigel Nicolson had commanded a platoon of thirty-five men but had always coveted the job of battalion intelligence officer, and so was delighted to be given the post shortly before leaving for North Africa. Crucially, it did not carry the negative stigma of being a staff officer, because he would always remain at the front with the battalion, yet he felt he was far better suited for the tasks involved than being a platoon commander. Under him were a sergeant and six other men, whom he immediately began to train, teaching them how to interpret maps and aerial photographs as well as Morse and semaphore, and how to mark up minefields. He also taught them interrogation techniques, how to gather information from civilians, weapon recognition, and how to write messages and reports. They had practiced these skills on a bemused Highland population, but now it was time to do it for real.

"Thank goodness you've arrived," the staff officer had told them at Beja, and hastily sent them forward to Medjez. A few hours after they'd moved into their new positions, Nigel spotted his first Germans of the war. Four or five tanks, "crawling like beetles" suddenly appeared across the plain in front of them.[419] As soon as they saw the Grenadiers, they opened fire and Nigel watched as sudden shots of flame sprang from their barrels and shells whistled toward them. With no tanks of their own, the Grenadiers hastily replied with mortars and machine guns, but their mortar officer was killed. "It was very alarming," admits Nigel. "To have someone shooting at you and seeing people killed. I was scared stiff."

Both sides had now temporarily run out of steam, although the Axis air forces continued to bomb and strafe without respite. On 12 December, Ike reported to the chiefs of staff, confessing that another pause was needed before the offensive resumed, but that a further, all-out attempt to take Tunis would be launched soon. CCB had been so badly mauled that it was to be withdrawn from the battle area and replaced with 18th Regimental Combat Team, who were to be moved up to Algiers as soon as the 97th Bomb Group had finished using their transport for a move of their own. The American bomber crews were being sent from Tafaraoui to Biskra, a flat, palm-lined town sitting in the desert beneath the Atlas Mountains, and a much better place from which to fly bombing operations. It was also closer to Tunisia. Ralph Burbridge and the other officers were quartered in hotels in the nearby town. Compared with Tafaraoui, the conditions were hugely improved, and not only did it rain less, but there also were fewer attacks by the Luftwaffe.

Then the rain stopped for a few days—"the weather is good, except for occasional showers," wrote Nigel Nicolson in a letter to his parents—and suddenly hopes rose that perhaps they would reach Tunis by Christmas after all. And by 19 December, the British 78th and 6th Divisions were at almost full strength—some 20,000 men—supported by nearly 11,000 US troops and 30,000—albeit poorly equipped—French.

But the Axis had also been further reinforced. In the middle of the month, General Jurgen von Arnim arrived from the Eastern Front to take command of what had become the Fifth Panzer Army. He now had nearly 40,000 troops at his disposal, the majority of which were German, as well as air superiority and generally better equipment than anything in the American or British armory. Despite this, the Allies remained confident. General Allfrey's plan was to advance south of the Medjerda Valley, along the Medjez-Massicault-Tunis road. Before the main assault, however, he considered it essential they take Longstop Hill, now in German hands and providing them with an excellent artillery observation post.

Longstop was not a particularly high hill, and to the north was dominated by a far more imposing range. But lying five miles northwest of Medjez on the northern side of the Medjerda Valley, its position was certainly a dominating one with far-reaching views to Medjez and to the south: precisely where Allfrey intended to launch his assault on Christmas Eve. From there, the Germans would be able to shell the Allied advance, disrupt supply lines and even use it as a footing from which to launch counterattacks. It had to be taken.

The Bowles twins were now bivouacked near Teboursouk, an Arab village southwest of Medjez, but it wasn't the 2nd Battalion that had been tasked with supporting the Coldstream Guards in capturing Longstop; that had been given to the 1st Battalion, who began moving up to Medjez on the night of 21–22 December. Instead, the 2nd Battalion readied themselves for Allfrey's main assault.

As the Coldstreams moved up to attack, the rain began falling once more. The men tried covering themselves with groundsheets but it didn't really work, and soon they were drenched to the skin, their woolen battle jackets and trousers weighing heavily against them. Mortar and shell fire were already pouring down among them as they began their advance up the hill. For most of the men, it was their first time in battle and as they scrambled up the slippery slope, mortar shells continued to burst around them, while arcs of machine-gun tracer streamed down from the ridges above.

Despite the heavy defense, the Coldstreams managed to seize the heights as planned. They were then to hand over to the Americans of the 18th Infantry, who were to occupy and hold the positions. The changeover was not smooth. The 18th were late reaching Longstop and the Coldstreams had already moved out by the time they too were scrambling up its western slopes. The guides who had been left to show them their positions were unsure about where they were, and as daylight arrived, it became clear that there was still a lot of hill ahead of them. From the Allied line of attack, the first summit appeared to be the highest and only one. But in fact, Longstop had no less than five ridges, as the hapless men of the 18th discovered—and the last three were still very much in enemy hands.

In their first encounter with the Germans, the Americans were treated to the kind of counterattack that had bedeviled British forces for so long. Early in the day, Company A, along with an anti-tank platoon, were completely surrounded and all but one officer and thirteen men were killed or captured. Telephone lines had been cut and many of the battalion's radio sets, sodden with rain, no longer worked. Nonetheless, with help from the artillery, the Americans fought back.

Overnight, the Coldstreams slogged up the hill again to reinforce the Americans, but it wasn't until after dark on Christmas Eve that they attacked the German positions again. Supported by mortars and machine guns of the Americans, they successfully took the next to last ridge. By the following morning, Christmas Day, the Americans had been further reinforced with a company of French infantry, but as the inevitable and heavy German counterattack began, both the French and the Coldstreams began to withdraw—the alternative was to face annihilation. Unfortunately, the message that they were pulling out never reached the Americans. Already severely mauled, the 18th were now exposed, outgunned, and outnumbered, and being blasted to smithereens. By 9 AM, runners were frantically scurrying across their positions with the orders to retreat. The battle for Longstop had failed, with the 18th Infantry losing 356 men. As the bedraggled remnants trudged back through the rain, the Germans—atop what they renamed "Christmas Hill"—began shelling Medjez.

"Ike is knee-deep in Frogs," noted Harry Butcher in his diary. Giraud was being difficult, demanding greater military control than the Allies would ever grant him in a million years, while both Clark and Ike were beginning to suspect Nogués was a "bad egg" and needed removing.[420] A change of scene was needed, so while the tragedy of Longstop was being played out, General Eisenhower, with Butch in tow, went up to the front to escape the politics and to see for himself how his Allied forces were doing. The bad weather made it unsafe to fly, so they set off by road early on 23 December, and by afternoon on Christmas Eve had reached Souk el Khemis, twenty miles southwest of Beja. A short way farther on, as they went to visit American troops and examine the lay of the land, Ike watched troops and trucks struggling through the mud and rain. Then one incident caught his eye. About thirty feet off the road, in a field that at first appeared to be full of winter wheat, a motorcycle had become bogged down. Four men were trying to pull it out, but in doing so only managed to slither into the mire themselves. This pathetic scene, as much as anything he witnessed that day, made Ike realize the hopelessness of their planned attack. Back at V Corps HQ in Souk el Khemis, Anderson told the allied commander what Ike already knew: that the attack should be postponed. Locals, he said, had told him that the rains usually got worse in January and February, not better. Anderson suggested a postponement of at least six weeks. Eisenhower agreed. "This was a bitter disappointment to Ike," noted Butch.

There was also the problem of command. Giraud was steadfast in refusing to allow any troops to serve under the British, and was pressing Ike to make him overall commander in the field. Anderson offered to resign—and was, wrote Butch, "most sporting in his efforts to find a solution."[421] Ike refused the offer, but suggested that perhaps he take over personal command at the front with Anderson keeping command of First Army in the north, Juin commanding the French in the center of the line, and Fredendall the Americans in the south. But as Harry Butcher put it, Ike already had "a million and one things to do as theater commander," without the additional burden of commanding his forces in the field.[422] Nothing had been resolved when a call arrived from Clark telling Ike to get back to Algiers right away. Darlan had been shot. By driving all night and on through Christmas Day, they reached Algiers by 6 PM, by which time Darlan's assassin, a youthful anti-fascist monarchist named Bonnier de la Chapelle, had already been tried and executed by firing squad.

On the last day of 1942, Harry Butcher recorded that "the Darlan thing passed over very quietly." At his funeral, Giraud knelt at the bier and shed a tear, having "reluctantly" taken over as leader of French North Africa. Ike, it was confirmed, would move his Advance Command Post to Constantine in the New Year, with Anderson still in charge of the First Army and with Clark commanding the French and Americans. "Haven't recorded the really amazing news," Butch added. "The fact is that Washington and London are coming to see us. The president, the prime minister, General Marshall, Admiral King, and various bigwigs are going to pow-wow at a place already recommended after investigation near Casablanca some time in January."[423] This was to be the Casablanca Conference, and with Ike's forces stuck in a muddy winter stalemate, there was much to discuss.

CHAPTER 19

Pause For Thought: January 1943

EVERY MAN HAS A LIMIT to how much combat he can take. Discipline and the even greater fear of letting down one's mates often help prolong a man's fighting capacity, but sustained exposure to maiming, death, and destruction, combined with physical fatigue, will inevitably take its toll eventually. Every man has a courage quota. For some, these reserves are considerable, while for others, they are less. Rest and recuperation are often enough to stock up the deficit, but the warning signs that a man is running low have to be acted on quickly. A sympathetic and observant medical officer could save a man's life, but while mental and physical exhaustion was considerably better understood than during the First World War, a tragic number of men were pushed too far, usually with tragic and far-reaching consequences.

Squadron Leader Tony Bartley had been flying operationally for almost three years, with only a short break as a test pilot for Supermarine, the designers of the Spitfire. He'd been tired before he'd reached North Africa, but the mud, rain, lack of facilities, and the added responsibility as a result had begun to seriously get to him. For solace he had turned to drink. He had always drunk a lot. During the Battle of Britain, particularly, when alcohol was still readily available, squadrons tended to either have a drink culture or not. Tony was with 92 Squadron and the pilots had played and drunk hard throughout that summer. There was little *joie de vivre* about his drinking now, however. On one occasion in early December, the rain had prevented them flying, so Tony and a couple of the boys had gone off on an expedition to a vineyard. There they had come across some Americans who had been badly shot up the day before and having traveled through the night, were now trying to set up a bivouac. The British pilots stopped, and the Americans complained that they had never once seen any friendly aircraft above them and that they had been strafed throughout the day. They were not impressed to discover that Tony and his fellow pilots were out hunting for booze. "It was a depressing encounter," noted Tony, "and we returned to our airfield with heavy hearts and a huge barrel of wine."[424]

Tony was drunk most nights and if there was no flying due to bad weather, he would often take himself with a bottle of whisky and head to a hotel in the hills. On Christmas Eve he was warned by the medical officer that he needed a break. Tony took the doctor's advice by taking a number of his pilots out on another bender. He was drinking to extremes, but it was his only means of relaxation and escape, and although all of his pilots were feeling the strain, Tony had been flying longer than any of them. The cumulative effect had begun to catch up on him. "I felt more tired this Christmas than I thought any man could ever feel," he noted. His reserves had almost run dry.[425]

Inevitably, matters soon came to a head. On 28 December, Tony once again led the squadron and they intercepted a formation of Me 109s and Ju 88s. Diving in behind the Messerschmitts, Tony drew up behind their leader and blew him up with one short burst of cannon fire, before turning on the wingman and setting him on fire. Later, as he circled to land again, he watched four aircraft crash on landing due to the state of the airfield. It was the final straw. On landing, he grabbed a bottle of whisky, drank half of it, then rang the air controller and told him to tell the group captain that he would accept no further responsibility for his pilots if they were forced to operate from where they had become sitting ducks. Soon after, Jimmy Baraldi, one of his flight commanders, found him, and Tony confessed that he'd finally shot his bolt. He could still fly and hunt and kill all right, but it was everything else. "Jimmy told me that I'd made the attack [that afternoon] like a man possessed," he noted, "and was heading for the biggest nervous breakdown ever."[426]

Jimmy was absolutely right and made Tony take the group captain's offer of some leave in Algiers. It wasn't enough to restore the tanks, however. Tony rejoined the squadron a week later, and a few days after that, was leading them against some FW 190s when something snapped, and he suddenly no longer knew where he was or what he was doing. Somehow, he made it back, but he now knew he was finished. The squadron doctor took him to see the group captain the next morning. On the way, they passed two ambulances that were burning on the side of the road. Pulling off to see if there was anything they could do to help, they skidded on the blood. But it was too late—the patients were all dead. They drove on to Souk el Arba and there the group captain agreed to let Tony go. Later, back with the squadron, Tony told the pilots he was no longer fit to lead them and that he was going back to England. "They sang, 'For he's a jolly good fellow,' and we all got good and drunk," noted Tony. Then he wrote his last sortie up in his logbook. It had been his 365th combat mission.[427]

Combat flying unquestionably placed pilots under considerable strain. Duke Ellington had flown about thirty missions when he began to doubt how long he could hack it. He and his good friend Bob Hoke were on leave in Cairo when Duke said, "Bob, this damn war is getting kinda scary. Shall we get our arses out of here?" Bob, it turned out, felt the same, and for a short while they actually considered running off. "Of course it never came to anything," says Duke, "and you have to keep going because you have no alternative." By the time he'd reached fifty missions, he felt better again, as though he had come to terms with the risks involved.

Duke and Bob Hoke kept their thoughts to themselves, but usually it was possible to tell pretty quickly if a pilot wasn't up to the task. Twenty-year-old Pilot Officer Christopher Lee joined 260 Squadron in January as intelligence officer and quickly realized that the pilots reacted very differently to combat flying. "Some seemed to be totally unaffected," he says. "There was a Scot in the squadron who never showed the slightest emotion. It was as though he'd been out for a walk. But there was a Canadian who had a thing about anti-aircraft fire. The others pulled his leg all the time." He could usually tell when people were affected by particular sorties, however, and realized that fear was no respecter of rank. "I'd see wing commanders coming back looking shaken," he says.

Billy Drake had to sack several pilots who had lost their nerve. This was termed LMF—lacking moral fiber. "I had no compunction about it whatsoever," he says. "We had a fair idea of how far we could go on, and that we were under a considerable amount of strain." If someone started to look washed out, Billy would give him a rest, but if that didn't do the trick, he would be quickly sent back to Cairo. "Particularly in the desert we relied on each other so much that we couldn't afford to have a weak link," he explains.

Tommy Thompson seemed to have particularly deep reserves of courage, having flown operationally for the best part of two years, including his ten-month stint on Malta. He was still flying most nights with 73 Squadron, although as he'd discovered during his brief stint as an instructor, it was pilots from his own side who could be the most dangerous. In early December, he had just landed when he saw another pilot heading straight for him, about to take off. Tommy braced himself for what seemed to be an inevitable collision, but just in the nick of time the approaching Hurricane lifted off the ground, clipping Tommy's propeller and roaring over just inches from his head. It was, he noted in his logbook, "a very shaky do for me!"

But Tommy and his fellow flight commander were becoming increasingly concerned about their CO, who had begun returning from night intruder sorties with wild claims about having shot up lorries and transport on the road, claims not substantiated by other pilots who would return from the same area having seen nothing. So they decided one of them should follow the CO on his next intruder. Tossing a coin for it, Tommy lost. As they'd suspected, he flew nowhere near any enemy targets. "He went out to sea at two hundred feet below radar," says Tommy, "circled for about three quarters of an hour, then fired his guns and headed back. He never spotted me because I was right under his tail."

Tommy landed just ahead of him and was in the intelligence tent when the CO came in to give his report. As usual, he claimed to have shot up a number of enemy vehicles.

"If that report goes to headquarters, I'm going with it," Tommy told him.

"Why's that?" said the CO.

"Because I've been sitting under your tail all evening and you haven't even been over enemy territory." The CO tore up his report and stormed out, but a few days later, it was Tommy who was posted, not the CO. "I was sacked," he says, a blemish that remained on his record. Fortunately for Tommy, he was posted to a Spitfire squadron and soon after that to Helwan as a Spitfire test pilot.

The tensions were also growing between Mary Coningham and General Montgomery, and now Mary was without his trusted Number Two and Chief of Administration. In the first week of December, Tommy Elmhirst received word that he was being recalled to London after two "enthralling" years in the Middle East. Before he went, however, he drew up the administrative plan for the next five hundred miles' advance to Tripoli. The cause of Mary's frustration was Monty's refusal to take any risks with his troops and his unwillingness to sufficiently help the Desert Air Force with supplies and fuel. Mary had feared that the panzer army would simply slip away from the El Agheila position before Eighth Army could begin their frontal assault. This was precisely what happened, Rommel once again ignoring Hitler's demand to fight to the last man. But Monty was in no hurry, preferring to steadily bring his army ever closer to Tunisia in strength, and having properly cleared the array of mines and booby traps always left in the Axis's wake.

Even so, the forward fighter squadrons had remained busy whenever the weather allowed, and they still found themselves running into formations of enemy aircraft. On one occasion in December, Billy Drake had been leading a mixed force of 112 Squadron pilots and Americans of 66

Squadron on a bombing raid when they'd been attacked by a number of 109s and Italians Macchis. Billy shot down one of each before finding himself being pursued by seven Messerschmitts, and wondering whether his career was about to come to a violent end. Cloud cover saved him, but when he emerged, he was attacked again and had to use every trick in his repertoire to dodge and weave and get himself out of trouble. By the time the skies cleared, he realized he was almost out of fuel and had to force-land with his wheels up among some forward reconnaissance troops of the 11th Hussars.

Once the enemy retreated from El Agheila, air operations lessened considerably, a cause of considerable frustration to the pilots of 112 Squadron who had now officially shot down 199 enemy aircraft since joining the Desert Air Force. Although there were almost daily bombing raids, their 200th victim eluded them, and instead they had to take solace from their sporting prowess: during a football match with the King's Royal Rifle Corps, they won 7–0, then later beat the Royal Engineers 5–0. They even won a game of baseball against the 57th Fighter Group. But to Billy's great disappointment, the squadron had still not claimed its 200th aerial victory when, on 16 January, his time with the squadron came to an end. Since arriving in May the previous year, he had shot down seventeen enemy aircraft and two shared, a record that had been bettered only by his predecessor. For the time being, his fighter days were now over. For the next few months, Billy's huge experience would be put to use helping to train the new pilots arriving in the Middle East and giving them an introduction to the very different demands of operational flying in North Africa.

With the new year, the Eighth Army seemed to change. The South Africans—Bill Eadie and Petrus Dhlamini included—had shipped out on 2 January, and the Aussies were due to sail at the end of the month. Mangal Singh, after three years in the Middle East, was also sent back home to India. A lot of the old timers had gone. Albert Martin noticed this change. Much was the same—the old battered 15 cwt trucks, bully beef, petrol-flavored water, and desert sores—but many of the faces were new. There were hardly any of the pre-war regulars left now; they'd been wounded, killed, or sent home. And while before, they'd gotten by with what little they'd been given, now they were swamped with new equipment, from guns and mortars to Gammon ("sticky") bombs. Albert sensed that the old days of roaming around the desert as an almost independent and freelance unit were over. He couldn't help feeling slightly discarded, as though the war that he had known for so long had been taken away from him. Whereas they'd always been in the front of any advance, they were now left behind at Timimi while the rest of Eighth Army moved on past El Agheila and toward Tripoli. Instead, they began training for fighting in more restrictive terrain—hills, mountains, towns. The kind of terrain they might find in Tunisia. "A shock to us all," wrote Albert. "We had known no other battlefield but the desert, so none of us was happy at what might lie in store."[428]

The triumphant days of the SAS in the Desert War were also coming to an end. They had performed well in support of the main fighting at Alamein by mounting raids against supply columns well behind the Axis front line, but by the time Carol Mather rejoined there were a lot of new faces and many of them had little experience or knowledge of the desert. Carol was to command a party and harass a fifteen-mile stretch of coastline sixty miles east of Tripoli, which included the port of Homs and its nearby airfield. Aerial photographs suggested there was plenty of good cover, but also that there were a number of settlements in the area, villages belonging to Tripolitanian Arabs. Unlike the Libyan Senussi, these were hostile to the Allies, which could make life tricky. The other problem was that of supplies. He and his party were expected to operate in the area for a month, but only had enough rations to last ten days. "You'll just have to live off your fingernails," Stirling told him cheerily. "Forage around and see what you can pick up in the Italian settlements."[429]

During their first day in the area they were spotted by an Italian roadblock and although they got away and found a suitably deep wadi and some caves in which to lie up and hide their kit, the following day an Italian patrol spotted their sentry. They had all hidden by the time the Italians found their makeshift camp, but were now left with only what they'd been carrying. Clearly, they would not be able to remain on the run for long. Carol and four of his men avoided detection for most of the next day, but the Italians were dogged in their pursuit, and, it seemed, had mounting numbers of Arabs to help them. By late afternoon Carol and his men were surrounded. They hid up an olive tree, and then in a ditch, but when grenades started to be lobbed at them they finally crawled out with their hands in the air. Carol's war in Africa was now over as well.

The journalist Ernie Pyle had arrived in North Africa toward the end of November, pining for his former wife, Jerry, whom he had determined to remarry. He felt no particular enthusiasm for this new assignment, and while the other journalists set off for the front, Ernie decided to stay put in Oran and continue what he'd begun in England: writing stories about the American boys and girls who made up this new adventure.

At the beginning of January, however, he took a trip down to Biskra to see how the bomber crews of the 97th were getting on. Biskra, he wrote,

was "Africa as we have pictured it back home," with sand, date palms, skies
of endless blue, and nights of a million twinkling stars. And although it did
sometimes rain there, that was pretty rare. "Soldiers who have lived knee
deep in the perpetual winter mud of the coastal belt call this the best place
in Africa."[430]

Apart from his time in London during the Blitz, this was the closest
Ernie had yet been to any action, and three hours after his arrival in
Biskra, he witnessed his first enemy air raid. Since there was no air-raid
siren, the alarm was called by ringing a dinner bell hung from a palm,
augmented by a system of sentries firing shots into the air. He was struck
by the randomness of the destruction caused—one man had the sights of
his rifle knocked out by a bullet, another discovered his water bottle had
been holed.

Ernie watched his first bombing raid take to the skies on 12 January.
Aircraft of the 414th and 341st Squadrons—Ralph Burbridge and the crew
of the *All American* included—flew off to attack the enemy airfield of Castel
Benito near Tripoli, their second mission in support of the Eighth rather
than First Army. By late afternoon the bombers began returning. "The sun
was lazy, the air was warm," noted Ernie, "and a faint haze of propeller dust
hung over the field, giving it softness." A red flare was fired by one of the
approaching Fortresses. As it landed and came to a halt, Ernie hurried over
and watched as the crew lowered their dead pilot through the hatch. No
one said very much, but the crew looked grave. Ernie, who had not seen a
dead man before, noticed how white the lifeless man's hands were. "Everybody knew the pilot," he wrote. "He was so young a couple of hours ago.
The war came inside us then, and we felt it deeply."

All the bombers had made it home bar one. Other returning crews said
they'd seen the *Thunderbird* in trouble, losing altitude and lagging behind
just after leaving the target. Since then, hours had passed, and the worst
had been assumed—and accepted. As dusk settled, Ernie had gone up to
the control tower to watch the sunset and to see whether there was any news
on an incoming raid—the Germans liked to attack at the end of the day.
Suddenly, far off in the distance, they saw a red flare flicker into the sky.
"Then we saw the plane—just a tiny black speck," wrote Ernie. It was flying
low and slow—so slow it appeared to be barely moving. "At that moment I
felt something close to human love for that faithful battered machine," he
continued, "that far dark speck struggling towards us with such pathetic
slowness." Inexorably, it closed ever nearer until it reached the edge of the
airfield, skimming over the tops of the parked aircraft and eventually
touched down. "And as the plane rolled on down the runway, the thousands
of men around the vast field suddenly realized that they were weak and that

they could hear their hearts pounding . . . Our ten dead men were back from the grave."[431]

Another who made a miraculous return from bombing Castel Benito was the South African, Cobber Weinronk. The bombers had gradually caught up with the rest of the Desert Air Force and had begun regular raids once more. Sunday, 17 January, had started badly for Cobber when he heard that his trusted top gunner, Tommy, had been taken off and replaced by a "sprog" who had yet to fly a mission. Cobber wasn't happy about this at all—he was superstitious about changing a crew member just before a raid, and usually such superstitions were accepted and observed. For example, one pilot who hadn't been able to find his mascot had been immediately taken off a raid by the CO until it had been found, so Cobber felt he was being hard done by, especially as Castel Benito was notoriously well defended and Cobber wanted the best crew available.

Just before he was due to take off later that evening, Cobber was reprieved. The new gunner hadn't arrived, so Tommy flew after all, and they took off as planned at around 7:40 PM. Since this was a night raid, the bombers were not expected to fly in close formations of eighteen aircraft, but rather operated individually. In the past, Cobber had tended to fly the bomb run between 10,000 and 12,000 feet, but this time thought he'd be clever and avoid the heavy ack-ack, and so flew in at 4,000 feet with only the light flak to contend with.

As they approached the enemy airfield, Cobber's navigator helped direct him over the target and then called, "Bombs away." But as Cobber leaned forward to pull the lever to close the bomb bay, they were suddenly hit by flak, shards hitting him in the face, left hand and arm. Blood gushed over him. He felt faint and nauseous and thought that he was about to die. "Bail out, bail out!" he shouted to the rest of his crew. He didn't see how he could make it, and didn't want them going down with him. His crew—men he'd flown with since arriving in the desert—jumped, and he was left on his own, the Boston already spiraling downward and rapidly losing height. A mental image of his mother opening the telegram entered his mind. Perhaps he should try and bail out too, but his arm was too weak and he was unable to get the pilot's door open. Then right over Castel Benito, it somehow occurred to him to put on his landing lights. Immediately the ack-ack stopped. They must have thought he was one of their own.

Now just four hundred feet off the ground, Cobber managed to pull out of the spin and open his side window. The cool air revived him somewhat and he decided he had to try and get as far from Castel Benito as he could. Making for the coast, his wounds began to hurt badly, but the nausea had worn off. Still bleeding badly, he passed a familiar marker. Soon after, he found himself approaching their airfield.

With his wheels jammed, he planned to belly-land, but as he dropped and approached the landing strip forgot that with the wheels retracted he would stall at a lower speed. As the airfield drew closer, he switched off the engine and petrol flow and waited. Normally, they touched down after the third flare, but the sixth had passed and he was still airborne. Pushing the stick gently forward he finally felt the belly of his Boston start scraping and grinding along the ground until eventually it came to a halt.

Medics rushed over to him and he was taken to see the MO, where he was given a couple of double scotches and his wounds tended. One piece of shrapnel had hit the ring on his finger and broken; it was the ring his father had given him just before he'd died. Cobber couldn't help thinking about his crew. "I'm satisfied that I did the right thing and brought my plane home," he noted in his diary, "but wonder what the powers that be will feel about it." For the time being, however, he was left to recover from his wounds, injuries that were bad enough to bring about an end to his time in North Africa. A couple of weeks later he flew to Heliopolis. After a brief period in a convalescent home, followed by leave in Palestine, Cobber was sent back home to South Africa.

Christopher Lee took over as intelligence officer of 260 Squadron in January, when the squadron's much-loved IO had been promoted and moved to 239 Wing. His was a hard act to follow for a six-foot-four, dark-haired twenty-year-old only just promoted to pilot officer.

"Put one foot wrong, my son, and you're out!" the CO told Christopher, and then added, "Right, let's go and get pissed."[432] In the officers' mess, he was introduced as the new "spy" and promptly put through the squadron initiation ceremony, which involved being de-trousered, having his shirt-tails set on fire, and being plied with an unspeakable number of drinks.

As Christopher soon found out, the squadron pilots were a typically eclectic bunch: there were South Africans, Canadians, Aussies, New Zealanders, and British among their number; even an American, known as "Ah Phuckett-ah," because of his habit of saying, "Agh, agh, fuck it!" every time his stammer got in the way of him telling a story. The Aussies seemed to particularly take to him. Christopher's father had been the first British officer to lead Australians in the last war, a fact that one of the adjutants remembered. "It made a hell of a difference," he admits.

He also quickly discovered that a great deal of authority and responsibility came with his new job. It was his task to keep all the pilots up to date about where the bomb line was and to make sure they neither attacked too far forward nor too far back. As the front was moving so rapidly, this was no easy task. He also fed information and intelligence to them, kept them up to date with what else was going on and interviewed each pilot after every sortie; it was up to him to analyze the information they told him and pass it on. "The responsibility was such," says Christopher, "that if I made mistakes people died."

The circumstances in which he found himself in the Western Desert were unusual. When he'd initially joined the RAF, he'd been sent to Rhodesia to become a pilot, but just before he'd been due to go solo, had been on a training session and flying at around 5,000 feet when he'd been struck by an intense headache and blurring in his left eye. On landing, he'd been sent to see the medical officer right away. It seemed there was something wrong with his optic nerve. There was no more precise diagnosis, but after a few days, he was told he would not become a pilot after all.

The RAF was clearly unsure what to do with him, so he was sent from one base to another with little to do until he eventually applied for some intelligence work. To his great surprise he was seconded to the Rhodesian police and made a warder at Salisbury Prison. He'd been there several months when he was sent to Durban and promoted to leading aircraftman (LAC) and eventually put on a boat to the Middle East. Reaching Port Said, Christopher was taken to a staging camp in the Canal Zone, arriving in the middle of an intense sandstorm. He had loathed the camp, where two NCOs in particular made the new arrivals' life a misery, forcing them to drill out in the intense summer heat. Christopher was singled out for having been to an English public school and given a host of impossible and menial tasks. "It was extremely unpleasant," he admits, although before long he was posted to the RAF base at Ismalia, where he finally began carrying out intelligence work for Administrative and Special Duties.

It was while at Ismalia—and having survived being stabbed in the neck by an Arab—that Christopher was attached to 231 Wing of Wellington bombers. Among a number of tasks, he would sometimes fly with the Wellingtons on their "milk runs," dropping propaganda leaflets out over Benghazi. "I can't imagine what good it did, but it was nice to be doing something different," he admits. And he was still with the Wing when the Battle of Alamein began. Even from the squadron landing grounds he could hear the barrage and see the whole sky lit up.

His arrival with 260 Squadron coincided with the renewed move forward along the coast. It seemed that no sooner had he set up his trailer than the squadron was off again. Occasionally he traveled by plane, but usually it was by 15 cwt truck, rattling along with the advance party to the next stop and hoping they didn't hit a mine or run into an Axis booby trap.

* * *

Also recently arrived in North Africa was Ernie Pyle's fellow journalist, Alan Moorehead. After his trip to America he had returned to Britain and had been initially surprised to discover the country bearing up well after more than three years of war. In London the buses and Underground appeared to be working with breezy efficiency, the people he met seemed cheerful and determined, while the military buildup struck him as truly astonishing. Britain was far from on her knees. And yet not all was as it seemed. Gradually, he began to discern an underlying frustration, similar to that felt in America. People he spoke to as he traveled around could not understand why the Allies had been dealing with Darlan, nor could they understand what was happening in North Africa. If such a large army had landed there, why was it being held up by a few Germans in a tiny corner of Tunisia? His voyage of political discovery in America and Britain had depressed him, but he hoped that by returning to the war in North Africa once more, he might find the answers to many of his questions. On the train from London, he changed back into his army uniform for the first time in four months. "It suddenly felt very warm and reassuring," he wrote.[433]

When Alan did finally arrive at the front in the first week of 1943, a number of his questions were soon answered. "It is no exaggeration at all to say that the average citizen in New York and London had not the remotest idea of what the fighting was like," he wrote later, "of who was doing it, of what weapons were being used, of the numbers engaged on both sides, of what local objectives were being sought or of the prospects for the future."[434] Moreover, as he pointed out, in the States it was widely believed (thanks to the initial landings) that the majority of troops doing the fighting were American, when in fact, it was largely a British operation. In most people's minds back home, the idea that Tunisia could be anything other than flat, sandy desert, was a hard concept to grasp. That their boys were struggling through hills, mountains, and thick, syrupy mud in driving and frequently freezing rain was incomprehensible.

It took him awhile to get used to this new battlefield too. In the desert, with its vast space and huge distances, the enemy had always seemed to him someone remote, "a red line on the map, a cloud of dust across the desert horizon." No-man's-land might be as much as twenty miles wide. He'd never really sense a battle as such, only bits of a battle—"all the rest vanished under clouds of smoke and dust." In Tunisia, however, he could lift his binoculars and see German soldiers moving about. Here, one looked down on positions, or even up to them, the combatants seemingly on top of one another. Alan was struck by the sense of congestion at the front, and the fact that every yard was dangerous: landmines and booby traps were everywhere. Behind a rocky crag, snipers perched; and zooming down the valley roads were the cursed enemy fighters, stifling these vital supply routes so that all driving had to be done at night and in the dark and with no headlights whatever.

And there was the mud. Even a car can turn a dirt track into a quagmire in no time at all, but with trucks, tanks, half-tracks, and the weight of an entire army, any kind of vegetation vanished amid the folds of sticky, knee-deep mud. "This perishing cold, this all-invading mud and this lack of hot food could exhaust and kill a man just as thoroughly as bullets," noted Alan.[435]

By Christmas, Lieutenant Nigel Nicolson had not taken off his clothes once in the fortnight since their arrival at "Grenadier Hill," a few miles southeast of Medjez. He was, he wrote to his mother, absolutely filthy. "It is a pleasure not to have to be tidy, but when I have no buttons left on my trousers, and only have dirty ditch water to wash in, because the clean water is too valuable, things are a bit squalid even for me."

Conditions were far from ideal even in Arzew. "It's really pouring down rain," wrote Margaret Hornback in a letter to her friend, Stout. "It sounds on the tent like it used to on the tin roof of our old house." Outside the rows of tents the ground around had turned to mud. Someone had said it combined the worst features of chocolate pudding and flypaper. Margaret thought that was a pretty good analogy. Earlier in the day a general had paid a call, and all he'd said was, "Mud, mud, mud."

After treating the wounded from the landings, life in the surgery unit had quieted down, so Margaret had been working on the wards of the old hospital instead. She'd been enjoying it, but her generally sunny outlook had taken a hit. At the beginning of December, she'd been told that Dick, her boyfriend from the journey over, was badly ill with pneumonia. Then just before Christmas, she'd received the news that he'd died. It hit her hard—his death seemed so particularly futile and it upset her greatly to think of him dying in a far-off land with no one he knew around him, not even other men from his company. "Seems the time was so short," she wrote, "and as I look back, we made so little of it."

They were not to stay in Arzew for long, however. With the recent fighting in Tunisia, they were needed closer to the front and so on 15 January, began the move to Constantine. Only a day after their arrival, they moved again, this time to a camp among the wooded hills north of Tebessa. For Margaret, the quiet days of walking the wards were over. Wounded began flooding in, Allied and German and Italian. As she quickly discovered, the enemy were young men just like their own. "They say if they could go home and tell their own people how they were treated here," she wrote to Stout, "the war would be over sooner." They were now operating entirely in tents. Margaret shared hers with another nurse. It was next to the operation tent, so they could be on call constantly. Facilities were basic, to put it mildly. All the surgery linen had to be washed by hand and then dried on lines strung between the tents. Since it seemed to be always either raining or dusty, it was next to impossible to get anything properly clean. Furthermore, the floor of the operating tent was just dirt—another hazard of being a mobile hospital.

At least the nurses now had the occasional shower, although it was not perhaps quite what they'd been used to. Out in the open, it was protected on three sides by sheets of metal and guarded by French soldiers. The fourth side was covered by blankets. The nurses would strip in what Margaret called a "refreshingly cool atmosphere." Then they stood under the showerhead, which was regulated by an Arab who understood no English. Waiting there naked and shivering expectantly, a flood of boiling water would suddenly burst out over them. They screamed so loudly that even the Arab could understand, the water was hastily turned off. Quickly lathering themselves, they then waited for more water—which, when it arrived, was as icy as it had been hot. "It's amazing, the lengths one will go to get clean," noted Margaret.

The war may have moved a long way west, but the hospitals were still busy in Alexandria and Cairo. One day in January, Sophie Tarnowska was at the offices of the Polish Red Cross when she received a telephone call from Sim Faversham, a British officer she had recently met at one of the many parties still going on in Cairo. "I have to see you right away," said Sim, and told her he would come straight over to her office. Sophie went downstairs and met him at the front door. "I probably shouldn't tell you this," Sim told her, "but I'm off tomorrow." He was heading back to the front, and explained to her that for the past fortnight he'd been visiting his brother-in-law, Richard Wood, who had been badly wounded and was in hospital. Would Sophie take over these daily visits? "He'll say you've only come because you feel sorry for him," he warned her, "but ignore him, and please keep visiting him."

Richard was the son of Lord Halifax, formerly viceroy of India, foreign secretary, and now British ambassador in Washington. Richard had been wounded on 30 December and both his legs had been amputated very high up. With a heavy heart, Sophie agreed. She was given permission to visit him out of hours—he was in a separate room—and would come in her Polish Red Cross uniform after finishing work. As Sim had warned, Richard was initially wary of her visits, but gradually their friendship grew. On one occasion, Richard showed her a letter from his mother, in which she explained that although she had the influence to pull strings and leave Washington to be with him every day in Cairo, it would not be fair to the many wounded who were not so fortunate. "I was very struck by that," says Sophie.

As Richard's condition improved, he was placed on a ward—much to his relief. Sophie continued to visit him and soon became known to all the men on the ward; and when Richard was allowed out of hospital, it was Sophie who took him. "He showed unbelievable courage," she says. "He had the bravery to face his terrible loss."

Arriving into the messy and complicated stalemate now developing in Tunisia were more and more troops. Lieutenant David Brown and the men of the 17th Field Regiment, Royal Artillery, had had a more exciting journey than most. Having safely crept through the Straits of Gibraltar, they were well inside the Mediterranean when their ship was struck in the middle of the night by a torpedo, although fortunately not critically. Nonetheless, eight men were killed and a number more wounded, and the ship, under heavy escort, had to make straight for Bougie, rather than Bone. "It was a bit queer after we'd been hit," wrote David in a letter to his wife, "waiting at boat stations for more to come. Our chaps are pretty good. Quite phlegmatic and bored about the whole thing—just annoyed at losing sleep."[436] On arrival at Bougie they hurriedly disembarked and headed for a transit camp nearby. There they had their first taste of North African rain, and although they were all soon drenched, David was so excited to have arrived on land that he wasn't too bothered about getting soaked.

Early on Christmas Day, they boarded another ship and set sail for Bone. The passage was a rough one, but did not have to be endured for long. They reached Bone later that evening and after only a few days, were sent up the line to Medjez. At 2 AM on 6 January, the regiment took over positions from 12 RHA and David found himself in action for the first time.

Twenty-six years old and standing over six foot tall with brown hair and pale gray-blue eyes, David cut a striking figure. Like most of the new officers and troops that were now arriving, he was not a career soldier by any stretch of the imagination and had circumstances been different, would never have imagined himself to be wearing khaki. Training in England had depressed him. He'd hated the atmosphere, which he thought was too like private school, even though he'd been to Rugby, one of the best-known private schools in England. "All frightfully hearty," he wrote, "with pipe and moustaches and all mad keen." The amount of work and study was also more than he'd anticipated, and although he wanted to do his bit and fight the Germans, he wished he didn't have to wear his brains out first. But most of all, he was homesick, and missed his actress wife and young daughter dreadfully. "I feel such miles away from you, darling," he wrote.[437]

Curiously, his homesickness had lessened the further he was from home, largely because he was busy all the time, and fascinated by the situation in which he found himself. Like most people, he was considerably more interested in the practical side of soldiering than the endless drill and study of artillery manuals. After three days at the front, he had acclimatized well. Based at the 13th Battery's command post (CP), his new home was a foxhole in a shallow wadi. "We are like moles," he wrote, "all tunnelling madly." Rather like the Western Front in the First World War, the men on both sides were burrowing into the ground and hoping to avoid the desultory shell fire that continued day and night. In this war, however, there was also the constant threat of aerial attacks. "One's pleasures are few," wrote David, "the next meal, sleep, and a smoke." He was supposed to have given up smoking—but life was too short, he told his wife, and when tired, he found a smoke a comfort.

On 9 January, the regiment spent the day fixing gun positions and working out the arcs of their indirect fire. In the evening, David, along with two other officers had to reconnoiter an Observation Post (OP) on motorbikes, but had some hairy moments when they became stuck in mud. A few rifle bullets whizzed by, but they were pretty sure they were being fired on by their own side. It rained all day, and despite wearing his black mac from home—"the best 37/6 worth I ever bought"—he and the men were all soaked through, with water filling their slit trenches and with no prospect of getting dry again. The novelty of being in Africa was already wearing thin. "I don't think the trenches in the last war were anything on this," wrote David.[438]

Also now in North Africa was Sergeant Bucky Walters of the 135th Infantry Regiment. They reached Oran, rather than Bone, on 2 January with little idea of what was going on or where they were headed. No sooner had they docked than Bucky had looked up and watched a dogfight in the skies above. Two Allied aircraft hurtled into the side of the nearby hills. Sure, he felt apprehensive all right, but also felt himself to be protected by a sensation of numbness. Nor was the 34th Division going to the front just yet. Despite being the first to reach Britain, and despite having had constant training ever since, it was felt that they needed even more before being sent to Tunisia. So while newly arriving British units were hurried east almost the moment they arrived, Bucky and his colleagues in the 135th were sent to Tlemcen, in western Algeria, to carry out yet more training and maneuvers. This was all well and good, but in all this time, Bucky had still barely even seen a tank. If they weren't going to be trained properly, then they might as well have been sent to the front right away. As most of the First Army were discovering, experience was the best training of all.

One thing the 18th Infantry Regiment had learned from Longstop was that the 37mm anti-tank gun was totally useless in modern warfare. As Henry Bowles points out, the 37mm was what they'd trained with and landed with and so, naturally, the troops using them had not thought twice about trying to knock out heavy guns and tanks with them. When this didn't work, it must have been something a shock. It is hard to understand why no one had thought to warn them it would be no good against the panzers.

The 18th Regimental Combat Team had been kept in the Medjez sector. On 30 December, they became attached to the British 6th Armoured Division. Conscious that feelings between British and Americans might be somewhat tense after the disaster at Longstop, Colonel Greer, the commanding officer of the 18th, made strenuous efforts to show appreciation and friendship toward Major-General Charles Keightly, CO of the 6th Armoured. This was exactly the kind of goodwill that would have been applauded by Ike, and indeed, worked wonders, for Keightly was of a similar mind and promised to send Greer some six-pounders and a number of anti-tank mines to help protect the 18th's new positions. Furthermore, Keightly promised to resolve any shortcomings affecting the regiment as soon as he could and to "do all in my power to get them put right."[439] Meanwhile, the Bowles twins were finding themselves taking up positions in the front line in Tunisia for the first time. While the 1st Battalion had been withdrawn from the front line to lick its wounds and gather strength once more, the 2nd was sent southeast of Medjez to relieve a British battalion. On 28 December, they moved into positions near Grenadier Hill, overlooking the Medjerda Valley and a crossroads known as Peter's Corner.

It was a strange time for the Americans. Under British command, they were given British rations, and, when they needed new clothing, British kit too. Pretty soon all Tom Bowles was left with was his GI helmet; the rest was all British Army serge. He was even given a new pair of British hobnail boots. "I didn't have a problem with it," says Tom. "The British were good fighters." Henry agrees. The only major difference as far they were concerned was the standard of food. "The volume was somewhat less than American rations were, you know," says Henry, although he loved the tea. "You had the tea, powdered milk and sugar and all you had to add was hot water," he says. "That tea they had really was beautiful."

Like everyone else, they dug in, got soaked, went out on patrols, and made their acquaintance with the Stuka and various Axis fighter planes. Soon their positions were linked with a complex network of zigzagging trenches not dissimilar to those of the Western Front in the previous war. By this time, a number of other—mostly British—units had been brought under Colonel Greer's command, including 16th/5th Royal Lancers, a squadron of the 2nd Lothian Horse, the 17th/21st Lancers and also Colonel John Frost's 2nd Parachute Battalion. It wasn't just the British who were doing all the commanding. Still, this had been a blow for Frost, not because he was under the command of the Americans, but because the rest of the parachute brigade had been withdrawn to prepare for another operation. Still badly under strength after the failed Oudna Raid, the 2nd Para Battalion had been left behind.

The lull in the fighting at least gave many of the green troops now in Tunisia a chance to learn a bit about being combat troops without having to take part in an all-out assault. Valuable lessons about mines, patrolling, and digging proper defenses made all the difference in the world. Desultory shell, mortar, and aerial attacks also gave them important experience of being under fire. This was particularly valuable for the 18th Infantry and other American units now in the front line, who had reached North Africa having had no training with live ammunition and little concept of what awaited them.

The inadequacy of American training was, in many ways, understandable: the Americans had far fewer instructors with any experience, they were mobilizing more men at greater speed than the British, and for much of their time had had insufficient equipment with which to train. In sharp contrast, however, British training was now much improved, partly because they were beginning to take note of the lessons learned in the Western Desert, and partly thanks to the battle school system developed by General Alexander and others. Lieutenant Peter Moore was a subaltern with the 2/5 Leicestershire Regiment, a standard infantry unit, which by 1943 was made up principally from wartime volunteers and conscripts. They were not in any way elite troops like the paras, nor from the top-drawer of line regiments like the Guards brigade. Yet both at his OCTU (Officer Cadet Training Unit) and subsequently with the regiment, Peter had carried out a number of all-arms and even inter-service exercises. During the previous summer, for example, he had taken part in a large training exercise in Scotland, in which one side launched a seaborne assault while the other defended, and which involved infantry, tanks, and artillery. Earlier on, while still at OCTU, he had watched a demonstration of a blitzkrieg-style attack along the sand dunes of the Lancashire coast. "It was extremely effective," says Peter. "A company of infantry was supported by artillery, mortars, waves of fighter-bombers, and tanks in attacking a high point in the dunes. Live ammunition was used by everyone. The noise was frightening and it was one of the best preparations for battle that I experienced." Once he was even made to eat lunch in an abattoir to get them used to seeing and smelling blood.

This disparity in training had been borne out in the recent fighting. It was one of the reasons why British generals were sending their own troops straight to the front while Bucky Walters' 135th Infantry was held back. What is harder to understand is why British and American training in Britain was not integrated in any way. The Bowles twins, for example, never once trained alongside the British, even though they were living alongside one another the entire time they were at Tidworth.

No one, however, could doubt the bravery of the vast majority of Americans, nor their willingness to learn, a fact reflected in the sheer number of "Combat Lessons Learned" memos that litter the records of the American units in North Africa. Unfortunately, there were a few more hard knocks to be taken in the weeks to come, setbacks that could and should have been avoided.

Peter Moore had turned twenty-one just a few days before setting sail for North Africa. Dark-haired, with a kind and good-humored face, he was, like David Brown, someone who would never have joined the army had it not been for the war. At school, despite loving all sports, he'd hated the obligatory Cadet Corps and had originally intended to pursue a career in agriculture, like his father, and to spend a life outdoors and in the countryside. He'd even spent a term at university studying agricultural science, before dropping out in order to try and join the RAF.

Poor eyesight had thwarted his plans, however, and so having turned nineteen, and now subject to being called up, he put his name down for the Leicesters, the regiment his father had served with in the First World War and to which he had been recalled again. After a brief period of basic training in the ranks, Peter was put forward for officer training, graduating in the summer of 1942 and finding himself a platoon commander in B Company.

He'd known they would be going overseas the moment it was announced that they were to parade before the king. It was well known that George VI liked to see every battalion before it was shipped abroad. Peter had been shocked by how ill the king had looked. His face had been rouged to give him color, but it had been a poor disguise. "It was terribly moving," wrote Peter, "and we all realized the enormous sense of duty of this man, insisting on wishing his subjects well before they departed for battle."[440] They had boarded their ship at Liverpool on Christmas Eve. Peter couldn't help remembering the last time he'd been along the waterfront there, in April 1939, when as a seventeen year old he was on his way back from a walking holiday in the Lake District. Now he was going to war.

They reached Algiers on 3 January. At once Peter was struck by the exotic smell of oranges and donkey bedding, and of the sight of little Arab boys running alongside them shouting, "Hey Tommy, jig-jig, m'amselle, dix francs!" They'd all been warned about the dangers of VD, and Peter, for one, was only too happy to resist the temptations of any jig-jig. He and a number of other officers did visit the "Sphinx" a few days later, however, it being a notorious brothel in the Kasbah in Algiers old town. Going there had already become recognized as an important *rite de passage* before troops headed off to the front. Peter thought the place looked like something out of *Arabian Nights*. The ground floor was strewn with divans and large cushions and scantily clad girls reclining on them. Neither Peter nor any of his friends wanted a girl to themselves; rather, they had come to watch the "exhibition," a floor-show that the madam told them would cost a hundred francs each. Having paid up, they were led to a small room with a padded bench around the walls and a large bed-size cushion in the middle. Peter looked around and saw there were about fifteen officers, from colonels to subalterns, sitting there expectantly. "We 21-year-olds waited with feelings of apprehension and dread," noted Peter, "because there had been a rumor that one was liable to be selected from the audience to be a partner as part of the act." With no experience of such matters, the very idea mortified him.[441]

Two girls—"disappointingly unattractive"—eventually appeared. Naked, one then strapped on a dildo and proceeded to demonstrate in broken English the lovemaking attributes of different nationalities. The Germans were the worst, followed by the British, Americans, and then French. By far the best, they told them, were the Italians. To Peter's relief, audience participation was neither offered nor demanded, and afterward, he left the room feeling rather shamefaced and sordid.

The battalion set off by train to the front on 10 January, a journey that would take two days. As they paused at a railway station along the way, Peter began thinking about home and his family. This made him feel momentarily homesick and depressed, and for the first time he began to think about his own mortality. So much uncertainty lay ahead of him at the end of the journey and he prayed that he would not let himself or anyone else down.

At the border railway station, they loaded themselves onto trucks and began the nighttime journey to the front. Peter sat with the driver, an old hand, who enjoyed telling new arrivals horror stories about traveling along what had already been dubbed "Messerschmitt Alley." It seemed that two

109s regularly patrolled the route and were known as "Gert and Daisy," after two popular cockney comediennes. The truck had no lights except for a small one at the rear, hung in such a way that it could only be seen at ground level. There was no sign of Gert or Daisy, however, and having safely negotiated Messerschmitt Alley, they then began climbing a mountain pass, from which there was always a sheer drop on one or other side of the road. It was a nerve-wracking experience. As Peter's driver desperately tried to keep up with the lorry in front, he sped up, faster and faster, hurtling round corners with alarming abandon.

By first light the ordeal was over, and the truck pulled off the road into a cork forest where the battalion was to concentrate before making their final move forward. The day was spent getting rid of excess kit and cleaning weapons, and then it was time to get into their trucks again and head off. They halted at Alouna Station in the north of the country near Sedjenane. The station building had already been flattened. In the distance, Peter saw artillery fire flashing in the night. In the faint night light, he could make out the grim outline of Sugar Loaf, Green Hill, and Baldy Hill, where the 36th Brigade had been halted nearly two months before. Leading his platoon to his designated area, Peter ordered the men to start digging in on the reverse slope of a slightly raised piece of ground. They had to work fast: each two-man slit trench was to be six feet deep, six feet long and three feet wide. It was cold and wet, the soil was heavy, thick clay and Peter could hear enemy reconnaissance aircraft buzzing overhead. By morning, he was exhausted, sodden, and covered in mud.

Admiral Cunningham had begun 1942 feeling very bleak about the future, but a year later, he felt there was cause for much optimism. He sensed their fortunes in the Mediterranean were on the turn. Even so, the first day of the new year had brought particularly heavy attacks on Bone, with over a hundred enemy aircraft bombing the port. Two merchantmen were hit and caught fire while the cruiser HMS *Ajax*, only recently arrived after a refit to join Force Q, was also hit and badly damaged, and a further ship, a minesweeper, was sunk. With enemy air raids on Bone continuing with almost daily regularity, doubts were soon raised about the wisdom of keeping Force Q based at Bone. "But I had to harden my heart," noted ABC, and insisted they stick it out rather than succumb to the enemy's game.

While Force Q was operating from Bone, the reconstituted Force K was once again based at Malta. More submarines had also joined the 10th Flotilla, but now that major Axis shipping routes were operating further west between southern Italy and Tunisia, it was decided to bring the 8th Submarine Flotilla from Gibraltar to Algiers, from where they could better attack enemy shipping. After their triumphant patrol in December,

Safari and her crew were posted back to the 8th Flotilla, reaching Algiers at the end of the first week in January. Although sorry to have to say goodbye to some of his friends, Ronnie Ward was delighted to leave Malta, with its terrible bomb damage, and lack of amenities, drink, and food. There had been little transport available on Malta, but at Algiers they were met by an amphibious jeep, one of two gifted by General Mark Clark, then whisked off to a party where there was not only champagne, but also a number of girls, the likes of which they had not seen since leaving Gibraltar the previous summer. And best of all, they were given a rest house just outside Algiers where the officers could relax and recharge their batteries. "Algiers was heaven," says Ronnie. "The villa was a lovely place. There was a beach and swimming and a kind of pub nearby—altogether it was bliss."

The 8th Flotilla operated mainly on the west and north of Sicily, and this was where *Safari* was sent on its first patrol operating from Algiers. Yet again, they were successful: two schooners sunk on 30 January, followed by a tanker and a steamer three days later. When it came to sinking enemy ships, *Safari* was in a league of her own.

Also now based in Algeria was the 10th MTB Flotilla—now at Bone—and like Ronnie Ward, Lieutenant Charles Coles was only too happy with his new change of address. They had been coast-hugging all the way from Alexandria, often neck and neck with Eighth Army. One time they had stopped for the night at a small fishing village and found the Italians had only just left—there was warm food still on the mess tables. They had then initially made for Malta, due to become an MTB base once more, but after a few days on the island, they were ordered to move on to Bone. The final run around the Cap Bon peninsula had been a bit hair-raising, but by traveling at night and lying up in sheltered positions during the day, they had avoided detection and safely made it to their new base, where they were to concentrate on anti-submarine patrols.

Shortly after his arrival, Charles was given a couple of days' leave and so borrowing an army jeep went off with a friend to explore the local countryside. He was surprised by how green and cultivated the countryside was around Bone. "Quite unlike the desert coast," says Charles. "Citrus trees everywhere." They stopped outside the gates of a very modern-looking farm and vineyard. Chickens were running about everywhere, so having not seen an egg for several months, Charles felt bold enough to ask the owner—he spoke French fluently—whether he might buy some eggs for his crew. Initially, the smartly dressed landowner was reluctant—everything was rationed and controlled, he explained. However, after chatting some more, the Frenchman invited them both in for some lunch. "It was a wonderful meal," says Charles. And when they left, they did so armed with no less than sixty eggs and a case of excellent wine.

Over lunch, the Frenchman—Monsieur Béghuin—told them that he had a yacht in the harbor at Bone, which, for security reasons, he was not allowed to visit. Charles offered to send over some of his crew to pump out the bilges and generally see that it was still in one piece. M. Béghuin accepted the offer gratefully and later confided that he had been the principal local intelligence agent for the British before the invasion. "They're an odd lot, your intelligence people," he told them. "I asked SOE for a radio operator and they sent me a Pole who didn't speak French." He then told them about another agent—his best, he said—who'd been operating in Bone, but who had been since put in prison by the Allies. Even worse, they had now taken on a pro-German character and sent him as a liaison officer to AFHQ in Algiers. Béghuin had been to the "authorities" but had gotten nowhere. Perhaps Charles could put in a word with the right people? Charles explained that he was not in intelligence and only very junior, but promised to do what he could.

It so happened that a few weeks later, Charles had some more time off while his MTB was being repaired and so was able to accept an invitation from M. Béghuin to a wild boar hunt west of Bone, near the front. It turned out to be a highly memorable occasion, not least because of the *Dejeuner de Chasse*, a picnic breakfast of proper coffee, chilled white wine, ham, fresh bread, and fruit. Charles had barely ever tasted such incredible food before, and certainly not since the beginning of the war. He soon discovered that most of the other guests were senior Algerian politicians, and that they were all anxious to explain to him the difficulties they were having with the Allied security services. He thoroughly enjoyed the hunting. "It was unbelievably exciting," he admits. Acting as beaters were colonial troops, mostly dressed in blue long-tailed tunics and bright red pantaloons, while not far away the continual sound of battle could be heard. To his great delight, Charles even managed to shoot and kill a boar, which he then took back with him. "I cut up this hairy, muscular wild boar on the dockside and distributed pieces amongst the crews," says Charles. It was the best meat they'd had in ages.

General Eisenhower and Harry Butcher flew to Casablanca on 15 January. It was another hairy flight. En route, one of their Fortress's engines started acting up and both men watched uneasily at the oil spewing out and over the wing. They were told to put on parachutes, and although they were saved the drama of jumping, by the time they finally came in to land a second engine was on its last gasp.

Another glad to reach Casablanca safely was Alan Moorehead. He had not initially been called back to Algiers, but desperate to know what was going on had followed anyway, only to find himself boarding another plane along with a number of fellow journalists. None of them had much idea of where they were heading or why, but were certainly perplexed by the American pilot's insistence on flying over the coastline of Spanish Morocco, especially once bursts of flak began rocking the aircraft. But to Alan's amazement, instead of taking immediate evasive action, the pilot began circling lower and lower as though about to land. Suddenly bullets started peppering the sky around them and hitting the aircraft. Alan stumbled along to the cockpit, but his shouts could not be heard. Meanwhile, one of his colleagues, a Canadian journalist called Edward Baudry, had his temple blown off by a bullet and blood and brains began spilling down the side of his face. One of the crew was also hit, and with what seemed like painful slowness the pilot finally turned out toward sea, bullets following after them.

They eventually landed at Port Lyautey—where the confused pilot had originally thought himself to be. Edward Baudry was taken off and then they continued to Casablanca, which, Alan noted, "was in the midst of a witches' brew of rumor and intrigue." Only once they reached their hotel were they told by a stern American general that "the biggest assemblage of high dignitaries ever gathered together since the war began" was taking place. Sworn to secrecy, they were warned not to even talk about it in their rooms for fear that they were being tapped.[442]

These "high dignitaries" included the president and prime minister as well as the combined chiefs of staff. The basis for the conference was a face-to-face discussion about future Allied strategy. Once again, the Americans found themselves outmaneuvered by the British, who had come far better prepared to fight their corner. After eighteen meetings at the conference, the net strategic outcome was the abandonment of a cross-channel invasion in 1943 and the agreement that an assault on Sicily—now code-named HUSKY—should be next on the list once North Africa was finally in Allied hands. Another important decision, and one that was made a proclamation at Roosevelt's insistence, was that the only terms the Allies would accept from Germany, Italy, and Japan were "unconditional surrender."

In between these debates there were also discussions about the current situation, which for Ike became increasingly uncomfortable. Over the past couple of weeks, he had begun to implement his command changes, including the establishment of his new forward command post for himself at Constantine. Recognizing that he still had to juggle command of his forces in Tunisia and the tasks of running AFHQ in Algiers, he appointed Brigadier-General Lucian Truscott to act in his absence at

Constantine. Clearly Ike was going to be spreading himself too thin, and in any case, Constantine was still two hundred miles from the front. Nor could he turn to Clark, who had taken over the newly evolving US Fifth Army, formed from the vast number of troops assembling in French Morocco and Western Algiers. This had left a vacancy over who was to command US II Corps, which Ike was now moving up towards the central Tunisian border.

Ike had recently chosen Major-General Lloyd R. Fredendall, who had commanded the American landings at Oran, and who, since then, had been acting as military governor of the area. It was to be one of the worst decisions Ike made during the entire campaign. Ike had not known Fredendall before the war, but he had been strongly recommended by Marshall, and that was good enough. Moreover, Ike had been impressed with the way Fredendall had handled the landings at Oran. Since then, however, Fredendall had done little to commend him. In particular, he had issued building contracts and appointments to well-known Vichyites, something that had caused something of a stir. It was also picked up on by Ernie Pyle after a tip-off from an American counter-intelligence officer in Oran, and he had not only written about it but had managed to get it past the censors. "Our fundamental policy," he reported, "still is one of soft-gloving snakes in our midst . . . We have left in office most of the small-fry officials put there by the Germans before we came. We are permitting Fascist societies to continue to exist."[443] This column became a news story in itself, not that Fredendall cared. When an American diplomat complained about these appointments, Fredendall gave him short shrift. "Lay off that stuff!" he told the diplomat. "What the hell do you know about it?"[444]

Loud and outspoken, Fredendall bullied his staff and was prone to jumping to conclusions from which he would not be swayed; he knew best. He was also rather too fond of a drink, had a bad habit of sending messages in a code known only to himself, and was openly critical of anyone he decided he didn't like. He was furthermore pathologically and quite openly Anglophobic. All in all, not the attributes needed for close cooperation with the French and British forces now in Tunisia.

Fredendall had taken over command of II Corps at the beginning of January and together with Ike, had come up with a plan to cut a swathe across central Tunisia, and then capture the ports of Gabes and Sfax and so cut the Axis forces in half, preventing Rommel from joining forces with von Arnim. Operation SATIN was to be an entirely American show, although French forces and the 1st Parachute Brigade (less Frost's 2nd Battalion) would also be placed at Fredendall's disposal. It was to be launched at the end of the month.

Ike enthusiastically presented this idea—along with his other command changes—during his day-long appearance at the Casablanca Conference. The operation had grown since its initial conception—final plans demanded 38,000 troops and a mind-boggling amount of supplies that the current system could not possibly deliver. The combined chiefs were not impressed, pointing out that Rommel now had 80,000 troops and von Arnim 65,000. Rather than split the two forces, a more likely scenario was that II Corps would be swallowed whole. Brooke also revealed that Ultra had discovered signs that Rommel was already sending the much-strengthened 21st Panzer up into Tunisia. With this bombshell, SATIN was promptly scrapped.

The following morning, Ike confessed to Harry Butcher that he had been "more or less bawled at" by Marshall for his poor presentation. Butch, who'd spent the previous day, on Patton's advice, being Ike's eyes and ears on the ground, talking to as many people as he could, had also become aware of malignant rumors doing the rounds. "I had heard a lot from the so-called lower levels," he noted, "but it seemed to me clear that the absence of clear-cut words of thanks from the president or the prime minister showed they had their noses to the political winds, and weren't going to be caught holding the bag for a general who had made an unpopular decision and hadn't yet gotten Tunisia." He quite openly warned Ike that his head was now in the noose.[445]

That same morning, Butch had met the president as FDR had sat in bed eating his breakfast. What was supposed to be a brief introduction became a proper conversation, much to Butch's delight. "The president said he was something of a father confessor to all the boys," recorded Butch, "and hoped to help Ike out of some of his political troubles while here."[446] FDR had also had a conversation with Ike the previous evening. Deciding he should be nothing but frank with the president, Ike told him that he realized it was the role of generals to sometimes carry the can, and offered to resign. But FDR was not going to fire him. Instead he asked him to name a date when the campaign might be over.

"May fifteenth," Ike blurted.

A few days later, back in Algiers, General Alexander confessed that when pressed over the same date, he'd suggested 30 May. The conference had gone much better for the British commanders, and Alex in particular. He'd been called to give an account of the developments in Libya and had impressed everyone, but most notably the president. Appearing tanned, healthy, and in desert garb of shorts and open shirt, he appeared every inch the fighting commander. And he brought good news, announcing that Tripoli was expected to be in Allied hands in the very near future. Both Churchill and Brooke were delighted. "His unspoken confidence was contagious," noted the prime minister. The contrast with the tired and jittery Eisenhower could not have been more obvious.[447]

The different showings by the two men and the contrasting successes of the two areas of their command gave Brooke the point of maneuver he needed to persuade the Americans to accept further changes. As far as Brooke was concerned, it was obvious that Eisenhower was simply carrying too much responsibility and had neither the tactical nor strategic experience required for such a position. Firm, centralized command was needed, not just to coordinate the American, British, and French forces in Tunisia, but soon the Eighth Army as well. So he suggested Eisenhower be promoted further and that Alex should become Ike's deputy and overall commander of Allied ground forces. At Alex's suggestion, these would be renamed Eighteenth Army Group, because it combined the numbers of both armies. "We were pushing Eisenhower up into the stratosphere and rarefied atmosphere of a supreme commander," noted Brooke, "where he would be free to devote his time to the political and inter-Allied problems, whilst we inserted under him one of our own commanders to deal with the military situations and to restore the necessary drive and coordination which had been so seriously lacking of late!"[448]

The British had their way with another important appointment too: Tedder was to become overall Allied air commander in the Mediterranean. There was good news for ABC, too, who was promoted to admiral of the fleet, the highest rank in the Royal Navy, and shortly after, reappointed as C-in-C Mediterranean Fleet. When it eventually came to HUSKY, British commanders would hold the plum jobs.

There was one last extraordinary episode to be played out at Casablanca. Alan Moorehead had been cooling his heels with the other reporters when they were taken to Anfa Camp a short way outside the city and to the villa where the conference had been taking place. After waiting for a couple of hours, they were led up the road to meet the prime minister and president. While Alan and the other journalists squatted in a semicircle on damp grass, FDR and Churchill sat on two chairs, with Giraud and General de Gaulle on either side of the president. Behind them stood diplomats and ministers. The sun shone and Churchill lowered his dark hat over his forehead. For both Frenchmen, this was torturous. De Gaulle was still smarting from the Allies' snub of leaving him out of the TORCH operations, while for Giraud, de Gaulle was nothing more than a dangerous upstart.

Roosevelt beamed, while Giraud and de Gaulle looked tense and uneasy. Then Roosevelt urged the two generals to stand and shake hands. "It was all rather embarrassing," wrote Alan, "like the first rehearsal of an amateur play."

Giraud and de Gaulle then trooped off, leaving the PM and president. Beckoning the reporters to close in around them, the leaders happily talked of the success of the conference. "The scene was irresistibly like a Sunday-school treat with the children gathered at the feet of their two schoolmistresses," wrote Alan. But he was all too aware of the great significance of the conference, and particularly Roosevelt's presence there in Casablanca. The Allies would be concentrating their efforts in the Mediterranean for the time being. "Returning on our plane to the front," noted Alan, "we knew that every effort was now going to be put into the Tunisian war, and that the Germans were going to suffer such a blitz as they had not yet seen outside Russia."

But not quite yet. Before this new resolve and all its accompanying changes could be put into action, General Ike and his Allied forces were to face one more devastating setback.

CHAPTER 20

Conflicting Personalities:
18 January–13 February, 1943

ON 23 JANUARY, the last day of the Casablanca Conference, a message arrived from Alex announcing that Tripoli had fallen. Rommel had abandoned the port and Eighth Army had walked in unopposed, providing the Allied troops with another massive opportunity to increase their personal war booty. At Stalingrad, the Russians were also now just days away from an astonishing victory. Things were looking up.

Despite an uncomfortable day at Casablanca, Ike had returned to AFHQ with a weight lifted from his shoulders. The new command arrangement pleased him, as had the president's vote of confidence. Even so, Alex and Tedder were not to take on their new roles until February or until such time that the campaign in Libya had been effectively wrapped up, and so in the meantime Ike hurried straight on to Constantine, where he called together his senior commanders to report on the new developments. With SATIN scrapped, he ordered Fredendall to use II Corps to conduct raids and take important vantage points, but stressed that their role was to be essentially defensive until Eighth Army had reached the Mareth Line. This was the next Axis defensive position after Tripoli, and lay some twenty-five miles beyond the Tunisian border. He also told Anderson that he wanted to keep as much of II Corps as possible together as a mobile reserve; it was not to be used to plug any more gaps in the line. He then turned to General Juin. "Do you approve of this plan?" he asked.

"Yes," Juin replied, "but the Germans will not remain inactive." For the French, any enemy thrusts in their sector could have serious consequences. They were still pitifully short of equipment—much more was needed of everything, Juin told him, from guns to radios. Ike assured him the Allies had pledged to "scrape the bottom of the barrel" in their efforts to provide his troops with better equipment. This was good news, Juin replied, but until it arrived, his forces were going to need help, especially in the Fondouk area, where there were two passes through the Eastern Dorsale.[449]

This rather thorny issue had not been resolved by the time Ike hurried back to Algiers, where Marshall and Admiral King were waiting to see him on their return from Casablanca. Marshall, in particular, was anxious to see for himself the difficulties facing his protégé. He was certainly not impressed with the rear-area service and supply units, which he thought were chaotic and being managed with a breathtaking lack of discipline. After instantly firing a number a senior officers, he decided the time had come to give Ike a major talking to about the nature of command. "Eisenhower," Marshall told him, "there is one thing that you must understand clearly. Retention under your command of any American officer means to me that you are satisfied with his performance. Any man you deem unsatisfactory, you must reassign or send him home!"[450] In other words, he needed to be tougher. Marshall also suggested he appoint a few officers that he knew and trusted to help him out. Ike leaped at the suggestion, quickly producing a list, top of which was his old West Point classmate, Major-General Omar N. Bradley. True to his word, Marshall had Bradley sent over at the end of February.

Despite this lecture, Harry Butcher felt Marshall's whole attitude to Ike was that of a father to a son. Certainly the chief had been shocked by how ill Ike had looked. Taking Butch aside, he said, "He may think he has had troubles so far, including Darlan, but he will have so many before this war is over that Darlan will be nothing. You must look after him. He is too valuable an officer to overwork himself."[451]

Since the beginning of the year, the front line had run from the north coast to Medjez, then to Bou Arada and all along the edge of the Eastern Dorsale, leaving the Axis in control of the long stretch of plains that ran from Tunis to the border with Libya. Although the Eastern Dorsale was not as high as the Grande Dorsale—the highest peaks were only some three thousand feet high—an advancing army could only really get across it through its four passes at Pichon and Fondouk, Faid and Maknassy. These were not narrow gorges with towering rock faces on either side, but rather stretched several miles wide, the mountains either side rising gently away from them. The Faid Pass, for example, was over five miles in width, and led the way to a vast open area of arid scrub crisscrossed by winding and often steep-sided wadis and broken up by long prominent mountain-like ridges that emerged from the plains around them.

These passes through the Eastern Dorsale were, however, held by units of the French XIX Corps. Watching these were Italian troops supported by German artillery and panzer detachments. Kesselring had quite rightly worked out that they would never lose Tunisia so long as they held these, and so ordered von Arnim to mount a series of attacks to take control of them and the Allied positions all along the Eastern Dorsale. These were launched on 18 January, with a diversionary attack by 10th Panzer Division in the north at Bou Arada. Juin's prediction had been spot on.

Bou Arada was where 17th Field Regiment was now based. Lieutenant David Brown was at the 13 Battery observation post when at first light he spotted around twenty-five enemy tanks approaching. The regiment, with its twenty-five-pounders dug well in, had clearly not been detected and when the enemy tanks were just eight hundred yards distant, the British guns opened fire and knocked out seven in just a few moments, while the remaining panzers began frantically positioning themselves into better cover. The regiment continued to pound away throughout the morning, with piles of shell cases mounting beside them. But having pinpointed the British guns, the Germans were not slow to begin counter-battery fire. "We had a hell of a battle," wrote David to his wife. "I hope never to be in quite such a tight spot again."[452] The panzers began withdrawing just after two that afternoon, but later, the regimental HQ was dive-bombed by fourteen Stukas. Even so, David was finding front-line action considerably more exhilarating than he'd imagined. Shooting up the enemy, he told his wife, was "the grandest sport in the world—you know how I love aiming at things, well, when the thing you are aiming at is a salvo of shells, and at the old Hun too, it's damn good fun." The pining and terrible homesickness he'd felt during the bleak days of training seemed to have all but vanished.

Mines, mud, and the good shooting of the British artillery ensured that 10th Panzer's attack did not get very far, but farther south, Axis infantry and a number of the dreaded Tiger tanks burst through into the Ousseltia Valley. The French, with their outmoded rifles and pop guns, were not so much forced back as completely overrun. The Axis captured 3,500, the equivalent of seven battalions.

Anderson believed the only way to stop the rot was to send British and American reinforcements, although it meant going against Ike's wishes. Ordering most of the British 36th Brigade to hurry to the rescue of the French, he also asked Frendendall to send CCB to help plug the gaps. Now in command of CCB was Brigadier-General Paul Robinett, who'd taken over after Oliver had been promoted and sent back home. His order from Fredendall was typically bizarre: "Move your command, i.e., the walking boys, pop guns, Baker's outfit and the outfit which is the reverse of Baker's outfit, and the big fellows to 'M', which is due north of where you are now, as soon as possible. Have your boss report to the French gentleman whose name begins with 'J' at a place which begins with 'D', which is five grid squares to the left of 'M.'"[453]

Once Robinett had finally deciphered this he set off for the Ousseltia Valley, and along with 36 Brigade, was able to stem the Axis advance, even though the CCB commander was struggling with yet more bizarrely coded messages from Fredendall—messages that ran completely counter to those issued by the French.

On 24 January, and with his limited objectives taken, von Arnim called off the offensive and his forces withdrew to their new positions. The speed with which the French had succumbed had been alarming. As Juin had forewarned, the French could no longer be expected to hold a stretch of the front. Retraining and re-equipping was now desperately needed. For this to happen, however, wholesale changes to troop deployments needed to be made, which Ike ordered Anderson to oversee in an "executive capacity." This way, he hoped he would not offend French sensibilities.

Among those ordered to plug the gaps were Colonel John Frost's 2nd Parachute Battalion, who since their escape from Oudna had been used as infantry around Medjez el Bab. On 4 February, they were suddenly moved to the Ousseltia Valley. With almost no support, they were expected to defend a stretch of the front littered with booby traps, mines, and rotting corpses from the recent fighting. Opposite them, they were told, were reportedly ten infantry battalions and a hundred tanks. It was bitterly cold, there was little cover and on his first morning, Frost woke up to discover he was literally frozen to the ground. Three days later they were moved again to near Bou Arada. This time they were given nearly three miles to defend. "Bearing in mind that by normal reckoning, a battalion front should not have been much more than a thousand yards," noted Frost, "it will be seen that our elongated front was much greater than was really desirable."[454]

Quite. This desperate attempt to plug a front line that was now far longer than was manageable, not only dissipated Allied strength but also meant further splitting up divisions, brigades, and regimental combat teams. Even the French began to see that their stance over Anderson was proving counterproductive, and so finally allowed Eisenhower to persuade them to accept Anderson's command. After all, Ike reassured them, Anderson was subordinate to him, and so any order the British general gave was really an order from him. With this now resolved, Ike was able to direct Anderson to take command of *all* Allied forces on the Tunisian front on the understanding that he promise to be polite and helpful to Juin and to be mindful of French honor at all times. Anderson, not the most naturally charming man in the world, promised he would try his best.

But by now units were hopelessly mixed up, and for the time being at any rate, there was little chance of unraveling them into some kind of uniformity and cohesion. Had the British and Americans trained a bit more together before leaving the UK, this might have been less of a problem, but because they hadn't, it took awhile before a battalion understood the British way of doing things, and vice versa. This confusion was obviously even worse when British and American units suddenly found themselves alongside the French. Such differences mattered less when the line was more or less static, but was asking for trouble when carried out in the middle of a battle, as had happened to Joe Furayter and the 5th Field Battalion when they had joined the British at Tebourba the previous November.

For the most part, the men couldn't have cared less who they were in the line with. The Bowles twins had no objection whatsoever to fighting alongside the British, nor even wearing British kit. Nor did Joe Furayter. Of course they were proud to be a part of the Big Red One, but if the division happened to be split up a bit, it was no skin off their teeth. The idea that this badly affected morale was tenuous reasoning on the part of the commanders—most GIs and junior officers accepted their lot with stoic fortitude and even at the best of times, knew little about what was going on much beyond twenty yards either side of them.

But this didn't mean carving up divisions was a good idea. It was impossible for a commander and his staff to oversee the development, deployment, and further training of a division if it was split to the four winds. Commanders like to command, not be left in the rear with nothing but a divisional HQ. Just as Francis Tuker had hated to see his 4th Indian Division split up into penny packets, so the American commanders—new to war and desperate to prove themselves—were distraught at having their divisions torn up and sent hither and thither. This was pretty much the fate of Major-General Terry de la Mesa Allen, the tough and uncompromising commander of the Big Red One, who by Christmas was "down to a couple of battalions and Joe Penici, the orderly who presses his pants."[455] His mood was not improved when he read a Summary of Operations report by Colonel Stewart-Brown, the Coldstream battalion commander at Longstop, in which he concluded, "I have nothing whatsoever to say against the Americans myself, except that they were unfitted and unprepared for the task that they were asked to perform, which would have been difficult for any battalion."[456] This was true: they were not experienced enough to take on the full force of a German counterattack. But then again, few new Allied troops were, while their equipment—particularly the 37mm anti-tank gun—had been hopelessly inadequate for the task. The rain, the lack of proper intelligence, and the novelty of fighting alongside British and French units had added to their difficulties. Longstop had been a hellish initiation. But to Allen, this was a gross insult and having conducted a report of his own, in which, unsurprisingly, the British fared less well, he went to confront General Allfrey of the British V Corps. Allfrey just shrugged and denied having seen or heard about Stewart-Brown's report, but the seeds of mistrust had already been sown.

The character of General Anderson did not help. Terse, dour, and rather humorless, he conformed almost to a tee to most Americans' preconceived notions of what British generals were like. His chief of staff, Brigadier McNabb, was cut from much the same cloth. This notion that all Brits were cold and condescending was, to some extent, ingrained in the minds of many Americans long before they ever came into contact with any of their new ally, and so it often took little to have those preconceptions confirmed. In history lessons they were taught about the War of Independence and the subsequent War of 1812, in which Britain was the old enemy. Harry Butcher admitted that he had arrived in England with many of the inborn prejudices common to any American raised and educated in the Midwest. "American officers and men who became acquainted with the British in England before TORCH had found that the lessons all Americans learn in their history books aren't true of the present day," he noted. "Believe it or not, the British are really not red-coated devils."[457] But Anderson had had little chance to get to know many of the American commanders he would be working with before reaching North Africa. Nor did he possess the kind of easygoing warmth or diplomatic skills to deal with men like Fredendall, who was gathering an increasingly large chip on his shoulder about the way the Americans were being pushed around by the condescending Brits.

This kind of negativity was not felt in the same way by the British—if there was an "old enemy" it was the French—although most British assumed that Americans were brash and loud in the same way that Americans thought that all British were aloof and cold. Of course there would always be conflicts of personality, but for the most part, once Americans and British got to know one another, they got on just fine. But that certain American commanders felt resentment at being given too little to do, and at having their forces divided and being under British command is entirely understandable, just as it is also understandable that a number of British commanders looked down their noses at their American counterparts for being too inexperienced and too outspoken. It's just that it didn't help.

Nor did the apparent lack of Allied air cover, still a common grouse up and down the line. Yet more and more aircraft were reaching the forward airfields, including the 33rd Fighter Group. Lieutenant Jim Reed and the rest of the 59th Fighter Squadron were the last of the three squadrons in the group to be sent forward. They finally left Casablanca on 8 January, after long weeks of little activity.

Since touching down in North Africa some seven weeks before, they had had a frustrating time, with little to do other than occasional patrols. The real trouble had begun when they were joined by the Lafayette Escadrill Squadron. These French pilots had lost most of their aircraft during the landings, and although the Americans didn't mind letting them use their P-40s occasionally, they strongly objected when they were told to hand them over for good just before Christmas. Jim watched sadly as his plane was repainted, "Renee" and the white American stars disappearing with the swish of a brush and replaced with French rondels. Nor was it just the aircraft they had to hand over: they were also told to give the French pilots their radio mikes, oxygen masks, and even their pistols.

Bored and frustrated, the boys of the 59th cooled their heels and wondered what the hell was going on. For want of something to do, Jim grew a moustache and then a beard, so earning himself the nickname "Walrus," which was added to the growing list of nicknames painted on their flight shack. The days passed slowly, the pilots tiring of hanging around the airfield, tormenting local Arabs, and playing endless games of cards.

When they did finally move forward, there were just five P-40s among thirty-four pilots, so most, Jim included, were unable to fly themselves there. "We sure did hate to ride to the front fighter fields in C-47 transports instead of our P-40s," he noted.[458] Their new airfield was Thelepte, near Feriana in Tunisia, from where the 58th FS had been operating for several weeks. Although in the Western Desert aircraft could just land somewhere and establish a new landing ground, this was not the case in Tunisia, where airfields had to be properly constructed. Thelepte was vast—aircraft could take off in any direction—but the contrast between this forward base and the easy luxury of Casablanca could not have been more marked. On their arrival Jim and the other pilots were told to start digging holes to live in, although tools with which to do this were scarce. Jim and three other pilots—Skippy White, Elton Posey, and Robert Smith—decided to share a hole, digging a trench four feet deep and somewhat smaller than two double beds, and with an entryway halfway along. Over the top at ground level they stretched their pup tents flat as a cover. There was no other sign of life around them other than patches of vetch. Water had to be brought up daily. Each man was given a canteen and one helmet full of water per day. Hygiene was to be put on the back burner.

After an uncomfortable night sleeping head-to-toe and in his heavy winter flying gear, Jim poked his head up out of his dugout at first light to see four 109s attacking their airfield patrol flight. This, he discovered, was as regular as clockwork. A few days later, the airfield was attacked four times: early in the morning by two lots of 109s, then by more fighter-

bombers a couple of hours later, and finally by ten Ju 88s in the middle of
the afternoon. With only four aircraft at their disposal, (the fifth was with
the maintenance team) the 59th were hastily scrambled to take on the Ju
88s. Jim was not flying, but it was a great day for the squadron as the four
pilots managed to shoot down eight of the enemy bombers, while the
neighboring French squadron claimed the last two. "This was a real
morale builder," noted Jim, whose dugout mate Lieutenant Smith had
been one of the triumphant pilots.[459]

But this was a rare high point in an otherwise difficult time. There was
little attempt to take the fight to the enemy; they were always responding
to enemy air attacks, flying patrols, or escorting light bombers, and only
ever strafing targets of opportunity. More aircraft did gradually arrive,
but the pilots found themselves outnumbered on most missions, while on
the ground the men were continually strafed and bombed. It was, Jim admits, "a very rough time." He himself was grounded for several weeks
with an infected thumb, but by the time the squadron was given a two-
week rest period on 8 February, Jim had lost all three of his "room" mates.
Skippy White had been forced to bail out behind enemy lines, Robert
Smith had been killed, and Elton Posey had come down in the middle of
a tank battle, although he did make it back a few days later. "My home in
the ground was very lonely during these times," wrote Jim.[460]

Some hundred and fifty miles farther north and suffering similar conditions were the men of 225 Squadron. The mud had made operations at
Souk el Arba impossible, so the engineers created another airfield for
them at Souk el Khemis, a dozen miles away, with different landing strips
all named after London railway stations. The RAF pilots dug their own
sleeping holes and latrines, just as Jim Reed and the Americans had
done. "Everyone mucked in," says Bryan Colston, who by this stage was
quite used to sleeping on a wooden camp bed below ground and eating
nothing but "compo" rations. "They were brilliant," he says of these
packed meals. "They came in a wooden box with practically everything
you wanted in them: a few cigarettes, Horlicks tablets, lavatory paper,
tinned beans, bully beef and McConnochies."

Bryan was by now A Flight commander, and carrying out a variety of
roles. The RAF in North Africa was beginning to take a tip from the
Desert Air Force's ability to multitask, and had started strapping bombs
underneath them when going out on Tac/Rs as well as performing other
tasks. At the end of December, for example, the squadron had been asked
to carry out a low-level attack around Pont du Fahs—no aerial reconnaissance was needed—and so Bryan had set off once more with Ken Neill,
his Kiwi wingman, and one other pilot, Sergeant Ash. Escorted by a flight

of Spitfires, they reached their targets just as some Ju 88s and escorting 109s were bombing the French. Within seconds a dogfight had developed, with aircraft turning and swirling around the sky. Bryan managed to fire a long burst at a Junkers, his Hurricane shuddering with the recoil. Bullets struck the bomber's wing, but Bryan had to break off to attack the tanks below. Swooping down toward them, he pressed down his thumb to fire only to discover his ammunition had run out just as he roared a few feet above them. "I got some terrific flak up my bottom," he noted in his diary, but managed to fly through to safety only to find himself being pursued by a 109. Quickly breaking away out of the mêlée, he shook off his pursuer and headed for home.

Reaching Souk el Khemis, with Ken Neill and Sergeant Ash alongside him once more, he saw enemy aircraft were attacking the airfield, but with no ammunition left there was little they could do. Realizing that safety was the better form of valor, they circled low around some nearby hills until the attackers had gone before finally coming back in to land.

It was increasingly obvious, however, that what they needed were Spitfires. "We knew we were so vulnerable," says Bryan of the obsolete Hurricanes, "and the Spitfire escorts didn't like it because we were so much slower than them, so they had to fly slower too." But in the second half of January, six Spitfire Mk Vs did reach the squadron and were given to Bryan's A Flight. Because of the shortage of time and fuel, the pilots were only allowed forty-five minutes in which to adjust to their new aircraft, even though not one of them had ever flown a Spitfire before. Twelve hours after receiving them, Bryan took off on a Tac/R with F/O Blackshaw, new to the squadron. The 111 Squadron were to escort them, but it was dusk and the light was particularly bad and so the mission was aborted. The Treble One Spitfires landed first, so by the time it was Bryan and Blackshaw's turn, the sky was almost pitch black. On what were only their second ever flights in Spitfires, they now had to land with a narrower undercarriage than they were used to, on a sandy landing strip in the dark and with no flare path. When they both touched down safely, it was with a sense of enormous relief.

With new airfields and gradually increasing number of aircraft, crews, and supplies reaching the front, and, crucially, the gaining of combat experience among the Americans in particular, the Allied air situation was slowly improving. Having two separate air commands with an imaginary dividing line was obviously pointless now that all the fighting was in Tunisia. Tedder had been urging for a unified Mediterranean air command, but in November what Eisenhower had needed was a senior staff officer to help him organize his air forces in Algeria and Tunisia, and to do so right away. With this in mind, Major-General Carl "Tooey" Spaatz arrived to join Ike in Algiers. Commander of the US Eighth Air Force in the UK, he had more experience of working with the British than most, having witnessed the Battle of Britain as the United States' "official observer." He wasted no time in making a number of changes, most notably insisting to Anderson that First Army end their effective control of the Allied air forces, a state of affairs that had led to blatant misuse of what limited air capabilities they had. It had been an army officer, for example, that had ordered the unescorted Bisley bombers to make their doomed attack at the beginning of December, despite protestations from the RAF wing commander.

With Spaatz taking a firmer control at the helm, he was able to activate the Allied Air Force at the beginning of January. It was a stop-gap, and nothing more, but it brought all Allied bombers—regardless of nationality—under the umbrella of the US 12th Air Force, while all fighter units and certain light bomber units came under control of the RAF Eastern Air Command. This was at least a step in the right direction.

Tedder's dream of a unified Mediterranean air command was finally agreed upon at the Casablanca Conference. Covering Algeria and Tunisia would be the Northwest Africa Air Forces (NAAF), commanded by Tooey Spaatz and further divided into various commands including Coastal and Training. The Strategic Air Command—the bomber force—was to be headed by Doolittle, but by far the biggest command was to be Air Support Tunisia, consisting of the majority of fighters and medium bombers already operating in Tunisia as well as the Desert Air Force. There was only one person who could conceivably command this new force: Mary Coningham.

Mary's new deputy was to be Brigadier-General Larry Kuter. Since helping to write the AWPD-1 paper, outlining America's basic plan for the employment of a strategic air offensive, Larry had been busy and at the very heart of the USAAF's planning for the future. After seven months working alongside General "Hap" Arnold as deputy chief of the Air Staff, he had been posted to Britain to command the 1st Bombardment Wing of the Eighth Air Force, but at the beginning of January he had been called upon by Tooey Spaatz to be his chief of staff in North Africa.

He'd only been at Spaatz's forward base at Constantine a few days when he discovered there were serious strains between army and air forces, particularly between the US fighter groups and II Corps. When the commander of the two fighter groups of the 12th Air Support Command (ASC) at Thelepte became ill, Spaatz sent Larry down to take over. He was appalled to discover that the US fighters were still flying purely at the demand of the army. "Fredendall had them parceled out here and there," noted Larry, "flying umbrellas and other piecemeal defensive chores." After meeting with the II Corps commander he began to understand why Craig was so ill. "Talking to Fredendall might make any airman delirious," he commented.[461]

On 21 January, Ike gave Larry temporary command of the embryonic Allied Air Support Command until such time as Mary Coningham could take over. This comprised the 12th ASC and the RAF 242 Group of front-line fighters and medium bombers. It so happened that Larry was not only fully up to speed with Mary's ideas on the use of air power in support of the ground forces, but in complete agreement. He was also increasingly aware that there would be no easy converts among the various army commanders battling it out in Tunisia. Fredendall was not alone in his misguided view of the use of the air support. This had been amply demonstrated at one of Anderson's planning conferences for Operation SATIN. At the meeting Larry had outlined his ideas, suggesting that the priority was to gain air superiority by concentrating on bombing and strafing Axis airfields, and pointing out that his aircraft could carry out reconnaissance work while they were at it. This plan was dismissed out of hand by the ground commanders. Fighters, they insisted, should continue to be used for standing patrols—"umbrellas"—during daylight hours. Larry was told quite emphatically that the ground troops could not withstand even one attack by the German Stuka and tank combination. The blitzkrieg was judged invincible. "It appeared to me," noted Larry, "that our troops had fallen victim to some very effective propaganda."[462] As he now realized, they faced a battle not only against the Axis air forces but also against the rigid mindset of the majority of the army commanders.

Arriving at the front at much the same time as Larry Kuter was thirty-three-year-old Lieutenant-Colonel Hamilton Howze, G-3 (operational planning) on the staff of "Old Ironsides," the 1st Armored Division. With the exception of those lost during the assault on Oran harbor, Combat Command B had been the only section of the 1st Armored to take part in the landings. The rest had languished in Britain, where they had been since their arrival the previous summer, until finally setting sail for North Africa in December.

The son of a major-general, Hamilton had entered West Point at eighteen and been commissioned as second lieutenant in the cavalry on his graduation four years later. Throughout the 1930s, the life of a cavalryman was spent on horseback, and it wasn't until after Pearl Harbor, when he was still a captain, that he managed to get transferred into an armored unit, and only in April 1942 that he joined the 1st Armored, soon after becoming G-3. With the massive pace of mobilization, professional officers suddenly found that after long years of no promotion they were being accelerated through the ranks, and so it was that when the division was shipped overseas, Hamilton wore the silver oak leaf of a lieutenant-colonel.

He'd been surprised when he'd learned that the Allies were going to invade Northwest Africa. As far as he'd been concerned, they'd come to Britain to prepare for the invasion of Europe, and when they finally reached central Tunisia under command of II Corps, he was concerned that they were hardly prepared for fighting in semi-desert conditions. In fact, he was worried about their state of training, period. Throughout the summer, this had been done primarily at company level but had been limited in nature. In Northern Ireland they soon found their room for maneuver severely restricted. "We were mostly tramping around the roads," commented Hamilton, "while pretending that we were fanned out on the countryside; we couldn't get onto the ground, with rare exceptions."[463] The local farmers wouldn't let them.

At the end of October, the remaining two-thirds of the division was sent to Crewe, in the north of England. They remained there a month, but as Hamilton admitted, during this time they barely trained at all. "We had no terrain to do it on," he said, "and besides, we weren't there; we were in the process of getting there, and then almost immediately got started to Africa." The journey by ship and across land was a tortuous one. On reaching Algiers, they were told they should have landed further west at Oran. So back they went, only to move eastward again toward Tunisia. By the time Hamilton and his commanding officer, Major-General Orlando "Pinky" Ward reported to Fredendall at II Corps HQ, the remainder of the division had done almost no training or military exercises in *over ten weeks*. What little they had learned in Northern Ireland was already being forgotten. It is hard to imagine how armored troops could have been less prepared for fighting the panzers.

By the third week of January, both Pinky Ward and Hamilton had considerable cause for concern. CCB, having operated independently of the division since the landings, had become battle-hardened compared with the rest of the division. "It sort of put us and the rest of the division headquarters at a disadvantage to have our subordinate command wise in the ways of battle," admitted Hamilton—especially when the commander of CCB was someone as ambitious and cocksure at Robinett.[464] Another and more serious difficulty, however, lay with Fredendall, who had already made it very clear that he had no time at all for Pinky Ward.

Action was not long in coming. Fredendall announced plans to capture Maknassy, and to do this had ordered Ward to further split up his division into little more than the bad old British-style Jock columns. In addition to Combat Command B, there was now CCA, CCC, and CCD, principally armor but with various other field artillery and infantry battalions swiped from both the 1st and 34th Infantry Divisions. "To our very great disappointment," noted Hamilton, "we remained split into widely separated parts."[465] CCB remained detached in the north, nominally under French control, while Fredendall issued detailed orders to the other three combat command teams, relegating Ward to little more than that of a message carrier.

On 23 January, he called for Ward and told him he wanted him to "knock the shit out of the Italians at Station Sened,"[466] a small enemy outpost between Gafsa and Maknassy and lying in a gap between the jagged ridge of mountains that separated the two towns. This was to blood some of the troops before the main assault began. Ward pointed out that this would give their hand away and show the Axis they were intending to thrust towards Maknassy, but Fredendall brushed aside such fears. The raid went ahead as planned the following day, with CCC capturing over one hundred Italian prisoners. But as Ward had warned, the Axis responded swiftly by sending reinforcements to Sened.

Fredendall still insisted on a further attack on Sened and Maknassy even though in the following days intelligence suggested the Axis were planning to take the Faid Pass. When the French appealed to him for reinforcements in the Faid area, he refused, telling them that by attacking Maknassy, he would draw enemy troops away from the pass. This never happened, because the Germans attacked first—during the early hours of 30 January, when the reconstituted 21st Panzer, sent up from the Mareth Line, swarmed over the Faid Pass and threatened to envelop the French garrison there with horrible ease.

The French immediately appealed to CCA, now based at Sbeitla, who passed on the request to Ward, sixty miles away at Gafsa, who passed on the request to Fredendall in his command post at Tebessa, who passed on the request to Anderson. Anderson agreed, but when Fredendall issued his orders to CCA—some five hours after the original request from the French—he told them to move forward, but only without weakening their defenses at Sbeitla. This was clearly an impossible task, but the CCA commander interpreted this as an order to split his force: half stayed put at Sbeitla, while the rest eventually got going toward Faid, harassed all the way by enemy aircraft. They eventually reached the Faid area late on 30 January, but rather than get stuck in right away, settled down for the night. By the time they attacked the following morning, thinly spread on two fronts and with two battalions of infantry supporting the tanks, the Axis had consolidated their positions and the Americans walked straight into the inevitable German anti-tank screen. Nine tanks were lost and a large number of infantry, who became jittery and disoriented in the face of Axis firepower and repeated aerial attacks. They tried again the following day, but once more the infantry got the jitters and lost any semblance of cohesion. In the meantime, a further thousand French troops had been taken prisoner. Indecision and desperate inexperience had cost the Allies the last of the passes along the Eastern Dorsale.

Despite the Axis attack, Fredendall was still determined to press ahead with his push toward Maknassy, an utterly pointless thrust in the present circumstances, which included capturing, rather than just raiding, the newly reinforced Sened Station. However, the news from CCA caused him to rethink, and so instead of attacking Sened Station with both CCC and CCD, he decided to send the former toward Faid to attack any enemy that might be either pushing southwest from Sidi Bou Zid or northward from Maknassy, and to let CCD attack Sened on their own. This was a terrible command decision: CCC was now doing neither one thing nor the other. So crucial was the Faid Pass, CCC should have been sent to help CCA with all haste, but by having it dithering in the plains south of Sidi Bou Zid it was achieving nothing, and consigning CCD to an even tougher battle at Sened Station.

Unsurprisingly, CCD's attack was a fiasco. Sened Station was only taken after two days of intense and costly fighting. Throughout this debacle, Pinky Ward was left as little more than a bystander, while Fredendall continued to command Ward's division in detail—and despite having not once ventured up to the front line. Incredibly, he had not even set foot in Tunisia, remaining resolutely at his HQ in Speedy Valley. "Never have so few been commanded from so far by so many," Ward confided to his diary.[467]

While the Old Ironsides were waking up to the harsh realities of modern warfare, the bomber offensive was continuing. Another of Tooey Spaatz's changes had been to insist that his heavy bombers attack Axis ports rather than willy-nilly targets dotted all over the Tunisian front. On Monday 1 February, at around ten minutes to eleven in the morning, the B-17 *All American* of the 97th BG took off from their airfield at Biskra. Pilot Lieutenant Ken Briggs pulled back on the control column as the bomber climbed steadily into the sky and then circled as it formed up, first with the other bombers from the 97th, and then with the other groups that were joining them, until there were no less than fifty in all, droning through the clear blue sky toward Bizerte. Major Coulter, the squadron leader, was leading. The *All American* was flying on his right wing.

Lieutenant Ralph Burbirdge always felt apprehensive as they took off; they all did. "No one felt too brave when you started a mission," he admits, although the intense camaraderie among the crew helped. "It was just like family—there really was a bond there," he adds. They had been to Bizerte before. The flight would take around two hours. Although he was the bombardier, Ralph also manned the .30-caliber machine gun protruding from the nose of the Fortress, and during the trip took the opportunity to test his gun, firing a few rounds harmlessly into the air. The whole sky appeared to be full of bombers, steadfastly heading on their way, white contrails streaming behind them.

It was 1:40 PM when the almost circular Lac de Bizerte homed into view, and beyond the wide arc of the coastline. Below was Bizerte, its jetties and wharves jutting out into the sea. Almost immediately, they saw groups of 109s climb into the sky, just as they'd done for the past six weeks. In the *All American,* no one spoke, each member of the crew concentrating intensely on the task expected of them. Ralph was manning his machine gun, waiting for a target to slip into range.

Now the 109s were upon them, diving out of the sun, machine guns and cannon fire spitting. Their own machine guns began to reply, reverberating and clattering through the B-17 as they did so. A couple of 109s spiraled earthward, black smoke trailing behind, but four of the Fortresses had been hit and were struggling to keep in formation, their only real hope of survival.

As the formation began the bomb run, the 109s left them alone, not daring to take on the flak that would open up any moment. Instead, they circled high in the sun, waiting for another chance to attack once the bombers turned for home. Ralph took up his position over the bombsight, peering down waiting for the target to appear. Thick black bursts of smoke peppered the sky as Ken Briggs ordered the bomb bay doors to be opened. This was always the worst part of any mission: they had to fly absolutely straight and level and with the fused bombs exposed to the tiny shards of shrapnel from bursting ack-ack fire. On they went, the Fortress jolting from the endless flak, until at last Ralph saw the target line up. Pressing down his thumb on the button, he called out "Bombs away," on the intercom.

With the bomb bay empty and with half their fuel now spent, the Fortress rose higher into the sky, then weaved from side to side, making the anti-aircraft gunners' task ever more difficult. But they still had to face the fighters again. Ralph had moved to take position by his .30 caliber. Away from the rest of the attackers were two 109s, climbing high into the sun, and then suddenly they were diving from twelve-o'clock high, seemingly straight for the *All American.* As Ralph poured bullets toward them, he watched the Messerschmitts, one behind the other, hurtling ever closer, their own lines of tracer spewing from their noses and wings.

The first 109 drew toward them and half-rolled just as Major Coulter's plane burst into smoke and begin spiraling uncontrollably toward the ground. The second fighter was riddled with bullets and instead of turning away, seemed to be heading straight into the *All American*. Ken Briggs rammed the control column forward in an effort to take evasive action. The Messerschmitt passed straight over his head, the Fortress jolting slightly.

"Pilot from top turret!" came an urgent voice over the intercom. "Pilot from top turret!"

"Come in top turret, what's the matter with you?" replied Lieutenant Briggs.

"Sir, we've received some damage in the tail section. I think you should have a look."[468]

Both Briggs and the copilot, Lieutenant Engle, found the Fortress was still flying okay, but the trim was not working, and she wanted to climb. But by throttling back the engines, they discovered they could keep her fairly steady, so Briggs handed her over to Engle and went back to see what had happened. He was stunned by what he saw: nearly three-quarters of the fuselage had been sliced in half. Jagged metal and wires were flapping in the air. Part of the wing of the Messerschmitt was still embedded in the tail of the plane.

When Ralph heard the skipper call everyone into the radio room, he clambered up from the nose to join the rest of the crew. Once gathered, Briggs told them they had a choice: either they bail out now, over enemy territory, or they could stay and hope the Fortress would keep intact. Briggs had already decided to keep going, and Ralph and the rest of the crew agreed to stay too, although they were all sent to an emergency exit ready to jump should they have to. "It was terrifying, though," admits Ralph, "wondering whether we were ever going to get back."

But the trusty Fortress held fast, and still leading the formation, they were the first to reach Biskra. Firing three emergency flares, they circled while the rest of the bombers landed, and then, with the runways cleared, they decided to try and get her down. Miraculously, she made it, her tail scraping along the ground until finally they came to a halt. "No business, Doc," Lieutenant Briggs called from the cockpit as the ambulance hurried to them. Not a single member of the crew had been injured.[469] As one of the 97th staff noted, "A Fortress really can take a beating and still fly."[470] A crew member of another Fortress took a photograph of the crippled *All American* as they flew back to Biskra, a picture that made the front page of the forces newspaper, *Stars And Stripes*. UNKINDEST CUT OF ALL, BUT BOMBER BEATS RAP ran the headline. "Boeing officials looked at the plane as it landed and said it was 'aerodynamically impossible to fly.'"[471]

The bombers had also returned believing they had successfully hit their target. One ship was seen to have been hit, while bomb blasts were also observed falling around the harbor installations. Even so, the Axis were managing to unload between 40,000 and 50,000 tons of supplies every month at Tunis and Bizerte. Since their goal was 60,000 tons per month at these two ports, the Allies were clearly not taking a great-enough toll. In fact, overall, 75 percent of Axis shipping was getting through, a figure that Ike knew was too high.

As Ultra revealed, the combination of narrow shipping and air routes from Italy meant that the Axis was able to continue building up strength. Promised divisions from the Eastern Front had not been forthcoming, but by 13 February, von Arnim's Fifth Panzer Army had 105,000 troops and over two hundred tanks, including eleven Tigers. Even so, the intelligence staff at AFHQ in Algiers concluded that the Axis's current supply situation allowed for only limited objectives and that a large-scale attack was unlikely. This was a fairly reasonable conclusion and one that was broadly accurate—on 7 February, for example, von Arnim warned the German High Command that his army was unfit for major offensive operations.

Enigma traffic was not as clear at the beginning of February as it had been, but in any case, the intelligence staff dealing with Ultra decrypts still had to tally them with other intelligence gathered by a combination of aerial reconnaissance, POW interrogation, reports from agents and ground observation. The efficiency of marshaling this information had not been helped by the muddled nature of the Allied command, but even so, it was clear the Axis was planning *something* for the middle of February, and from Ultra decrypts of 1 February, this appeared to be an attack involving von Arnim's 10th Panzer Division and Rommel's 21st through the Fondouk-Ousseltia area.

Rommel's star had waned considerably in recent months, however, and there is no doubt that he was still held in far higher esteem by the Allies than the German and Italian High Commands. Even the Fuhrer was disillusioned with his former favorite. At the end of November, Rommel had visited Hitler and told him that if the supply situation was not radically improved, North Africa would have to be abandoned. This did not go down at all well, and Rommel was treated to a full-fledged tirade, reminding him that a sizable bridgehead had to be maintained "for political reasons."[472]

Against the methodical, solid wall of Monty's Eighth Army, Rommel simply had no answer, however. Successive defensive positions were abandoned, leaving Eighth Army to untangle the latest web of mines and booby traps: El Agheila, then the Buyarat Line, then Tripoli itself. For some time, Rommel had been pressing for a retreat into Tunisia, where his German-Italian Panzer Army could link with Fifth Panzer Army. The Italians, to whom Rommel had always been answerable—on paper at any rate—did not see the military sense in this, only the disappearance of their last African conquest. "Resist [Tripoli] to the last," Mussolini told him, "I repeat: resist to the last."[473]

Eighth Army had reached just short of Tripoli by 19 January, and Monty began preparing an encircling maneuver, the tactic he had adopted whenever the panzer army halted. Rommel again felt that the best option was to retreat into Tunisia, and so called a summit with Kesselring and the Commando Supremo, demanding a definite ruling on whether he could abandon Tripoli. The Italians would not give him one—they needed to check with Il Duce first. Mussolini's answer the following day was predictable: they must stay and fight. But two days later, with Eighth Army's encircling movement already under way, Rommel decided to make his own decision and ordered Tripoli to be abandoned, telling Cavallero, the Italian chief of staff, "You can either hold on to Tripoli a few more days and lose the army, or lose Tripoli a few days earlier and save the army for Tunis. Make up your mind."[474]

Anything that could not be taken with them was, as far as possible, destroyed. The port installations were also mined and blown up, and the usual box of booby-trap tricks left for the new incumbents. And by leaving Tripoli, Rommel *had* given himself a breather. Monty needed to reorganize and regroup once more, to bring the long trail of his forces up together, and to clear and reopen the port.

Nonetheless, Rommel paid the price for disobeying his superiors. He'd been ill for some time. The violent headaches and "nervous exhaustion" were taking their toll. At 5:59 AM on 26 January, he left Libya for the last time and crossed into Tunisia. Six hours later, he received a message from the Commando Supremo informing him that he was to be relieved of his command due to his ongoing sickness. The only caveat was that he could decide the timing of his departure.

Why Rommel failed to leave immediately is not entirely clear, but it appears that the chance for an all-out attack on the Americans and the opportunity to leave Africa with his reputation bolstered, if not restored, was too good a chance to miss, and so he began suggesting that his own panzer army as well as von Arnim's should launch a combined attack on Gafsa. If they hit the Americans sufficiently hard, then the Axis might be able to deal with Eighth Army along the Mareth Line without interference. This idea had been rejected, but on 8 February, a more limited attack on Gafsa was proposed. The following day, however, Rommel met with both von Arnim and Kesselring. The Axis had their own personality issues: von Arnim and Rommel loathed each other; but at this meeting they did manage to agree on a policy for attack, one that was readily encouraged by the ever-optimistic Kesselring.

The last word from Ultra related to the decisions of 2 February, but a week later those plans had become completely out of date. Between them, Rommel and von Arnim had decided on a joint attack after all, although both would maintain their separate commands. The aim was to cripple the Americans, enabling Rommel to then deal with Eighth Army without interference. Despite Kesselring's belief that they could push the Allies back as far as Tunisia, neither Rommel nor von Arnim shared this view. Operation *Frühlingswind* was to be a limited action after all.

The 48th Evacuation Hospital operated a leapfrogging system not dissimilar to the one used by Tommy Elmhirst for the Desert Air Force. The idea was that one unit went forward and took in the wounded closest to the action, then when that was full, it would begin to evacuate the patients while the other unit leapfrogged and began the process all over again. Now, however, both units were in the front line: the 1st Unit at Thala, and the 2nd at Feriana.

The 2nd Unit had moved on 27 January into an old French outpost barracks block, one story high and with holes in the roof and windows that had long ago forgotten what it was like to be filled with glass. The corpsmen attached to the unit had filled in the holes with canvas and bits of cardboard, but with the weather as it was, any kind of building, whatever the state of disrepair, was preferable to operating out of a tent.

The nurses, as ever, had to live in pup tents outside, but Margaret Hornback was getting used to this new kind of lifestyle. They were now as near to the front line as they'd ever been and uncomfortably close to the airfield at Thelepte, a magnet to enemy air attacks. With this in mind, they decided they should make themselves a giant cross that they could then place on the ground to show that they were a hospital. Painstakingly, the nurses sewed together fifty-four white sheets into a giant cross and then laid it out three hundred yards in front of the barrack blocks. In no time an American air force officer had hurried over and demanded to know what the hell they thought they were playing at. The nurses explained.

"That flag there you're bragging about," snarled the officer, "is not a Red Cross flag. When a white flag is put out on the ground like that it means the surrounding area is an airfield under construction."[475]

The nurses soon had this confirmed, but to make the kind of flag they needed would require another forty sheets and a hundred yards of unbleached muslin, and once again, it would all have to be sewed by hand, at night, and whenever there was a lull. They stuck to their task, however, everyone pitching in, and it was soon finished. The corpsmen painted on a large red cross and then they laid it out and prayed it would not blow away. "If anything happens to that cross," one of the nurses commented, "I'll take a chance on the bombs before I help make another."

Margaret was still working as a nurse in the operating room and with the fighting they soon found themselves pretty busy. The hospital could hold a maximum of two hundred patients. Those not too badly wounded were debrided—any infected tissue was removed—then were hurriedly shipped to an evacuation hospital further back, while the surgical team dealt with the most serious cases. This included an Italian soldier with a gangrenous leg—their first such case. Shortly after, another case arrived, and this time it was a GI. Because of the risk of contamination to the operating room, both amputations had to be carried out in specially pitched tents outside the barracks.

The weather continued to be miserable. "We had a tiny fall of snow today—our first," wrote Margaret on 6 February. "The wind seems awfully cold." Not only that, it sent flurries of sand swirling around the hospital. "There's always an inch of sand over everything, even if you've just cleaned," noted Margaret. One night there was a particularly bad storm, and the wind howled so strongly that the cook tent blew away and the wards were filled with sand that had been blown through gaps in the roof and walls. The amputees' tents stood firm, however, but while the Italian was recovering well, the GI was losing his battle. Hour by hour the stench got worse, until it became almost unbearable. The nurses did what they could, but the day after the storm, the American boy died.

Harry Butcher accompanied Ike to his meeting with Anderson on 1 February, which was held around the hood of a car on a windy day at Tulergma airfield, near Constantine. Anderson pointed out that the line was becoming worryingly thin now that the French had been all but pulled out. They were supposed to be preparing for an offensive in the north, but instead were struggling just to hold the line and respond to Axis thrusts. So Anderson suggested they should make Fredendall call a halt to his Maknassy drive and bring II Corps back into a mobile reserve. Ike agreed—clearly there was no point frittering away American forces with futile aggressive operations that seemed to cost dear and gain little. "Hereafter," noted Butch the following day, "they are to hit only when they know that they have heavy superiority."[476]

At varying times, both Anderson and Ike had talked of the need to pull back to the Grande Dorsale. This would have shortened the length of the front, brought them closer to their airfields and supply lines and given them the passes through the mountains to form strong defensive positions. Here, they could have built up their strength with far greater ease. Neither, however, seems to have quite had the courage of their convictions, presumably fearing the loss of face and confidence this might cause. Instead, Ike ordered Anderson "not to leave the French unsupported in isolated positions and to concentrate his mobile forces in the south so that he may counter any enemy move immediately."[477] The problem was that he couldn't really support the French and keep his forces concentrated, and so 1st Armored remained divided into the four different combat commands, and, for the most part, in the plains. Anderson was facing the same quandary as Ritchie at Gazala, and responding in exactly the same way: trying to cover the entire front, and in so doing, splitting his forces into more and more penny packets—penny packets that could all too easily be gobbled up one by one by a more concentrated Axis force.

Amongst those now bivouacked in pup tents outside Gafsa were the US Army Rangers. Since the opening few days of the invasion, the Rangers had found themselves left behind in Algeria—where they had carried out further training and guarded Arzew. Since they were undoubtedly the best-trained US infantry unit in the invasion force, the decision to keep them in reserve was a somewhat odd one, but Fredendall certainly had plans for them now. Despite orders to go on the defensive, the II Corps commander could not shake off his obsession with Sened, which was now back in Italian hands, and so on 9 February told Colonel Darby that he wanted the Rangers to raid the outpost, with the aim of causing as much havoc and destruction as possible and capturing some prisoners.

At midnight on 10 February, three companies, E, F, and Bing Evans's A, with the headquarters mortar company in support, loaded onto trucks and began the winding journey up into the jagged mountains to the south of Sened Station. Twelve miles from Sened, the trucks came to a halt and the men clambered out. The plan was to walk cross country to within about four miles of the Italian outpost, lie up for the day, then attack under the cover of darkness.

The Rangers had practiced this exact kind of operation time and time again. Bing Evans felt apprehensive yet confident. Each man carried nothing other than his rifle, grenades, ammunition, first aid, and a small amount of rations, while on the back of each man's helmet was a strip of white tape to make it easier for the man behind to see the one in front in the dark. Reaching their lying-up position without any difficulty, they spent the following day carefully watching the outpost. It lay on a long ridge, overlooking the railway station. There was a barracks block and various gun positions, but no gates or perimeter wire. The Rangers would be able to walk straight on in.

As darkness fell, they blackened their faces, checked their rifles, and then, at around 11 PM, as the moon dropped, moved a mile farther forward and then moved out into position, each company spreading out in a long line abreast so that they could attack simultaneously and give the impression of being of far greater number than the 180-man force they really were. A Company was on the left of the line. Bing Evans had ditched his helmet in favor of his light olive drab wool cap. Underfoot, the ground was stony—each step had to be taken carefully—and the smell of sage wood wafted strongly on the cold night air.

The orders were not to fire until they were right in among them; they did not want to give the game away, and even if the Italians did open fire, in the darkness they knew their aim would almost certainly be high. Sure enough, around a hundred yards from the outpost, an Italian sentry began to fire—and fired high. Moments later, the Rangers were upon them. One group of Rangers ran straight into the barrack block, where sleepy, disoriented Italians were just beginning to wake up. With their commando knives, the Rangers cut the Italians' throats.

Outside, flares were arcing into the sky. Suddenly, the place was lit up and Bing Evans turned and saw an Italian emerge from the shadows and rush toward him. "He was intent on killing me," says Bing, "and I looked into his eyes and saw they were big and frightened and bewildered and I just couldn't pull the trigger on my forty-five. I froze." Then a shot was fired and the Italian slumped in front of him. Bing turned and saw Tommy Sullivan. He'd saved his life.

The mayhem continued, then, under cover of their mortars, they slipped away again into the darkness. One Ranger had been decapitated by a shell, but the rest managed to get away, including twenty wounded. With them were eleven prisoners. The damage they'd inflicted on the Italians was considerable: at least seventy-five dead, several guns destroyed, and long-lasting psychological damage. "Our job was to make the enemy uneasy and wary," says Bing. "There's a difference fighting a cocky enemy and one that's apprehensive."

It was now about two in the morning and it was essential they get back to their positions before daybreak. Their task was made harder by the need to carry many of the wounded, but as Bing points out, adrenaline and the thought of being caught out in the cold drove them on. "We didn't think about being tired," he says.[478]

They all made it safely back, and on finally reaching their bivouac, Bing suddenly felt exhausted and drained of emotion. They'd had two nights without sleep, had walked twenty-four miles over rough terrain and been involved in an intense hand-to-hand action with the enemy. But the

Rangers had proved that amongst II Corps there were some troops who were now not only well trained but combat experienced too.

Headquarters of the 1st Armored Division was now in a large prickly-pear cactus patch just west of Sbeitla, a town still dominated by the ruins of an ancient Roman city. "This was not quite as undignified and impracticable as it sounds," commented Hamilton Howze. "The plants were some ten feet high, providing considerable cover in the bare, flat terrain."[479] It even offered some protection against aerial attacks. Axis dominance of the air had come as something of a shock to Hamilton, and his confidence had not been improved when he'd visited the 33rd Fighter Group at Thelepte. On the bulletin wall in the mess was a brightly colored ad for an American aircraft manufacturer which had been cut out from a magazine. The catchline ran: WHO'S AFRAID OF THE BIG BAD FOCKE WULF? Someone had written SIGN BELOW. Every pilot had added his name.

Hamilton could understand why the new boys had found coming under aerial attack so alarming. He'd been frightened himself the first time, desperately flinging himself flat into a tire rut, even though it was only an inch or two deep. But he had also realized that in most cases, the damage caused by Stukas, in particular, seemed far worse than it actually was. The British had produced a booklet called *How To Be Bombed,* which, while never denying the terrifying effect of bombing and strafing, listed many statistics to reassure the reader that the odds of surviving an aerial attack were actually pretty good. "In my job as G-3," noted Hamilton, "I took pains to get one of those booklets for issue to each man in the division."[480]

He was well aware that the division was not sufficiently trained and that they had not performed well in the recent fighting, but he also had great faith in Ward and felt that with encouragement and the opportunity to command his men properly, his boss would soon turn things around. And at least their men had now been blooded. Fredendall did not share Hamilton's faith in Ward, however. Relations between the two had further broken down. Any suggestion Ward made, Fredendall immediately dismissed: when Ward asked for some aerial reconnaissance, the II Corps commander told him to mind his own business. "He is a spherical SOB, no doubt," noted Ward. "Two-faced, at that."[481]

"Fredendall's judgment was made on very infrequent visits of his staff officers to the forward area, and no visits at all by himself," noted Hamilton Howze.[482] Instead, Fredendall continued to stay put in his command post at Speedy Valley, situated deep in a narrow gorge in the rock and which could only be accessed by a single-lane track. Not content with the natural cover this offered, the II Corps commander had organized over two hundred engineers to excavate two tunnels deep into walls of the ravine. For several weeks, his staff worked to the accompaniment of pneumatic drills as his underground headquarters painstakingly took shape. Speedy Valley was eighty miles from the front and only very rarely visited by enemy aircraft. That such a bunker was taking precautions to ridiculous extremes, or that the engineer battalion employed to build it might have been better used elsewhere does not appear to have entered Fredendall's increasingly wayward mind.

Pinky Ward's frustration increased. CCB remained attached to the British and CCD in reserve, while Fredendall's tight control over the rest of the division continued. He did eventually visit Ward at the command post near Sbeitla on 10 February, but it appears to have had little impact on his decision making. On 2 February, Anderson had ordered Fredendall to keep a "small force" in the Faid area to back up the remaining French—another halfhearted measure, but one that was based on Anderson's belief that any future Axis attack through the pass would be merely a diversionary, small-scale thrust. But rather than leave Ward—as divisional commander—to make his own dispositions, Fredendall gave him a directive for the use of CCA and CCC that was so specific and so rigid as to make Ward almost irrelevant; he had become a supernumerary. In particular, Fredendall singled out two hills either side of the Faid Pass as the two key features for the defense of the area to the west of the pass. On the Djebel Ksaira he placed one battalion of infantry, while on the Djebel Lessouda he positioned a further infantry battalion as well as a single battery of artillery and a few tanks. The two hills were ten miles apart, too far to be mutually supporting. As a result, the forces placed on them could not avoid operating in isolation of each other. A mobile reserve was also to be kept in the vicinity of Sidi Bou Zid, but these were now of insufficient size to be able to offer much resistance. CCC, meanwhile, was to remain deployed further north, protecting the Fondouk area. Even a small Axis force of all arms would have little difficulty picking off these penny packets one by one.

Hamilton Howze was outraged—as was Ward—seeing this directive as not only deliberately insulting but also military madness, belying just how little Fredendall knew about mobile warfare or understood about the terrain in which he expected them to fight. By contrast, Fredendall completely ignored the French forces of the Constantine Division, who came under his command. Also hopelessly split up, they were scattered throughout the area: some occupied positions near Sbeitla, another group were at Fondouk, while others were still stationed at Gafsa and Feriana. General Welvert, the French commander, tried to make suggestions, pointing out that should they need to withdraw, his troops would need transport to do so. But such concerns appear to have fallen on deaf ears.

* * *

Ike also failed to show the courage of his convictions over Fredendall, who was by now a complete liability, as the Allied C-in-C was well aware. He'd already sent a warning note to Fredendall telling him not to stay in his command post. "Speed in execution, particularly when we are reacting to any move of the enemy's, is of transcendent importance," he wrote. "Ability to move rapidly is largely dependent upon an intimate knowledge of the ground and conditions along the front." Then came the warning, echoing Marshall's words to him a week before: "Generals are expendable, just as is any other item in the army."[483] There was no need for a warning, however. Fredendall should have been fired without one. This letter appears to have stirred Fredendall into visiting Ward's cactus patch but little more, as Ike discovered during his visit to the front on 13 February.

These had been strange and trying times for the Allied commander. He was desperate to get at the enemy, to launch the offensive and snatch Tunis, but what could he do? "I don't suppose people at home can understand why things aren't moving quicker," Lieutenant David Brown had written in a letter to his wife. "But if they were here, and realised conditions generally, among them the very big transport difficulties, they would appreciate the situation."[484] He was echoing Ike's thoughts exactly, but few in America or Britain *did* understand. The *Daily Oklahoman* had claimed that "Mud is a silly alibi." In England there were reports that there was increasing bitterness between British and American troops. Elsewhere in the press there was much speculation that Ike was about to be fired. Furthermore, his initial relief about the new command structure agreed at Casablanca had been dampened by a directive from the combined chiefs that specified the duties expected of Alex and Tedder when they took on their new roles. Ike saw this as a direct challenge to his authority. As supreme commander (as he was about to become), he and he alone, he believed, should be issuing orders to his subordinates.

Then suddenly, on 12 February, he'd arrived back at the villa in Algiers only for Harry Butcher to offer him his congratulations.

"What for?" he asked.

"On being a full general," Butch replied, then explained how earlier he'd heard it on the grapevine. Following up the story, he had discovered it was true.[485]

"Goddammit," said Ike, "that's a hell of a way to treat a fellow. I'm made a full general, the tops of my profession, and I'm not told officially!" Shortly after, his wife Mamie phoned. It *was* true—Marshall had told her himself.

Now, on Saturday, 13 February, he was back near the front as a four-star general, and approaching II Corps HQ for the first time. He heard the din of hammers and drills coming from Fredendall's command post long before his car actually reached the entrance. Truscott had warned his boss, but the sheer scale of the complex and amount of time being wasted on its construction shocked Ike deeply. Approaching a young engineer, Ike asked if he'd helped prepare the front-line defenses first before working on these bunkers. "Oh, the divisions have their engineers for that!" came the reply. With a sinking heart, Ike then continued with an all-night inspection of the front lines. He found minefields that hadn't been planted, forward positions inadequately prepared, and 1st Armored Division still spread in penny packets. Worse was to come. Robinett, the CCB commander, was visiting Ward at the cactus patch when Ike arrived, and told him that his reconnaissance parties had repeatedly ventured through the Fondouk area and found no evidence of any Axis military buildup. He had, he told Ike, reported this several times to his British superiors.

Ike left the cactus patch and drove on with Pinky Ward to Sidi Bou Zid to see the CCA command post. Just before midnight, he got out and strode off into the dark on his own, then paused a moment in the cold, still night. The biting winds and snow flurries of the previous few days had died down. Above him, the sky was clear and twinkling with stars, while the light from the moon outlined the shadows of the Djebel Lessouda to his left and the Djebel Ksaira to his right. Up ahead loomed the Faid Pass, that vital link to the plains beyond—the plains that held the key to victory in Tunisia.

Ike's small inspection party began heading back before dawn. There had been little to cheer the Allied C-in-C, and he determined to get changes made without delay. After being held up at Sbeitla, and again when his driver fell asleep at the wheel and ran them into a ditch, they eventually managed to get going again and reach Speedy Valley. But by the time they arrived, Ike learned that the Axis had already begun their attack through the Faid Pass. For the moment, it was too late to make any changes.

CHAPTER 21

Rommel Strikes Back: 14–22 February

AT 5 AM, von Arnim's 10th Panzer Division began clanking and rattling through the Faid Pass. The wind was blowing again, whipping up sand in the early light of dawn, and visibility was bad. Tanks from a company of the 1st Armored Regiment rumbled out at dawn as normal to establish a defensive screen in front of the pass, only to come face to face with the German panzers, who had rolled over poorly laid rows of mines without any trouble at all. The leading American tank was hit almost immediately, and with it the radio link to the artillery dug in on the Djebel Lessouda. Brushing aside the American armor, 10th Panzer split, beginning its envelopment of the djebel. The foremost of the infantry knew about what was going on when, just after 7 AM, panzers appeared below them and Stukas and fighter-bombers above. In moments, both tanks and aircraft were pounding the stunned Americans in a master class of armor and air cooperation.

More aerial attacks followed throughout the morning, including one on the battalion of fifty-one Shermans sent forward by CCA to counterattack. But while 10th Panzer had come through the Pass, 21st Panzer had swept up through Maknassy and the Maizila Pass, twenty miles to the south, reaching Sidi Bou Zid by early afternoon. Smoke and dust from bombs dropped by the Stukas and fighter-bombers added to the American confusion. Shermans were blowing up into raging infernos of angry flames one after the other as they came into range of the 88mms. An American artillery battalion, equipped with First World War 155mm Howitzers, discovered, as the Notts Hussars had found back at Gazala nine months before, that these were hopeless as anti-tank guns; and like the South Notts Hussars, in very little time there was nothing left. The battalion was simply blown away. By five o'clock, the two prongs of the German forces had linked up two miles west of Sidi Bou Zid, ensnaring anything left in between. The troops on Djebel Lessouda were trapped. So too were the men on Djebel Ksaira. Of the fifty-one Shermans that had attempted a counterattack, just seven remained.

Only piecemeal news from the fighting reached the cactus patch, but Ward was already bitterly regretting not withdrawing from the area much earlier. With the remains of CCA streaming back from Sidi Bou Zid, Ward asked Fredendall for urgent reinforcements. The II Corps commander immediately asked Anderson to release CCB. A situation report (sitrep) issued at 4:20 PM had warned "enemy tk strength SIDI BOU ZID now 70–90. Additional 30 tks moving NW." This should have made it pretty clear this was no sideshow,[486] but at First Army HQ they had placed too much faith in Ultra, and persisted with their theory that the main Axis assault would still come through Fondouk. Consequently, they refused Fredendall's request, allowing just one battalion from the 1st Armored to be released and hurriedly sent down toward Sbeitla.

Even with this extra battalion and with CCC, which had also been sent south, Ward was still wondering how he was going to be able to defend Sbeitla from two highly seasoned panzer divisions when worse news arrived. At around 8 PM, Fredendall had received a message from Anderson telling him to concentrate on "clearing up the situation [at Sidi Bou Zid] and destroying the enemy." In other words, he was expecting Ward to launch a counterattack. Without checking the viability of this order, Fredendall merely repeated to Ward Anderson's request verbatim. Hamilton Howze could not believe what he was hearing. "This was insanity," he noted. As Fredendall—and Anderson for that matter—knew, the best they could manage by the following day was a cobbled-together force of CCC and one further tank battalion. Lying in wait for them were not only nigh on a hundred tanks, but also the accompanying artillery and anti-tank guns. "General Ward didn't like it, and neither did I." But neither man had the courage to contest it further, something that Hamilton regretted ever after, "even at the cost of my commission."[487]*

To the west, Private Ray Saidel had spent St. Valentine's Day driving his truck to a depot in Clairefontaine, an eighty-mile round trip from Tebessa. Most driving was done at night, at breakneck speeds and with no lights, ferrying ammunition, fuel, and troops to II Corps bases at Ferian, Gafsa and Sbeitla, but this had been a day trip. It had been good to see where he was going for a change.

---

*It has been suggested that Ward thought there were only forty German tanks now in Sidi Bou Zid, but his diary for 14 February states quite clearly that he estimated the German strength to be one hundred tanks, two battalions of infantry and some artillery.

No sooner had Ray arrived back at the 1st Provisional Truck Company HQ than he was told to turn around, fill up with gas, pick up some extra fuel cans, and pull into line to head down to Gafsa right away. His dog tags were checked and he was told to take a rifle and some ammunition. He couldn't think what was going on; to the best of his knowledge, the front had been quiet for days.

Ray had only been in Tunisia a few weeks, one of a number of replacements earmarked for the 1st Armored Division. Landing at Oran, they had been taken to the Replacement Depot, and then the following day, 120 of them had been called out and told that they were to take sixty trucks up to the front. Although during his training he'd driven jeeps, half-tracks, and even tanks, he'd never had a go in a truck before. It took him a while to get the hang of the heavy steering and deep clutch, so there was a fair amount of gear crunching until he eventually began to master the art of double declutching such a large vehicle. The drive was made trickier thanks to the heavy cargo of tank tracks, which on the winding mountainous roads tended to make the truck swerve. Still, the seven-hundred-mile, six-day journey to the front gave him the perfect opportunity to adjust to his new role.

From Manchester, New Hampshire, on the East Coast of the United States, Ray was the eldest of three, although by the time he reached North Africa, he was still only eighteen. His father was Lithuanian, having arrived in America when he was just twelve years old. Ray's mother was half Lithuanian and half Irish, so Ray happily conformed to the polyglot nature of many of those serving in the armed forces. A precocious kid, he had become politically motivated at a very young age. As a Jew, and with a left-wing uncle, Ray developed a vehement hatred of fascism and Nazism. "The biggest disappointment in my life at the time was not being old enough to go to Spain," he admits. In high school he had organized political demonstrations and petitions, and this had continued when he'd begun university. Word had preceded him, and he was immediately asked to join the Student Defense Committee. But when America entered the war, Ray had no hesitation in volunteering right away, and was one of the very few to do so for moral and political reasons. "I just felt we had to beat these people," he explains. "I had no doubts at all."

While at university, he'd joined the ROTC—"practically every young guy there was in the ROTC"—and so during his initial training he was soon singled out and brought before the board with a view to becoming an officer. He passed with no problem, but hit a brick wall when it came to the security check. His politics at school and college had been noted and he was refused entry to officers candidate school and sent back to the ranks. "I was probably very fortunate," he says. "Survival rates for young tank officers were not good."

Now he was part of a convoy heading toward Gafsa. As the light began to fade, the column of trucks trundled through the winding passes to the east of Tebessa and then over the Grande Dorsale until they dropped into the plains around Feriana. Although they'd made the trip before, they had never done so with empty trucks; and although they were familiar with the route, the lead truck managed to take them on a wrong turn so that they were heading toward Sbeitla, in the opposite direction from Gafsa. By the time they realized their mistake and turned the trucks around again, they were nearly three hours behind schedule. The officer in charge, Lieutenant Hurwitz, could not be found, but they continued on their way regardless. When they finally turned on to the Gafsa road, they noticed large groups of troops and vehicles trundling past them back toward Feriana. To begin with, Ray assumed they must be part of a large troop movement, but as the road became more and more congested with trucks and half-tracks crammed with French and American troops, he began to realize something more sinister was going on. "I'd seen the movies of the retreat in France," he says, "and what I saw here was the same." Soldiers were clutching onto the fenders, roofs, hoods—any way they could get a ride. Those without a ride were tramping along the road. It was a particularly dark night, and Ray was worried he was going to hit someone, but discovered that by having the windshield down, his left hand holding open the door, and with one foot on the running board and the other on the throttle, he could just about see enough to be able to keep going. "The stream of humanity passing our window was like looking at a horrible motion picture," noted Ray.

The terrible congestion was delaying them even more, so having battled their way for twenty miles, the leader halted to talk things over. They were by now hours late. They reckoned at least a division had already passed them, as had stragglers and civilians. Several trucks had also recently gone by them with just a handful of soldiers aboard. Certainly, their convoy was the only one heading toward, rather than away, from Gafsa. For a moment, they couldn't decide whether to keep going or turn around, but in the end agreed they should keep going; that was their order, after all. With the road finally beginning to clear, the convoy headed off again. It was then that Ray hit a mule cart. It had been in the middle of the road, and before he knew what was happening, Ray had smashed straight into it, and a French soldier was flung onto his hood, and bounced off again. "I didn't stop," admits Ray. "I couldn't. It was pitch dark and I had most of the convoy behind me, all hurtling at top speed."

They eventually approached Gafsa in the early hours of the morning. Fires were burning in the town, and occasional explosions rang out, with bursts of light showering vividly in the night. One mile short of the town, they were stopped by a military policeman who wanted to know what the hell they thought they were doing. Didn't they know the Germans were about a mile the far side of town and trying to outflank them? "There's Kraut tanks only two hundred yards away," he told them. "We're trying to mine the road, so get the hell out of here before you're all trapped." Ray could now hear them, the rumble of diesel engines and squeaking of tank tracks. These were the forward elements of Rommel's Afrika Korps who had moved up from the Mareth line and had begun their march toward Gafsa just a few hours before.

Hurriedly, they turned around. Ray had been one behind the leader, but now was second from last as the convoy took off again. Traveling at top speed—about 60 mph—and hunched over the wheel, Ray strained through his glasses at the dark road ahead. He was driving more by intuition than any real knowledge of the road. They were only fifteen miles from Gafsa when the first thin streak of dawn appeared on the horizon. Daylight meant Stukas and strafing Messerschmitts, a terrifying prospect. They knew they now faced a terrible race against time.

Driving around a bend, Ray was distracted by an infantry patrol at the side of the road. Swerving, he hit an abandoned truck loaded with furniture and other belongings, and went into a ditch. He managed to reverse it out all right and told the patrol to jump aboard—but they refused. These were Rangers, ordered to bring up the rearguard of the retreat. Further up the road were some Senegalese troops from the abandoned truck, and although he could speak neither French nor Arabic, Ray managed to persuade them to jump aboard. Unfortunately, the crash had badly affected the steering and his truck was now veering hideously to the right. This rapidly grew worse until he could no longer drive it at all. Ray was only too thankful that there was still one truck behind him. He hailed it down, and they were about to blow up the wrecked lorry with a thermite grenade when suddenly Lieutenant Hurwitz appeared in a jeep. "Don't!" he yelled at them. "We'll recapture this ground tomorrow."

Grabbing his rifle and a blanket, Ray scrambled into the back of the last truck along with the Senegalese, and off they sped again. At Thelepte they were bombed and strafed, but managed to keep going unscathed, and headed back to the comparative safety of the mountains, finally reaching Tebessa just after noon. They had lost thirteen of the thirty trucks, and killed a number French troops and Arab civilians on the road. Ray had not been the only one to have had a fraught time. "It was chaos," he says.

Meanwhile, Ward's meager armored force was preparing to ride into the valley of death. Finally assembled and ready to begin at midday, they began across the plain toward Sidi Bou Zid, thirteen miles away. The ground was largely flat, sandy, and interspersed with thick vetch and cactus, but despite coming under repeated aerial attack, the bulk of the column pushed forward without too much difficulty, passing through the first wadi and village of Sadaguia and across another wadi a short distance farther on. They began to come under fire, but were warned that an Allied air strike would shortly arrive, and so slowed their pace. But the promised strike never materialized. In the meantime, the Americans had managed to knock out four 88s and were making good progress toward the third wadi, just four miles west of Sidi Bou Zid. This ditch, although only around ten feet deep, was nonetheless impassable except at a few points. The leading formation of tanks had begun funneling itself toward the main crossing when the enemy guns started firing with greater intensity. Now strung out in a long line, they were sitting ducks. Stukas appeared, screaming down on top of them and sending up mountains of the dust, dirt, and sand and adding to the suddenly mounting sense of confusion. As the dust began to settle, the Americans saw to their their horror that panzers were now rattling toward them from the north. Turning to face this assault, they then discovered they were being attacked from the south as well. Mayhem and panic struck the column as they realized they'd be drawn into a carefully prepared trap. All semblance of order and cohesion evaporated as tanks and half-tracks desperately tried to fight their way out. Flames and pitch black smoke began billowing into the sky as the Shermans blew up. Tank crews leaped from their tanks, some already ablaze, others running for their lives only to be cut down by machine-gun fire. It was another annihilation. Mission completed, the panzers then sat back and waited for their next orders.

Survivors scrambled back on foot, saved only by the smoke and dust that screened the battlefield. Around two hundred men managed to escape from Djebel Lessouda during the night, but the rest were captured, as were nearly all those on Djebel Ksaira. Tanks continued to burn as darkness fell, and although much of the artillery made it safely out of the carnage, the plain facts were that the 1st Armored Division had suffered the worst two days in its history: 98 tanks, 57 half-tracks, 29 guns, and 500 men had been lost. A hundred of its tank crews, together since the beginning of the war, had been blown away in one of the harshest lessons of war.

Anderson, meanwhile, had by now accepted that the Axis advances through Sidi Bou Zid and Gafsa were indeed the main enemy assault, and had begun to realize that he should have withdrawn to the Grande Dorsale at the beginning of the month when he'd had the chance. Late on 15 February, he suggested a wholesale withdrawal toward the mountains, although he hoped to be able to hang on to Feriana, Kasserine, and Sbeitla. Ike agreed, and the order was issued at five that afternoon. Reporting later to Marshall,

Ike tried to paint as positive a picture as he could and assured him, "I expect to strain every nerve to hold the line covering Feriana-Sbeitla."[488]

But Feriana was already being evacuated almost the moment he issued his new orders. Margaret Hornback and the other nurses and staff at the 48th Evacuation Hospital had spent two days watching anxiously as more and more of their army seemed to be trundling past. After a brief lull a few days before, their little hospital was once again heaving. Then at half past eight on the fifteenth, orders came for them to leave as well. By midnight they were packed, closed and ready to go, every single tent taken down, every piece of equipment loaded and every single patient lifted into a truck or an ambulance. Margaret and the other thirty nurses piled into two two-and-a-half-ton trucks and began the tortuous nighttime journey over the narrow mountain road that would lead them to Algeria.

Several hundred miles away, important events were also unfolding, although of a less dramatic or violent nature. While Montgomery regrouped at Tripoli, he decided to hold a conference of allied commanders in which they could discuss and share ideas and lessons learned from the recent fighting. It was not a bad idea. Attempts by the planners and commanders of TORCH to learn from those in the Middle East had been conspicuously absent, and it was about time ideas were disseminated more freely across the various Allied commands.

Monty had also been busy writing pamphlets for his generals and for the greater good in general, who he felt could benefit from his winning ways. On 15 February, the opening day of the conference, he sent General Brooke a copy of *High Command at War*. "This, and the previous one on conduct of battle," he assured Brooke modestly, "give the answer as to how we have won our battles in the Eighth Army."[489] The turnout at Tripoli, all things considered, was impressive, with a number of generals flying in from Britain. Bedell-Smith, Ike's COS, was there, as was Patton, who noted ruefully that he was probably the oldest and, as a mere major-general, the lowliest in rank. Alex and Tedder were also in attendance, but Monty was disappointed by the poor showing from Tunisia. "I had hoped to get over here Anderson, Allfrey, the British div comds, and some American div comds," he told Brooke. That they might have had their hands full staving off the Axis assault does not seem to have crossed his mind.

On the first day, Monty led the discussions, in which he gave a long talk about the various obstacles he had faced since the beginning of the Battle of Alamein and how he had overcome them. But he concluded by talking about the use of coordinated air power, the subject that had been top of the agenda in his pamphlet *High Command in War*. For all Monty's bragging and despite the spat with Coningham, he had, to his credit, never denied the important part the Allied air forces had played in his ground victory. Larry Kuter had discovered this a couple of weeks before. At the end of January he had met Tedder and Mary in Algiers as they traveled en route to England for two weeks' leave. Mary had impressed him with his enthusiasm and obvious charisma and by his brief discourse on the use of air power, with which he heartily concurred. Mary had also told him that he was not going to offer "air support" to anyone and so was renaming their new command the "Northwest African Tactical Air Force." Both he and Tedder had also suggested to Larry that he visit Monty and the new C-in-C of the Desert Air Force, AVM Harry Broadhurst. This he did right away. "My visit was revealing and reassuring," he noted. "In private, Monty spent a couple of hours with me extolling the concept. They had proved the soundness of their tactical air force doctrine."[490]

Now, at Tripoli, Mary was given a platform by Monty, in which he could properly articulate these ideas into a semi-formal creed. "The doctrine that we have evolved by trial in war over a period of many months," Mary began, "could, I think, be stated in its simplest form as follows: the soldier commands the land forces, the airman commands the air forces; both commanders work together and operate their respective forces in accordance with a combined army-air plan, the whole operations being directed by the army commander." As he pointed out, the army fought on the ground along a front that could be divided into many sectors. But the air front was indivisible. The army had one battle to fight: the land battle. But the air had two: first it had to beat the enemy in the air, then it could go into battle against the enemy land forces "with maximum possible hitting power." They lived in a technical age, he told them, and there was much for every soldier, sailor, and airman to learn about their professions. "In plain language," he continued, "no soldier is competent to operate the air, just as no airman is competent to operate the army."

Mutual support, he told them, was the key. "Sedada is a good example of the standard that we have reached," he said, a site halfway between Benghazi and Tripoli and one which the previous December had been earmarked as a possible landing ground. Advance units of the 7th Armoured Division had arrived there one evening and by the following morning had cleared a landing strip, equipped it with anti-tank guns, motor transport, and fuel and soon after two fighter squadrons landed. From there, they bombed targets just forty miles east of Tripoli. By the time they had landed again, more fuel, ammunition, and maintenance teams had also flown in. These transport planes could then be used to fly wounded soldiers back to hospitals in the rear. They had given passage to 5,800 in this way during the past three months. "You can imagine the effect on the morale of the army," Mary added, "when it is known that badly wounded cases, if trundled over the desert, very often die." In this, Sam Bradshaw would have heartily agreed.

He also pointed out that another reason the air commanders should make the decision of what and where to bomb was that they often had a better appreciation of the targets on offer. He gave an example: an army unit at the front reports a concentration of two hundred enemy vehicles and armor, but their request for an air attack is turned down. Perhaps fifteen miles away, however, an even bigger concentration of enemy armor is discovered, which, from experience, they know might well affect the whole course of the battle some time later. "The smaller formations of the army must understand that penny packets of air are a luxury which can only be afforded at certain times, and that judgment on the question of targets is the result of agreement between the army and air commanders, and in accordance with the army commander's broad directive on priority."[491]

Experience, as Mary and Monty both pointed out, had proved the rightness of this doctrine, yet Patton, for one, remained unimpressed and unconvinced. In the US Army, the air corps—and now the air force—was part of the army, rather than a separate service, there to support the needs of the ground forces first and foremost. While most British commanders in Tunisia begrudgingly accepted the independence of what Mary called a "tactical air force," most American commanders vehemently disagreed. Ike endorsed the policy, but, Larry Kuter believed, was not convinced. Overcoming the hearts and minds of such men was going to be an enormous task, as both Tooey Spaatz and Larry were aware. Frustrating though it was, Spaatz told him to bide his time, to try and keep his air forces together and to wait until the arrival of Alex and Mary and others to reach Tunisia. Then the battle to change the entire concept of air power into what Larry felt certain was a winning formula could begin.

Briefly, the Axis offensive paused. They had not expected such sweeping successes. On the evening of 15 February, von Arnim told Rommel that he would not be returning 21st Panzer to him as planned, because Gafsa had already been taken. Instead, he was going to mop up around Sidi Bou Zid on the sixteenth and then move on Sbeitla and northward to Fondouk the day after that. For his part, Rommel had spent the day not with his advancing panzers, but at the Mareth line instead. For a while, he seemed to be struck with a rare bout of indecision, telling his Afrika Korps that he might have to send some of the attached Italian troops back to shore up his southern defenses. Conscious that the clock was ticking, he was expecting Eighth Army to march forward any moment.

But as he set out toward Gafsa early on the morning of Monday, 16

February, he saw a road full of his own trucks, troops, and tanks, and his confidence soared once more. With the cheers of his troops ringing in his ears, a far more ambitious plan began to take shape in his mind. Rather than pulling back part of the Afrika Korps, he would reinforce it and push on to Feriana. Then he could either fork left toward Tebessa or head north to Kasserine and link up with von Arnim.

The following day, the seventeenth, his forces surged on down the Gafsa-Feriana road. By the afternoon they had reached and taken Feriana and were marching on toward the airfield at Thelepte. Jim Reed and the 59th Squadron were still out of the line resting, but the remaining fighters there had hurriedly taken off while the ground crews set the fuel dumps ablaze and then hastily jumped into their trucks and headed for the safety of the mountains. The Rangers were the last men to leave Thelepte, and looked on in disgust as thirty-four unserviceable aircraft were still burning, the columns of smoke billowing into the air. With the Axis tanks hard on their heels, they then headed off to make a stand up at the Dernaia Pass on the road to Tebessa.

Meanwhile, at the cactus patch, Ward had at long last been reinforced with CCB, which had in turn been reinforced with a British tank battalion. By 16 February, they had reached Sbeitla and were bracing themselves to take on von Arnim's forces any moment. Earlier in the afternoon, the remnants of CCA had also fallen back to the town; 10th Panzers' pause at Sidi Bou Zid had given them a much-needed respite.

It was not until after dark that evening that the panzers began probing their way toward the town, although this was still a day before they'd initially planned. CCA were refueling at supply dumps when the first tank shells screamed overhead and began landing among their command post. Hamilton Howze was still at 1st Armoured's command post when he heard the sound of shells exploding. Then, shortly after, he heard further, even louder explosions and saw the sky burning fiercely. CCA were already beginning to withdraw in panic and had begun the demolition of their supply dumps. "It looked and sounded as though the whole damned world was blowing up," noted Hamilton. With information hard to obtain, Ward called through to Fredendall and warned him that they were unlikely to able to hold on to the town. After a heated argument between the II Corps commander and Anderson, they agreed to allow 1st Armoured to withdraw after eleven the following morning. The situation was not as bad as it first appeared, however. Robinett, with his now seasoned troops, had told his men to hold firm, and soon after, the panzers had called off their attack.

During the night some semblance of order had been restored to CCA, and in fact, the panzers did not attack again until noon the following day.

They had been distracted by attempts by the stranded US infantry to escape from Djebel Ksaira. When they did move forward, they were met by Robinett's well dug in force, who managed to hold out until after five that evening. Having expected the worst, the Allies were only too relieved to discover that someone, at last, was standing up to the mighty German assault.

Nor did the panzers pursue the retreating Americans with any great vigor. After blowing the water mains, destroying bridges, and mining the roads, the American forces were able to make good their escape. The French in the area had withdrawn earlier in the morning, and now, as darkness fell once more, the remnants of CCA headed toward Sbiba, while CCB, along with Pinky Ward, Hamilton Howze and the headquarters of 1st Armored made their way to Kasserine and then on through the Kasserine Pass. It was now up to others to stem the Axis advance.

By now, Anderson had begun issuing movement orders to many of his front-line troops, hurrying them down to block three passes through the Grande Dorsale: at Kasserine, Thala, and Sbiba. On the morning of 17 February, much of the British 6th Division was told to get moving and to take up positions in the pass to the south of Sbiba. This included the Guards Brigade. Nigel Nicolson had now been promoted to brigade intelligence officer and to the rank of captain—"In a way flattering," he wrote to his parents, "but in a way it takes one down in the estimation of one's friends—for one is irretrievably a Staff Officer." In order to excuse the greater luxury he now enjoyed, he was determined to work his socks off.

Also joining the Guards at Sbiba was the 18th Regimental Combat Team. By the time of the launch of the German offensive, the 18th had spent forty-eight days in the Medjez sector, entirely under British control, and without any relief whatsoever. Not one unit had been taken out of the line. At the beginning of February, they'd been transferred to the 78th Division, but on moving to Sbiba, the Americans once again came under the control of the British 6th Armoured. With the Guards taking up positions astride the Sbiba-Sbeitla road, facing south, the 18th were to dig in a short way behind and to the east in support, all three battalions strung out in a line across the valley.

The Americans reached their positions in the early hours of Thursday, 18 February, and immediately set to work digging their foxholes. At Company G's lines, Tom Bowles began hacking and shoveling furiously. Like all the men, they now knew how important it was to be properly dug in before the Stukas and Messerschmitts paid them their first compliments of the day. Then the mortars had to be set up and ammunition brought forward. There was no time to waste at all. At Colonel Sternberg's battalion command post, Henry Bowles was also busy. As a wireman in Company HQ, his task was to lay down the telephone lines between battalion headquarters and the various company HQs before he could start thinking about his own safety. This meant teaming up with a buddy and scurrying across the entire battalion positions in the dark, on unfamiliar ground, with a large reel of wire. Since battalion HQ was at least half a mile behind the forward companies, this meant he and his buddy had to cover a fair amount of ground. It was not easy.

Joining the 18th were two regiments from the 34th Division, including Sergeant Bucky Walters' 135th Regiment. They had finally reached the front on 8 February and over two successive nights took over positions that had been held by the French. Bucky had made the journey from Algiers sitting in a jeep with the company captain and the heavy weapons company following behind with their 37mm pop guns and a few 50mm as well. As they'd dropped into Tunisia for the first time, they had been welcomed by enemy fighter planes swooping low and strafing them. "We started to have our first test of what it was like being in the infantry," says Bucky. It had both snowed and rained as they'd trundled through the Atlas Mountains, and he'd spent most of the journey feeling bitterly cold. "We didn't have the proper clothing either so suffered a bit," he admits. Like most troops who'd passed that way before him, Bucky was discovering North Africa was quite different from the place of his imagination.

Once at Pichon, they gained their first introduction to mud. "The trench foot started right off," says Bucky. "We had shoes and leggings. The shoes would get soaking wet, and there was no way of drying them." Most of the French had left by St. Valentine's Day, but a unit of French irregulars had stayed behind. These were Moroccan Berber-speaking natives, mountain troops known as *Goums*. Soon after his arrival, Bucky and a number of others in the company were taken out on a night patrol by one of the outgoing French officers. Leading them over particularly rough countryside, he eventually halted in a cave, where a number of Goums were sheltering with their horses. Bucky was shocked. "There was no sign of any rifle or pistol," he says, "just knives." And around their necks were strange-looking necklaces—made of ears. "They used the left ear of the German they'd killed," says Bucky, "and they kept them round their neck."

On 17 February, they had come under attack from the 10th Panzer, who had been sent up toward Fondouk and Pichon by von Arnim. The American artillery had fired without letup and held the panzers at bay, but at seven in the evening, the first of the American units was told to pull back toward Sbiba, some thirty miles away. Bucky and his battalion were not given the order to go until six the following morning. There was almost no transport available, so most of the men had to travel on foot.

Once again, it was the gunners who saved the infantry as they fell back. "We were being harried all the way," says Bucky, "but our artillery was holding them off. They were leapfrogging backward and they saved us over and over." As they slogged back in retreat, there was little chance for a rest, but with the rumble of tanks in the distance they hardly needed urging on. By 11 PM that night, they were finally digging in at their new positions alongside the 18th Infantry, but for Bucky, it had been a numbing first taste of combat. "That retreat," he says, "was a terrible nightmare."

Also on the move were the 2/5 Leicesters. Orders to head south and link up with the 26th Armoured Brigade were only received at one in the morning on 18 February, but they were told to get going right away. The first trucks were under way at around 5:30, but they faced a long journey over rough and muddy roads in broad daylight, a potentially extremely dangerous undertaking. Fortunately for Lieutenant Peter Moore and the other men of the battalion, the journey was uneventful. Rain followed them most of the way, but for once no one grumbled; the low cloud and mist kept the Stukas and enemy fighters at bay. They reached Thala, another mountain pass town some twenty miles west of Sbiba, at around eight that night, but then were told they would be moving farther south to reinforce the Americans at the Kasserine Pass. "We waited interminably through the night," noted Peter Moore, but by morning the news was not good. In fact, it was very grave indeed.

After capturing Thelepte, Rommel had continued on toward Kasserine but instead of finding von Arnim's forces, the road had been empty. Then news arrived that 10th Panzer was now up near Fondouk, in the opposite direction. Rommel was furious. He sensed a crushing victory was there for the taking, but needed another panzer division. By midday on 18 February, he'd formulated a plan to drive on Tebessa. There they would find all the supplies they needed to keep going and strike deep into the Allied rear. He knew it was an all-or-nothing gamble, and contacted von Arnim demanding he take personal control of 10th and 21st Panzer immediately. Von Arnim refused, so Rommel appealed to Kesselring and the Commando Supremo in Rome. Two hours later, Kesselring gave him the provisional go-ahead. "I feel like an old cavalry horse that has suddenly heard the bugles sound again," he commented that evening.[492]

To Rommel's great chagrin, however, the eventual reply from the Commando Supremo was a compromise: Rommel was handed command of 10th and 21st Panzer, but ordered to head northward to Le Kef first, not Tebessa, with its implications for a further drive toward the coast. "This was an appalling and unbelievable piece of short-sightedness," railed Rommel, who knew that by driving north, rather than west, his forces were more likely to run into Allied reinforcements.[493]

But orders were orders, and for once, Rommel obeyed. Rather than take the road for Tebessa, where the Rangers were dug in and waiting, the Afrika Korps were sent toward the Kasserine Pass, while 21st Panzer headed for Sbiba, and 10th Panzer, recalled from Fondouk, awaited developments at Sbeitla.

Although Pinky Ward was desperately regrouping his shattered 1st Armoured Division at Tebessa, there had been neither the time nor troops available to properly defend the Kasserine Pass, a mile-wide valley that separated the Grande Dorsale and the open plains of the Foussana Basin beyond. Through it ran a road, railway, and the River Hatab. At the top of the pass the road forked—right to Thala, left to Tebessa. Holding it on the morning of 19 February were the 26th Infantry Regiment of the Big Red One and a combat engineer regiment. Neither had much in the way of heavy firepower, and so had to rely on the all but useless 37mm anti-tank gun and mortars. Nor had they had much combat experience or the kind of training necessary to take on the Afrika Korps.

As it was, the Americans did rather better than might have been expected, and although they had been pushed back, the attackers were unable to force their way through the pass. Rommel had launched his assault on two fronts, however, and while the Afrika Korps were attacking at the Kasserine Pass, the 21st Panzer Division moved up toward Sbiba. Dug in against them was a more formidable and by now combat-hardened force: the 1st Guards Brigade, three battalions of the US 34th Division, the US 18th RCT, a further British cavalry regiment and the 2nd Hampshire Battalion. Since their arrival, the 18th and Guards Brigade, in particular, had dug themselves into a strong defensive position, with a highly effective minefield laid in depth in front of them and lined with thick entanglements of wire.

It was raining hard when, at 10 AM, enemy tanks began approaching the line in front of the Coldstream Guards. An hour later, infantry were spotted clambering out of their trucks farther down the road, and then more panzers appeared. By 1:30 PM, there were twenty-four of them—including five Tigers—but they were struggling through the Allied minefields and unable to find the weak spot in the line. During the morning they tried the Guards' positions, but after losing a number of tanks, turned their attentions in the afternoon to the 2nd Battalion of the 18th Infantry. More and more panzers kept appearing, until just before five o'clock, as many as thirty were bearing down on the 1st and 2nd Battalion positions, closing to within six hundred yards of the Americans. Company G found themselves as the main line of resistance (MLR). Tom Bowles' mortar team fired shell after shell at the panzers, which were making no greater progress against the 18th Infantry than they had the Guards. No amount of firepower from the enemy tanks could budge the resolute GIs. Henry Bowles and his wiring buddy were scuttling to and fro mending damaged telephone wires, concentrating on the job in hand and trying not to think about the enemy shells pounding their lines. Behind, the British seventeen-pounders, linked to the American positions, gave them unwavering support

Together, the Allies were holding the line in an action that showed how much both units—British and American—had progressed since the humiliation of Longstop. There was now no confusion between the battalion commanders. The lines of defense had been properly prepared, and each man knew exactly what he had to do. Suddenly the mighty German panzers did not look quite so formidable after all.

The 18th never wavered. By dusk, the 21st Panzer Division began rumbling back into the encroaching darkness. Seven tanks were left in front of the 18th Infantry's positions. Later, under cover of darkness, a patrol from Company G broke cover, and armed with bazookas, finished off the four tanks lying disabled directly in front of them. Had Ike seen their performance that day, he would have been rightly proud.

The excellent Allied defense at Sbiba persuaded Rommel on that rain-sodden day to abandon any further attempt to try and force his way along this route. Instead, he planned to resume his offensive the following day through the Kasserine Pass. And this time he had more success. The Americans had made a heroic stand, and the 10th Rifle Brigade an important delaying action, but by midafternoon on 20 February, the Axis had broken through into the Foussana Basin. There, their forces split, with the Italian Centauro Armoured Division pushing toward Tebessa, while the 10th Panzer, having joined the Afrika Korps the previous day, began trundling up the road to Thala. As the Panzers advanced, so the 10th Rifle Brigade had continued with their fighting withdrawal, falling back toward the 26th Armoured Brigade, now some miles south of the Leicesters and blocking the road to Thala.

Having spent the previous day awaiting firm orders, the 2/5 Leicesters had finally moved to their forward positions late on the twentieth, only to be told to withdraw to a new line just a few miles south of Thala. At first light on 21 February, they found themselves getting out of their trucks once more and moving into a number of small hillocks that overlooked the valley road. Peter Moore's B Company was to take up positions on a knoll behind A Company, while on the other side of the road, C Company was to dig in behind D Company. Supporting them were several Royal Artillery detachments and a couple of sections of mortars. It was raining hard and bitterly cold. They'd had almost no sleep for two nights and Peter's woolen greatcoat felt damp and heavy. Nor was he exactly sure what was going on. The previous morning, news had filtered through that the enemy was pushing through the Kasserine Pass, but whether the reinforcements that had been sent down to help had stopped the Axis advance was not clear.

Meanwhile, Peter and his platoon did their best to dig in, but up on their knoll, the ground was hard and stony, and the soil thin. "There was no question of digging the normal two-man, six-foot-deep slit trench of the training manuals," noted Peter, especially when their only means of doing so was with the standard issue entrenching tool, which consisted of a six-inch pick and small nine-inch shovel. While he hacked away at the rock, Peter listened to the dull, continuous thud of artillery fire in the distance, which, as the day progressed, grew ever closer. Aircraft were also active. Ahead of them, Stukas were screaming as they dived over the battle. "No orders came," noted Peter. "We spent the whole of that day digging, watching and waiting."

What Peter had been listening to was the battle unfolding between the British and Axis armor farther on down the road. The 10th Panzer had resumed their advance that morning and had then clashed with the 26th Armoured Brigade. Slowly but surely, the British armor was pushed back, ridge by ridge. By the middle of the afternoon, vehicles of all kinds began to stream past the Leciesters' positions, nose to tail and in no kind of order. The Leicesters watched anxiously, listening to the sound of gunfire inching ever nearer. The ground had now begun to quiver as shells exploded, and suddenly the rapid chatter of machine guns could be heard. Peter began to feel increasingly vulnerable. There were no deep minefields in front of them, nor any form of anti-tank defenses. And they were lying in slit trenches that were still far too shallow—Peter had managed to carve himself a hole of only a couple of feet deep and six feet long. None of his men had fared much better. They all knew about the German technique of driving a tank over a trench then spinning it around to crush the poor soldiers below.

Sherman tanks were even now joining the exodus, as the British armor withdrew through the Leicesters' positions. An American jeep towing a 37mm gun pulled over in the road below Peter's position. "Are you stopping?" asked one of the Yanks.

"Yes," Peter's men told him.

"Then I guess we had better stop too," he replied and the two of them quickly set up their gun directly in front of Peter's platoon.

As dusk began to settle, a Sherman approached A Company. When it was right upon them a German, rather than an Allied trooper, shouted from the turret, "Surrender! Die panzers are here!" He was promptly shot through the head and the captured Sherman retreated, but shortly after, three Mk IV panzers advanced and opened fire, hitting the mortar ammunition truck and setting it ablaze. Mortar bombs exploded and screamed from the fire, but two of the panzers were then hit in turn. The third hastily disappeared back into the darkness.

Hurrying toward Sbiba were more reinforcements, including the artillery of the American 9th Division, having traveled from Oran at breakneck speed. Also now approaching Thala was a long column of trucks carrying the Guards Brigade from Sbiba. A few miles short of the town, Captain Nigel Nicolson watched an isolated American troop carrier approach their convoy of trucks. "He's right behind us!" yelled one of the GIs as they passed. As they entered the town, Stukas swirled overhead and bombed the place. Nigel was looking after the American war correspondent, Virginia Cowles, and noticed that everyone but her ducked as the first bombs landed. Then the brigade moved to the south of the town, started digging in and waited for the inevitable creak and clank of approaching panzers.

First, though, the enemy had to get past the Leicesters and their supporting artillery. For half an hour after the first panzers had approached, the Leicesters waited apprehensively. There was no movement from down the road and their positions became shrouded in an eerie stillness. Perhaps, Peter wondered, they had beaten them off for the night, but then he heard the sinister squeaking of tank tracks from somewhere in the inky black night ahead of them. "There are few sounds more blood chilling," wrote Peter, "than that of the unseen enemy tanks edging forward in the darkness." Suddenly, revving engines filled the night air, and then there were voices too—German voices—and not just from ahead but from their flanks as well. Very lights shot into the air like fireworks, showering their positions in phosphorescent light. And then the Germans opened fire, shells from the panzers whistling through the air and mingling with the chatter of machine guns. Tracer seemed to be coming from all angles, as the Leicesters desperately fired back. Behind them, the Allied guns sent out their salvoes in return. Shells screamed, machine guns coughed and sputtered, men shouted. The noise was absolutely deafening. Peter was surprised by how much the Germans used flares. He could see the enemy weaving and moving their way forward. A German tank clattered forward almost directly in front of Peter's position and then was hit and set on fire. "One of the crew started to scream," says Peter, "and he screamed and screamed for at least a quarter of an hour." He also heard the death cries of the Americans as their

37mm was overrun. Despite the din, the anguish of dying men still rose above the sound of bullets, shells, and mortar fire.

Peter's small piece of high ground was now being raked with machine-gun fire. He had not only lost contact with the rest of the company but his entire platoon as well. The Bren had stopped firing and so had any rifle fire. Ahead of them, A and D companies had clearly been overrun. Peter felt pinned to the ground. Bullets cracked just over his head, while shells and mortars continued to explode terrifyingly close around him. He could not tell exactly what was happening but was aware from shouts and continuing fire that the enemy were moving on around them. His brain felt numb, incapable of terror, as though he were watching with a kind of strange detachment. He was struck by the sheer professionalism of the Germans and as their awesome firepower continued around him, he couldn't help thinking about the Home Guard back in Britain. They wouldn't stand a chance.

Then, almost as quickly as the firing had begun, it stopped. Gingerly, Peter peered up from his slit trench. In front of him, the German tank was still burning, but he could not see or hear any sign of the rest of his platoon. Then he heard German voices nearby. He'd been told that Germans would fire into slit trenches and so he waited, convinced they would soon discover him and then shoot him dead.

But nothing happened, and so he eventually raised his head again. Just five yards away, a small group of German soldiers were sitting smoking, so Peter feigned death and waited some more, hoping they would move away. Only they didn't; they stayed where they were, so Peter decided he would have to try and creep away. As quietly as he could, he slowly slipped off his much-loved greatcoat and then his webbing. The slightest noise would have spelled disaster, but not once did the soldiers turn around, and so inch by inch, Peter wriggled and wormed his way toward some open ground to his left, fully expecting to be discovered and shot at any moment. Eventually, he reached the cover of the hill and gently getting to his feet, slipped away into the night.

Behind him, lorries and tanks burned, glowing brightly. The moon had now risen and he could see quite clearly. Climbing up the hill and away from the scene of battle, he reached a plateau and ran into a herd of goats and their Arab owner. Offering him a cigarette, Peter tried to ask him the way to Thala. For a few minutes, they sat together in the still, moonlit night, smoking. "I thought of the extraordinary contrast with the inferno I had just experienced a mile or so away," noted Peter. "It could have happened on a different planet."

He continued walking, down a steep valley and up the other side, across farmland until eventually he drew near to Thala. By noon the following day, he had found the main Kasserine-Thala road, north of their old positions. Groups of British soldiers were taking cover from aerial attacks among the high cactus hedges that ran alongside, but someone told him the Leicesters were only a short way farther down the road. Ten minutes later, he found the rest of B Company, and there he discovered that of the four battalion companies, B had fared the best. And despite his earlier fears, most of his platoon had also managed to get away safely.[494]

The Germans had also suffered, particularly from the artillery behind the forward infantry positions. One battery of twenty-five-pounders had knocked out no less than six panzers, and having overrun the Leicesters' positions, the Germans had gone no further and had eventually withdrawn. When a small counterattack had been launched early in the morning, it had met only the rearguard of the retreating 10th Panzer Division.

The Axis advance had finally run out of steam. Robinett had further enhanced the reputation of his CCB by successfully seeing off the Italian assault toward Tebessa. While Peter Moore picked his way toward safety on the morning of the twenty-second, Rommel drove up the road toward Thala. After consulting with his commanders he concluded that the Allies had grown too strong for his attack to be maintained. At around one o'clock that afternoon, he met Kesselring, and together they agreed to call off the entire offensive and to withdraw in stages. Kesselring then offered him the chance to command the army group that was being formed from the two panzer armies. "Apparently, as a result of the Kasserine offensive, I had ceased to be *persona non grata*," noted Rommel. He accepted warily, although he still intended to return to Germany in the near future for medical treatment. Of first importance, however, was his need to get back to the Mareth line, where he planned to take on the Eighth Army one more time.

At Thala, news began to filter through that the Germans had gone. It had been a bitter night for the Leicesters, their first battle since the evacuation from Dunkirk back in 1940. What had struck Peter Moore was how confused and chaotic it had been. At OCTU, he'd learned elaborate command procedures for action, and yet had not uttered one of those orders. Moreover, right up until the moment the captured Sherman had appeared, he'd been thinking they were getting ready for a counterattack. The assault by the panzers—a division that had been personally led by Rommel earlier in the day—had come as a complete shock. Over three hundred men—nearly half the battalion—had been either killed, wounded, or captured.

Later during the day, the battalion padre, along with several officers and a pioneer platoon to bury the dead, gingerly returned to the battle-scarred knolls only to find scavenging Arabs scurrying away as they approached. Most of the dead had already been stripped of their clothing. One discovery struck a deep chord with Peter Moore. Among those killed the previous night was Jim Pickard, a friend who had joined the 2/5 Battalion the same day as Peter. He had been stripped, his little finger cut off and his signet ring stolen.

All along the new front line, the Allies slowly discovered that the enemy had gone. As usual, however, the Axis had protected its withdrawal with extensive booby traps and mines. Captain Nigel Nicolson had cautiously taken Virginia Cowles forward and past the sight of the Leicester's stand. At one point, on either side of the road, were the two halves of a British soldier, ripped apart by an exploding mine.

Lieutenant-Colonel Hamilton Howze trailed British tank units as they began moving back up the road toward Kasserine. Reaching a crossroads, his jeep was stopped by a British military policeman who told him he could go no farther because the road ahead was heavily mined.

"How do you know?" Hamilton asked.

"Well," he said, "if you look, you'll see a little pile of dead Arabs and camels in the road. That shows it's mined."

"What about the area to the right of the road?" suggested Hamilton.

"Look to the right," said the MP politely, "and you'll see more dead Arabs and camels."

"Well, how about to the left?"

"I'll let you know presently," the MP told him. "I see another party of Arabs and camels coming up now."[495]

Twenty-first Panzer had also left a devil's garden of mines as they'd retreated from Sbiba back toward Sbeitla. Sergeant Bucky Walters had gone forward on a patrol soon after the Germans had gone. Fortunately for him, they had driven out in two jeeps, and Bucky was following the first. He watched it drive down into a hollow, then there was an explosion. The jeep had hit a mine. One of the officers had been wearing his helmet with his chin-strap down and the blast had knocked back his helmet and as it had jerked backward, the strap had ripped his face clean off. "So from that point on," says Bucky, "we never wore our chin straps down." As Eighth Army had been discovering every time they restarted their pursuit of the panzer army, so the Allies in Tunisia were now learning that it paid to proceed with caution.

No sooner had the Axis called off their offensive than the rain that had made life a misery for all the combatants finally stopped. The bad weather had hampered air operations on both sides, although once again, the Axis, with their superior numbers and all-weather airfields, had dominated. Bryan Colston and the pilots of 225 Squadron had been grounded throughout much of the past week. On 22 February, they had tried to move to Tebessa in support of the Americans there, but rainstorms had forced them back. Finally, however, on the following day, they had managed to get airborne. Leading a large formation of twenty-four Spitfires and ten Hurri-bombers, Bryan attacked the retreating panzer army in the Kasserine Pass. Although a number of their aircraft were hit by flak, Bryan personally managed to hit three trucks and cratered the road. The efforts of the fighters was supported by heavy bombing raids. Ralph Burbridge and his crew in their new Fortress also pounded the pass. Rommel later said these attacks were "of a weight and concentration hardly surpassed by those we had suffered at Alamein." It probably would not have surprised him to know that the architect of the air offensive at Alamein, Air Marshal Sir Arthur Coningham, was now in charge in Tunisia.

The Kasserine Pass was reoccupied on 24 February, the Allies feeling their way back up along the mine-infested roads and tracks and battling over destroyed bridges. The Allies had suffered a humiliating defeat, but in terms of casualties, the Axis losses had been as bad, and were felt more keenly. Even so, over 6,000 Americans had been killed and wounded in the fighting, and a further 3,000 taken prisoner. The biggest casualty had been 1st Armored Division, which had lost around half its number.

Back home in the USA, the news of the defeat was received with stunned shock. "You folks at home must be disappointed at what happened to our American troops in Tunisia," wrote Ernie Pyle. "So are we over here. Our predicament is damned humiliating . . . we've lost a great deal of equipment, many American lives, and valuable time and territory—to say nothing of face." Yet, he assured them, there was still not the slightest doubt that they would fling the Axis out of Tunisia. It was, he added, also important to put things in perspective. "One thing you folks at home must realize is that this Tunisian business is mainly a British show. Our part in it is small. Consequently our defeat is not as disastrous as to the whole picture as it would have been if we had been bearing the major portion of the task."[496]

This was true enough, but it didn't stop the soul-searching, or the recriminations, which had begun even before the offensive was over. "The defeat has made all hands realize the toughness of the enemy and the need of battle experience," noted Harry Butcher on 20 February.[497] Certainly it was true that the biggest casualties had been among the least experienced troops, and there is no doubt that combat experience was the best teacher.

Nonetheless, the inadequate nature of American training prior to reaching North Africa had been ruthlessly exposed by the Germans.

But the "greenness" of American troops was only a part of it. Not even seasoned troops would have fared much better at Sidi Bou Zid, when the American armor was pitched against the prepared defensive positions of a force considerably larger than their own. "One good man simply can't whip two good men," noted Ernie Pyle. The real problem lay not so much with the troops, but with the commanders.

Throughout the battle, Fredendall had continued to make a complete hash of his command, issuing orders without any real appreciation of what was happening. He had been quick to move out of the still incomplete bunkers at Speedy Valley and farther back, into a mansion owned by a Vichy businessman, and there had continued to act in increasingly erratic and bizarre ways. On one occasion, an artillery officer had been ordered to see him and had arrived as quickly as he could, straight from the front and covered in mud. But Fredendall had kept him waiting until he'd finished his dinner of beef and ice cream. The II Corps commander had also continued to completely ignore Ward. On 20 February, for example, he bypassed the divisional commander and ordered Robinett to counterattack with CCB toward the Kasserine Pass, an order that would have seen an armored column head once more into the waiting jaws of a larger enemy force; even after Sidi Bou Zid, Fredendall hadn't learned. After an impromptu meeting with Robinett, he appeared to have had a change of heart, but by that time had already succumbed to defeatism, telling Robinett, "There is no use, Robbie, they have broken through and you can't stop them."[498]

At this point, the Allied command structure had begun to rapidly disintegrate. Anderson had become convinced that Fredendall was incapable of sorting things out, and so had ordered another British commander, Brigadier Nicholson, to the front to help take control, even though his chief of staff, Brigadier McNabb, was already forward with the troops and liaising with Robinett. Then Major-General Ernest Harmon, commander of 2nd Armoured Division in Morocco, also arrived to lend a hand. Fredendall had tried to have Ward sacked, and Ike initially agreed, ordering Harmon up to the front to take over. But while Harmon had been flying east, Ike changed his mind, having heard from Truscott that Ward had done well at Sbeitla. Instead, Eisenhower told Fredendall that Harmon should be regarded as his deputy and "a useful senior assistant."[499] On arriving at Fredendall's new mansion, Harmon had been told to take over tactical command of II Corps and to use Ward's staff. An already confused command structure was now an appalling tangle.

In the meantime, Robinett quietly circumnavigated most of these senior commanders, and after consulting with Brigadier Dunphie of the

26th Armoured Brigade and Brigadier McNabb, drew up plans for a co-ordinated defensive stance, plans that would soon pay off. That they were able to cut through this jumbled chain of command and stream of orders and counter-orders and actually successfully hold the Axis onslaught at bay, was a credit to men like Robinett and Dunphie, and the troops under their command.

"There are two things we must learn," wrote Ernie Pyle. "We must spread ourselves thicker on the front lines, and we must streamline our commands for quick and positive action in emergencies." He may not have been a fighting man, but there was certainly much to be said for his prognosis. What the Allies needed was firm and vigorous leadership. Fortunately, they were about to get it.

PART IV

SHOULDER
TO
SHOULDER

"General Ike insisted that there be created
in our Army a feeling of partnership
between ourselves and the British."
Commander Harry Butcher

CHAPTER 22

Alex & Mary Take Control: 22 February–20 March, 1943

GENERAL ALEXANDER ARRIVED in Algiers on Wednesday, 17 February, around the same time that Rommel's panzers were storming onto the airfield at Thelepte. After a brief chat with Ike the following morning, he hurried to the front, anxious to check out the lay of the land as quickly as possible. In pouring rain he and his small party landed at Tulergma airfield near Constantine and then, after briefly setting up his first North African tactical headquarters, he headed off to inspect the front. It was bitterly cold and he still only had his desert uniform, although fortunately had also brought their "goonskins"—heavy sheepskin-lined jackets rather like the RAF Irvin. With this and his high peaked cap and plastic eye-shields, Alex looked more like a German officer than a British one. Still, his appearance was certainly distinctive: he looked every inch the fighting general.

And well he might. He was, after all, by some margin the most experienced general in North Africa. He had witnessed war—both success and defeat, triumphant advances and ignominious retreats—at all levels. Under turbulent skies and through the mud and rain, he motored from one headquarters to another. There he spoke with the commanders and their staffs and in between watched the streams of troops and vehicles crowding many of the roads. He had seen such signs of chaos before and knew that here in Tunisia, their armies had lost confidence and were coming apart at the seams. "The general situation is far from satisfactory," he wrote to Brooke on 19 February. "British, American and French units are all mixed up on the front, especially in the south. Formations have been split up. There is no policy and no plan of campaign. The air is much the same. This is the result of no firm direction or centralized control from above . . . We have quite definitely lost the initiative."[500]

That same day, he wired Ike, proposing to take over right away, a day earlier than planned. Ike agreed immediately, and so without further ado,

Alex issued orders—as he had on taking command in Egypt—that there would be no more withdrawals, with certain key positions to be held at all costs. Anderson was ordered to concentrate his armor at Thala, and he also asked Monty to move some of his forces up to the Mareth line as soon as he possibly could to exert pressure on the Axis, a plan that worked with almost immediate effect and which helped persuade Rommel that his forces were needed once more in the south. "Well done—I am greatly relieved," he told Monty on the twenty-second, then added, "I have seen enough in the short time available to be very shocked."

In his address at Tripoli, Mary Coningham had pointed out that "the fighting efficiency of a service is based upon leadership, training and equipment."[501] Well, Alex had few concerns over the standard of equipment, but plenty about the quality of leadership and training, particularly with regard to the Americans. Fredendall's HQ had horrified him. No one seemed to have any real appreciation of what was going on or to be doing their jobs properly. He thought Fredendall's COS was "dithery," while the II Corps commander impressed him even less, appearing "utterly shaken" and with no ideas about how to improve the situation.[502] It was unfortunate that his first view of American troops was of those retreating from the Kasserine Pass, but to him these men appeared terribly underprepared for war, and this had a profound affect on his view of their fighting potential. They were, he told Brooke, "so badly trained. This is the case from top to bottom, and of course entirely inexperienced."[503] Had he known the truth about the training of Ward's 1st Armored Division, he would have been absolutely appalled. The pity, though, was that these first glimpses did not demonstrate the American ability to learn quickly. Had he seen the 18th Infantry in action at Sbiba, for example, his view might have been entirely different, and considerably more optimistic. As Admiral Cunningham pointed out, "They were at much the same stage as were the British a year after they had entered the war, young, inexperienced, and apt to be thrown off their balance the first time they went into action." But he, too, already knew enough about the Americans to realize they would soon catch up.[504]

Alex's initial impressions were reinforced by a report conducted soon after by staff at 18 Army Group HQ. Between 22 and 25 February, they toured the front much as Alex had done. They agreed that CCB was a good outfit. II Corps HQ, on the other hand, "was the least impressive HQ we visited, in every way." Conversely, Pinky Ward's HQ "was much more impressive, being well laid out in a good covered site. The operations appeared to be completely under control and the HQ working smoothly."[505] This was as much to do with Hamilton Howze and the rest of the senior staff as it was Ward. The British 26th Armoured Brigade exuded calm control, they reported, but the team had felt uneasy at the large number of closely concentrated vehicles, making easy targets for any aerial attack. This was a fault that Alex had also noticed all along the front.

Like Alex, the team did not visit the troops of either the 34th or 1st Infantry. Again, this was a shame. They might have drawn different conclusions. They did talk to a number of troops involved in the fighting at Kasserine Pass, however. From such statements, it became clear that in that battle, mines had been insufficiently laid and inadequately covered; anti-tank guns had opened fire at too great a range, and troops had not been properly dug in. Security was generally terrible. Even Monty confirmed this. "I have been listening on my 'J' to all American chat on the air during the battle," he told Alex. "It is all in clear, without any attempt to disguise it or to use simple codes."[506]

But, the team reported, morale remained good among most troops, including the Americans. "They appeared to be more critical of their leaders than we normally are, and to realise the mistakes which had been made. It has been something of a shock to them to find that lavish equipment alone is not enough to win a battle."[507] This was an opinion echoed by none other than Ernie Pyle. "We have got it into our heads that production alone will win the war," he wrote. He even wondered whether the Kasserine setback might not have been a bad thing in the long run. "It is all right to have a good opinion of yourself, but we Americans are so smug with our cockiness. We somehow feel that just because we're Americans we can whip our weight in wildcats."[508] Nonetheless, most of the US officers the team spoke with showed admirable honesty and humility, expressing their wish to profit from the recent fighting and openly admitting their lack of experience. "Yes! Such a spirit is most praiseworthy," scribbled Alex. "It is up to us to help them."

Alex sent this report to Brooke, noting that the shortcomings described were "all the obvious weaknesses which will appear when untrained and inexperienced troops take the field for the first time."[509] There was now much work to be done if he was to fulfill his earlier prediction of an Allied victory in North Africa in May. He set to work immediately. On his first day in the job, he announced that American, British, and French forces were to be organized into their own sectors, and all battalions and regiments returned to the command of their own divisions. Static troops were to hold the line, while any armored and motorized troops were to be withdrawn and grouped into mobile reserves. There would be re-equipment and intensive training for *all*, and as soon as possible. Meeting with Ike on 22 February, he suggested they should try and benefit from the vast experience of Eighth Army, and so proposed sending battle-hardened soldiers to join II Corps as liaison officers. The Americans were also to be given British six-pounder anti-tank guns to replace their 37mms. Lastly, there was to be no more failure. Any future offensive operations had to be guaranteed of success.

It was this final assertion that dictated his plan for the defeat of the Axis armies in North Africa. It seemed to him that there were several clear factors that should affect his decision-making. The first was that Axis troops were still pouring into Tunisia at a rate of a thousand troops a day. These forces would continue to rise unabated unless the supply line between Tunisia and Sicily could be cut off. ABC's naval forces in the Mediterranean, especially the submarines, were once again doing well, but Alex knew that to really seriously affect Axis supply lines, they needed to gain air superiority, which at present they most certainly did not have. This air superiority could only be achieved by taking enough airfields close to the Tunisia-Sicily air bridge—in other words, along the coastal plains the far side of the Eastern Dorsale, south of Enfidaville and north of Gabes. There were only two realistic means of reaching these plains in force: through the Gabes Gap to the south, or through the Fondouk Pass in the middle. The latter he dismissed as too risky; it held many of the same risks of Operation SATIN. Rather than take the chance of being enveloped by two panzer armies, he decided to crush the two of them together into a vice in the Tunis bridgehead. Eighth Army was the most experienced, battle-hardened and confident of his forces. It made perfect sense to launch the next Allied offensive with the best team available. That meant Eighth Army.

"The campaign would be divided into two phases," he wrote. "In the first, the main objective would be to get Eighth Army north of the Gabes Gap where it would gain contact with First Army and gain freedom of manoeuvre to develop its superiority in mobility and firepower . . . In the second phase, the efforts of both Armies would be directed towards securing airfields which would enable us to develop the ever-growing strength of our Anglo-American air forces. When we had achieved that, we should be able to co-ordinate to the full the striking power of all three services in drawing a tight net round the enemy's position."[510]

It was to Larry Kuter's great relief that Alex, like Monty, appeared to not only recognize the importance of airpower and of gaining air superiority, but also that he fully supported the tactical air doctrine. It made a refreshing change from the majority of ground commanders he'd come across since arriving in North Africa. As if to underline this point, Alex insisted on having his tactical HQ next door to that of Mary and Larry at NATAF, initially in Constantine, but from mid-March at an encampment among scattered olive trees in the hills fifty miles further south at Ain Beida. Both Alex and Mary had their caravans brought up, while the rest of the staff—Larry included—made their homes in tents. In addition to a bed and locker, Larry also had a desk and telephone in his. At the center of the encampment was a large khaki and camouflaged marquee. This was their operations center, and was dominated by a large, waist-high horizontal map. This marquee, noted, Larry, "was the heart of ground-air cooperation and collaboration."[511]

Larry had been at Forward HQ on 18 February when at 9 AM he had received a message warning him that the newly promoted Air Marshal Coningham would be arriving to take over command of the Northwest African Tactical Air Force (NATAF) in fifteen minutes' time. "He came in full of steam," Larry noted, and promptly issued an order prohibiting any further defensive umbrellas unless by written authority of NATAF. Copies were sent straight away to all the ground commanders and at higher levels. When Larry suggested they send an officer to First Army HQ to discuss the coordination of airfield construction and future ground operations, Mary replied, "To hell with that. We'll set up the airfields and 1st Army will conform to our plan."[512]

Mary had then disappeared back to Algiers to collect the rest of his staff, including Tommy Elmhirst, who had still been in the UK and worrying about what his next posting might be, when Mary had rung him out of the blue asking him to be his Chief of Administration at NATAF. "Nothing could have pleased me more," noted Tommy. He and George Beamish, once again Mary's Senior Air Staff Officer (SASO), had reached the front on 19 February, and were told in typical Coningham style that their task at NATAF was to "Set up HQ, take over command of all forward air forces, both British and American, fuse them, reorganise them and get command of the air over Tunisia. Then help the soldiers to run the Germans out of Africa before May."[513] Simple.

Immediately, both 18th Army Group and NATAF commanders began messing together. Tommy had detected an air of despondency to begin with, prompted by the huge task ahead and the critical battle situation. The only exceptions had been Mary and Alex, who never once showed anything other than good humor and confidence. Alex cheerily told them that whenever he started a new job, it was always in the middle of a retreat. "He was quite imperturbable," noted Tommy, "and a very pleasant and cheerful mess mate—more than I could ever say of Monty."

Mary's old desert routine was soon reestablished. Every morning at 8 AM there were "Morning Prayers," where his senior staff would meet to talk through anything that needed discussing. In the evening, before joining Alex and his staff for dinner, there would be a drink in Mary's caravan. This way, everyone was kept fully up to speed, while at the same time forging a strong sense of teamwork and friendship. Tommy immediately found himself working harder than he'd ever done in his life. The administrative side of NATAF was in a hopeless mess. "The only thing that was really first class was the fighting spirit of both British and American aircrews," wrote Tommy. "All they needed was to be organized and directed."[514] By working from 8 AM until midnight every day, within two weeks the squadrons had been moved into wings, a day bomber group had been formed, new airfields had either been built or were under construction, ancillary units had been moved forward to where they would be of most use to the fighting units, lines of supply had been straightened, fuel and ammunition dumps had been established, and spares had been brought up from Algiers. He also discovered that American flying efficiency was being held back by a shortage of lorries, so that supplies were not coming forward quickly enough. Soon after, Ike and Bedell-Smith visited their HQ, and over lunch Tommy was able to collar "Beetle" about the matter. "The Air Corps [sic] got their lorries within the week," noted Tommy.[515] Another time, Tommy was at Thelepte talking with one of the senior American officers there. It was cold and damp, and the American apologized for not being able to offer Tommy a drink, but explained that it was forbidden. A couple of days later, Tommy sent him a bottle of rum. "Thereafter," he noted, "our friendship and cooperation prospered exceedingly."

Life was certainly improving for the 33rd Fighter Group. Jim Reed and the 59th FS were finally given new P-40s. Jim wasted no time in painting "Irene II" on the engine cowling. They'd all been given the latest P-40L version, lighter and faster, but with only four machine guns rather than six. They soon added two more and at the end of February moved up to a new airfield at Berteaux in Algeria, close to the Tunisian border. Every single pilot in the 33rd now had their own aircraft, a first since arriving in North Africa. From now on, they would rarely find themselves outnumbered by the enemy.

Jim's plane had needed a bit of work on it, so he had joined the rest of the group a few days later, but he soon managed to get his new P-40 just as he wanted. "She's doing all right now," he wrote to his girlfriend, "even if the score is still even. She usually does as she is directed, because she knows who's boss." By the beginning of March they were training for the new roles required of them: the regime at NATAF no longer wanted fighters who could only fight other fighters. They needed their pilots to multitask, to escort the bombers on missions over Axis airfields and to dive-bomb as well. The 33rd practiced hard, dropping single five-hundred-pound bombs and fragmenting cluster bombs, and flying with various bomber formations. They were also beginning to change the way they flew together as both squadrons and as a thirty-six-plane fighter group. Before, they'd always flown in the by now outmoted vic—or *V*—formation. Instead they decided to fly line abreast, in a long stretched-out line, so there was no longer any need for the vulnerable tail-end Charlie. To fend off enemy attacks they worked out a system similar to that developed by Billy Drake at 112 Squadron, whereby a number of aircraft would be detailed to fend off the attackers while the rest continued with their escort duty. Whatever the size of the formation, whether it be in squadron or group strength, the aircraft would be staggered in height. If flying in a three-squadron formation, the lead squadron would be in the center, while the other two would be slightly behind, with one a bit higher and the other slightly lower. The difference in height meant that all aircraft could easily turn together, simply by the two outside squadrons swapping places. "This formation proved very successful for the 33rd Fighter Group," noted Jim.[516]

At Algiers, ABC was already busy planning for the invasion of Sicily, but at sea, his naval forces continued to do what they could to disrupt Axis shipping. The 10th MTB Flotilla were still patrolling the coastline, but on 24 February, two MTBs were given the task of laying mines off the island of Galite, on the approaches to Bizerte. One of those was Charles Coles' MTB 262. "We'd never laid mines before," admits Charles, "and we hated seeing the torpedo tubes coming off." There were other warning signs that the mission might be jinxed. As they carried out their normal engine trial before heading off on the mission, the flotilla engineer discovered there was something wrong with the starting mechanism. The auxiliary engines wouldn't start either, so the engineer told them to change all the batteries. While this was happening, Wagstaff, his Number One, told him, "Charles, I've the worst case of gyppy tummy I've ever had. Of course I'll come, but I'll be sitting on a bucket all the time." Charles excused him, and took along the spare Number One instead, a new officer with no operational experience at all. To make matters worse, his leading motor mechanic then appeared with a badly cut hand, so he too had to be excused from the trip.

Charles had just returned to active duty after a two-week leave of absence. The political figures he had met during his boar hunt had invited him to Algiers. The navy had given him permission to go and then told him to spend two weeks, researching their grievances and writing up a report. However unorthodox this might have been, he had finally finished his assignment that very morning. To begin with the journey went well, but they were halfway between Bone and Galite when the other MTB flashed "Slow Down!" and came alongside 262 to explain that one of their engines had blown and that they were going to have to turn back. Two-sixty-two should have returned to Bone with them. The golden rule was never to operate alone, in case anything went wrong, as it sometimes did. But they were now so close to Galite that Charles decided to carry on. "I confess," he says, "I disobeyed orders, but it would have been ignominious to have gone back with the mines still on board."

On reaching Galite, they saw there was a small lighthouse. Five hundred yards away, they cut the engines and allowed themselves to drift in silently on the wind. Charles's idea was to get to within a hundred yards of the target, drop the mines, and then creep away on their quieter auxiliary engines. If necessary, they would have to start the main engines—with their explosive roar. Charles knew that the moment the Italians heard anything they would direct the lighthouse beam onto them, so told the Oerlikon gunner to be ready to immediately shoot out the light should the need arise.

"Everything seemed to be going all right," says Charles, "but it was all very tense." In due course, they reached their target and were ready to lay the first mine, so Charles ordered the auxiliary engines to be started at low revs. Nothing happened. Charles waited anxiously, the boat drifting ever closer to the mouth of the harbor. "For God's sake, go and see what's going on," Charles whispered to the new Number One. Moments later he came back and said, "The batteries are not responding at all." Charles then told the engine crew to try the auxiliary engine again. But once more, it remained silent. The telegraphist suggested they take out the HT wireless battery—hoping it might offer just enough power to kick-start the auxiliary. The minutes ticked by and the crew barely dared breathe as the MTB slowly drifted away from the harbor entrance and almost scraping the rocks along the coast. "By this time we could see the blades of grass waving in the wind on the shore," says Charles. After about an hour, and with a cold wind getting up, they had drifted clear of the island. They made a jury-rigged sail from various bits of tarpaulin and with this they managed to head about a mile from the island.

But as Charles was well aware, they were not going to get very far without engines, and once the sun rose, they would soon be spotted. Assembling the crew on deck, Charles told them they were going to have to sink the boat: they were carrying new secret equipment on board and could not risk it falling into enemy hands. He told the coxswain to blow the self-destruct hole in the bottom of the boat, which he did. Soon the water was up to their knees, but 262 was still very slow settling in the water due to the buoyancy from the half-empty fuel tanks. They tipped the mines over the edge without the detonators and set a couple of depth charges to blow at twenty feet under the water. By this time, they were about twenty to thirty miles from the north coast of Tunisia, almost on a level with the front line. On board, they kept two fairly primitive and untested dinghies, but Charles thought that with luck, they might just be able to paddle to safety. Prepared to do battle should they arrive on the enemy side of the line, he loaded hand grenades and a Bren gun aboard each craft.

Assembling the crew on the fo'c'sle, Charles explained his plan to the crew. He also felt it was his duty to lead them in a rather hesitant rendition of the Lord's Prayer. Then he thanked them all for their devotion to duty through many hazardous experiences, and wished them a safe passage during the hours ahead. The coxswain—against all medical advice—then asked for some rum. Charles acquiesced and then they cautiously clambered into the dinghies and started to paddle slowly away. But the sea was too rough and the dinghies too light. They started to take on water and when still only a short way from the MTB, the first became waterlogged and sank, followed soon after by the second. It was a dark February night, and the sea was icy cold. Charles shouted to the crew to try and swim back to the half-sunk boat, and to help one another. But two of the crew could not swim and their lifejackets made progress difficult. Charles then asked for the two fittest men to head back to the MTB as fast as they could and take the detonators out of the depth charges. Should they explode, it would mean certain death for all of them. Fortunately, the two spare first lieutenants were able to get back on board as Charles ordered and reached the charges before it was too late. Most of the crew managed to make it back to the MTB and were pulled aboard—most, but not all. One man simply disappeared forever; another was to drift ashore on Sicily many months later.

A new plan was needed for the survivors. Charles decided to now keep 262 afloat until dawn; with any luck they would still all be alive and then they could review the situation. Fortunately, the MTB was still sinking slowly—the scuttling charge had not been heavy enough. Throughout the rest of the night, the exhausted crew pumped and baled, managing to reduce the rate of sinking. They even tried to block the hole at the bottom of the boat with a rug wrapped around Wagstaff's beloved wind-up gramophone. Charles had rarely been allowed to even borrow it—despite their perilous situation, he was unable to help smiling as he helped wedge it like a cork into the damaged hull.

Dawn came with a fine, clear, sky and a calmer sea. MTB 262 was now very low in the water: there was nothing more they could do to save her. Only about half a mile away was the island of Galite, once home to a small colony of French fishermen, but now held by Italians. Once again,

Charles assembled the rest of his crew on the fo'c'sle and held their second farewell ceremony in under twelve hours before suggesting they all take to the water again and try to swim to the island all roped together. It seemed to be their only option. With the two strongest swimmers in the front and the nonswimmers at the back, they set off, singing rude songs and even hymns in an effort to boost their morale. They'd been in the water a while when Charles saw 262 lurch downward amid foam and hissing bubbles—the bow with "262" painted on it turned skyward, then slowly slid beneath the waves. "It was," says Charles, "the only time I wept—albeit silently—during the war."

He was not sure how long they remained swimming in the water, but there came a moment when he heard an engine approaching. "I was convinced it was an MTB come to rescue us," he says, "and in my relief I must have passed out." The next thing he knew, he was waking up to find himself cuddling a slightly warm body. "When I came to, I realised he was a member of my crew who must have just died. We were in the bottom of a French fishing boat, with an Italian Carbinieri in the stern with his semiautomatic pointing at us." The coxswain and one other survived the swim, but both the stoker and the spare mechanic had been among those drowned. Ironically, they had been the best swimmers.

When the crew failed to return for breakfast, strings were pulled and Spitfires sent out to look for them—the squadron leader was a pre-war friend of Charles's. Nothing was found. MTB 262 was already at the bottom of the sea. Four of the crew were dead and Charles and the other survivors were now prisoners of war.

Before Alex's plans could be put into action or any wholesale reorganization undertaken, he found himself confronted with a further Axis assault—this time in the North. Von Arnim, without warning Rommel, his new army group commander, gained permission from Kesselring to launch Operation Oschenkopf, a three-pronged attack to push the British back in the north. The main central strike force was to seize the railway station of Sidi Nsir and the valley westward that led all the way to Beja, while in the north another assault was to drive the British back from Green and Baldy Hills towards Djebel Abiod. Another attack farther south was directed towards Medjez el Bab.

Oschenkopf was launched on 26 February and immediately came up against stiff opposition from the 5th Hampshire Battalion and 155 Battery of the 172nd Field Artillery Regiment. Both had only recently arrived in Tunisia and this was their first engagement. They were twelve miles farther east from the rest of the brigade, who were holding positions at Hunt's Gap, the mouth of the valley and the last defensive position on the road to

Beja. All day long this tiny British force held off the full force of a German armored corps—which included Tigers, Mk IVs, paratroopers, and infantry equivalent to three battalions—in a last stand that was every bit as remarkable as that at Snipe, five months before. But by nightfall, the position had been overrun. All the British guns had been destroyed, although they had fired to the last man and to the last round. Nine gunners made it to safety along with 120 men from the 5th Hampshires. The rest had all been either killed or wounded. Although reports on the number of enemy tanks knocked out vary, it was certainly a significant number and the action forced the Germans to delay any further advance for forty-eight hours. And in that time, the British were able to hurriedly bring up more reinforcements.

Further south, the Herman Göring Division had launched their attack on Medjez and Bou Arada, where both the 17th Field Regiment and 1st Parachute Brigade were based. Early on 26 February, the 2nd Battalion heard intensive fighting away from the left flank, where the 3rd Battalion were positioned. By nine, they were coming under fire themselves, and Colonel John Frost could see large numbers of sticklike infantry advancing down the slopes opposite them. "They looked very small and ineffective in the distance," Frost noted, "so we took up our places at the command post with a feeling of alarm." He knew his men were ready, however. They had built up large stocks of ammunition, were dug in properly and their defensive fire plan coordinated with the supporting French artillery. Moreover, his men were fit, fresh, and knew exactly what they had to do, and although the different companies were necessarily spread out because of the wide section of front they'd been ordered to hold, the gaps in between were covered by machine guns and mortars. The German attacks got nowhere. "The situation at nightfall," noted Frost, "was that we with our French supporters were intact and sound in every way, but the enemy were scattered about in front of, and between, our forward company positions."[517] During a day of long fighting, the 2nd Parachute Battalion had suffered just one man killed and two wounded. During the night, Frost listened with satisfaction to the sound of grenades and Stens cutting apart the still night air as his raiding party went hunting for prisoners. By dawn, they had over eighty Italians in their hands. Of the enemy there was no sign. A day later Frost's men handed over their positions to the Americans.

A few miles north of the paras, the 17th Field Regiment were supporting the infantry of 38th Brigade. They too found themselves mainly faced with an assault by Italian infantry supported by German panzers. Here, too, after initial success, the enemy was forced back. The British gunners also had ready a carefully prepared fire plan. Helping to direct this fire was David Brown, who had spent the day at the battery observation post. On one occasion, the entire regiment had managed to get twenty-one rounds from their twenty-five-pounders in amongst the advancing infantry in the space of ten minutes, no mean achievement. "We've had a lot more action in which we were pretty successful," wrote David a few days later.[518] His wife had been sending him newspapers, but although any kind of news only rarely reached them, he had heard about the Russian success at Stalingrad. It had given them all a great lift.

While the thrusts on Bou Arada and Medjez had failed, von Arnim had not yet given up on his major assault toward Beja, and on 28 February, his forces set off again from Sidi Nsir toward Hunt's Gap. Facing this latest onslaught were the battered 2/5 Leicesters.

After being overrun at Thala, the 2/5 Liecesters had been reformed into two companies and were then sent to Beja on 25 February to rejoin 46th Division. There, they were to be given a chance to refit. After a long overnight journey, they had arrived to the welcome news that they were being given seven days' rest at Teboursouk. It was not to be, however. By mid-morning on the twenty-sixth, news began reaching them of the latest German assault, and so the Leicesters were hurriedly sent up to Hunt's Gap. Beja had to be saved at all costs as it commanded the Allied lines of communication and supply to the entire northern front.

Despite the grim news, there was one cause for optimism, however. "For the first time, while waiting in Beja that day," noted Peter Moore, "we saw impressive Allied air activity. Waves of medium bombers, British and American, flew over escorted by fighter aircraft, British Spitfires and Hurricanes and the American twin-boomed Lightnings."[519] One of the Spitfires Peter saw zooming overhead was that flown by Bryan Colston—225 Squadron was now in action every day bombing enemy airfields as well as enemy ground forces. On 28 February, Bryan flew no less than three sorties during what he called a "big bombing day" over the German forces moving toward Hunt's Gap. Along with 241 Squadron, they dropped 64,000 pounds of bombs between their first and last mission. Despite facing heavy flak, it was, says Bryan, "a bumper day dive-bombing the Hun."

The Leicesters moved up through Hunt's Gap that night, B Company moving to Frenchman's Hill, while C Company took up positions at Montaigne Farm, ahead and to the right, and began digging in. This time, they had been thoroughly briefed about their role, which was to be purely defensive, and so they were determined to establish their positions properly. Dawn proved what good positions they were. Ahead, Peter could see a long area of swaying grassland, a mile or so wide, protected on either side by long ridges of high, mountainous hills. The single-track railway from Sidi Nsir continued beneath them, while to the left of their position the road wound its way up from the valley. Montaigne Farm, a cluster of white, flat-roofed buildings, was perched on a gently curving spur that strutted out into the centre of the valley. From there, the Leicesters were given commanding views. More important, so too were the twenty-five-pounders and heavy 5.5-inch guns digging in behind.

At first light, Peter saw and heard the approaching enemy, and recognized the now unmistakable square-shaped hulk of the Tiger Mk VI with its 88mm gun. Artillery fire and the new heavy British Churchill tanks repulsed this first attack, but from then on and for the entire week the Leicesters spent at Montaigne Farm, the men in their slit trenches suffered a particularly uncomfortable time. Peter was already becoming familiar with the various types of shell fire. With normal artillery, they had learned that whenever they heard the report, they would count to ten and then brace themselves for the rushing scream of the descending shell. Mortars were even more frightening. They would hear the *tung, tung, tung, tung, tung* of five mortar bombs being dropped down the mortar, then would wait six or seven seconds until they whistled down upon them, counting each explosion and praying they would not be torn apart by a direct hit. The 88s, on the other hand, fired and arrived almost simultaneously. "This was easier to bear than the long drawn-out wait for the indirectly fired gun or mortar," noted Peter. During that first day at Montaigne Farm, Peter managed to find the time to scrawl a note to his parents, who had recently sent him a parcel of socks, soap, writing paper, and pajamas. "There is absolutely no need to worry about me," he assured them, "because we are living very well and having a fine time."[520]

Under a hail of high explosive and jagged shards of white-hot metal, Peter and the Leicesters held firm. The Germans reached the ground directly in front of them, but got no farther despite repeated infantry and armored assaults. It was during the defense of Hunt's Gap that Peter suffered what was his worst day of the entire war. From first light, the terrible sound of mortars being loaded drifted up to their positions. Peter was sharing a slit trench with Sergeant Ragg, and the mortars appeared to be falling almost vertically from the sky. Sustained mortar and shell fire rained down on them with increasing intensity all day. Whenever he thought they were being given a respite, the *tung, tung, tung* of the mortars began again. They couldn't move. They simply had to stay where they were and endure the repeated and relentless wait for each bomb and shell to explode. "By the end of a day of this form of torture," wrote Peter, "crouched in your slit trench, awaiting the coup de grace, you are literally gritting your teeth, clenching your hands together and tensing your whole body to avoid giving way to involuntary shaking." It was obvious that later they could expect another infantry assault, and sure enough, as darkness fell, flares were sent up and

showed the Germans readying themselves to attack. The artillery sent down
a withering barrage, however, after which one of the officers spoke through
a loudspeaker demanding the Germans surrender or face another heavy
blast of artillery. The Germans turned down the offer. The guns boomed
again, the ground trembling as the night was ripped apart by the ear-
shattering din and flash of fire. After this, the chance to surrender was offered again, and on this occasion, thirty Germans walked in with their hands
up, while the rest withdrew. The Leicesters were learning that when stout
hearts occupied properly dug-in positions and were supported by plenty of
well-trained artillery, it was very difficult for the enemy to break them.

After ten days of continuous action at Montaigne Farm, the Leciesters
were relieved by another battalion of the Hampshires. They were delighted
to be away from there, not just because of the intensity of the enemy attacks,
but also because the battlefield around them had become littered with dead
cattle, goats, and pigs, and the smell had been appalling. Their respite was
short-lived, however. After one day out of the line at Beja, they were hurriedly sent to help stem the northernmost enemy attack. In the early hours
of 11 March, without having had any kind of chance to recuperate, they
took over the positions of the 3rd Parachute Battalion on some high
ground amongst the dense cork forests near Temara. On their right were
Colonel John Frost's 2nd Parachute Battalion, who had already helped repulse two major enemy assaults since reaching the Cork Wood four days before. The contrast with the rolling grassland of Hunt's Gap could not have
been starker. Stukas and Focke-Wulfs roared and swirled above them, while
the sounds of rifles and machine-gun bursts could be heard from amongst
the forests around them. "It was like jungle warfare," says Peter.

For several days, he watched and listened as the battle in front of them
grew ever more intense. He was particularly in awe of the paras. "They were
superb," he noted, "aggressive and enterprising soldiers and officers who
fought with tremendous élan and made us feel very pedestrian in comparison."[521] During the fighting, Frost's Paras had managed to capture so many
German machine guns that each section now had an MG 34. The sound of
these weapons ripping through the forest made Peter think the enemy was
doing all the fighting. It was slightly unnerving.

The Germans attacked heavily again on 16 March, aiming their blow at
the French battalion on the left of the Leicesters. The Frenchmen were soon
overrun, and once their position collapsed, the Leicesters, and then the
paras, found their own positions were enveloped in turn, until they too
were forced to pull back, Frost's men covering the withdrawal to three bare
hills some four miles west, known as the Pimples. Peter Moore and his men
began taking up their new positions on "Leicester's Pimple" in heavy rain

during the night of 19–20 March. Spirits were low as they began hacking once more in the dark into the hard, wet rock. At first light Peter's heart sank even further when he realized just how vulnerable they were. "It was the highest feature in the area, completely bare of trees, scrub and rocks, just closely cropped turf," noted Peter. It was impossible to dig in properly. To make matters worse, they were told they had to defend it to the last man.

Having successfully covered the withdrawal from the Cork Wood, Frost's men were placed in reserve while fresh infantry battalions were brought up to the Pimples. The new arrivals came under heavy mortar attack, as did the Leicesters. For much of the day, Peter could barely move. "We could only lie on our stomachs and pray," he noted.[522] Sure enough, the enemy attacked again that night. Peter was very conscious of the order for No More Withdrawal, but after C Company HQ was over-run, it was clear this was an impossible order. Chaos ensued as the Leicesters began retreating down a narrow track leading away from the Pimple. Peter had no idea what was going on, but then grenades started exploding all around him and ahead of him he saw some German soldiers charging toward him shouting, "*Hände Hoch! Hände Hoch!*" "There was nothing for it," he wrote. "I was on my own. I turned and fled down the track, firing my revolver as I ran." Safety lay on the far side of a fast-flowing flooded river. Reaching the water's edge, Peter heard a voice say, "Who's that?" It was Tony Cripps, commander of C Company. Both agreed the river would be too cold and the current too strong to give them much of a chance. There was, however, a bridge a short way up-stream, and so inching past German troops, they crawled along the riverbank, frequently stopping and desperately holding their breath as enemy soldiers passed within feet of them. Once they reached the bridge, they couldn't be sure it wasn't already posted with Germans, so in the darkness they strained their eyes and listened intently. Since neither of them could see nor hear anything, they agreed to take a chance and hope for the best. The risk paid off. Tiptoeing across the bridge, hoping they wouldn't suddenly be exposed by the glare of a flare, they reached the other side and soon after found the remains of the battalion. Both Peter and Tony felt bitterly disappointed that Leicesters' Pimple had fallen without a fight. "At the time I felt ashamed of what I regarded as my own performance in not fighting to the last man last round, as we had been ordered," says Peter. "I did not question then the right of my commanders to put us in what I later realized were impossible positions. I was only aware that I was fighting for the honor of my regiment and that I had let it down."[523]

But Peter was being hard on himself. Moreover, the attack marked the limit of the German advance. The next day, the 1st and 3rd Paras managed to push the Germans back and retake the Pimples. Sedjenane might have fallen, but the more important Djebel Abiod had been held.

Peter had seen little of the RAF, but despite the continued bad weather, they had done much to support both the defenses of Hunt's Gap and Djebel Abiod. Two twenty-five Squadron was busy throughout this time. On 6 March, Bryan Colston had taken off on a Tac/R in poor weather and low cloud. His Merlin engine was already sounding below par when he dived on some enemy trucks. Flak opened up and he was hit in the tail, although this did not prevent him banking hard and turning back to strafe two German staff cars with his cannons. "I shall never forget one German machine gunner who continued firing at me as I attacked," noted Bryan. He could see the man, crouched over his gun; and saw him keel over too, raked by Bryan's bullets. "A very brave enemy," he added. But Bryan's Spitfire had now been hit in the engine as well. It was a nerve-wracking journey back. The damage to his tail had affected his elevators and rudder, but worse was the rising oil pressure in his engine, and he wondered whether he would be able to make it back to Souk el Khemis. "Had difficulty in the circuit," he recorded in his diary, "but landed safely. The aircraft was completely u/s." This was extraordinary understatement: with damaged controls and an engine that could seize at any moment, landing the Spitfire in such conditions was, to put it mildly, very, very dangerous indeed.

Rommel had been scornful of von Arnim's efforts, and particularly irritated to discover that fifteen of the nineteen Tigers that had gone into action had been lost—Tigers that would have been infinitely more effective in the open terrain of southern Tunisia. Now in charge of the renamed Italian panzer army was the Italian General Messe, like von Arnim a veteran of the Eastern Front. While the Fifth Panzer Army was launching its offensive in the north, Messe had been preparing a spoiling attack on Eighth Army.

There was sound reason for this. On Alex's request to support First Army and the Americans, Monty had hurriedly brought up both 7th Armoured and the 51st Highland Divisions from Tripoli to the border town of Medenine, some twenty-five miles south of the Mareth, but it had left him "off-balance," and meant he was running dangerous logistical risks. If ever there had been a time to hit Eighth Army and deal them a painful blow, it had been during the ten days these two divisions lay isolated at the front.

Fortunately for Monty, however, Messe had not been able to act quickly enough. Elements of 10th and 21st Panzer had been used by von Arnim in the north, and until they could be brought farther south, Messe was unable to attack. As it was, his plan was fraught with risk, and involved sending the

Afrika Korps around the Matmata Hills, which bordered the western edge of the Mareth Line. This would enable them to attack Monty's forces from the west and south around Medenine, while a mixed German-Italian group launched a holding attack from south of the Mareth line. Rommel was not especially enthusiastic about the plan but felt there was little choice; the alternative was to sit back and mark time until the full weight of Eighth Army was brought to bear against them.

The Desert Air Force were now in Tunisia. At the beginning of March, 73 Squadron were at El Assa, just six miles from the Tunisian border. Still on night-fighter duties, Johnnie Fairbairn was nonetheless having an easier time of late. They had discovered large quantities of Italian wine and after the long, dry trek across the desert, the pilots were ready to let their hair down. "Today blokes have been really getting their heads stuck into Itie wine," recorded Johnnie in his diary, "passing out like ninepins all day." They had also managed to lay their hands on a softball bat and a rugby ball. "The mess," Johnnie noted, "looks like a school sports day with all the events going on at once."

On 26 February, Johnnie felt the very first signs of spring. The icy wind had dropped and he spent much of the day sitting outside his tent soaking up the sun, and watching the day fighters roaring overhead. Camels grazed close by their tents, while at the nearby well, Bedouin Arabs and their children came and went, laughing, chattering, and paying the airmen very little attention. "Felt quite at peace with the world," he noted.[524]

There was no question that the Desert Air Force had control of the air in this corner of Africa, but the Axis air forces were still capable of turning up and spoiling the show, as Christopher Lee discovered shortly after 260 Squadron crossed over into Tunisia. He'd been standing on the edge of their landing strip gazing out into the distance when suddenly a loud explosion snapped him out of his daydreaming. Spinning around, he was horrified to see a gas pump bursting into flames. Four Me 109s were dive-bombing them. When another bomb landed only 150 yards away, Christopher began running.

The nearest cover was a small vehicle, so he dived underneath only to discover three others had had the same idea. Hastily getting to his feet again, he sprinted toward another. He hadn't reached it, however, before the blast of the next bomb hit him in his behind. "It was like being hit with a shotgun from thirty yards," he noted. "The stuff penetrated and stitched my trousers to my buttocks." Once the enemy planes had gone, Christopher staggered over to see the MO. After perfunctory treatment, he was standing by a truck wondering whether he would ever be able to sit down again when two senior officers approached. One of them was none other than the C-in-C Allied Mediterranean Air Command, Air Marshall Tedder. "What's all this bloody nonsense going on here?" he asked, then without waiting for a reply, added, "There's been an aerial attack." Christopher was then subjected to a grilling about precisely what had happened, but in truth, there was very little to tell. "And what were *you* doing while this was going on?" Tedder asked him. Christopher explained that he'd tried to hide underneath a small truck. "Kept them off, did it?" inquired Tedder.

"No, sir, I stopped a bit of blast," Christopher replied.

"Oh? Where?"

"In my backside, sir."

Tedder laughed, but for Christopher this somewhat humiliating experience had been no joking matter. "I advanced toward the enemy's last redoubt in North Africa," he wrote, "with my arse on fire."[525]

By 5 March, Monty had most of Leese's XXX Corps in place at Medenine, including the New Zealanders. Holding three miles of a new and hastily drawn front line were the Maori. Maiki Parkinson had been happy to be on the move again. Tripoli had been nothing special: a sun-bleached city short of just about everything and with a harbor that was only slowly being brought back into some kind of order. Nor had wharf fatigues been much fun. C Company also had a new CO—Captain Peta Awatare. "He was brilliant," says Maiki. "He could be a bad-tempered bastard, but he was a great company commander," and a most definte improvement on Pull the Pin.

The New Zealanders reached Medenine late on 2 March and the following day began digging in some three miles east of the town and facing west toward the Matmata Hills. Here the ground was still desert—rocky, sandy, and interspersed with rough vetch and scrub. Theirs was the southern flank of the line and their role was to defend the airfields and supply dumps building up behind them.

Also taking up battle positions were the Sherwood Rangers, although along with the rest of 22nd Armoured Brigade, they were being held in reserve, behind the Guards in the center of the line. On 4 March, they leaguered in a garden surrounded by oak, olive and fig trees and which was scented by wildflowers. As at Alam Halfa, Monty had ordered them to stay where they were and not be drawn out. Instead, a powerful artillery and anti-tank screen was drawn up, including Harold Harper's 107 Battery, and also including, at long last, some 3.7-inch guns, specifically to be used in the anti-tank role. The infantry were warned that should an attack come, they too were to lie low until the anti-tanks guns opened fire. These had been placed well forward with the aim of dealing with the tanks before they reached the infantry. Seventy thousand mines were hastily laid in the northern part of the line, but there were none in front of the New Zealanders, just a single line of wire.

"From air reports it appears that the Germans are going to attack from the north," noted Major Stanley Christopherson in his diary on 5 March. Monty had known the Axis attack would be launched the following day, although his intelligence had not known the exact direction of the assault. First light on the sixth brought with it a cold mist. Axis long-range artillery from the hills signaled the start of their attack, but the panzers were debouching from the hills cautiously, unsure in the mist exactly where the British positions were. Maiki Parkinson was in a muddy slit trench manning a Bren when he and his mate suddenly heard German voices ahead of him. Then the mist began clearing and there, rumbling down from the ridge ahead of them, were hordes of German tanks. At this, Maiki's mate fled, leaving Maiki to man the Bren on his own. Now that the mist was lifting he could see everything perfectly. His slit trench was on a slight ridge in the ground overlooking a wadi in which the anti-tank screen was waiting. He now watched more tanks spreading out in front of him, while lorried infantry followed up behind. Unsure whether the sergeant manning the six-pounder in front of him could see what was happening from in the wadi, Maiki yelled out, "Hey, Sarge! Tank coming!"

"What do you mean, you stupid bastard?" the sergeant shouted back.

"Tank!" shouted Maiki again. The 10th Panzer got to within four hundred yards of the New Zealanders before the Kiki gunners opened fire. "I could feel the ground shaking," says Maiki, who watched one then two tanks, blow up. A third was hit by a mortar bomb. "Lucky shot," says Maiki. "The shell went straight down the open turret."

The Sherwood Rangers remained behind the line all day. Several men were wounded by shards of flying shrapnel, but none of the injuries was particularly serious. Trooper Shewell broke his leg when his armored car went over a mine. He was an American who had volunteered to fight for the British, although had recently asked to join II Corps. "The Colonel has agreed," noted Stanley, "and has further promised that when we do join up with the Americans, he personally will take him over there in his jeep."

Maiki Parkinson barely fired his gun all day. "I just watched the shells scream over and the guns blasting away at the tanks," he says. All along the line, the story had been the same: the panzers had hit a wall of concentrated artillery fire. The only British tanks to be used had been a few Shermans brought up to help the 1/7 Queen's and who operated from static, hull-down positions. The 1/7 Queen's accounted for twenty-seven tanks alone. In all, Messe had lost fifty-two.

As night fell, the British pushed forward and further artillery fire made life difficult for the Axis recovery parties. "All attacks easily held," signaled Monty to Alex, "and nowhere has enemy had any success . . . My tanks losses are nil. All my troops delighted enemy has attacked Eighth Army, as it is exactly what we wanted."[526] Monty's crowing was understandable. The Battle of Medenine had been a disaster for the Axis. "The cruelest blow," noted Rommel, "was the knowledge that we had been unable to interfere with Montgomery's preparations. A great gloom settled over us all."[527]

The following morning, the Sherwood Rangers broke leaguer, and Stanley Christopherson sent out half his squadron to mop up. "They got one prisoner," noted Stanley, "who turned out to be a Pole but in appearance looked to be the usual blonde, well-made, thick-necked German." When later questioned, the Pole confessed he'd been forced to fight for the Germans, which was why he'd given himself up. He wanted to fight for the Allies instead. The recce party also came back with other trophies: a pair of coveted black panzer trousers, a pair of "Canadian bathing drawers, size 34, I suppose captured from the Americans," and a notebook with detailed drawings of American equipment. Stanley also noted his thoughts on the battle. The Axis had not properly reconnoitered beforehand, he thought. "This only goes to prove once again," he scribbled, "that the antitank gun will always beat the tank." Stanley and the rest of the Sherwood Rangers had reached the front the previous summer every bit as green and undertrained as the US 1st Armored when they'd reached Tunisia. Battle and the success of Eighth Army were making them wise to the ways of modern warfare.

Rommel had already asked Messe and von Arnim for appreciations of the situation. Both felt a bridgehead in the north—with a shortened front and with both panzer armies operating together—was their best chance now of maintaining a foothold in Tunisia, particularly since they were only receiving around 70,000 of the 120,000 tons of supplies needed to supply the 350,000 fighting troops they now held among them. Rommel agreed and so suggested to Commando Supremo and the OKW that Messe withdraw as far as Enfidaville and that they attempt to maintain a one-hundred rather than four-hundred mile front around Tunis instead. Kesselring was against this idea, believing the accompanying loss of airfields would prove disastrous. So too was Hitler, but only because it seemed to him that Rommel was going back on earlier assurances. With the defeat at Medenine and his new plans discarded, Rommel decided the time had come to take his postponed medical treatment. On Wednesday, 9 March, the Desert Fox flew to Rome, leaving Africa for the last time. It would now be left to von Arnim to face Allied forces that were growing in strength with every passing day.

* * *

Alex aimed to have the new command system up and running by 8 March. At that point, First Army would consist of the British V Corps, while the French XIX Corps and US II Corps would come under direct command of 18th Army Group. By that date, the Allied forces would be ready in their new positions and sectors.

Anderson was still in charge of First Army, but only just. Alex had also wondered why the front had not been shortened before the Axis offensive. As Churchill pointed in a letter to him, "Nobody cared about these places whose names they had never heard of until they were lost. A kind of false front manoeuvre might have been very clever."[528] Ultimately all decisions and responsibility fell on Ike, and he was the first to hold his hand up for what had happened at Sidi Bou Zid and Kasserine, but Alex was neither able nor willing to start pointing fingers at his new C-in-C. Furthermore, although Ike had guided Anderson with regard to his troop dispositions, he had been shocked to discover on the eve of battle just how thinly they had been spread. This had been Ike's first view of the extended front. Anderson, on the other hand, was forever traipsing up and down the front, diligence that did him credit. But like Ritchie before him, he should have known that by dealing in penny packets he was asking for trouble. He could—and should—have suggested shortening the front to Ike, but never did so. The similarities with Ritchie did not end there. As Alex also recognized, Anderson did not have the force of character to gel his troops together. Alex, like Monty, believed commanders needed to create an "atmosphere" in which staff and subordinates all follow the chief's firm and clear leadership. From the moment Alex reached Anderson's HQ, he knew this was lacking. He even asked Monty if he could spare Leese. Anderson's neck was saved only because Monty wanted to hang on to his XXX Corps commander. With US II Corps taken out of his control, Anderson was given another chance.

Fredendall's inadequacies as a battlefield commander had been glaringly revealed by the recent fighting, although for a while it seemed as though Ike intended to keep him in position as well. Even on 1 March, the supreme commander was writing to Fredendall saying, "There is no question in my mind of you having proved your right to command a separate and fairly large American force on the battlefield."[529] That was blatant nonsense; as Marshall had warned, Ike needed to be tougher with his subordinates. Alex would certainly have sacked Fredendall on the spot, but had refused to get involved in what he now considered an American matter. However, when Ike later asked him what he thought of Fredendall, he replied, "I'm sure you must have better men than that."[530] Instead, it was left to Ike's other senior American commanders to bring down the axe on the II Corps commander. General Harmon, on his way back to Morocco told Ike bluntly, "He's no damn good."[531] Later, he went further, saying Fredendall was a "common, low son-of-a-bitch," and a "physical and moral coward."[532] Equally unimpressed with Fredendall was Major-General Omar Bradley, Ike's old friend from West Point, sent over to North Africa by Marshall at Ike's behest, and now at II Corps HQ. On a visit to II Corps, Ike took Bradley aside. "What do you think of the command here?" he asked him.

"Pretty bad," Bradley told him.

"Thanks Brad," said Ike. "You've confirmed what I thought."[533]

Fredendall left II Corps in the early hours of 7 March. Back in the US he would receive a third star and a training command, but he never took to the battlefield again.

Three days earlier in Morocco, General George S. Patton had already been given the nod to take over II Corps. Ike had felt that if anyone could take the Corps by the scruff of the neck, gel it together, and turn it into an effective fighting force, it was Patton. Nonetheless, he had his reservations as well: Patton's impetuosity and disapproval of what he saw as Ike's cow-towing to the British were well known. Only a month before, Ike had felt obliged to write to him to warn him to "count ten before you speak."[534] Harry Butcher had recently spent an evening with him and Patton had told him how disappointed he had been not to have been given command of II Corps from the outset. "He felt he was the logical man to chase Rommel," noted Butch, "had a great desire to personally shoot Rommel, and had all the spirit that goes with the job."[535] Patton was to be denied this chance, but his appetite for killing Germans would soon be pressed upon every man in II Corps.

The other problem was that Patton was also already busy with preparing the newly formed US 7th Army for the invasion of Sicily. However, with Bradley as deputy corps commander, and with Patton's promise that he would behave himself, Ike felt the appointment of his old friend—albeit a temporary one—was a risk worth taking. Furthermore, on their first formal meeting, Alex and Patton appear to have struck some kind of rapport. "[He] was very friendly and complimentary in his remarks," noted Patton, "stating that [he] wanted the best corps commander he could get and had been in-formed that I was the man."[536] Shortly after, Patton wrote glowingly about his new British commanding officer. "What a man," he wrote to his wife when he heard about Alex's long life of soldiering. "I like him very much."[537]

By the middle of March, cohesion had been brought to the front. Succes-sive Axis offensives had been halted. Valuable experience had been gained and confidence was visibly increasing. In the southern sector, the Americans were recovering well. The Bowles twins and the 18th Infantry had said farewell to the British, and had been re-equipped with American uniforms, while Joe Furayter and the 5th Field Artillery Battalion had parted company with the French. All were now back with the Big Red One, while Bucky Walters and the 135th were also now together with the rest of the 34th Red Bull Division and in positions southwest of Fondouk.

Ray Saidel, meanwhile, had been posted to the 1st Armored Division. In the aftermath of Kasserine, the division badly needed to rebuild its strength. Ray was sent to Company G of the 1st Armored Regiment, and because of his machine-gun training back in the States, became a .30-caliber gunner on an armored half-track. "When I got there," he says, "we didn't have anything, not even a single half-track. But within two weeks we were completely re-equipped as a company and heading back through the Kasserine Pass."

Pinky Ward finally had the whole of 1st Amored under his command, while Hamilton Howze was thrilled to learn that Fredendall had been fired and replaced by Patton, a man whom he had known as a boy but also whom he greatly respected as a soldier and general. "He was profane and colorful," noted Hamilton. "More importantly, however, he was aggressive and bold . . . He shook up II Corps Headquarters by getting it off its behind and fining everybody for poor saluting or appearing without a helmet; he shook up divisions by telling them that he wanted to see more dead bodies, American as well as German."[538] Patton's new rules about dress and saluting applied to every man in II Corps, and included the wearing of ties and full uniform at all times. Despite what Hamilton says, this was, unsurprisingly, not at all popular with the men. As far as Bing Evans was concerned, Patton was a show-off. Ray Saidel was of much the same opinion. "He was just arrogant," he says. "Everyone disliked him." Bucky Walters agrees. "The infantry hated him. They didn't like him at all. We knew he was a glory seeker." The Bowles twins were more charitable. "He was OK," says Tom. But whatever the men thought of him, no one now doubted who was in charge of II Corps. "He spread the word almost immediately that there was now a new commander present," says Hamilton Howze, "and I think that had a very salutory effect on the Corps."[539]

In the British sector, the front was stabilizing once more. Lieutenant David Brown was still finding the art of gunnery of great interest. "I spend a lot of spare time improving myself as a gunner," he told his wife, then added, "I am very keen on promotion now, I reckon I've done enough at the gun end, and love being at the OP. I am due for captain fairly soon." He was rather enjoying the war: it was exciting and the comradeship was intense. His chief concerns were not his personal safety, but his personal discomfort: he now had boils on his hands and neck, infected scratches, and the rain was getting to him. For three days in the middle of March, it poured solidly on their positions and he got soaked through. "It makes life rather sordid," he wrote. Worst of all, however, was his hunger, a not uncommon problem for tall men like himself. The rations and meals he was given were never enough, and he found himself fantasizing over the food he used to get at home. "Wish I hadn't such a big appetite," he added. When his wife wrote to him about her role as the Fairy Queen in a pantomime, he replied wistfully, "Wish I had a theatrical late supper to look forward to," and then added, "Gosh I am hungry."[540]

For the most part, Captain Nigel Nicolson was also enjoying himself. He was good at his job: not for nothing had he been promoted. His situation reports—sitreps—were becoming famous throughout the Guards Brigade and beyond for their eloquence and incisiveness, and he never shied from going out into the firing line to gather information. He also found the task of interrogating German and Italian prisoners enormously fascinating, not least because it revealed that the Axis forces were vulnerable and decidedly beatable. The Italians, he wrote in a letter to his parents, were just as he'd imagined: "Hopeless, charming, loquacious, dirty and puzzled." One Italian was asked what he thought of Mussolini. "I don't like the Duce at all," he told Nigel, "because he stays in bed and sends me to the front." Another told him that his entire battalion wanted to desert, and would have, but most were scared the Allies would shoot them. "The Germans, of course, are much better," he added, although among their number were plenty of Poles, Yugoslavs, and even French who were generally reluctant combatants. "The Panzer Div is not, however, the unconquerable dragon that we had always imagined," he wrote, "and on one or two occasions I have seen it looking particularly foolish." Self-belief was vital as the Allies readied themselves for the next offensive.

Alex had given all his commanders—Anderson, Monty, and Patton—very clear directives. In the north, Anderson was to regain certain pieces of land, but would otherwise concentrate for the moment on holding the line and retraining. Monty was to break the Axis along the Mareth line; this next big offensive was to begin on 20 March. Patton was to retake Gafsa and the airfields at Thelepte, establish a supply base to ease Eighth Army's logistical problems, and, it was hoped, draw off some of the enemy troops from the Mareth line.

Alex was happy to give Monty an almost completely free hand in the planning of Eighth Army's operations, but decided to keep Patton on a much tighter leash. His reasoning was irreproachable. He knew the American commander was an indomitable fighter, but also believed he was "a horse that you had to keep a rein on—a dashing steed that always wanted watching."[541] The way to turn II Corps into an effective fighting force, Alex believed, was to give them achievable goals that gave them fighting experience and also built up their confidence. He was determined not to let Patton push II Corps beyond their capabilities and have them knocked back again, recognizing that another Sidi Bou Zid could have disastrous and far-reaching consequences. General Doc Ryder's 34th Division was to take control of the northern half of II Corp's sector toward Fondouk; Pinky Ward's 1st Armoured was to take Thelepte, while General Terry Allen's 1st Infantry Division were to capture Gafsa, and, if the conditions were right, the oasis of El Guettar, ten miles farther southeast. Under no circumstances was Patton to push beyond the Eastern Dorsale—not yet, at any rate. Predictably, Patton found such restrictions frustrating, but Bradley felt they were justified. "Better, I thought, that we learn to walk before we ran," he wrote later, "and I believe for all his tough talk, Patton believed that too."[542] Certainly his diary entries suggest this was true. He was worried about the state of his troops. He thought discipline was slack—as had Alex. "If men do not obey orders in small things," he noted in his diary, "they are incapable of being led in battle." The 34th Division, he noted, had "too defensive" in attitude. 1st Armoured was "timid." The newly arriving 9th Infantry Division was yet to be tested, but at least he thought the Big Red One was good. It was certainly the most experienced. "I cannot see what Fredendall did to justify his existence," he noted. "Have never seen so little order or discipline."[543]

By the middle of March, Alex had reason to feel sanguine. His air forces were operating well and his ground forces properly established, with the command structure now clear. The days were getting longer and at long last the rains were beginning to lessen. The time had come for the Allies to take the offensive once more.

CHAPTER 23

Left Hook:
17–31 March, 1943

LIEUTENANT RANDY PAULSEN was one of a number of officers and enlisted men who were transferred from the 3rd Division in the wake of Rommel's offensive. Randy was sorry to be leaving—the 3rd Division had been his home since graduating from officer school. He knew little of what had been going on in Tunisia, although like just about every other American on the planet he'd heard something about a place called Kasserine Pass.

When he eventually reached the Big Red One, he was none too impressed either. Assigned to Company F, he was taken over to see the company first sergeant, a huge, imposing man, a pre-war regular named Merrill. Merrill showed not the slightest interest in his new officer. "Sergeant," said Randy, "isn't it customary to stand to attention when you're speaking to an officer?"

Merrill eyed him and said, "I've been standing to attention longer than you've been in the army." Randy couldn't believe what he was hearing. "I thought, my God, what the hell kind of guy is this?" he says. Merrill then turned around and yelled, "Spinney!" Captain Spinney was the company commander. Randy was even more astonished. "I'm thinking, the first sergeant calls the company commander by his last name?" says Randy. "Jesus Christ, I thought, this is a great outfit." Spinney appeared. "What d'you want?" he asked Merrill.

"The new lieutenant's here. Where do you want him?"

"Put him in the weapons platoon," Spinney told him.

A little while later, Spinney appeared again and took Randy to see the battalion commander, Colonel Ben Sternberg. The colonel was wearing fleece-lined flying boots and walking with a cane because his feet had frozen. "You can imagine what I was thinking of the big First Division," says Randy, "where the sergeants don't pay attention to you, the company commanders do what the sergeants want and the battalion commander can hardly walk. I wondered what the hell I'd got into."

In the desert, new personnel were joining the 2nd Rifle Brigade too. Under the six-year repatriation rule, most of the remaining pre-war professionals were now being sent home, which left Albert Martin and the others in the class of 1940 as the senior veterans in the battalion. One of those leaving was Albert's great mate Paddy. He'd not seen England for seven years and rather than feeling over the moon at the prospect was decidedly gloomy, worrying about what he would find after such a long time away and whether he would find it easy to adjust to a more settled existence. He'd been so long with the battalion he could hardly remember any other kind of life.

The new replacements that had arrived were generally older too— not the fresh-faced, highly impressionable eighteen- and twenty-year-olds that Albert and his contemporaries had once been. Most were married, had left secure jobs and had joined up with less enthusiasm than Albert had done. It was the task of men like Albert, younger but wiser in the ways of war, to show them the way.

On 1 March, 2 RB finally dismantled the camp at Tmimi where they had been based all year and began the fourteen-hundred-mile journey to the front. It was a dull, cold day as they set off, with greatcoats buttoned, collars up, and groundsheets wrapped around them. "We looked anything but an army intent on victory," noted Albert. Eighty-five miles were covered that first day; ninety the next. Each day they managed between seventy and a hundred miles, over often rocky and difficult terrain, past Benghazi, El Agheila, then Sirte, and eventually Tripoli. And all along this epic route were the signs of battle and war: burned-out vehicles, stacks of lifted mines, shell cases, and rough lines of makeshift crosses.

By the time they crossed into Tunisia, thirteen days later, Albert was beginning to think gloomily of their imminent return to action. Rations had become short. They were all low on cigarettes and in need of a beer and a bit more sleep, and began grousing about the failure of the First Army and the Americans to wrap up the campaign already. On 14 March, they took over positions northwest of Medenine. The monotony of the journey was behind them and their minds once more turned to the job in hand. On his second day back at the front, Albert was told to lead his section to lay markers for a night bombing run on enemy artillery positions in the low hills to the northwest. Bearings were taken during the afternoon and empty ammunition boxes laid ahead of their positions where the markers were to start. Then in the early hours, they moved out, the platoon commander in a jeep and Albert and his section in a truck with a six-pounder on the back, and loaded up with a stack of four-gallon petrol cans cut in half and three jerry cans of petrol. They found the box markers and then drove along a straight bearing for exactly 1.2 miles—bringing them within 1,000 yards of the enemy guns. At this point they stopped and began placing the petrol cans in a stright line, six feet apart with a few inches of petrol in each. Then came the nerve-wracking part. The bombers were due in about a minute, so they could delay lighting the petrol no longer. Immediately they were lit up in the darkness. "I felt extremely vulnerable," noted Albert, "expecting any second a ferocious riposte." Leaping into their vehicles, they sped off, but to their relief neither shells nor bullets followed them. All they could hear was the roar of bombers overhead and shortly after, a mass of explosions.

Also now at the Mareth line was General Francis Tuker and his 4th Indian Division. He and his headquarters team had reached Medenine on 11 March, and at a meeting with Horrocks, he was told that once again "they" intended to split his division up. "In that case, I would like to be relieved of my command," Tuker told him. "I can accept this misuse of my division no longer."[544] The following day, however, he was asked to visit the army commander for tea, and as they sipped their brew, Monty told him that he'd put his foot down with Horrocks and wanted Tuker's division concentrated and to take part in the forthcoming battle. For Tuker, it was a minor triumph.

1/2 Gurkhas had already arrived ahead of the rest of the division, and had immediately been put to good use. Nainabadahur Pun found himself patrolling the Matmata Hills on a nightly basis, making the most of the Axis fear of the kukri. On the night of 14–15 March, Nainabadahur Pun, along with the entire battalion, investigated the El Djouamea Pass, a narrow gorge through the heart of the Matmata mountains. During that one night, they covered nearly forty miles and returned with a number of prisoners. The following evening, Nainabadahur Pun was out again, this time attacking a German machine-gun outpost. Not a single shot was fired: the Gurkhas had crept up silently and overrun the position using only their kukris. Nine Germans had had their throats cut, while the rest of the position ran off screaming into the night. Accompanying the Gurkhas that night had been George Lait, an American war correspondent, who then wrote up an account of the raid in gruesome detail. When the story ran in the US, the Gurkhas suddenly became news. "Why have I not been told of these Gurkhas before?" one American editor complained.[545]

The Mareth Line was based along the northern edge of the Wadi Zigzaou, a dried, and sometimes deep, riverbed, largely impassable to any kind of vehicle, even tanks. In places, its cliffs were sheer and as much as twelve feet deep, while along its northern edge was a long network of pillboxes, bunkers and connecting trenches, built, ironically, by the French before the war to keep the Italians out of Tunisia. Concrete gun positions covered every approach across the Wadi Zigzaou and stretched twenty-two miles into the Matmata Hills, a long and dense range of mountains that ran north-south and protected the left flank of the line.

Monty had begun planning his attack on the Mareth line weeks before Messe had launched his assault at Medenine and had been exploring ways to outflank the Axis defenses. The French had suggested there was no route through the hills that could be used by massed armor and heavy vehicles, but the intrepid Long Range Desert Group had found a way around behind the back of them. It meant a long 160-mile journey, but would eventually lead into a narrow pass, just a couple of miles wide, between the northern end of the Matmata Hills and the Djebel Tebaga. Beyond was the village of El Hamma, the gateway to the plains west of Gabes. This was the Tebaga Gap, and had been recognized as a key pass centuries before by the Romans. The remains of their fortified wall was now defended by the Axis, but Monty hoped that a left hook around the Matmata Hills and through the gap would draw off a large amount of Axis forces, especially armor, and bring his forces around behind the Mareth line where they would be able to cut off any retreating forces. For this task, he created the New Zealand Corps, made up of Freyberg's New Zealand Division, but also 8th Armored Brigade and a newly arrived French Force led by the inspirational and enigmatic General Leclerc.

The main assault, however, was to be along the eastern flank of the Mareth line and would be carried out principally by 50th Division. The aim was also to draw enemy reserves to this part of the line. As at Alamein, the main thrust was covered by XXX Corps, with the 1st and 7th Armoured Divisions of X Corps as a mobile reserve ready to push through any breech of the line.

General Leclerc's L Force of Free French had joined Eighth Army in Tripoli, where he had been welcomed by both Alex and Monty. Leclerc's was a remarkable story. As France had collapsed in June 1940, he had returned home to his family chateau outside Paris, collected his wife and six children and fled to their retreat near Bordeaux. His children had still been sleeping when, before dawn on 3 July, 1940, he had told his wife, "Courage, Therese. Our separation may be long," and had then set off on a bicycle to continue the fight against the Axis.[546] Managing to reach England, he joined de Gaulle, and immediately changed his name from Philippe de Hautecloque to Jacques Philippe Leclerc in order to protect his family. They had not heard from him since, although they had listened in complete ignorance to the exploits of General Leclerc and his Free French forces in Central and West Africa. In the autumn of 1942 he had been in Chad, and collecting together 555 Frenchmen and 2,713 Colonial and African troops, began the long march north across the Sahara to join Montgomery, clearing, with his meagerly equipped force, any Italians that crossed his path. It was a quite breathtaking achievement.

By 10 March, L Force had been reinforced with a handful of six-pounders, Bofors and a couple of Shermans and had clashed with a German armored reconnaissance force at Ksar Rhilane, fifty miles southwest of Medenine and behind the Matmata Hills. With the help of the RAF, L Force had easily seen off the Germans, leaving a dozen armored cars, guns, and forty trucks smouldering in the desert. They were still there, guarding the planned route of the left hook, and waiting to join the rest of the New Zealand Corps that was beginning to form up for their epic march.

The Maori, along with the rest of 5th Brigade, gathered ten miles southwest of the small town of Ben Gardane on 12 March. Maiki Parkinson had no idea where they were headed or what they were doing, but in the trucks with them were six days' rations and water, and petrol for six hundred miles. The New Zealand silver fern emblem had been painted over on all their trucks and equipment and they had been ordered to remove all cap badges and titles from their uniforms. From there the battalion was dispersed along a stretch of over fifty miles on the southwest side of the Matmata Hills, hidden and lying low in the hope that neither they nor the rest of the force would be spotted by the enemy.

On 13 March, Major Stanley Christopherson had been taking part in the brigade shooting tournament. For several days beforehand he'd hoped the battle would not begin before the competition, and he'd not been disappointed, although C Squadron had lost out to the Staffs Yeomanry in the Crusader category. For their efforts, the victors had won a whole sheep. Then the following day they received orders to head off to join the New Zealanders in the left hook around the Matmata Hills, traveling on transporters until the ground became too rough. The Sherwood Rangers arrived at their forming-up positions in the early hours of the sixteenth. By now there were 27,000 men, and many hundreds of trucks, tanks, and other vehicles scattered across the rough country of the southern Matmata Hills, waiting for the signal to begin their march north.

That same day, Private Johnny Bain had been involved in early sparring as the Gordon Highlanders took part in attempts to push the Italians back from their outposts among the minefields ahead of the Mareth line, an Operation labeled CANTER by General Leese. This was largely successful, and far more so than Operation WALK, the attack by the Guards Brigade on Horseshoe Hill, the one dominant feature along this stretch of the line. It was supposed to have been lightly defended, but had in fact been reinforced by the German 90th Light Division. Moreover the area around it was thick with mines. These had become increasingly sophisticated in recent months and were no longer just the old soup-plate and plunger style. There were long, rectangular Italian "N" mines; heavy Tellermines; paratroop anti-tank mines that looked like soup bowls; there were also the fiendish German "S" mines, filled with ball-bearings and which sprang chest high and then exploded; and limpet mines shaped like Chianti bottles. Some were now covered in plastic or wood and were invisible to mine detectors; others were designed to explode only after being crossed several times. Trip wires and booby traps were now so sophisticated that almost any object when touched might spell death. The two Guards battalions attacking Horseshoe Hill managed to gain most of their objectives, but not the hill itself, an important observation point. Inadequate reconnaissance and intelligence meant the Guards were slaughtered. Over five hundred men were lost. Later, over seven hundred mines had to be lifted in order to bury the corpses of sixty-nine Grenadier Guardsmen.

But despite their failure to capture the hill, Monty still intended Leese to launch his attack on the main Mareth line on 20 March, and for the New Zealanders to start moving toward the Tebaga Gap the day before. With a bit of luck, they would both push through to victory on 21 March.

A couple of hundred miles away, the Americans were beginning their march on Thelepte and Gafsa. Never one to be held back by political correctness, Patton had termed his operation "WOP." The new II Corps commander felt torn, however. On the one hand, he desperately wanted to be tested in battle against the Germans, but at the same time, he knew he'd not had much time in which to prepare the 90,000 troops now under his command, and was worried that they weren't ready. The best he could do was to try and boost their confidence and crank up their aggressive spirit by offering dramatic pep talks. "Our bravery is too negative," he warned them. "We must be eager to kill, to inflict on the enemy—the hated enemy—wounds, death, and destruction. If we die killing, well and good, but if we fight hard enough, viciously enough, we will kill and live. Live to return to our family and our girl as conquering heroes—men of Mars. The reputation of our army, the future of our race, your own glory, rests in your hands. I know you will be worthy."[547]

Whether this kind of rabble-rousing did spur his men into a state of fever-pitched aggression is unclear. Such talks certainly left no lasting impression on the Bowles twins, who cannot remember one word that Patton ever spoke to them, but certainly the American advance began promisingly. The Big Red One took Gafsa after an overnight march on 17 March and then headed on to El Guettar, which was taken by the Rangers the following day. The Axis had retreated almost without a fight, moving to positions just east of El Guettar among the razorback pink hills either side of the road to Gabes.

Colonel Darby then sent out patrols of his Rangers to locate the enemy defensive positions. Bing Evans was now a lieutenant, having received a battlefield commission, and was given the task of leading one of the patrols, while Lieutenant Walt Wojcik led the other. The key to the enemy position, they quickly discovered, was the narrow, rocky valley that cut through the hills toward Sened Station, known as the Djebel el Ank Pass. In places only a few hundred yards wide, it led to the mountain village of Bou Hamran, but funneled into it were large numbers of the Italian Centauro Division, with guns ranged and covering the Gafsa-Gabes road. On the first night, Bing and his men probed the enemy positions. "The whole night long, we repeatedly advanced until we drew their fire," he says, "then we withdrew into the darkness and pushed forward somewhere else." This showed Bing where the enemy were strong and where they were a bit weaker. "They seemed worried about my patrol," says Bing. "They had no idea we were just ten men." Just as important, they were acting as a diversion while Wojcik and his men worked out a route through the rocky slopes that would bring them into the rear of the Italian positions.

The following night, the Rangers moved in force along Wojcik's route through the mountains. It was six miles of rocky and dangerous terrain, but they were used to such nighttime marches by now, and in the early hours, the moon came out so that the jagged peaks were silhouetted against the sky and their way bathed in soft, milky light. At dawn they were all in position, overlooking the rear of the Italians' positions. As Wojcik had promised, the enemy guns, which they could see dug in beneath them, were all facing the opposite direction. The first rays of sunlight hit the jagged tops of the mountain behind them, and then Darby, echoing Colonel Frost's rallying cry, blew his bugle, and the Rangers, yelling and shouting like Dark Age barbarians, charged down the slopes, while others covered them with machine-gun fire. "They didn't know what had hit them," says Bing. Emerging from foxholes and tents, the stunned Italians were completely taken by surprise. Groups of Rangers sped from one gun position to another, shooting, knifing, and capturing over two hundred prisoners. At the same time, the 26th Infantry pushed straight along the road, and with the Italian guns silent, took the pass easily, along with over seven hundred prisoners.

A pall of blue-gray smoke now hung over the valley. The Rangers had not lost a single man in the entire attack. The 18th Infantry fared almost as well. While the Rangers had been stealing through the mountains, a few miles farther south, the 1st Battalion of the 18th Infantry had pushed forward over flat, mine-infested land with no cover, and at dawn caught the Italians napping once more, securing Hill 336, a key feature overlooking the Gafsa-Gabes road. Later in the morning, Randy Paulsen and the Bowles twins were in action with the 2nd Battalion, attacking with the 3rd around a long ridge running north of the road and overlooking Djebel el Ank. The confused and surprised Italians threw in the towel, surrendering in droves, and so the Americans, despite aerial attacks and heavier resistance, pushed on eastward, establishing a firm line along the foothills of the next ridge of mountains that ran north-south some fourteen miles east of El Guettar. They had lost just fourteen men all day.

While Bing Evans and the Rangers had been stealing through the mountains of Djebel el Ank, the New Zealand Corps had begun stealing around the Matmata Hills toward the Tebaga Gap. Maiki Parkinson noticed plenty of enemy reconnaissance planes. "They must have seen us all right," he says. Their efforts to remain inconspicuous were not helped by the French colonial troops of L Force. "Those bastards would shoot every time a plane came over," says Maiki, "even with rifles, the stupid idiots." He was not impressed. "They were rough, wild-looking bastards, unshaven and dirty." Nor were efforts to keep the left hook a secret helped by Howard Marshall of the BBC who reported on 23 March that "a British armoured column has out-flanked the entire Mareth position after a forced march of over 100 miles over the desert." Alex was furious. "This is very wrong after what I had told the press," he told Ike, "and makes one despair that they will ever have any sense. How can any intelligent man give out the whole plan as Howard Marshall has, without realizing that he was giving the whole show away?"[548]

Then one evening, just as Maiki's column was breaking their daytime leaguer to begin the nighttime march, they were strafed by American P-38s, who flew over them so low that Maiki could easily see the stars underneath the wings and on the fuselage. "Shit, their map reading was terrible," he says.

Meanwhile, the infantry of the 50th Division had begun Operation GALLOP against the Mareth line. Monty had left Leese to plan the details of the attack, which was a solidly unimaginative affair. The enemy defenses were formidable, both in terms of mines and firepower, and although reconnaissance and intelligence about the opposition along the eastern edge of the line had been excellent, Leese had announced his assault with the division's artillery firing a barrage that had little hope of causing much damage to the thick concrete gun positions overlooking the Wadi Zigzaou. To make matters worse, the armor supporting the infantry were obsolete Valentines, of which only one in five had a six-pounder gun; the rest were armed with two-pounders, about as much use against concrete as throwing mud. For some reason, Leese had not thought to use Shermans with their 75mm gun and ability to fire a mixture of HE and solid shot. To make matters *even* worse, the rain that had been pouring down in the west had run down the mountains and hills, making the dried-up riverbed not quite so dry after all, so that far from galloping across the wadi, the armor failed to clear the first fence. As a tank tried to cross a low point in the wadi, it sank up to its turret, blocking the way for any others. By daylight, only four more Valentines had made it across.

While the gallant infantry—almost to a man from the north and northeast of England—managed to take their objectives and establish a bridgehead, engineers worked all day to build fascines* across the wadi. As dusk fell, the Tynesiders, along with their four tanks, began the job of extending their gains, but instead of sending over as many anti-tank guns as possible with which to fight the inevitable armored counterattack, Leese ushered over more Valentines. By the time a further forty-two had made it across, the fascines were wrecked and the wadi once again impassable.

Then the rain finally reached the coastal areas, grounding the Desert Air Force, which had been ready and waiting to support 50 Division's attack. Through the rain, and the smoke and mist that hung over the battlefield, the tanks of the 15th Panzer emerged. They had covered a serious amount of miles in recent weeks, but this had little effect on their shooting: by dusk, over thirty outgunned Valentines had been knocked out of the bridgehead and all but pushed back into the mire of the Wadi Zigzaou.

Earlier in the day, Leese had asked Tuker whether some of 4th Indian's sappers might help build two crossings from a combination of fascines and steel plating. Tuker sent his 4th Bengal Sappers, 12th Madras Sappers and division miners. Amidst an ear-splitting din and torrent of bullets, they set about their task. Ramps were cut, fascines laid, and ballast spread, and then a steel roadway was laid on top. Before dawn the two causeways had been finished. Few people seemed to know what was going on. The congestion around the crossings, both that night and since the beginning of the battle, had torn wires to bits, while wireless radio had proved singularly ineffective. While more troops and—at last—Shermans and Grants arrived

---

*Fascines are bundles of sticks and other material used for filling in ditches or wadis such as at Mareth.

ready for a further attack, news reached them that there had been a change of plan. In the early hours of the morning, Monty had decided to call off the assault on the Mareth line and reinforce the New Zealanders with 1st Armoured Division instead.

It had been a busy few days for the gunners of the 7th Medium Regiment, RA. In 107 Battery, Harold Harper and his gun crew had been called upon to fire one stonk—bombardment—after another. They also came under heavy counter-battery fire themselves. On one such occasion, as the shells began crashing into their positions, Harold dived into a shallow slit trench. Suddenly he felt a terrific burning sensation coursing down his back. By then, he'd seen many dead and wounded men and as the fluid trickled over, he was certain that his time had come. But much to his surprise, a few minutes later he was still alive and when the shelling stopped, was able to pick himself up without any difficulty. He then discovered that the cookhouse nearby had received a direct hit. What had been running down his back was not blood, but a shattered tin of hot stew.

The Axis had also been hastily redeploying their troops. The left hook *had* been detected, and so Messe had ordered most of his German 164th Division out of the Matmata Hills to reinforce the Italians at the Tebaga Gap, where they were to be joined by 21st Panzer. They had not arrived, however, by the time the forward elements of the New Zealand Corps reached the entrance to the Tebaga Gap. The Sherwood Rangers had been among the first to make contact with the enemy, their tanks firing indirectly at the enemy artillery. Alongside them, New Zealand troops were also using captured 88mms, much to the delight of everyone who saw them. It was the first time the Sherwood Rangers had seen action without Colonel Kellett as CO. He had been promoted to Deputy Brigade Commander. His departure had been felt keenly; Kellett had become something of an institution, beloved by the men.

During the night the New Zealanders forced a path through the minefields at the mouth of the Tebaga Gap, but Freyberg had not felt confident enough to push his armor through in the darkness. By dawn, the chance of a quick breakthrough had gone. German troops had reached the Italians and had set up machine-gun posts and artillery and anti-tank positions on the high ground. It was a bitterly cold morning as Stanley Christopherson led C Squadron through the New Zealanders, only to come under fire immediately. "The shelling was extremely unpleasant," noted Stanley, "not only for ourselves but even more so for the echelons and gun positions in the rear. The enemy held wonderful observation posts." Stanley's tanks still managed to knock out a 50mm gun, capture some prisoners, and push out of the congested area around the old Roman wall, but having crossed a wadi, they got little further. "We came across a fairly intensive screen of 50mm," noted Stanley, "and it was pretty obvious the high ground was held." RAF tank busters roared overhead, and the valley became shrouded in an array of different-colored smoke and dust, from exploding shells, burning vehicles, yellow smoke signals put up by the British for the RAF, and pink smoke signals put up by the Axis for the benefit of the Luftwaffe. During the afternoon, they heard via the RAF that enemy tanks were maneuvering behind the high ground now in front of them. Stanley decided to climb out of his tank and lead some of his troopers on a stalk around this ridge. Unbeknown to him, a German tank crew the other side of the ridge had had the same idea. "As a result we both came face-to-face," noted Stanley, "had one quick look and beat a somewhat hasty and undignified retreat back to our respective tanks." Then news arrived that Colonel Kellett had been killed. Earlier in the morning, as his old regiment had been pushing forward, he'd been shaving in his tank turret when a shell burst nearby and he had been struck by a shard of shrapnel. His old regiment was stunned.

After their efforts at Djebel el Ank, the Rangers were taken out of the line. As they came from the mountains and headed back to El Guettar, Patton and General Terry Allen passed them on their way to the front. By this time, Bing Evans had four days' growth of beard, no tie, and a muddy and soiled uniform. "Patton stopped me and read the riot act," says Bing, who seethed with anger at being so publicly admonished. Fortunately Colonel Darby intervened. "Darby put Patton straight," says Bing. "He said, 'Look, General, this guy hasn't seen a razor, hasn't looked at water, hasn't had a chance for water. They've been fighting from mountain top to mountain top and you're asking him to wear a tie!' He backed off."

There was still much for the Americans to do, however. While the Big Red One was holding the new line southeast of El Guettar, Pinky Ward's 1st Armored Division were pushing forward to the north of the mountains toward Sened Station. Patton had wanted his armor to capture Sened on 19 March, but heavy rains had once again brought terrible delays. Patton himself had driven the forty miles to see Ward, but it had taken him three hours. "He is in a sea of mud," Patton noted on reaching Ward's command post.[549] Ward's plan was for a two-pronged attack, with part of his armor attacking Sened along the road from Gafsa while another part put in a surprise attack through the hills to the northwest. Ray Saidel was now a part of CCA, who were to attack along the road from Gafsa. It had been a tortuous journey down from Thelepte, and it wasn't getting any easier by 21 March. Their column had been attacked several times by enemy aircraft and once by their own P-38 Lightnings. When they heard the strafing at the back of the column, everyone in Ray's half-track jumped over the side and ran into the field—except Ray, who stayed on the .30 caliber and began firing furiously at the lead aircraft."

Also traveling with the column was journalist Alan Moorehead. He had accompanied the Big Red One to Gafsa and had been impressed with Patton and his pearl-handled revolvers. "Go down that track until you get blown up," Patton had told his ADC as they had approached the town. "The ADC set off in his jeep," noted Alan, and soon they were all trundling after him.[550] But he noticed more caution amongst CCA as they now struggled toward Sened. Alan was surprised to notice the alacrity with which the column halted and then leaped for safety the moment the faint buzz of aircraft engines could be heard. "Most of the vehicles were equipped with heavy machine guns," he commented, "and the men would have felt very much better firing them than they did taking cover among the wildflowers."[551] Ray Saidel agreed.

By the time they finally reached Sened Station late on 21 March, having struggled through mines and mud, the outpost had already fallen to CCC and a regiment of 9th Division's infantry. Opposition had been light, but the Americans had been able to notch up another minor victory, and their confidence was growing, just as Alex had hoped it would. He had already changed Patton's orders once. On 19 March, with Gafsa and El Guettar taken, he had instructed Patton to push on and take Maknassy, and then to send a light armored force through the Eastern Dorsale for a raid on the enemy airfields at Mezzouna. Alex was mindful that there was always balance to be weighed between responding to the changing demands of the Allied offensive, and not overstreching II Corps. For example, Monty had told Alex as early as 11 March, when outlining his plans for the Mareth Battle, that an American thrust towards Maknassy "would be of greatest value."[552] Now, however, with XXX Corps struggling along the Mareth line, he asked Alex for an even more ambitious effort from the Americans, suggesting they push through in force into the plains beyond Maknassy to cut the Gabes-Sfax road. Alex refused, but on 22 March, did change his orders to Patton a second time, telling him to prepare a strong armored force ready to push through to the plains should the situation change and warrant the risks involved in such a thrust. Patton was hugely disappointed, and saw it as a deliberate attempt to ensure that any Axis defeat remained a British triumph. This was absurd; no one could have been less of a glory seeker than Alex, and, within a few days, his decision to keep the reins tight on II Corps would be entirely justified. So far, the American offensive had been almost entirely against Italians. When the inevitable German reinforcements arrived, then Patton's men would be properly tested.

In the meantime, as Leese's attack on the Mareth line was failing, Ward's men marched on Maknassy, only to find the Axis had already left. His reconnaissance troops then discovered that enemy rearguards to the east of the town were holding the pass through to the plains. It is possible that a big effort might have dislodged them, but his men were exhausted, and mindful of Alex's orders, he called a halt. Certainly Ray Saidel felt that none of them in the 1st Armored Regiment were in a fit state to fight. They were still lagging behind the rest of the division, bivouacked halfway between Sened and Maknassy—and were to remain there for another three days, bogged down as the rain continued to pour. Streams were overflowing, their bivouac was sodden, and Ray, for one, was fed up. Most of their time was spent trying to dislodge tanks that had become bogged down. "We were out of rations for two days," he noted, "weak from the weather and soaked to the core. Everyone was miserable. Everyone was tired . . . Morale was at an all-time low."

Morale wasn't exactly at fever pitch among the British struggling along the Mareth line. "This battle's a mess," wrote General Tuker on 23 March. "It has been badly fought by XXX Corps and 50 Div. I've made up at least six plans of attack and not yet been put in and not likely to be for a bit." But although disappointed not to attack north across the Mareth line as had originally been the plan, Tuker was now given another task for his two infantry brigades. Monty envisaged another, smaller, left hook, this time through rather than around the Matmata Hills. No other troops in Eighth Army were better trained for such a task.

As Tuker had already planned for such an operation, he was able to get cracking right away. His 7th Brigade loaded up and set off through Medenine, before heading southwest towards the hills. They were to cross through the hills south of Kreddache, and then turn northward and double back down the Hallouf Pass. Meanwhile, 5th Brigade was to enter the hills from the east slightly farther north, and push straight through the pass. Tuker intended that the two brigades would then link up, having squeezed out any enemy forces, and push north together toward Techine, emerging behind the Mareth line through the village of Beni Zelten. He was anxious to get on with the job as quickly as possible: the sooner they emerged from Beni Zelten, the better their chance of cutting off the enemy from the Mareth line before it had a chance to escape through the Gabes Gap.

"But now came a sad disappointment," wrote Tuker. Just as 5th Brigade were entering Medenine on their way to the Matmata Hills, 1st Armoured were also passing through on their way to join the New Zealand Corps. "We had previously reconnoitered every possible way round that beastly village," noted Tuker, "and there was none." They were stuck, as hundreds of tanks, trucks, and other vehicles trundled through, and then were held up again as a brigade from 7th Armoured followed on the tail of the rest of the British armor. Tuker was fuming. The delay had cost him twenty-four precious hours, and so Nainabadahur Pun and the rest of 5th Brigade did not push into the mouth of the Hallouf Pass until the night of 24–25 March.

The Big Red One was now dug in along a twelve-mile line. In the north, covering the "Gumtree Road" that ran through the Djebel el Ank, were the 26th Infantry. In between, as far as the Gafsa-Gabes road, were the 16th Infantry and the 3rd Battalion of the 18th. South of the road, the ground rose again. Here, on the night of 22–23 March, the 2nd Battalion of the 18th Infantry was hurriedly moved across to join the 1st Battalion. This had been no easy task. The slopes here were so precipitous that guns had to be winched into position. Tom Bowles discovered that he and his colleagues in Company G had been given an isolated stretch of high ground on the Djebel Berda, overlooking another spur that lay on the northern side of the road. They immediately began digging in, but it was hard work on such rocky ground. Both battalions were expected to attack the Italian positions later that morning.

But as they were digging in, strange deep rumblings could be heard coming along the road from the east. Gradually they grew until it became clear they were listening to the sounds of engines. A mist had settled along the valley beneath them, so that even though the first sliver of sunlight was creeping over the valley opposite, Tom still could not see clearly what it was that was rumbling toward the American lines. Suddenly tracer cut across the sky, then more, followed by the deep, resonating report of larger guns. As the sun rose, so the mist cleared, revealing a valley full of tanks, armored vehicles, artillery, and trucks. The 10th Panzer Division had arrived.

Henry Bowles had barely started wiring between the various companies before the panzers formed up and began their advance straight on down the road. Both he and his brother now had ringside views as the Germans swept past in front of them toward El Guettar. Both the 5th and 32nd Field Artillery Battalions had been sited on Hill 336, captured two days before. At A Battery of the 5th Field Battalion, Joe Furayter was with his crew by their gun when news arrived from D Battery, a bit farther forward, that the enemy was coming. "They could hear all this rattling of tanks coming and the next thing they knew, they were looking down the barrel of a German panzer," says Joe. "They reported enormous amounts of tanks, infantry, trucks, self-propelled artillery—all kinds of things." Both artillery battalions immediately opened fire, Joe bringing up shell after shell. The enemy column then broke between the 3rd battalions of the 16th and 18th Infantry, rolling over their foxholes, then swiveling and crushing the infantrymen below. Those who were able to fell back, but it soon became clear that the artillery on Hill 336 was also about to be overrun. "We were getting low on ammo," says Joe, "and then the order came to abandon our guns. They were dug in and we couldn't get them out in a hurry." Having spiked most of their howitzers, the artillerymen ran to their trucks and hastily withdrew.

But just as the Germans threatened to repeat their slaughter at Sidi Bou Zid, so they came in for a shock. Having continued their surge forward, it was the panzers who had found themselves faced with a wadi running across their path. It was they who were being led into the trap of a well-prepared anti-tank screen on the other side of this ditch. The violence of the battle was ferocious. Round after round screamed across the narrow stretch of land between the panzers and the waiting Americans. Amidst the dust and smoke, eight panzers were knocked out as they struggled through the thick rows of mines laid across the Wadi Keddab. Another thirty were destroyed by the American tank destroyers and artillery. By midmorning, under cover of a hail of enemy artillery shells whistling down among the US positions, the panzers turned and withdrew. The Americans cheered to see them go, but they'd suffered heavily for their success: one tank destroyer battalion, for example, had lost twenty-four of its thirty-six guns.

Stukas continued to screech overhead, hurtling so close the Americans felt they could reach out and touch them, while enemy shells hurtled down the valley, exploding relentlessly as the defenders scuttled about bringing up more ammunition and reinforcements. Bing Evans and the Rangers were hastily brought into line along the Wadi Keddab next to the 16th Infantry. Meanwhile, the two battalions of the 18th, still on the slopes of the Djebel Berda, also braced themselves. They had become almost completely cut off from the rest of the division.

A radio intercept warned that 10th Panzer was preparing to attack later that afternoon, and sure enough, at 4:30 PM, a heavy attack by Stukas was followed by another assault. Again, the Germans came straight down the valley, with no attempt at concealment. This time, the panzers hung back behind the infantry. It was an inexplicable tactic from a division as experienced as 10th Panzer, likened by Colonel Darby, who was watching with his Rangers, to an attack in the American Civil War. When the Germans were within 1,500 yards, the American gunners opened fire, sending over one booming salvo after another. Black smoke as the shells exploded showed they were deliberately bursting before they hit the ground. They fell like flies. "My God," muttered Patton, who had been watching the German assault, "it seems a crime to murder good infantry like that."[553] For the second time that day, the Germans were forced to withdraw. At Sbiba, American infantry had helped repulse a panzer division. Now the Big Red One had done it again, but this time on their own.

Moreover, the Germans had only fallen back, however, not withdrawn entirely, and the following day, began digging in alongside the Italians and nibbling away at the American forward positions, especially along the Djebel Berda, where the two battalions of the 18th Infantry were still stranded from the rest of the division; the Wadi Keddab was some two miles to their west. Most isolated of all, however, were Company G, dug in on a different spur to the rest of the battalion. "We were on a peak about a quarter of a mile ahead of everyone else," says Tom. From his position he could see German tanks in the valley beneath him. "We couldn't go nowhere," he says. They were beginning to run short of supplies. In among the rocks there was a pool of water. When they'd first moved in, they'd used it for washing both themselves and their clothes. Now they were drinking it. Enemy mortars had been lobbing in amongst them ever since they'd arrived, but there were now German troops on their right overlooking them from the higher ground of Djebel Berda. Throughout the day, the mortar fire had been intensifying, every explosion spattering shards of lethal metal and rock splinters. "They were picking us off one at a time, for all of the time," says Tom.

On another rocky crag a short distance to the west of Tom was Company F. Randy Paulsen had also seen the German tanks in the valley below and saw that as dusk fell, they'd formed into a leaguer and had begun cooking on little fires. He reported this to Captain Spinney, who told him to fire on them. Randy pointed out that all he had was a few mortars and .30 caliber light machine guns. Spinney repeated his order. "Fire on them," he told Randy. So Randy returned to his weapons platoon and repeated the order. "Lieutenant, those are .30-caliber lights," his sergeant said, looking at their machine guns.

"I know," said Randy resignedly.

"You'd better dig in deep," his sergeant replied. Sure enough, the moment they fired, the Germans jumped into their tanks and swiveled their turrets around. Their shells soon found their range. "I lost two guns," says Randy.

By this time, over at Company G's positions, Tom Bowles's sergeant, Nels de Jarlais, had been wounded, so he and his friend Giacomo Patti, an Italian American from Brooklyn, decided they needed to try and get him out of there. It was evening, and the light was fading. Mortars and machine-gun fire continued to burst and chatter nearby. They picked their way carefully down to the aid station and collected a stretcher, then clambered back around the front of the hill. "Probably the only reason we weren't shot was because we were carrying the stretcher," says Tom, who could hear the strange sound of motorbikes in the valley beneath him. Having made it safely back to their positions, they were just putting the sergeant on the stretcher when word arrived from their listening post that the Germans had just about surrounded them and were about to attack.

By now it was almost dark. Since being in Tunisia, Tom and his buddies had noticed that darkness fell quickly, and in the time before the moon rose, the Germans often liked to carry out their attacks. So it was this night. Suddenly flares were whooshing into the sky, lighting up their positions, and troops from the 10th Motorcycle Battalion were clambering up the slopes beneath them yelling *"Heil Hines!"* "Don't know what that meant," says Tom. There was no question of getting the sergeant out now, however. Taking off the scarf around his neck, Tom rolled it up and and put it under Sergeant de Jarlais' head to make him more comfortable. "D'you think we can hold 'em?" the sergeant asked him.

"Yeah, we can hold 'em," Tom replied, then hurried back to his mortar. He would not see his sergeant ever again. Tom quickly began firing, but he had just thirty-six mortar bombs left. Enemy mortars were landing all about him, exploding with an ear-splitting din followed by the whiz and hiss of flying rock and shrapnel. The motorcycle battalion was getting ever closer to their positions. Tom saw one mortar land in a foxhole. One of the sergeants clambered out of his dugout. "Dees!" shouted Tom, "Don't go over there!" but his warning was ignored. Moments later another shell hurtled down, just twenty yards in front of Tom, killing both Sergeant Dees and the wounded man instantly. Then Patti hurried over. "The lieutenant says we're going to surrender," he told Tom. "Let's get out of here."

"When one of the officers says that," explains Tom, "you're on your own. You can do as you please." They scrambled over the rocks, slid down a small cliff and fell into a pool of water, but got themselves out and away to the comparative safety of Battalion HQ. "I never hated anything so much in all my life as leaving those guys up there," admits Tom. "And we had to leave the sergeant up there too. I still don't know whether he made it or not . . ."

His brother Henry, however, was unaware that Tom had managed to escape, and so with two of his colleagues set out to try and find him. He'd heard Company G had come under heavy fire all day and was worried about his twin brother. In the dark and with the rain pouring down, they scrambled up through the rocks toward Company G's position, then suddenly heard German voices. One of Henry's friends said, "Looks like we're caught here. Shall we give up?"

But it was dark and all three were wearing captured German ponchos, so Henry said, "No. Let's just turn around and head back the way we came." The ploy worked. Not a single German so much as spoke to them.

The following morning, Henry was back at battalion HQ when he was told to get a wire to Company E, so he and his old buddy, Blake C. Owens, gathered up another spool, and armed with a field telephone, began laying a line toward the Company E command post. The firing of the previous night seemed to have quieted down, but desultory shell and mortar fire continued to explode among the battalion positions. Henry and Blake were trying to cover as much ground as they could by scrambling along a small wadi, when suddenly they found themselves being shot at from the general direction of Company E's positions. Henry had a raincoat rolled up and tied on the back of his belt, so to begin with, he thought they must have been mistaken for Germans, with their raincoats looking like German gas mask canisters. "So I waved at them and they stopped," says Henry. On they went a bit farther, but then the firing began again, bullets pinging and ricocheting uncomfortably close by. Henry waved again, and once more they stopped. They scurried on a bit farther, but sure enough, the firing began again. They could see the shots were coming from some rocks just ahead of them, so they ran and dropped behind the safety of a large boulder, bullets whistling over their heads and pinging into the other side of the rock. Frantically, Henry wired up his phone and put a call in to headquarters. "We're trying to get to E Company up here," Henry told them, "but there's somebody shooting at us."

"E Company?" came the reply. "They've already left that position." Unbeknownst to Henry and Blake, E had been moved to higher ground in the early hours of the morning. "You better get out of there quick," they were told.

"We can't," Henry told him. "We're out in the open here."

"Just wait a minute, kid," said the man on the other end. "The artillery liaison officer's right here. You can talk to him."

The LO came on the phone and asked Henry whether he thought he could direct their fire onto the enemy position.

"I can try," Henry told him. Shortly after, two shells whistled over but landed short. "Raise up two hundred yards," Henry told him from his crouched position behind the rock.

"All right," said the LO, then added, "Now when you hear those shells coming in, you get out of there."

"And boy, when we heard that whistling we took off," says Henry. "The Germans still shot at us a couple of times, but we zigzagged down and managed to get away." Both men were later awarded the Silver Star for this action. "For escaping, I guess," says Henry.

Later that afternoon, the 1st and 2nd Battalions finally withdrew

from their isolated positions along the Djebel Berda. Although reinforced by the Rangers, they had not been gaining ground, and by midnight on 25 March were back in reserve in El Guettar. Tom's Company G
had been all but wiped out. A few others had escaped, but most had been
either captured or killed. The other companies had suffered heavily too,
since the offensive had begun. The loss of these crucial positions along
the Djebel Berda would come back to haunt General Patton in the days
to come.

Patton had been pleased to see the Big Red One beat back 10th
Panzer, but he was an offensively minded person, and more interested in
attacking rather than defending. What he really wanted to see was 1st Armored take the Maknassy Pass. He'd been annoyed that Pinky Ward had
not pushed on in strength as soon as he'd taken the town. In fact, he was
beginning to doubt Ward had enough drive and force of personality to
lead the division. During his attack on Sened, Ward had spoken to Patton
and told him he'd been fortunate not to lose a single officer that day.
"Goddamit Ward, that's not fortunate," Patton replied. "I want you to get
more officers killed."

"Are you serious?" said Ward incredulously.

"Yes, Goddammit, I'm serious," snapped Patton. "I want you to put
some officers out as observers well up front and keep them there until a
couple get killed."[554]

Early on the twenty-third, the pass was still weakly held, but just as
Ward's forces seemed to be breaking through, German reinforcements—
Rommel's former personal guard—arrived. Only eighty strong, this tiny
German force stiffened Italian resolve and kept Ward's forward infantry
battalion at bay. "Ward has not done well," Patton noted in his diary that
day. By now more German reinforcements were arriving—including eight
Tigers—and their position in the pass strengthened with every hour. By
evening on 24 March, 1st Armored still hadn't forced their way through,
and when Patton found out, he rang Ward and told him to personally lead
the attack the following morning on a crucial hill that overlooked the
pass, and to not come down again until he'd captured it. "Now my con-
science hurts me for fear I have ordered him to his death," noted Patton,
"but I feel it was my duty."[555]

Pinky Ward did not die, but as they were approaching the crest of the
hill, he was wounded in the eye. Covered in blood, he crawled back down
the hill and continued to direct artillery fire, but the summit could not be
held. Shortly after, he called off the attack. Both Bradley and Robinett
met him at his command post and were somewhat shocked at his appearance. Dried blood caked his face, while across his back was a narrow red

line where he had been seared by a bullet. "I think I have made a man of Ward," noted Patton later.[556]

CCA had not been involved in the attack on the Maknassy Pass, but on 25 March, were brought out of their bivouac area and told to protect the northern flank of the division along the Wadi Leben, a few miles south of a small mining town called Meheri Zebbeus. Ray Saidel and his half-track crew drove down into their new positions in broad daylight, and clambering out of their vehicles, started digging in. Shells soon screamed toward them as the enemy artillery adjusted their range. "Unfortunately for us," noted Ray, "our artillery was in the same wadi and it drew counter-battery fire and bombers like molasses does flies." Around noon on his second day there, Ray was catching a brief nap when he was woken by the sound of machine-gun fire. Looking up, he saw twelve Stukas peeling off for their dive directly above him. "Yeah, I was scared," he admits. He started to run down to the bottom of the wadi where there was a slit trench but had only gotten halfway down when the first bomb landed about twenty-five yards away. Ray flattened himself into the ground, but several pieces of shrapnel cut holes through the top of his helmet. "How I escaped being hit is beyond me," he noted. As soon as the Stukas had gone, he immediately set to work deepening his gun post so he could get greater elevation. When twelve Ju88s roared over later that afternoon, Ray was ready, and poured 250 rounds into them. "I could see that they were going right in," he noted.

The Wadi Leben was, in fact, a number of dried river channels, which gave CCA a natural network of wide trenches. Machine-gun posts had been set up along the Americans' main defensive positions, but every night, MG teams were sent forward and set up overlooking a further wadi several hundred yards in front of them. This was to protect their principal line from a potential night infantry attack. In addition, listening posts were also sent out, beyond the nighttime machine-gun positions. Teams of two would slither forward a couple of hundred yards and lie down close to the Axis front line. While one strained into the darkness and listened, the other tried to sleep. Then they would swap roles until, just before first light, it was time to scamper back again.

During the day, back in their main positions, only one post in three would be on duty, while the other two teams slept and rested. "I pulled MG posts most nights," says Ray, "and listening posts on others." It was impossible to ever sleep properly, however. Nuisance shells would be sent over at least every two hours, just to keep them awake. Ray and Sergeant Lowrey found this intensely frustrating, and felt they should do something—anything—to try and get those guns. After talking it over, they hatched a plan for the two of them to creep out into no-man's-land and see what they could find out. Initially their plan was dismissed out of hand; although night patrols were widely used by the infantry, CCA was inexperienced at holding a static line and not so ready to adopt tactics and techniques that were normally accepted as run of the mill. However, a couple of days later, Ray and Lowrey were summoned to the Command Post and told to get themselves ready to go out on their planned patrol. Their orders were to head about a mile to their right where the 16th Engineers were based. There they would find a railway line that led to the mining town. They were then to head along by the railway and try and find out where the enemy's forward positions were. "But don't engage them," they were told. "Just find out where they are."

Having armed themselves—in Ray's case, with a Tommy gun, a borrowed .45 revolver and a number of grenades—they set off. The engineers were holding an iron bridge that had been blown up and which had collapsed into the wadi. Having reached the sappers, Ray and Lowrey quizzed them about minefields and asked them not to shoot when they came back. Then off they went, down into the wadi, then along for about thirty yards before clambering up the other side into enemy territory, the railway on their right. No matter how quietly they moved in that still, dark night, Ray thought they were not being quiet enough. Every noise seemed horrendously amplified. The water in his canteen was swishing about, so he got rid of it. Then the strap on his Tommy gun seemed to be chinking against something. He threw that away too. They had gone about three hundred yards when they heard voices, so they flattened themselves on the ground and waited. After about an hour, and with nothing stirring, they got going again, pushing forward another hundred yards or so. Suddenly they heard more voices and the chink of metal directly in front of them. Ray and Lowrey froze, then lowered themselves to the ground. Directly in front of them, only about twenty-five yards away, was a German machine-gun post.

Ray had his Tommy gun ready and silently prepared his grenades, but after a couple of hours' lying there, he heard the Germans changing their MG team, so leaned over to ask Lowrey what the time was. As he did so, their helmets chinked. "Boy, they were on the ball," says Ray. "Almost at the same instant a green flare went up right over us." Ray pushed his head down into the ground and prayed. "There was no cover, nothing."

Miraculously, they were not spotted, but they knew they needed to get out of there soon because the moon was due to rise and when it did, they would be silhouetted into the easiest targets imaginable. "After another half hour, we just stood up and gradually walked away," says Ray. When they'd inched back about fifty yards, they quickened their pace, eventually reaching the wadi again, and hoping their own MG posts wouldn't cut loose. They didn't, and the two of them were able to calmly make their way back to their lines.

After they'd reached their own positions and reported their limited findings, Ray suddenly felt absolutely exhausted. "The suspense was worse than being fired at," he scribbled in his diary. "Every second of those hours was packed with more than ten years of normal life!!"

Meanwhile, further south, Eighth Army was preparing to launch its main assault on the Tebaga Gap. Horrocks had reached the New Zealand Corps ahead of the rest of his armor and was coolly received by Freyberg, who not surprisingly resented having the X Corps commander breathing down his neck. Although Monty had not put either one of them in charge, together they managed to draw up some plans, which they then sent off to the army commander. All were rejected, because in the meantime, Monty had accepted a plan by AVM Broadhurst, now commanding the Desert Air Force, who was proposing to take Mary Coningham's air doctrine one stage further by saturating the Tebaga Gap with his entire bomber force, followed by reams of low-flying fighter-bombers. Working in conjunction with the artillery, they would effectively become part of the barrage, and help to blast a way through for the infantry and armor. Both Freyberg and Horrocks thought the plan worth trying, but made it clear they would not be ready until 26 March, a day later than Monty had hoped.

By evening on the twenty-fifth, most of Horrocks's force had reached the Tebaga Gap, despite a fraught and uncomfortably hurried journey. Among those at the rear of the column were 2 Rifle Brigade, and as far as Albert Martin was concerned, the journey had been one of the most uncomfortable of his life. Progress had been painfully slow, partly because of congestion and partly because of the very difficult terrain over which they were traveling. Albert found their surroundings "a confusing mixture of desert and fertile plains between dominant hills, some with sheer cliff sides; then wadis steep, deep and strewn with boulders that defied intrusion by either wheeled or tracked vehicles."[557] The flat, featureless desert of old was now behind them for good.

The riflemen may have been cursing their slow progress, but the fact that so many men, guns, and armor had reached the Tebega Gap was no small achievement. The Maori had not been in the initial attack on the Gap—that had been left to 6th Brigade—but on the eve of battle on 25 March, they were told they would be leading the right flank of the infantry assault. The Maori company commanders had all been to Brigadier Kippenberger's briefing, and Peta Awatare returned and told his men the plan. "Peta came round and said, 'You know what, we're going to attack to-

morrow afternoon,'" recalls Maiki. "I thought, shit, we're in for a pounding. It was the first daylight attack I was to be in and I wasn't happy about
it." Their attack was to be preceded by the heaviest air assault ever attempted by the Desert Air Force; the enemy would have to return fire with
the sun in their eyes, and the infantry would be advancing with the tanks
of the 8th Armoured Brigade, but Maiki would have gladly foregone all
these advantages for the protective darkness of night.

The Maori moved up to their start line overnight. Broadhurst's preliminary air assault began with his entire night-bombing force pounding
the enemy positions. Albert Martin, some miles in the rear, heard the explosions of their bombs as he got his head down for his first proper sleep
in forty-eight hours. He found the sound relaxing rather than disturbing,
knowing they were for the enemy and not him. There was no chance of
sleep for the forward troops, however, as bomber after bomber roared
overhead and the earth shook with each explosion.

Dust was being whipped up through the valley by the khamseen blowing in from the south as the Sherwood Rangers trundled forward around
the Roman wall to their start line a couple of hundred yards farther on, directly in front of the Maori. The 28th (Maori) Battalion were now lined up
in their battle formations. A and B Companies were to lead; C Company to
follow behind, mopping up. The aim was to penetrate some three miles, although they were to pause roughly halfway, at the foot of a gentle rise in the
ground known as Point 209. This was then to be taken by C Company, with
D Company following behind to help.

Just before 3:30 PM, the Tebaga Gap was quiet, save for the occasional whistle and thud of shell fire. Then, at half past three exactly, orange flares denoting the forward lines of the infantry and armor
whooshed into the sky. Moments later, droves of bombers roared over,
carpet bombing the enemy positions, which disappeared in a cloud of
thick dust and smoke. Following behind was the first relay of fighter-
bombers, swooping in at zero feet, dropping their bombs and then strafing anything that moved. Wave after wave arrived and tore up and down
the valley so that there were always at least two squadrons of fighters over
the area at any time. Duke Ellington and the boys of the 57th Fighter
Group were among the squadrons used in this way. There was little opposition from the Axis air forces, but by flying so low, they were dangerously exposed to flak and small-arms fire; most of the fighters that made
it back did so with bullet holes and flak damage riddled all over their aircraft. Duke had been flying low along the deck when he was hit and saw
a huge hole in one of his wings. Hurrying out of the fray, he headed for
the coast and out to sea. As soon as he was sure he was behind British
lines, he turned back in and landed at an RAF resupply unit. "When I

landed," says Duke, "the British sergeant took a look at my bird and said, 'Damn Yank, you've got a problem here.'" His P-40 Warhawk was also gushing fuel from a ruptured tank—he had been extremely lucky not to run out of fuel over the sea. To his surprise, the sergeant asked him whether he wanted another plane. Eager to get back, Duke jumped at the chance. The cockpit was configured slightly differently for British use, but Duke quickly got his bearings and set off to join the rest of the 57th. By now he'd been missing for several hours and was presumed to have been shot down. "My appearance," says Duke, "with a new plane was hard to explain."

At four o'clock, two hundred field and medium guns opened their barrage, and the three battalions of the 8th Armoured Division and three battalions of Kiwi infantry began their advance. On the right, Major Stanley Christopherson moved off, leading his squadron of Crusaders, while behind him Maiki Parkinson started to walk forward. The barrage was lifting at a rate of one hundred yards per minute for the first 1,000 yards, and Stanley found this an extremely uncomfortable experience: the great strength of the Crusader was its speed, but now they were moving at a snail's pace. Ordnance was flying everywhere, screaming and whistling overhead. Ahead of them was nothing but smoke, dust, and explosions, but this did not stop the Axis artillery firing shell bursts through the barrage and over the tanks.

The attackers reached the first objective without too much difficulty, a number of the Maori catching rides on the backs of the Sherwood Rangers' tanks—although not C Company, who soon found themselves falling behind. As they pushed forward, there was plenty of evidence of a hasty retreat: paper flapped in the wind, abandoned trucks lay in perfectly good working order. There was even an enemy regimental aid post, although no sign of any patients left behind. Then as the forward tanks and leading companies reached the rise of Point 209, they were forced to bunch up as they veered around to the left side of it. Suddenly, concealed anti-tank guns opened fire. B Squadron, to Stanley's right, bore the brunt, three Shermans blowing up in quick succession. Maiki also saw the tanks get hit. "They knocked their turrets clean off," he says. Stanley raked the positions with his machine gun and main gun and even lobbed grenades as they rumbled past, but enemy fire continued. "They were sitting pretty in the hills," says Maiki, who was stumbling forward into a shower of bullets and razor-sharp shards of metal. He saw a number of men fall nearby. "That's me done," said one man close by Maiki, and then dropped dead. He watched another Maori fall, then another, but as they took cover at the base of the rise, his section was miraculously still in one piece.

For a short while they paused as they braced themselves for the assault.

It was now clear that what they had thought was Point 209 from the start line was actually only a lower rise of the feature; the hill, in fact, had two significant rises and was thus much deeper and more heavily defended than they had thought; their view had shown them a false summit. Along the other side of the valley, the advance stumbled on with the rolling barrage, leaving the Maori, and C Company in particular, to take out the hill. And they would have to do it alone: the artillery was supporting the main attack. "Nor was there a smokescreen," says Maiki. "I couldn't understand why not, because it had worked so well at Alam Halfa."

Peta Awatare quickly organized his men. The 13 Platoon were to work their way around the hill to the right, 14 Platoon to the left, while 15 Platoon—including Maiki and his section—were to head straight up from where they were toward the summit. The lower slopes were comparatively steep and rocky, and the enemy machine-gunners dug in at the top of the first rise were unable to get an angle on the Maori below them. "That's probably what saved us," says Maiki. He could see tracer pouring down over their heads from an MG post on the ridge immediately above them. For the moment they were pinned down where they were. Maiki turned to Paul Te Kani, his section leader, and said, "Have you got a grenade? We can get this bastard. If we crawl up round the side here, he won't see us." But Paul didn't have one. They could hear fighting just to their left where Lieutenant Ngarimu and his platoon were attacking another German position. Mo Ngarimu had already taken out two MG nests single-handedly and his men another two, and had cleared their side of the first ridge. They were now pinned down on the slopes below Point 209, while Maiki and the rest of 15 Platoon were still stuck below the first ridge.

By now it had begun to get dark, and then suddenly someone hollered out that the Germans were coming down the hill toward them. "We thought they were attacking us," says Maiki, so when they appeared Paul opened fire with the Bren. "He cut them down," says Maiki, "only when we looked at them, we realized they had no guns." They'd been coming down to surrender. One of them, a young lieutenant was crying and calling for his mother. "The tears were running down his face," says Maiki. "Christ, it was awful. I took off my great coat and laid it over him, but he died later in the night."

In the heavy fighting above them, the Maori had suffered heavily for their gains. Among the casualties, Mo Ngarimu had been wounded twice, and Peta Awatare once in the leg. Both refused to go down to the regimental aid post, insisting they stay with their men, but Awatare's leg got so bad that after organizing their defenses, he finally relented and Lieutenant Jackson of 13 Platoon took over. Scrabbling back down to 15 Platoon, he said, "Right, one of the Bren gunners go and give Mo a hand." Paul and Maiki volunteered.

Moving around to their left, they were clambering up the slopes where Ngarimu's men had advanced when the enemy started lobbing mortars instead. One landed right in front of Maiki and Paul. Maiki was cut above the eye and in the crook of his arm, while Paul was hit in the leg and on his trigger finger. Blood was running over Maiki's eye and down his nose, and both were cursing. "Shit, we've got to get out of this, Parky," said Paul. But the mortars were still dropping behind them, barring their way. "We can't, we'll have to keep going," Maiki told him, so they continued to scramble up the slopes until they saw a machine-gun nest twenty yards in front of them that hadn't already been destroyed by Mo's men. Paul sprayed it with the Bren, and then they dropped to the ground. Maiki called out in Maori, "Are you there?"

"Who's that?" replied Ngarimu.

"It's Parky and Paul," shouted Maiki. "We've come to give you a hand."

"What I need is ammo and grenades."

By now the mortars had quieted down, and so they clambered back down again and told the Battalion Sergeant-Major that Mo was in urgent need of ammunition. "All right," he told them, "I'll see to it."

Paul and Maiki were still bleeding, so Maiki said, "Let's get the hell out of here. We've done our bit." Paul agreed, and finding some rocks at the foot of the hill they sat down and rested.

The rest of the advance had reached its objective, with the tanks of the 1st Armoured pelting through 8th Armoured Brigade around six o'clock that evening. By 7:30 PM, they had broken through 21st Panzer and were some four miles down the valley. The Sherwood Rangers had halted as darkness fell, but could see there was still fighting on Point 209 behind them and to their right; the situation still seemed to be confused. Stanley Christopherson felt they had done well, though, having accounted for six tanks, and two 88mm and 50mm guns. A number of men had been killed, however, including Stanley's friend Sam Garrett, another stalwart of the regiment.

Meanwhile, on Point 209, the Germans had launched a counterattack on Mo Ngarimu and his men. This had been thrown back, as the Maori threw their last grenades. Over the screams of the German wounded, the Maori started chanting *E koe*, their traditional taunt for when a wrong had been requited. Another assault was also repulsed, Ngarimu rallying his men once more and hurling stones now that they had run out of grenades. Then, just as the Germans were about to withdraw for good, Ngarimu was killed, shot while leading his men forward once more. For his extraordinary heroics that night, Mo Ngarimu was awarded a posthumous Victoria Cross.

The Sherwood Rangers eventually leaguered, as they'd been ordered, along their final objective, some two miles from the start line. It was an uncomfortable place to spend the night. Fires from burning tanks flick-ered, silhouetting them against the night. Nearby was a knocked-out Ger-man tank, whose headless commander hung limply from the turret. In the darkness they could hear the rumble of a tank engine and so expected a counterattack any moment. Only at dawn did they realize they'd been listening to another casualty of the battle. With its engines still running, a lone Mk IV was idling where it had stopped, its crew all dead. The rising sun also revealed to the astonished Sherwood Rangers the sheer levels of destruction achieved the previous day. Across the battlefield lay the wreckage of blackened and contorted tanks and vehicles, and among them the bodies of the many dead.

With dawn, the Maori were at last able to get some help from the ar-tillery, which was soon directed onto the German positions. A smokescreen was finally used so that C Company and D Company could change places. Both sides continued to exchange fire, but the Germans had had enough. First sending some men forward to request urgent medical aid, they soon after surrendered entirely. Around noon, a long procession wound its way down the hill, some walking, others in the arms of comrades and a number on stretchers. The bloody and bitter fight for Point 209 was over.

The rest of the Battle for Tebaga Gap was over too. The 1st Armoured were now just three miles south of El Hamma, although they were unable to push on through and take the town as planned. Bad weather, blowing dust storms over the plain, plus a hastily cobbled-together anti-tank screen from the remnants of 15th and 21st Panzer and the 164th Light Divisions, halted the British tanks. It was here that Albert Martin and the 2 Rifle Brigade faced their first serious engagement since returning to front-line action. Earlier they'd passed through the debris of the battle at the rear of the ar-mored column. During a brief pause, Albert had added to his collection of booty as he and his mates scavenged pistols, binoculars, and Iron Crosses. Then they found a black metal document box. Prizing off the padlock they discovered it was full of Bank of Tunis notes. Looting was considered fair game by both sides, but nicking a pay box was a different kettle of fish, so over a quick cup of tea, they pondered what they should do. With hot tea inside them, they eventually decided to keep it—after all, who was going to know?—so divided it out between them, each man ending up with a thick wad of notes in his backpack.

Now south of El Hamma, the riflemen were coming under uncomfort-ably close shell fire as they set up their six-pounders and began firing in re-turn. For another day, Horrocks' forces were held up, by which time Messe had begun withdrawing his forces from the Mareth line. Few can have been more disappointed than General Tuker. His Indian Division had been fighting hard in the Matmata Hills. Nainabadahur Pun had found himself fighting an elusive enemy. No sooner did they overcome one rearguard than they found their progress slowed by collapsed roads, mines, and booby traps. By the time they finally emerged through Beni Zelten and onto the plain north of the Mareth Line, the enemy had gone. They had performed well, however; Tuker had reason to be proud of his men. But as he'd feared, the delay in Medenine had cost them. "This operation was put on forty-eight hours too late at least," he noted bitterly. "We've missed him after all our sweat and trouble."

Earlier on 25 March, Alex had visited Patton. He still believed the American commander needed to be closely controlled, but the developing situation required another change of orders. With the success of the Big Red One and with Monty's main thrust now coming through the Tebaga Gap, Alex felt it made sense for II Corps to try and push on down toward Gabes. He hoped that by releasing the 9th Infantry Division to support the Big Red One, they might be able to clear a now weakened enemy from the mountains running east from El Guettar, and then send the 1st Armoured down to cut off the enemy as they retreated from the Tebaga Gap.

Patton drove up to 1st Armoured's HQ near Maknassy on 27 March to explain the new plan to Ward. He also wanted to see their forward positions. Lieutenant-Colonel Hamilton Howze was assigned to guide him. With Hamilton in a jeep and Patton in a glaringly conspicuous command car, they drove toward the front until they were stopped by engineers clearing mines. Hamilton walked over to Patton's command car and explained they could go no farther.

"To hell with that," Patton told him. "Let's go. Ham, lead the way!"

"I figured this was possibly my last act," noted Hamilton, but on they went, past the astonished engineers. A light tank then joined them and shortly after duly hit a mine. Much to Hamilton's relief, this finally persuaded Patton to have a change of heart, and very gingerly they turned around and went back the way they'd come.

Patton's attack down the Gafsa-Gabes road was finally launched on the night of 28–29 March. The 1st Division, including the 18th Infantry, pushed the enemy back down the Gumtree Road that led from Djebel el Ank, but could not take the high point that overlooked the Gafsa-Gabes road. This was where the 9th Infantry attacked and their inexperience soon got the better of them. In the dark, they assaulted the wrong objectives and discovered, as many Allied troops had before them, that prizing out German troops from strong positions was an extremely difficult task. With no immediate breakthrough, but sensing there was still a chance that an eastward thrust by the Americans might force the Axis to quickly abandon their next line of defense north of Gabes, Alex decided to order

II Corps to make another push from El Guettar, and so changed his orders for a fourth time. This time he instructed Patton to bring some of his armor down from the Maknassy area to El Guettar, and from there launch a lightning armored raid, supported by the 9th Infantry, in one last effort to break through to Gabes. But it wasn't to be. Much to everyone's frustration, 10th Panzer fell back just 5,000 yards and then held fast.

The enemy had slipped away again. While the Americans were being held at El Guettar, the Axis had held up X Corps at El Hamma just long enough to allow the main bulk of their forces from the Mareth line to slip through the Gabes Gap behind them, so that by the time the rest of New Zealand Corps joined Horrocks' armor, the chance to cut them off had passed. On 29 March, the Highland Division, advancing over the Mareth line, linked up with 1st Armoured once more in Gabes. As at Alamein, Eighth Army had won the battle, but had failed to destroy the enemy army.

CHAPTER 24

Joining Hands:
1–18, April 1943

COMMANDER HARRY BUTCHER had not set foot in America since leaving with Ike the previous June, but early in the morning on Wednesday, 17 March, having spent eight days covering nearly 10,000 miles, he touched down in Washington once more and made straight for the Wardman Park Hotel, where his wife and daughter were currently living.

"Hello gals," he said casually, as the door opened. "The next day," noted Butch, "Ruth said her knees had quaked so vigorously that she had two charley horses. Bev cried."[558] It was hardly a relaxing trip, however. To begin with, Butch was laid low with a bug, and then was unleashed into a whirlwind of meetings and parties without ever having had a chance to get over it properly. General Marshall also wanted to see him. How was Eisenhower? the general wanted to know. Fine, Butch told him, although he confessed that he had yet to find him a masseur. Marshall told him that a delegation from General MacArthur had come over from the Pacific and was now in town. Of particular interest were the new air-to-surface tactics being developed by the US air forces out there. "I told General Marshall that our air people in the North African theater are always on the lookout for new and better methods of attack," noted Butch, "and that I would tell his story to Ike." Marshall also told him that Ike was not to waste any time on political machinations or defending his past actions. "The general said that Ike's rise or fall depended on the outcome of the Tunisian battle," recorded Butch. "If Rommel and Co. are tossed into the sea, all quibbling, political or otherwise, will be lost in the shouting of the major victory." The president was more reassuring, however, impressing upon Butch that he and the whole country was not only right behind Ike, but confident of his success in North Africa.

All this Butch dutifully reported back to his chief on his return on 4

April. He had felt somewhat relieved to get back on the plane again. "I couldn't stand the pace of the home front," he noted. Ike was delighted to have him back—he had missed him—but if he was pleased with Marshall's and FDR's vote of confidence, he was disturbed by Butch's view of popular opinion. "Most of the critics assume we have 'won the war', and are now quivering for fear we are 'losing the peace,'" Butch told him. "The hardships of our combat troops, the quality of the Axis fighters in Tunisia, and the supreme effort that will be required finally to shove Rommel [sic] into the sea are lost in the swirl of wishful thinking that an early victory is inevitable."[559] From a PR point of view, Butch felt their AFHQ had been picking up the habit of reticence from their British colleagues and that they should be more open about the realities of fighting against the Axis. "We must recognize that our theater is in competition with every other theater for equipment and attention," Butch told him. And Ike agreed. "I rather think that my press relations people ought to help a little on this matter," Ike told Marshall, "by emphasising the toughness and skill of the German, both in offensive and defensive battle."[560]

Meanwhile, on the battlefront, the Allies were clawing back the land they'd lost during the earlier Axis offensives. Most of the action might have been taking place in the south, but the north and center parts of the line had not been inactive—not in any way, for while Patton and Monty were launching their major attacks at El Guettar and the Tebaga Gap, two other assaults were being made—at Temara in the north, where an effort was being made to recapture Sedjenane, and on the Fondouk Pass in the center of the line. Both were coordinated to ensure von Arnim's forces were kept occupied and unable to hurry to bolster Axis defenses in the south, although Alex hoped that by taking the Fondouk Pass, armor could then pour through into the plains as and when the enemy started to retreat through the Gabes Gap.

Although the Red Bull Division initially took some high ground overlooking the pass, they had begun their attack with only two infantry battalions, and suffered the usual difficulties faced when assaulting Axis troops dug in to advantageous mountainous positions. After four days of bitter fighting, their attack was called off, the men of the Red Bull falling back several miles.

The attack in the north went rather better, despite heavy rain that was to last for nearly a week without letup. Anderson had massed his 46th Division as well as a number of French troops, although it was once again the parachute brigade who led the way, taking their objectives forty-eight hours before anyone else. This marked the end of a difficult period for Colonel John Frost and his men of the 2nd parachute battalion. He had lost over

150 men during the retreat to the Pimples, while the drive to capture Temara and Sedjennane had involved particularly brutal and difficult fighting against equally skilled German parachute troops. Churchill had written to Alex earlier in March questioning the wisdom of continuing to use the paras in an infantry role rather than for airborne operations, but time and again during the Tunisian campaign they had proved their exceptional tenacity and skill. And here, in the wooded, hilly north, the quality of the fighting troops counted for everything.

After two days, when the paras reached their final objective in the Cork Wood around Temara, Frost was left with just 160 men. But despite such crippling losses, Frost himself was in great heart, happy that his men had performed so well and that they had achieved all that had been asked of them. With them were around a hundred German and Italian prisoners, and when the double rum ration arrived that Frost had ordered, the paras shared it freely with the men they had so recently been fighting. Later that evening, they held an impromptu concert, and Frost was most impressed with the vigor with which the Germans and Italians sang. The following day, when one of their German prisoners was taken to the Corps interrogation center, he was asked where he had spent the previous night. "Singing and drinking with my comrades of the English *Fallschirmjäger*," he replied.[561]

Frost had discovered he had little hatred for the enemy. They were, he realized, much like themselves, with the same fears, worries, strengths, and weaknesses. "We had met no cases of 'Hunnish frightfulness,'" he noted, "and on the whole they were a chivalrous foe." He was also interested to hear from prisoners about conditions on the Eastern Front. One wounded German officer told him that the relentlessness with which the Russians pushed their men forward defied belief. "You simply cannot kill them quickly enough," the officer told him. "Even when the scene of carnage in front of our positions is indescribable, still they come, and eventually you have to move to avoid being trampled on."[562]

There were several reasons why the paras had proved to be such good fighting men. One was obviously their level of training. Another was their high morale and pride—throwing in the towel was simply not part of their culture, and mental toughness became a point of honor. At one time during the attack on Temara, Frost was under such intense attack and the enemy so close, that he ordered his men to fix bayonets. "The very act of fixing bayonets struck a wonderful note among all ranks," he noted, "and morale reached a peak." Most men would have been scared witless in such circumstances, but instead one of his men simply picked up a tray of captured Italian grenades and handed them around, joking, "Cigarettes? Choclates?"[563]

But another reason was their ability to adapt to the environment in which they found themselves, a skill shared with the LRDG and SAS. Frost had instilled in his men the importance of keeping clean and fit at all times despite appalling conditions, and had evolved a drill that made maximum use of a small bowl of hot water which he insisted each man use every day, even though this meant taking it out of their precious drinking ration. First they would shave with it, then wash their face and neck, followed by armpits. After putting their shirts back on, they turned to their feet, giving particular attention to the area between their toes. "Finally off with the pants so that one could squat over the bowl to deal with nether regions," noted Frost. Undignified this might have been, but once he had set the example, there was no excuse for anyone else. This daily routine quickly paid off. Few of his men suffered the kinds of sores and other skin troubles that affected men like David Brown and so many others in Tunisia.

At Bou Arada, David was still suffering from sores, and although he was now based in a dilapidated farmhouse and had a bed in which to sleep, he was being eaten alive by bedbugs and lice. And he was still hungry. "It is nearly teatime, thank goodness, I'm starving," he wrote in a letter to his wife on 21 March. "Lunch is no sort of a meal at all. Cheese or jam and a few biscuits and what is left of the bread . . . Wish I was just going to have a Castle Park tea, what a pig I'd make of myself. I'll never say no to scones and pancakes again. The thought of one makes my mouth water." Then he added, "Or potatoes, I could eat any amount of those too."[564]

Sergeant Bucky Walters felt he was slowly acclimatizing, however. He had not been involved in the Red Bulls' attack at Fondouk—the 1st Battalion of the 135th Infantry were held in reserve—but he was learning how to make the most of their rations and to keep warm. He had stitched together two blankets into a kind of sleeping bag that made the most of his body heat. His feet were suffering from the wet, but he, too, made sure he did his best to keep his nether regions clean if nothing else. "The filth and dirt—you just got used to it," he says, "even though this was an utter change and different kind of existence to the one we were used to. But we adapted pretty well, especially the farm boys from Minnesota. They were a pretty rugged bunch." And young too: at twenty-two, Bucky was one of the oldest in his company. "You're pretty adaptable at that age," he says.

Farther south, Eighth Army were also adjusting to their new environment. Albert Martin was conscious that this new landscape was very different from the desert of old. They were going to have to learn new ways of fighting from now on. The Gurkhas could not have been happier, however. "Morale was high," says Nainabadahur Pun. Not only were the hills and mountains more familiar to him than the wide open desert, most of the

Gurkha officers and senior NCOs were highly experienced in mountain warfare. "Many of them had served on the Northwest Frontier," he says. "We had great trust in our British officers and knew they listened to the advice and experience of our 'gurus.' Nainabadahur Pun was also a great admirer of Tuker. "We had enormous faith in him," he says, "and were tremendously proud that he was originally an officer in 1/2 Gurkha Rifles." The feeling was entirely mutual. Tuker *knew* his Indians could achieve great things, and for once it looked as though they were going to be given a major role in the next battle.

Messe's forces had fallen back to the Akarit Position, the last practical defensive line in Southern Tunisia. It was here that the so-called Gabes Gap was at its narrowest. Eighteen miles north of Gabes town, the plains were just five miles wide, before rising into a craggy salient, firstly the high ground of the Djebel Roumana, a whale's-back hump some five hundred feet high, and then the jagged and rocky peaks of the Zouai Heights and Fatnassa Hills, an imposing jumble of ridges and pinnacles, which in places towered as much as nine hundred feet over the plains below. These features alone made this narrow stretch of land a formidable natural defense, but running across this stretch were not only minefields and an anti-tank ditch, but also the often deep and steep-sided Wadi Akarit.

Most of Eighth Army was now a few miles south of the enemy defenses in the dusty, stunted-grass dunes north of Gabes. General Tuker immediately recognized that gaining control of the high ground of the Zouai Heights and Fatnassa Hills was the key to the forthcoming battle; in mountain warfare, gaining the second highest peak is of little value. But if it could be achieved, they would then command the entire position and Eighth Army would have a wonderful opportunity to burst through and encircle the Axis forces once and for all. Wasting no time, Tuker began sending out patrols. "All we wanted to know," he wrote, "was whether our men thought they could, on a starry, moonless night, perhaps using the odd flare, the Bofors direction shoots on selected points, and a very occasional artillery concentration at call to fix their position—whether they could scale those sheer cliffs and infiltrate right through to seize all the heights by daylight." His patrols confirmed what he had hoped: it could be done.

On 2 April, Tuker was summoned to XXX Corps HQ for a planning conference. Driving along to the meeting, Tuker was reminded of Captain Popham's infiltration into Gwalior fort in August 1781 during the First Anglo-Marathan War. He had done so during the dead of night and had captured the stronghold with a handful of men. The same principle applied now. All he had to do now was persuade his senior commanders.

Monty, however, had immediately discounted an attack on the Zouai

Heights and Fatnassa Hills as impossible, deciding instead to attack with two divisions—the Highland pushing over the Wadi Akarit and across the coastal plain, and 4th Indian seizing the low ground between the Djebel Roumana and the Fatnassa Hills. X Corps was to once more wait in reserve ready to burst through any gap. But it was because it seemed so impossible that Tuker felt certain his men would succeed; achieving surprise was one of his principal tenets for securing any victory.

As the plan was explained by Leese, Tuker kept silent. He was not going to get into an argument before a gathering of officers. But afterward, having talked to General Wimberley of the Highland Division, the pair of them went to see Leese alone, and Tuker then assured him that his division would take the massif before the main assault was due to begin at 4:30 AM on the morning of 6 April. He also urged him to bring 50 Division into the center of the line and stressed his belief that his men could also build a crossing over the westernmost part of the anti-tank ditch. Leese agreed to Tuker's suggestions and set off at once to discuss it with Monty. "Eighth Army conceded all our points," noted Tuker.[565]

As dusk fell on Monday, 5 April, an early sickle moon hung in the sky. Both 5th and 7th Brigades immediately began their approach march. Nainabadahur Pun was amongst those in 1/2 Gurkhas who were chosen by Tuker to lead the silent attack. They were to strike at the Zouai Heights. "After a very long march into the hills, we split into company groups," says Nainabadahur Pun. "It was a very slow and difficult move as absolute silence had to be maintained and it was very dark." Scouts moved stealthily ahead of them as they crossed several ridges. C Company were the first to encounter the enemy, when they came across an Italian sentry who was asleep. A quick swish of the kukri ensured he never woke again, then the Gurkhas leaped into the first machine-gun nest and cut down the unsuspecting defenders.

Nainabadahur Pun was slightly below when he heard the enemy alarm being raised. Wild firing suddenly tore the silence of the night apart. "To watchers in the plain below came an eerie sound," noted the division history with relish, "an excited whimper not unlike hounds finding scent—as the Gurkhas, swarming over the high ground, guided each other with shrill voices."[566]

With the rest of A Company, Nainabadahur Pun attacked Point 275, singled out beforehand as a key objective. "Everything was very confused," he says. "The enemy opened fire with everything—artillery, mortars, machine guns." But their firing was wild and inaccurate and the light of explosions and flares only helped to illuminate their positions to the attackers. Screams of the dying soon rang out over the sound of gunfire. Point 275 was captured just after midnight. By 2 AM, the Zouai Heights were in Gurkha hands.

Meanwhile, D Company had discovered a ravine studded with enemy outposts and crammed full of anti-tank guns, machine guns, and mortar positions. Leading two sections, Subedar Lalbahadur Thapa reached the leading sangar and cut down the enemy there without challenge, but then every gun post along this narrow pathway began to open fire. Without hesitation, Lalbadahur Thapa dashed from one gun position to another, leading his men through a sheet of bullets, grenades, and mortar bombs. Leaping into one MG nest, he personally killed two men with his kukri and the other two with his pistol. By the time he reached the last enemy position, he had only two men left with him, but he slashed two more men dead, and the rest of the defenders fled in panic. For this action he won the Victoria Cross.

With the Zouai Heights captured, the 1/4 Essex—one of Tuker's two English infantry battalions—led the 11th Field Regiment and their artillery working parties up to take over the enemy positions. Tuker aimed to have seventy-two guns in place by dawn. Meanwhile the 1st Royal Sussex—his other English battalion—were making good progress on the Djebel Meida, another ridge of peaks overlooking the low ground through which 50 Division was due to pass.

Much to the relief of Private Johnny Bain, the Gordon Highlanders were in reserve for the main attack. They'd only been told just before setting off to their forward positions, although Johnny had already learned not to crow about such good fortune. Fate could play tricks, and many a man had been killed by a freak shell or booby trap far from the main fighting. Like the Gurkhas, they had all marched up to their forward positions in the dark, and in silence, apart from the occasional cough and the tramp of boots on the stony ground. On reaching the foot of Djebel Roumana, the Gordons had begun digging in, while 152 and 154 Brigades prepared to make their attack. Mortar bombs soon started dropping among them, filling the cool air with the pungent smell of cordite, but Johnny continued digging furiously. Soon he and his mate had scooped out enough earth to enable them to crouch fetally in their hole. This done, and with their Bren set up in front of them, Johnny had taken first kip, his knees up and chin resting on his chest. He had no difficulty in getting to sleep this way; he'd done so in far worse conditions.

At 4:15 AM, a 496-gun barrage began and 50 Division and 51 Highland set off as planned, the Seaforth Highlanders passing over Johnny and the rest of the Gordons. From their slit trenches, they softly wished the assault infantry luck, watching them silently and steadfastly advance in the murky darkness. As soon as they were out of sight, the first rip of the Spandaus rang out over the still night air.

Fifty Division ran into heavy artillery fire and soon became pinned down. Hurrying to help were a platoon of Tuker's 1st Royal Sussex, who on the far left flank charged the Italian positions and captured four of their anti-tank guns. They immediately turned them around and began firing at the enemy batteries and mortar teams.

By the first streak of dawn, the 4th Indians had taken most of their objectives, just as Tuker had promised they would, and at his divisional headquarters, he was receiving news from the fighting with increasing excitement. At around 7 AM, Major-General Harding of the 7th Armoured Division visited him to tell him that thousands of prisoners were streaming in. At 7:35 AM, Tuker told XXX Corps that all first objectives had been taken. Now there really was nothing stopping X Corps from charging through and cutting off the Axis forces by a right thrust to the coast. Horrocks arrived soon after, and Tuker told him at 8:45 AM that the way was clear and that immediate action could finish the campaign in North Africa. "Now was the time to get the whips out and spare neither men nor machines," Tuker told him.[567] While Horrocks was still at 4th Indian HQ, the news arrived that Tuker had been waiting for since dawn: his sappers had crossed the anti-tank ditch. A complete breakthrough had been achieved. The path was clear for the British armor. X Corps' passage was being further improved with every minute, as the 4th Indians continued clearing the Fatnassa Hills. By 10 AM, Tuker's men were about to break out into the plains behind the enemy front line. Six enemy infantry battalions had simply ceased to exist, while a further six had been cut adrift in the hills to the west and were completely paralyzed.

There and then, Horrocks made a request to Monty for permission to put in X Corps immediately. Monty gave it, and the X Corps commander told Tuker he was going to send through his armor at once, using 4th Indian's crossing as well as the one now open on the boundary between 50 and 51 Divisions. Shortly afterward, from their commanding positions in the hills, Tuker's men could see the entire battle unfolding. They saw the first British tank columns head forward. They saw the enemy artillery pulling out. They saw that the only fighting was on the right, in 51 Division's sector. All this they gleefully regaled to Division HQ, which was in turn passed to XXX Corps and X Corps. Their attack had run like clockwork. The surprise had been total and now a decisive victory was there for the taking.

* * *

Eisenhower had visited Monty for the first time in North Africa on 31 March, and had "a most interesting time" being given a tour of the Mareth line before all the debris of battle had been towed away. He was not much taken with the Eighth Army commander, however. "He is unquestionably able, but very conceited," Ike wrote to Marshall. "He is so proud of his successes to date that he will never willingly make a single move until he is absolutely certain of success."[568] This was true. Monty had been irascible and had rubbed people up the wrong way long before he ever reached North Africa, but if his ego had reached new levels after Alamein, it was now out of control in the wake of his Mareth victory. His belief in his own preeminence was total. "I like Eisenhower," he told Alex. "But I could not stand him about the place for long; his high-pitched accent and loud talking would drive me mad. I should say he was good probably on the political line; but he obviously knows nothing about fighting."[569] Ike did not speak with a high-pitched accent; his voice was strong and quite deep. Monty, however, did, and was notorious for it. Nor was he in any real position to make judgments about Ike's capabilities; rather, his assessment was suspiciously similar to Brooke's.

In his letters and notes, he wrote as though his authority was absolute, no matter to whom he was writing. Eighth Army was always "his." References were always made to "my" artillery; "my" tanks; "I" have given Rommel a bloody nose. His notes to Alex were frequently bossy and dictatorial in tone. "It is *vital* to keep the Americans their side of the agreed boundary," he wrote on 8 April. "Please impress this on the Americans, French, and everyone else. Keep clear of my area." Alex was used to this. He knew Monty would never change, and he took no notice of his dictatorial tone. If he agreed with Monty, he acted upon his suggestions; if he did not, he ignored them.

Alex could do this because he *was* Monty's commanding officer. But his corps commanders could not. Lumsden had "bellyached" (disagreed with him) and had been sacked after Alamein. Horrocks and Leese were his lieutenants, men who carried out his wishes without impunity. This was fine so long as any plan was Monty's and so long as he kept firm control and command at all times. The problem during the drive through the Tebaga Gap had been that Monty had not been commanding the left hook of the battle. He had been some way from the main action and had left the drive through to El Hamma to Horrocks. And Horrocks lacked the confidence and strength of character to make potentially risky or costly decisions. Monty's mantra of proceeding only when victory was guaranteed had rubbed off too strongly; his autocratic style of command hindered initiative.

The same was now true at Wadi Akarit. Monty had left the running of the battle largely to Leese and Horrocks, and once again Horrocks dithered. Not until 1 PM did the first tanks of 8th Armoured Brigade start nosing across the 4th Indians' anti-tank ditch, some *four and a quarter hours* after Tuker had told Horrocks the coast was clear. The Sherwood Rangers had been formed up and ready to move much earlier in the morning, when they were bombed by their own side—but casualties were light. Stanley Christopherson was told that they were being held up by strong anti-tank fire at the end of the pass. This was simply not true. German anti-tank guns were lurking at the far end of the valley behind the Djebel Roumana, but as Tuker was quick to point out, these were comparatively few in number and no match for the hundreds of tanks and guns available to X Corps and the New Zealanders, who had been placed temporarily under X Corps' command. At 9:20 AM, Tuker had even sent his trucks over the anti-tank ditch to resupply his forward infantry—and they had done so without so much as a scratch. At regular intervals, Tuker sent through increasingly "peevish" inquiries as to why on earth X Corps wasn't pushing through, until at 4 PM, he was told X Corps was now going to wait until dawn the following morning, moving behind another massive air bombardment and barrage. Tuker was appalled. His men had done all the hard work, and X Corps was being handed the battle on a plate. That Horrocks was prepared to so feebly squander it begged belief.

Meanwhile, to the right, the Highlanders were facing vicious counterattacks. Bitter fighting continued all day and into the evening along the ridge and the wadis below it, fighting that could have been largely avoided had X Corps pushed through. Johnny Bain had remained in his hole for much of the day, occasionally seeing figures moving about in sticklike clusters. As normal, no one along their line was really sure what was going on. Johnny watched and waited in a state of trancelike indifference, something he'd noticed would come over him whenever he was close to the action. By nightfall, the fighting seemed to die down.

Throughout the afternoon, Nainabadahur Pun and the men of the 1/2 Gurkhas had fought off repeated efforts by the Germans to retake the Fatnassa heights; they were now holding a 3,000-yard mountainous front. The enemy had made no progress, however, and at the end of the day the entire division had lost only around four hundred men. While this had been going on, the Axis commanders had been discussing their options. Messe believed they could hang on, but von Arnim was more pessimistic. In the end, it was the commanders of the 15th Panzer and 90th Light Divisions who had the casting vote, and they believed they should retreat overnight or face annihilation.

During the early hours, the air and artillery bombardment began, but on empty Axis positions. At 7 AM on April 7, X Corps finally passed through the 4th Indian and 50th Divisions' fronts. Once again, Eighth Army had won the battle but failed to finish the job. "Here, in this spot," wrote Tuker, "the whole of Rommel's [sic] army should have been destroyed and Tunis should have been ours for the taking. Again the final opportunity and the fruits of our victory have been lost."[570]

That morning, Johnny Bain and the Gordon Highlanders had crept up over the Djebel Roumana, unsure at that stage whether the enemy was still there or not. The dead were scattered across the hillside. Johnny stumbled by a lifeless Seaforth Highlander. "There's one poor bastard's finished with fuckin' an' fightin'," said his friend. "Already the flesh of the dead soldiers, British and enemy, was assuming a waxy theatrical look," wrote Johnny, "transformed by the maquillage of dust and sand and the sly beginnings of decay."[571] Then men in his own section started bending over the bodies, turning them over with their boots and taking watches, rings, and any other valuables they could find.

Johnny watched this for a moment, then simply turned away and began walking back down the hill. No one stopped him, and he later picked up a ride all the way back to Tripoli. On the Djebel Roumana, Johnny had realized he'd had enough of fighting. And so he deserted.

Alan Moorehead had been having a busy time, flitting from one part of the front to another, but on 7 April, he was near Medjez el Bab, where 78th Division were beginning another assault. He had noticed that in the past couple of weeks the efforts of the Luftwaffe had been considerably on the wane; he'd barely seen a Stuka for days. But as he and a fellow reporter drove toward Testour, ten miles southwest of Medjez, yellow tracer bullets suddenly began spitting either side of them. The driver immediately slammed on the brakes and skidded to a halt, and they all leaped out as a 109 roared past only twenty feet over their heads. At the same time, a nearby Bofors crew opened fire, hitting the Messerschmitt on its underside. Alan watched as it flew on, rose slightly, and then banked before belly landing among a field of wildflowers.

They rushed toward the aircraft, but the Arabs had gotten there first. The pilot had made an attempt to get away and hide, but was quickly found and marched back to his machine with his hands behind his head and a pistol pressed into his back. "He was a strikingly good-looking boy," wrote Alan, "not more than twenty-three or four, with fair hair and clear blue eyes." He was searched and his pistol taken from him, and then everyone stood back. The pilot looked suddenly alarmed. "He stiffened and the hand holding the cigarette was tensed and shivering," noted Alan, who had realized that the pilot thought he was about to be shot. "Little globes of sweat came out in a line on his forehead and he looked straight ahead."

But he was not executed, nor was he ever going to be. Someone moved toward him, and motioned the pilot to come with them. The relief on his face was unmistakable. But for Alan, it had been an illuminating experience. "This actual physical contact with the pilot," he wrote, "his shock and fear, suddenly made one conscious that we were fighting human beings and not just machines and hilltops and guns . . . But now, having captured a human being from that dark continent which was the enemy's line, one wanted to talk to the pilot and argue with him and tell him he was wrong."[572]

Air reconnaissance and intelligence soon showed that the Axis were pulling out of the El Guettar massif and Maknassy areas as well, and that same day, 7 April, II Corps finally linked up with Eighth Army on the Gafsa-Gabes road. Alex had already anticipated such a retreat and on 4 April, had ordered another attack through the Fondouk Pass. He now had General Crocker's British IX Corps in Tunisia, and since the Red Bull Division was already to the west of the pass, it made sense to use both forces together, with Ryder's men temporarily under Crocker's command.

Crocker's background was with tanks rather than infantry; the 6th Armoured Division—of which the Guards Brigade was the mobile infantry—were the backbone of his corps. Doc Ryder's men had had the least combat experience of all II Corp's forces, while the British 128 Brigade that was loaned to Crocker had to be brought out of training at 18th Army Group's Battle School early, but Alex hoped that overwhelming strength would see them through. Unfortunately, however, Crocker's plan was faulty, largely because he ignored Tuker's tenet that the highest ground needs to be captured first. The attack was actually to be made through two passes: the Pichon north of the Djebel Rhorab, the Fondouk to the south. This high ground in the center thus dominated the position, but although it was to be pasted, it was not on Crocker's list of objectives. General Ryder, whose men were to pass to the south of the Djebel Rhorab, was not happy about this, and so gained permission to start his attack early in the morning of 8 April, and under the cover of darkness.

Sergeant Bucky Walters in 1st Battalion, 135th Infantry, was once again in reserve, following on behind the 3rd Battalion, who were to lead the assault against the high ground to the south of the Fondouk Pass. To their right was the 133rd Battalion, but from the outset, their attack was mired in confusion. Rather than begin their attack at 3 AM, as planned, they finally got going some two hours later. At 6:30 AM, the leading troops gave the signal that the artillery barrage should start. A number of the shells fell short, hitting their own men, but the Red Bulls pressed on. By now the Axis troops in the hills above them were fully awake to the attack and began finding their range on the advancing troops with ease. At

7:30 AM, the American advance was halted entirely; an air bombardment was due to start half an hour later, and the infantry was concerned not to be within the 2,000-yard bomb line previously agreed. Unbeknown to them, however, Corps HQ had already canceled the air attack precisely because it was worried the Red Bulls had already advanced too far.

All this time, the poor infantry were milling around, wondering what was going on and offering themselves as sitting ducks. Another artillery barrage began at 9:30 AM, but by this time it was too late. It was now broad daylight, and the Americans were coming under heavy attack. Bucky had not been far behind the assault troops. "Our advance was delayed once, then twice, then three times," he says. "We could feel that somebody who was issuing orders wasn't doing their job properly." All he could see was a number of hillocks from which enemy fire was pouring down amongst them. "We were right in front of them in open skirmish order. It was like World War I." Then they reached the enemy minefields. Bucky's lieutenant trod on a mine nearby. "I saw him go," says Bucky, who by now hadn't the faintest idea what they should be doing and what the hell was going on. Instead, the advance ground to a halt and the Red Bulls began hastily digging foxholes. "It was pretty flat as we advanced," says Bucky. "We'd have been entirely wiped out if we'd gone any further. It was murderous and a terrible, terrible piece of strategy."

One twenty-eight Brigade had had an easier time. Their advance had begun on time and their objectives, against weak opposition, had been taken. By late afternoon they had turned south with a view to taking Djebel Rhorab. But with the Red Bulls' attack grinding to a halt, Crocker ordered his tanks of the 6th Armoured Brigade to go and help the Americans. They arrived just as 34th Division's own armor was renewing their attack. More confusion followed, but later the Red Bulls' armor made another attempt at an advance. Reaching the foot of the massif ahead of them they were then shot to pieces by the 88s. They were short of leadership, not courage.

Overnight, Alex ordered Crocker to send in 6th Armoured in force, and to smash through the pass whatever the cost. The Americans also launched another attack, and this time Bucky Walters was in the main assault, accompanied by a tank-destroyer battalion. "Men were getting hit by small-arms and shrapnel," says Bucky. "The enemy was firing air bursts—they were terrible." Time and again, Bucky and his men hit the dirt, before eventually crawling to a hillock and finding some disused foxholes. There he watched one tank after another get hit. "They were coffins," says Bucky. "The 88s were devastating." At one point he looked down into his foxhole and saw an ant and wished he could be the same size.

The Djebel Rhorab was eventually taken at great cost by the Welsh Guards later that afternoon. Watching them from the high ground facing the pass was Captain Nigel Nicolson, who was amazed to see them advance in long lines over open ground, crouching down as they ran forward. "In the closing stages of the infantry attack, I suddenly observed fifty of the enemy rise from their trenches, throw down their arms, and advance down the hill with their hands up, led by their officer," he later wrote to his parents. Meanwhile, to the south, 6th Armoured had launched their assault. Many of the tank crews had assumed it would be their last day—the odds of surviving the enemy guns seemed so slim. But they'd set off all the same, their spearhead led by a young squadron leader of the 16th/15th Lancers. Moving in a wide open formation they pushed forward, shell fire soon whistling around them. "There's a hell of a minefield in front," reported the squadron leader. "It looks about three hundred yards deep. Shall I go on?"

"Go on," came the reply, "Go on at all costs."[573]

They did so, losing twenty-seven tanks in the process. The squadron leader was killed, but it could have been very much worse. As darkness fell, however, they stopped, because word had arrived that 10th and 15th Panzer were moving up. This was not the case; what had been spotted was the flank guard protecting the panzer divisions as they continued their escape northward. The following morning, 6th Armoured pushed through into the plains, and the Red Bulls finally captured the high ground to the south of the pass. But by then, the Axis had largely evaded the Allies once again.

Bucky Walters felt deeply dispirited. The division had lost nearly eight hundred men, but he felt they'd performed badly and let everyone down. "We had some good officers, and some good men," he says, "but at that time we weren't that battle-wise and our chain of command had broken down somewhere . . . Our officers were brave men, but they didn't have the experience to keep us moving." In contrast with Colonel John Forst, Bucky also felt that they suffered for not feeling any hatred toward the enemy. "We didn't hate them because before Fondouk we hadn't seen too many of our men being mangled and killed by them. Now, when you see your buddies being killed, a sense of anger develops, and anger gives you a kind of impetus to start hating the enemy, and once you have that you start becoming a better soldier."

This was a sentiment that Alex certainly agreed with, as did Patton, but although the Red Bulls' failure at Fondouk was as much to do with Crocker as it was Ryder, this joint operation caused Patton to explode with indignation, especially when word reached him that the British press had been particularly critical of Doc Ryder's men. "God damn all British and all so-called Americans who have their legs pulled by them," he wrote, and then confided to his diary, "I feel all the time that there must be a show-down [with the British] and that I may be one of their victims. Ike is more British than the British and is putty in their hands."[574]

This was written in private and when his blood was up; Patton was always a highly emotional man. Like most people, he resented criticism of his own people, but despite this, his view of much of II Corps was extremely similar to that of Alex. The problem was that Alex tended to tar them all with the same brush, which was harsh on the Rangers, who were now a class act, and also the Big Red One, which was developing into a fine infantry outfit. Nonetheless, both agreed that all too often the Americans had lacked "drive." "34 Div would have captured the high ground south of Fondouk if they had gone all out at the first attempt," concluded Alex in his report on II Corps' recent operations.[575] This was a criticism Patton frequently directed at 1st Armored. "I have little confidence in Ward or in the 1st Armored Division," he noted on March 28. "The division has lost its nerve and is jumpy."[576] The very next day, Alex echoed these sentiments in a letter to Monty. "The trouble, as I have said, is with the troops on the ground who are mentally and physically rather soft and very green. It's the old story again—lack of proper training allied to no experience of war."[577] Two days after that, with II Corps unable to force a breakthrough along the El Guettar massif, Patton recorded, "Our people, especially the 1st Armored Division, don't want to fight—it is disgusting."[578]

Alex's report also concluded that there was "at present a lack of confidence in their officers by the ORs because they feel they don't know their job. This, of course, affects discipline."[579] Again, this was a concern Patton felt too. Larry Kuter had met up with Patton just after Fondouk. "He said that he had lost 286 junior officers because most of them had to do the work that sergeants and corporals should have been trained to do," recorded Larry. "He concluded tearfully, 'I still couldn't make the sons of bitches fight.'"[580]

On 2 April, Alex had written to Patton suggesting Ward be replaced. Although Patton did not know it at the time, Alex had done so only at Eisenhower's insistence. Patton was in agreement, although resented Alex's involvement. "I should have relieved him on the 22nd or 23rd [march]," noted Patton, "but did not do so because I hate to change leaders in battle, but a new leader is better than a timid one." By now, however, Patton was already in a thoroughly bad mood, frustrated by British interference and annoyed that Eighth Army were getting all the glory while his II Corps had been given little thanks for holding off two panzer divisions that would otherwise have been confronting Monty's men.

And he was particularly annoyed that Eighth Army seemed to be getting the lion's share of the air support available. Matters came to a head on 1 April, when some German aircraft attacked one of Patton's observation posts, killing three men, including his ADC, of whom he was particularly fond. As Patton later admitted, this radio post had not been regularly moved, enabling the Germans to get a fix on it. But that evening, through grief, anger, and mounting frustration, he added to his daily sitrep, "Forward troops have been continuously bombed all morning. Total lack of air cover for our units has allowed German air forces to operate almost at will," and then sent it off with a much wider distribution than normal.[581]

Larry Kuter saw the sitrep that night at Ain Beida, but thought little of it, thinking it so obviously exaggerated and emotional that no one would pay the slightest bit of attention. The following morning, however, he got another surprise. Mary Coningham had read Patton's complaint and had become increasingly incensed and so wrote a detailed response and sent it to everyone on the original message.

> Total enemy effort over 2 CORPS GUETTAR Front. 0730 unspecified number of fighters. 0950. 12 Ju87s. 1000. 5 Ju88s and 12 ME 109s of which some bombed. Total casualties four killed, very small number wounded. Our effort up to 1200 hours. 92 Fighters over 2 CORPS front. 96 Fighters and Bombers on enemy aerodromes concerned. On SFAX, 90 Bombers at 0900. For full day, 362 Fighters, of which 260 over 2 CORPS.

Mary then finished by adding, "12th AIR SUPPORT COMMAND have been instructed not to allow their brilliant and conscientious air support of 2 CORPS to be affected by this false cry of 'Wolf.'"[582]

These were potentially serious allegations from both camps. Kuter met both Tedder and Spaatz at Thelepte on 3 April to discuss Patton's claims. Tedder, particularly, was furious with Mary and was insisting that he apologize. They then drove on to Gafsa to meet Patton, who Larry thought seemed belligerent and unrepentant. "Patton appeared to me to act like a small boy who had done wrong, but thought that he would get away with it," Larry noted.[583] Alex phoned while they were there and told Patton that he'd read Mary's message and that the II Corps commander had asked for it. Spaatz also sided with Mary, telling Ike a couple of days later that "Coningham's trouble was all caused by Patton's distribution of his sitrep of April 1st, and that in view of its accusation notice had to be taken of it."[584]

On Tedder's insistence, Mary later withdrew his signal and the following day visited Patton to apologize in person. Patton was initially wary, but Mary seemed sincere and they eventually shook hands and then lunched together. "We parted friends," noted Patton.[585] But both Ike and Tedder had been angered by the whole episode. Tedder had felt it could have led to "a major crisis in Anglo-American relations," as did Ike.[586] But this wasn't about Anglo-US relations: Mary had been defending the US 12th Air Support Command. Rather, it was an argument over doctrine, air versus army. It was Ike and Tedder who turned it into a nationality spat instead. Once again, Ike felt he had to rebuke Patton, reminding him of the importance of maintaining Anglo-US unity and appealing to him to strike a sensible balance: yes, he expected Patton to show complete loyalty to Alex, but this did not mean he should not express his views and concerns to his commanding officer whenever he felt it was necessary. To a hothead like Patton, however, such a rebuke merely underlined his belief that Ike had sold out to the British.

But even the considerably calmer and more rational General Omar Bradley had been hurt by British criticism, and had been deeply upset when, on 19 March, Alex's COS, Dick McCreery, unveiled plans for the final conquest of Tunisia, which was based on the assumption that once the Axis was squeezed out of the Gabes Gap, it would rapidly retreat to the next obvious defensive line at Enfidaville in the north and only forty miles south of Tunis. Since Eighth Army would be already in the plains and was by some margin the most experienced force within 18th Army Group, it was logical that it should be the hammer against this line of defense. First Army was already in the north, so Alex thought to use it in conjunction with Eighth Army in a strike from the west. II Corps, in the south, would play no role. It was one occasion where Alex's diplomacy skills faltered. Bradley, especially, was outraged, because he knew that by then he would be II Corps commander. For the next few days, he seethed with anger every time he thought about Alex's plan.

Such feelings of Anglophobia and even anti-Americanism should not be overplayed, however. Any group of commanders can rub each other up the wrong way and make decisions others feel angry and frustrated about. There were as many tensions among American commanders as there were directed to the British, and vice versa. Of course, national pride played a large part, but then so did pride of one's service, or division, regiment or squadron. And below command level, such feelings were less apparent. Among most American troops, Anglophobia was almost nonexistent, and while many in Eighth Army undoubtedly felt they were superior to the Americans, they also believed they were a cut above those in First Army too. Alan Moorehead recorded an incident where a First Army soldier had gone up to an Eighth Army sergeant and said, "Hullo! Pleased to see you. I am from the First Army."

"Well, you can go home now," came the reply. "The Eighth Army's here."[587] But Eighth Army's superiority complex was rather like that of a supporter of football club at the top of the league when meeting a fan from a club at the bottom, and with regard to the Americans should not be confused with anti-Americanism. Bucky Walters felt that criticism of the 34th Division was, in some ways, justified, and yet he never heard any British soldier ever grumble about them. "They didn't criticize," he says. "They did whatever they could for us." As Guards Brigade intelligence officer, Nigel Nicolson, for example, found little evidence of any ill feeling between American and British troops. He felt that after Sidi Bou Zid, they had rallied well. "There is no bitter feeling left behind," he noted. "Nothing like a German-Italian relationship." He told his parents that "one of the most enjoyable half hours I have spent" was with an American officer as they had traveled together back through the Kasserine Pass.

As it happened, Bradley had decided to press his case that II Corps should be given a role in the final push, and on 22 March, had appealed to Ike in person. Ike had agreed with him and asked Alex to reconsider, which he did, announcing his new plans for the final push on 7 April. II Corps would operate on the northern flank of First Army, but without the Big Red One. Finally recognizing that this division was the most battle-trained, Alex wanted them withdrawn for intensive amphibious training so they could lead the HUSKY assault. Bradley also had his way with regards to the Red Bull Division. After Fondouk, Alex felt they should be withdrawn and sent off to his newly established battle school for intensive training, but Bradley believed that this would be too humiliating. "Give me the division," he pleaded, "and I'll promise you they will take and hold their very first objective." Alex was struck by Bradley's passion. "Take them," he replied after some consideration. "They're yours."[588]

Bradley took over command of II Corps on 15 April, allowing Patton to return to Morocco to prepare for HUSKY as originally planned. Alex had already sent a letter of congratulations to II Corps for the Americans' role in holding at bay two panzer divisions in very difficult country, but this was not enough to quell Patton's mounting feelings of bitterness and resentment. "I hate to quit a fight but feel that I had best do so," he confided in his diary, "as I fear that on the north flank, where Alexander has put us, there is no future . . . I fear the worst." His influence on II Corps had been considerable, but his exit was timely, for Patton had become far more of a hindrance than a help in the Allied quest for outright victory.

After Fondouk, Nigel Nicolson followed the 6th Armoured Division through the pass and into the plains. On 11 April, the holy city of Kairouan was taken. At about the same time, one of the patrols from the Derbyshire

Yeomanry met up with men of the Eighth Army. "That was our first link," Nigel wrote to his parents breathlessly. "A few hours later, an armoured car, painted russet brown, and covered in dust, drew into our headquarters. Out of it jumped a young man dressed in corduroy trousers, a sort of [battle] blouse, suede shoes and a beret. 'I have brought you orders from the Eighth Army,' he said."

Eighth Army's advance had not been entirely smooth sailing, however, although for a number of different reasons. The 7th Medium Regiment were suffering after having covered nearly 2,000 miles across North Africa. Harold Harper was still using the same gun that had seized up on the opening night of Alamein. It was still firing all right, but the trucks and other transport were now in a terrible way. "It was a case of make-do and mend," says Harold, but breakdowns were a constant hindrance to speedy progress, so he was much relieved to hear that they would soon be given a period of rest and a chance to re-equip.

There had been marauding enemy tanks protecting the enemy's rear-guard and also repeated air attacks. Albert Martin and 2 Rifle Brigade were traveling northward toward Sfax, through cornfields and olive groves. He was sitting up front in the truck, with his mate Tug driving, four men in the back, and their six-pounder gun towed behind, part of a long column of trucks and vehicles. Albert had never got used to moving in such a fashion; he preferred the old ways of the desert, where they'd traveled in wide-open order.

Suddenly Dennis shouted from the back, and Tug slammed on the brakes. Three 109s had swooped over them and were spitting bullets and cannon shells at their column. "When that happens you scarper," says Albert. "Believe me, you scarper." Albert just made it, the puffs of dust kicked up by the bullets inches behind him. Tug made it as well, but of the others, one was killed and the rest seriously wounded. A number of trucks were hit and already in flames. "Now that shook me up," admits Albert, "because one minute there were six of us and the next there were just two." Albert and Tug did what they could, and then to their relief, the medics took over. Tug drove the truck off the road and into an olive grove, where they brewed tea and smoked incessantly. "We lost our nerve for a bit," says Albert. He had seen so many deaths during his years in North Africa, and so much destruction: bodies blown to smithereens, charred corpses, every horror imaginable, and he'd barely batted an eye. But this attack had a profound and lasting effect on him. "Friends and colleagues are not shielded from danger simply because they are friends and colleagues," he wrote later. "In war you just have to set aside the normal human feelings. Not much time to grieve when they become casualties if you are to keep a hold on reality, to continue to do your job and keep yourself alive."[589] Albert soon calmed down; after twenty-four hours in the olive grove, he was once more back on the road, ready to fight again. He was a man with deep reserves.

For one so cautious in battle, it was curious that Montgomery could never resist a chance for a flutter. Visitors to his headquarters often found themselves drawn into small wagers, and if they lost, Monty was always unstinting in collecting his dues. Bedell-Smith had unwisely been persuaded by Monty to give him a B-17 and an American crew if he captured Sfax by 15 April. "Have captured Sfax," Monty signaled to Ike on 10 April, "send Fortress."[590] Ike was initially mystified and ignored the message, but a few hours later, Monty sent another follow-up message, once again calling in his prize. There were obviously far better uses for a fully-trained crew and their B-17, but Monty insisted. "Goddam it," growled Ike, "I can deal with anybody except that son of a bitch."[591]

Nigel Nicolson managed to get permission to visit Sfax, driving over in an armored car, the only spare vehicle. He thought the plains were uninteresting country, but enjoyed the vast array of wildflowers that had now appeared and which gave the air a strong scent of honey. Eighth Army had already moved on, and so Nigel followed them to Sousse, thrilled to be able to see their triumphal progress. By the time he reached the center of town, a large Union Jack was already fluttering from the hotel that had previously been the Axis headquarters. For months, Sousse had been visited regularly by Allied bombers—both Willie Chapman and Ralph Burbridge had made several trips over the city—and now the town lay in ruins, the port "a forest of masts and funnels sticking up." Houses had been smashed, rubble littered the streets and even the palm trees looked as though they'd been blasted by a particularly vicious hurricane. "One felt slightly ashamed," wrote Nigel, "but interested all the same, that our bombs make as much mess as the Germans'." He was, however, in time to see Monty accept the official surrender of the town. Mounting a pile of rubble, the army commander addressed the crowd, which included a number of officials who had only just crawled from their cellars and shelters and were still covered in dust. Nigel thought his speech was contemptuous—Monty told the people how glad they must be to have been liberated by the famous Eighth Army, despite the Allies' efforts to destroy their city. "I hated Monty from that moment," wrote Nigel.[592]

On 14 April, HMS/S *Safari* returned from a patrol, which was, according to Captain Fawkes, CO of the 8th Flotilla, "outstanding amongst so many outstanding patrols carried out by this fine submarine."[593] Six, possibly seven vessels had been sunk and destroyed. Around 5 PM on April 10, *Sa-*

fari had been in the Gulf of Cagliari, off the coast of Sicily, when they had spotted a convoy of three merchant ships, including one tanker. Accompanying these were a minesweeper, several E-boats, destroyers, and aircraft. Despite this formidable protective force, Bryant decided to attack as though there were no escort at all, firing two torpedoes at the cargo liner, and two at the tanker. Anxiously they waited, then several minutes later heard the explosions as all four hit home. By now well below periscope depth, the crew could nonetheless hear the telltale creaks and groans of ships breaking up.

They immediately came under heavy and sustained depth charging. *Safari* dived, but hit the bottom of the sea at only 270 feet and then became stuck. It was a nerve-wracking time, because they were only a mile off shore, and the moment they tried using the main motors to free themselves, they were heavily depth charged again, the boat shaking with the blast. Although lying still in one position when under attack was dangerous in the extreme, there was nothing for it but to sit it out until dark, when Bryant at last thought it was safe to blow the main ballast tank and climb once more. Even so, a hunting craft spotted the telltale bubbles and promptly sent down a further ten depth charges.

Despite this unnerving experience, Bryant decided to spend another day, the third in a row, in the area. "This was very risky," admits Ronnie Ward, "but we all trusted Ben implicitly." And this contemptuous daring paid off. The third ship in the convoy had since run aground—presumably due to its haste to try and get away from *Safari* the previous day. Two torpedoes sent her to the bottom. E-boats then peppered the sea with a further twenty-one depth charges, all more powerful and larger than the submariners had previously been used to. But once again, they managed to slip away. "The valor, daring and skill displayed in this patrol," Fawkes continued, "is done little justice by the wording of the patrol report."[594]

The submarines from both the 8th and 10th Flotillas were doing better than they had the previous winter: fifteen vessels were sunk between them in March, and their total for April was to be a further seventeen. Royal Navy surface ships, however, had not sunk a single thing in March. For the Allies to draw the North African campaign to a speedy conclusion, they needed to make a far larger dent in the Axis supply line, and this could only really be achieved by air power.

Admiral Cunningham knew this and so did General "Tooey" Spaatz. On taking over command of the air, Spaatz had wasted no time in getting to know ABC and trying to do what he could to help the naval effort. "Admiral," Spaatz had told him on a visit to ABC's HQ, "I've just come to tell you that we don't know a darned thing about this business of working over the sea. Will you help?" Of course, Cunningham replied. "I already held Spaatz in high esteem," wrote ABC later, "but that simple remark of his endeared him to me more than ever."[595]

The two had worked closely ever since. Doolittle's heavy bombers continued to paste Axis-held ports. Ralph Burbridge and his crew had quickly been given another Fortress and along with the rest of the 97th Bob Group, had begun bombing not only Tunis and Bizerte, but ports in Sicily and southern Italy as well. These relentless attacks did not come without a price, however: from their arrival the previous November up to 19 April, the 97th had lost 201 killed or missing, and from only three squadrons.

Losses were mounting in the 98th Bomb Group as well, now part of General Brereton's 9th US Air Force. The 98th were operating almost entirely from Benina Main, near Benghazi, and were attacking across the Mediterranean to Naples, Messina, and other Italian ports. Willie Chapman gradually lost one good friend after another. In March, his good buddy Moose Anders came down over Naples. "You learned to accept casualties in a combat unit," noted Willie, "however, this one hurt a little more than most."[596] He and Moose had been friends and had been flying alongside each another since before Pearl Harbor.

Since January, when Paul Francis had been transferred, Willie had been first pilot on the "Dasiy Mae." As more men had arrived from the US, there had been greater opportunities for each crew to take regular leave in Cairo, but despite these respites, he was now rapidly approaching the three hundred combat hours that constituted a completed tour of duty. On 2 April, however, when both the 98th and 376th were scheduled for a maximum effort over Naples, Willie had a few more missions to fly before it was his turn to head back to the USA.

The weather was not ideal, with low cloud across most of the Mediterranean, but they still managed to find Naples during the last light of day with what appeared to be good bombing results and no casualties. The return trip, however, was more complicated, and approaching Benghazi, Willie found himself flying in dense cloud, relying entirely on his instruments and hoping they didn't collide with any other returning B-24s. Willie decided to come in lower than normal, almost at zero feet, telling his crew to keep a sharp lookout for the white caps of the sea. As luck would have it, they emerged through the cloud at around two hundred feet and eventually spotted the North African shoreline. From there, Willie turned them in toward Benghazi, taking care not to fly into any barrage balloons that hung over the port.

As he was finally approaching Benina Main, Willie heard another pilot, "Booster" McKeester, calling for information about weather, landing instructions, and wondering what the hell was going on. Both ground control and Willie tried to contact him, but his radio appeared to be operating only one way. As Willie landed, he was still trying to get through. Both Booster and the other officers in the crew were good friends, and he was worried. Heading over to the control tower, he followed reports from their ground radar, which was tracking Booster's plane. His B-24 was observed over Tobruk—also shrouded in cloud—and was picked up by British radar, their plane tracked some distance over the sea east of Tobruk toward Cairo. Then all contact was lost. A search mission was carried out the following morning, but nothing was found. "The Mediterranean Sea remained calm and silent," noted Willie, "and never to my knowledge revealed any information regarding Booster, his crew, or the missing B-24."[597]*

With the assistance of the other air commands, however—9th Air Force included—NATAF was able to considerably increase the tempo of its air operations. "We just have to make a success of things in front," Mary told his staff. "We have turned everyone upside-down behind, and the only way of proving to them that the new brooms are an improvement is to produce results at the front." Tommy Elmhirst felt that by the beginning of April they were doing just that, and was now very satisfied with what he termed their "New Order."[598] So was Larry Kuter. "As our air attacks on Luftwaffe airdromes began to increase, their attacks on our ground forces began to diminish."[599] Their strategy was paying off.

They were, however, still having difficulty persuading certain army commanders to come around to their doctrine of the use of air power. On 14 April, Ike visited Ain Beida to discuss plans for the final push. Also there were Patton, Bradley, and Mark Clark. Tooey Spaatz had also been asked to attend but his plane had had to make a forced landing and he'd missed it. Once more, it had been left to Alex to defend Mary Coningham's air policy. He insisted that the army and air forces plan their operations together on a co-equal basis and then carry them out in coordination, even though both Patton and Clark, in particular, were still dead against this. Later, Spaatz arrived and Larry Kuter also joined the discussions, but the arguments had not abated until Ike told the assembled commanders that he was getting Goddamned tired of hearing the ground forces claiming they needed control of the air. "One would believe that our case had been settled," noted Larry. From then on, however, there was no more argument. Patton and Clark might not like it, but they had now lost their control of the air forces for good.

---

*Another B-24 was lost during the same raid, the "Lady Be Good" from the 376th BG. It was eventually discovered intact many miles south in the Libyan Desert in 1959. The crew had tried to walk to safety but failed, all but one of their bodies eventually being recovered.

In the meantime, more and more aircraft and equipment were arriving. The 225 Squadron were now equipped entirely with Spitfires. Also being used in the theater for the first time were Spitfire Mk IXs, a considerable improvement on the Mk V and the equal of the latest 109s and 190s. Larry Kuter also managed to arrange for a new American radar unit to be installed on 242 Group's headquarters. This new model was much more powerful than anything the RAF could lay their hands on and provided cover for the entire northern half of Tunisia and beyond the Cap Bon Peninsula.

Crucially, this meant they now had advance warning of Axis aircraft coming into the Tunisian bridgehead. Over several meetings from 7–10 April, Hitler and Mussolini reaffirmed that Tunisia was to be held at all costs, and so continued to pour in supplies and reinforcements. But with the numbers of ships being sunk increasing, they had to rely more and more on the air bridge, using Ju 52s and the huge six-engine Messerschmitt 323s to ferry this lifeline across the sea from Sicily and southern Italy. When the weather was favorable, these enemy air armadas would frequently make two trips in one day. From the many sources of intelligence now available to them, NATAF began to get a picture of when these missions might occur, and so with Spaatz and Mary's approval, Larry began preparing to intercept this air bridge using as many Allied aircraft as possible, code named FLAX. The first proper FLAX operation took place on 5 April, when in the morning long-range American P-38 Lightnings shot down thirteen enemy aircraft northeast of Cap Bon. A further eleven were knocked out of the sky by P-38s operating over the Sicily Straits. Fourteen enemy aircraft were destroyed during attacks on airfields in Sicily and a further eighty-five damaged. Helping NATAF over Sicily were Air Marshall Keith Park's forces on Malta, who were now bombing and strafing the Axis airfields on a daily basis.

By now, the 33rd Fighter Group was based at Sbeitla. Lieutenant Jim Reed had flown his first mission from there on 7 April, dropping fragmentation cluster bombs on a mountain road jammed with Italian vehicles and equipment. Jim had seen there was plenty of light flak, and although they had been asked to strafe the enemy once they'd dropped their bombs, they had not done so. This would have meant two sweeps over the same target, a practice the Desert Air Force never observed and which, understandably, Jim's CO, Colonel Momyer, was reluctant to do. Jim flew a repeat performance that afternoon, but by the third mission of the day, the group had been *ordered* to strafe after the bomb run. "The end result," noted Jim, "was that most of our planes were shot up." Five aircraft never made it back, and several others returned with landing gear hanging down and holes torn out of the wings and fuselages. "This was a case of someone giving orders who did not know what they were doing," noted Jim.[600] After that, the order was clarified: they were to strafe only if they saw a separate target.

The 33rd moved again on 12 April, this time to Ebba Ksour in the plains near Kairouan. At last Jim felt he was leaving behind the memories of mountains, mud, and rain. "The country around our new home is beautiful," he noted in his diary.[601] Flight Lieutenant Johnnie Fairbairn of 73 Squadron felt much the same. The fighters of the Desert Air Force were also moving up into the plains. "After all the sweaty months in the desert," noted Johnnie, "it was great to find trees and flowers everywhere." Pitching his tent in the middle of a peach orchard, he was thrilled to find an abundance of green, unripe fruit hanging heavily over him. He was also pleased to be able to hear the dawn chorus once more, a sound that had eluded him in the desert. Even better, cigarettes and alcohol arrived in plentiful numbers, and before long there was even a piano in their mess tent. "We began to enjoy the spoils of war," he noted."[602]

Two sixty Squadron was now near Kairouan. For Christopher Lee, the journey up through the Gabes Gap was particularly unpleasant. "We came through a dense array of stricken machines and men, still smouldering," he wrote, "and while I'd become used to wreckage and death, the smell that hung over this devastation was a real wrench in the guts."[603] He was concerned not to let any of his pilots see these scenes of carnage at close quarters. After all, a fair amount of it had been down to their efforts in the air. He didn't want it to weigh too heavily on their consciences. Air combat tended to be an impersonal affair: it was the plane, or truck, not the individual flying or driving it. It was best to keep it that way.

The boys of the 57th Fighter Group were also now up in the plains, at a new airfield three miles down the road from El Jem, home to one of the largest and best-preserved Roman amphitheaters in the world. Duke Ellington was now a flight commander in the 65th Fighter Squadron, and early on 18 April—Palm Sunday—they got intelligence that there might be a large force of German aircraft bringing over supplies to Tunisia. Relishing the prospect, Duke put himself on the first mission of the day, patrolling over the Cap Bon area looking for transports. He went up a second time, but still saw nothing. Then at 5 PM, the 57th sent off its final mission of the day, 46 aircraft in all from all three squadrons, although on this occasion Duke stayed behind. Accompanying them was another US fighter squadron, the 314th, with a Spitfire top-cover provided by the RAF's 92 Squadron.

This time, the 57th struck lucky. Droning toward them at low altitude and in perfect formation of sixty-five Ju 52 transports, escorted by over twenty German and Italian fighters. They were first spotted many miles offshore: it was a fine afternoon, and the setting sun glinted off their surfaces. "They were the most beautiful formation I've ever seen," said one pilot. "It seemed a shame to break them up as it looked like a wonderful propaganda film."[604] But break them up they did. While the Spitfires and the 64th FS stayed aloft to fend off the fighter escort, the rest peeled off and dived, jumping on the cumbersome transports in a mass of blazing gunfire. As the Americans swept over them, some of the Junkers blew up in midair, while others plummeted into the sea; some fluttered from the sky like leaves; others limped on trailing smoke. The American pilots could barely contain their excitement. Larry Kuter was listening to the fight unfold on 242 Group's radarscope. "All conversations were in the clear," he noted. "Code names of units and targets were forgotten . . . From my electronic view, the scene resembled the feeding frenzy of our Atlantic Coast bluefish."[605]

In what became known as the Palm Sunday Turkey Shoot, the 57th, along with their Spitfire and 314th FS colleagues, shot down seventy-four enemy aircraft. While Duke Ellington was thrilled that the 57th had done so well, he was absolutely gutted to have missed out. "I had two guys in my flight who I'd just finished putting through the training program and who had only been with the squadron a couple of weeks, and both got victories," says Duke, then adds, "Damn! That was our first big battle and I missed it."

Even more galling for Duke was that later that night, their airfield was attacked by Ju 88s. Duke leaped out of his tent only just in time, flinging himself into the nearest slit trench—only in his confusion he went for the wrong one and ended up lying in the squadron latrines. When the raiders had gone and he returned to his tent, he found it riddled with pieces of shrapnel.

For the Allied commanders, however, the Turkey Shoot couldn't have come at a better time. Only a few days before, Ike had been stunned to learn about the level of bad press they were getting back home in the States, where it seemed that II Corps was being blamed by American journalists for not securing a more decisive victory over the Axis during the recent fighting. "This has had a most disheartening effect at home," Ike told Bradley, "and apparently morale is suffering badly."[606] Well, now the journalists had something good to write about for a change, and news of the 57th's exploits soon spread across America.

Since the Battle of the Mareth Line, 519 Axis aircraft had been shot down, and nearly twice as many destroyed or damaged on the ground. Allied losses in the same period had been 175. At last, the Allies were masters of the air. With that secured, the final push for victory could begin.

CHAPTER 25

Endgame:
19 April—13 May 1943

AS COMMANDER of 18th Army Group, Alex certainly had a lot on his plate. He had to clear the Axis from North Africa, help prepare for HUSKY, deal with the hundreds of messages—often conflicting—that arrived on a daily basis, and manage the personalities and egos of his commanders. But if the strain ever got to him, General Alex never let on. Harold Macmillan, the British resident minister in Algiers, was astonished by his unflinchingly calm demeanor. "The whole atmosphere of the camp," he wrote in his diary during a trip to Ain Beida, "is dominated by his personality—modest, calm, confident."[607]

Alex never lost his temper—not publicly at any rate—and over dinner, Tommy Elmhirst no longer had to introduce topics for discussion to keep the conversation going. Instead, the banter flowed easily, turning to any number of subjects: the right way to drive pheasants in flat country, for example, or the pros and cons of Gothic versus classical architecture— "all very lightly touched and agreeable." Rarely did anyone talk shop, least of all the Army Group commander.

And everyone *liked* him, even Patton. "Alexander proved all that I had heard," wrote General Bradley some time later, "a patient, wise, fair-minded, shrewd, utterly charming professional soldier with a firm strategic grasp of the whole Mediterranean-North African Theatre." Like both Ike and Patton, Bradley had also been initially somewhat awed by Alex's combat record, but despite feeling frustrated by British military dominance in Tunisia, he never held this against his commander. "He had been thrust into a difficult position in Tunisia," noted Bradley, "a job requiring utmost tact, diplomacy, tolerance and discretion. He was clearly the man for the job and he bore the responsibility with disarming modesty."[608] Also impressed with Alex was his American aide, Major Ted Conway, who accompanied him on many of his trips around the front, in-

cluding any visits to II Corps. "He could talk better to generals than anyone I ever saw," says Conway, who later became a general himself. "How
could you harness up Montgomery and Patton and Bradley and Anderson on the same team?" says Conway. "The answer was that you had to be
an Alexander to be able to do it and make it work."[609] Yes, there were
plenty of tensions, but with a lesser commander than Alex, those conflicting personalities may well have proved disastrous. Conway noticed that
Alex often brought his commanders around to his way of thinking
through coercion and suggestion. Written orders were often preempted
by personal visits and discussions. Harold Macmillan also picked up on
this technique, when he accompanied Alex on a visit to see Bradley just
before the El Guettar offensive. "He did not issue an order," noted
Macmillan. "He sold the American general the idea, and made him think
he had thought of it all himself."[610]

He was now faced with coercing his forces into an effective plan for victory. By mid-April, there was no doubting the eventual conclusion in North
Africa despite Hitler's orders to the contrary. Alex now had at his command
nineteen divisions with which to crush von Arnim's severely depleted fifteen divisions, and over 1,000 tanks compared to the enemy's 150, not to
mention the crucial factor of air superiority. But his plan of attack still
needed to be the right one if it were to quickly overcome the German capacity for strong and effective defense. Montgomery had showed time and
again what could happen when victory was not absolute. Both Ike and Alex
had assured Roosevelt and Churchill that the campaign would be over in
May. They could not afford to let it drag on a day longer than necessary.

Ike had already encouraged Alex to change his original plan to include
II Corps, a decision he not only accepted but now fully endorsed, but his final orders for Operation VULCAN, which he announced on 12 April, were
different again from those sketched out a few weeks before. They were
based on his improved assessment of the terrain. In the north the ground
was mountainous and hilly and led to Bizerte. This was to be II Corps' objective, but their route did not lead to Tunis, the key to winning the campaign. In the south, the terrain was even worse. Blocking Eighth Army was
the Enfidaville position, not dissimilar from Wadi Akarit: it ran along a narrow stretch of plain, and then was flanked by jagged mountain peaks. The
difference was that it was here that the plains ended. Northward all the way
to Tunis, the land was mountainous in the extreme, the point at which the
Grande and Eastern Dorsales met.

Only in the center of the front was the terrain more manageable: the
Medjerda Valley and to the south of its southern ridge, the Goubellat Plain.
This was still difficult country in which to fight, as the Allies had discovered
at the beginning of the Tunisian campaign, but from Medjez to Djedeida—

the gateway to Tunis—the Allies would have to travel twenty miles. From Enfidaville, that distance was fifty. "Main effort in next phase operations will be by First Army," Alex signaled to Monty on 11 April, "Preparations already well advanced for attack earliest date 22 April."[611]

There had been a number of changes in II Corps since their efforts in the El Guettar-Maknassy area, and not just in the change of their commander. General Harmon was once again back in Tunisia, having taken over from Ward at 1st Armored Division. Like Patton, Harmon was a cavalry man and also like Patton, a good horseman and polo player. The similarities did not end there: he also swore like a trooper, wore knee-high cavalry boots and had a passion for war and soldiering. Bringing with him his own staff, Harmon relieved Lieutenant-Colonel Hamilton Howze of his job as G-3. Instead, he moved across to the 81st Reconnaissance Battalion.

Shortly after Harmon arrived, he took his officers back to Sidi Bou Zid and gave them a talking to. No criticism was expressed about Fredendall or Ward or any other commanders involved in that defeat. But he did tell them that he expected the division to perform at a much higher level than it had previously. "I can tell you that quite a number of the officers of the division resented it," said Hamilton, although he was not one of them; he accepted that they could and should have done better. They would soon get their chance to put the record straight, and this time, Hamilton would not be at division HQ, but out in the field, leading his own men into battle.

Also passing over the earlier battlefields was Ray Saidel and the 1st Armoured Regiment, who by early April were bivouacked at the foot of Djebel Lassouda, along the mouth of the Faid Pass. One day, Ray and several of his buddies went to have a look at some of battle debris that remained from the slaughter at Sidi Bou Zid, and soon came across the remnants of their own company. "As soon as we passed the first tank we knew what the story was," noted Ray. "The boys were still inside. The smell told us that." Taking a look inside, Ray saw the remains of one man on the assistant driver's seat. In tank after tank, the story was the same. Nearby was one grave of a tank man who had obviously been killed as he tried to escape. His body had been so lightly covered that bits of clothing were sticking out through the sandy soil. Between them, they accounted for fifteen out of their company's seventeen tanks. On many, the painted nicknames were still discernible through the blackened paintwork: War Daddy, Maggy, Donald Duck, Marie, Tornado, Stuggle Buggy, and Mrs. MacArthur. "Although these hunks of crisp, burned flesh were once members of our company," noted Ray, "it was hard to believe that they had ever been alive." Not far away, they also discovered the enemy gun positions. Some of the 88mms had been just two hundred yards from the tanks.

The 1st Armoured Regiment was soon after withdrawn into reserve near Tebessa, but most of II Corps was making its way northwards. The 18th RCT began the long trek northward on 17 April, taking over from the British in the early hours of the 20th. The 2nd Battalion moved into positions held by the 6th Black Watch. Lieutenant Randy Paulsen was now in Company G, transferred along with a number of other men to bolster the survivors of the rout on Djebel Berda. He and his new company commander, Lieutenant Jeffrey, drove up in separate jeeps to arrange the changeover, and were surprised to discover the Scottish battalion were down to about a company in strength. They found the acting commander sitting with his back against a ramshackle building. He'd been wounded and was barely able to stand, but did offer them a drink from a silver hip flask and cigarettes from a silver cigarette case. Around them was open grassland, largely devoid of cover. They were in the mouth of a valley, christened by Bradley as the Mousetrap, as an ever-present reminder of the dangers they would find lurking along its course. To their south lay the range of hills overlooking the Medjerda Valley that marked the new boundary between II Corps and First Army. To the north loomed the Djebel Ang range of hills that dominated Sidi Nsir and the Djoumine Valley. Before the Americans could drive to Mateur and then Bizerte, the highest points on these two ranges would have to be taken.

Following them was the 48th Evacuation Hospital, moving to a cork grove near Tabarka on the north coast, and Margaret Hornback, for one, was glad for the change of scene. "This region seems a lot like home," she wrote, "green fields and large herds of cattle." They'd been busy during the fighting around El Guettar, but as summer approached were now dealing less with battle wounds and more with malaria and other diseases. One malaria sufferer was Captain "Andy" Anderson, an American gunner, and the two of them found themselves drawn to each other. In her letters home, Margaret was coy about him. "No, I'm not in love with him," she wrote some time later, "he's younger than I but a grand person and oceans of fun." Understandably, the nurses were popular wherever they went. "American tent hospitals in the battle area seem to be favorite hangouts for correspondents," noted Ernie Pyle. "The presence of American nurses is alleged to have nothing to do with it." Ernie reckoned that the fifty-six nurses of the 48th were about the most veteran outfit in the whole of II Corps, and were living just like soldiers. "They have run out of nearly everything feminine," he added. "They wear heavy-issue shoes, and even men's GI underwear."[612] He asked them what they'd like from home. Cleansing creams, tissues, shampoo, and underwear were the items top of their list, which Ernie dutifully reported in his column. Sure enough, not long after, these luxuries reached the nurses. "We've just received a half pound of cold cream and a big box of Kleenex," wrote Margaret a couple of weeks later.

The whole Allied front seemed to be moving in anticipation of the final push. Peter Moore and the 2/5 Liecesters had been shifted from the Djebel Abiod area in the far north—the Sedjenane Valley now lay in the northernmost part of II Corps' sector. The task of reclaiming Green and Baldy Hills was to be given to the US 9th Infantry Division, ably assisted by the colonial troops of the French Corps D'Afrique. While American trucks were bumping along the roads northward, the Leicesters and the rest of 46 Division were rattling southeastward toward the Bou Arada area, where they were to join Crocker's IX Corps in the thrust through the Goubellat Plain. As they bounced their way southward over obscure tracks to avoid observation, Peter noticed that for the first time, they weren't swimming in mud. Instead, his lungs were filling with choking dust.

The division would be fighting their next battle without the parachute brigade, however. Much to Colonel Frost's disappointment, the paras had been withdrawn back to Algiers, where they were to begin preparing for HUSKY. "It seemed rather galling to be missing the glorious end," noted Frost, but as General Alex cheerfully revealed to them, the Germans had begun calling them the Red Devils. It was a singular honor: few troops were ever granted such distinctions by their enemies.

As the Leicesters drew into their concentration area near Bou Arada, they saw Eighth Army troops for the first time. These were the men of the 1st Armoured Division who had been brought across to join IX Corps. Peter noticed them immediately—they were conspicuous by their weather-beaten and tatty appearance and by the desert brown camouflage of their vehicles. Among them was Albert Martin and the men of the 2nd Rifle Brigade. Albert had been frankly stunned when he'd heard the news of their transfer, as was just about everyone else in the battalion. They were outraged, and the mood became distinctly ugly. Two days of route marches with full kit was their punishment for this spontaneous revolt, but then they were on their way, on a long detour through the Kasserine Pass where the remnants of the earlier battle remained for all to see and then northwards on a long, wide arc to Bou Arada. En route, the riflemen also met their first Americans. "In no time at all we were lifelong buddies," noted Albert. A certain amount of swapping took place and the riflemen were delighted to be able to get rid of some of their loot—especially the Lugers and Iron Crosses—for what seemed to them to be vast sums of money. Their packs full of gum, sweets, and cigarettes, they continued on their way.

When they joined up with the rest of IX Corps, Albert was astonished to see the First Army men properly attired with steel helmets, full web-bing, buttons done up and still wearing European olive drab. In contrast, the riflemen looked a mess: their vehicles stripped to the superstruc-ture, a few caged chickens in the backs of their trucks, and wearing little regulation uniform among them. "The men of the two British armies never did get used to one another," noted Albert.[613]

Lieutenant David Brown and the 17th Field Regiment were now with 36 Brigade facing Longstop Hill in the Medjerda Valley. They had been in action almost every day that month as 78th Division chipped away at the Axis defenses in preparation for the main assault. The gunners had certainly noticed the improvement in air cover. Rather than the constant menace of old, enemy aircraft only occasionally buzzed over them in quick hit-and-run dashes. They were also working closely with 225 Squadron, who had almost entirely reverted to their former tactical re-connaissance role. Although carrying out occasional Tac/Rs over Tunis and Bizerte to observe enemy shipping, Bryan Colston was spending much of his time flying alternately over the Bou Arada and Medjerda Val-ley areas, carrying out low-level photographic sweeps of enemy positions.

David Brown was in good spirits because he'd at last been promoted to captain and because they were finally advancing. His days were busy. During their time at Bou Arada he'd had plenty of time to read—he'd de-voured E. M. Forster's *Howard's End*—and had even been teaching him-self German. There was little chance to rest now. Sometimes they'd carried out two moves a day, an exhausting business, as it meant packing everything up, loading up the guns, moving forward a few hundred yards, then carrying out the same procedure in reverse. "It has been quite excit-ing," he wrote to his wife, "especially advancing over half-cleared mine-fields. One hears a bang, and turns around to see the vehicle immediately behind one blown up. The old Jerry leaves his beastly mines everywhere." He had, however, had a chance to air his German on some prisoners that had been brought in. "They told me," he added, "how much they didn't appreciate our fire."[614]

Eighth Army might not have been in the driving seat for Operation VUL-CAN, but Alex still wanted them to provide "continuous pressure" along the Enfidaville Line in order to draw off troops from First Army's sector. That meant harrying the line and keeping the Axis forces there busy and under pressure. Monty was now suffering from a bad case of overconfidence combined with diminishing interest in the campaign, now that Eighth Army had been consigned to a supporting role. However, believing there were only eight German battalions shoring up weak Italian troops along the Enfidaville position, he was anxious to have a crack at it before Operation

VULCAN was launched. "All my troops are in first-class form and want to be in the final Dunkirk," he told Alex.[615]

Now preoccupied with planning for HUSKY, Monty once again left matters to Horrocks. The two key features along the line were the imposing massif of the Djebel Garci and the hills around Takrouna. The former was made up of imposing 1,000-foot peaks, which rose steep and unbroken from the flat plains to the south. Roads ran either side of it, but it was obvious they would be heavily mined. Furthermore, the massif was bare and offered little cover to any advance, and was a far more serious obstacle than the hills at Wadi Akarit. Moreover, the element of surprise necessary for such an attack had already been used. Takrouna, on the other hand, was only a few hundred feet high. Its south-facing side was almost sheer, although around to the right and behind, the slopes were more gentle, with an Arab village built up on several levels beside a zigzagging climbing track. Perched on its summit were a smattering of buildings and a white mosque. Several hundred yards away to the right was the Djebel Bir, also steep sided and with a precipitous final climb to the top. Both hills sprang from the flat plains as dramatically as the Himeimat feature at Alamein. Behind, a mile to the northeast, was the Djebel Ogla, a similar-sized hill. The Arab villagers had gone, and all three were now swarming with enemy mortar teams and machine-gun nests. On Takrouna the buildings provided excellent defensive cover. Not only was there no hope of disguising any advance on these features, they were sufficiently close to one another to be supporting. Any attackers would be met with a hail of converging fire.

While 7th Armoured Division were tasked with "demonstrating" to the west of the line, and 50th Division charged with holding the coastal sector, Horrocks ordered Freyberg's New Zealanders to take Takrouna and Tuker's 4th Indians to capture Djebel Garci. Once Tuker's men had achieved this, they were to make their way northeast across another, even higher set of peaks and cut in toward the coast road to Bou Ficha. It was a plan that had been made by Monty without properly assessing the terrain or the opposition, or even sufficiently taking account of the troops he had available, the same charge that had earlier been made against Fredendall before Sidi Bou Zid. Tuker, as was his way, had sent patrols out as soon as he arrived within shouting distance of the Enfidaville Line. It soon became clear that Monty had seriously underestimated the strength of the opposition facing them. Tuker's intelligence suggested there were at least twenty battalions and that they were all dug in on the south sides of the features, facing out across the plain. Secondly, he was unable to get ahold of any pack mules, essential in such circumstances for carrying equipment into the hills. The Axis had beaten them to it. As it was, at least a quarter of his infantry would be required to act as porters; there was no chance of taking any transport across such terrain. Thirdly, there would be a strong moon on the night of 19–20 April, when they were supposed to attack, making their approach even more conspicuous. Freyberg was as equally unhappy as Tuker about the prospect of an attack on Takrouna; even Horrocks had severe reservations. At the planning meeting, however, Monty swept these objections aside. The attacks were to go ahead as ordered.

Nainabadahur Pun had been wounded a couple of days before, while dug in to the south of the line. He had left his slit trench to relieve himself when the enemy had opened fire, mortaring their positions. Unable to get back to his trench, he'd dived for cover, but had been hit by shrapnel in three places in his leg. Fortunately, no bones had been broken and he was quickly whisked away to a field dressing station and then to a field hospital. But for him, like many of his colleagues in the ensuing battle, his war in North Africa was over. In view on what was to come in the next few days, his was a lucky escape.

The 4th Indians began their attack at 9:30 PM on April 19. The Essex men broke their way through the outposts and were then followed by the Rajputana Rifles and 1/9 Gurkhas. Clambering up the steep slopes, they attacked one machine-gun post after another and soon found themselves caught up in heavy fire and intense hand-to-hand fighting. The assailants were forced to work their way upward yard by yard, around craggy crests and across gullies, mortars, and small-arms raining down upon them without respite. Tuker's men gained their second VC of the month, awarded to Havildar Major Chhelu Ram of the Rajputana Rifles. The fierceness with which the Indians fought was extraordinary. One Gurkha survivor, Jemadur Dewan Sing, recorded how he chopped off a German soldier's head with his kukri, then cut down two others. Attacking a fifth, he was himself wounded between the neck and shoulder. His hands were now slippery with blood and in tussling with a number of Germans, he lost his kukri. "One German beat me over the head with it, inflicting a number of wounds," he recounted. "He was not very skillful, however, sometimes striking me with the sharp edge but oftener with the blunt." Wrestled to the ground, he pretended to be dead. He couldn't see anything, because his eyes were full of blood, but still managed to get to his feet and rejoin his platoon the moment he sensed the enemy had forgotten about him. "My hands being cut about and bloody," he continued, "and having lost my kukri, I had to ask one of my platoon to take my pistol out of my holster and to put it in my hand. I then took command of my platoon again."[616]

Dawn broke with the mountains wreathed in smoke. The Indians had gained their first objective, but this was only a toe on the Djebel Garci, and all morning the enemy continued to lob mortars as Tuker's men tried to consolidate what gains they'd made. As their commander had forewarned, the massif had been considerably more strongly held than the army commander was prepared to accept. "We've got about 300-odd prisoners and must have inflicted about 1,000 casualties," he noted. "Our losses are about 400." Counterattacks continued, repulsed every time by the Indians and supported by eleven artillery regiments who continued to pound the enemy positions. Clearly, however, there was little chance of gaining any more ground, not swiftly at any rate. Tuker thought their small foothold in Djebel Garci was not worth the eighty-odd casualties a day they could expect to suffer; Horrocks thought otherwise. "Bad plan," noted Tuker.[617]

The New Zealand attack went in the same night as the 4th Indians. The Maori were given the task of taking Tekrouna itself, and also Djebel Bir. When Maiki Parkinson heard about the plan earlier that day, he couldn't believe what he was hearing.

"Who the bloody hell suggested that?" said Maiki, once the platoon sergeant had explained their task. "We've got the Desert Air Force, all the bloody artillery, all Eighth Army's tanks. Why have we got to go up there? Why can't we just go round the bastards? What the hell's going on?"

"Have you finished?" said his sergeant. Maiki nodded. The sergeant looked at him. "Tell you what," he said. "You go back to battalion headquarters. You're LOB. Have a rest."[618]

But Maiki refused. "We'd just got reinforcements from New Zealand. I knew most of them—been at school with them, and had gone hunting with them. This was their first bloody battle. I couldn't let them go in while I stayed behind." His friend Paul Te Kani then came over to him and put an arm around Maiki's shoulder. "I'm glad you're not going back," he said. "But I'm sad too."

"So am I, Paul," said Maiki.

The battalion held their normal pre-battle service—a few hymns, and some prayers and thoughts from the padre—then as darkness fell they prepared to set off. Paul told Maiki to keep an eye on three of the new fellows in their section. "Look after them, Maiki," he told him. B Company had been tasked with attacking Takrouna from the south, where the rock face was its most sheer. On their left were 21 Battalion. A Company were to take Djebel Bir, and C the right of Takrouna and the land in between. There was confusion from the outset. In front of Takrouna were heavy minefields and dense cactus plantations. A barrage had been laid on, but it rolled forward far faster than the men could advance. Soon their shells were landing far ahead of them and were of little use, as were the three tanks allotted to help clear a passage through the cactus. "Jesus Christ," says Maiki. "They were bloody useless. As soon as they went over these bloody great cactus, they sprang back up again." And the tanks simply drew enemy fire, bullets clanging and pinging into them. The moon was up, flares streaked across the sky, and tracers screamed over and into the advancing infantry. Maiki and his three new boys soon lost sight of Paul and the rest of the platoon, and were struggling to make their way through. Eventually they worked their way out of the cactus plantation and into a wheat field. Crossing through that and then some olive groves, they eventually emerged at the base of Takrouna, taking cover by a ledge under its lower slopes. For the moment they were quite safe. "You stay here," he told his three charges, "while I go and try and find the others."

Working his way around, he came across a Bren Carrier, which had just made it through with stacks of extra ammunition. Maiki could see fierce fighting going on both on Djebel Bir and on the lower slopes of Takrouna above him, but then heard voices and suddenly Sergeant Manahi from B Company appeared, scrabbling down toward him. He needed help carrying the ammunition up to where he and eleven other men were attacking up the most precipitous side of the hill. "Get some men together will you?" he asked. Maiki was worried that he didn't really have the authority. He was only a private and didn't want to be responsible for getting anyone killed. If Paul had been with him, he'd have been able to tell them what to do, but they still hadn't found him. When he went back for the others, however, they insisted on helping, and so they began lifting the boxes out of the carrier and carrying them up the slopes. "It was difficult," says Maiki. "These were two-to-a-box jobs, and the slopes were bloody steep." They were aiming for the first level of buildings, where B Company had a foothold, but all the time mortars and grenades were being slammed down into them. Even so, they made it in one piece, handing over the boxes to the B Company men. Maiki paused for a moment, his back against a building. He had only been there a few moments when a bullet ricocheted off a wall and hit him in the leg. "The bastard went straight through the top of my thigh," says Maiki.

"Look, we're all right now," Manahi told him, having seen his wound. "You get on back down." With the help of the new boys, Maiki did just that, reaching the comparative safety of some rock at the foot of the hill. His wound was not good, but he was worried about Paul—he hadn't seen him since they'd set off and so thought he'd try and look for him. He now had a better sense of his bearings and knew roughly where Paul had told him they were to aim for. Telling the new boys to stay put, he staggered off.

But there was no sign of Paul, or any of the rest of C Company. Having decided he should try and get back to the others and rest up his leg, he had begun stumbling back when a mortar bomb whistled down and landed right next to him. "Jesus Christ, it was just as though someone had stuck a searing hot iron on you," says Maiki. "The bomb inflated like a tire and blew out." Blasted to the ground, his leg was just hanging on by a bit of skin. "The blood was pissing out, just pumping out," he says. Fully conscious still, he tried to lift himself up and do something to stem the flow, but he was rapidly losing strength, and the weight of his pack, his Tommy gun, and ammunition, was too much. He tried to undo his belt but couldn't. He fell back. "I just lay there. I had my right hand inside my groin and I could feel the bone. I wasn't in pain. They say your life swims before you . . . I started thinking of home."

Maiki was still conscious when he heard a voice, and looking up, saw two stretcher bearers. With some difficulty they managed to lift him up onto the canvas. "I can't do anything here, Parky," one of them told him. "It's too bad." They took him to a trench and then eventually, by ducking and dodging the bullets, back to the regimental aid post. And there Maiki finally passed out.

"I attacked the Enfidaville position on night 19/20," Monty wrote to Alex on 21 April, even though he was in Cairo at the time. "Fighting was very heavy. A lot of Boche were killed."[619] So too were a lot of his own troops. Djebel Bir was taken on the twentieth, and Takrouna finally cleared the following day. At one point, two Maori had reached the summit by scaling hand-over-hand up telephone cables. There they captured an astonished German radio operator and artillery observer. Later, Italians—who offered stiff resistance throughout—hurled grenades into a building sheltering the wounded, and the survivors went berserk, even hurling the enemy over the rock face. Elsewhere, the New Zealand attacks had met heavy resistance, and while most reached their initial objectives, 21 Brigade had to be withdrawn after the first night of the attack.

News of the Maori assault on Takrouna quickly filtered through Eighth Army, recounted with something close to awe. "In my opinion," wrote Horrocks some years later, "it was the most gallant feat of arms I witnessed in the course of the war."[620] But their success had come at a bitter price. One of the dead was Maiki's great friend Paul Te Kani. His scattered body had been found later as they'd cleared the battlefield. "They told me they picked him up in pieces," says Maiki.

Monty's attempt to break through to Tunis had failed, but it made Kesselring and von Arnim believe they could be attacked in any sector along the front at any time. In this, they were quite correct, as they were about to find out. Crocker's IX Corps were the first to strike in the center. At midnight on 22 April, two hundred guns opened up ahead of 46 Division's advance. Their immediate goal was the hills that barred the way to the

Goubellat Plain. The Leicesters were down to three of their usual four companies and were in reserve, and while Peter Moore was comforted to know that the attack was being supported by such large numbers of artillery, he had come to learn that being in reserve was often an ominous situation. "It meant you were going to be hurled into action wherever a crisis arose and with very little preparation," he noted. For two days they watched the battle, as firstly 6th Armoured, and then 1st Armoured, pushed through, littering the plains on either side of the high ground. On 23 April, they moved up from their concentration area, following behind the tanks and preparing for any counterattack. But none came, although it was clear their advance was not progressing as speedily as Crocker had hoped.

The Guards Brigade were also following behind 6th Armoured's tanks, and once again, Captain Nigel Nicolson was able to watch the armor press on across the open plain. He noticed they all lurched forward and then halted. A belch of thick smoke suddenly appeared from the turret of one of them—this had been hit by an 88mm. "The other tanks then scurry around like a farmyard full of hens," wrote Nigel, "and try to get into position behind hills where the 88 cannot hit them, but they can hit the 88. All this is a very quiet affair. There is very little shooting, and the whole thing is very clumsy. Tank battles are not in the least bit slick." He then watched the infantry push forward and try and shoot at the 88 and its crew. Germans then hurriedly brought up a half-track, hooked the 88 to the back of it and began withdrawing. This was the cue for the tanks to open fire again as their target scurried off. Then the armor pushed on forward again.

In this way, Crocker's armor made slow and steady progress, but they had been unable to advance more than a few miles and there were still pockets of resistance on the high ground. On the twenty-fourth, the Leicesters, along with the Sherwood Forresters, were suddenly called upon to attack a cluster of hills known as the Djebel Bessioud. The plan was for the Leicesters to storm one ridge, the Forresters another.

To avoid a long march, the Leicesters were taken under the cover of darkness by recently arrived Churchill tanks, clinging desperately onto the flat area behind the turret and above the engine as they lurched and climbed to the start point. There they synchronized their watches and, staring into the darkness, waited on the grassy slopes for Z-hour. On the stroke of midnight, the Leicesters and Sherwood Forresters stood up from where they'd been lying and began marching toward the German positions, which in the case of the Leicesters were just eight hundred yards away. They covered the first two hundred without any opposition, but then the Spandaus began drilling out their fire. Flares hissed into the sky, but so far Peter and the rest of C Company, on the right flank of the hill, had not been seen. Their presence was not left undiscovered for long, however. Another flare burst above them, and machine-gun bullets crackled over their heads. Everyone dived for the ground, but once the flare died down, they began to organize themselves for a final charge. One platoon was to give covering fire while the other two pushed around to the right. Then a green flare was shot into the sky and all four companies charged at once. "As we charged, the Spandaus fell silent," noted Peter. "Even the splendid young men of the Hermann Göring Division had had enough." They took a handful of prisoners, but the rest had fled.

By dawn, the Forresters had also taken their hill. Peter Moore's C Company quickly set up their mortars but were out of range of the retreating enemy. The hill, however, gave the Leicestershire men a commanding view. Peter Moore looked out across the wide sweep of the Goubellat Plain, with its tranquil-looking fields of corn and groves of fruit trees. Out of sight on the horizon was Tunis. At first glance, the path seemed tantalizingly clear, but appearances were deceptive. Crocker's armor had forced back 10th Panzer some six miles, but if anything, German resistance here was stiffening rather than weakening, and there were still a number of hills that needed clearing, most particularly the Djebel Kournine, known as the "Twin Tits." American Mitchell bombers were called in to help, two waves of twenty-five. Peter was not envying the Germans, but then he watched in disbelief as the B-25s dropped their bombs on their own side. Once again it was the hapless Hampshires who bore the brunt; they had been jinxed throughout the campaign by incidents of friendly fire.

As the Leicesters attended an Easter Sunday service in a grassy bowl on their captured high ground, Peter could sense the campaign was drawing to an end. There would be one last effort, however. That night, Peter found himself marching across the dried salt lake and then climbing up the precipitous Twin Tits, unsure of what they would find there but expecting to meet German resistance at any moment. Miraculously, it was empty and the following day the Leicesters were withdrawn. It was to prove an unfortunate decision. Crocker's drive had run out of steam, and in the lull, the Twin Tits were reoccupied by the Germans, who wasted no time in defending it heavily. On 29 April, 2nd Rifle Brigade were given the task of storming the position at night. Although defended by only around thirty Germans, the bare and coverless slopes were now littered with mines, booby traps, and trip wires. Albert, manning a six-pounder on the lower slopes, could only gaze at the black hulk of the mountain and try and work out what was going on. But all they could see was a mass of tracer, star shells briefly lighting a patch of the battle and then fading, and bright, sudden, explosions as mines detonated or wires were tripped. But although the riflemen were within shouting distance of the summit, they were unable to clear the final rock face.

"We were a somber group," noted Albert, "as we returned empty-handed to our positions." [621]

Over the hills to the north of IX Corps, General Allfrey's V Corps were preparing to launch their own two-pronged attack along the ridges of hills that overlooked the Medjerda Valley. On 20 April, Captain David Brown took the chance to write a long letter to his wife. He often fretted about money and was anxious that they should be trying to save something for later. This was hard, he knew, but he urged her to try and manage. "We'll have a super nest egg after the war is over," he wrote. "I look forward to it very much."

He was tired. It had been a hectic few weeks—during the last stretch of fighting he'd gone seventy-two hours without sleep. Right now, he'd had enough of the Medjerda Valley, and especially of tramping up and down the mountains. "I've been a bloody mountain goat lately," he grumbled. The battery's only means of transport to their gun positions on the high ground were pack mules, of which there never seemed to be enough. "You carry 60lb wireless sets, batteries, food, water and every damn thing up the mountain yourself," he wrote. "All this with no sleep and any little packets Jerry may be sending over." More than at any time since arriving in North Africa, David was feeling the tug of home; he wished he could be back in London, or anywhere in England, where spring would be bursting out once more. "Goodbye for now, darling," he finished off. "Much love to you and Carola, and your mum and pats to the wee chap, and regards to all." Then having added his regards to everyone else he could think of, added, "And big hugs and kisses to you, my darling."

The following day, the entire regiment moved up to new positions in preparation for 78th Division's attack on Longstop. "What a legend Longstop had become," wrote Alan Moorehead, who was there. He hoped to watch its capture. "For five months it had lain right in the front line, the fortress of the Medjeda Valley, the locked gate on the road to Tunis." As he climbed the hills before it and looked across at this stubborn crest, he likened it to "a great two-humped bulk that heaved itself out of the wheat fields like some fabulous whale beached on the edge of a green sea."

During the night of 22 April, the 17th Field Artillery began firing concentrations onto the enemy positions on Longstop. Between them and the other divisional artillery, they managed to bring 154 guns to bear, but despite their efforts, the attacks the following morning met predictably stiff resistance. As troops and Churchill tanks began crawling up the slopes of Longstop on this sunny Good Friday, the battlefield soon became shrouded in smoke and dust and it was hard for anyone to follow quite what was going on. Alan Moorehead looked out and through the smoke watched Churchill tanks climbing unbelievably steep terrain "like toys."[622] Dot-like infantry scurried across the uplands while equally toy-like pack mules drudged up hill tracks.

David Brown was one of the dots that Alan had been watching. Sent up ahead with the assaulting troops, he and several other gunners had been given the task of trying to establish a forward observation post, and by early afternoon, despite intensive mortar and machine-gun fire, he had managed to reach the main summit along with the infantry of 36 Brigade. He got no farther. Soon after, he was killed, his body discovered later during a lull in the fighting. David had been shot through the head.

Administratively, Alex had placed II Corps under Anderson's command, but this did not worry Bradley. Alex had outlined the II Corps mission in fine detail, to which Bradley concurred entirely, making any interference from Anderson very unlikely. Nonetheless, Alex had further put the II Corps commander's mind at rest by paying him a visit and assuring him that should he ever receive an order, suggestion, or request from First Army to which he objected, he was to feel free to refer it back to him. Alex did not view Bradley as a loose cannon like Patton.

Bradley had realized that the army campaign in Tunisia was all about capturing the high ground. His attack was launched the day after First Army, on 23 April. First on the list was a series of high points, all close to one another and from a defender's point of view, all mutually supporting, so they needed to be attacked simultaneously. He gave the task to the Big Red One. The only hill that actually dominated the mouth of the Mousetrap—the Tine Valley—was Hill 350, the objective given to the 2nd Battalion of the 18th Infantry. Intelligence had told them that the enemy was strongly dug in along the reverse slopes, while a cluster of buildings known as Windmill Farm on the forward slopes was held by a few enemy outposts.

After softening up the Germans with artillery fire, Company G launched a bayonet charge at Windmill Farm in the last hour before dawn. It was another bloody and costly night for the company. The farm was far from being lightly held, and the attackers met far stronger resistance than they'd expected. "We'd lost so many men we had to pull back," says Randy Paulsen, "but as we pulled back, the Germans came over the hill and counterattacked us." Randy had been lying flat on the ground, aiming his new carbine, when the enemy appeared. A big German lieutenant lunged toward him. Squeezing the trigger, Randy put one round straight through him. But then the carbine jammed. Randy desperately tried to pull out the offending bullet, ripping a fingernail in the process, but unable to dislodge it, had to give up and run for his life. "In fact, I took a couple of rounds through the pack on my back and didn't even know it," he says. "I don't think I was ever scared, though. I think I was more petrified. I didn't think I'd ever get back." Tom Bowles was another from Company G who'd managed to get back to safety that day. "We lost a lot of good men there," he says. In fact, they'd lost 40 percent of their number.

Despite further counterattacks, the hill was eventually secured later that day. Elsewhere, the Big Red One was also making progress. Enemy positions were slowly but surely overrun, ground out through dogged persistence and weight of arms. By 26 April, Bradley's men had slugged their way forward about five miles, but then they, too, became bogged down. The Germans, leaving reams of mines and the usual booby traps in their wake, had dug in particularly firmly on the highest mountain in the area, Djebel Tahent—or more simply, Hill 609. This feature, more rugged than most of the hills in the area, dominated both the Djoumine and Tine Valleys.

It occurred to Bradley that the capture of Hill 609 was the perfect opportunity for the Red Bull Division to redeem themselves. "Get me that hill," he told Doc Ryder, "and no one will ever again doubt the toughness of your division."[623] Ryder's men began flushing out the lower hills on 28 April, then supported by heavy artillery launched their main assault the following day. Time and again, the Red Bulls stormed the peak, only to be pushed back. At Bradley's suggestion, Ryder tried a fourth attempt, but this time supported by tanks. The British Churchill tanks had proved particularly good at forcing their way up steep terrain, and this had a knock-on effect. Suddenly commanders were being more adventurous in the use of tanks in hill country. On the morning of 30 April, the Red Bulls assaulted Hill 609 again, the accompanying tanks pounding the enemy mortar and machine gun nests with shell after shell. By afternoon, the Americans had taken the summit. Counterattacks were successfully beaten off, and by 2 May, all of Hill 609 and the neighboring high ground was occupied by the victorious Red Bulls. Both sides had fought with exceptional tenacity; one German prisoner told his captors that in the final assault on the thirtieth, they had lost 50 percent of their men.

Following their progress was Ernie Pyle. When he'd reached North Africa, his columns had been syndicated to 42 newspapers throughout the USA. Such was his growing popularity, however, that the figure was now over 120. Even in London excerpts were being printed. He couldn't understand it—as far as he was concerned, he was doing little more than writing letters home. But at a time when there was no television and little film coverage, his efforts to paint a picture about what their boys were up to brought it home to millions of Americans more clearly than anyone else in the theater.

"I love the infantry because they are the underdogs," he wrote. "They are the guys that wars can't be won without." One day during the Red Bulls' assault on Hill 609, he watched a column of men returning from the front line, traipsing down a winding mountain track. "Their walk is slow," he noted, "for they are dead weary . . . Every line and sag speak of their inhuman exhaustion. On their shoulders and backs they carry heavy steel tripods, machine-gun barrels, leaden boxes of ammunition. Their feet seem to sink into the ground from the overload they are bearing." He was shocked by their appearance. "Their faces are black and unshaven," he continued. "They are young men, but the grime and whiskers and exhaustion make them look middle-aged." His heart ached for them.[624]

Bucky Walters was one of those blackened-faced, battle-weary, infantrymen who'd been in the thick of the fighting on Hill 609. From the outset, when they'd moved through the Big Red One and into position on the lower hills, he'd felt better equipped to deal with the battle ahead of them than when they'd been at Fondouk. "We'd become hardened, absolutely," he says. "We had developed quite a bit of hate and anger toward the enemy. Seeing your buddies get killed—you become dulled. It's a numbness. And the fact that you're still alive makes you somehow still able to go on, I guess." Ernie Pyle noticed this change, too, among the soldiers he spoke to. "He wants to see the Germans overrun, mangled, butchered in the Tunisian trap," he noted, then added, "Say what you will, nothing can make a complete soldier except battle experience."[625]

Bucky Walters agrees. A lot of the uncertainty at Fondouk had come from not knowing what to expect; they'd never advanced together into the waiting jaws of an Axis defensive screen before. New boys joining the Eighth Army, for example, would be sent to a section in which there were several old timers, veterans who had experienced what it was like to be attacked by Stukas, to advance at machine guns or be shelled and mortared without respite. The Red Bulls had had to discover these things together, as one. The shock had been appalling.

But now they knew. At Fondouk, Bucky had learned to distinguish between the different sounds of shell and small-arms fire. He had learned that Stuka attacks were usually directed at tanks and artillery more than infantry, and that with air bursts, the shrapnel usually went in one direction. Air bursts, particularly, were still terrifying—"You tasted fear," he says—but there was no longer any uncertainty about what they were doing. Each man knew his task and what he had to do to try and achieve it.

Bucky was still with the heavy-weapons company, and spent much of the battle for Hill 609 alongside the company commander carrying out forward observation work. It was while working his way up toward an OP that he came under a Stuka attack. "We all jumped in a little wadi," he says, "and the son of a gun hit not too far away and the blast lifted us right out, about

four or five feet, and dropped us onto the bank again. Not a mark on us."
Shrapnel could cover quite a wide area, especially from an 88mm. By the
end of the battle for Hill 609, Bucky's uniform was full of holes, his body
covered in small welts and burns. They also came under fire from the *nebel-
werfer,* or "Screaming Meanies"—multiple rocket launchers—for the first
time. "The noise was terrible," he says. "It was deafening, a horrible sound.
It seemed as though there were fish swimming over your head and going
around in circles." But they quickly realized that despite their terrible wail,
these charges were to be the least feared of German explosives.

"We did a pretty good job on Hill 609," says Bucky with some satisfaction. General Omar Bradley agreed. As he'd hoped, their victory restored
the division's self-confidence. "No one ever again would question its
courage," he noted. At AFHQ, both Ike and Harry Butcher had been following events on Hill 609 particularly closely. The Red Bulls' success,
Butch thought, was "another indication that after greenness is overcome
by actual battle experience, our American troops fight very well."[626] But the
consequences of this American epic also had a decisive effect on the course
of II Corps' campaign. With its loss, the Axis decided to pull back to a
tighter bridgehead around Bizerte. In the far north, this enabled the 9th
Infantry, who had been pushing forward slowly alongside Koeltz's French
troops, to finally capture Green and Baldy Hills on 1 May. Moreover, the
Tine Valley—the Mousetrap—was now clear for Harmon's armor to push
its way forward. Bizerte beckoned.

All the while, Mary Coningham's air forces never let up, flying an average
of 650 sorties a day. Only on 24 April, when rain and low cloud once more
interfered, did that figure drop. Bombers and fighters continued their relentless attack: airfields, supply columns, infantry, tanks, and artillery positions were bombed and strafed without mercy.

The 33rd Fighter Group were as busy as at any time since they arrived
in North Africa. On 20 April, Jim Reed was flying as wingman to the
group's CO, Colonel Momyer. Their mission was to bomb an enemy airfield near Tunis, but unfortunately, just before they reached the target, Jim
was hit in the wing by some light flak, knocking out the three machine guns
in his right wing and giving him quite a scare. Unsure how badly he'd been
hit, he immediately released his bomb into an Arab field. Their practice
was for everyone in the flight to drop their bombs the moment the leader
did, and obviously confusing Jim for Colonel Momyer, the other pilots began dropping their bombs too. Momyer immediately ordered them back to
base, with Jim landing first as an emergency. "I sure took a lot of kidding
for a while about this mission," says Jim. "Some funny things and some serious things happen in war. I don't know which this was."[627]

Jim still managed to fly three days later when most of the air forces were grounded, and again the following day, this time on the lookout for Stukas. Flying at only five hundred feet, he was given a bird's-eye view of the battle below. "Big shells were streaking across the ground, from one tank to another," he noted in his diary. "I saw one large tank explode and burn . . . smoke was everywhere."[628]

Bryan Colston was also busy, flying every day. They now had a few P-51 Mustangs, the latest American fighter planes built on behalf of the British. He, too, was getting to see much of the battle, flying over the IX Corps sector on 24 April—"an amazing sight," he recorded. The heavy bombers also continued to pound the enemy's port facilities and targets further afield. On 27 April, the 97th Bomb Group flew their 100th over-seas mission, with Tooey Spaatz on board as an observer. Since that first mission, they had had 1,878 encounters with the enemy and had shot down 181 enemy planes. Ralph Burbridge had been on their first and was on their hundredth too.

Longstop was eventually cleared of all enemy forces on 27 April, but as in IX Corp's sector, their strike either side of the Medjerda had run out of steam. Alex had recognized that First Army's drive needed fresh impetus and had begun thinking about bringing most of Crocker's armor over to join 78th Division in an all-out charge through the Medjerda Valley. On 30 April, he visited Monty at Eighth Army Tactical HQ. Montgomery had been in Cairo on a HUSKY conference and while there had come down with tonsillitis. Although recovering, he was not in the best of form. His head told him that any further strike through the coastal sector would be a wasted effort, but his vanity made him unable to resist another chance to be first in Tunis. Both Freyberg and Tuker repeatedly told both he and Horrocks that this was foolish and that the drive from Medjez was the most effective course open to them, but their arguments fell on deaf ears. Monty's one concession was to cancel 4th Indian's part in the plan. Instead, Horrocks launched 56 Division on the coastal strip on 28 April. These Lon-doners were inexperienced in battle and had only recently arrived at the front after a thirty-two-day trek from Kirkuk in Iraq. Their attack was bloodily beaten back.

Even Monty had to concede that any further thrust along his front would be pointless and acquiesced when Alex cancelled his further plans to attack up the coast. Instead, Alex told him, he wanted Monty to dispatch the best troops he could spare for the renewed strike through the Med-jerda Valley. Monty nominated 4th Indian and 7th Armoured Divisions, along with 201st Guards Brigade, the nucleus from which Eighth Army had been formed back in 1940. "It was particularly appropriate," noted

Alex, "that the two divisions which had won our first victory in Africa, at Sidi Barrani, should be chosen for the main role in our last victory, the battle for Tunis."[629] When General Crocker had been wounded the previous day, Alex had originally had Freyberg in mind to take over IX Corps for this final thrust. Monty, however, was adamant that it should be Horrocks. On this matter, it was Alex's turn to acquiesce.

Tuker was delighted with this outcome. It was what he'd hoped for all along, and secretly felt that it was his constant badgering of Monty and Horrocks that had also persuaded Alex to adopt this course. In this he was mistaken, but he was certainly able to have a significant bearing on the course of the battle. At last, his senior commanders were listening to him. It had been a long time coming, but General Tuker was about to be given the chance to implement the tactics and principles of modern warfare, which he had studied so carefully for so long, in a major and decisive battle.

The Americans, meanwhile, were drawing ever closer to Bizerte. The 48th Evacuation Hospital—now enlarged and renamed the 128th—had moved nearer to the front and was now encamped around the battered railways station at Sidi Nsir. Once more, the staff were frantically busy tending and caring for the sick and wounded. Margaret Hornback was used to seeing the horrors of war, but it did not stop her mourning the men who were mangled and killed in the process. Just before they'd headed north, she'd been taken to see the southern battlefields before they were cleared away. "American troops were plotting the graves there," she wrote. "Ours on one side of the road, the Germans on the other. You remember that little poem, *Under the Willow the Blue, Under the Laurel the Gray?* Same kind of boys on both sides. What a pity!"

While the 9th Infantry and the Corps D'Arfrique Francais pushed cautiously along the coast, General Harmon's 1st Armoured Division pressed on down the Mousetrap. On 3 May, CCA had taken Mateur, a sizable market town on the Bizerte road. Now with the 81st Reconnaissance Battalion, Lieutenant-Colonel Hamilton Howze was one of the first to enter the town. Two days later, he was still with the advance guard pushing through the hills toward Ferryville, a French town nestling on the southern banks of the Lac de Bizerte. Under cover of a low ridge, Hamilton drove forward in his jeep, then got out and walked up toward the crest. Before he reached the top, however, he encountered an American lieutenant about the same age as he, but with weathered, crinkled skin, and four of his front teeth missing. It turned out he was a ranchhand from Texas, and had only reached the front the previous evening. Hamilton then asked him if he knew where the nearest Germans were.

"Oh, right over on the next ridge," he replied.

Hamilton thought this unlikely, so said, "How do you know?"

"You can see them," the Texan told him. "The whole damn ridge is covered with them."

Hamilton was certain this was nonsense, but as he stepped over the crest of the ridge he saw that the lieutenant was right. Less than a mile away, the hill was heaving with Germans—ten times the number he'd seen throughout all the previous four months. Through his binoculars, he could see them hurriedly digging in and bringing up anti-tank guns. "I was flabbergasted," he noted, "but my new friend wasn't at all—it seemed quite normal to him."[630]

The following day, once the rest of the armor had caught up, CCB attacked but were heavily repulsed. Hamilton was then called for by Harmon to take command of the 2nd Battalion 13th Armoured Regiment after the previous CO was wounded, and was told to prepare another assault. Ordering support from all the division's artillery, Hamilton led his tanks forward under a heavy smokescreen, quickly overrunning the enemy's forward positions. From his Sherman, Hamilton looked down from his turret on a number of Germans huddled in their gun emplacement. He felt exhilarated and scared in equal measure—this was his first action as a battle commander.

They crested the next rise and came under heavy enemy fire once more as the Germans began lobbing high-angle shells into them. Hamilton's tanks were taking some damaging hits and soon became bogged down. He knew he had to get them moving again, but his radio was now on the blink. There was nothing else for it but to clamber out of his turret and hurry over to every tank in turn, banging on the hatch and shouting orders to each commander. "This is a poor way to issue orders," he observed, "but we got moving and once underway restored our order and momentum." As they set off, the shell fire died away, so they pushed on, inching ever closer to Bizerte until darkness fell.

To the west, CCA were also finding their path checked by a series of counterattacks. In the early hours of 7 May, Ray Saidel and the men of the 1st Armoured Regiment found themselves on the receiving end of long-range field artillery. The very first shell to land amongst them did so just 150 yards from Ray's half-track. This was followed by more and more screeching over and bursting all around them. "It was the first time I really felt sure our number was up," he noted in his diary. For over two hours, the shelling was heavy and persistent and Ray felt that sooner or later an explosion was bound to get them. The blast of one nearby shell lifted Ray off the ground. As he slammed back down again, he smashed the frames of his glasses. For the next few months, he had to wear them wrapped in adhesive tape.

At dawn, Hamilton Howze had half expected to discover that his lea-guer was surrounded, but in fact there was no sign of the enemy, and so he led his tanks on to Ferryville. The 1st Armoured Regiment also reached the town later in the afternoon. Unlike most of the Arab towns they'd been through since arriving in Tunisia, Ferryville was thoroughly French in both appearance and population, and as they trundled through, the streets were lined with cheering people. "I dare say there were very few GIs that day who didn't have a lump in their throat," noted Ray. He certainly did.

On his arrival at Medjez el Bab, General Tuker had gone to Horrocks's HQ, where he heard the new IX Corp commander's battle plan. This was essentially a dawn attack supported by a barrage. Tuker said nothing at the time, but then carried out his own reconnaissance of the battlefield along with his divisional artillery commander. The extent of the hills overlooking the proposed line of advance made it clear to him that a day-light attack would be a huge error. At the next conference he pressed his views, suggesting, 1) a night attack with artillery to cover the noise of their advance and to pave the way; 2) massive *concentrations* of artillery, rather than a barrage, pinpointed onto one target after another; 3) one thou-sand rounds per gun, which Tuker had discovered was perfectly feasible, and not 450 as Horrocks was suggesting; and 4) plenty of air photo-graphs beforehand in order to accurately provide detailed analysis of en-emy positions.

In what Tuker described as "a battle of wills," he won nearly all his points. Horrocks argued that not enough men were trained for a night at-tack; Tuker replied that his infantry would do this on their own, guaran-teeing that by dawn he would have tanks, anti-tank guns, mortars and machine guns in amongst the enemy's forward positions to make sure the rest of the infantry succeeded easily in the final punch. He did, however, have to accept a "token" barrage, but managed to ensure that his own ar-tillery commander was allowed to run the whole artillery plan for the bat-tle. "I urged this as the perfect infiltration battle," noted Tuker.[631]

In the event, Operation STRIKE went almost entirely as Tuker had hoped. After dark on 5 May, massed formations of night bombers arrived, followed by the devastating artillery fire: 450 guns blasting one position af-ter another, slinging 16,600 shells in under two hours. Nigel Nicolson, who had climbed up Grenadier Hill to follow the attack, was astonished. "The shells whistle over your head at the rate of eight or ten a second," he told his parents. "The gun flashes jump up out of the darkness and the explod-ing shells on the crest of the enemy position flower a few seconds later into a ruby tulip." Then, in the early hours the following morning, the 4th Indians attacked through thick, reedy grass, and with the noise of the artillery and with the lack of moon, gained the crucial advantage of surprise. With bayonet and kukri, they finally broke the German will. One panzer grenadier regiment was almost entirely annihilated in the holocaust. As dawn broke, the infantry could be seen swarming all over their objectives, the Churchill tanks lurching behind them through wheat fields speckled with bright red poppies.

That morning Grenadier Hill was busy as officers and commanders, politicians and journalists, all took their seats to watch the final act in the African drama. Mary Coningham was among them and looked up as, at 7 AM, the first of his bomber and fighter formations filled the sky above him, roaring over to complete the coup de grace. Accompanying him was Harold Balfour, undersecretary of State for Air. "I never realized what complete air superiority meant," he said, "until I saw this example of military and air movements carried out without the slightest attempt by enemy aircraft at interference." Hundreds of bombers and fighters flew over, while farther north, the Desert Air Force attacked airfields around Bizerte in support of II Corps. By noon, NATAF had carried out 1,200 sorties. "I was worried all day lest the petrol and bombs on the forward airfields would give out," noted Tommy Elmhirst, "but I had no complaints."[632]

Alex had ordered that every effort should be made to pass the two armored divisions through on the same day as the infantry attack started, but yet again, Horrocks was slow to push his armor forward.[633] "He had sworn that he would send it through at 0700 hours," complained Tuker. "At last at about 1100 I got him to move." Even then, Horrocks did not push hard for Tunis, ordering his tanks to stop for the night at Messicault, some fifteen miles to the southeast.

But this was of little consequence. The Axis was beaten, crushed by the overwhelming air-army combination. Tunis fell on May 7, as did Bizerte. The following day, all available Allied shipping was sent to patrol off Cape Bon. "Sink, burn, destroy," Admiral Cunningham signaled to them. "Let nothing pass." This prepared operation was given the code name RETRIBUTION. "I knew most of the destroyer captains," wrote ABC. "Some of them, and many more of their ships' companies, had endured the agony that our men had had to face during the evacuations from Greece and Crete two years before."[634]

For the next few days, sporadic fighting continued up in the rocky ground of the Cap Bon Peninsula, but mostly in the rocky ground north of the Enfidaville position where much of the Axis forces were trapped. In Algiers, Harry Butcher noted that Ike was rather nonchalant at the news of imminent victory; the supreme commander had long since moved on to planning the next invasion. Butch, however, was overjoyed. Congratulations poured in: from the president, from Marshall, from the prime minister. Few, however, touched Ike more than the letter from General Anderson. "This is a personal and not an official letter," wrote Anderson, "written to one who, like myself, was in this party from the beginning, and who has tasted the bitter as well as the sweet." He assured Ike that it would remain "one of his proudest memories" to have been "so intimately connected with the US Army." Ike immediately forwarded it to Marshall, "so that you may personally have some evidence of the soundness of the cooperative spirit that is animating the principal combat officers in this theater."[635]

Many of the men who had fought so hard throughout the campaign were unable to enjoy the spoils of victory. The Big Red One never reached Bizerte or Tunis, for that matter. On 9 May, they were relieved and sent back to Algeria, where they were to be deployed, ready to embark for Sicily. Albert Martin had also left Tunisia. A few days after the attack on the Twin Tits, he was told to report to Geneifa in Egypt, where he was to become an instructor in the anti-tank training wing; his time in the front line was over. He left his battalion amidst a sudden flurry of enemy shell fire. As the truck was pulling away from their positions, he suddenly remembered he'd left his knapsack of loot on his old truck, but as he looked back he saw it receive a direct hit. Rueing his bad luck, Albert began the two-thousand-mile journey back across North Africa.

The end in Africa brought little joy to Maiki Parkinson. As the victorious Allied troops marched into Tunis, Maiki was coming out of his coma at a military hospital in Tripoli. In the bed next to him there was a young soldier about the same age who'd had his leg cut off at the thigh. "I'm sad to see you've lost a leg," Maiki said.

"You'll get a good pension, though," the soldier replied.

"Will I?" said Maiki. And then the penny dropped. "I looked down, and oh Christ, I couldn't stop crying," he says. "Realizing my leg had gone was the most devastating thing that's ever happened to me."

As it turned out, ABC's naval forces had little seeking or destroying to carry out: only around eight hundred men were captured sailing away in light vessels and dinghies. Most had been trapped in Tunisia. Prisoners clogged every road around the Tunis bridgehead. Hamilton Howze had motored forward in his jeep early on 8 May only to drive straight into a large bivouac of German troops, all of whom were armed. "We regarded them with trepidation," noted Hamilton, "after all, the day before, they would have killed us—but were happy to note that each unit displayed a white rag tied to a stick."[636] On the way into Bizerte, Ray Saidel also watched agog as "thousands and thousands" tramped down the road toward them.

For Tommy Elmhirst, too, the sheer number of prisoners seemed astonishing. "I met one column of about two thousand under the charge of six British Tommies," he noted. "At its head were fifty or so German and Italian officers, the younger ones looking happy, the older ones, much bemedaled, trudging sullenly up a dusthill in the midday sun, carrying bags containing all their worldly belongings." Nigel Nicolson had never been busier, interrogating as many officers as he could manage and spending the rest of his time with a headset on, listening to vast numbers of messages flooding in. Final figures vary, from 275,000, according to American figures, to 238,243 as registered by the British. At any rate, around a quarter of a million, a huge figure, and one that matched Axis losses at Stalingrad. Total Axis casualties during the entire North African campaign were over half a million.

Fittingly, it was General Tuker to whom the Axis commander finally surrendered on 12 May, having motored up to von Arnim's HQ along with General Allfrey of V Corps. Tuker, especially, looked a sight, but that had ever been Eighth Army's way: worn pullover with no medal ribbons, battered drill trousers, and dusty suede desert boots; in contrast, von Arnim was dressed immaculately. Messe followed suit, signing the surrender document the next day. Appropriately enough, last to throw down their arms were the Afrika Korps.

For some, it seemed hard to believe the war in North Africa was finally over. The Sherwood Rangers had been stuck at the Enfidaville position for several weeks, facing an obstinate enemy. Suddenly, almost without warning, the front collapsed and they were on the move again, rounding up prisoners and equipment. "Somehow it is extremely difficult to fully realize that the war out here is finished," noted Stanley Christopherson, whose thoughts had immediately then turned to the future. "I am afraid that home leave appears to be out of the question," he added, "but still, one never knows." He was right, although they would be seeing England before many of those in North Africa.

At about 6 PM on 12 May, Nigel Nicolson was driving his jeep along the coastal road near Hammamet, to a point where the First and Eighth Armies were finally coming together. A ruined bridge lay across the riverbed, but the sappers were already there, busily finishing off the construction of a Bailey bridge in its stead. As Nigel waited to cross, he noticed an Italian corpse beside the bridge abutment, the belt of his machine gun trailing in the dust beside him. Just then, a staff car drew up, and out stepped General Alexander. Nigel had never seen him before, but stepped aside as Alex walked up to the lip of the wadi. For a while the general stared at the sandy bottom, and then he stepped over to the Italian machine gun, put the toe of his boot under the magazine, and shoved it, toppling it into the riverbed. "It was a gesture of finality," observed Nigel, "but it was something more. It expressed all his loathing for the wastage of war, and his contempt for the adulation of which he was then the hero."

The general then turned, walked back to the car and in a cloud of dust was gone. He'd not uttered a word.

The following day, at 1:16 PM, Alex sent a signal to Churchill. "Sir, it is my duty to report that the Tunisian campaign is over. All enemy resistance has ceased. We are masters of the North African shores."[637]

POSTSCRIPT

AT THE VICTORY PARADE through Tunis on 20 May, it was the 135th Infantry who led the American contingent, chosen for the courage and resolve they'd shown in capturing Hill 609. Bucky Walters was there, marching in time to "Stars and Stripes Forever." He felt somewhat refreshed, having spent a couple of weeks swimming in the deep blue Mediterranean at Bizerte. "Boy, that was paradise!" he says.

Bucky had come a long way since the day, just over a year before, when he'd bid a tearful farewell to his father. But then so had the entire Red Bull Division. They'd gone from being green, wide-eyed country boys from the Midwest, training with wooden rifles, to battle-hardened combat veterans, ready for the next big test: the invasion of Italy.

The final year of the campaign in North Africa had seen both Allies transformed. In the summer of 1942, Britain had been at her lowest ebb, a nation still stunned by the defeats of the first years of war, only slowly waking up to the realization that they'd left their war preparations a little too late. Their commanders in the field were hopelessly behind the times and so was much of their equipment. In the heat and sand of the desert, they had tried to fight a colonial war with colonial tactics and it hadn't worked. German professionalism had glaringly shown their deficiencies.

The Americans too had entered the war woefully underprepared. Their armed forces had been forced to spring out of the ground fully formed. That they were able to contribute so significantly to the war in North Africa was nothing short of a miracle, but to expect them to perform on an equal footing with the enemy was a hope too far. An army needs experience, at all levels.

Nonetheless, the two nations had, together, produced a team that could beat the Axis powers in Europe. American muscle was helping Britain's war capabilities, while British experience was guiding the novice American forces in the ways of war. As the Americans had shown in North Africa, they were willing to learn fast and by the end in Africa were proving that they could absorb the humiliation of defeat and emerge better and stronger. In achieving this, however, they were fortunate to have two men whose leadership helped them incalculably. Few would have thought at the beginning of 1942 that Eisenhower would be supreme Allied commander in little more than a year, yet he turned out to be an inspired choice, a man whose single-minded determination and insistence on maintaining Allied unity gelled two alien nations together. Under his command, Britain and America cooperated on the biggest seaborne invasion the world had ever seen, and on the battlefield, worked together with closer ties of shared command than either nation had ever attempted before.

Alexander also deserves credit. From the moment he arrived in the Middle East, Britain never retreated again. He handled Montgomery superbly and enabled the difficult and irascible Montgomery to work to his best potential. It says something about Alex that he was the only senior commander Monty never argued with. Later, as Army Group commander, Alex guided the Americans forward, while the divisions and tensions in command that had threatened to undermine this grand alliance were replaced by a sense of cohesion and singleness of purpose. His achievements have often been overshadowed by some of the glory seekers who served under him. Alex was never one to blow his own trumpet, but he deserves greater recognition than he has often been given. The Allies had much to thank both these men. Under their direction, the Allied experiences gained in North Africa made the future invasions of Italy and Normandy possible; and made victory against Nazi Germany not only possible, but also probable.

Many lessons were learned in North Africa. By the end of the campaign, Britain had shaken off many of her earlier mistakes. Her equipment had improved considerably: the Churchill tank, although not without its faults, was a marked improvement on anything they'd produced before, while they were now equipped with first-class anti-tank guns—the six- and seventeen-pounders—the most important weapons on the ground throughout the campaign. They were also beginning to employ the correct tactics to defeat the enemy: the final assault was, as Tuker claimed, an ideal example of how to use superior strength to devastating effect. He was only ever employing the basic tenets of warfare, but these had often been forgotten amidst the dust and smoke. Britain was learning how to win wars again.

Of great significance was the development of air power, and in this, the Allies were able to gain serious tactical advantage over the Germans for the first time. Although the Germans had developed the notion of army-air cooperation, demonstrating it with devastating effect during the blitzkriegs of 1939 and 1940, they had never expanded these ideas further. Mary Coningham, along with his small staff at the Desert Air Force and ably supported by Air Marshal Tedder, soon caught up and then overtook the Luftwaffe. The Luftwaffe never had the system of support that the Desert Air Force established—and in this, Tommy Elmhirst deserves his place in history too. Moreover, the Luftwaffe did not share the same culture as the Allied air forces, where personal scores counted for little against the combined effort of the squadron, wing, group, and even air command. The Germans were always held back by their willingness to idolize their aces and *experten*. Nor did the Germans ever adopt the policy of close cooperation as endorsed first by Mary and Monty and then by Mary and Alex. It was a system, however, that would be used by Britain and America alike until the end of the war and beyond, whenever there was a land battle to be won. Aircraft would also be specially developed for ground support. North Africa had shown that the feared Stuka was now almost as obsolete as the Hurricane. What was needed was a fast, powerful and strong air-to-ground fighter plane. This would be the Hawker Typhoon, originally designed to replace the Hurricane as an air-to-air fighter but later modified. At Falaise, a year later, this aircraft almost single-handedly finished off the German forces in Normandy, its rockets, cannon, and machine guns causing a devastating holocaust as the encircled enemy tried to make their escape.

In America, the tactical air doctrine was officially endorsed on 21 July, 1943, when the US War Department Field Manual was significantly altered with regard to the use of air power. This was, said Colonel Momyer, commander of the 33rd Fighter Group in Tunisia and later an air force general, "the emancipation proclamation" of tactical air power.[638] A key player in securing this change was Larry Kuter, who returned to Washington soon after the end in Africa and ensured that the work of NATAF impacted heavily on the way Americans viewed future warfare. A sign of any good tactical development is its longevity; the principles established by Mary *et al* are still used to this day.

British pride had been restored by victory in North Africa, while it had given the Americans much-needed confidence and, crucially, experience. It also heralded the end of the German-Italian partnership. Italy soldiered on, but with the loss of Africa, the writing was on the wall, as Hitler had known it would be. In July, the Allies invaded Sicily, and again they were victorious. On 3 September, Italy surrendered. From then on, the war in Europe was against Nazi Germany only.

Many of the commanders who fought in North Africa continued to lead the Allied forces to the very end. Eisenhower continued as supreme commander for Sicily and then returned to London to plan, at last, for the invasion of Northern Europe. His stature had grown significantly by the end of the North African campaign, and after the wobble of the early days of 1943, his authority was never seriously questioned again. He continued to hold sacrosanct the importance of Allied unity, although this would be tested time and again before the war was won. It was on his word that Operation OVERLORD—D-Day—was launched on 6 June, 1944. He remained as supreme commander, with Tedder his deputy, until the end of the war, receiving the German unconditional surrender, as stipulated at Casablanca, in the early hours of 7 May, 1945. Also there to witness the final victory was his trusted aide, Harry Butcher. The two remained together throughout the war. Afterward, Butch returned to the world of broadcast media, moving to California where he launched both a radio and television station. He saw a lot less of Ike, but the two remained good friends. Butch died in 1985. Ike, on the other hand, continued in the army, becoming chief of staff and then chief of NATO land forces in Europe before eventually turning to politics. In 1953, he became the thirty-fourth president of the United States, serving two terms before retiring to his farm at Gettysburg. He died on 28 March, 1969.

As commander of 15th Army Group, Alex commanded the Allied invasion of Sicily and then that of Southern Italy. He was still at the helm in Italy when the war ended. Since arriving in North Africa, he never lost another battle of which he was in command. By the end of the war, he was a field marshal and afterward was made a viscount, and became Governor-General of Canada, a post he held until 1952. He made an unhappy foray into politics, briefly joining Churchill's government as Minister of Defense, and was given an earldom, choosing the title Earl Alexander of Tunis, after his most famous victory. He died in June 1969, a few months after his good friend General Eisenhower, and was buried in the parish church of his Hertfordshire home in southeast England. At the head of his gravestone lies a single word: ALEX.

Both Montgomery and Patton led the respective Eighth and Seventh Armies in Sicily, their rivalry testing Allied relations once more. Patton was briefly disgraced for slapping an American soldier suffering from shell shock, but returned to lead the US Third Army in Normandy and Northern Europe, eventually commanding the main Allied advance into Germany. He was killed in a car accident in December 1945. Monty commanded all Allied ground forces on D-Day and later headed the 21st Army Group. Time and again he threatened to undermine Allied unity, stretching Ike's patience and clashing again with Patton. It was his idea to launch the airborne operation MARKET GARDEN, an uncharacteristically high-risk strategy, which failed and dogged his reputation forevermore. One of the principal reasons for the disaster at Arnhem was the failure of XXX Corps, led by General Horrocks, to link up with the airborne troops in time. Monty should perhaps have known that of all people, Horrocks was not the best person to lead any force in a hurry, although on that occasion, he was less to blame. After the war, Monty became CIGS, but in retirement continued to rub his former colleagues the wrong way, particularly with his memoirs, an extraordinarily one-sided and vainglorious account of his life. He died in 1976.

General Omar Bradley was also in Europe at the end, commanding the US First Army, and then the US Twelfth Army Group. After the war, he went on to become Army chief of staff. He died in 1981. Both General Ritchie and General "Pinky" Ward also returned to battlefield command in Europe: Ritchie as a corps commander, to which he was much better suited, and Ward as a divisional commander; he was to capture Munich in April 1945. Nor was the Auk's reputation threatened for long by his dismissal from Africa. He was reappointed as C-in-C of India in June 1943, playing a key role in the eventual victory in the Far East. Promoted to field marshal in 1946, he kept a dignified silence when Monty criticized him heavily in his memoirs, but continued to hold the loyalty of many of the Eighth Army originals. He died in 1981, aged 97.

General Tuker's frustrating war continued: his victory at Medjez el Bab, for which he was the architect but for which he was given too little credit, was to be his finest moment. He did well both in Sicily and southern Italy, but then, one day in March 1944, at the height of the battle for Cassino, he collapsed, suffering from rheumatoid arthritis. Returning to England, he recovered and was posted back out to the Far East, taking over first as army commander in Ceylon, then commanding IV Corps against the Japanese at Mandalay. After the war, he took over as GOC-in-C Eastern Command, India, under the Auk, and was promoted to lieutenant-general, also receiving a knighthood. After independence, he retired to Cornwall, where he planned to farm. Sadly, his illness soon returned, and by 1960, he was wheelchair-bound, left only with his ability to write, a skill he continued to use until his death in 1967.

Of the air commanders, Mary Coningham commanded the Second Tactical Air Force during D-Day and thereafter in Northwest Europe until the end of the war. He too continued to battle against Monty. After the war, he was made head of the RAF's Flying Training Command. He later suggested that in London and New York there should be statues of Rommel, "for his great contribution in directing the training of the US and British armies." There was something to be said for the idea. Mary retired—after thirty years in the service—in 1947. His life was tragically cut short, however, in January 1948, when the transatlantic flight from Lisbon on which he was a passenger crashed into the Atlantic and was never seen again. Tributes poured in from around the world. "It was to him personally more than to anyone else that we owe the initiation and development of the joint land-air technique," claimed Tedder. For Tommy Elmhirst, Mary's loss was a crushing blow. "To have heard him speaking every morning through those exciting years at his 8-am staff meetings and again every evening to have discussed with him, over a gin in his caravan, the events of the day was an education in itself," he wrote.[639]

Tommy, happily, had a much longer life. After working alongside Mary until the end of the war, he joined the Air Ministry as director of intelligence before taking over the post of chief of Inter Service Administration in India, serving under the Auk. He stayed on after independence as C-in-C Indian Air Forces. He retired in 1950, becoming governor of Guernsey, in the English Channel Islands, from 1953 to 1958. Thereafter he retired for good, spending his time fishing, writing, and with his wife, children, and grandchildren. Tommy died, aged 86, in 1982.

Larry Kuter also continued to rise up the ladder after his time in North Africa, ending the war in the Pacific. In 1955, he became a full general, becoming head of Far East Command two years later and then in 1959, commander of the North American Defense Command. He retired from the air force in 1962 and died in 1979.

But what of the men—and women—who slogged their way across North Africa? Like many of those who commanded them, a large number continued to serve elsewhere—in the Far East, in Italy, and in Northwest Europe.

Sam Bradshaw later fought with the Eighth Army through much of the Italian campaign. Toward the end of 1944, he was badly wounded again, and was eventually sent home to England, when he stepped on English soil for the first time in four long years. He did not stay long, however, and was posted to Northwest Europe for the last few weeks of the war. He stayed in the army, later receiving a commission, and retired as a major. Married, with seven children he now lives in Wigan, a town west of Manchester. Former chairman of the Eighth Army Association, Sam has done much to foster good relations with veterans of the Afrika Korps, a number of whom are now close friends.

Harold Harper returned home to the UK soon after the end of the Tunisian campaign, but in July 1944 was posted to Normandy where he became battery sergeant-major of 426 Battery, serving through France, the Netherlands and into Germany, where he remained after the end of the war to help run POW and refugee camps. In 1946, he was discharged and joined Boots the Chemist, a drugstore chain, in the accounts department. He stayed with Boots for forty-six years. He still lives in Nottingham, England, where he has been actively involved with the South Notts Hussars Regimental Association and Museum for a number of years.

The Sherwood Rangers spent the summer of 1943 in Africa and were then posted back to Britain to prepare for D-Day. By then, Stanley Christopherson was commanding the regiment and had become a lieutenant-colonel. He was to lead them with distinction. Few regiments demonstrate the development of the British army during the Second World War more than the Nottinghamshire Sherwood Rangers Yeomanry. Even by June 1944, the Sherwood Rangers had become a slick, highly trained outfit, the amateurism of their early days in the Middle East long since gone. They continued through Normandy and Northwest Europe until the end of the war, after which the regiment was disbanded along with so many others. Stanley Christopherson married, had three children, and returned to the bar, where he continued his civilian life as a highly successful barrister. He died in 1996.

Another who served in Normandy was Johnny Bain. After deserting at Wadi Akarit, he was caught and put in a military prison and only released in order to fight again in France. He survived the war and on returning home changed his name to Vernon Scannell, becoming a highly acclaimed and award-winning poet, novelist, and playwright. He now lives in North Yorkshire.

Rifleman Nainabadahur Pun recovered from his wounds and went on to serve with 1/2 Gurkhas throughout the Italian campaign, including the long, bitter, battle of Cassino. After the war, he returned to Nepal, where he was given three months' leave. He then decided to ask for a permanent discharge, which he was granted, only to later rejoin in 1949, serving with the Royal Engineers in the Brigade of Gurkhas. After retiring in 1959, he went back to the mountain village of his birth, where he married two wives and had five sons and three daughters. He lives there still.

Joe Madeley saw further action in the Far East, fighting his way through New Guinea and ending the war in Borneo. "It was a different kind of war altogether," he says, although felt the Japanese were no match for the Germans as fighting soldiers. After the war he returned to the family farm but, having spent four years fighting, found life a bit slow. He worked in the motor industry and later as a production manager for RCA Records, and was responsible for bringing Abba to Australia. "I tried Elvis, but he wouldn't come." He now lives in New South Wales and has two children, five grandchildren, and fifteen great-grandchildren.

A number of First Army men saw action in Italy. Nigel Nicolson also remained with the Guards Brigade throughout the campaign. He left the army soon after the war and had a long and varied career as a politician (where he served as a Conservative MP alongside Field Marshal the Earl Alexander); as a publisher, founding the publishing house Wiedenfeld and Nicolson; and as a writer and journalist. In 1973, he published the authorized biography of Alexander. He died at Sissinghurst Castle, in Kent, England, in September 2004. Peter Moore also served in Italy and Greece right up to end of the war. When it was over, he returned home, went to Cambridge University, lettered in rugby and then began a long career as a farmer and agricultural advisor. He married and had three sons, and lives just the other side of the Leicestershire border, in Derbyshire county, northern England.

John Frost served in Sicily and in Southern Italy, and most famously took part in the failed attempt to secure Arnhem Bridge, since renamed John Frost Bridge. After spending the last few months of the war as a POW, he returned to Britain, remaining in the army until he retired in 1968, and rising to major-general. During the war, he won the Military Cross and two Distinguished Service Orders. His last years were spent as a beef farmer in Sussex. He died in 1993.

The Bowles twins, Randy Paulsen, Bing Evans, Bucky Walters, and Joe Furayter all served in Sicily. Bing Evans was captured at Anzio. He spent much of the remainder of the war as a POW, although managed to escape twice. He was eventually sent back to the US, where his fiancée, Frances, was still waiting for him. They married two weeks after he reached home, in August 1945. He then went to college and spent much of his career working in agriculture and the construction business. He has three sons, is still blissfully married to Frances and lives in a small town in southern Indiana.

Bucky Walters served throughout the Italy campaign. By the time Bucky made it home, his father had passed away and his younger brother had been killed. Putting himself through college, thanks to the GI Bill, he became a history teacher. He married and had two sons and has spent much of his life back in New Jersey, where he still lives. The 1st Armored Division did not take part in the invasion of Sicily, but CCA took part in the landings at Anzio. Ray Saidel then remained fighting in Italy until the end of the war. He also made it home in one piece and went into the automobile business, running his own dealership in Manchester, New Hampshire. He also built and raced cars. A man of many parts, in the 1970s, he went to Israel to cover the war there as a journalist for his local paper. He has three children and a number of grandchildren, still paints and even occasionally races motorcars.

Hamilton Howze led the 13th Armored Regiment at Anzio and later the following summer took over command of CCA. He remained in the army, having a long and distinguished career and rising to the rank of full general in 1963, when he commanded the US Third Army. Earmarked to lead US forces in the invasion of Cuba in 1962, he also became a pioneer of army air-mobility during his time as director of Army Aviation. Working for the Bell Helicopter Company after leaving the army in 1965, he eventually retired to Texas. He died in 1998.

The Bowles twins, Randy Paulsen, and Joe Furayter were all with the Big Red One on D-Day. Henry and Tom Bowles, by then both in HQ Company, landed on Easy Red on Omaha Beach shortly after 9 AM on 6 June. Henry was seriously wounded on 7 June and sent back to England. His injuries could have given him a ticket home, but he decided home was with his brother, and so rejoined Tom in HQ Company in time for the Battle of the Bulge. They were in Czechoslavakia when the war came to an end. Returning to Alabama, they became electricians. Both married; Tom has five sons and Henry two daughters. They still see plenty of each other, but while Henry still lives in northern Alabama, Tom has moved to Lake Charles, Louisiana. Joe Furayter also survived D-Day and the Battle of the Bulge, following the Big Red One's flag from Oran to Czechoslavakia and ending the war without ever having suffered so much as a scratch. He returned home and went back to being a coal miner. He married and had one daughter and still lives in Pennsylvania.

Randy Paulsen also went right through, later commanding Company L of the 2nd Battalion, 18th Infantry. In April 1945, he accepted the surrender of more than 4,000 troops, including an SS general, when they took the town of Thale in the Harz Mountains of Southern Germany. Soon after, he was sent home on leave but when that was over was unable to get back to the First Division, and so he left the army and returned to his prewar job in newspaper advertising with the *New York Daily News*. He married, had two daughters, and continued to serve part-time with the National Guard. After living nearly his whole life in New York, he finally retired to Florida, where he still lives.

During the brief lull after the end in Africa, Margaret Hornback spent quite a lot of time with her boyfriend, Andy. Both were then posted to Sicily, but while he continued fighting in Italy, the 128th was eventually shipped back to England to prepare for the Allied invasion of Normandy. Margaret then followed the soldiers to France and spent the rest of the war in Northwest Europe. She was due to meet Andy, who had come up from the South of France, in Paris in the autumn of 1944, but he never showed up. She later learned he had died of malaria. After the war, Margaret returned home to Shelbyville, Kentucky, where she continued nursing. She never married, but dedicated herself to the care of others at her local hospital and also, briefly, in the Gaza strip during the 1970s. She died in 1998.

For some, however, the fighting ended in North Africa. Mangal Singh returned home, continued serving as a signalman in Burma and remained in the Indian Army after independence until retiring in the 1960s. He then moved to England, living in London and taking a job as a factory worker. Since retiring permanently, he has spent his time living between London and India. After returning to South Africa, Petrus Dhlamini was later sent to Italy, where he once again continued to work as a driver. He was posted back home again toward the end of 1944 and then joined the South African railway police, remaining with them for thirty-three years. He married and had seven children, although, tragically, three subsequently died. He now lives in Soweto.

On his return to South Africa, Bill Eadie became a pioneer carpenter, then later an instructor. After the war, he was discharged, and joined India Tyres, for whom he worked for the rest of his career, living with his wife and three children in Benoni, near Johannesburg. He died in 2000, aged 93.

Carol Mather escaped from his POW camp in Northern Italy, walking hundreds of miles south to join the advancing Allies. Sent home to England before D-Day, he rejoined Montgomery's staff, remaining with Monty until the end of the war and winning an MC (Military Cross). After the war, he stayed in the army, rising to lieutenant-colonel, and then entered politics, serving as a Conservative MP from 1970 to 1987. He was later knighted and now lives in Gloucestershire, England. He remains close friends with two of his old SAS companions: George Jellicoe (Earl Jellicoe), and Stephen Hastings. Stephen remained in the Middle East until fit again for active service. He then joined SOE (special operations executive) and was parachuted into Northern Italy to help the partisans around Piacenza during the final months of the war, winning an MC for his efforts. After the war, he spent several years in occupied Austria before joining the Foreign Office, serving in secret intelligence. He too became a Conservative MP, serving from 1960 until retiring in 1983, and was also knighted. Until recently, he was still indulging his lifelong passion for horses, regularly hunting (he won a number of cross-country races), and also breeding racehorses at his home in Northamptonshire. He died in January 2005.

Ray Ellis also escaped from his POW camp in Northern Italy, and then went into hiding, sheltered by an Italian family until he was eventually repatriated and sent home. After five years away at war, he initially struggled to adjust to life back in England. In due course, however, he was discharged, married, and had three daughters. Ray trained as a teacher and later achieved his ambition of becoming a headmaster. He still lives in Nottingham and is an active member of the South Notts Hussars Association.

Albert Martin remained as a "base wallah" at Geneifa until early

1945, when he eventually sailed for home. It was only a homecoming of sorts: the family house had been destroyed during the Blitz. Albert ended his soldiering as an instructor back at Winchester Barracks, and was discharged in 1946. He married, had two daughters, and spent the rest of his professional life working in the electricity business. In 1993, he returned to Tunisia and revisited the Djebel Kournine, the sight of his last action. This time, he reached the summit. He died in January 2005.

Maiki Parkinson pleaded not to be sent home, dreading the reaction of his friends and family when they saw he'd lost a leg, but he had to go, and left North Africa in 1943. He stayed in Wellington for a while, recuperating and slowly coming to terms with his disability. Not until after the war did he finally return home. There he met his wife, had eight children, and returned to a life of farming. He still lives in Opotiki.

Not all the airmen continued to serve in Europe, but most did. Willie Chapman had completed his three hundred hours just before the end of the campaign, leaving North Africa on 6 May. After getting married, he was later posted to 9th Bomb Group in the Pacific, a B-29 Superfortress Very Heavy Bombardment Unit, where he served as a pilot and staff officer. After the war, he settled in California and had a long career in the engineering and construction business. He has a son and daughter and still lives in California. Ralph Burbridge's career with the 97th BG continued until after the start of the Italian campaign, by which time he'd flown a phenomenal fifty-two combat missions. He returned home in late 1943, spending the rest of the war as an instructor. Ralph now lives in Arizona and Seattle.

Jack "Cobber" Weinronk spent the rest of the war as an instructor. Afterward, he eventually took over the family furniture business in Port Elizabeth. He married and had four children and continued to fly into his seventies. Cobber died in 2003. Tommy Thompson left the RAF to join BOAC before the war's end, remaining a commercial pilot until his retirement from British Airways in 1975, by which time he'd become the most senior pilot within his fleet. He now lives in Hampshire, in southern England. After the end in Africa, Johnnie Fairbairn spent over a year as an instructor, first in Egypt and then in Southern Italy, before returning to combat flying with 213 Squadron, SAAF. Soon after, he crashed while carrying out a low-level attack over Yugoslavia and was presumed to have been killed. His parents were informed of his death and even held a memorial service for him. In fact, he had become a POW and made a good recovery from his injuries. After the war, he and his brother, Alan, became partners in the family law firm in North London, Johnnie's clients including Tottenham Hotspur Football Club. He died in 1981.

Christopher Lee also served in Italy, remaining there until the end of the war. Afterward, he became an actor. During a long and successful career, he has starred in many films, including several as Count Dracula, in the Bond movie *The Man with the Golden Gun, The Wicker Man,* and more recently as Saruman in *The Lord of the Rings* and as Count Dooku in *Star Wars.* He lives in London.

After leaving Tunisia, Tony Bartley returned to England and after a period away from combat flying, became attached to the 70th Fighter Wing of the 9th US Air Force, covering the Normandy landings and later following them to the Pacific. After the war, he also pursued a career in films, following his wife, the actress Deborah Kerr, to Hollywood, where he became a screenwriter and production executive working for CBS and a number of other film and television companies. Later he moved to Ireland with his second wife. He died in 2001. Billy Drake also continued to work closely with the Americans. After his stint instructing in the Middle East, he took over the Qrendi Wing on Malta before and during the invasion of Sicily, and then later returned to Britain to take command of the Second Tactical Air Force Typhoon Wing under Mary Coningham. Later he joined Ike's Operations Staff at the Supreme Headquarters Allied Expeditionary Force (SHAEF), where he remained until the end of the war. Afterward, he stayed in the RAF until retiring as a group captain in 1963. He now lives in Devon.

Duke Ellington also flew in Italy and remained in the air force after the war, serving at the Pentagon, then at various training posts, before becoming a night-fighter squadron commander in Japan. Married, with five children, he retired as a colonel and has lived in California ever since. Jim Reed was rotated back to the States in November 1943, after taking part in the capture of Pantelleria and the invasions of Sicily and Southern Italy. On returning home, he married his girlfriend, Irene. He still lives in Tennessee.

Soon after the African campaign was over, Bryan Colston almost died of typhoid. He recovered but was sent home in November. After a brief period instructing, he took command of 695 Squadron, flying Spitfire Mk XVIs. Leaving the RAF after the war, he went to university and became a chartered surveyor. He married, had three sons, and now has "innumerable" grandchildren and two great-grandchildren. He lives in Somerset, England.

Charles Coles spent the rest of the war in various POW camps, and then was drafted into MI9, interviewing former prisoners and survivors of the Nazi death camps who had been Allied secret agents in escape organizations. Returning home, he remained in the Royal Navy Reserve, and began his career with the Game Conservancy, a job that took him all around Europe and led to a number of books and articles on game, wildlife, and farming. Married, with a son and daughter and now three grandchildren, he lives in the New Forest, near Southampton. Ben Bryant left *Safari* at the end of April 1943, and Ronnie Ward followed soon after, going back to Britain to take his Perisher submarine course before commanding his own boat. After the war, he stayed in the Royal Navy, rising to lieutenant commander before embarking on a new career as a specialist holiday operator: Ronnie was one of the first people to offer tours of China. Now retired, he lives in Buckinghamshire, near London. *Safari* also survived the war, although was sunk on her way to scrap in January 1946; she rests somewhere on the seabed southeast of Portland Bill in Southern England, and has become a popular site for divers.

After his time attached to the Eighth Army, Pierre Messmer moved to Algiers, where he joined de Gaulle's staff. He returned to France after D-Day and was with de Gaulle at the liberation of Paris. Later serving on de Gaulle's government as minister of defense, he became prime minister of France in 1972, until replaced by Jacques Chirac two years later. He still lives in France. Susan Travers was finally parted from General Koenig when he, too, was ordered to Algiers to join de Gaulle. Her time with the Free French was not over, however, and when they were sent to Italy, where they were attached to the US Fifth Army, Susan went with them as an ambulance driver. She also served with them during the invasion of Southern France in August 1944 and was still with the 13 DBLE when the war finally came to an end. Afterward, she was briefly reunited with Koenig, then military governor of Paris, but the love of her life was lost to her. After being inaugurated officially as the only female member of the French Foreign Legion, in August 1945, and with a military medal and *Légion D'Honneur* to her name, she was posted to Indochina. While there she became pregnant and married her lover, a Frenchman and fellow Legionnaire, Nicholas Schlegelmilch. They had two children and in 1950, when Nicholas left the Legion, they moved back to France. There she remained until her death in Paris in 2003.

Sophie Tarnowska stayed in Cairo until the end of the war. There she married William Moss, an SOE agent, and later, author of the bestseller *Ill-Met by Moonlight*. They eventually moved to London, where she still lives. Cecil Beaton continued to prove himself to be one of the most versatile photographers around. After an affair with Greta Garbo, he continued to work around the world and gained new acclaim for his set design and costume work, most notably for the film *My Fair Lady*. He was later knighted and continued to work up until his death in 1980.

The journalists Ernie Pyle and Alan Moorehead remain among the most celebrated of war correspondents. Ernie followed the GIs to Sicily and Italy, and then to Normandy and Paris before taking himself off to cover the war in the Pacific. He was killed by a machine-gun bullet on the island of Okinawa in April 1945. Alan Moorehead also followed the Allied armies to Italy and Normandy, and remained in Northwest Europe until the German surrender in May 1945. After the war, he wrote a number of celebrated and award-winning histories and travel books, as well as a biography of Montgomery. The three books comprising the *African Trilogy* are still in print and remain a classic account of the campaign. He died in 1983.

Most of the towns and cities so familiar to the Allied forces in North Africa have changed almost beyond recognition, but much of the battlefields remain curiously untouched. In Egypt, the patch of scrub at Burg el Arab where Monty, Mary, and Co. set up their headquarters has now been engulfed by hotels and holiday homes for wealthy Egyptians, but the sea is still as brightly turquoise as it ever was. Even Alamein itself has grown, although the original railway station building is still there, unkempt but much the same as it was back then. A new road has been laid through the Australian sector, but the blockhouse remains, dusty and battered.

It is possible to travel the length of the Alamein line, but Bedouin guides are needed. People are still killed every year by mines, and piles of them, detonated by the side of a desert track, are a common sight. Horseshoes of stones mark the place where guns once stood, and at any point one can still find shards of shrapnel, rusted British petrol cans, broken bottles and other debris from the battles that have never quite been cleared.

Although the Western Desert is more heavily populated—along the coast at any rate—than it was during the war, its vastness and relentlessness can still easily be appreciated. On and on it stretches, mile after mile, rarely changing, save for an occasional and sometimes dramatic rise in land. The logistical problems that faced both the British and Axis can only be truly appreciated when the vast distances between Egypt and Libya are experienced firsthand.

In Tunisia, the pillboxes and trenches of the Mareth Line remain largely intact, if not overgrown, as does Rommel and Messe's bunker a few miles behind. After the Western Desert it is easy to see how the Eighth Army thought even this southern part of the country was green in comparison, but this is still a dusty and bleak part of the world, as is the El Guettar massif. One glance at the high, jagged crests, and it is easy to see why this was a comparatively straightforward place to defend but a very hard place to attack. Further north, around Sidi Bou Zid, it is still possible to follow the path of the American armor on 15 February, 1943. There are no tanks there now, but the wadis—except for a very few places—remain as impassable as they were then.

Even in the more heavily populated north, there is much that remains the same: Longstop and the Medjerda Valley, Sidi Nsir, Hill 609, the Pimples and Twin Tits—they're all there, completely recognizable to anyone who fought back then, still surrounded by cork forests, wheat fields, and plains of grass. Even Takrouna and the Djebel Bir look every bit as intimidating as they must have to Maiki and the other Maori that April night in 1943. Climb to the top of Djebel Bir, and Italian machine-gun positions can still be seen, hacked out of the rock, while opposite, the village perching on top of that strange hill has hardly grown at all.

Perhaps a more moving reminder, however, are the large numbers of war cemeteries that mark the progress of the Allied armies: Alamein, Halfaya-Sollum, Tobruk, Knightsbridge, Benghazi, Tripoli, Sfax, Enfidaville, Beja, and Massicault, to name but some. They are all, without exception—both Allied and Axis—exquisite places, carefully tended havens, their peace and tranquillity a sharp contrast to the violence in which the men buried there died. They are also unbearably sad places.

The cemetery at Medjez-el-Bab, just southwest of the town, is particularly wistful. Here, 2,524 British and Commonwealth lie dead, their bleached white headstones fronted by bright flowers and guarded by rows of eucalyptus trees. From their branches, hundreds of birds seem to sing a shrill dirge without respite. In row 1B, grave 14, lies David Brown, "lieutenant," aged 28 years—in death he reverted to his substantive rank. Perhaps these places are tiny corners of England, or New Zealand, or India, but the moment one walks out of the gates or looks out across to the hills that were once so bitterly fought over, it is impossible not to be reminded that these men remain a long, long way from home.

GLOSSARY

ACV	Armored Command Vehicle
AFHQ	Allied Forces Headquarters
AFV	Armored Fighting Vehicle
AWPD-1	Air War Plans Division—team set up to prepare the USAAF's war policy in July 1941
Big Red One	US 1st Infantry Division
Bir	Desert well or water cistern
Brigade Group	Self-contained fighting unit consisting of infantry, armor, artillery, and engineers
C-in-C	Commander-in-Chief
CCA	Combat Command "A"
CCS	Combined chiefs of staff
CGS	Chief of the general staff
CIGS	Chief imperial general staff
COS	Chief of staff
CRA	Commander, Royal Artillery—the senior artillery officer in a division
DA	Director angle
DAF	Desert Air Force
DAK	Deutsche Afrika Korps
Deir	A depression
Djebel	Hill or mountain
DMI	Director of Military Intelligence
DMO	Director of Military Operations
DMT	Director of Military Training
GHQ	General Headquarters
GPO	Gun position officer

GSO 1/G-1 (US)	Senior general staff officer 1
HE	High explosive
LAD	Light aid detachment
LCA	Landing craft assault
LO	Liaison officer
LOB	Left out of battle
LRDG	Long Range Desert Group
LSI	Landing ship infantry
LST	Landing ship tank
MGRA	Major-general Royal Artillery—senior RA officer at army headquarters
MLR	Main line of resistance
NAAF	Northwest African Air Forces
NATAF	North African Tactical Air Force
NCXF	Naval commander Allied Expeditionary Force
OCS	Officer Candidates School
OCTU	Officer cadet training unit
Old Ironsides	US 1st Armored Division
OP	Observation post
OP/AC	Observation post assistant to the commander
OPD	Operations Division
Red Bull	US 34th Infantry Division
RAAF	Royal Australian Air Force
RAP	Regimental aid post
RCAF	Royal Canadian Air Force
RHQ	Regimental headquarters
ROTC	Reserve Officer Training Corps
RTR	Royal tank regiment
SA	South Africa
SAAF	South African Air Force
SASO	Senior air staff officer
SP Artillery	Self-propelled artillery
Tac/R	Tactical reconnaissance
Trigh	Track, road
WPD	War Plans Division

Code Names

AGREEMENT	Raid on Axis oil installations at Tobruk and Benghazi carried out on 13 September, 1942
BOLERO	Plan for buildup of American troops in United Kingdom

CANTER	Preliminary assault on forward Mareth Line positions, March 1943
CRUSADER	British offensive, Western Desert, November 1941
FLAX	Allied air operation to disorganize the enemy's system of air transport to Africa, April 1943
GALLOP	50th Division assault of Mareth Line, 20 March, 1943
GYMNAST	Original plan for British landing in French North Africa
SUPER GYMNAST	Plan for Anglo-US landings in French North Africa (later to become TORCH)
HUSKY	Plan for capture of Sicily
LIGHTFOOT	Opening phase of Battle of Alamein
JUPITER	Proposed Allied invasion of Norway
ROUNDUP	First plan for invasion of Europe
SATTIN	Allied plan to drive between German armies in Tunisia, January 1943
SLEDGEHAMMER	Plan for Allied landing in Cherbourg peninsula in 1943
STRIKE	Final phase of 1st Army's assault on Tunis and Bizerte, May 1943
SUPERCHARGE	(i) Last phase of Battle of Alamein (ii) British attack at Tebaga Gap, March 1943
TORCH	Allied landings in French North Africa, November 1942
VULCAN	18th Army Group offensive to destroy Axis forces in Tunisia, April–May 1943
WALK	Guards Brigade attack on Hill Horseshoe at Mareth Line, 16 March, 1943
WOP	US II Corps advance on Gafsa and El Guettar, March 1943

NOTES

1. There were exceptions. Major George Patton, for example, was among the forefront of those advocating a greater US preparation for tank warfare.

2. Cited by Churchill in *Grand Alliance: The Second World War Volume III*, p. 538.

3. Ibid, pp. 538–9.

4. In May 1941, Brigadier J. M. Whiteley had been sent to Washington with a list of stores that were needed by the British in the Middle East. It was a long one, and included not just tanks and guns, but also equipment as diverse as barbed wire, workshop equipment, and even typewriter ribbon.

5. *The Story of the Famous 34th Infantry Division* by Lt. Col. John H. Hougen.

6. Kuter Papers, United States Air Force Academy.

7. Cited by Laurence S. Kuter, Autobiography, p. 170, Kuter Papers, US Air Force Academy.

8. Cited by Stephen E. Ambrose in *Eisenhower: Soldier and President*, p. 46.

9. *Crusade in Europe* by Dwight D. Eisenhower, p. 17.

10. Ibid, p. 25.

11. Eisenhower's diary, 4/20/1942.

12. Ibid, p. 4.

13. *Ashcombe: The Story of a Fifteen-Year Lease*, p. 74

14. Diary, September 1939.

15. Ibid.

16. Diary, May 1942.

17. *Hellfire Tonight* by Albert Martin, p. 3.

18. *Apres Tant de Batailles . . . memoires* by Pierre Messmer, p. 16

19. Ibid.

20. Ibid.

21. *Near East* by Cecil Beaton, p. 52.

22. Ibid, p. 57.

23. Cecil Beaton's diary, May 1942.

24. Ibid.

25. General Auchinleck, 21 March, 1942, cited in *Auchinleck: A Critical Biography* by John Connell, p. 482.

26. General Auchinleck, 27 April, 1942, in his paper to the Middle East Defense Committee, cited in *Auchinleck*, p. 488.

27. Cited in *Fourth Indian Division* by Lt.-Col. G. R. Stevens, OBE, p. 124

28. *Long Life* by Nigel Nicolson, p. 84.

29. *Sherwood Rangers* by T. M. Lindsay, p. 3.

30. Ibid.

31. Ibid, p. 8.

32. *Notes from Theatres of War No. 4: Cyrenaica, November 1941/January 1942,* prepared under the direction of the chief of Imperial General Staff. These papers were drawn up in London, but on the advice and experience drawn from Auchinleck and his staff in Cairo.

33. *Near East* by Cecil Beaton, p. 49.

34. Cited in *The North African Campaign, 1940–43* by W.G.F. Jackson.

35. *Approach to Battle*, p. 17.

36. Cited by Paul Fussell in *Wartime*, p. 4.

37. *Once a Hussar,* by Ray Ellis, p. 107.

38. Ray Ellis, IWM 12660.

39. Between November 1940 and December 1941, no fewer than 11,797 Spitfires were built—compared with 8,442 Hurricanes.

40. *Diary of an Ordinary Fighter Pilot* by John Fairbairn, p. 9.

41. Tuker in a letter to General Hartley, Deputy C-in-C, Indian Army, 23 June, 1942, IWM Tuker Papers. Tuker complained, "This is a suitable place to talk about the pernicious Inf Bde Gp system which I have always hated and always opposed . . . It leads to chaos, confusion, dispersion, unbalancing of armies and chaotic planning."

42. *Once a Hussar* by Ray Ellis, p. 108.

43. Ibid, p. 111.

44. *Hellfire Tonight*, p. 127.

45. TNA CAB 44/97.

46. Ibid.

47. *Eastern Epic* by Compton Mackenzie, p. 544.

48. Cited by John Ferris in *The British Army, Signals and Security in the Desert Campaign, 1940–42*, featured in *Intelligence and Military Operations*, edited by Michael I. Handel.

49. *Diary of an Ordinary Fighter Pilot*, p. 10.

50. Harold Harper, IWM 10923.

51. Ray Ellis, IWM 12660/29.

52. *Once a Hussar*, p. 115.

53. Harold Harper, IWM 10923/10.

54. *The Rommel Papers*, p. 207.

55. TNA CAB 44/97.

56. TNA CAB 44/97.

57. Ibid.

58. Ibid.

59. *The Rommel Papers*, p. 212.

60. Cited by J. Connell, p. 532.

61. TNA CAB 44/97.

62. Elmhirst Papers, Churchill College.

63. Connell, quoting letter to Ritchie of 20 May, 1942.

64. Like Harold Harper, General Messervy had been captured on 27 May, but he too had managed to escape.

65. TNA WO 201/379.

66. *The Rommel Papers*, p. 214.

67. Cited in *Billy Drake, Fighter Leader*, p. 45.

68. TNA AIR 41/26.

69. TNA AIR 23/904.

70. *Tomorrow to be Brave*, by Susan Travers, p. 21.

71. Ibid, p. 80.

72. Cited by Tony Geraghty in *March or Die*, p. 246.

73. Koenig, in *Ce Jour-là*.

74. *Tomorrow to be Brave*, by Susan Travers, p. 161.

75. Ibid, p. 4.

76. The photograph of the original document is reproduced in *Tomorrow to be Brave*.

77. Cecil Beaton, diary, 30 May, 1942.

78. Cecil Beaton, diary, 30 May, 1942.

79. Cecil Beaton, diary, 31 May, 1942.

80. *Near East* by Cecil Beaton, p. 27.

81. *Alan Moorehead* by Tom Pocock, p. 19.

82. *Daily Express*, 2 June, 1942.

83. *African Trilogy* by Alan Moorehead, p. 349.

84. Ibid., 355.

85. Ray Ellis, IWM 12660.

86. *Once a Hussar* by Ray Ellis, p. 117.

87. Ray Ellis, IWM 12660.

88. TNA CAB 44/97.

89. Ibid.

90. *Once A Hussar*, p. 118.

91. Ibid, p. 119.

92. Ibid.

93. Ibid.

94. Ibid.

95. Ibid.

96. Ibid.

97. Ibid.

98. *Approach to Battle,* p. 124.

99. Letter from Tuker to General Hartley, IWM Tuker Papers.

100. Ibid, p. 127.

101. Cited in *Auchinleck,* p. 548.

102. *Diary of an Ordinary Fighter Pilot,* pp. 11–12.

103. TNA AIR23/1346.

104. TNA AIR 41/26.

105. *Billy Drake Fighter Leader,* p. 45.

106. *Tomorrow to be Brave,* p. 165.

107. *Après Tant de Batailles,* p. 98.

108. Ibid, p. 99.

109. Ibid, p. 101.

110. *Tomorrow to be Brave,* p. 172.

111. Ibid.

112. Ibid.

113. Cited in *March or Die* by Tony Geraghty, p. 261.

114. Ibid

115. *Hellfire Tonight* by Albert Martin, p. 132.

116. *Tomorrow to be Brave,* p. 161.

117. Ibid.

118. Field Marshal Lord Alanbrooke, *War Diaries,* 16 April, 1942.

119. Cited in *Turn of the Tide* by Arthur Bryant, p. 314.

120. Cited in *Eisenhower: Soldier and President* by Stephen E. Ambrose, p. 57.

121. Cited in *Eisenhower* by Carlo D'Este, p. 306.

122. Cited in *Calculated Risk* by Mark Clark, p. 19.

123. *The Papers of Dwight David Eisenhower (DDE),* diary 26 May, 1942.

124. Diary, 4 and 5 June, 1942.

125. Cited in *Cecil Beaton* by Hugo Vickers, p. 261.

126. *Diary of an Ordinary Fighter Pilot,* p. 13.

127. *Daily Express,* 9 June, 1942.

128. *Daily Express,* 11 June, 1942.

129. TNA CAB 44/97.

130. Cited in *Auchinleck,* p. 562.

131. TNA WO 169.

132. TNA WO 201/379.

133. *The Second World War Volume IV* by Winston Churchill, p. 331.

134. *Auchinleck,* p. 578.

135. Elmhirst Papers, Churchill College.

136. Ibid.

137. TNA AIR 27/873.

138. TNA AIR 41/26.

139. Elmhirst Papers, Churchill College.

140. Cited by Roskill in *The War at Sea, Vol. II*, p. 43.

141. Captain Smith was killed by a shell fired from the quayside shortly after the evacuation order was given.

142. *The Rommel Papers*, p.232.

143. Ibid, p. 233.

144. *Daily Express,* 22 June, 1942.

145. *The Times*, 22 June, 1942.

146. *Daily Express,* 23 June, 1942.

147. Cited in *The Memoirs of General Lord Ismay*, p.257.

148. *A Sailor's Odyssey: The Autobiography of Admiral of the Fleet Viscount Cunningham of Hyndhope*, p. 460.

149. Ibid, p.461.

150. Ibid, p. 465.

151. *Crusade in Europe*, p. 58.

152. Cited in Ibid, p. 60.

153. Butcher Diary, 8 July, 1942.

154. *War Diaries*, p. 276.

155. TNA AIR 23/1397.

156. *Billy Drake, Fighter Leader,* p. 47.

157. TNA AIR 23/1398.

158. *The Rommel Papers*, p.241.

159. Rommel's men had no trouble whatsoever adapting to British guns. This, again, pours water on the notion that British gunners would need time to learn how to use the 3.7-inch anti-aircraft gun.

160. Cited in *Cairo at War* by Artemis Cooper, p. 192.

161. Diary, 1 July, 1942.

162. *African Trilogy*, p. 383.

163. Ibid, p. 385.

164. *The Second World War Volume IV,* p. 344.

165. *Armoured Fighting Vehicles in the Mediterranean Theatre 1939–1945*, report by Colonel Gordon Hall.

166. American pursuit groups were renamed fighter groups in May 1942, although the prefix P for "pursuit" was kept as a label for fighter aircraft, e.g., the P-40 Kittyhawk and later the P-51 Mustang.

167. *Booster McKeester and Other Expendables* by Willie Chapman, p. 65.

168. *The Times*, 18 June, 1942.

169. TNA AIR 23/1397.

170. *Infantry Brigadier,* p. 139.

171. *Auchinleck* by John Connell, p. 628.

172. *The Rommel Papers*, p. 246.

173. TNA WO 169/4509.

174. *Near East,* p. 134.

175. Diary, 2 July, 1942.

176. *When the Grass Stops Growing* by Carol Mather, p. 35.

177. Ibid, p. 49.

178. Ibid, p. 82.

179. *The Drums of Memory* by Stephen Hastings, p. 43.

180. Ibid, p. 47.

181. *When the Grass Stops Growing* by Carol Mather, pp. 83–84.

182. *The Rommel Papers,* p. 250.

183. TNA AIR 41/50.

184. RUSI Journal, Vol. 91.

185. Cited in *Middle East 1940–1942: A Study in Air Power* by Philip Guedalla, p. 200.

186. *Diary of an Ordinary Fighter Pilot,* p. 14.

187. TNA AIR 23/1398.

188. Elmhirst Papers, Churchill College, Cambridge.

189. TNA AIR 23/1398.

190. These fliers are all kept in a scrapbook at the National War Museum, Johannesburg.

191. *Hellfire Tonight,* p. 144.

192. Ibid, pp. 145–146.

193. *A Sailor's Odyssey,* p. 465.

194. Diary, 8 July, 1942.

195. Ibid.

196. Cited in *Eisenhower,* by Carlo D'Este, p. 316.

197. Diary, 9 July, 1942.

198. *The Papers of Dwight David Eisenhower* (henceforth DDE), *Vol. I,* p. 379

199. Cited in *Rommel's Intelligence in the Desert Campaign* by Hans-Otto Berendt, p. 170.

200. *When the Grass Stops Growing,* p. 84.

201. Cited in *The Phantom Major* by Virginia Cowles, p. 193.

202. Ibid.

203. *The Drums of Memory,* p. 54.

204. Ibid.

205. *Daily Express,* 14 July, 1942.

206. *Daily Express,* 23 July, 1942.

207. Butcher Papers, Eisenhower Library.

208. Butcher Diary, 22/7/1942.

209. Ibid, 23/7/1942.

210. *The Second World War, Vol. IV,* p. 404.

211. Cited in *The Phantom Major,* p. 197.

212. Ibid, p. 61.

213. Ibid, p. 64.

214. Cited in *Rangers in World War II* by Robert W. Black, p. 4.

215. Col. Kelly American Veterans Oral History Project, University of Kentucky.

216. DDE, p. 435.

217. Ibid.

218. Butcher Diary, 4 August, 1942.

219. *With Prejudice*, p. 348.

220. *Booster McKeester and Other Expendables*, p. 72.

221. Ibid, p. 77.

222. Ibid, p. 81.

223. *The Vaulted Sky*, p. 42.

224. Ibid, p. 44.

225. Brooke Diary, 28 July 1942.

226. Elmhirst Papers, 5/2.

227. Cited in *Auchinleck*, p. 698.

228. *African Trilogy*, pp. 421–423.

229. *The Alexander Memoirs*, p. 16.

230. Lt-Gen Sir William Jackson, who served under Alexander in Tunisia, once wrote that his integrity "was so obvious to everyone who met him at any stage in his career."

231. Cited in *Alex* by Nigel Nicolson, p. 26.

232. Cited in *The Full Monty* by Nigel Hamilton, p. 131.

233. Cited in *Eisenhower*, p. 409.

234. *My Three Years with Eisenhower*, p. 45.

235. Cited in *Grand Strategy*, p. 119.

236. *My Three Years with Eisenhower*, p. 45.

237. Ibid, p. 47.

238. Ibid, p. 41.

239. Ibid, p. 51.

240. *The Alexander Memoirs*, p. 12.

241. At the time, this post was still called Brigadier General Staff, or BGS.

242. *Memoirs* by Montgomery of Alamein, p. 97.

243. Ibid, p. 99.

244. *Alexander Memoirs,* p. 19.

245. TNA WO 32/13256.

246. *Operation Victory,* by Freddie de Guingand, p. 136.

247. Elmhirst Papers.

248. IWM 10923.

249. Tuker Papers.

250. IWM 3942.

251. *The Second World War, Vol IV,* p. 464.

252. Elmhirst Papers.

253. Ibid.

254. Rommel Papers, p. 233.

255. Cited in *Supreme Gallantry*, p. 182.

256. *The Memoirs of Field Marshal Kesselring*, p. 112.

257. *My Three Years with Eisenhower*, p. 64.

258. Butcher Diary, 16 August, 1942.

259. *My Three Years with Eisenhower*, p. 65.

260. Tuker Papers.

261. IWM 10923.

262. *The Second World War IV*, p. 489.

263. Butcher Diary, 2 September, 1942.

264. *Sherwood Rangers*, p. 31.

265. Ibid, p. 32.

266. *Alamein to Zem Zem* by Keith Douglas, p. 110.

267. *The Vaulted Sky*, p. 55.

268. *The Rommel Papers*, p. 279.

269. *The Vaulted Sky*, p. 56.

270. *28 (Maori) Battalion* by J.F. Cody, p. 218.

271. *The Rommel Papers*, p. 282.

272. Elmhirst Papers.

273. Ibid, p. 47.

274. Butcher Diary, 29 July, 1942.

275. Butcher Papers.

276. Butcher Papers.

277. *A Short Guide to Great Britain*.

278. Eisenhower Library.

279. Cited in *Cunningham* by John Winton, p. 278.

280. *My Three Years with Eisenhower*, p. 55.

281. *Ernie Pyle in England*, p. xi.

282. *Washington Daily News*, 30 December, 1940.

283. *Ernie Pyle in England*.

284. *Washington Daily Post*, 10 October, 1942.

285. *Washington Daily Post*, 16–19 October, 1942.

286. Letter to Paige Cavanaugh, 8/8/1942, Lilly Library, Indiana University.

287. *African Trilogy*, p. 440.

288. TNA AIR 23/1315.

289. *African Trilogy*, p. 442.

290. *The Second World War IV*, p. 487.

291. *Butcher Diary*, 3 September, 1942.

292. Cited in *My Three Years with Eisenhower*, p. 75.

293. Cited in *4th Indian Division*, p. 188.

294. *Hellfire Tonight*, p. 55.

295. *The Drums of Memory*, p. 87.

296. Ibid, p. 89.

297. TNA WO 32/13256.

298. Cited in *My Three Years with Eisenhower*, p. 82.

299. TNA CAB 79/57.

300. CHAR 20/80.

301. *War Diaries*, 9 September, 1942.

302. CHAR 20/80.

303. *Hellfire Tonight*, p. 162.

304. *Hellfire Tonight*, p. 163.

305. Elmhirst Papers.

306. *The Vaulted Sky*, p. 54.

307. *Billy Drake, Fighter Leader*, p. 53.

308. Butcher Diary, 19 October, 1942.

309. DDE Vol I, p. 627.

310. Cited in Butcher Diary, 18 October, 1942.

311. Butcher Diary, 20 October, 1942.

312. *Diary of an Ordinary Fighter Pilot*, p. 17.

313. *Diary of an Ordinary Fighter Pilot*, pp. 17–18.

314. *Hellfire Tonight*, p. 166.

315. *The Memoirs of Field Marshal Montgomery*, p. 119.

316. TNA AIR 41/50.

317. Cited in *Montgomery and the Eighth Army*, p. 68.

318. *My Three Years with Eisenhower*, p. 115.

319. DDE Vol I, p. 604.

320. *A Sailor's Odyssey*, p. 476.

321. *My Three Years with Eisenhower*, p. 78.

322. Butcher Diary, 17 October, 1942.

323. *The Vaulted Sky*, p. 76.

324. Elmhirst Papers.

325. CHAR 20/81.

326. IWM 10009/4.

327. Elmhirst Papers.

328. Ibid.

329. CHAR 20/81/87.

330. Taken from the poem *Baptism of Fire* by Vernon Scannell.

331. *Hellfire Tonight*, p. 170.

332. *Après tant de Batailles*, p. 126.

333. Ibid, p. 130.

334. Elmhirst Papers.

335. *Tomorrow to be Brave*, p. 204.

336. *Après tant de Batailles*, p. 133.

337. *Hellfire Tonight*, p. 171.

338. *The Vaulted Sky*, p. 80.

339. *Hellfire Tonight,* p. 172.

340. *When the Grass Stops Growing,* p. 178.

341. Cited in *Last Stand!* By Bryan Perrett, p. 118.

342. *Hellfire Tonight,* p. 174.

343. Ibid.

344. TNA WO 169/5055.

345. *The Crusader: Eighth Army Weekly,* 9 November, 1942.

346. Cited in *The Rifle Brigade in the Second World War 1939–1945* by Major RHWS Hastings, OBE, MC, p. 174.

347. *Hellfire Tonight,* p. 178.

348. Elmhirst Papers.

349. TNA AIR 27/873.

350. *War Diaries,* 29/10/1942.

351. *The Memoirs of Field Marshal Montgomery,* p. 132.

352. CHAR 20/81/134.

353. *A Sailor's Odyssey,* p. ☐☐☐.

354. *When the Grass Stops Growing,* p. 178.

355. *The Vaulted Sky,* p. 84.

356. *Rommel Papers,* p. 317.

357. Elmhirst Papers.

358. Elmhirst Papers.

359. *The Fighting 33rd Nomads, Vol. 1* by James E Reed, p. 74.

360. Ibid, p. 53.

361. *The Vaulted Sky,* p. 86.

362. *Approach to Battle,* p. 259.

363. *When the Grass Stops Growing,* pp. 185–7.

364. Ibid, p. 185.

365. *Cited in Coningham,* p. 115.

366. *Rommel Papers,* p. 328.

367. TNA WO 216/7517.

368. MHI Direct Air Support in the Libyan Desert.

369. *Recollections* by Air Marshal Sir Thomas Elmhirst, p. 78.

370. CHAR 20/82.

371. *My Three Years with Eisenhower,* p. 135.

372. Cited in *Calculated Risk,* p. 94.

373. *My Three Years with Eisenhower,* p. 140.

374. *My Three Years with Eisenhower,* p. 144.

375. *Calculated Risk,* p. 98.

376. *A Sailor's Odyssey,* p. 486.

377. *My Three Years with Eisenhower,* p. 145.

378. Cited in *Heroes from the Attic,* p. 68.

379. *My Three Years with Eisenhower,* p. 148.

380. DDE, Vol II, p. 675.

381. *The Patton Papers, 1940–1945*, edited by Martin Blumenson, p. 97.

382. TNA ADM 199/1839.

383. *Patton Papers*, p. 109.

384. Ibid., 109.

385. Ibid, p. 110.

386. *Ciano's Diary*, 8 November, 1942.

387. *Germany and the Second World War, Vol. VI* by Horst Boog et. al., p. 794.

388. *Calculated Risk*, p. 115.

389. *Cunningham*, p. 284.

390. Ibid, p. 123.

391. *A Sailor's Odyssey*, p. 501.

392. *The Fighting 33rd Nomads, Vol. I*, p. 54.

393. *Smoke Trails in the Sky*, by Tony Bartley, p. 90.

394. TNA WO 106/2728.

395. Ibid, p. 94.

396. *My Three Years with Eisenhower*, p. 165.

397. *The Second World War, Vol. IV*, p. 567.

398. *A Sailor's Odyssey*, p. 502.

399. Ibid, p. 571.

400. *The Vaulted Sky*, p. 100.

401. Elmhirst Papers.

402. Cited in *Coningham*, p. 123.

403. *Diary of an Ordinary Fighter Pilot*, p. 23.

404. This conversation is recounted verbatim by Carol Mather in *When the Grass Stops Growing*, p. 196.

405. *Smoke Trails in the Sky*, p. 109.

406. *My Three Years with Eisenhower*, p. 168.

407. *Crusade in Europe*, p. 132.

408. *A Sailor's Odyssey*, p. 505.

409. Ibid, p. 506.

410. TNA WO 175/526.

411. Cited in *Men of the Red Beret*, by Max Arthur, p. 62.

412. *A Drop Too Many*, p. 96.

413. Cited in *Men of the Red Beret* by Max Arthur, p. 65.

414. DDE, Vol. II, p. 792.

415. *Smoke Trails in the Sky*, pp. 112–114.

416. *My Three Years with Eisenhower*, p. 183.

417. *Battle History of the 1st Armored Division*, p. 97.

418. IWM 10009/04.

419. *Long Life*, p. 91.

420. Butcher Diary, 20 December, 1942.

421. *My Three Years With Eisenhower*, p. 195.

422. Butcher Diary, 21 January, 1943.

423. Ibid, p. 197.

424. *Smoke Trails in the Sky,* p. 120.

425. Ibid, p. 128.

426. Ibid, p. 132.

427. Ibid, p. 141.

428. Ibid, p. 188.

429. *When the Grass Stops Growing,* p. 202.

430. *Washington Daily News,* 20 January, 1943.

431. *Washington Daily News,* 21 January, 1943.

432. *Tall, Dark and Gruesome* by Christopher Lee, p. 91.

433. *African Trilogy,* p. 456.

434. Ibid, p. 497.

435. *African Trilogy,* pp. 511–512.

436. IWM 83/16/1.

437. Ibid.

438. Ibid.

439. Cited in *American Iliad* by Robert W. Baumer with Mark J. Reardon, p. 73.

440. *No Need to Worry* by Peter Moore, p. 20.

441. Ibid, p. 28.

442. *African Trilogy,* p. 539.

443. *Washington Daily Post,* 4 January, 1943.

444. Cited in *An Army at Dawn,* by Rick Atkinson, p. 273.

445. Butcher Diary, 20 January, 1943.

446. Ibid.

447. *The Second World War, Vol IV,* p. 605.

448. *War Diaries,* p. 365.

449. Butcher Diary, 18 January, 1943.

450. Cited in *Eisenhower: A Soldier's Life,* p. 386.

451. Butcher Diary, 26 January, 1943.

452. IWM 83/16/1.

453. NARA RG 407/E427.601.

454. *A Drop Too Many,* p. 117.

455. "Find 'Em, Fix 'Em, and Fight 'Em, II" by A. J. Liebling, *The New Yorker,* 24 April, 1943.

456. TNA WO 175/487.

457. *My Three Years with Eisenhower,* pp. 205–206.

458. *The Fighting 33rd Nomads, Vol I,* p. 107.

459. Ibid, p. 160.

460. Ibid.

461. Kuter autobiography, p. 283.

462. Kuter autobiography, p. 272.

463. Hamilton Howze, Senior Officers Debriefing Program, interview 1973, MHI.

464. Ibid.

465. *Thirty-Five Years and Then Some: Memoirs of a Professional Soldier* by Hamilton Howze.

466. Ward Diary, 23 January, 1943, MHI.

467. Ward Diary, 29–30 January, 1943, MHI.

468. *The Hour Has Come: The 97th Bomb Group in World War II*, p. 80.

469. Ibid, p. 81.

470. AFHRA GP-97-SU-RO (BOMB).

471. *Stars And Stripes Africa,* 5 March, 1943.

472. Cited in *Germany and the Second World War, Vol.VI: The Global War,* p. 813.

473. Ibid, p. 815.

474. *The Rommel Papers,* p. 389.

475. *GI Nightingale* by Theresa Archard, p. 73.

476. *My Three Years with Eisenhower,* p. 219.

477. DDE, p. 936.

478. *Heroes Cry Too,* p. 121.

479. *Thirty Five Years And Then Some,* MHI.

480. Ibid.

481. Ward Diary, 8 February, 1943, MHI.

482. *Thirty-Five Years and Then Some,* MHI.

483. DDE, p. 940.

484. IWM 86/16/1.

485. Butcher Diary, 15 February, 1943.

486. TNA CAB 106/894.

487. *Thirty-Five Years and Then Some,* MHI.

488. DDE, p. 956.

489. Liddell Hart Centre for Military Archives, Alanbrooke Papers, 14/62.

490. Larry Kuter autobiography, p. 275.

491. TNA AIR 23/1709.

492. Cited in *The Trail of the Fox,* p. 246.

493. *The Rommel Papers,* p. 402.

494. Peter Moore's account is taken from his published work *No Need To Worry,* and an unpublished memoir, *Khaki and Gown.*

495. *Thirty-Five Years and Then Some,* MHI.

496. Pyle mss. III, 25 February, 1943.

497. Butcher Diary, 20 February, 1943.

498. *Armor Command* by Paul Robinett, p. 175.

499. *Northwest Africa: Seizing the Initiative in the West* by George F. Howe, p. 471.

500. TNA WO 214/11.

501. TNA AIR 23/1709.

502. Howe interview with Alexander, MHI.

503. Alanbrooke Papers, 6/2/17.

504. *A Sailor's Odyssey,* p. 519.

505. TNA WO 204/6999.

506. TNA WO 214/18.

507. TNA WO 204/6999.

508. Pyle mss. III 24 February, 1943.

509. TNA WO 204/6999.

510. Alexander Dispatch, p. 870.

511. Kuter autobiography, p. 279.

512. Kuter Diary, 18 February, 1943

513. Elmhirst Papers.

514. Ibid.

515. Ibid.

516. *The Fighting 33rd Nomads, Vol. 1*, p. 217.

517. *A Drop Too Many*, p. 122.

518. IWM 86/16/1.

519. *No Need to Worry*, p. 49.

520. Ibid, p. 55.

521. *No Need To Worry*, p. 57.

522. Ibid, p. 60.

523. Ibid, p. 61.

524. John Fairbairn *Diary*.

525. *Tall, Dark and Gruesome* by Christopher Lee, pp. 94–95.

526. TNA WO 214/10286.

527. *The Rommel Papers*, p. 416.

528. CHAR 20/107/18.

529. DDE, p. 1002.

530. Alexander interview with Howe, MHI.

531. *Combat Command* by General Ernest Harmon, p. 120.

532. Harmon interview with Geoffrey Howe, MHI.

533. *A General's Life* by Omar Bradley and Clay Blair, p. 137.

534. DDE, p. 938.

535. Butcher Diary, 7 February, 1943.

536. *The Patton Papers*, p. 181.

537. Ibid, p. 186.

538. *Thirty-Five Years and Then Some*, MHI.

539. Hamilton Howze Senior Officers Debriefing Program, MHI.

540. IWM 86/16/1.

541. Alexander interview with Howe, MHI.

542. *A General's Life*, p. 142.

543. *The Patton Papers*, pp. 188–189.

544. Tuker Papers.

545. Cited in *Fourth Indian Division*, p. 208.

546. Cited in *Is Paris Burning?* By Larry Collins and Dominique Lapierre, p. 60.

547. *The Patton Papers,* p. 187.

548. Eisenhower Papers.

549. *The Patton Papers,* p. 194.

550. *African Trilogy,* p. 551.

551. Ibid, p. 552.

552. TNA WO 214/18.

553. Cited in *An Army At Dawn,* p. 443.

554. Ward Papers, MHI.

555. *The Patton Papers,* p. 197.

556. Ibid, p. 198.

557. *Hellfire Tonight,* p. 203.

558. Butcher Diary, 8 April, 1943.

559. Ibid.

560. Butcher Papers.

561. *A Drop Too Many,* p. 167.

562. Ibid, pp. 137–8.

563. Ibid, p. 163.

564. IWM 86/16/1.

565. *Approach to Battle,* pp. 318–20.

566. *4th Indian Division,* p. 222.

567. Cited in *Fourth Indian Division,* p. 225.

568. Butcher Papers.

569. TNA WO 214/18.

570. Tuker Papers.

571. *Argument of Kings,* p. 22.

572. Ibid, pp. 563–4.

573. *African Trilogy,* p. 567.

574. *The Patton Papers,* p. 218.

575. TNA WO 214/18.

576. *The Patton Papers,* p. 199.

577. IWM BLM 1/88.

578. Coincidentally, at that time Ike had received a letter from General "Hap" Arnold's son, a former aide, who was now a gunner at the front. He also recognized that the level of training played a large part in the fighting quality of their forces and that a lot of new US troops were arriving "trained but not properly trained." What was needed, Arnold's son suggested, was much greater realism during training—"to hell with blank ammo." This was why Alex had introduced the battle schools in Britain and again in North Africa.

579. TNA WO 214/18.

580. Kuter autobiography, p. 287.

581. Cited in *A General's Life,* p. 147.

582. Cited in Kuter autobiography, p. 285.

583. Kuter autobiography, p. 286.

584. Spaatz Diary, Library of Congress Manuscript Division.

585. *The Patton Papers*, p. 208.

586. *With Prejudice*, p. 411.

587. *African Trilogy*, p. 578.

588. *A General's Life*, p. 150.

589. *Hellfire Tonight*, p. 208.

590. Alanbrooke Papers, 14/16.

591. Cited in *An Army at Dawn*, p. 466.

592. *Long Life*, p. 95.

593. TNA ADM 199/1839.

594. TNA ADM 199/1839.

595. *A Sailor's Odyssey*, p. 512.

596. *Booster McKeester and Other Expendables*, p. 176.

597. Ibid, p. 187.

598. Elmhirst Papers.

599. Kuter autobiography, p. 288.

600. *The Fighting 33rd Nomads*, p. 251.

601. Ibid, p. 270.

602. *The Diary of an Ordinary Fighter Pilot*, p. 31.

603. *Tall, Dark and Gruesome*, p. 96.

604. Cited in *Fighters Over Tunisia*, p. 322.

605. Kuter autobiography, p. 289.

606. DDE, p. 1093.

607. *War Diaries: The Mediterranean, 1943–45* by Harold Macmillan, 21 March, 1943.

608. *A General's Life*, p. 134.

609. Interview with General Theodore J. Conway by Colonel R. F. Ensslin, MHI.

610. *The Blast of War* by Harold Macmillan, p. 246.

611. TNA WO 214/18.

612. Ernie Pyle column, 20 April, 1943.

613. *Hellfire Tonight*, p. 211.

614. IWM 86/16/1.

615. Cited in *The Mediterranean and Middle East, Vol. IV*, p. 402.

616. Cited in *Fourth Indian Division*, pp. 237–8.

617. LOB—left out of battle.

618. Tuker Papers.

619. TNA WO 214/18.

620. *A Full Life* by Lt.-Gen. Sir Brian Horrocks, p. 162.

621. *Hellfire Tonight*, p. 215.

622. *African Trilogy*, p. 585.

623. *A General's Life*, p. 156.

624. Ernie Pyle column, 3 May, 1943.

625. Ibid, 22 April, 1943.
626. Butcher Diary, 30 April, 1943.
627. *The Fighting 33rd Nomads, Vol I*, p. 271.
628. Ibid, p. 283.
629. Alexander Dispatch, p. 881.
630. *Thirty-Five Years and Then Some*, MHI.
631. TNA CAB 140/145.
632. Elmhirst Papers.
633. Alexander Dispatch, p. 882.
634. *A Sailor's Odyssey*.
635. DDE, p. 113.
636. *Thirty-Five Years and Then Some*, MHI.
637. CHAR 20/111.
638. *Air Superiority in World War II and Korea*, USAF Warrior Studies, p. 36.
639. Both cited in *Coningham*, p. 25.

BIBLIOGRAPHY & SOURCES
Unpublished Sources

ARCHIVES

Academy Libraries, United States Air Force Academy, Colorado
Papers of General Laurence Sherman Kuter, including unpublished autobiography.

Air Force Historical Research Agency, Maxwell, Alabama (AFHRA)
The Command and Employment of Air Power; US Air Force oral history interview,
General Laurence S. Kuter; unit history & war diary of 97th Bomb Group;
war diary of 415th Squadron; unit history & war diary of 33rd Fighter
Group; war diary of 59th Fighter Squadron; unit history & war diary of
98th Bomb Group; war diary of 414th Squadron; unit history & war diary
of 57th Fighter Group; war diary of 65th fighter Squadron.

The British Library, London
Papers of Admiral Cunningham of Hyndehope; maps: GSGS-4225, Tunisia,
1:50,000, 1942 & 1943; GSGS 4386, Egypt & Cyrenaica, 1:250,000, 1942.

Churchill College Archives, Cambridge
Papers of Winston S. Churchill, including correspondence with General
Alexander; papers of Admiral Cunningham of Hyndehope; papers of Air
Marshall Sir Thomas Elmhirst, including unpublished autobiography and
recorded memoirs.
Miscellaneous editions of *The Crusader: Eighth Army Weekly*.

CMI Documentation Centre, Department of Defence, Pretoria
Regimental diary of Regiment President Steyn; service record of William
Eadie; service record of Petrus Dhlamini.

Collindale Newspaper Archive, London
Daily Express, May 1942–May 1943; *The Times*, May 1942–May 1943; *Daily Telegraph*, May 1942–May 1943.

Dwight D. Eisenhower Presidential Library, Abilene, Kansas
Papers of Harry S. Butcher, including unexpurgated war diary; the papers of
    Dwight David Eisenhower.

Gurkha Museum Archives, Penninsular Barracks, Winchester
Citations of 1/2 Gurkha Rifles; Papers of J. P. Cross.

Imperial War Museum, London (IWM)
Diary and papers of Field Marshal Viscount Montgomery of Alamein; Papers of
    Lieutenant-General Sir Francis Tuker; letters of Lieutenant D. E. Brown;
    diary of Sergeant J. R. Harris; letters of Reverend F. J. Brabyn.

Imperial War Museum Sound Archives, London (IWM)
General Alexander, Christmas address 1944; Tony Bartley; Ronald "Ras"
    Berry; Richard Brooks, RNVR; Russell Collins; Ray Ellis; Gunner Green-
    wood; Field Marshal Harding; Harold Harper; Vernon Scannell.

**Library of the Joint Services Command and Staff College,
Shrivenham, Wiltshire**
Notes from the Theatres of War, prepared under the direction of the chief of
    the imperial general staff:
    No. 4: Cyrenaica, November 1941/January 1942
    No.14: Western Desert and Cyrenaica, August/December 1942
    No. 16: North Africa, November 1942–May 1943

Liddell Hart Centre for Military Studies, King's College, London
Papers of Field Marshal Viscount Alanbrooke.

The Lilly Library, Indiana University, Bloomington, Indiana
Letters and newspaper columns of Ernie Pyle.

Manuscript Division, Library of Congress, Washington DC
Papers and diary of General Carl Spaatz.

The Military History Institute, Carlisle Barracks, Pennsylvania (MHI)
Memoirs, *Induction into the Armed Services,* by Robert Bond; papers & unpub-
    lished autobiography, *Thirty-five Years and Then Some,* of General Hamil-
    ton Howze; diary of Robert M. Marsh; papers and diary of General
    Orlando Ward.
Army service experience questionnaires: Robert M. Marsh; Robert Moore.
Interview with Field Marshal Alexander by Dr. Sidney Matthews; interview with
    Air Marshal Sir Arthur Coningham by Forrest C. Pogue; Interview with
    General Theodore J. Conway by Colonel R. F. Ensslin; interview with Gen-
    eral Hamilton Howze by Lieutenant-Colonel Robert Reed; report, *Direct
    Air Support in the Libyan Desert,* 1942; reports on operations of 18th RCT in
    Tunisia.
Military Intelligence Service, Campaign Study No. 4: *The Libyan Campaign,
    May 27–July 27, 1942.*

The National Archives, Kew (TNA)

AIR FORCE: Air Historical Branch Official Histories: May 1942–May 1943; NATAF daily intelligence summaries; NATAF orders of battle; Western Desert operations; AOC-in-C correspondence with PM, Secretary of State, and CAS; Operation SUPERCHARGE; RAF Western Desert War Diary 1942–43; Operation TORCH preliminary operations; information on enemy air forces dispositions etc.; US reinforcements to Middle East; AOC-in-C dispatches and reports 23 October, 1942–16 February, 1943; AOC-in-C dispatches and reports, May–July 1942; demi-official correspondence of Tedder; Western Desert Air Force Tripoli to Tunis; American aid: correspondence with Washington; reports and appreciations on the war situation; AHQ Western Desert correspondence; PM & CAS correspondence; number of pilots & aircraft available for Fighter Command; Fighter Command aircraft strength; Australian Spitfires diverted to Middle East; Spitfire reinforcement policy; Western Desert correspondence; Advance AHQ Western Desert operational instructions; Western Desert Air Force reports and appreciations; report on enemy air tactics, 1940–1943; PM & Tedder re: German claims against Americans; Air Marshal Sir Arthur Coningham's address at Tripoli Conference, February 1943.

RAF OPERATIONAL RECORD BOOKS: 73 Squadron; 111 Squadron; 112 Squadron; 225 Squadron; 24 SAAF Squadron.

WAR DIARIES: XXX Corps; X Corps; XIII Corps; 4th Armoured Brigade; 8th Armoured Brigade; Nottinghamshire Sherwood Rangers Yeomanry; 2nd Battalion Rifle Brigade; 4th Indian Division Signals; Leicesters; 1/2nd Gurkha Rifles 1942; 1 RTR; 6 RTR; 17th Field Regiment, RA; 2nd Parachute Battalion; 5/7th Gordon Highlanders; 7th Medium Regiment.

ROYAL NAVY: North Africa: ABC missives re: French and Eisenhower; History of Naval Intelligence including TORCH; 10th MTB Flotilla awards; patrol reports of HMS/S *P.211* (*Safari*).

CABINET PAPER OFFICIAL REPORTS: Section I, Ch J: Gazala and Fall of Tobruk; El Alamein, 24–26 October; El Alamein 29 October–1 November.

OTHER: 9th Australian Division report of operations at Alamein; 9th Australian Division report of operations Lightfoot; Report on 9th Australian Division at Alamein; SAS (L Detachment) report of operations, May 1941–July 1942; SAS report of operations up to 1943; 2nd Rifle Brigade Account of Snipe action; El Alamein: notes with maps on final breakthrough; 4th Indian Division orders, instructions, etc.; lessons from Battle of Egypt; Western Desert tactical training notes by General Tuker; correspondence between General Tuker and Brigadier C.J.C. Moloney; translation of German war diary; landings in North Africa: combat narratives, Office of Naval Intelligence, US Navy; Portuguese minister: German, Spanish, French attitudes to Allied landings; Eighth Army change of corps commanders, June 1942; Eighth Army RA—lessons learned from campaign; Eighth Army deception schemes, October 1942; lessons learned from operations September 1941–August 1942; Report on Battle of Alamein; Operation TORCH, Eighth Army activities; Tactical HQ Eighth Army May–Aug 1942; Tactical HQ Eighth Army logs Oct–Dec 1942; Tactical HQ Eighth Army logs July 1942; Main Tactical HQ September–December 1942; Main Tactical HQ August 1942; Main HQ August 1942; GS (Ops) August–December 1942; Eighth Army commander's conferences; Alexander correspondence; Alamein to Tunis report by Captain Wynne; correspondence between PM and Montgomery, 1950s; army commander messages to troops and brief summary of battle; lessons learned from Alamein to end in Tunisia; Battle of Alamein by Colonel Fryer; maps of Alamein and troops positions; report on the Battle in Tunisia; First Army operations; First Army Operation Instructions Nos 1–15; Alexander papers; report of Southern Sector of First Army; battle diary of Lieutenant-General Neil Ritchie.

The National Archives and Records Administration, College Park, Maryland (NARA)

UNIT HISTORIES, RECORDS AND WAR DIARIES: II Corps; 1st Armored Division; 1st Infantry Division; 34th Infantry Division; 18th Regimental Combat Team; 135th Infantry Regiment; 1st Armored Regiment; 1st and 3rd Ranger Battalions; 81st Reconnaissance Battalion.

MISCELLANEOUS: *Welcome to the 135th Infantry; Mission Accomplished: Africa, Sicily, Italy;* transcript of interrogation with General von Arnim; German-Italian panzer army expose and estimate of the Mareth position; interview with Colonel P. C. Hains III; George F. Howe correspondence with Colonel Robert I. Stack, Colonel John K. Waters; George F. Howe questionnaire for General Charles Ryder, General Mark Clark; interview of General Mark Clark by George F. Howe; General Orlando Ward correspondence with Lieutenant-Colonel J. D. Alger and his comments on Official History.

FILM: Tunisian victory, 1943; desert victory, 1943; artillery shelling enemy positions, 1943.

New York City Public Library, New York City

The New Yorker magazine, December 1941–May 1943; *The New York Times,* December 1941–May 1943; *Stars & Stripes Africa,* December 1942–May 1943.

St John's College, Cambridge

Diaries of Cecil Beaton.

Second World War Experience Centre, Leeds

Oral history interviews: Charles Coles; James D'Arcy Clark; Earl Jellicoe; Peter Moore; Geoffrey Wooler.

South African National Museum of Military History, Johannesburg, South Africa

Diaries and papers of William (Bill) Eadie; *Non-White Personnel in the SA Artillery: 1939–1045, And Today* by Colonel L. A. Crook; *Historical Survey*

of the Non-European Army Services Outside the Union of South Africa, Ed.
Noelle Cowling; Zulu call to arms.

Tank Museum Archives, Bovington Camp, Dorset
Armoured Fighting Vehicles in the Mediterranean Theatre, 1939–1945 by Colonel
Gordon-Hall; Special Supplement to AFV Technical Report No.1—Fight-
ing Efficiency; Department of Tank Design—Origin and Organisation.

University of Kentucky Oral History Program, Lexington, Kentucky
American Veterans Oral History Program Interviews: General William Buster;
Curtis Fultz, Margaret Hornback, Andrew Kiddey.

INTERVIEWS & PERSONAL RECOLLECTIONS

Ken Anderson—33rd Field Artillery, 26th Combat Team, 1st Infantry Division
James D'Arcy Clark—Queen's Own Yorkshire Dragoons
Major Sam Bradshaw—6th Royal Tank Regiment
Charles Coles—Tenth MTB Flotilla, RN
Dick Bowery—31st Field Regiment, RA
Henry Bowles—18th Infantry, 1st Infantry Division
Tom Bowles—18th Infantry, 1st Infantry Division
Ralph Burbridge—414th Squadron, 97th Bomb Group
Willie Chapman—415th Squadron, 98th Bomb Group
Squadron Leader Bryan Colston, DFC—225 Squadron, 242 Group
Wing Commander Hank Costain, MBE—154 Squadron, 242 Group
Bob Cullen—1st Field Artillery, 1st South African Division
Alf Davies—1st Royal Tank Regiment
L. Gordon Delp—60th Fighter Squadron, 33rd Fighter Group
Petrus Dhlamini—Regiment President Steyn
Group Captain Billy Drake, DSO, DFC , DFC (US)—112 Squadron, 239 Wing
Joe Furayter—5th Field Artillery Battalion, 1st Infantry Division
Christopher Lee—260 Squadron, 233 Wing
Colonel Edward "Duke" Ellington—65th Fighter Squadron, 57th Fighter
    Group
Ray Ellis—South Notts Hussars, RHA
Warren "Bing" Evans—1st and 3rd Ranger Battalions
Bob Hall—16th Infantry, 1st Infantry Division
Ted Hardy—2/3rd Field Company, 9th Australian Division
Harold Harper—South Notts Hussars, RHA, and 7th Medium Regiment, RA
Sir Stephen Hastings, MC—SAS
Earl Jellicoe, MC—SAS, SBS
Robert Kolowski—135th Infantry, 34th Infantry Division (interview by
    Matthew Parker)
Xavier Krebs—Moroccan Tirailleurs (interview by Jane Martens)
Joe Madeley—2/13th Battalion, 9th Australian Division
Mangal Singh—4th Indian Division Signals
Albert Martin—2nd Rifle Brigade

Sir Carol Mather, MC—SAS and Montgomery's staff
Bill McInnes—26th Battalion, 5th New Zealand Brigade
Len Meerholz—1 SAAF Squadron
George Monroe—92 Squadron, Desert Air Force
Sophie Moss (*nee* Tarnowska)—Polish Red Cross, Cairo
Nainabadahur Pun—1/2 King Edward VII's Own Gurkha Rifles (interview by
     Major Peter Ridlington)
Ken Neill, DFC—225 Squadron, 242 Group
Nigel Nicolson—3rd Coldstream Guards and Guards Brigade
Maiki Parkinson—28th (Maori) Battalion, 5th New Zealand Brigade
Frank Read—172nd Field Artillery, RA
Captain Jim Reed—59th Fighter Squadron, 33rd Fighter Group
Randolph Paulsen—15th Infantry, 3rd Infantry Division, and 18th Infantry,
     1st Infantry Division
Raymond Saidel—1st Armored Regiment, 1st Armored Division
Vernon Scannell—5/7 Gordon Highlanders
Dennis Scott—38 Squadron
Captain ARF "Tommy" Thompson, DFC—73 Squadron
George Vaughan—5th Hampshire Regiment
Frank Vidor—1/4th Hampshire Regiment
Edward "Bucky" Walters—135th Infantry, 34th Infantry Division
Ronnie Ward—1st Lieutenant, HMS *Safari*
George Williams, CBE—608 Squadron

UNPUBLISHED DIARIES, MEMOIRS, ETC.

Beckett, Frank. *Algiers to Austria with the First and Eighth Armies.*
Christopherson, Stanley. Diaries, 1941–1943.
D'Arcy Clark, James. Letters to his parents.
Colston, Bryan Colston. Diary, November 1942–May 1943: *Recollections of
     Wartime Experiences.*
Deniston, Dale R. *Memories of a Combat Fighter Pilot: World War II and Korea.*
Eadie, Colonel J. A. *The War Diary of Colonel J. A. Eadie, DSO, TD, DL.*
Ellington, Edward "Duke." *Summary of WWII Experience.*
Ellis, Ray. *Once a Hussar: Being an Account of Some of the Events in the Service Life
     of Ray Ellis, Who Was Once a Hussar.*
Elmhirst, Air Marshal Sir Thomas, KBE, CB, AFC. *Recollections.*
Fairbairn, John. *The Diary of an Ordinary Fighter Pilot,* copyright Fairbairn
     2004 (for further information: *enquiry@fighterpilotdiary.com* (www.fighter
     pilotdiary.com). Diary, 1943–1944.
Hirst, Fred. *A Green Hill Far Away.*
Hornback, Margaret. Letters, 1942–1943.
Kernaghan, Stan, DFC. Papers, letters, logbook.
Martin, Albert. *Diaries, 1941–1942.*
Merewood, Jack. *To War with the Bays: A Tank Gunner Remembers, 1939–1945.*
Moore, Eric. Diary, 1943.

Nicolson, Nigel. Letters to his parents, 1942–1943.

Reddish, Arthur. *A Tank Soldier's Story.*

Reed, James E. *A P-40 Pilot Speaks: Fifty-Five Years Later.* Letters.

Saidel, Raymond. Diary, 1943.

Schwartz, Gerald. Correspondence with author.

Published Sources
OFFICIAL HISTORIES

Agar-Hamilton, JAI & Turner, LCF. *Crisis in the Desert,* OUP, 1952.

Boog, Horst, et al. *Germany and the Second World War; Vol. IV: The Global War,* Clarendon Press, 2001.

Cody, J. F. *28 (Maori) Battalion,* War History Branch Department of Internal Affairs, 1956.

Craven, W. F., & Cate, J. L., Eds. *The Army Air Forces in World War II, Vol. II; Europe: Torch to Pointblank, August 1942 to December 1943,* University of Chicago Press, 1949.

Howard, Michael. *Grand Strategy, Vol. IV,* HMSO, 1972.

Howe, George F. *The Mediterranean Theater of Operations: Northwest Africa: Seizing the Initiative in the West,* Office of the Chief of Military History, Department of the Army, 1957.

Institute of the Royal Army Service Corps. *The Story of the Royal Army Service Corps, 1939–1945,* G. Bell & Sons Ltd., 1955.

Maughan, Barry. *Australia in the War of 1939–1945: Tobruk and El Alamein,* Collins. Australian War Memorial, 1966.

Orpen, Neil. *War in the Desert,* Purnell, 1971.

Playfair, I. S. O. *The Mediterranean and the Middle East, Vol. III,* HMSO, 1960.

Playfair, I. S. O. & Moloney, CJC. *The Mediterranena and the Middle East, Vol. IV,* HMSO, 1966.

Pogue, Forrest C. *US Army in World War II: European Theater of Operations; The Supreme Command,* Office of the Chief of Military History, Department of the Army, 1954.

Richards, Denis, & Saunders, Hilary St. G. *Royal Air Force, 1939–1945, Vol. II: The Fight Avails,* HMSO, 1954.

Roskill, Captain S. W. *The War At Sea, 1939–1945: Vol. II: The Period of Balance,* HMSO, 1956.

Scott, J. D. & Hughes, Richard. *The Administration of War Production,* HMSO, 1955.

Wardlow, Chester. *US Army in World War II: The Transportation Corps: Movements, Training and Supply,* Office of the Chief of Military History, Department of the Army, 1956.

BOOKS

Addison, Paul & Calder, Angus, Eds. *Time to Kill: The Soldier's Experience of War in the West, 1939–1945,* Pimlico, 1997.

Alanbrooke, Field Marshal Lord. *War Diaries, 1939–1945,* Weidenfeld & Nicolson, 2001.

Anon. *Artillery Training Volume III,* HMSO, 1928.

———— *Combined Operations,* HMSO, 1943.

———— *The Eighth Army,* HMSO, 1944.

———— *RAF Middle East,* HMSO, 1945.

———— *The Rajputana Rifles in World War 2 up to the End of the Campaign in Tunisia,* Dhoomi Mal Dharam Das, Delhi.

———— *The Rise and Fall of the German Air Force, 1933–1945,* Public Record Office War Histories, 2001.

———— *Special Forces in the Desert War, 1940–1943,* Public Record Office War Histories, 2001.

Alexander of Tunis, Field Marshal Earl. *The Alexander Memoirs, 1940–1945,* McGraw-Hill, 1962.

———— *Despatch: The African Campaign from El Alamein to Tunis, from 10 August, 1942, to 13 May, 1943,* Supplement to the London Gazette, 3 February, 1948.

———— *The Paintings of Field Marshal Earl Alexander of Tunis,* Collins, 1973.

Altieri, James. *The Spearheaders,* Popular Library, 1960.

Ambrose, Stephen E. *American's at War,* Berkley Books, 1998.

———— *Eisenhower: Soldier and President,* Pocket Books, 2003.

———— *The Supreme Commander: The War Years of Dwight D. Eisenhower,* Doubleday, 1970.

———— Intro. *Reporting World War II: American Journalism, 1938–1946,* Library of America, 1995.

Anderson, Roy C. *Devils, Not Men: The History of the French Foreign Legion,* Robert Hale, 1987.

Archard, Theresa. *GI Nightingale: The Story of an American Army Nurse,* Norton, 1945.

Arthur, Douglas. *Desert Watch,* Blaisdon Publishing, 2000.

Arthur, Max. *Men of the Red Beret: Airborne Forces, 1940–1990,* Hutchinson, 1990.

Atkins, Peter. *Buffoon in Flight,* Ernest Stanton Publishers, 1978.

Atkinson, Rick. *An Army at Dawn: The War in North Africa, 1942–1943,* Little, Brown, 2003.

Austin, A. B. *Birth of an Army,* Victor Gollancz, 1943.

Awatare, Arapeta. *A Soldier's Story,* Huia, 2003.

Bacon, Admiral Sir Reginald, et al, Eds. *Warfare Today,* Odhams Press, 1946.

Barnett, Correlli. *Engage the Enemy More Closely,* Penguin, 2000.

Barr, Niall. *Pendulum of War: The Three Battles of Alamein,* Cape, 2004.

Bartley, Tony. *Smoke Trails in the Sky,* Crecy, 1997.

Baumer, Robert W. with Reardon, Mark J. *American Iliad: The 18th Infantry Regiment in World War II,* Aberjona, 2004.

Beaton, Cecil. *Near East,* Batsford, 1943.

Behrendt, Hans-Otto. *Rommel's Intelligence in the Desert Campaign,* William Kimber, 1985.

Bidwell, Shelford. *Gunners at War,* Arrow, 1972.

Bidwell, Shelford & Graham, Dominick. *Fire-Power: British Army Weapons and Theories of War, 1904–1945,* George Allen & Unwin, 1982.

Bierman, John & Smith, Colin. *Alamein: War Without Hate,* Penguin Viking, 2002.

Bierman, John. *The Secret Life of Laszlo Almasy, the Real English Patient,* Penguin Viking, 2004.

Billiere, General Sir Peter de la. *Supreme Courage: Heroic Stories from 150 Years of the Victoria Cross,* Little, Brown & Co., 2004.

Birkenhead, the Earl of. *Halifax: The Life of Lord Halifax,* Hamish Hamilton, 1965.

Black, Robert W. *Rangers in World War II,* Ballantine, 1992.

Blomfield-Smith, Denis, compiled by. *Fourth Indian Reflections,* privately published, 1987.

Blumenson, Martin. *Kasserine Pass,* Playboy Paperbacks, 1983.

——— *The Patton Papers, 1940–1945,* Da Capo, 1974.

Blumenson, Martin, and Stokesbury, James L. *Masters of the Art of Command,* Da Capo, 1990.

Bowman, Martin W. *USAAF Handbook, 1939–1945,* Sutton, 2003.

Bowyer, Chaz. *Men of the Desert Air Force,* William Kimber, 1984.

Bowzer, Chaz, with Shores, Christopher. *Desert Air Force at War,* Ian Allen, 1981.

Bradley, Omar N. *A Soldier's Story,* Henry Holt, 1951.

Bradley, Omar N. & Blair, Chay. *A General's Life,* Simon & Schuster, 1983.

Brendon, Piers. *The Dark Valley: A Panorama of the 1930s,* Pimlico, 2001.

Brereton, Lewis H. *The Brereton Diaries,* William Morrow & Co., 1946.

Brooks, Stephen, Ed. *Montgomery and the Eighth Army,* The Bodley Head, 1991.

Brookes, Andrew. *Air War over Italy,* Ian Allen, 2000.

Brown, Robin. *Shark Squadron: The History of 112 Squadron, 1917–1975,* Crecy, 1994.

Brown, Russell. *Desert Warriors: Australian P-40 Pilots at War in the Middle East and North Africa, 1941–1943,* Banner Books, 2000.

Bryant, Ben. *One Man Band,* William Kimber, 1958.

Bryant, Arthur. *The Turn of the Tide,* Collins, 1957.

Budiansky, Stephen. *Air Power: From Kitty Hawk to Gulf War II: A History of the People, Ideas and Machines That Transformed War in the Century of Flight,* Viking, 2003.

——— *Battle of Wits: The Complete Story of Codebreaking in World War II,* Viking, 2000.

Bungay, Stephen. *Alamein,* Aurum, 2002.

Butcher, Harry C. *Three Years with Eisenhower,* Heinmann, 1946.

Cardozier, V. R. *The Mobilization of the United States in World War II: How the Government, Military and Industry Prepared for War,* McFarland, 1995.

Carmichael, Thomas N. *The Ninety Days: Five Battles That Changed the World,* Bernard Geis Associates, 1971.

Carver, Michael. *Dilemmas of the Desert War: A New Look at the Libyan Campaign, 1940–1942,* Batsford, 1986.

——— *El Alamein,* Batsford, 1962.

—— *Out of Step: The Memoirs of Field Marshal Lord Carver,* Hutchinson, 1989.

—— Ed. *The War Lords,* Little, Brown & Co., 1976.

—— *Tobruk,* Batsford, 1964.

Center of Military History. *The War in the Mediterranean,* Brassey's, 1998.

Chamberlain, Peter, & Ellis, Chris. *Tanks of the World, 1915–1945,* Cassell, 2002.

Chandler, Alfred D. Jr., Ed. *The Papers of Dwight David Eisenhower, Vols. I–V,* Johns Hopkins Press, 1970.

Churchill, Winston S. *The Second World War, Vol. III–IV,* Cassell, 1951.

Ciano, Count Galeazzo. *Ciano's Diary, 1937–1943,* William Heinemann, 1947.

Clark, Mark W. *Calculated Risk,* Harper, 1950.

Clarke, Rupert. *With Alex at War: From the Irrawaddy to the Po, 1941–1945,* Leo Cooper, 2000.

Clayton, Phil & Craig, Tim. *The End of the Beginning,* Hodder & Stoughton, 2002.

Clifford, Alexander. *Three Against Rommel: Wavell, Auchinleck, Alexander,* Harrap, 1943.

Close, M. C, Major Bill. *A View from the Turret,* Dell & Bredon, 2002.

Connell, John. *Auchinleck: A Critical Biography,* Cassell, 1959.

Cooper, Artemis. *Cairo in the War, 1939–1945.* Penguin, 1995.

Cooper, Johnny. *One of the Originals,* Pan, 1991.

Covington, Sargeant Robert L. *The War Diaries, Pocahontas Press, 1998.*

Cowles, Virginia. *The Phantom Major,* The Companion Book Club, 1958.

Creveld, Martin van. *Supplying War: Logistics from Wallenstein to Patton,* Cambridge University Press, 1995.

Cross, Air Chief Marshal Sir Kenneth "Bing," with Orange, Prof. Vincent. *Straight and Level,* Grub Street, 1993.

Cross, J. P. & Buddhimann Gurung. *Gurkhas At War: In Their Own Words: The Gurkha Experience 1939 to the Present,* Greenhill Books, 2002.

Cunningham of Hyndhope, Admiral of the Fleet Viscount. *A Sailor's Odyssey,* Hutchinson, 1951.

Curtiss, Mina, Ed. *Letters Home,* Little, Brown, 1944.

Daniell, David Scott. *Regimental History of the Royal Hampshire Regiment, Vol. III, 1918–1954,* Gale & Polden, 1955.

Darby, William O., with Baumer, William H. *Darby's Rangers: We Led the Way,* Presidio Press, 1980.

D'Arcy-Dawson, John. *Tunisian Battle,* Macdonald, 1943.

Davis, Keneth S. *The American Experience of War, 1939–1945,* Secker & Warburg, 1967.

De Guingand, Major-General Sir Francis. *Generals at War,* Hodder & Stoughton, 1964.

—— *Operation Victory,* Hodder & Stoughton, 1960.

Deighton, Len. *Blood, Tears and Folly,* Pimlico, 1995.

D'Este, Carlo. *Eisenhower: A Soldier's Life,* Henry Holt, 2002.

Dickinson, Arthur P. *Crash Dive: In Action with HMS Safari, 1942–43,* Sutton, 1999.

Dodds, Wayne, Ed. *The Fabulous Fifty-Seventh Fighter Group of World War II Alias America's Flying Circus Alias The Gang*, Walsworth Publishing, 1985.

Doherty, Richard. *The Sound of History: El Alamein, 1942*, Spellmount, 1942.

Doolittle, General James "Jimmy," H., with Glines, Carroll V. *I Could Never Be So Lucky Again*, Bantam, 1991.

Douglas, Keith. *Alamein to Zem Zem*, Faber & Faber, 1966.

———— *The Complete Poems*, Faber, 1988.

Drake, Group Captain Billy, with Shores, Christopher. *Billy Drake, Fighter Leader*, Grub Street, 2002.

Dugan, Sally. *Commando: The Elite Fighting Forces of the Second World War*, Channel 4 Books, 2001.

Dunning, Chris. *Courage Alone: The Italian Air Force 1940–1943*, Hikoki, 1998.

Duke, Neville. *Test Pilot*, Grub Street, 2003.

Duke, Neville, & Franks, Norman, Ed. *The War Diaries of Neville Duke*, Grub Street, 1995.

Eade, Charles, Ed. *Secret Session Speeches by the Rt. Hon. Winston S. Churchill*, Cassell, 1946.

———— *The Unrelenting Struggle: The Second Volume of Winston Churchill's War Speeches*, Cassell, 1942.

Eisenhower, Dwight D. *At Ease: Stories I Tell to Friends*, Eastern National, 1969.

—*Crusade in Europe*, William Heinemann, 1948.

Eisenhower, John S. D. *Allies: Pearl Harbor to D-Day*, Da Capo, 1982.

Ellis, John. *The Sharp End: The Fighting Man in World War II*, Pimlico, 1993.

———— *The World War II Databook*, Aurum, 1995.

Geraghty, Tony. *March or Die: France and The Foreign Legion*, Grafton, 1986.

Gilbert, Martin. *Road To Victory: Winston S. Churchill, 1941–1945*, Minerva, 1989.

Gulley, Thomas F., et al. *The Hour Has Come: The 97th Bomb Group in World War II*, Taylor, 1993.

Fisher, David. *The War Magician*, Berkley, 1983.

Fleischer, Wolfgang. *An Illustrated Guide to German Panzers, 1935–1945*, Schiffer Military History, 2002.

Fletcher, David. *Crusader and Covenanter Cruiser Tanks, 1939–45*, Osprey, 1995.

———— *The Great Tank Scandal: British Armour in the Second World War, Part 1*, HMSO, 1989.

Flower, Desmond & Reeves, James, Ed. *The War, 1939–1945*, Da Capo, 1997.

Flynn, G. Jesse. *Heroes from the Attic: A History of the 48th Surgical Hospital/128th Evacuation Hospital, 1941–1945*, Butler Books, 2003.

Forty, George. *Tanks Across the Desert: The War Diary of Jake Wardrop*, Sutton, 2003.

———— *British Army Handbook, 1939–1945*, Sutton, 2002.

———— *The Desert War*, Sutton, 2002.

———— *German Infantryman At War, 1939–1945*, Ian Allen, 2002.

———— *US Army Handbook, 1939–1945*, Sutton, 2003.

Foster, Philip. *A Trooper's Desert War*, Wilton 65, 1994.

Franks, Norman. *Aircraft Versus Aircraft*, Chancellor Press, 1998.

—— *Dark Sky, Deep Water,* Grub Street, 1997.

Fraser, David. *And We Shall Shock Them: The British Army in the Second World War,* Hodder & Stoughton, 1983.

Frost, Major-General John. *A Drop Too Many,* Buchan & Enright, 1982.

—— *Nearly There: The Memoirs of John Frost of Arnhem Bridge,* Leo Cooper, 1991.

Fussell, Paul. *Wartime: Understanding and Behaviour in the Second World War,* Oxford, 1989.

Garber, Max & Bond, P. S. *A Modern Military Dictionary,* P. S. Bond, 1942.

Gardiner, Juliet. *Overpaid, Oversexed & Over Here: The American GI in World War II Britain,* Canopy Books, 1992.

Gardiner, Wira. *The Story of the Maori Battalion,* Reed, 1992.

Gleeson, Ian. *The Unknown Force: Black, Indian and Coloured Soldiers Through Two World Wars,* Ashanti Publishing, 1994.

Graham, Desmond. *Keith Douglas: A Biography,* Oxford University Press, 1974.

Gunston, Bill. *The Illustrated Directory of Fighting Aircraft of World War II,* Salamander Books, 1988.

Guderian, Heinz. *Panzer Leader,* Penguin, 2000.

Guedalla, Philip. *Middle East, 1940–1942: A Study in Air Power,* Hodder & Stoughton, 1944.

Hamilton, Nigel. *The Full Monty: Montgomery of Alamein, 1887–1942,* Penguin Press, 2001.

—— *Monty: The Battles of Field Marshal Bernard Montgomery,* Hodder & Stoughton, 1986.

Handel, Michael I., Ed. *Intelligence and Military Operations,* Cass, 1990.

Harrison, Frank. *Tobruk: The Great Siege Reassessed,* Brockhampton, 1999.

Harrison Place, Timothy. *Military Training in the British Army, 1940–1944: From Dunkirk to D-Day,* Cass, 2000.

Hart, Peter. *To the Last Round: South Notts Hussars, 1939–1942,* Leo Cooper, 1996.

Hart, Stephen Ashley. *Montgomery and the Colossal Cracks: The 21st Army Group in Northwest Europe, 1944–45,* Prager, 2000.

Hastings, Major RHWS. *The Rifle Brigade in the Second World War, 1939–1945,* Gale & Polden Ltd, 1950.

Hastings, Stephen. *The Drums of Memory,* Leo Cooper, 1994.

Hayward, Brigadier P. H. C. *Jane's Dictionary of Military Terms,* Book Club Edition, 1975.

Heckstall-Smith, Anthony. *Tobruk: The Story of a Siege,* Anthony Blond, 1959.

Heiber, Helmut, & Glantz, David M, Eds. *Hitler and His Generals: Military Conferences, 1942–1945,* Enigma Books, 2003.

Hess, William N. *B-17 Flying Fortress Units of the MTO,* Osprey, 2003.

Hillson, Norma. *Alexander of Tunis,* WH Allen, 1952.

Hinsey, FH. *British Intelligence in the Second World War,* HMSO, 1993.

Hirshon, Stanley P. *General Patton: A Soldier's Life,* HarperCollins, 2002.

Hogg, Ian V. *The Guns, 1939–45,* Macdonald, 1969.

Holland, James. *Fortress Malta: An Island Under Siege, 1940–1943*, Orion, 2002.

Holmes, Richard. *Battlefields of the Second World War*, BBC, 2003.

—— *Bir Hacheim: Desert Citadel*, Ballantine, 1971.

—— *Firing Line*, Pimlico, 1994.

Holloway, Adrian. *From Dartmouth to War: A Midshipman's Journal*, Buckland Publications, 1993.

Hooton, E. R. *Eagle in Flames: The Fall of the Luftwaffe*, Brockhampton Press, 1997.

Horrocks, Lieutenant-General Sir Brian. *A Full Life*, Collins, 1960.

Houghton, Squadron Leader G. W. *They Flew Through Sand*, Jarrolds, 1942.

Howe, George F. *The Battle History of the 1st Armored Division, Old Ironsides*, Combat Forces Press, 1954.

Hougen, Lieutenant-Colonel John H. *The Story of the Famous 34th Infantry Division*, The Battery Press, 1949.

Howlett, Peter. *Fighting With Figures: A Statistical Digest of the Second World War*, HMSO, 1995.

Hoyt, Edwin P. *The GI's War*, Cooper Square Press, 2000.

Ireland, Bernard. *The War in the Mediterranean*, Pen & Sword, 2004.

Irving, David. *The Trail of the Fox: The Life of Field Marshal Erwin Rommel*, Book Club Associates, 1977.

Ismay, Hastings. *The Memoirs of General Lord Ismay*, Viking, 1960.

Jackson, W. G. F. *Alexander as Military Commander*, Batsford, 1971.

—— *The North African Campaign, 1940–43*, Batsford, 1975.

James, Lawrence. *Warrior Race: A History of the British at War*, Abacus, 2002.

James, Macolm. *Born of the Desert: With the SAS in North Africa*, Greenhill Books, 2001.

Jenkins, Roy. *Churchill*, Pan, 2002.

Jones, R. V. *Most Secret War: British Scientific Intelligence, 1939–1945*, Hamish Hamilton, 1978.

Jörgensen, Christer. *Rommel's Panzers*, Reference Group Brown, 2003.

Keegan, John, Ed. *Churchill's Generals*, Abacus, 1999.

—— *The Second World War*, Pimlico, 1997.

Kelly, Orr. *Meeting the Fox*, Wiley, 2002.

Kemp, Anthony. *The SAS At War, 1941–1945*, Penguin, 2000.

Kemp, P. K. *Victory at Sea*, White Lion Publishers, 1957.

Kesselring, Field Marshal Albert. *The Memoirs of Field Marshal Kesselring*, Greenhill Books, 1988.

King, Ernest J. *Fleet Admiral King: A Naval Record*, Norton, 1952.

King, Michael. *Maori: A Photographic and Social History*, Heinemann, 1983.

Kippenberge, Major-General Sir Howard. *Infantry Brigadier*, Oxford University Press, 1961.

Klein, Harry. *Springbok Record*, South African Legion of the British Empire Service Legion, 1946.

Knickerbocker, H. R., et al. *Danger Forward: The Story of the First Division in World War II*, Society of the First Division, 1948.

Knox, MacGregor. *Hitler's Italian Allies: Royal Armed Forces, Fascist Regime and the War of 1940–1943*, Cambridge University Press, 2000.

Kohn, Richard H., & Harahan, Joseph P. *Air Superiority in World War II and Korea*, USAF Warrior Studies, 1983.

Konstam, Angus. *British Motor Torpedo Boat, 1939–45*, Osprey, 2003.

Kurowski, Franz. *Hans-Joachim Marseille*, Schiffer Military History, 1994.

Lambert, John & Ross, Al. *Allied Coastal Forces of World War II, Vol. II: Vosper MTBs & US Elcos*, Conway, 1993.

Latimer, Jon. *Alamein*, John Murray, 2002.

Lee, Christopher. *Tall, Dark and Gruesome: An Autobiography*, Gollancz, 1997.

Lewin, Ronald. *The Life and Death of the Afrika Korps*, Batsford, 1977.

—— *Rommel as Military Commander*, Batsford, 1968.

—— *Ultra Goes to War: The Secret Story*, Hutchinson, 1978.

Liddell Hart, B. H. *The Other Side of the Hill*, Cassell, 1948.

—— Ed., *The Rommel Papers*, Collins, 1953.

Linderman, Gerald F. *The World Within War: America's Combat Experience in World War II*, Harvard, 1999.

Lindsay, T. M. *Sherwood Rangers*, Burrup, Mathieson & Co., 1952.

Longmate, Norman. *The GIs: The Americans in Britain, 1942–1945*, Hutchinson, 1975.

Luck, Hans von. *Panzer Commander*, Cassell, 2002.

MacGibbon, John. *Struan's War*, Ngaio Press, 2001.

Mackenzie, Compton. *Eastern Epic Vol. I: September 1939–March 1943*, Chatto & Windus, 1951.

Macksey, Major K. J. *Afrika Korps*, Ballantine, 1968.

Macmillan, Harold. *The Blast of War, 1939–1945*, Harper & Row, 1967.

Majdalany, Fred. *The Battle of El Alamein*, Weidenfeld & Nicolson, 1965.

Manning, Olivia. *The Levant Trilogy*, Penguin, 2001.

Massimello, Giovanni, & Apostolo, Giorgio. *Italian Aces of World War 2*, Osprey, 2000.

Mather, Carol. *When the Grass Stops Growing: A War Memoir*, Leo Cooper, 1997.

McCallum, Neil. *Journey With a Pistol*, Gollancz, 1959.

McGregor, John. *The Spirit of Angus*, Phillimore, 2002.

McGuirk, Dal. *Rommel's Army in Africa*, Airlife, 2003.

McKee, Alexander. *El Alamein: Ultra and Three Battles*, Souvenir Press, 1991.

Mellenthin, Major-General F. W. von. *Panzer Battles*, Futura, 1977.

Mercer, Derrik, Ed. *Chronicle of the Second World War*, Longman, 1990.

Messenger, Charles. *The Second World War in the West*, Cassell, 2001.

Messmer, Pierre. *Apres Tant Des Batailles*, Albin Michel.

Miller, Lee G. *The Story of Ernie Pyle*, Viking, 1950.

Minterne, Don. *The History of 73 Squadron Part 2, November 1940 to September 1943*, Tutor, 1997.

Moen, Marcia & Heinen, Margo. *Heroes Cry Too: A WWII Ranger Tells His Story of Love and War*, Meadowlark Publishing, 2002.

Monahan, Evelyn M., & Neidel-Greenlee, Rosemary. *And If I Perish: Frontline US Army Nurses in World War II,* Knopf, 2003.

Molesworth, Carl. *P-40 Warhawk Aces of the MTO,* Osprey, 2002.

Montgomery, Field Marshal Viscount, of Alamein. *Memoirs,* Collins, 1958.

Moore, Peter. *No Need to Worry: Memoirs of an Army Conscript, 1941 to 1946,* Wilton 65, 2002.

Moorehead, Alan. *African Trilogy: The Desert War 1940–1943,* Cassell, 1998.

———— *The Desert War,* Hamish Hamilton, 1965.

Morley-Mower, Wing Commander Geoffrey. *Messerschmitt Roulette,* Phalanx, 1993.

Mortimer, Gavin. *Stirling's Men: The Inside Story of the SAS in World War II,* Weidenfedl & Nicolson, 2004.

Moss, W Stanley. *Ill Met by Moonlight,* Harrap, 1950.

Murray, Williamson. *Luftwaffe: Strategy for Defeat, 1933–45,* Grafton, 1988.

Neillands, Robin. *Eighth Army: From the Western Desert to the Alps, 1939–1945,* John Murray, 2004.

Nesbit, Roy C. *The Armed Rovers: Beauforts & Beaufighters over the Mediterranean,* Airlife, 1995.

Nicolson, Nigel. *Alex,* Weidenfeld & Nicolson, 1973.

———— *Long Life: Memoirs,* Weidenfeld & Nicolson, 1997.

98th Bomb Group (H) Veterans Association. *Force For Freedom: Legacy of the 98th,* Turner Publishing, 1990.

Orange, Vincent. *Coningham: A Biography of Air Marshal Sir Arthur Coningham,* Center for Air Force History, 1992.

Owen, Roderic. *The Desert Air Force,* Arrow, 1958.

Pack, SWC. *Invasion North Africa,* Ian Allen, 1978.

Padfield, Peter. *War Beneath the Sea: Submarine Conflict, 1939–1945,* Pimlico, 1997.

Palmer, John. *Luck on My Side: The Diaries and Reflections of a Young Wartime Sailor, 1939–1945,* Pen & Sword, 2002.

Peniakoff, Vladimir. *Popski's Private Army,* Cape, 1950.

Perrett, Bryan. *Last Stand! Famous Battles Against the Odds,* Cassell, 1998.

———— *Panzerkampwagen IV Medium Tank, 1936–45,* Osprey, 1999.

Piekalkiewicz, Janusz. *The Air War, 1939–1945,* Blandford Press, 1985.

———— *Rommel and His Secret War in North Africa, 1941–1943,* Schiffer Military History, 1992.

Pitt, Barrie. *The Crucible of War: Auchinleck's Command,* Cassell, 2001.

———— *The Crucible of War: Montgomery and Alamein,* Cassell, 2001.

Pocock, Tom. *Alan Moorehead,* Pimlico, 1990.

Porch, Douglas. *Hitler's Mediterranean Gamble: The North African and the Mediterranean Campaigns in World War II,* Weidenfeld & Nicolson, 2004.

Price, Dr Alfred. *Spitfire Mark V Aces, 1941–45,* Osprey, 1997.

Pyle, Ernie. *Brave Men,* Henry Holt, 1943.

———— *Ernie Pyle's England,* McBride, 1941.

———— *Here Is Your War: The Story of GI Joe,* World Publishing Company, 1945.

Ranfurly, Countess of. *To War with Whitaker: The Wartime Diaries of the Countess of Ranfurly, 1939–45,* Mandarin, 1995.

Reed, James E. *The Fighting 33rd Nomads In World War II, Vol. I,* Reed, 1987.

Reynolds, Leonard C. *Dog Boats at War: Royal Navy D Class MTBs And MGBs, 1939–1945,* Sutton, 2000.

Ripley, Tim. *Wehrmacht: The German Army in World War II, 1939–1945,* Brown Reference Group, 2003.

Roberts, Owen. *31st Field Artillery Regiment RA,* 1994.

Robinett, Brigadier-General Paul McDonald. *Armor Command,* McGregor & Werner, Inc., 1958.

Rolf, David. *The Bloody Road to Tunis,* Greenhill Books, 2001.

Rutherford, Ward. *Kasserine: Baptism of Fire,* Ballantine, 1970.

Saunders, Andy. *No. 43 "Fighting Cocks" Squadron,* Osprey, 2003.

Scammell, William. *Keith Douglas: A Study,* Faber & Faber, 1988.

Scannell, Vernon. *Drums of Morning,* Robson Books, 1992.

—— *The Tiger and the Rose: An Autobiography,* Hamish Hamilton, 1971.

—— *Of Love & War: New and Selected Poems,* Robson Books, 2002.

—— *Argument of Kings,* Robson Books, 1987.

Scutts, Jerry. *Bf 109 Aces of North Africa and the Mediterranean,* Osprey, 1995.

Shephard, Ben. *A War of Nerves: Soldiers and Psychiatrists, 1914–1994,* Jonathan Cape, 2000.

Sherwood, Robert E. *The White House Papers of Harry L. Hopkins, Vol. I & II,* Eyre & Spottiswoode, 1948.

Shorer, Avis D. *A Half Acre of Hell: A Combat Nurse in WWII,* Galde Press, 2000.

Shores, Christopher, & Rings, Hans. *Fighters over the Desert,* Neville Spearman, 1969.

Shores, Christopher, Ring, Hans & Hess, William. *Fighters over Tunisia,* Neville Spearman, 1975.

Simpson, Rear Admiral GWG. *Periscope View,* Macmillan, 1972.

Simpson, J. S. M. *South Africa Fights,* Hodder & Stoughton, 1941.

Sinclair-Stevenson, Christopher. *The Gordon Highlanders,* Hamish Hamilton, 1968.

Smeeton, Miles. *A Change of Jungles,* Rupert Hart-Davis, 1962.

Soutar, Monty. *28 Maori Battalion, 23rd National Reunion,* 2002.

Spick, Mike. *Luftwaffe Fighter Aces: The Jagdflieger and their Combat Tactics and Techniques,* Greenhill Books, 1996.

Spooner, Tony. *Supreme Gallantry: Malta's Role in the Allied Victory, 1939–1945,* John Murray, 1996.

Sprot, Aidan. *Swifter than Eagles,* The Pentland Press, 1998.

Starns, Penny. *Nurses at War: Women on the Frontline, 1939–45,* Sutton, 2000.

Steinbeck, John. *Once There Was a War,* Penguin, 1994.

Stewart, Adrian. *North African Victory: The Eighth Army from Alam Halfa to Tunis, 1942–1943,* Penguin, 2002.

Summersby, Kay. *Eisenhower Was My Boss,* Dell, 1948.

—— *Past Forgetting: My Love Affair with Dwight D. Eisenhower,* Golden Apple, 1984.

Sutherland, Jonathan. *World War II Tanks and AFVs,* Airlife, 2002.

Tedder, Lord. *With Prejudice,* Cassell, 1966.

Terraine, John. *The Right of the Line,* Wordsworth Military Library, 1997.

Thompson, Julian. *Lifeblood of War: Logistics in Armed Conflict.* Brassey's, London, 1991.

———— *Ready For Anything: The Parachute Regiment at War, 1940–1982,* Weidenfeld & Nicolson, 1989.

Thompson, R. W. *Montgomery,* Ballantine, 1974.

Thorpe, D. R. *Eden: The Life and Times of Anthony Eden, First Earl of Avon, 1897–1977,* Chatto & Windus, 2003.

Timpson, Alastair. *In Rommel's Back Yard: A Memoir of the Long Range Desert Group,* Leo Cooper, 2000.

Tobin, James. *Ernie Pyle's War,* Kansas, 1997.

Travers, Susan, with Holden, Wendy. *Tomorrow to be Brave,* The Free Press, 2001.

Tuker, Sir Francis. *Approach to Battle,* Cassell, 1963.

———— *When Memory Serves,* Cassell, 1950.

———— *The Pattern of War,* Cassell, 1948.

Tyldon, Major G. *The Armed Forces of South Africa, 1659–1954.*

Verney, Major-General G. I. *The Desert Rats,* Hutchinson, 1955.

Voss, Capt Vivian. *The Story of No. 1 Squadron SAAF,* Mercantile Atlas, 1952.

Warlimont, Walter. *Inside Hitler's Headquarters, 1939–45,* Weidenfeld & Nicolson, 1964.

Warner, Oliver. *Cunningham of Hyndhope: Admiral of the Fleet,* J. Murray, 1967.

Warner, Philip. *Auchinleck: The Lonely Soldier,* Sphere, 1982.

Weinronk, Jack "Cobber." *The Vaulted Sky: A Bomber Pilot's Western Desert War Before and After,* Merlin Books, 1993.

Weal, John. *Jagdgeschwader 27 "Afrika,"* Osprey, 2003.

Westwell, Ian. *1st Infantry Divison,* Ian Allen, 2002.

Wheal, Elizabeth-Anne, and Pope, Stephen. *The Macmillan Dictionary of the Second World War,* Macmillan, 1989.

Whiting, Charles. *Disaster at Kasserine: Ike and the 1st (US) Army in North Africa, 1943,* Pen & Sword, 2003.

Whitlock, Flint. *The Fighting First: The Untold Story of the Big Red One on D-Day,* Westview, 2004.

Willmott, H. P. *The Great Crusade,* Pimlico, 1992.

Wingate, John. *The Fighting Tenth,* Leo Cooper, 1991.

Winterbotham, F. W. *The Ultra Secret,* Book Club Edition, 1974.

Winton, John. *Cunningham: The Greatest Admiral Since Nelson,* John Murray, 1998.

———— *The Submariners: Life on British Submarines, 1901–1999,* Constable, 1999.

Woerpel, Don. *The 79th Fighter Group over Tunisia, Sicily and Italy in World War II,* Schiffer Military History, 2001.

Wright, Patrick. *Tank,* Faber & Faber, 2000.

Wynn, Humphrey. *Desert Eagles,* Airlife, 1993.

Young, John Robert. *The French Foreign Legion,* Thames & Hudson, 1984.

MAGAZINES & PERIODICALS

Anon. "Libyan Letter," *Field Artillery Journal*, Vol. 33, No. 3, March 1943.

Benson, Col. C. C. "Some Tunisian Details," *Field Artillery Journal*, Vol. 34, No. 1, January, 1944.

Bidwell, Shelford. "Wadi Akari," *War Monthly*, Issue 12, March 1975.

Blumenson, Martin. "Difficult Birth of a Grand Alliance," *Army*, December, 1992.

Burba, Lieutenant-Colonel E. H. "Battle of Sidi Bou Zid: 15 Feb. 1943," *Field Artillery Journal*, Vol. 33, No. 9, September, 1943.

—— "Sidi Bou Zid to Sbeitla, February 14–17, 1943," *Field Artillery Journal*, Vol. 34, No. 1, January 1944.

Carver, R. M. P. "Tank and Anti-Tank," *RUSI Journal*, Vol. 91, 1946.

Coningham, Air Marshal Sir Arthur. "The Development of Tactical Air Forces," *RUSI Journal*, Vol. 91, 1946.

Creveld, Martin van. "Rommel's Supply Problem, 1941–42," Vol. 119, 1974.

Drummond, Air Marshal Sir PRM. "The Air Campaign in Libya and Tripolitania," *RUSI Journal*.

Elmhirst, Air Vice-Marshal Sir Thomas W. "The German Air Force and Its Failure," *RUSI Journal*, 1946.

——"Lessons of Air Warfare, 1939–45," *RUSI Journal*, 1947.

Harding, Field Marshal John. "The Day Alexander Locked up His Airmen," *Sunday Times*, 22 June, 1969.

Heaton, Colin D. "Jimmy Doolittle: The Man Behind the Legend," *World War II*, March 2003.

Johnston, Mark. "The Blockhouse, El Alamein," *Australian War Museum Journal*.

Lanza, Colonel Conrad H. "Finale in Tunisia," *Field Artillery Journal*, Vol. 33 No. 7, July 1943.

—— "Perimeters in Paragraphs: Tunisia, February 17 to March 19, 1943," *Field Artillery Journal*, Vol. 33, No. 5, May 1943.

—— "Perimieters In Paragraphs: Tunisia, March 20 to April 19, 1943," *Field Artillery Journal*, Vol. 33, No. 6, June 1943.

Lodge, Major Henry Cabot Jr. "The Enemy In Africa," *Cavalry Journal*, Nov–Dec, 1942, Vol. LI, No. 6.

Newton, Robert A. "Ambushed by the Afrika Korps," *World War II*, September 2002.

Oliver, Major-General Lunsford Errett. "In the Mud and Blood of Tunisia," *Collier's*, April 17, 1943.

Pago, Colonel Douglas J. "El Guettar: March 25–April 8, 1943," *Field Artillery Journal*, Vol. 33, No. 9, September 1943.

Patch, Jim. "A Relic of the Long Range Desert Group," *After the Battle*, Number 44, 1984.

Philipsborn, Martin, Jr. & Lehman, Milton, "The Untold Story of the Kasserine Pass," *Saturday Evening Post*, February 14, 1948.

Raymond, Major Edward A. "Slogging It Out," *Field Artillery Journal*, Vol. 34, No. 1, January, 1944.

Thompson, Lieutenant-Colonel P. W. "Close Support in Tunisia," *Field Artillery Journal*, Vol. 33, No. 7, July 1943.

INTERNET

www.afvinteriors.hobbyvista.com US/British M3 Medium Tank, 'Grant'Part I
———— M4A£ Medium Tank, 'General Sherman', Parts I & II
www.britain-at-war.org War Memories of Derek Jackson

MAPS

Egypt & Cyrenaica 1;250,000
GSGS 4386 Compiled, drawn and reproduced by 512 Field Survey Company, RE
Sheet 3: Sollum & Tobruch
Sheet 14: El Daba

Tunisia, 1:50,000
GSGS 4225 Compiled, drawn and reproduced by 512 Field Survey Company, RE

Tactical Pilotage Charts
Algeria, Italy, Spain, Tunisia, 1:500,000
TPC G-2A, G-2D, G-2C
Egypt & Libya, 1: 500,000
H-4A, H-4B, H-4D, H-4C; G-3D; H-5A

Agypten 1:100,000
Ed-Daba, El Alamen
Department of Survey and Mines, Germany, 1939

Ordnance Survey
Tunisie, 1: 2,000,000
Copied from French Map, 1936
Alger-Bizerte, 1:2,000,000
1943

Prepared and published by the Defense Mapping Agency, St Louis, Missouri

ACKNOWLEDGEMENTS

This book could not have been written without the help of a great many people, most notably the veterans mentioned in the text and their families, who without exception cooperated freely and beyond what could be reasonably expected: Ken Anderson; Jenny Altschuler; Dick Bowery; Henry Bowles; Tom Bowles; Tim Bowles; Hazel Boylan; Sam Bradshaw; Ralph Burbridge; Willie Chapman; David Christopherson; Charles Coles; Squadron Leader Bryan Colston, DFC; Wing Commander Hank Costain, MBE; Bob Cullen; James D'Arcy Clark; Alf Davies; L. Gordon Delp; Petrus Dhlamini; Group Captain Billy Drake, DSO, DFC, DFC (US); Colonel "Duke" Ellington; Ray Ellis; Elaine Paulsen Evans; Frances Evans; Warren Evans; David Fairbairn; Joe Furayter; Jennifer Kernaghan and Mrs. Stanley Kernaghan; Christopher Lee; Bob Hall; Ted Hardy; Harold Harper; Sir Stephen Hastings, MC; Robert Hornback; Earl Jellicoe, MC; Robert Kolowski; Xavier Krebs; Joe Madeley; Mangal Singh; Albert Martin; Sir Carol Mather, MC; Bill McInnes; Pete McInnes; Len Meerholz; George Monroe; Sophie Moss; Nainabadahur Pun; Ken Neill, DFC; Adam Nicolson; Nigel Nicolson; Maiki Parkinson; Frank Read; Captain Jim Reed; Ida Paulsen; Randolph Paulsen; Marcy Roberts; Raymond Saidel; Vernon Scannell; Dennis Scott; Gerald Schwartz; Marnie Terhune; Tommy Thompson, DFC; George Vaughan; Frank Vidor; Bucky Walters; Ronnie Ward, DSC; Sarah Weinronk; and George Williams, CBE.

I would also like to thank the various staffs of the archives around the world who helped put me in the right direction and offered guidance and advice. In particular, I would like to thank the following: Dr Christopher Dowling, Roderick Suddaby and his team, Richard Hughes and Laurie Milner, at the Imperial War Museum in London; Jeffrey Suchanek at the University of Kentucky Oral History Program; Steve De Agrela at CMI

Documentation Centre in Pretoria; Erika Dowell at the Lilly Library, Indiana University; Gavin Edgerley at the Gurkha Museum in Winchester; Mark Wilson and Michael Elliott of the Sherwood Rangers Yeomanry Museum; Eric Marenga, Hamish Paterson, and Rowena Wilkinson at the South African National Museum of History in Johannesburg. I would also like to particularly thank Dr. Monty Soutar at the History Group at the Ministry for Culture and Heritage in New Zealand, and Arthur Blake in South Africa for their enormous help.

Particular thanks also go to Major-General Julian Thompson and Robert Boyle for their military expertise; and to Trevor Chaytor-Norris and James Petrie for accompanying me on trips to Egypt and Tunisia respectively. Major Peter Ridlington traveled on foot through the hills of Nepal to interview Nainabahadur Pun, while Jane Martens conducted interviews in France and researched Pierre Messmer—special thanks go to them. I am also enormously grateful to Professor Jeremy Black and to my father, Martin Holland, for reading through the manuscript and for their suggestions. I am also indebted to Lalla Hitchings, who transcribed nearly all of the interviews I conducted with the veterans—thank you.

I would also like to thank the following: John Agius; Major Jon Bartholomew; David Berry; Giles Bourne; Artemis Cooper; Mr. Dhatt; Lieutenant-Colonel David Eadie; Lieutenant-Colonel Patrick Emerson, OBE; John Evans, secretary of the Hampshire Regiment Comrades Association, Southampton Branch; Frederick Galea; Emma Gardner; Herb Harper, 98th BG Association; Mo Harper; James Hitchings, Mark Hitchings, Tom Hitchings; Tim Holt; Kitty Jenkins; Lieutenant-Colonel Hugh Keating, curator of the Hampshire Regiment Museum; Mr. R. A. Morris; Edward Neubold, 79th FG Association; Major Tim O'Leary; Mr. Seitz, 98th BG Association; Captain Trevor Rowbotham, RN; Erika Rubel; Christopher Shores; Barry Soutar; Captain John Taylor, Rajputana Rifles Association; Guy Walters and Rowland White.

Enormous thanks are also due to Emma Parry at Fletcher & Parry; Jonathan Burnham, JillEllyn Riley, and all who have helped at Miramax Books; to Jane Bennett, Barry Clark, Jane Harris, Melanie Haselden, Rachel Smyth, and everyone else at HarperCollins; Peter Wilkinson for producing the maps; Michael Cox for his brilliant editing; and Ed Jespers, Jo Cooke, Clare Conville, and the team at Conville and Walsh. However, special thanks go to three people: Patrick Walsh, Trevor Dolby, and my wife, Rachel.